# NIRVANA

# NIRVANA THE BIOGRAPHY

EVERETT TRUE

DA CAPO PRESS
A Member of the Perseus Books Group

Printed in the United States of America.
Cataloging-in-Publication data for this book is available from the Library of Congress.

First Da Capo Press edition 2007
Reprinted by arrangement with Omnibus Press
ISBN-13 978-0-306-81554-6
ISBN-10 0-306-81554-0

Published by Da Capo Press
A Member of the Perseus Books Group
www.dacapopress.com



10 9 8 7 6 5 4 3 2 1

**For Charlotte and Isaac**

# CONTENTS

# INTRODUCTION

Have you noticed how the rock establishment all wear Ramones T-shirts now?

From Eddie Vedder to Jessica Simpson to the Chili Peppers, all the way through the Baby Gap generation, they wear the mark of a dead band like a badge of approval, now it's acknowledged the Ramones accepted their status as Rock Outsiders with true stoicism: like they're hoping that wearing the T might somehow help some of the Ramones' natural flair for music transfer across. Fat chance. If you don't know now, you never will.

None of them wears a Nirvana T-shirt. Not one.

Leave that to the kids – the eight-year-olds who weren't even alive while Kurt Cobain was around: the 12-year-olds desperate for peer approval and fed up with the blandishments of the mainstream media: the 15-year-old Goths lounging round city centres, studiously bored, frightened of the encroaching adult world. They understand how it feels to be unloved, confused, misunderstood, betrayed by those in positions of authority who only ever claim to be helping you. The kids understand.

Stories need to begin somewhere.

Mine is a jumble, a confusion of nightclubs and pranks that turned out wrong; names and faces that went in one eye and straight out the other; nights that began drunk and ended in amnesia; crawling around airports on my hands and knees; punching walls with bare knuckles; shaved heads on rooftops underneath a red moon; laughter and screaming and – caught up right in the centre of it all – music; loud and plentiful and spontaneous and unpolished and beautiful and thrilling. I keep reminding myself. This is a book on Nirvana. Not Kurt Cobain. The gossip stories, the conspiracy theories have all been laid out in detail and by folk far more qualified to talk about these matters than me – folk with a vested interest in history and shifting units and keeping the myth alive. It was the butler. Every Agatha Christie fan knows that. The butler did it. If not him, then the nanny was responsible. Easy access, you see. The drugs took their toll. It was hereditary. Must've been the nanny. Maybe the wife's responsible. Words get added on top of words until all semblance of reality is gone, smothered under cynical rewrites and well-meaning anecdotes from the past.

". . . the Melvins were going on tour and so Kurt invited me down.

He's like, 'Hey, they gave us these apartments to live in, come down any time you want, come down for the weekend, Shelli is down here with Krist.' They kept calling and saying, 'When are you coming, when are you coming?' Finally, one weekend I decided to go down. We planned to meet up at this Butthole Surfers/L7 show at the Hollywood Palladium, and from there we would go to the apartments. We flew in, rented a car, got lost and ended up at the club. We got there really late. We found Kurt, and Krist was super drunk. He either got a DUI [driving under the influence of alcohol] that night or almost ran someone over in the parking lot. Then I remember Courtney – someone who I had heard about and read about for years via other people I knew who knew her or were married to her. She was around . . ."

This is a book about Nirvana. I have to keep reminding myself. Nirvana. Schoolyard friends Kurt Cobain and Krist Novoselic formed the band in Aberdeen, Washington during the mid-Eighties through a mixture of boredom and a love for music. There wasn't much else going on. Home life sucked; nothing to do but watch TV – *Saturday Night Live*, *The Monkees*, late night sci-fi films. The logging industry that had helped spawn their home town had long moved elsewhere in its search for cheap labour. Life was a succession of dead-end jobs, cleaning up hotel rooms and waiting on tables. Punk rock beckoned – punk rock and Olympia, Washington. Form a band. Why not? If it feels good, do it.

"Living in Olympia when I was 20 years old, I lived in a town where every band either had no bass-player or else it was keyboards and a singer, or someone singing along to a recorded tape or with just a guitar player. All we heard from the rest of the world was, 'You're not legitimate, that's not real rock'n'roll,' particularly from the big city next door, Seattle. They would laugh at us like, 'You can't play your instruments, you don't know what you're doing, that's not rock'n'roll.' In the days of hardcore, it'd become so that if you weren't Black Flag, or some derivative of Black Flag, people would laugh at you for claiming to be punk rock. Today, kids live in a world where duos in particular are the thing like The White Stripes and Lightning Bolt – both big and small, duos or laptop artists like RJD2 are the norm in the post-*Pitchfork* world. We led the fight that made this possible. I laughed at the old people when I was 20 who said they'd paved the way for us and I can't really expect the 20-year-olds now to understand that Godheadsilo made it possible for most of these bands today, or Beat Happening or Mecca Normal. They suffered all the degradation, the hard work that never paid off, the years of ridicule, so that other bands could . . ."

Nirvana went through several line-up and name changes, losing and gaining drummers, moving cities as circumstances dictated – before rubbing up on the wrong side of celebrity culture. They had a naïve belief in the power of spontaneity. They released three albums during their lifetime and momentarily changed a few million people's worlds. They appeared on MTV a lot, and helped prop up and reinvent a decaying patriarchal music industry they professed to despise, much as the punk rockers had done two decades before. Reading Festival, the headline slot, was memorable. There was a benefit for Bosnian rape victims at the Cow Palace in San Francisco that stood out. Several small tours playing the clubs of the US and Britain and Europe helped hone their destructive tendencies. Kurt and Krist and Dave. Kurdt and Chris and Chad. Pat and Lori, and Earnie Bailey the ever-smiling guitar technician, and Alex MacLeod the acerbic Scots tour manager, and Craig and Monte and Anton and Nils, and Susie and Charles and Jackie and John and Janet and Danny, and Jon and Bruce from Sub Pop records . . . a lot of names, sure, though probably not as many as most large corporations shifting millions of units around the world. Nirvana: what a great live band!

"We started kind of raging and destroying our gear a lot, but we didn't do that right off the bat. It was probably about the third show. I didn't do it on purpose. I just joined in with what was already going on. But it was fun. It wasn't like we said, 'OK Krist, you jump really high and throw your bass in the air and have it knock you out; and Kurt, you get down on the floor and do the worm.' It was that we were so sick and tired of the big rock – all the arena rock and special effects and all that that entailed wasn't what we were about."

Stories need to start somewhere, but of course they never usually do.

This is a book about Nirvana. Nirvana were a band who understand the primary rule of rock'n'roll: that spontaneity is at the heart of all great rock music, that you need to be able to react instantly to circumstance and context, that the idiot boards and sound-bites television saddled us with lead to a deadening of the senses. Art constantly changes. That's why it's art. It's not there to be documented and pored over in stuffy galleries and libraries. Except everyone needs a vocation. Everyone needs a little history so they can understand their own situation better. And someone sure deserves a royalty settlement for the design on all those T-shirts . . .!

"I think he suspected her of cheating on him with Evan Dando and Billy Corgan. Was she? I think so. I mean, define cheating. Did they get fucked up and make out one night? That counts to a husband who's wondering. Was it a real affair? No, probably not. The one intense moment, and we're jumping ahead here, was when he called me from Italy, and I was in London with Courtney. We were late to see him. We were three weeks late. He was really serious and calm and like, 'I know that you don't get in the middle of our stuff and I know you don't take sides, but can I ask you something as your friend?' I was like, 'Yeah.' He goes, 'Is she cheating on me?' It was serious, no nonsense. I remember thinking, 'I think that she is,' but I didn't say that. I didn't know for sure and what if I had said, 'I think, maybe?' I don't think I could have saved him from anything if I did say yes.

"We had been putting off going to Europe. We came down to LA for a couple of days because she had to do something. She immediately got two bungalows at the chateau – one for me and Frances, and one for her. She rented a car for me the second day. After what felt like a couple of weeks, I stopped asking when we were leaving every day. She kept putting it off and I was like, 'Well, tell me when you want to go.' I don't remember how long we were there, but I remember he was calling, going, 'Are you coming or what?' I'd be like, 'Hey, I'm coming. When Courtney's ready to come, I'm coming.' I don't remember how long we were there, but I do know that I saw the hotel bill when we left, and it was for $37,000."

I have to keep reminding myself. This is a book about Nirvana.

I slip and there's sweat pouring down my shirt, legs kicking at the side of my face as another fan clambers up on stage to leap off pursued by five angry security men, sunlight blowing through eyes and temples that still hurt way too much from the night before, body a welter of cuts and bruises. What do you understand from your own brief lifespan? Did you touch others? Affect those around you? How? Why? Was it the music, the lifestyle, the projected myth that other people who never even knew or met you decide to place around a few random actions and interactions? Those in charge can never hope to understand Nirvana: most of us aren't winners, don't end up exploiting the rest for all they're worth. Most of us struggle to get by, confused by what we perceive to be out there, life a series of disappointments and putdowns. Is it that difficult to understand Nirvana's appeal? They captured the *zeitgeist*: the disaffection of their generation. And because Kurt killed himself, they remain true to that spirit, consequently resonating with *all* alienated teenagers. Kurt Cobain never got past the stage of being an angry, betrayed teenager.

"Die young, leave a good-looking corpse," ran the conventional wisdom as I grew up. Kurt Cobain left one of the best-looking corpses around.

"I was a junkie for 10 years. Heroin makes you forget about everything else going on in the world. It makes you forget about the fact your band isn't getting as much attention as another band, or that you have to go to work throwing fish around Pike Place Market. It's pure comfort. It's fucking great. And then later on, it turns on you. And yes, you steal your friend's Sub Pop 45 collection and take old ladies' purses and steal from your places of employment. You sell your own stuff first, of course: you don't jump right into criminal activity. And we lost a lot of great friends and a lot of great musicians to it. I got lucky: I lived. And I stopped, eventually. The appeal is weird, and the danger involved is strange too, because it's not like we don't know what's going to happen, but when you start, you don't think it's going to affect you. We're such pompous egotistical assholes. We think it won't happen to us."

This is a book about Nirvana. Punk rock. It's a book about the betrayal of Olympia, and how – just when you're beginning to think there is light at the end of the tunnel, that it may just be possible to help change the world for the better, so that the ones with quieter voices get a chance to be heard – the world up and whacks you in the face. The corporations win. So ignore them. Don't get involved. Step outside the mainstream, the conventional day-to-day and create your own communities, your own alternatives that don't need or seek approval from the adults, the outside world. The saddest thing about the Ramones was the way the group never felt validated until they'd been inducted into the Rock And Roll Hall Of Fame. After two decades of having their vision and sound and career thwarted, the Ramones felt vindicated because the selfsame bunch of assholes responsible deigned to recognise their talent *long after it ceased to matter.* The saddest thing about Nirvana was that the industry wholeheartedly embraced them even while making snide jokes and innuendo behind their back: Kurt Cobain wanted to view himself as an outsider, but how outside can you be when you're selling eight million records?

"Kurt had one of those voices that could sing the telephone book and make it sound real and convincing. Nirvana frustrated me so much once they got famous: how could that band make as many mistakes as they made? Once they got a little bit of success, it was like, 'Oh my God, you're doing everything wrong!' I never liked the production on *Nevermind*, it sounded like Eighties big rock. I don't like Grohl's drumming at all. He's a hard-hitting, pounding drummer. I like things with more finesse. I liked Chad's drumming for Nirvana, a little sloppier and a little looser. It swung more."

This is a book about Nirvana. Forget melodies or virtuosity or image or marketing or any of that textbook stuff. It's important, but anyone can do that. That's just research. If you can't react to the situation you find yourself in – whether it be by leaping on to the back of a bouncer who's beating the shit out of one of your fans, stopping a song entirely because the crowd is singing along, or messing up the intro to The Hit Song so completely it's unrecognisable – then you probably shouldn't be on stage at all. Play to yourself and your mum in the living room, spend years honing your craft in a recording studio with soft lights and wood panelling, but don't pretend to be a live rock band. It's the thin line that separates the mediocre from the great, The Vines from The White Stripes, Coldplay from Oasis, grunge catwalk chic (Offspring, Muse, Alice In Chains) from Nirvana. CDs and videos mislead: they can never hope to recapture the feeling you get when you experience something live, blood pounding in your temples, hair a matted, sticky mess. They are only documents, fading snapshots of a time that is already fast disappearing from memory, preserved only in celluloid and in digital sound and *Behind The Music* specials . . .

"We didn't have contracts. The standard etiquette was handshake deal, but over and above that, we did not have the money to hire an attorney. I reflect back on Nirvana's signing and sometimes it seems divinely orchestrated to me. For one thing, I wasn't at my house when Krist showed up that night. I was at my neighbour's, and for some reason I'd decided, 'I need to step out of the house.' And the moment I stepped outside, Krist walked up. If I had stepped out of the house a minute later I would have missed him, and he would have woken up sober the next day and probably not threatened to beat me up over the contract. Little things add up to big things. But he demanded a contract and he was intimidating. He was drunk and big and very aggressive. So I called up Jon and said, 'You've got to get this guy signed, cos he is pissed. This is something that has to happen.' Krist was in the room when I was talking to him, 'Get the contract. This guy is gonna kick my ass, OK?' So he went to the library and Xeroxed a contract out of some book, and used some whiteout and filled in some names. It was a 10-cent contract with no lawyer. When they signed it in the office, I remember thinking, 'This could be a significant moment.' It was the first time Sub Pop had signed a group."

Once they'd shed their temporary fourth member, Nirvana shows were raucous, genius, a jumble of blurred emotions and shattered strings – Chad Channing pounding his way through another floor tom like he was Dale Crover, Krist perpetually drunk and wreaking havoc, Kurt inviting wasted friends up on stage to sing while he sat himself down behind the drum kit and proceeded to hammer the audience's objections into silence. Encores got refused, got played out with no strings or guitars because every instrument in the place had been trashed, got spun out into painful abstractions of sound. Nirvana on record were the least of anyone's worries . . . since when did such a fun live band become massive?

"Oh, there was always a food fight. It was inevitable. These guys were like children. There was egg throwing, food fighting, putting CDs in the microwave, it was just ridiculous. After we got thrown out the *Nevermind* record release party we all went over to Susie's house and dressed the Nirvana guys up in dresses and put make-up on them and danced around the house and I think that was the night that Kurt was slingshot-ing eggs off of Susie's porch at the neighbours' cars. Kurt Bloch made a huge mountain of CDs in the living room and people started running at them. There was a bottle of pain medication on top of the refrigerator, and Kurt and I saw it and were like, 'Oh! Those look good!' So we took the rest of the bottle, and he and I decided it would be fun to jump from the bedroom window on to the roof of the garage next door. I remember sitting in that window just laughing and laughing, and then Susie or somebody wouldn't let us jump and we were pissed, like really mad that somebody was not going to let us do something so ridiculous. The next day Dylan came over and picked up Kurt to go shoot guns. They used to buy big hunks of meat at the store, big hams, and go out in the woods and . . ."

SHUT UP! SHUT UP! This is a book about Nirvana. You don't want anecdotes, hearsay. Personal journals should remain personal. Have you ever stopped to think that there might be a human being at the heart of all this? That not everything should be public property? Think about what you're saying, with all your talk of conspiracies, of drugs, of arguments and exploitation. Nirvana were a band. A fucking great live band that also benefited from some judicious radio-friendly production and the fact their lead singer had baby-blue eyes. All the other stuff is extraneous. Listen to the music. Listen to the music. Why do you feel the need to know more?

Do you remember Kurt saying anything about Courtney that night?

"He was sort of mumbling stuff about her. There was some talk about her trying to get him to go with her but he didn't want to. My friend Alex kept a journal back then, and she recently emailed me a quote from Kurt from that night that might've been about Courtney: 'I want to meet a woman twice as intelligent and half as jaded as I am.' So we went back to the apartments and it was quiet for a little while and then chaos ensued. There was a drunken English guy there and he was walking through the bushes. I don't remember why we were outside, I just remember this very drunk English guy yelling, 'I love Courtney Love. I love Courtney Love.'

Then he'd fall into the bush and we'd have to pick him up. 'I love Courtney Love. I want to marry Courtney Love.'"

Were you awake for most of that night?

"Well, Krist started throwing furniture out the window. He threw an ashtray and it hit Alex in the head on its way out. She started crying and he was so apologetic. I remember the apartment being trashed. Krist was the biggest and so he could pick up the biggest things: the coffee tables and the couches. The next day Alex and I went into Hollywood. I bought a guitar. I got an old tattoo covered that I'd wanted to get covered forever. There was a big party with Jennifer from L7, but Kurt didn't want to go, so he and I stayed home and watched TV. He wanted to finish lyrics and we watched a really cool cartoon that blew our minds – *Night Flight*. And then he wrote something down."

SHUT UP! SHUT UP! This is a book about Nirvana.

"Dress was not a big concern in Seattle. It still isn't. There's a picture of an early audience in '83, that I call the 'stray dogs from every village'. There is no uniform sense of style at all. There's a little bit of hippie, some glam, there's the trench coat, the flannel coat. One boy's got the leather jacket with the Sid Vicious pin on it, a little bit of punk. We just liked thrift store clothes. It was an amalgamation of stuff. It started to split up into camps. The Mudhoney camp was more into peg trousers and old school penguin shirts. A little more garage rock."

SHUT UP! SHUT UP! This is a book about Nirvana.

"While we were doing the demos, the cops came by. It was the only noise complaint we'd had at that studio in five years. It's an old building, with triple walls. It's soundproofed. And yet Dave was so loud there was a noise complaint from a house three doors away. I was out in front talking to the police. The cops said, 'You guys need to turn it down.' I was telling them, 'You guys know who Nirvana is?' I'm trying to explain to the cops that I've got Nirvana in here, and I'm trying to explain to Nirvana that I've got the cops outside. I'm going, 'What a time for the cops to show up – I'm doing demos for Nirvana. Jesus Christ, I'm going crazy!' What am I going to tell the band? We have to stop? It's a studio! The studio's been there since the Seventies."

None of this ever happened, and Kurt is still somewhere out there, nestling underneath a bridge in blue-collar America laughing at us all.

"All right, let's start with this: page 185. He says that I said, 'Kurt said to me, "Look! You can see their little arms and pieces floating in the tank."' Talking about the tadpoles that we had brought back from the quarry and he had in his aquarium in the apartment. And he says, 'A young man who used to save birds with broken wings was now delighting in watching tadpoles being devoured by turtles.' Kurt didn't throw the tadpoles in his tank thinking they were going to be killed by the turtles. He wanted them to grow up to be frogs. It was a mistake of reasoning on his part because he could have probably figured out that they would get devoured by the turtles and, yeah, he did point out the pieces of them to me, but I wouldn't say he was delighting in it, I would say he was horrified by it. And then he dumped that stuff out in the backyard and, yes, he was irresponsible, but I wouldn't say . . . I mean this makes him out to be some kind of a sadist. Which is just totally wrong."

Enough already.

This is a book about Nirvana. Some guy took drugs and killed himself. Some guy began looking outside the rock arena for fulfilment and moved into politics. Some guy fell in love with rock'n'roll and there he remains. Some guy never left home and is still on an island with his wife and kid, building studios in the air.

Welcome to the world of Nirvana.

# PART I

# UP

## CHAPTER 1

# Welcome To Aberdeen

*Hi, Everett*
*Most of my experience with Aberdeen is driving through it on the way to, or back from, a nice weekend on the coast. I have eaten at a couple of diners and fast food joints there, but that hardly makes me an expert on the place. One noticeable thing is that as soon as you leave Aberdeen and hit Hoquiam, the houses and streets are nicer. It's nothing fancy, it's just that the same kinds of houses are no longer rundown, and the yards, for the most part, are better kept. The towns merge into each other and if it weren't for the 'Welcome To Hoquiam' (or Aberdeen) signs, you wouldn't know that you were in one town or the other.*

*Aberdeen is a small (and small-minded) white trash town with high unemployment and, as such, isn't remarkably different than thousands of other small white trash towns with low employment across the US. If the environment of Aberdeen created Kurt Cobain, then there should be tens of thousands of Kurt Cobains. But there aren't. I don't think there's anything special, or especially bad, about Aberdeen. There are worse places with worse vibes – like Butte, Montana for instance. Butte hasn't produced a tortured soul – at least one that got out of there, unless that's what drove Evel Knievel to jump across the Snake River Canyon.*

*Love, Mark Arm*[1]

THE story of Nirvana begins in Aberdeen, in the US state of Washington.

Let me level with you.

I know little about the pasts of individual members of Nirvana. You'll discover some stuff about that in this book, but plenty more in others. I'm not good on history or bullshit. I'm not good on straightening out facts so rigidly they cease to bear any semblance to meaning. I've always preferred first-hand experience, first-hand recollections, even if this necessarily leads to contradiction and confusion because no two people view the same event in the same way, not collating together a jumble of assorted views and giving prominence to the most famous among them.

The salient facts about Nirvana's most famous member are well known by now: Kurt Donald Cobain was born on February 20, 1967 in Grays Harbour Community Hospital. His 21-year-old father Don worked as a mechanic at the Hoquiam Chevron garage; his teenage mother Wendy got pregnant just after graduating from high school. The family moved to central Aberdeen from Hoquiam six months after Kurt was born. Kurt had an imaginary childhood friend, Boddah, whom he created at the age of two, and would later believe to be real, listening back to the echo of his own voice on his Aunt Mari's tape recorder.[2] He was the centre of attention in an adoring family; there were seven aunts and uncles on his mother's side alone. A sister, Kimberley (Kim), was born when he was three. His relatives nurtured his musical leanings and his burgeoning artistic talent, presenting him with a ready stream of paintbrushes and a Mickey Mouse drum kit. Uncle Chuck played in a band and had some large speakers in his basement studio.

As an infant, Kurt would draw cartoon characters (Aquaman, Creature From The Black Lagoon) and sing Arlo Guthrie's 'Motorcycle Song'. The family would go on toboggan rides together. Kurt was later diagnosed as hyperactive and claimed to have thrown 7-Up cans full of pebbles at passing police cars, even from the age of six.

The singer died at the age of 27, victim of a self-inflicted shotgun blast.

Some like to question this last fact because some like to read conspiracy into everything around them: figure out that it's unfair that life rewards the avaricious and pushy, that those on top most often end up on top because they have so few scruples and are willing to trample on whomever it takes. Or maybe they just like a good story, no matter how hollow its basis. Some would be wrong. But hey, we'll try and remain open-minded to everything . . . perhaps Kurt wasn't born in Grays Harbour hospital, Aberdeen after all? No wait. That's verifiable. Other people were present.

Unlike suicide.

*Leg,*
*Hi. Have only been to Aberdeen once. Remote, desolate . . . working class. Lumber town? What's fascinating to me is: how unlikely the odds are of an act coming from, truly, The Middle Of Nowhere . . . to becoming the world's biggest band in . . . four years?*
*Bruce*[3]

Aberdeen is an isolated community situated in the south of America's most north-western state[4], an hour west of the state capital Olympia and just south of the Olympic Peninsula, home of the most formidable mountain range on the Pacific Coast. It's in an area that travel writers like to describe with the clichéd phrase 'outstanding natural beauty'. In Washington State's case the epithet is justified: mountains (the Olympics, the Cascades) and rivers and ocean inlets and vast fields of trees all wind round one another, locking and interlocking and taking the breath away on a sunny day – which it rarely is. You wouldn't know about beauty if you were born in Aberdeen, though: the town is dominated by its lumber mills and sawmills, and especially the towering Rayonier Mill, pumping white smoke from 150 feet in the sky.

Aberdeen is a Scottish name, meaning 'confluence of two rivers': the town is located on the banks of the Chehalis and Wishkah rivers. For a hundred years, Aberdeen was a timber mill town on a bay, Grays Harbour, at the foot of the mountains. By the late Seventies, the region ran out of trees to cut down, and all businesses of any size were shuttered. The grand department stores downtown were emptied of merchandise and reborn as flea markets selling old books, magazines and second-hand clothes for a nickel a pound. In its heyday in the early twentieth century, Aberdeen was home to a population of more than 50,000. It now boasts less than a third of that. It's a dying town. Aberdeen in 2006 is pretty much unchanged from back when a teenage Kurt Cobain used to spray incomprehensible graffiti in alleyways.

Unemployment's high in Aberdeen: unemployment and alcoholism and the suicide rate.[5] There's little for youth to do except run around drunk and light small fires in disused junkyards, or pick the psychedelic mushrooms that grow in the fields around the edges of town. Initially, Aberdeen prospered because its logging industry was serviced by a railroad terminus and seaport that engaged men who squandered their wages in its saloons and bordellos. But successive American governments in the Sixties and Seventies systematically ran down the railroads; the logging industry became decentralised and sailors started looking elsewhere for their pleasures after a crackdown on prostitution in the Fifties. Sounds grim, but Aberdeen is no different to anywhere else in small-town America – if it's not logging, it's strip-mining or oil-drilling, though nowadays it's more likely to be corporate chains like Wal-Mart moving in, leeching the heart out of a small community and moving out again once they've sucked it dry.

"Aberdeen was apocalyptic in the way old industrial towns are when the economy dies and there is no money or jobs," explains Olympia musician Tobi Vail.

When people talk about 25 per cent of the US population being near or below the poverty line[6], they're talking about Aberdeen. The difference between Aberdeen and the similarly depressed Olympia is that Olympia is rich enough to have a homeless community. Vagrants simply don't bother coming to Aberdeen – they know there's nothing for them there. It's simple US economics: the side of America politicians never like to talk about. You don't have many rights, just the right to exist. No one wants to know you because you're not rich or powerful enough to be part of any political agenda. You don't vote so you don't count. It's not like there isn't beauty around Aberdeen, though. You can find a veritable treasure trove trawling through its thrift stores and church halls – but you need to focus, like the camera blowing on an empty carrier bag at the end of *American Beauty*.

That's one point of view.

Others feel there's plenty to appreciate about the town.

"I don't think it's fair to say Aberdeen's inhabitants don't appreciate its beauty," comments former K recording artist Rich Jensen. "Aberdeen's raw wildness – its lack of structure – is one of the main things that keeps them there; the freedom to take a leak off your porch in the moonlight; the pleasures of rolling a junked car into a ravine and shooting at it periodically over a summer or two. I think the residents and working people of rural towns enjoy the quiet: the eagles that rest in the tops of the pines, the smell of sea air at dawn, etc – and they extract a satisfaction in believing that they deserve the charms of their rugged landscape because they work there, they belong there, they know what the place is, where the bones were broken, not like the aesthetes from the cities who see only a shallow, sunny afternoon's image of the land."

Imagine a grey, rainy afternoon in the Pacific Northwest.

As we set out from Olympia to Aberdeen on a highway that weaves through densely forested and hilly terrain, we're playing the obligatory Nirvana soundtrack followed by the theme music from *Twin Peaks*.[7] There are few stops along the way and the only signs of life are a handful of scattered farms, dilapidated barns and the occasional abandoned, sometimes half-built, breeze-block building whose purpose is ambiguous. Before you reach Aberdeen, there's a small town called Montesano. This is where Kurt lived with his dad for a time. The man working at the Chevron station immediately identifies us as 'big towners'. He knows we aren't from the area because he knows everyone in the town. He explains that most people pass through here on their way to the big casinos in Ocean Shores. If it wasn't for the constant drizzle and gusty winds, we could probably comfortably traverse the city limits in an hour by foot.

Kurt's dad's old home is on Fleet Street, not too far off the freeway (there again, nothing is). The house is of modest size and well-kept, just a few houses away from the end of the street – a dead end – which leads to a repair shop that services cement trucks and construction equipment. The nearby railroad tracks appear to be derelict. A bike ride away is the combined junior high/high school where Kurt went for his freshman year. There is a small baseball field across the street, and a parking lot that could probably accommodate 20 cars or SUVs.

Driving into Aberdeen, it's hard to tell whether the sky is covered in fog, clouds or smoke from the smokestacks. Dense forest appears to surround the freeway and the river, but on closer examination the area is barren behind the first layer of trees. There is a logging factory immediately to the left, across the water. Timber is stacked up and stretches out in piles for several acres. What little traffic there is can be attributed to trucks toting lumber, RVs and station wagons. As we cross the city limits, we get to see the new, improved Aberdeen sign. As of April 2005, the Kurt Cobain Memorial Committee erected a new board with the words 'Come As You Are'[8] added to the bottom of 'Welcome To Aberdeen'. There's nowhere convenient to pull off the main stretch of road to take pictures, so we do what a few others have already clearly done (tyre marks as evidence), stopping on the narrow hard shoulder.

Near the bridge there's a Scenic Overlook point that perversely overlooks lumber-yards and smokestacks. There is a Wal-Mart with American flags adorning its façade, a McDonald's with its familiar yellow arch, Taco Bell, Ross and Pizza Hut – the corporate images from a thousand American malls giving the temporary illusion of a successful, commercial area. Once we drive on a mile or so further, however, across another bridge, the picture is entirely different. Many of the homes are boarded up and businesses closed down. A pretty even mix of mom and pop stores litter the town's main shopping area, and the neighbourhoods are mostly small houses situated close together, decked out in the faded pastel colours popular in the Seventies. The rain, the constant cloud, the fumes and the distant rumble of Highway 12 create a tepid pall across the town. The city seems worn out.

If it was sunny, you could imagine kids gathering in the park to play among the sea lion statues that shoot water from their mouths.

Our first stop is underneath North Aberdeen Bridge, a short road span that straddles the Wishkah River where legend has it that a runaway Kurt Cobain slept during the winter of 1985. We park on the dead-end street where Kurt's family lived (First Street), walk one block down to the crest of the bridge, climb through some overgrown brush and weeds and skittle down an embankment to its underbelly. There's no official monument: instead there's a few empty beer cans, some faded graffiti . . . *I ♥ Kurt, cobaincase.com, Kurt Rests in Heaven, 20 hour drive to see your bridge – we love you Kurt, Kurdt*[9]*: am I stupid for writing on this walright now, or is it still OK to? Your music is a gift to us all . . .* piles of cigarette butts and some random bits of trash. It seems almost cosy down here, with a surprising amount of shelter and refuge from the rain. Like the names of so many American rivers, Wishkah sounds exotic, a throwback to the Native Americans who would have bathed in, washed in and drank from its waters – but this is a brown and murky Wishkah, littered with broken wood and pilings jutting out from the surface. The woods reach all the way to the banks of the river.

The First Street residence is covered in chipped paint and surrounded by unkempt rose bushes. It's not deserted, but the house and its neighbours are eerily quiet. Where is everyone? An overweight kid wearing a Grateful Dead T appears from the house across the street. He eyes us suspiciously from his front porch. We decide to move on as his painfully overweight mother emerges from their home, an equally suspicious look on her heavy face.

Down the street, there's a clerk inside a spacious Thriftway shop explaining to a customer that 60-year-olds and over get their discount on Tuesdays only. The store sells everything from used wire hangers to fabrics, old trophies, folders and binders, clothing, baskets, tins and cheap Halloween decorations. There is a shelf with old romance novels, self-help manuals and a wide variety of religious works. The clerk sees us taking notes and asks us, dryly, what we're doing. We explain that we're just going around learning about Nirvana. She says: "Oh right, Nir-van-a. Is that the guy that died?"

We walk around the corner to 'the shack' where Kurt and Matt Lukin lived: it's now completely unliveable (perhaps it always was), the windows boarded up and the roof caved in. The paint is stripped away and there are nails protruding from several surfaces. Graffiti on the side says, 'Cripts Rule'. They could at least spell it right. Other vacant, decaying houses surround the shack, as if one diseased house has infected the rest. There is one well-kept home decorated with 'Support Our Troops' and 'United

We Stand' stickers[10], but mostly this particular street is uninhabited . . . left to fall by the wayside.

Kurt and Krist's high school, Aberdeen High – home of the Aberdeen Bobcats – is housed in an unexpectedly small building; two, maybe three, storeys high. A fire occurred recently in the historic wing, apparently caused by students attempting to burn school records. The absent wing has been replaced with a gravel parking lot, with spaces for cars marked on the rocks with spray paint. This building looks like a large cinderblock, prison-like . . . anyone seeing it for the first time might well be tempted to drop out, just like Kurt. A large yellow and blue painted rock rests on a platform. It's hard to figure out its significance – maybe Aberdeen's take on abstract art?

We visit Judy's, an antique book and record shop next door to Krist's mom's old hair salon, which is across the street from what used to be the YMCA where Kurt worked. The place seems closed because the doors and windows are entirely blocked with books, but Judy sees us and lets us in. She's not usually open on Wednesdays, she says. Judy remembers the Nirvana guys coming in quite often, mostly buying records. She says Shelli (Krist's ex-wife) sometimes bought games, and Krist's mom would do her hair.

Aberdeen feels lethargic. The products in the antique shops sum the place up: overused, dirty and neglected. There are billboards and marquees spouting bible verses and religious propaganda: it's that sort of a town. There's even a pastor on the sidewalk, waving to oncoming traffic as if beckoning them into his church, like those guys who wear sandwich boards or chicken costumes to advertise the daily specials.

This is the reality that Kurt Cobain – and childhood friend Krist Novoselic (of Croatian heritage and also the product of a broken home) – was born into. A place that maybe once existed, once had a heart and bustling soul but is now just another white trash trailer stop off the freeway, a place you'd never visit in a million years unless you had a reason to.

"Aberdeen was real scary: redneck, hell town, backwoods, like a village or a big city for lumberjacks," Krist told me in Nirvana's first mainstream interview in February 1989. "You see Jack Nicholson in *Easy Rider* talking about rednecks? About how if they see something different they don't go running scared, they get dangerous. Aberdeen's like that. But they were so bone-headed, why shouldn't we be different from them?"

"Aberdeen was really out there," comments former Nirvana drummer Chad Channing from the relative security of his present-day house on

Bainbridge Island, a ferry-ride away from Seattle. "It was a total logger town or something, you know? It's this place I could never picture living in. These people just seemed to work all day and drink all night. It seemed kind of rundown. It's a place on the verge of not being a town any more. Why did you go there and why is this place – how is it existing? What keeps it running?"

A lot of towns are like that in America.

"Well, it makes you wonder," he replies. "In every small town there are usually people who have lived there their whole lives. Aberdeen's one of those towns where I couldn't imagine doing that. How could you do that? Down the road you could be in your seventies or eighties. 'I've been here all my life.' 'Geez, I'm sorry – you're not dead yet?' "

Kurt Cobain was eight when his parents divorced, the reasons predictably similar to those of thousands of other couples caught in the same predicament. They married too young, and the harsh economic pressures of trying to keep their small household together drove them apart. Don Cobain changed jobs in '74, and took an entry-level job into the timber industry – office work at Mayr Brothers – but at $4.10 an hour, less than he'd been earning as a mechanic. The Cobains would frequently borrow money from Don's parents, Leland and Iris. Kurt became increasingly wayward, and his father tried to keep him in line, inflicting almost daily psychological punishments – thumping him on the chest with two fingers – and, of course, there was the famed 'lump of coal' Christmas present, wherein Don and Wendy threatened Kurt he'd only receive a lump of coal in his Christmas stocking if he continued fighting with his sister. It didn't happen – it was meant as a joke – but it left enough of an imprint on a young Kurt for him to claim later that it did, that on Christmas morning one year he found a lump of coal by his bed instead of a five-dollar Starsky and Hutch gun.[11]

"My story is exactly the same as 90 per cent of everyone my age," he told *Guitar World*. "Everyone's parents got divorced. Their kids smoked pot all through high school, they grew up during the era when there was a massive Communist threat and everyone thought they were going to die from a nuclear war. And everyone's personalities are practically the same."

The year before the divorce was, by all accounts, pleasurable for the Cobains – there was a trip to Disneyland south of Los Angeles, and a visit to the hospital where Kurt's broken arm was reset after some boisterous rough-and-tumble with Don's brother Gary had gone too far; even the unlikely image of Kurt stepping out as a baseball player in his local Little

League team. It was suggested that his hyperactivity might be due to attention deficit disorder. Food colourings were removed from his diet, followed by sugar. When that didn't work and he was still marching round the house banging a drum and screaming at the top of his voice[12], he was placed on Ritalin for three months.

It was the divorce that really changed Kurt's perspective on life. Almost overnight he became withdrawn. His mother Wendy told Nirvana biographer Michael Azerrad that Kurt became "real sullen, kind of mad and always frowning and ridiculing". On the wall of his bedroom in June 1976, a few months after the divorce, Kurt scrawled, "I hate Mom, I hate Dad, Dad hates Mom, Mom hates Dad, it simply makes you want to be sad," with caricatures of his parents to one side. The divorce was acrimonious: Wendy wanted to split from Don because she felt he wasn't around very much; Don contested the split and remained in a state of denial for a considerable period afterwards. Both parents admitted they used the kids in the war between them. Wendy got the house and the kids; Don was granted the 1965 Ford pick-up truck; Wendy got the 1968 Camaro; Don was instructed to pay $150 a month child support.

Don moved into his parents' Montesano trailer. Kurt hated his mom's new boyfriend, who was prone to violent fits and whom he called "a mean wife-beater" (he once broke Wendy's arm). Soon after the divorce he asked to live with his dad. Don was granted custody in June 1979. For the remainder of his formative years the troubled child was bounced back and forth between parents and relatives. Kurt began to develop stomach problems, caused by malnutrition. Initially, Kurt felt buoyed by the close relationship developed through necessity between father and son, even though Don's idea of a bonding experience was to take him to work. Later, he felt betrayed after Don remarried – to Jenny Westby, who had two kids of her own, of whom Kurt felt intensely jealous.

From being a happy, outgoing kid, Kurt became incredibly insecure.

## NOTES

1 Mark Arm: singer with Mudhoney, the archetypal late Eighties Seattle band for whom the term 'grunge' was coined. Arm was a major influence on Kurt Cobain.

2 Mari – sister to Wendy – claims to be the first person to have placed a guitar in Kurt's hands, when he was two. She was 15 years old, and played guitar herself. "He turned it around the other way because he was left-handed," she told Seattle journalist Gillian G. Gaar.

3 Bruce Pavitt, founder of Sub Pop records. Leg is a reference to my stage name, The Legend!, which is how I was first introduced to many in this story.

4 Strictly speaking Washington is the most north-western state in the contiguous 48 states. Let's not forget Alaska.

5 Aberdeen's suicide rate was twice the national average in 1991, at 27 people per 100,000. In July '79, one of Kurt's great-uncles, Burle Cobain, committed suicide (gunshot to the abdomen). Five years later, Burle's brother Kenneth shot himself in the head. By choosing to die the way he did, Kurt – either knowingly or unknowingly – chose the perfect Aberdeen death.

6 *Financial Times* magazine, May 18, 2005.

7 Kurt described his home town as being like "*Twin Peaks* . . . without the excitement." In actuality, *Twin Peaks* was filmed 162 miles up the road at the rather picturesque blue-collar holiday resort Snoqualmie Falls.

8 'Come As You Are' was the second single lifted from *Nevermind*.

9 Kurdt was the spelling Kurt first gave to his name in Nirvana. He also briefly spelt his surname Kobain.

10 Olympia's nearest neighbour is an army base, Fort Lewis.

11 The 'Bean' in his daughter's name, Frances Bean Cobain, is a reference to the lump of coal – Kurt's own spin on his imaginary childhood present.

12 Cartoon images spring to mind. First, there's Charlie Brown in *Peanuts*, cast adrift on his pitcher's mound, the eternal optimist despite all the evidence to the contrary – and then Calvin, the insatiable hyperactive kid with his imaginary friend, the toy tiger Hobbes, in Bill Watterson's brilliant Nineties *Peanuts* equivalent, *Calvin And Hobbes*. In one four-panel strip, Calvin can be seen hammering nails into the dining-room table. His mother screams at him: "WHAT ARE YOU DOING?" Calvin stops for a minute, considers and then looks up at her, all innocence, and says, "Is this a trick question or what?"

CHAPTER 2

# Don't Want To Be Confused

1. *The Melvins are not heavy metal.*
2. *They are conceptual artists working in a pop vein.*
3. *Think Boredoms, Sonic Youth, Captain Beefheart.*[1]
4. *There is no better band. Equally good, yes, but better, no.*
5. *They are completely misunderstood by fans and critics.*
6. *They are hilarious.*
7. *They are sadists.*
8. *They are highly intelligent.*
9. *They are punk, not hardcore. Think Sex Pistols, Dead Kennedys, not Fugazi or Bikini Kill.*[2]
10. *They were influenced by The Wipers.*[3] *This is what they have in common with Beat Happening.*[4] *The Wipers and the Melvins were influenced by Hendrix.*[5] *This is what they don't have in common with Beat Happening.*
11. *If Northwest music was split into a chart of influences, most bands could be traced back to The Wipers, the Melvins, Jimi Hendrix or Beat Happening. Nirvana was influenced by all four. The other two ingredients were desperation and The Beatles.*

(Taken from www.bumpidee.com)

LIFE wasn't much fun for Kurt Cobain, post-divorce.

Kurt refused to eat with his new family; joined the school's wrestling team on the insistence of Don but refused to fight back on the day of the big tournament, sitting on the mat with his arms folded; didn't want to go hunting; wore a pageboy haircut and bell-bottom jeans; and doodled constantly in class. He watched *Close Encounters Of The Third Kind* and recounted its dialogue word-for-word to his stepbrother James; made his own Super-8 snuff movie at the age of 11; talked about becoming a big rock star and going out in a blaze of glory like Jimi Hendrix . . . no big deal, many kids are overtly concerned with death and attention. He was left-handed, artistic in a town that viewed art as the closest thing to gay (his mother later forbade him from hanging around with a gay friend); he smoked the marijuana that grew around Montesano.

Musically speaking, Kurt's taste wasn't improving: some might view his progression from liking the odd Beatles record to championing Journey's heinous early Eighties album *Evolution* as a step backwards. Ironically, he would later compare rivals Pearl Jam to the self-same stadium rock band when seeking to dismiss their music as holding no credibility whatsoever. Maybe teenage boys should be banned from listening to rock music: it'd sure put paid to the careers of such ageing wannabe juvenile delinquents as Velvet Revolver and anyone still impressed by Mick Jagger's pout. In 1981, Kurt began life as a freshman at Montesano High School. In a clearly doomed attempt to please his dad and not stand out from his peers, he joined the football and track teams.[6]

In February, Uncle Chuck decided it was time to buy Kurt a proper teenage birthday present. It was to prove a decisive turning point. "I was offered the choice once between a guitar and a bicycle for my birthday," he told me eight years later – before adding mendaciously, "so I took the bicycle.[7] Why did I start playing music? Boredom, I guess. I wanted to be able to play the drums," he added, referring to his old childhood toy. "I still do."

The guitar was cheap, second-hand and Japanese – a Lindell – but it was more than enough for Kurt. He called up his Aunt Mari to ask if the strings should be strung alphabetically. He carried it with him everywhere as a badge of pride, even though he could barely play it through the tiny 10-watt amp Chuck also gave him. In March 1982 – after having been moved down to the basement – Kurt decided to leave his dad's house: first, he went to his paternal grandparents' trailer, then on to his Uncle Jim's house in South Aberdeen. He found Aberdeen intimidating compared to Montesano.

"There are actually about a hundred *really* small towns in south-west Washington," Tobi Vail explains. "I lived in Naselle, WA, which is one hour south, and to us Aberdeen seemed really big – they had city buses, a library, a post office, a handful of restaurants and stores; stuff that rural places don't have."

Uncle Jim smoked pot and had a hipper record collection than his brother Don: The Grateful Dead[8], Led Zeppelin and The Beatles; stoner musical influences that Kurt absorbed, encouraged by older school buddies sporting tie-dyed T-shirts and feathered hair who'd drop by to mooch off Jim's food supply. "I just thought they were cooler than my geeky fourth-grade friends who watched *Happy Days*," Kurt told biographer Azerrad.

From Jim's, Kurt was passed around from relative to relative – including Uncle Chuck's where the young Cobain began taking guitar lessons from one of Chuck's bandmates, Warren Mason. Mason found Kurt a proper guitar – an Ibanez costing $125 – and tuition began in earnest: such classic rock standards as 'Stairway To Heaven'[9], 'Louie Louie'[10] and AC/DC's 'Back In Black' being among the first songs learned.

In '82, Kurt moved back into his mother's house at 1210 East First Street and was transferred to his parents' old school, Aberdeen's Weatherwax High. Once again he felt like an outcast, a situation probably aggravated by his choice of class – commercial and basic art, where he'd draw crude cartoons of Michael Jackson, sperms and Ronald Reagan, and make rudimentary Claymation movies.

"I was a scapegoat," the singer told music journalist Jon Savage, "but not in the sense that people picked on me all the time. They didn't beat me up because I was already so withdrawn. I was so antisocial that I was almost insane. I wouldn't have been surprised if they had voted me 'Most Likely To Kill Everyone At A High School Dance'."

Wendy had started dating younger men, and delighted in sunbathing in her bikini: Kurt was embarrassed by the attention his mom would get and hit any friend who'd joke about it – which many of them did, especially as his mom bought them beer and let them stay over. In February '83, Kurt turned 16 and passed his driver's test. Several weeks later, he saw his first rock show: Sammy Hagar[11] at Seattle Center Coliseum.[12] Impressed by the show's theatrics he turned up at school the next day wearing a Hagar T-shirt. He was later to feel embarrassed at his teenage proclivity, but he certainly didn't deny his past as has since been claimed. This is how he described the event to me:

"Everyone was passing round pot and I got really high and lit myself on fire. I had a Bic lighter in my sweatshirt pocket and I was watching Sammy, swinging upside-down from the rafters, mocking everyone else who was holding their lighters above their heads. I looked down and petrol had spilt out everywhere and my shirt was on fire. It went well with the piss-stained pants. I got those before the show when we drank a case of beer and got stuck in a traffic jam. There was nowhere to go so I peed my pants in the back of the car.

"In the bathroom there was a passed-out, drunken seventh grader lying in the piss trough. People relieved themselves on him throughout the concert, not even caring. There were these two girls cutting lines of coke on a small mirror when, all of a sudden, a drunken man fell behind their chairs and vomited all over their laps. The girls had their boyfriends beat up the drunken coke killer."

Journalists would attempt to make something out of the fact that Kurt Cobain – like 99 per cent of his peers in small town America – saw some butt rock band at his first ever show; and even caught UK hard rock/metal outfit Judas Priest at the Tacoma Dome the same summer. Kurt also once owned an REO Speedwagon album. So what? Doesn't mean he'd found his calling: just that he didn't know where to look. It wasn't until mid-'83 that Kurt discovered what he'd – unknowingly – been searching for.

It was during that summer that Kurt Cobain discovered the Melvins – and through the Melvins, the world of punk rock. "I remember hanging out at Montesano, Washington's Thriftway," he wrote in his journal[13], "when this short-haired employee box-boy who kinda looked like the guy in Air Supply handed me a flyer that read: 'the Them festival, tomorrow night in the parking lot behind Thriftway. Free, live rock music'." The employee in question was Melvins' singer Buzz Osborne, an older pupil at Montesano High. Melvins had formed the year before[14], playing the sped-up hardcore that was in fashion among US bands such as Dead Kennedys and the Minutemen.[15]

"I showed up with stoner friends in a van . . ." Kurt continued. "They played faster than I had ever imagined music could be played and with more energy than my Iron Maiden records could provide. This was what I had been looking for. Ah, punk rock."

Nirvana historians conflict over what happened next: in one account, it's claimed that Buzz passed along copies of over-feted US rock magazine *Creem* to Kurt. In others, Kurt claims to have had a subscription to *Creem* at the age of 12, following the exploits of The Sex Pistols as they disintegrated on their calamitous tour of the US in January 1978. Excited, he took out a copy of the only 'punk' record on offer at Aberdeen's library, The Clash's sprawling, mediocre triple album set *Sandinista*.

"I blame that record for not allowing me to get into punk rock faster than I wanted to," he told me later. "When I got that, I said, 'If this is punk rock I don't want to have anything to do with it.'"

Whatever the truth, there's no denying that the Melvins – Buzz Osborne with his shock-headed afro; hard-pounding drummer and Neil Young lookalike Dale Crover; and heavy drinking bassist Matt Lukin – were to change Kurt's life irretrievably. Buzz gave Kurt a mixtape of underground US punk bands, mostly Californian hardcore like Flipper, MDC[16] and Black Flag.

The first were a seminal dissonant psychedelic punk band from San

Francisco, closer to conceptual art than rock music. The influence of their menacing debut single, 'Love Canal'/'Ha Ha Ha' (1981), can clearly be heard in the Melvins – slowing down the thrash and becoming even stranger. The second were more notable for their fierce polemic – the anti-police 'I Remember' and anti-capitalism 'Corporate Death Burger' – than their music. The testosterone-charged Black Flag, meanwhile, took the raw directness of the Ramones, merged it with rhythmic changes and topped it off with lyrics that dwelt harshly on alienation, loneliness and paranoia. 1981's *Damaged* is a benchmark of US punk rock – the aggression in its grooves frequently spilled over into fist-fights at live shows.

Popular legend has it that the first song on Buzz's tape was Black Flag's apocryphal 'Damaged II', with singer Henry Rollins screaming, *"I'm confused/ I'm confused/ Don't want to be confused."*[17]

"With Melvins, context was everything," Dawn Anderson, former editor of Seattle fanzine *Backlash* explains. "The Eighties were very anti-rock, and a lot of us thought it was great that these guys were willing to completely lose their heads and rock out without the slightest embarrassment. At their early shows there would always be some whiney hipster standing next to me saying, 'I can't tell if they're kidding or not!' They totally blew those people a new asshole.

"I partied with them a time or two," she continues. "I bonded with Buzz over pro-wrestling. I was a suburban heavy metal gal, and never met too many people I could talk about things like that with. I remember a party where Matt Lukin almost blew up my house. 'Oh, you mean this is *real* dynamite? Sorry.' Later, he spilled orange juice, got down on all fours and licked it off my rug. He'd charm every girl who walked in the room by saying, 'Is that your head or did someone crap on your shoulders?' I thought he was great."

"Melvins were kids from Aberdeen who'd come up to the hardcore shows in town [Seattle]," explains Mudhoney guitarist Steve Turner. "They stood out because we didn't see them anywhere else but they looked like anybody: short hair, Converse, Vans. Matt had dyed hair. The top dog hardcore band was The Accused, but the Melvins were faster and tighter. Then everyone started reaching for other music . . . and they reached further. Black Flag influenced them to do that. Black Flag was just huge."

Black Flag slowed their music down – notably on 1984's *My War* – so Melvins slowed their music down. But Melvins took it to extremes: an unbelievably dense, sludgy grind, that on 1987's thunderous *Gluey Porch Treatments* album helped inspire a new musical form, grunge.

⋆ ⋆ ⋆

The greatest pop music is throwaway. There to be listened to one moment and discarded the next. I can understand musicians not liking to be told this, but critics have for too long indulged them on this point. Many bands have only one idea, and most not even that. The rest of their career is then spent in a hopeless quest to recapture the initial buzz. Why else do so many musicians turn to excess drink and drugs after a few years in? It's because they have no way of *feeling* otherwise.

I love Melvins because they are loud, basic and primal. That's it. They've had their one idea and they're not budging from it. They want to rock, and they do just that, with no consideration for taste or sales or carving out a place in history. It's the real grunge. Together, the Melvins have a knack of slowing time down so each note seems to last an eternity. This is indubitably a good thing, if only because life is too short.

Melvins received attention because Nirvana were fans, but even without their patronage they would've attained cult status. Bands as focused as that always do. Even their fiercest enemies have to admire their singularity of purpose. Through their inexorable grind, the Melvins provided a sense of community to Aberdeen friends who felt outside of their peers. Everyone needs to feel special and if that means supporting a band few others understand, all the better.

In the Eighties, while Lukin was still in the band, Melvins scared and confused the hardcore punks by playing even heavier chord sequences than Flipper. Not in a guitar store show-off way, more like James Brown or Ted Nugent where everybody played the same thing: the music was one huge power riff. Dale Crover hit the drums so hard he would wear gardening gloves, underwear and nothing else on stage.

"They were like nothing you'd seen before," explains Mudhoney drummer Dan Peters. "They were great performers – Matt gave it his all, Buzz was totally rocking, while Dale would sit behind his cobbled-together drum kit that looked like it was tied together with baling wire. They wore furry-collared Levi's vests. Somehow I got a vibe on them. When Matt joined Mudhoney, I was shitting my pants. Mark and Steve were in Green River and I'm like, 'Eh, whatever,' but I was like: 'I'm going to be in a band with the guy from the Melvins!' [Green River were Mark Arm and Steve Turner's pre-Mudhoney Seattle band, notable for containing a couple of future members of Pearl Jam, releasing the first Northwestern record on Sub Pop records, the *Dry As A Bone* EP, and for being *the* proto-grunge group of the Eighties.]

"The first practice we had with Matt was killer," Peters continues. "I was 20 and still not old enough to buy beer. Matt comes down with a buddy of his and we're like, 'Let's go to the store and buy some beer before practice.' Matt's like, 'Sounds good,' grabs a half case of beer and is like, 'Got mine!' I was like, 'Well, I'm not of age, but I'll take one of those!' "

In America, you're deemed old enough to drive a car and fight for your country long before you're allowed to down an alcoholic beverage in public. Fake IDs are a way of life: this restriction directly affects rock shows – most small gigs take place in bars where under-21s are not allowed. Hence the rise of all-ages shows championed by Fugazi and Beat Happening.

"The first time I saw Melvins was amazing," says Tom Hazelmyer, boss of Amphetamine Reptile records. The Minneapolis label was home to a circus of the insane during the Nineties, where singers would stab themselves in the ass with large crucifixes while singing about salvation and serial killing, where it was as important to be a showman as to rock out. Best-known bands on AmRep included Helmet[18], Cows[19] and the libidinous Nashville Pussy.

"It was in Seattle '84," Haze continues. "Some friends from back home were playing – Hüsker Dü.[20] All of a sudden the opening band starts up, the Melvins. What the fuck! They were doing the same stuff as now but hardcore speed. It was insane."

Melvins played a major role in Nirvana's career. You can trace their influence through to latter-day Nirvana improvisational encores such as 'Endless, Nameless', where the trio would take a riff and build upon it for as long as it took. Most importantly, it was via the Melvins that Kurt met his future bassist, lanky Aberdeen resident Krist Novoselic.

"One of the first times I met Krist was at Bob Whittaker's[21] cabin on the Washington coast," recalls Seattle photographer Charles Peterson. "We were having a bonfire on the beach and Krist drank a good portion of a bottle of whiskey. As the whiskey went down, a piece of clothing came off. By the end of the evening he was naked on the beach, running up and down. The rest of us were all bundled up. I was freezing. And he was like, 'Whoa,' running and singing."

How would you describe Krist?

"Goofy," responds Kelly Canary, former singer with Seattle all-girl chaos band Dickless. "Back then he was just the big, tall guy that fell on stuff. He was like the Chevy Chase of grunge."

Krist Anthony Novoselic was born in Compton, California on May 16, 1965, the first-born of Croatian immigrants Krist and Maria.

Krist Novoselic senior first fled his childhood village of Veli Iz in 1955[22] in an attempt to escape Marshall Tito's communist rule. The 17-year-old walked 74 miles north along the Adriatic coast with three other men. After four days they reached Trieste, Italy where they were thrown in jail for three months. He was later held in a refugee camp for six months before signing up to work on a tugboat on the River Rhine – reaching America six years later. After briefly living on the East Coast, he began fishing for tuna, mackerel, salmon and squid. Soon after, he moved to Gardena, CA where he got a job driving a truck delivering Sparklets drinking water. Maria came out to join him a year later.

Two other children were born after Krist: Robert and their younger sister Diana. During their pre-teen years, the brothers felt no real affinity towards their peers and soon resorted to vandalism: "Robert and I were kind of big boys and we used to get into trouble," Krist told Michael Azerrad. "Slash tyres, stuff like that. My dad would just have to whip us, because that's all he knew how to do. We were scared of him. But it wasn't like he was an abuser. It was action and reaction."

The move to Aberdeen in 1979 – necessitated by rising California property values and the attraction of ready work for Novoselic senior as a machinist in one of the town's lumber mills – was not met with wholehearted approval by all the family. Aberdeen had a sizeable Croatian community, but compared with Gardena it seemed like an East European town to Krist: people were judgemental; the clothes were dated – flares compared to Krist and Robert's straight-leg Levi's. Aberdeen High School kids listened to the Top 40 but Krist preferred Black Sabbath, Led Zeppelin and Devo.[23] The Novoselic family moved into a house on Think Of Me Hill, so named because there had been a sign promoting 'Think Of Me' tobacco on the spot several decades earlier.

The young Krist – six foot seven, gangly like Joey Ramone skipped a couple of generations – would have looked out of place in even the most liberal of cities. In Aberdeen he must've stood out like a ballad on a Black Flag record. Kurt recalled seeing him sabotaging Aberdeen High assemblies: he described him as a "really clever, funny, loudmouth person [that] everyone laughed at, even though he was smarter than them".

Krist grew depressed in the small, rainy, provincial surroundings of Aberdeen: "I couldn't get along with those kids," he complained. "They were assholes. They treated me really badly."

In June 1980, concerned for his state of mind, his parents sent Krist to live with relatives in Croatia, then still part of Yugoslavia. There, Krist became fluent in Croatian and even heard some punk rock – The Sex

Pistols, Ramones, and local bands. Not that it made too much of an impression.

"The slick, canned sounds of mainstream heavy metal didn't appeal to me," he wrote in his autobiography, 2004's *Of Grunge And Government, Let's Fix This Broken Democracy*. "Yugoslavia had a home-grown scene with good, diverse music. But when I returned to the US, I found that it was hard for punk to make its way to Aberdeen because of its geographic isolation."

Frustrated on his return by the stupidity of the Aberdeen kids who treated him like some sort of a freak, Krist became a heavy drinker and began to smoke marijuana. He wasn't even known by his native name in Aberdeen – he spelt his name Chris in a forlorn attempt to fit in. He went back to the original spelling in 1992 in a show of solidarity with his native Croatia when Yugoslavia dissolved amid some of the most terrible and bloody fighting seen in Europe since World War II. Indeed, one can trace Krist's present-day championing of voters' rights and discriminated-against people to his parents' homeland's turbulent history.

After several months of partying, Krist got a job at Taco Bell. He started saving, eventually having enough for a car, a guitar and a pair of stereo speakers. Alongside brother Robert, he began taking guitar lessons from Warren Mason[24], but soon quit and retreated to his bedroom where he'd spend days picking out B.B. King riffs.

Then he, too, met Buzz and Matt of the Melvins. There's a great story in Azerrad's *Come As You Are* about when Lukin first caught sight of Krist at the Taco Bell: "There was a big, tall, doofy guy back there," Lukin recalled, "singing along to the Christmas carols they were playing on the Muzak." Via the Melvins, Krist discovered punk bible/fanzine *Maximumrocknroll*. Through its pages, he was introduced to the activism of politically charged hardcore bands like Minor Threat.

"As a badge of my independence, I dressed differently from the status quo, and unlike some punks, I didn't dress dangerously," he explained in his autobiography. "I didn't have a Mohawk or a studded leather jacket. I didn't throw away my Aerosmith or Led Zeppelin records either."

It was around this time that Kurt first registered Krist – via Robert, who brought him round to the Novoselic house. Kurt asked what the noise was coming from upstairs: "Oh that's my brother," Robert replied. "He listens to punk rock."

Tell me the story about when you first heard about Nirvana.

"When I lived in Seattle as a teenager during the Eighties, I went to every fucking show that happened," begins Slim Moon, founder of Riot Grrrl label kill rock stars[25] and ex-neighbour of Kurt Cobain. "Good or bad, that was my life. A friend would drive me to the shows, even if they were in Bellingham or Anacortes or Bremerton or Olympia or Tacoma or Ellensburg. Green River was the biggest band in town, but the Melvins were the one that the cool kids like us liked the best. In 1986, I became aware there was a much cooler music scene in Tacoma and Olympia. There was Girl Trouble [Tacoma's answer to The Cramps[26] – a stripped-back, blue-collar, garage rock band that used to hang out at a café shaped like a teapot], there was Beat Happening, there were a bunch of other bands . . .

"Hardcore was taking over in Seattle," he continues. "There were all these early grunge bands: people playing hard rock or glam or metal, influenced by a non-stop wave of punk from California and Texas. Every weekend there'd be four hardcore bands playing. The Seattle all-ages scene had tons of violent moshing and pit action. It became hard for me to find friends that were into music other than hardcore. If you went to Olympia, there was tons of dancing and contact, but the contact was friendly. Instead of flying elbows and people getting bruises and cuts, it was bashing into each other and rolling around on the floor and having this great sense of community.

"At a warehouse community space called GESCCO[27], we started getting bands like the Melvins. Meanwhile, I started going to a lot of parties. The Melvins were such gods that if they were in the house, we were always aware of it. So I went to this party at the Dude Ranch with my friends Dylan Carlson and Kurt Flansberg and his girlfriend Tracy Marander, who lived in Tacoma. And there was Krist Novoselic. We knew Krist because he always drove the Melvins around. He was like their roadie. He had this zebra-striped VW van, so you always knew when the Melvins were there. There was always a crowd of these Aberdeen guys – these inbred, scary, loser, freako weirdos – who would go wherever the Melvins went.

"Dylan and me were walking up the driveway having an animated conversation about Big Black[28], when I see this guy walking towards us. I'd seen him before: he was one of the Melvins' hangers-on and he always wore the same grey trench coat. He went, 'I like Big Black,' and kept going. He said it in a self-aware way, like he knew we thought he was just one of these losers that hangs out with the Melvins. He was trying to tell us, 'I'm cooler than that, I've heard of Big Black.'

"That was the very first thing that Kurt ever said to me.

"The next memory I have of Kurt was at GESCCO. Melvins were playing and they needed an opening band. Buzz was like, 'Can my project band[29] play?' We couldn't figure out their name exactly from his phone conversation, so some of the flyers said Brown Cow and some said Brown Towel. There were ads on the TV where a woman would hold up a towel and go, 'How can you tell if a brown towel is clean?' But the name could also have been inspired by the 'How now brown cow?' playground chant. I'm not sure anybody knew – and they only played this one time. Buzz played guitar and Kurt was singing, but he wasn't playing guitar. I think Dale was the drummer . . . it was just Buzz playing with one of those crazy Aberdeen guys.

"The Melvins also had a band called The Meltors where they would play covers of Mentors songs. Krist Novoselic would be their singer.[30] The Melvins were always doing goofy stuff like that; opening for themselves or having their friends sing.

"I wish I could say the first time I saw Kurt sing was a brilliant performance. I can't. I just know I saw it. I have a visual picture. It's Kurt in a trench coat in a big empty room, risers borrowed from the college; Buzz with his little Les Paul and one of those flower-shaped rubber things from the bath so you don't slip was stuck on his guitar, but I don't remember the music. About that time I started a band with Dylan, Mike Nelson [aka Mikey Dees, singer with fiery Olympia punk band Fitz Of Depression] and Kurt Flansberg called Nisqually Delta Podunk Nightmare.

"The first Nirvana show that I remember, I did not see. Tracy was a part of our crowd. Then there was this new girl who worked at the coffee shop everybody went to, Tam Orhmund. Tracy and Tam became best friends. One day I heard that Tracy and Tam both had huge crushes on one of the Melvins kids in Aberdeen, Kurt Cobain. They both decided he was going to be their next boyfriend so they went down to Aberdeen to visit him and Krist.

"I'd known Krist for years as the one cool Melvins guy, but I didn't know Kurt during that time. So I went with them to Aberdeen to see Dale Crover's new band – that's how we were talking about it. Dale's band was going to play at this party because his parents were out of town. The house was full of scary Aberdeen people, mostly heavy metal people. Earlier that day, we went by the house where Kurt was living – it was a squat. I was disgusted by it and we were only there for a couple of minutes. I saw the turtles in the tub and I was like, 'Well, where do they bathe?' Then we went thrift shopping. The show itself was boring and scary and nothing was happening. It was just this one project band. I'd seen lots of parties where project bands had played. It was like, 'OK, Dale Crover is going to play really good drums and these other two losers are going to fuck around and play blues scales.'

"Once I saw it, I realised, 'This is not a band playing, this is everybody getting wasted and then there's going to be a jam session.' After three hours I got tired of it so we left and went to the Smoke Shop and had coffee. Then the band that turned into Nirvana played. I'm pretty sure that was their first show but I didn't see it because I got tired of waiting. Two weeks after that, they played at the Tacoma Community Theater. I think they played with us, and they were called Skid Row[31] for that show."

What was Krist like back then?

"Tall and drunk."

Any particular habits?

"Yeah, getting up on a table and dancing on it till it broke, or setting off a fire extinguisher in a crowded apartment until nobody could breathe and ruining the party. He would call drunken people bitches and think it funny, but he would get people mad instead. He would get so drunk he would inevitably do something inappropriate. The Melvins loved having people like that around – people who would inevitably make a fool of themselves."

## NOTES

1 Three highly individual and idiosyncratic artists. Boredoms play a frequently hilarious but always deadly earnest Japanese noise-skronk-thrash that often threatens to topple over under the weight of its own ingenuity. Sonic Youth define US independent rock music (OK: Sonic Youth, Beat Happening and Ian MacKaye). And Captain Beefheart was notable for melding manic, twisted and alien dance rhythms to blues-rock at a time (the Seventies) when having a moustache virtually condemned you to a life of pomp mediocrity.

2 Ian MacKaye – through Fugazi and his Washington, DC label Dischord – gave voice to a thousand thrashing emo rockers at a time when youth was frowned upon. MacKaye refused to be co-opted, and almost by accident invented 'straight edge' via his first band Minor Threat: the attitude that says music alone is enough for the body (certainly not drugs or alcohol, being capitalist inventions to keep the worker satiated). Dead Kennedys were the US answer to the acidic anger of Sex Pistols two years on, tackling politics head on with such singles as 'Holiday In Cambodia'. Bikini Kill were three girls and a boy from Olympia, WA inspired by DIY culture and the pressing need to right the patriarchal hegemony of rock'n'roll.

3 "The Wipers started Seattle grunge rock in Portland, 1977," Kurt told me. "Their first two albums were totally classic, and influenced the Melvins and all the other punk rock bands. I write very similar lyrics to [singer] Greg Sage. Sage was pretty much the romantic, quiet, visionary kind of guy."

4 From Olympia. Beat Happening's music was a mix of warmth, hostility and gladness straight out of the adult-rated version of *Huckleberry Finn*. Poignant and direct, deceptively childlike, the trio mixed dark metaphor with fuzz tone. Much of the music that you read about in these pages follows on directly from their two-chord, no bass, call to arms.

5 Jimi was a native of Seattle: a statue honouring him still stands, rather incongruously, at one end of Capitol Hill.

6 Apparently, Kurt was a fast sprinter.

7 Or perhaps I amended the quote myself to make it read funnier. There was a lot of that going on back in those days.

8 Two reasons why the UK will never understand America: The Grateful Dead and The Dave Matthews Band.

9 'Stairway To Heaven' was the staple try-out riff in guitar shops across the Western world for nearly two decades, although some shops would levy a £5 fine for playing it. In a weird twist of fate, 'Smells Like Teen Spirit' briefly replaced it at the start of the Nineties.

10 Appropriately enough: The Kingsmen's raw-assed 1963 version of the garage classic 'Louie Louie' is one of the most famous rock songs associated with Washington state (even though The Kingsmen themselves were from Portland, Oregon).

11 Sammy Hagar was an Eighties soft rock star renowned for his 'poodle' hairdo. He later joined Van Halen.

12 Kurt himself claimed to have seen Hagar play when he was in the seventh grade, which would have made Kurt 12 and the year 1979.

13 Kurt's journals were made public after his death by his wife, against his express wishes.

14 Melvins took their name from an Aberdeen Thriftway shop assistant's name tag.

15 San Pedro, CA art punk group featuring bassist Mike Watt, heavily influenced by Captain Beefheart – the Minutemen's early songs were frantic, angular one-minute bursts of aggression and humour.

16 Short for Millions Of Dead Cops, Millions Of Dead Children or perhaps Millions Of Damn Christians.

17 Rollins was notable for his tattoos and fiercely misogynist statements. A talented poet and stand-up comedian, he went on to become an MTV presenter and currently performs for US troops in Iraq and Afghanistan.

18 The Minutemen were a clean-cut early Nineties metal band from NYC – often confused with grunge. Singer Page Hamilton had formerly been in the far more interesting, sonically dissonant, feedback-heavy Band Of Susans.

19 Singer Shannon enjoyed playing trumpet wearing nothing more than a big hat and a bigger smile. Cows were almost avant-garde in their shuddering, feral blast of noise matched to surprisingly melodic pop structures.

20 The triumvirate of Hüsker Dü, The Replacements and R.E.M. helped invent 'alternative rock' in the Eighties by adding a soulful, melodic edge to their abrasive punk influences. Particularly awesome is Hüsker Dü's 1984 album *Zen Arcade* and their mind-blowing cover of The Byrds' 'Eight Miles High' (also 1984). The Replacements played exuberant, blues-tinged rock, shown off to great effect on their debut album, 1981's *Sorry Ma, Forgot To Take Out The Trash*. Even R.E.M. were OK, once upon a time . . .

21 Bob Whittaker was Mudhoney's manager for years, and is currently R.E.M.'s tour manager: anyone who knows him could see his drunken fingerprints all over the 2004 Peter Buck 'air rage' incident.

22 He fled it a second time a few months after retiring there in 1991 when the Serb artillery started pounding the nearby town of Zadar, returning in 1994.

23 Great band, and surprisingly mainstream; Akron, Ohio's Devo ploughed a staccato, spasmodic groove with mordant satirical lyrics similar to that of David Byrne's art school punks Talking Heads – their debut album, 1978's *Q: Are We Not Men? A: We Are Devo!*, is pure warped genius.

24 Warren was also Kurt's guitar tutor.

25 The title's lower case is deliberate: reflecting kill rock stars' disdain for the machinations of the recording industry.

26 The Cramps were one of the great early US punk bands: dressed in fetish gear and wallowing in the same primal slime that spawned Sixties garage outfits such as The Rats and The Sonics.

27 GESCCO was run by Beat Happening's Bret Lunsford and Olympia artist Lois Maffeo, among others. According to Slim, GESCCO was "just a dumb acronym to impress the college into giving us some funding. Actually," he adds, "it stands for Greater Evergreen State College Community Organisation – nobody knew that, I'm just a total nerd."

28 Producer Steve Albini's relentless, superb, drum machine-led, Eighties noise band. When Big Black split, he formed the equally uncompromising Rapeman with Scratch Acid's David Wm Sims. Both bands were brutal in their minimalist, almost industrial beats and malevolent lyrics – and gave vent to the paranoia of urban living with strictly focused bursts of rage: incessant, nasty and oddly tinny.

29 Project band – like a one-off or a side-project.

30 The Mentors were a joke Eighties hardcore band that had (crap) songs about sex and related topics. Their singer, El Duce, claimed to have been offered $30,000 by Courtney Love to "snuff Kurt Cobain" in the 'documentary' *Kurt And Courtney*. El Duce was so clearly taking the piss out of the filmmaker, the guileless Nick Broomfield, it's painful to watch.

31 Skid Row was originally named after Yesler Way, a steep street leading down to the Puget Sound in Seattle. Lumberjacks used it as a ramp for sliding timber to a sawmill. It became synonymous with down-and-outs during the Thirties.

## CHAPTER 3

# Class Of '86

HERE's the problem in writing a Nirvana biography: Kurt liked to construct myths around himself. It was part of his appeal. I recall being at the Cobain residence a few times when his biographer Michael Azerrad called up; Kurt would shout up the stairs to Courtney and myself, asking if we had any stories we wanted to pass on. Kurt exaggerated certain aspects of his childhood, ignored other parts and sometimes downright lied. Often he would do this to give additional weight to songs: so he would talk about living underneath a bridge in Aberdeen because it tied in with the lyrics to 'Something In The Way'. Fact or not, it's a great image.[1]

There's an apocryphal story about how Kurt claimed he bought his first guitar in return for the proceeds of some recovered guns. The strange thing is, Kurt never actually claimed this – but the falsity provided a useful stopping-off point for one journalist to pontificate about Kurt's story-telling abilities. And now, because it's been written that Kurt made the claim, the supposition that he was lying about that moment is now itself part of the myth. Confusion is layered on top of confusion. In reality, Kurt pawned the guns and spent the cash on an amplifier. The guns were dragged out of the Wishkah after his mother Wendy had thrown them in after a particularly volatile fight with her second husband Pat O'Connor. She was scared she might kill Pat if his guns remained in the house. So did Kurt buy a guitar with the proceeds, or an amp?

Does it even matter?

The second problem is – obviously – Kurt is dead. Others are at liberty to manipulate history in favour of how they would prefer Kurt to be remembered. He can't refute it. One biography portrays his mother as promiscuous and uncaring. But Wendy had refused to talk to the book's author: was the writer exacting revenge? In Kurt's own words, his mother wasn't so bad. Did Kurt kill a cat as has been claimed, or is this merely an example of the singer's later infatuation with Sex Pistols' bassist Sid Vicious? There's a famous line in Sid's version of 'My Way' that goes,

*"To think . . . I killed a cat"*. Killing animals seems very out-of-character for him, but Kurt isn't around to disprove the charge. And did he molest a "half-retarded" (his words) girl when he was 16 – his school called in the cops after her father complained – or was he simply guilty of exaggerating a certain incident in his own journal? It is possible to lie in your own diaries.

Rock stars and actors – or those who manage and promote them – have always created myths to enhance their image, whether it's simply a year or two clipped off a singer's real age or a more elaborate romanticising of a mundane childhood. Kurt wasn't the first to invent a past. Bob Dylan, Jim Morrison, Keith Moon . . . they all did it. It's an accepted tradition.

Never let the truth get in the way of a good story.

In December 1982, Kurt brought a guitar along to his Aunt Mari's house in Seattle, where she'd moved after marrying – and with the help of her bass, some spoons and a suitcase[2] made his first musical recordings.[3] The sound was bare. "Mostly, I remember a lot of distortion on guitar, really heavy bass and the clucky sound of the wooden spoons," she told *Goldmine* writer Gillian G. Gaar. "His voice sounded like he was mumbling under a big fluffy comforter, with some passionate screams once in a while. It was very repetitious." Mari later revealed that she'd told Kurt he was welcome to use her computer drummer if he wanted. "I want to keep it pure," he replied.

Kurt called this recording 'Organised Confusion' – a name he would later sport on one of his home-made T-shirts.

Being a nightclub performer, Mari Earl left her equipment set up in a corner of the dining room. "Kurt was probably about 10 when he started asking if he could play my guitar and sit behind the microphone," she said. "I don't have any vivid memory of what he sounded like, but he was very careful not to damage the equipment."

Soon, Kurt was developing a strong desire to get a band together, partly fuelled by revenge fantasies.

"When I was about 12," he told me in 1992, "I wanted to be a rock'n' roll star. I thought that would be my payback to all the jocks who got all the girlfriends all the time. Girls wouldn't even look at me when I was a little kid growing up, or at least until I was 15. I had this attitude that someday I'll be a rock star and be able to get girlfriends. But I realised way before I became a rock star, when I was a punk rocker, that that was stupid. That was just because I was a geek."

It took him a while to discover the right vehicle for his talents. Early on,

Kurt had auditioned for the Melvins, but failed. In the meantime, he began writing his own songs – 'Wattage In The Cottage', 'Ode To Beau' (a song poking fun at a fellow classmate who'd killed himself) and 'Diamond Dave'.

In August '84, Kurt drove up to Seattle to see Black Flag with Buzz Osborne and Matt Lukin. One Nirvana book wrote that Kurt claimed in "every interview he did later in life" this was the first concert he saw. This is more myth making, perhaps fuelled by the journalist's desire to make Kurt Cobain seem less cool. Cobain never claimed anything of the sort: but by writing that he did, it makes it look like he was overtly concerned with making himself seem cooler than he really was.

In April '84, Kurt lost his virginity in the haphazard way that teenagers often do. Stung into action by his stepfather's boasts of how sexually active he'd been at Kurt's age and how Kurt must be a 'faggot', Kurt picked up a couple of girls at a party and took them back home. One passed out drunk: the other, Jackie Hagara (whose own boyfriend was in jail), stripped off and joined Kurt in bed. Right at that moment, his mother walked in and unceremoniously threw the teenagers outside into a raging storm. The threesome walked over to Jackie's friend's house – just as they arrived, so did Jackie's boyfriend. (Sounds unlikely? Don't question the myth!) Kurt ended up sleeping with Jackie's friend.

Wendy didn't want him back.

Kurt's possessions were packed into rubbish bags: the next four months were spent flitting between friends' houses – a cardboard box on Dale Crover's porch (where the Melvins also rehearsed) – and hallways in Aberdeen apartment buildings. He even returned to his birthplace, Grays Harbour Community Hospital, where he'd crash out in the waiting room with a friend. He then moved back to his dad's place in Montesano, where Don persuaded Kurt to talk to a navy recruitment officer, pointing out that at least they'd provide shelter and food. Kurt spoke to the officer once and then refused to see him again.

It's been claimed that Kurt flirted with religion, encouraged by his friend Jesse Reed, whose parents Dave and Ethel were born-again Christians.[4] Whatever the truth, Kurt moved into the Reeds' spacious North River house that autumn.

Dave wasn't a typical Christian youth counsellor. He'd been playing rock music for two decades; he was the saxophonist in cult Sixties garage band The Beachcombers[5]; and there was plenty of musical equipment around. It soon became obvious, however, that things weren't working out – Kurt skipped lessons to smoke pot and, by May 1985, dropped out of high school altogether, rejecting the idea of a possible art scholarship. Kurt was a bad influence on Jesse, convincing his impressionable friend to skip classes. Dave Reed got Kurt a dishwashing job but it didn't last.

It was at the Reed residence that Kurt first jammed with Krist: nothing auspicious, just a few bad heavy metal licks and a couple of artless Cobain originals, Kurt and Krist and Jesse fooling around . . .[6]

Krist Novoselic graduated from high school in 1983, a few months after meeting future wife Shelli Dilly, whom he first encountered after he overheard her praising The Sex Pistols' album *Never Mind The Bollocks* – she recognised him as the "class clown-type guy, always joking". Soon afterwards, Shelli dropped out to work at McDonald's, while Krist got a job at the Foster Painting Company.

Shortly after his graduation, Krist's parents divorced. Around the same time, he had his jaw wired shut for six weeks to correct severe under-bite. Lukin recalled dropping by his house the day Krist had the surgery: "His head was totally swollen up," he told Michael Azerrad, "like a fat oriental baby. It was like seeing the elephant man."

"You fuckers," Krist cried, having been woken from his anaesthetised slumber. By March 1985, Krist and Shelli were dating – he got laid off and gradually moved into Shelli's apartment: no phone, no TV, and all adornments and furniture bought at thrift stores. By December they'd moved into a larger, more run-down house – briefly relocating to Phoenix, Arizona the following March in search of work – before settling on an apartment above a garage in Hoquiam, where they became vegetarians.

Meanwhile, Kurt got himself thrown out of the Reed residence after an incident where he forgot his key, and either smashed a window or kicked down their door to get in. Once again, he was homeless. On June 1, 1985, Kurt moved into an Aberdeen apartment with Jesse Reed where he continued to write songs ('Spam', 'The Class Of '85'). The flat was tiny, enlivened by pink walls and a mutilated blow-up doll decorated with shaving foam swinging in the window, dirty plates stacked up in the sink, shaving cream fights, writing on the walls and stolen lawn furniture.

Later, Nirvana would revel in their earlier reputation as freaks.

"[Jesse and I] were branded Satan worshippers back home," Kurt told me in 1990. "This girl came knocking on our door looking for a wallet and she goes, 'You know what all the other kids told me in the neighbourhood? Don't go in there, they worship the Devil.' That's why nobody ever bothered us in redneck country. We would neither confirm nor deny satanic affiliations.

"Maybe it was those desecrated cemetery pieces buried in our front yard," the singer added – jokingly – in the same interview. "But you didn't have to do anything to be considered extreme back there. Just take a lot of acid."

Jesse and Kurt were asked to remove the doll by a local sheriff; a more serious brush with the law occurred the same summer after Kurt was caught graffiti-ing the SeaFirst bank with the words "Ain't go no how watchamacallit" with a red marker pen. He was fingerprinted, fined $180 and given a 30-day suspended sentence.

"Kurt was a completely creative persona – a true artist," Krist wrote in his autobiography. "When I first met him, he had just got a job and found his own place. What a den of art/insanity that was. He tried to make his own lava lamp out of wax and vegetable oil (it didn't work). He sketched very obscene *Scooby Doo* cartoons all over his apartment building hallways. He made wild sound montages from obscure records. He sculpted clay into scary spirit people writhing in agony. He played guitar, sang and wrote great tunes that were kind of off-kilter. Kurt held a sceptical perspective toward the world. He'd create video montages that were scathing testimonies about popular culture, compiled from hours and hours of watching TV."

Kurt had two temporary part-time jobs: as a janitor at Aberdeen High where he dressed in brown overalls, and as a swimming instructor for kids at the local YMCA.[7] The work didn't last long, and neither did the apartment – after three months Jesse moved out to join the navy. Kurt stayed till late autumn. Then, unemployed and homeless, he convinced the Shillinger family to take him in. Dad Lamont was an English teacher at Aberdeen High, while son Steve was a heavy metal kid who liked to party hard, who'd noticed Kurt because he'd scrawled Motörhead[8] on his folder. He moved in during the winter of 1985, and stayed on their sofa for the next eight months.

The Shillingers had six kids and were used to taking in strays. Usually, concerned parents would call to check up on their offspring: Wendy and Don didn't. "Kurt kept his sleeping bag behind the couch," Lamont Shillinger told one interviewer, "and was put into rotation on the family chores. I don't believe that either his mother or stepfather attempted to make contact with us the entire time he was there." Steve's brother Eric played guitar, and Kurt jammed with him through the family stereo on Iron Maiden[9] songs.

In December 1985, Kurt formed a band with Melvins' drummer Dale Crover on bass and Greg Hokanson on drums called Fecal Matter. They played original material and, depending on which history you believe, they either did or didn't play one show, supporting Melvins at a Moclips beach bar. Whatever. Hokanson didn't last long, so it was Cobain and Crover, driven by Lukin in his blue Impala, who went down to Seattle to record a demo on Aunt Mari's four-track TEAC deck.

With Crover behind the drums, the session lasted a couple of days. Early versions of 'Spank Thru' and 'Downer' were recorded, alongside 'Sound Of Dentage', 'Laminated Effect', 'Bambi Slaughter', 'Class Of '86', 'Blathers Log Dinstramental' and several untitled songs – but not 'Suicide Samurai', as has been erroneously reported. "There was a song that was among his lyrics he never did record on that particular tape," Aunt Mari remarked in the documentary *Kurt & Courtney*. "It was called 'Seaside Suicide' [sic] and it left me with an impression he had possibly tried suicide before."

"The drums were strong and forceful," Mari told Gillian G. Gaar, "and Kurt was playing some pretty good bass by then. The guitar riffs were fast and furious, with a powerful hook. The lyrical content was rebellious and angry. Mostly slams against society in general. Kurt didn't like the social ladder in school. Kids thinking they were cool because they wore the 'right' clothes or were handsome or pretty, or had money."

Copies were dubbed on to cassette, entitled *Illiteracy Will Prevail*. The cover featured a Cobain-drawn picture of flies buzzing round a pile of shit, there to illustrate a lyric from 'Class Of '86', *"We are all the same/ Just flies on a turd"*. Fecal Matter split up shortly after, despite yet another incarnation featuring Osborne on bass and original Melvins' drummer Mike Dillard.

Meanwhile, Kurt – bored with life in Aberdeen – stepped up his petty vandalism, fuelled by Bad Brains' *Rock For Light*, and frequent acid trips.

"Hell," I wrote back in *Melody Maker* in 1991, referring to a series of conversations I'd had with Kurt while we skipped out of commercial radio interviews in Philadelphia, "you even told me something of your past in Aberdeen, how you would get bored out your skull and go round and break into people's homes, trash them, not steal anything, just trash them, graffiti the walls, break up the furniture, smash the adornments – anything for a thrill, the buzz. Sounded pure James Dean[10] to me. You mentioned the buzz you get from the after-effects of your troublemaking, the exhilaration of being confronted by a truckload of angry officials."

With Steve Shillinger in tow, Kurt changed a Pink Floyd mural to read Black Flag, and spray-painted many a back alley in Aberdeen. He'd brag to Steve how he was going to be in a band "bigger than U2 or R.E.M.", and continued making silent Super-8 movies.[11] Kurt loved the skewed, melancholic pop of Michael Stipe's R.E.M., but like all punks scorned the self-righteous preening of U2 as being derisive bombast on a level with Bruce Springsteen. On May 18, 1986, after having been found wandering on top of an abandoned building, Cobain was charged with trespassing and being a minor in possession of alcohol: he was thrown in jail when it was discovered that he hadn't paid the fine from his previous conviction. He stayed there for eight days, unable to raise the bail.

Kurt has said he first did heroin in the summer of '86, after checking out the opiate Percodan: "It was really scary," he told Azerrad. "I always wanted to do it – I always knew that I would." Other versions of his story place his introduction to the drug at around 1990.[12] Kurt was drawn to the drug partly because of its forbidden nature; also because it's supposed to induce a euphoric high and he was on the lookout for new drugs to try; but mainly for its seedy glamour, its association with rock stars like Iggy Pop. He claimed he knew it was OK to take because it was in short supply in Aberdeen and hence it would be impossible to become hooked.

What kind of damage does heroin do to people?

James Burdyshaw [ex-Seattle grunge band, Cat Butt[13]]: "Oh my God . . . Well, there's a line in a Jon Spencer[14] song, where he says, *'You look like a vampire'*, talking about somebody close to him that has a really bad habit. That's sort of what it's like. It's like you've been bit with a weird blood disease. It makes you a night creature, and taking heroin becomes your number one priority. It's always in your mind, and no matter what you do or say or how you act, your goal is to get it and get on it and when you're on it you don't give a shit about anybody or anything, just being high and blazed out of your head."

Have you done heroin?

"Yeah."

Can you describe the feeling of being high?

"It's not like doing a hallucinogenic where your mind does weird things and you start thinking about how your father beat you or how beautiful everybody is. It's just this weird sort of numbing sensation, like if you overdose on about four or five painkillers. Imagine doing that in an IV. You get this warm feeling in your brain and your skin, and you get really loopy and lethargic. It's a painkiller – it's like morphine, only it's street morphine."

Heroin has got an incredibly bad rep – why do people take it in the first place?

"That's part of it. The thrill of danger, the unknown . . . At first it was kind of scary, the whole concept of sticking a needle in your arm and injecting something liquid, but then, when you're young and you're fearless of drugs if you're into them, you think, 'Wow, this is a kick.' You're obsessed with the idea of doing the same chemicals as your heroes. Some addicts deny this, but that's bullshit. When you're young and stupid you totally want to follow your idols, and I think that listening to Lou Reed and John Lennon and the Stones and John Coltrane . . . the list goes on and on and on, Johnny Thunders, Sid Vicious, Ray Charles . . . it's almost like a rite of passage, like if you don't do this somehow you're not a suffering musician."

Why is it that Seattle has such a strong association with the drug?

"Before heroin became popular and a lot of people who ended up on Sub Pop records started taking it, the drugs of choice were MDMA and psychedelics and ecstasy. That's what the kids were into, but the gnarly guys did heroin so everyone got interested in that. The kids who would never think about doing heroin in 1986 thought it was cool the following year. Friends influence friends. Kurt was one of the last people to use. Everybody else was doing it before him. He was a pot-smoking, drinking guy when I met him. The only reason why I think he fell in love with it so much was because of his background in Aberdeen. He needed the numbness. And if you fall in love with the numbness . . . you're in trouble."

Kurt's drug usage increased his sense of paranoia and anger. He developed nervous tics: cracking his knuckles, scratching his face compulsively. He began to imagine that everyone he knew had it in for him – whether true or not. He grew ever more distrustful of 'outsiders' (ironically enough, mirroring his town's general attitude towards the rest of the world) and retreated more and more into his music and opiates.

The singer's falling out with the Shillingers in August 1986 had an air of inevitability to it. Matters came to a head after a particularly bloody fight involving both Eric and Steve. The next morning, Kurt paid Steve $10 to transport his belongings to Dale Crover's house. Once again, he was homeless. Kurt survived the next month by sleeping in the library during the day and crashing at friends' houses at night. Sometimes, he'd sleep in Krist and Shelli's van: sometimes he'd sleep at his mother's, unbeknown to her, while she was at work: other times it would be in the apartment above Krist's mother's hair salon.

That September, Kurt convinced his mother to loan him $200 so he could pay the deposit and a month's rent on 1000 1/2 East Second St., Aberdeen ('the shack'). The house was decrepit – and, after Kurt moved in with new housemate Matt Lukin, everywhere the smell of discarded, rotting food and stale beer. Fortunately, Lukin was a skilled carpenter. A hole was drilled in the floor, underneath Kurt's bathtub of turtles placed in the middle of the living room, to drain away the foul-smelling water. The arrangement wasn't entirely successful: the water merely collected in stagnant pools beneath the house.

Living with a Melvin meant that Kurt got to hang out and jam on a regular basis with both the band and their regular coterie of hangers-on. The shack soon gained a reputation as a party house.

Kurt took a job as a caretaker at the Polynesian Hotel in Ocean Shores: he wasn't the most reliable of workers, frequently he would just kip down in one of the guests' rooms and dream about the day he would have his own rock'n'roll band and get revenge on all the people who treated him like dirt.

"Aberdeen is a terrible, gross place that smells like vanilla," says former K records co-boss Candice Pedersen. "We would drive down, and meet Dale and Buzz who worked out in Montesano, then go over to Kurt and Matt's house. The weird thing is there were no girls. Those people dated girls but they didn't hang out with girls. So you'd go to these parties that weren't really parties, more like people just sat around drinking beer. We'd be the only girls there. It was only Shelli who was a girlfriend. A lot of the Aberdeen folks thought we were weird."

Where would you hang out?

"Not really anywhere. At the house," replies Candice. "The people in the periphery were what would have been called burnouts in high school. In a very small town, you're identified early on if you're a burnout, or a slut, or a jock. Kurt worked at some disgusting hotel, and that's where I learned about everything gross that happens there: rooms would be trashed or there'd be condoms everywhere."

Let's get back to Skid Row, the band Kurt formed with Krist . . .

"Skid Row was really cool," says Slim Moon. "I thought their songs were all right. They played really heavy. Kurt was totally glammed out – he was in platform shoes, like a parody of a glam costume. You have to remember we're talking 1987 here, at the height of Guns N' Roses[15] and [hair metal band] Poison.[16] Their songs were basically riffs. They'd play a riff for a long time and Kurt would scream into the microphone, then he'd drop the guitar and play with the digital delay and make crazy noises instead of a guitar solo, and then he'd pick the guitar back up and play the riff some more and scream some more. Right away, he was a showman.

"Because Dale Crover was their drummer and Dale Crover was the heaviest drummer in the universe, they were great just playing a riff, then a solo, then a riff and ending. The songs weren't like verse, chorus, verse; they were riffs – they were unfinished bits.

"Soon after that, GESCCO got notice from Evergreen[17] that they'd realised their insurance didn't cover off-campus activities so they cut off their funding. We only had four days' notice, so I hastily put on a show and got this band from Tacoma, my band Nisqually Delta Podunk Nightmare and Skid Row to play. Krist was so drunk and being so dumb, it looked like Skid Row wouldn't be allowed to play. We appealed against the decision on three levels: this band is really great, we'll make him calm down . . . and who cares? It's the last show ever. What can he do, get us closed down? They did play, and it was just as I described. Then there are so many Nirvana shows after I can't remember the sequence any more."

### Addenda: Matt Lukin's butt

Did you ever count the number of times you saw Matt Lukin's butt?

"Oh God . . ." laughs Mark Arm's old girlfriend, Carrie Montgomery. "My son and his friend were talking about picking up a dollar bill with their butt cheeks and I thought of Matt instantly. How many times did I see Matt carry a quarter in his ass across the room? Really a bad influence, too. He wasn't just destructive, though; Krist Novoselic was the same. Those Aberdeen guys were just crazy, they were like animals – almost hippie-like, but crazy. Olympia was the same. Aberdeen was hippie-redneck, while Olympia was more hippie-hippie.

"Mark would keep a diary while he was on tour and he'd write me a lot of letters . . . something I learned about Matt Lukin that I never ever wanted to know was that when he takes a shit, he's afraid to have the toilet water splash back up on him, so he'd line the water with strips of toilet paper. Yeah. This is a guy who'd walk around naked in front of whoever and carry a quarter between his butt cheeks but he didn't want any toilet water to splash on his ass. Where does this person come from? What kind of an environment creates this person? But such a great guy, so nice, never any malicious intent."

## NOTES

1 "I've been up there," says Seattle resident Candice Pedersen. "There's the train tracks to Olympia and you might end up staying overnight on them. That myth could be true."

2 Kurt played drums in the school band.

3 Possibly. *Come As You Are* also mentions an abortive attempt with two school friends, jamming in an abandoned meat locker in the woods, Kurt playing a borrowed right-handed guitar.

4 Krist was also supposed to have attended the same church, Central Park Baptist, but only 'for the girls'.

5 The Beachcombers released several 45s including 'Purple Peanuts', 'Chinese Bagpiper' (1963), 'Tossin' And Turnin'' (1964) and 'All To Pieces' (1965). Kurt's Uncle Chuck played with them for a while, and they also turned in a very creditable version of 'Louie Louie', as evinced on their 1997 reunion CD *The Legendary Beachcombers, Live In The Great Northwest.*

6 Krist also played in several of the Melvins' satellite bands – such as The Stiff Woodies, whom he fronted. The Woodies had a revolving line-up including Kurt on drums.

7 Kurt later cited his stint working with children as the best job he ever held.

8 Motörhead were perhaps the greatest heavy metal band ever: British contemporaries of Ramones. I once saw singer Lemmy bust all four strings on his bass with the opening chord to 'Ace Of Spades'. Without missing a beat he threw the instrument away, a roadie slipped a new bass over his head and the band continued. Metallica couldn't have existed without Motörhead's influence.

9 Iron Maiden are a UK heavy metal band, best known for song titles like 'Bring Your Daughter To The Slaughter' and their mascot Eddie.

10 James Dean: leather-jacketed teen star of iconographic Fifties film *Rebel Without A Cause.*

11 One Super-8 film unearthed in recent years seems to be typical: a 10-minute short, filmed in '84 by Kurt, Krist and Dale Crover on the streets of Aberdeen, known as the 'Horror Movies'. The camera flicks between a turtle, a bloody hand, Kurt dressed in a Mr T mask, a scary female statue, some of Kurt's Claymation, Kurt cutting his own throat with a fake knife, a picture of someone jerking off to people passing by, various dogs . . . all to a Melvins soundtrack.

12 This certainly ties in with what James Burdyshaw says later in the chapter about Kurt being "one of the last people to use". Again, it's impossible to know.

13 "The most disorganised band in Seattle," recalls producer Jack Endino. "Cat Butt once did an entire session with me where they were so drunk that they had to come back and re-record it all."

14 Jon Spencer fronted groovy hate-fuck Eighties NYC noise band Pussy Galore, and fronts present-day blues revivalists The Blues Explosion. Pussy Galore also spawned the all-girl STP and Royal Trux, among other bands.

15 The sprawling *Appetite For Destruction* was released in '87, selling 20 million

copies, and spawning the monster, lighters-waving hit 'Sweet Child O' Mine'.

16 Ironically enough, Sebastian Bach's heavier hair metal Skid Row sounded like a cross between those same two groups. Their moment of fame came in 1991, with the US number one album *Slave To The Grind*, before the grunge bands eclipsed them.

17 Evergreen is Olympia's hippie college, an oasis of liberal thought and teaching in redneck surrounds.

## CHAPTER 4

# Gentle Sound, Half-finished Town

*"Gentle sound/ Half-finished town . . . drinking water from wells/ Watching shows, kiss and tell/ Walk down the railroad tracks/ Never look back"*

– 'Olympia', The Legend!, 2000

SO everyone's seated on the floor, lights turned off, banging water bottles in accompaniment to the chant-song from Al, Tobi and Amy on stage, myself squat-legged in the middle of the audience sometimes breaking into a fresh verse of the old gospel spiritual, room stunned into silence and – gradually – more and more voices joining in. *"There's a man going round taking names/ There's a man going round taking names/ He's taken my father's name/ And he's left me crying in vain/ There's a man going round taking names."*

Tobi and Amy's voices swell and fade in the current of emotion, my voice cracking, my eyes downcast, people coming in at the back of the room looking for the music's source. I wonder whether I should lie fully stretched out on the floor but decide not. My voice soars once more through the disharmonic groundswell of emotion as I come in with the line, *"Death is the name of that man/ Death is the name of that man . . ."*

(Everett True's weblog, September 12, 2004, www.planbmag.com)

Olympia, WA isn't the most beautiful of places on first sight.

Sure, there's the state capitol up on the hill, imposing with its dome and white pillars; the old railroad tracks leading down to the beautiful woodland of Priest Point Park; timber houses without kerbsides or fences so one unruly garden merges into the next; the boardwalk and moored boats down by the organic supermarket; apartments occupied by punk rock librarians who don't need alcohol for an excuse to party, just good music (alcohol doesn't hurt either); the tiny park next to Starbucks with its deserted bandstand; the crumbling Capitol Theater; the docks; the muddy riverbanks; framed papercuts on coffee shop walls; fountains that double as water sculptures; backroom bars with dollar beer and cheap cocktails; cosy co-ops with retro clothes shops and fanzine and comic book stores nestling up to one another; disused temples that house independent record labels; Evergreen State College up in the hills with its gloomy concrete architecture and manicured lawns, home to KAOS radio.

Sure there's all that.

But you have to know the city to appreciate it – to find the spontaneous house parties where earnest, engaging solo artists still perform, the secret water pumps, the working men's clubs that hold underground rock festivals, the hipster bars and late-night redneck drinking establishments, the bewildering array of Outsider music and art.

Step off the Greyhound bus – two hours along Interstate 5 from Seattle, past Mount Rainier, one stop in Tacoma and one in Fort Lewis – and you find yourself in a cramped, small building filled with downcast people, shuffling along. The economy isn't great in Olympia: mostly the work is either in Seattle or at the nearby Boeing aeroplane plant, little reason to stay in town if you're not a student or musician. The weather isn't good for tourism either: it *rains*, and when it's not raining it's overcast. The shops have all seen better days, and in recent years the downtown area has been besieged by an influx of vagrants: Tacoma and Aberdeen are too poor to make hassling worthwhile, Seattle too rich. Once you get outside the four blocks that comprise downtown, the place is deserted. Sometimes, Olympia feels like the town in *Back To The Future*.

Opposite the Greyhound depot is the Ramada Hotel where Madonna was rumoured to have stayed when she played the Tacoma Dome. (No one would have thought of looking for her there!) We set off in search of the K offices, walking past The Martin apartments, once home to K records' founder and Beat Happening frontman Calvin Johnson, also any number of Olympia musicians and artists such as Tobi Vail, Al Larsen, Nikki McClure, Lois Maffeo, Stella Marrs, Kathleen Hanna, Candice Pedersen . . . in fact pretty much the whole of the nascent Riot Grrrl movement that started out of Olympia's 1991 International Pop Underground festival. Tobi was one of the last to go, finally moving out after a 2001 earthquake damaged the building's foundations.

We walk down State Street along the old train lines to the sprawling warehouse that is home to K. Downstairs is a large room stacked with shelf after shelf of independent CDs and vinyl and T-shirts. Upstairs are a few sparsely furnished offices and a massive hall that serves as the Dub Narcotic recording studio – where Calvin has recorded pretty much everyone from Jon Spencer Blues Explosion to The Gossip[1] to . . . well, if The White Stripes didn't record here it was an oversight on Jack White's part.

Back downtown at kill rock stars, Tobi Vail is weighing parcels of merchandise to be sent out. An open-plan office overlooks an area stacked high with CDs and vinyl. Circular metal tubes cross the ceiling. At one computer sits Tobi's sister Maggie with her Alsatian dog Jackson, listening to Ramones on iTunes, while label owner Slim Moon sits a few desks down, arranging with a pal to go to a basketball game. A few more musicians and interns good-naturedly hurl insults at one another. Someone mentions going for a beer: we clutch our heads and groan.

Last night was a riot of drinking and dancing, one boy racing up the side of walls on 4th, Maggie leading the entire crowd at the Brotherhood on to their feet. Asses were waggled and tail-feathers shaken. Then it was over to the gay bar for a quick last orders, before Tobi's battery-powered toy record player took over and we played the 'Mystery 45' game. I'd hold a record up, dim in the light, and go, "What's this I'm holding in my hand?" And then the room would explode into a frenzy of chanting and percussion, until the atmosphere was deemed sufficiently excited for Chris O'Kane to flip another record on – Rachel Sweet, Black Flag, Patrik Fitzgerald, Judy Nylon, Bangs.[2]

This is the town where Kurt Cobain received his schooling in 'cool' punk rock, 15 years ago. It sure hasn't changed much.

"I moved to Olympia from Kirkland in 1987, to study politics and philosophy," explains Ian Dickson, former Sub Pop computer tech savant. "Evergreen doesn't have degrees. You just graduate when you have the right number of credits. I was a big fan of music, and an avid reader of *The Rocket*, especially Bruce Pavitt's column on local bands."

*The Rocket* was a Seattle music paper that started in 1979 as an insert in the *Seattle Sun*. Ostensibly devoted to the Pacific Northwest, it was more notable for featuring out-of-town acts like Bruce Springsteen on its cover at the height of the first grunge explosion.

"My girlfriend Nikki [McClure] had already moved down," Ian continues. "She was heavily involved with the rock scene, as was I. We were huge U-Men[3] fans. I was really into Melvins and Sonic Youth, that whole hard noise scene. Bruce turned us on to Beat Happening, and we started corresponding with Calvin in high school. That's how we got to discover [Calvin and Tobi's band] The Go Team, and compilations like *Let's Together* and *Let's Kiss* . . ."[4]

Calvin wrote you letters?

"Oh yeah, he would write us back – or Candice would, on his behalf," Ian laughs. "In those days they'd always respond, on a little piece of stationery that had the K stamp."

What did you like about K?

"The whole DIY concept appealed to us most. There was something about the Olympia rock scene that was so much more appealing than Seattle. Even Earth, which people probably think of as a Seattle band, was an Olympia band. Earth was the ultimate distillation of the Olympia aesthetic, even more than Nirvana. In fact, Nirvana and Earth and Beat Happening are like the same band; there's no talent to speak of on a technical level. It's all this raw expression of emotion."

Many friends consider Earth to be one of the greatest bands ever. They're primal, extreme, minimal and LOUD. Scary. Dense. Earth made it over to the UK for a show in the mid-Nineties. It was Dylan Carlson and Ian Dickson. Five minutes before the show was due to begin, Dylan walked up to the amplifier, plugged it in and left his guitar resting against it – so it started feeding back. He went back down and sat in the audience. Forty-five minutes later he turned his amp off, end of show.

The Seattle thing was much more testosterone-led . . .

"It's almost working class versus middle class," Ian says. "Seattle was way more working class. It was all about drinking beer and pounding dope and playing . . . metal. The U-Men bridged that gap, because Scratch Acid[5] and Live Skull[6] and that whole art thing influenced them. But most of the Seattle bands were either straight up hardcore or metal. In Olympia, people were doing experimental stuff. Even the bad bands would be interesting. You'd go to a show and be like, 'Oh my God, what are they doing?' Calvin had a massive influence. You wouldn't have wanted to be in that downtown Olympia scene unless you were into that aesthetic."

What was the aesthetic?

"It was The Go Team aesthetic," replies Ian. "I'll play one song and then switch instruments and then play another. Anybody can do it. Anybody should do it. You should do it now. It doesn't matter how good you are. And you should express your nature, whatever that happens to be."

"The Go Team was four people fighting for the back of the stage," laughs Olympia musician Al Larsen.[7]

"My whole point of view in music has been about inclusiveness," explained Calvin in cult UK magazine *Careless Talk Costs Lives*. "Making things accessible, making things open. I'm not saying, 'Play your instrument badly,' which is how it's been interpreted. I never said that. All I said is that the expression should be the emphasis rather than the technical skill."

It was Heather's voice in 1985 that first drew me into Beat Happening. That and the bare graphics on their debut album: the cat on the spaceship! The band was Heather, Calvin, Bret – no bass, no stated instrument and no last names. The Greg Sage production was sparse. That, I could relate to. I've always hated extraneous noise, especially unnecessary drumming. In the mid-Eighties, I would sing on stage either a cappella or with minimal backing myself and was made to feel a freak for doing so.[8] It was so nice to hear people halfway across the world doing the same.

Calvin's deep-throated voice and Bret's minimal guitar reminded me of early Cramps. Beat Happening played with a rigid structure that was both highly formalised and formal. Many people have mistaken their Richard Brautigan[9]-like schoolyard imagery and dry humour for naivety: Kurt Cobain stated the reason he got the K logo (a shield round the letter K) tattooed on his arm was to "try and remind me to stay a child". However, there was nothing naïve in Calvin's ability to manipulate crowds. Beat Happening delighted in inverting convention: his band was truly subversive in the way they superficially sounded so innocent yet were anything but. Childish dreams often have their dark side.

Calvin is one of the three most powerful performers I've seen.[10] He reminds me of Johnny Rotten – he has the same manic, intense stare, the same way of intimidating an audience, the way he'd move so close to them. That'd be why he was once knocked cold by an ashtray hurled during a Fugazi support slot.

"You know the first time you hear out-there jazz?" asks Slim Moon. "Your brain goes, 'That's not music.' It was the same the first time I heard Beat Happening. As minimal as they were, I was like, 'These people must be 12, they have no fucking clue what they're doing, and they probably just wrote these songs today.' I was really offended. But the first independent record I bought was 'Our Secret' [BH seven-inch]. I walked into Fallout Records [Olympia] and I was like, 'Tell me what to buy.' Bruce Pavitt [future Sub Pop boss], who was working there at the time, told me to buy that single. I really liked the Calvin song. I listened to that song all the time. It sounded like music. Somehow it didn't connect that this band was that same horrible band. The next time I saw Beat Happening I realised there was no bass-player. Then I started to get that vocabulary of how to understand it."

"There were two sides to Beat Happening," says Mark Arm. "The Heather side and the Calvin side. Their shows were funny, great, sometimes infuriating, depending on who you are. They could totally piss people off."

Do you think Calvin was a big influence on Kurt?

"I'm sure of it," the Mudhoney singer replies.

How did it manifest itself?

"His 'K' tattoo, embracing stuff like Daniel Johnston[11] and The Raincoats."

Do you think Calvin influenced Kurt's attitude at all?

"I don't know. Kurt was pretty reserved. When he and I would hang out it was like two introverts in a room."

"I feel like that concept of being an outsider has basically formed my life and the idea of being included no matter what your 'problem' is," Calvin says. "That confrontation is not about showing how much cooler I am than other people, it's about confronting their privileged point of view, that they have the right to exclude me. It's not like, 'I'm so cool. I can piss you off.' It's, 'I'm doing what I want to do. Now, why does that piss you off?'"

It was while Kurt was living at the shack that he fell under the influence of Olympia. He journeyed up to the city as an unpaid Melvins' roadie, carrying Buzz's amp when they played one of the state capital's tiny, community-led punk clubs.

Aberdeen's underground scene was minuscule: when Krist eventually agreed to start rehearsing with Kurt, a year on from being given the Fecal Matter tape, pretty much anyone who had a quiff would come to visit their practice space (an empty flat above Krist's mom's beauty parlour). It was the only place to go. For equipment, the pair – plus 'some jock guy', Bob McFadden, on drums – used a cheap mic and beat-up guitar amp; Krist had given his old one to Matt Lukin in return for Matt bailing him out of jail after an incident involving some rednecks in a parking lot. Krist and Kurt didn't like their new hangers-on: they referred to them disparagingly as 'the Haircut 100 Club' after the lightweight British pop band of the same name.

Kurt didn't like the people who were hanging out at the shack, either: most would be under age drinkers with little respect for the place. Kurt was more into acid, or pot. "He was totally into getting wasted, whatever the time of day," Krist recalls. "He was a real mess."

In the early spring of 1987, Matt Lukin left the Melvins when Buzz decided to quit drinking momentarily and that Melvins should become a 'dry' band. Matt was like, "No way." Buzz then used the excuse of a move down to California to say the band was breaking up. (They weren't.)

Kurt also began to fall out with his flatmate. Matters came to a head when he laid masking tape down the centre of the house, and informed Matt that he was forbidden to cross the line. It was too bad the bathroom was on Kurt's side. Lukin moved out, and Dylan Carlson moved in. Carlson was a self-taught genius with wild, unkempt hair, a messy beard and strong views on life. Kurt tried to find him a job, laying carpets – it didn't work out, the boss at Kurt's workplace in the Ocean Shores hotel was too drunk to open the door to them. The pair became best friends.

"I first met Dylan in '85," recalls Rich Jensen. "He must have been 13 or 14. He was a dark kid. He was like – if William S. Burroughs is an icon of darkness – a little William S. Burroughs kid. I had a sense he came from a rural, gun-toting family. He was kind of fun, but he had this very dark character. I knew kids in high school who were into carburettors in cars and amps and computers or whatever. Guns and heavy metal and weird religions were Dylan's categories."

"Dylan was fucking nuts, God bless him," remarks Seattle musician Kelly Canary fondly. "Once I asked him what he'd been doing. He was like, 'Oh, I realised I didn't know anything about teeth so I went to the library and learned about teeth.' That was Dylan. He didn't know anything about teeth, so he spent five hours in the library learning about teeth."

"One time Dylan was passed out," Slim Moon – also a former member of Earth – recalls, "and nobody else was home. Krist was banging on the door, but it was locked. So he crawled up the back of the house to a second storey window, when suddenly he saw a double-barrelled shotgun right in his face. Dylan always kept a gun under his bed. Dylan used to talk about how he wanted to kill people and how if he didn't make it as a rock star, he'd have to become a serial killer. He had this dog that he found on the beach that was burnt. He set it up as an altar near his bed. It was this burnt dog with candles and rosaries and this other pseudo-religious iconography."

Kurt first met Tracy Marander while living at the shack.

"Tracy was awesome," says Tobi Vail. "She was one of those punk girls that every scene has, who knows more about music than most guys and totally nurtures the scene but gets no credit for it because nurturing isn't valued, although people need that kind of love and support. She was really into girl bands – there weren't many then. I think I found out about Frightwig[12] through her. She documented Northwest punk shows for years in photographs. She should put out a book. She had a great sense of style and a lot of guts. She was older than me and I totally admired her. She was tuff. She really did take care of him . . ."

Tracy and her friend Tam Orhmund were unlike Aberdeen girls: Tracy sported a zebra-stripe coat and bright red hair. She changed her hair colour a lot: from shocking punk to thick wavy dark brown with bangs – later, she'd look like a typical Olympia indie kid; tights, clumpy shoes, flowery skirt, cardigan pulled down over the hands. She was larger than Kurt, who would dress himself in layers of clothes, Pacific Northwest style (because then you can remove each layer as it gets less cold or rainy). Kurt and Tracy first met a year earlier, outside an all-ages punk club in Seattle, the scene of one of Kurt's under age drink busts: it took a while for Tracy to convince Kurt she wanted to date him. The two bonded over their pet rats: Kurt had a male one called Kitty that he'd reared from birth and given free run of the shack.

"Tam and Tracy were totally punk-looking – and Aberdeen is all plaid shirts and baseball caps," recalls Candice Pedersen. "We'd all drive up to Aberdeen together, and listen to music – Black Sabbath, Kiss. We'd stay up all night, listen to music and drive home. It was pretty innocent."

"Tracy was super sweet," says Ian Dickson. "She worked at the food court at Boeing and took care of Kurt *entirely*."

Kurt stayed on at the shack for two months after Lukin moved out. Then, in the autumn of 1987, Tracy moved from Tacoma to a new apartment at 114 1/2 North Pear St, Olympia, and Kurt moved in with her. Tracy made Kurt lists of tasks to do while she was out at work, leaving them pinned everywhere – to the fridge door, cupboards and walls. Stuff like, "Do laundry, mop floors, clean cages, get shopping, vacuum." The usual.

"The first time I met Kurt was when we knocked on his door to talk to Tracy about moving into the apartment," relates Ian. "I was 19. He was a couple of years older than me. I had the most powerful first impression of him because he was so sweet. He brought us coffee to where we were sitting on the steps. Nobody did that at our house. It sounds totally normal, but he was like, 'You guys want some coffee?' and I was like, 'Oh my God! It's Kurt Cobain! He's in Nirvana!' And of course, you know, they weren't even called Nirvana then . . .

"The front door opened on to a kitchen and a big room," he continues. "There was a huge rat cage with these different levels and a giant rat called

Sweetleaf [probably named after the Black Sabbath song]. The apartment was crammed full of stuff he'd collected. They had cable, which was weird – nobody had cable back then. He would channel surf for days. This was back when Jerry Springer was starting and there were all these Christian channels. There was this thing they called *The Power TV*, these Christian weightlifters that'd do stuff like, 'In the name of Jesus!' and smash bricks with their elbows. He'd make tapes of them and inter-cut them with weird scenes he'd find elsewhere on the dial. We were like, 'Oh my God. You've done way too much acid and got way too much time on your hands.'"

Kurt would stay at Nikki McClure's house while she was away. He was a good houseguest – he kept the place clean and tidy, much to her surprise. "It was probably because he was so timid, and didn't cook," she explains.

"There was one time I came to Kurt's house and saw him in the kitchen," she continues. "When he saw me he was like, 'Oh good! I'm cooking! Would you like some?' He was making this Rice-a-Roni stuff out of a box with random ingredients mixed in." Nikki wasn't tempted by his offer – not only was the food unappealing but the place was a mess and Kurt kept a rabbit in a cage above the fridge.

"Kurt was a hermit. He kept weird hours," she says. "They were a presence at parties, though: especially Krist. He would sit there with two jugs of wine – one in each hand – and he was just so big!"

Tracy's apartment was decorated with a defaced Paul McCartney poster, Kurt's mutilated dolls and paintings – anatomical models, religious artefacts. "He'd make incredibly detailed sculptures out of stuff he'd find in thrift stores," says Slim. "A strange mix of pop culture ephemera and clay sculpture."

"I didn't mean to make the dolls look evil," Kurt told me in 1992, "but somehow they always ended up that way. I liked Goya[13] a lot." The singer painted the bathroom blood red, writing RED RUM[14] on one wall. Outside in the backyard, the pair placed strings of cheapo Fifties lights. Pictures of meat intermingled with those of diseased vaginas in a particularly gruesome montage on the fridge. "He was fascinated by things that were gross," Tracy explained to one journalist. One of Kurt's skeletal self-paintings hung on the wall. The apartment was small, cramped; smelly and fly-infested because of all the pets . . . but it was home.

"There was the rat, a bunny rabbit and a cat," remembers Dickson. "The cat would have sex with the rabbit and it would cause the bunny's vagina to invert and so Kurt would have to take a pencil and push the vagina of the rabbit back in. I'd come up and say, 'Hey, what's going on?' And he'd be like, 'Oh my God, I'm so glad you're here! I'm going to push the bunny's vagina back in!' I was like, 'What are you talking about?' He's like, 'Yeah! Check it out!' He had this cool fish tank that took up one side of the apartment that these turtles lived in. They'd haul themselves out the tank . . ."

Did they have posters on their walls?

"They had junk," he says. "You could never tell what was trash and what wasn't. Things would be ripped out from magazines and taped up. He read *NME* and *Melody Maker*, bought on import from Positively Fourth Street."

"Kurt made audio collages from the kinds of records you get for a dollar at garage sales," Slim says, "everything from TV actors doing really schmaltzy covers to instructional things or dog noises and Halloween records. On the other side of the first Nirvana demo was something called 'Montage Of Heck' that was like half an hour of audio collage."[15]

Kurt took a job as a cleaner and, with the little money he earned, bought a second-hand Datsun car. He'd practise guitar, watch TV, write in his journals and create art. Mostly, he was unemployed.

"Candice told me about this guy in Olympia that everyone thought was a genius," recalls former K artist Rich Jensen, "who just hung around in his room listening to Seventies music all day – serious butt rock."

If that's the case, how did The Vaselines[16] and all the others come about?

"Kurt admired Calvin," Rich replies. "Calvin is a student of youth culture – a serious student, from World War II on, into films and music and the whole rise of an industry centred around teenagers. Calvin could have earned multiple PhDs on that topic. My impression was that Kurt learned about those bands through mix-tapes, passed down to him, possibly from Calvin via Tobi."

"Olympia is a small town with amazing resources, specifically KAOS radio," states Bruce Pavitt. In 1979, Pavitt moved from Chicago to study in Olympia. There he wrote a column on US independent rock for *Op*, and in 1980 started a fanzine called *Subterranean Pop*, dedicated to the same music. It lasted for a couple of years and was followed by some tape compilations. In '83, he moved to Seattle and started a monthly column in *The Rocket* and a biweekly radio programme, both called *Sub Pop*.

"KAOS had the most comprehensive collection of independent music of any radio station in the United States," he continues. "And that's because John Foster, who was the music director, specifically pushed for a priority system for independent record labels. That meant, if you were putting out your own record, you were guaranteed to get airplay on

KAOS. From that collection of music, he put out *Op* magazine, which specialised in independent music.[17] So, from the late Seventies on, Olympia became a magnet for independently produced records. KAOS had the mother lode library in the universe of independent punk records. Because of that library, there were a handful of people who had access to a wide body of information: Calvin Johnson, a few others and myself. If you were involved in the music scene in Olympia, chances were you knew about records that people in Seattle didn't.

"There was a higher degree of sophistication in Olympia, an almost academic approach to punk rock. That's what I studied at Evergreen State College. I hung out at the KAOS library, studied their records and got college credit for it. Anybody going through Olympia at that time was most likely bumping into Calvin Johnson or doing interviews on KAOS – or in Kurt Cobain's case, being interviewed by Calvin Johnson on KAOS. Even though Kurt was from Aberdeen, the fact that he was sitting in the KAOS record library could not help but influence his approach to music.

"There was also a real purity about the vision coming out of the Olympia scene, a high level of integrity, while the Seattle scene was more about business. Kurt was schooled in Olympia. Kurt made money in Seattle. That's how I would define it. And Kurt probably partied in Tacoma. But when talking about Olympia, it is crucial to mention *the honouring of the feminine*. Female punk bands like The Slits and The Raincoats[18], and obviously The Marine Girls[19], were highly valued and that helped lead into a lot of the Riot Grrrl stuff. That's really a key to Kurt's personality, his honouring of the feminine. Whereas in Aberdeen it was about hard rock, whether it was metal or punk, a lot of what Olympia was about was, 'We're going to dig through the crates and find female punk stuff that isn't quite as popular.' "

I used to break it down that Olympia is a mod town, and Seattle is a rocker town. Another definition is that Olympia is hardcore as defined by Ian MacKaye and the LA bands of the early Eighties, whereas Seattle is more punk, as defined by The Sex Pistols and the British bands of the late Seventies. As much as punk disrupted things, it was always trying to work within the mainstream, whereas hardcore didn't see any point in engaging with the mainstream. Punk is an attitude. Hardcore is a lifestyle. The first seeks to subvert society. The second aims to live outside of it.

"Exactly," agrees Bruce. "Calvin and I go way back. He was the only other person to work on *Sub Pop* when it was a fanzine. I envisioned Sub Pop as kind of a networking tool. I was interested in having different regional scenes that were isolated due to lack of media to connect. I've always been interested in the synergy that happens when people or scenes come together. Hence the *Sub Pop* magazine being set up so that all records were reviewed from a regional perspective. And then I started putting out cassettes – and the *Sub Pop 100* compilation – with artists from different scenes from around the country.

"K started out as a vehicle for Beat Happening recordings, and it grew from there. In both cases, the personalities and interests of Calvin and myself came through in what we were doing. K's vision was to establish Olympia as a vibrant alternative scene. And although *Sub Pop* started out in Olympia and moved to Seattle, it was more about looking at things nationally, trying to facilitate sharing music between scenes. *Sub Pop* morphed into a label that promoted what was going on in Seattle. And from that, it reached out once again with the Singles Club and started working with bands from all over the country.

"Kurt was very influenced by Calvin's championing of obscure independent artists, and Thurston Moore [Sonic Youth guitarist] influenced him the same way. I remember visiting Kurt down in Olympia, trying to convince him to sign an extended contract with Sub Pop. I spent eight hours at his house. As a diplomatic gesture, I brought down copies of The Shaggs[20] record, and a Daniel Johnston disc, just to let him know in a symbolic way that Sub Pop supported alternative music. A couple of years later I saw him in *Rolling Stone* in a Daniel Johnston T-shirt."

My T-shirt!

"Your T-shirt!" Bruce exclaims surprised. "Well, I turned him on to Daniel Johnston. So I appreciated the fact he used his celebrity to promote some of the most obscure and independent music out there. Even though his music didn't always reflect that. I mean, just wearing the Daniel Johnston T-shirt was huge!"

Yeah, it got Daniel signed to Atlantic.

"Yeah, but what it really meant was, 'Even though I am the biggest rock star in the world, I am going to champion the least appreciated artist on the planet.'"

On their final US tour, they took Half Japanese[21] as support.

"That's great," says Bruce, smiling. "That is a real demonstration of the Olympia influence. Half Japanese was a huge influence on Calvin and me. Seattle wasn't listening to Half Japanese. Olympia was. This is important: Kurt's conflict of wanting to be the biggest rock star in the world but at the same time wanting to be a fully independent artist in control of his career. It can be seen in the relationship between Olympia and Seattle. Olympia was about valuing integrity. Seattle was about becoming successful. Sub Pop reflected those tensions as well. Because Sub Pop grew out of Olympia and wound up in Seattle."

It was during early 1987 that Krist and Kurt began practising with Aaron Burckhard.

Aaron was a bit of a 'character': he was one of the Melvins' cling-ons, worked at Burger King, boasted a moustache, lived with a divorced mother on benefits, had been in a couple of accidents – once as a passenger in a vehicle that drove through the front window of a local shop, another time when a car he was in caught fire after it rolled over, killing its driver. But he played the drums – albeit a kit comprised of a few bits of his own, a few bits of Dale Crover's and a music stand. Basically, Burckhard was a straight metal kid more interested in getting drunk than practising, which irritated Kurt immensely. He was becoming more and more driven with each rehearsal: "There wasn't much to do," said Burckhard, "except drink beer, smoke pot and practise. Every night we'd do our set three or four times."

By this point Krist was into incense, tie-dyed T-shirts and psychedelic Sixties rock: hippie music. One of his favourite albums was *Shocking Blue At Home*, the 1969 heavy rock album by Dutch band, Shocking Blue.[22] Kurt agreed to cover their song 'Love Buzz'; the interpretation accordingly influenced by his then-favourite bands like Butthole Surfers and The Meat Puppets.[23] It wasn't the first cover the pair had attempted: early on, Krist and Kurt played numerous cover versions, including Led Zeppelin's 'Heartbreaker' and Creedence Clearwater Revival's epic 'Bad Moon Rising' – in fact, they'd briefly formed a Creedence covers band called The Sellouts that fell apart once they realised they wouldn't make any money from it.[24]

House parties were in vogue. So it seemed natural that the trio would play their first show at one.

In March 1987, Kurt, Krist and Aaron headed out to Raymond, a tiny isolated community, 30 minutes' drive from Aberdeen. The band was determined to make an impression on an audience they all considered redneck (apart from Burckhard who described them as 'yuppie', perhaps reflecting his own world view), and the Raymond kids in their Def Leppard[25] T-shirts, lumberjack shirts and mullet hairdos were thrown by the band's appearance. To Raymond residents, Aberdeen kids seemed like 'big towners'. "We scared the hell out of everyone," laughed Burckhard. "Kurt was climbing all over the furniture, pouring beer over the couch."

Krist covered himself in fake blood and jumped out of a window while playing his bass, drunk on Michelob; Shelli and Tracy pretended to make out with the bassist while Kurt introduced 'Spank Thru' as 'Breaking The Law' (later to become one of MTV cartoon critics' Beavis & Butt-head's favourite phrases). Other songs played included 'Downer', 'Pen Cap Chew' and 'Hairspray Queen', plus 'Heartbreaker'. Despite Krist pissing on cars from atop their van, and Shelli getting in a fist-fight with one of the local women over a broken necklace, the band went down OK.

Such extreme music always attracts some measure of support.

In April 1987, Nirvana did their first radio session – a live midnight performance at Olympia's KAOS, with producer John Goodmanson. John hosted the Monday night rock show (mostly SST-type bands[26]), a four-hour block back-to-back with Donna Dresch. He'd seen Kurt play the week before, supporting his and Donna's band Danger Mouse[27] at the closing night of GESCCO.

"I thought Nirvana was awesome," says Goodmanson. "They were like an Olympia band. They were obviously the best of the Northwest rock bands – they transcended the whole Seattle Seventies cock-rock macho thing. So we invited them in.

"There wasn't much banter," he continues. "They were like, 'Are we still on the air?' after every song. Kurt had a tiny Fender amp, like something your uncle would buy you at a guitar store. He was playing around with the same Boss delay pedal I had – very un-punk rock. It was very minimal, like around 11 songs. I could barely afford the tape to record on, so a couple of them were cut off when they were talking about where to go get soda pop."

Early on, Nirvana often played the Community World Theater in south-east Tacoma. CWT was a converted porn emporium in a white trash neighbourhood, kept running through the enthusiasm of local punk rockers. Mostly, bands played for nothing.

"I saw all the early Nirvana shows at Community World," recalls ex-Seaweed[28] singer, Aaron Stauffer. "They sounded like a heavy metal Scratch Acid. Kurt told me he enjoyed watching 'Faces of Death' movies on mushrooms. These mushrooms called liberty caps grew in many places throughout the fall, so any punker worth his or her salt would be tripping a lot for free throughout October.

"It was hands down the coolest rock theatre I've been to," Stauffer continues. "I played my first shows there reading poetry until the owner's brother told me I would never get a girlfriend until I learnt some chords.

Myself and many other local punks would show up and work for free, sanding and painting, making our theatre happen! There was a Melvins' show where Krist got up and sang a bunch of classic rock songs (Kiss, Judas Priest) for the encore. He yelled, 'Punk rock is dead and gone, but rock' n'roll will still live on,' into the mic as he took the stage."

On stage, Kurt wore crushed velvet bell-bottoms, a Hawaiian shirt and platform shoes, and sometimes attempted coordinated jumps similar to Danger Mouse.

"The first time I ever saw Nirvana was at the Community World," recalls Ian Dickson. "I went with Slim and Dylan. There were eight people in the audience. But man, all of us, as soon as they came on and started playing – I think it was 'School' – our jaws hit the floor. Like, 'Oh my God! This is it!' We'd seen the Melvins, we've seen Green River and The U-Men, but the opening note of the fucking first Nirvana set I ever saw was like, 'This is the shit.'"

It was during 1987 that Kurt began experiencing severe stomach pains – quite probably exacerbated by his drug use, Vicodin (a painkiller) and codeine. "It's burning, nauseous, like the worst stomach flu you can imagine," he told Azerrad in *Come As You Are*. "You can feel it throbbing like you have a heart in your stomach. It mostly hurts when I eat."

The condition would haunt Kurt to the end of his life.

Kurt and Tracy's move to Olympia coincided with Krist and Shelli moving to Tacoma where the bassist found work as an industrial painter, working in aircraft factories and paper mills. The band briefly fell apart – so Kurt sent Krist a letter encouraging him not to let all their hard work go to waste. Krist remembers the note being quite formal: "It was like, 'Come join the band,'" he told a local journalist. "'No commitment. No obligation (well, some).'"

Tacoma is a blue-collar town located midway between Seattle and Olympia, similar to Aberdeen, but "more violent" (Kurt). Although Tacoma has its own beauty spots – the train ride alongside the placid Puget Sound, for example – it's notorious locally, mostly because of the 'Aroma of Tacoma', a pungent, burnt rubber smell that assails the nostrils as the city looms into view. It's also home to the most polluted bay on the West Coast – Commencement Bay.

"It's the sawmill," laughs Candice. "Olympia used to be really bad, too, you could see faeces in the water. Tacoma had an air of danger or depravity that you didn't see in Olympia, although there was certainly a pocket of not-healthy stuff in Olympia going on at the time. I would have lived in Tacoma but there were no good jobs. Tacoma was very punk, very lower-middle class. Girl Trouble was an atypical band. When we were growing up, we were really poor, but it was a different kind of poor, it wasn't city poor. That had a play in the kind of music and partying that took place there. It was much more traditional punk."

"People from Tacoma got a lot of respect from Olympia in the mid-Eighties," says Pigeonhed's Steve Fisk.[29] "If Seattle is New York, Tacoma is New Jersey. New Jersey doesn't need New York. People talk different and have lower rent concerns and priorities. Maybe that's what made Girl Trouble easier to relate to than Soundgarden, if you were from Olympia."

The two bands were contemporaries. "Girl Trouble *are* Tacoma," explains Seattle musician James Burdyshaw. "They're Sixties garage hounds. They love The Cramps, The Sonics, The Wailers and goofy TV like *The Banana Splits*." Soundgarden, meanwhile, started in the mid-Eighties after guitarist Kim Thayil moved down to Olympia specifically to be part of the KAOS/*Op* scene. Odd, considering how heavily influenced by Led Zeppelin Soundgarden were. Not so odd, considering how cool – in their attitudes towards women especially – Soundgarden were for a heavy metal band.

"But Kurt went to Tacoma as well," says Candice, "because that's where Tracy lived. Then Tracy came to Olympia because it was less expensive. Their choices were made by where their girlfriends were. I don't think it was a philosophical choice. It was a reality."

"Tacoma is a little more sleepy and grittier than Seattle. It's a quasi-city," says Burdyshaw. "My memories of going to Tacoma are all weird keg parties with heavy metal guys and punks and normal kids drinking together."

So Kurt moved into an apartment with Tracy. Was that the one you were living next door to with Dylan?

"It was a house converted to three apartments," corrects Slim. "I had lived with Dylan in this place called the Alamo. I lived on a porch, then I had my own apartment that I got just for Jean Smith[30] and after she dumped me I went back to living with groups of people. Nisqually Delta Podunk Nightmare had broken up because Dylan heard the first Melvins album and declared he would never play guitar again, moving back to Seattle in despair. So I started this new band Lush, then Dylan moved back and we had an empty room, so he moved in with us.

"I was the weirdo that hung out sober while everybody else got plastered. Tracy and Shelli almost never got to hang out because they had the graveyard shift at Boeing [Shelli later took a job at the same cafeteria as Tracy]. They'd get off work at six in the morning and go to King Solomon's Reef, for Longshoremen's happy hour, and get drunk, and then go to sleep. When they were home, and if Kurt wasn't feeling sorry for himself, or having band practice, we'd go to parties. We were teenagers, it was social."

Why did he feel sorry for himself?

"He was a mopey guy. Except for when he was doing the thing he was born to do, or he was loaded and being hilarious, he was either depressed, or quiet, or introverted. There was a ton of record listening. Me and Dylan listened to a lot of crazy jazz and King Crimson and Uriah Heep and some metal like Metallica. There was a lot of classic rock like Led Zeppelin and AC/DC. I liked Beat Happening and The Vaselines, Talulah Gosh.[31] I wasn't scientific about it. We loved X[32] and the bands that were written about in *Forced Exposure.*[33] That was much more the world that enchanted Kurt: Big Black and Killdozer[34] and Scratch Acid and Sonic Youth."

**Addenda 1: Olympia vs Seattle**

Most of the literature about Nirvana portrays them as being a Seattle band. Do you agree?

"Well . . . they weren't from Seattle," mulls Steve Fisk. "Some bands came to Seattle and changed their sound. Whatever they were, Nirvana were like that already when they got here. Nirvana were big and fuzzy and metal-like because they hung out with the Melvins. Do you think of Melvins having more to do with Olympia than Seattle?"

Of course I do.

"There's your answer. You should have seen the shit I gave the guys putting together that TV show.[35] I told them, 'What, you're coming to Seattle to talk about *Nevermind*? Why, because they won't talk to you in Olympia, where Kurt had real friends? Or haven't you figured that out yet?' During the Eighties, the same 100 people would travel an hour to see a show in Washington. Calvin would put on these weekend tours that lasted a month: Girl Trouble, Beat Happening and Danger Mouse. Everybody would get together on the weekends and play each other's hometowns. One weekend they'd play Eugene, another weekend Olympia, another Bremerton. They weren't playing big cities because they weren't from big cities. For me, the world was two things: from Seattle, or not from Seattle. There was Tacoma with the garage rock thing and Boise's got the clangy guitar sound. There really weren't bands that sounded like

Seattle in Olympia. You had to go into Portland to find a band that sounded like it was from Seattle."

What separated Olympia from Seattle and the other regions?

"Nobody played solos in Olympia – ever. Even if something happened between the second chorus and the third verse, it was more of a rhythmic thing. There might be some single string guitar playing in there, but it wasn't a solo. Also, having no bass-player meant that you were not going to be a conventional band."

Doesn't the bass traditionally provide the sexual element in rock music?

"The kick drum is a little more sexual than the bass."

Obviously, the fewer instruments you have to play, the easier it is to form a band.

"Olympia is all about Tobi Vail throwing her drink across the room and saying, 'Damn it, let's make a record.' Then you go do it right then and there. A bass is heavy. Not only is it heavy to play, but also the actual gear you have to plug the bass into is expensive and heavy, whereas some guitar amplifiers are cheap and small and crappy. The smaller the guitar amplifier, the better it sounds at a low volume. There you've got your Olympia aesthetic. No bass, nothing complicated, and a guitar that sounds great when you turn it all the way up and you can still play in your apartment, hopefully without bugging anybody."

What would you say the K records aesthetic is?

"A friend told me about how he'd been playing Frisbee on the courtyard of Evergreen State College and he had his shirt off. Another Evergreener, a man, had come up and casually said, 'It's a sunny day. I notice you've got your shirt off.' He goes, 'There are a lot of women out here. They'd probably like to take their shirts off too. Maybe you ought to put your shirt on. What do you think?' Olympia was a place where one man would tell another man to put on his shirt to support women's inability to take off their shirts. Talk about subjugating your own ego: 'The only way the world's going to get any better is if the men get together and give the women a chance.' And it's so condescending and so stupid and so un-feminist, but that's kind of the mentality of an Evergreener. And so Kurt, trying to be cool and fit in, trying to be an upright, moral human being, got some third-hand version of how to be an Evergreener."

How did you meet Calvin?

"It was 1978. I'd just moved to Olympia. My friends there, the people who ran KAOS and *Op* magazine, were telling me how they had kids with their own radio shows. Calvin was one of them. Someone described him as this really mean punk rock kid: 'He'll walk in and he'll be in such a bad mood that he won't even play the news. He'll just get on the air with some surly voice and play records. He's a real jerk.' The first time we met, I suspect he was trying to figure out if he could trust me because I had long hair. He was wearing girl-watcher shades and sported serious spiky hair. It was 1980.

"I later recorded him in The Cool Rays. The Cool Rays played half covers and half originals. Just like Beat Happening, there was a soft-spoken guitar-player who was the brains behind everything, the guy that made the music stuff happen. Calvin always needed a six-string guide."

Why do you think Calvin has such an influence?

"He picked one thing he was good at, and did it. He did it really well, did it all the time, and lucked out. The adults did all the paperwork. Calvin was a very young person, surrounded by six older people who really knew what they were doing. By the time Calvin was 30, these people had lives, but Calvin was still running strong in the philosophy and ideals of the time. KAOS was really important, *Op* as well. So why was Calvin? He's charismatic, a very good dancer. I don't know how he talked the world into starting these two-piece bands and singing about bunnies and picnics."

Nirvana was an Olympia band. Do you believe that?

Al Larsen: "I don't know. Olympia is not very together ever, it seems like."

Rich Jensen: "Personally, I thought they were an Aberdeen band that wanted to be an Olympia band."

Al: "Hey, wow. Black Flag, Screaming Trees, Beat Happening, The Vaselines, The Pastels . . . I was working with some of these pieces in Some Velvet Sidewalk, and putting them together. And Nirvana worked with some of these same pieces in a really pleasing way."

Screaming Trees were a windswept, psychedelic noise band, whose members met in an Ellensburg detention centre. The Conner brothers (guitar and bass) weighed 300 pounds each, and their dad was the local school principal – so they were easy targets for redneck humour. Singer Mark Lanegan has one of the great Pacific Northwest nicotine-laced voices, and a penchant for trouble. Kurt Cobain, for one, was heavily influenced by Lanegan's laconic world-view, drug use and musical preferences.

Rich: "'Swap Meet' is one of my favourite Nirvana songs, because that's an Olympia song, not a Black Sabbath song."

Al: "I think that your central contention for your book is probably really good, but Rich and I won't be able to agree with you. It doesn't mean you're not right. It just means you can't have us saying it."

Rich: "I disagree. They're a rural Washington band whose image of the artistic cultural Valhalla was Olympia but they never quite managed to fit it in with their sound because they grew up surrounded by shit-kickers."

**Addenda 2: Sonic Youth**

The first time I saw the NYC quartet was in 1983 for their *Confusion Is Sex* album, when they filled The Venue in Victoria, London with a cacophonous maelstrom of mangled sound that still reverberates, more than two decades on. Through the Eighties, I loved them because they sounded like none other (1986 – *Evol*, 1987 – *Sister*, 1989 – the incredible *Daydream Nation*; and especially the chilling collaboration with New York performance artist Lydia Lunch, 'Death Valley '69'). I remember seeing a 1985 show of theirs in Woolwich, south London where the sound engineer decided he needed to leave early and started dismantling the PA system around the New York band. It didn't faze them one bit. Shorn of microphones, the band continued to play one of the most exhilarating, frightening wall-of-guitars instrumentals I've ever heard.

At the start of the Nineties, the NYC quartet changed gear. Listened to now, albums like 1990's *Goo* and 1992's *Dirty* with their bubblegum pop sensibilities don't sound so out-of-line with the previous albums, but at the time it felt like a minor revolution was taking place. Not so much for the music, more for its source: Geffen records. If Sonic Youth could worm their way into the heart of the beast then surely anyone could?

So it proved. Before Sonic Youth signed to Geffen, 'alternative rock' and MTV grunge didn't exist. Check your history books.

"Our whole scene was under their shadow," comments Slim Moon. "They've remained 'the band' forever. They're royalty. If Sonic Youth had only made three or four records, they might be part of a list of the greatest American bands. Considering they've made 20 years of great records, they pretty much left everybody in their dust."

"*Sister* [Sonic Youth's 1987 album] is more bad acid trips I never took," stated Courtney Love to me in 1992, "plus physics or psychics, Philip K. Dick, astronomy, best bending of English and football, no boyfriends at all, no girlfriends either, lots of cigarettes and bad drugs, a frozen spring in a room all alone for six months not talking to anyone except the regulars at the strip bar. Bad wine and the same old stinky old nightie and trench coat, big holes in my shoes all over NYC, until I got bag lady blisters and I had this record, anti-depressants don't work now. Times Square is sick, I gotta go back to LA, maybe I'll stop listening to this damn velvet shiny light Josephine Wiggs' [Breeders bassist] sticky New York dark. I can't get the rats out of my hair, angels are dreaming of you."

It's easy to take Sonic Youth for granted: whereas their peers who split up long ago are re-forming and cashing in, the Youth have maintained an astonishingly high musical standard – never static, always fluid, bringing on board only their second new member in 15 years with Chicago's Jim O'Rourke in 2002 on *Murray Street*. If Sonic Youth had split after *Dirty* and got back together in 2005 they'd be making a million bucks a year too.

I had a minor epiphany in Portland, winter of 2004, when watching the Sonic Youth compilation video with M. Ward. The songwriter turned to me and said, "I think they're as good as Nirvana." For him it was the highest compliment.

I looked at him, dumbstruck.

How could he even begin to compare the two bands?

. . . So Thurston Moore's leaning over the front of the stage, lanky, his instrument howling with distortion; one moment he's sawing at the edge of an amplifier and throwing his guitar into the galley; the next he's pulling a speaker across the stage, lacerating sound. Steve Shelley slumps down low over his drums, spent, hammering out the occasional roll of distant thunder; Lee Ranaldo races across to the wings to pick up another Fender to mutilate; saxophonist Mats Gustafson blows deep squalls of dementia. Kim Gordon walks off stage, bored by the boys' indulgence. Over on the far side, Jim O'Rourke sways back and forth like a drunken Nick Cave, cracking his guitar lead (or possibly a steel tape measure) like a whip, lashing layers of noise with every swirl of his arm.

Suddenly there's a blur of movement, and next thing anyone knows Thurston has been brought crashing to the ground, arms thrown up too late to protect himself, as a member of Detroit's noise overkill lords Wolf Eyes hurls himself on to his back. For a moment he rides Thurston, cruising on a wave of elation: the next it's all over, folk shaking their heads at the sheer unpredictability of the performance. How do they keep their music so fresh? We were making jokes about their name – Sonic 'Youth' – over a decade ago; Kim Gordon's been like the coolest person in rock for easily that time; and yet their sound continues mutating, challenging and inspiring wave upon wave of disparate artists. It's no exaggeration to claim that without Sonic Youth *Plan B* magazine and the community that fuels it would not exist. Wolf Eyes. Lightning Bolt. Nirvana. Part Chimp. Pussy

Galore. Huggy Bear. Liars. Afrirampo. Pavement. Sonic Youth is a primary source for all these bands.

Last year's *Sonic Nurse* album is as emotionally charged as 1984's scouring *Bad Moon Rising*. The tension still rises. The momentum grows.

(*Plan B* issue 7, 2005)

## NOTES

1 The Gossip are a relocated Olympia band: singer Beth Ditto has a bluesy vibrant voice to rival Etta James.

2 Bangs are Maggie's own Ramones/Joan Jett-inspired Olympia trio.

3 Seattle's answer to The Birthday Party's warped suburban take on Iggy Pop: The U-Men had elements of garage rock, The Sonics and The Fall, The Cramps, voodoo, mysticism, art rock, boogie-woogie. Guitarist Tom Price later joined Cat Butt and then Gas Huffer.

4 *Let's Together* and *Let's Kiss* were tape compilations of Pacific Northwest bands put together by Calvin, and sold via his fledgling K distribution network.

5 Scratch Acid were from Austin, Texas, contemporaries of Butthole Surfers and Big Black – ribald squalls of abrasive noise and churning riffs.

6 Live Skull were early East Coast contemporaries of Sonic Youth. Singer Thalia Zedek later fronted the powerful narcoleptic Sub Pop band, Come.

7 Al Larsen: singer with Some Velvet Sidewalk – they played a heavy, primal grind not dissimilar to Nirvana, but more directly personal. "Some Velvet Sidewalk was a mixture of reading William Blake and taking classes in Critical Theory," explains Al. "History is fucked up."

8 Dylan once told me he'd been inspired to form Earth after seeing The Legend! perform live – sandwiched between Nirvana, Tad and Screaming Trees in Portland's Pine St Theatre, 1990. "Well, if *that* guy can do it . . ."

9 Richard Brautigan was a US writer, best known for *Trout Fishing In America* – full of child-like wonderment and metaphors. Born in Tacoma, Washington. Committed suicide in 1984, age 49.

10 The other two most powerful performers, in case you're wondering, are Courtney Love in the early Nineties and Nick Cave in his Birthday Party days.

11 Daniel Johnston is a troubled singer-songwriter who used to hawk his home-made cassette tapes round the streets of Austin, Texas. Has spent his adult life in and out of mental institutions: once after he pushed a woman out of a second-storey window, believing her to be possessed by the devil. His songs are deeply personal, deeply affecting.

12 Frightwig were an all-female San Francisco punk band, similar to Flipper.

13 Goya was a classic Spanish oils painter, masterful user of light, notorious for his 'Black Paintings' created at the end of his life and still some of the most disturbing, intense images ever committed to canvas.

14 Murder spelt backwards – a reference to Stephen King's *The Shining*.

15 Snippets of 'Montage Of Heck' appeared on *Bleach* and *Incesticide*.

16 The Vaselines were a minimal and alluring Eighties Scots boy-girl duo heavily influenced by The Pastels and The Velvet Underground – sexually charged where most of their C86 contemporaries paraded their lack of libido almost as a badge of pride. Nirvana famously covered a couple of their songs.

17 The non-profit Lost Music Network (LMN) published *Op*. Hence K records: K – LMN – OP.

18 Two brilliant and interlinked British all-female punk bands: The Slits supported The Clash on their 1976 *White Riot* tour and experimented with heavy dub and reggae sounds, although some purists prefer their earlier all-out sonic noise assaults. The Raincoats matched a scratchy violin to fragile, spaced-out feminist lyrics and a jagged, jarring sound. The bands shared a drummer, Palm Olive – and a mutual mistrust from the bone-headed English audiences of the time.

19 The Marine Girls: an early Eighties school project that spawned two minimal, melodic and charming all-girl pop albums; plus a career in soporific chart music for Tracey Thorn. They split because, as singer Alice Fox put it, "Tracey wanted to write ballads for estate agents, [songwriter] Jane [Fox] wanted to throw ping-pong balls on to xylophones."

20 The Shaggs: an early Seventies US troupe, often regarded as primary exponents of Outsider Music in their naïve, fumbling and quite charming attempts at pop music. "They were all sisters," Kurt told me in 1992, "with their evil uncle making plans for them. I heard this one live song, where they must have been playing a day-care centre, and the screams in the background are louder than the music. The Shaggs are an archetypal K band."

21 If you're looking for a band that comes closest to capturing the secret heart of Nirvana's music, then you should listen to NYC's Half Japanese.

22 Formed in 1967, Shocking Blue's 'Venus' topped the US singles charts in February 1970 and reached number eight in the UK. They split in 1974.

23 Both the Buttholes and The Meat Puppets disseminated Americana with a warped, wired and explosive psychedelic take on the blues. During the Eighties, Butthole Surfers were seriously out there: full-on acid-fuelled dementia that bubbled over with schizophrenia, backwards tape loops and heavy metal. Frontman Gibby Haynes was like Middle America's worst nightmare. Thoroughly recommended is 1987's *Locust Abortion Technician*.

24 Creedence were a San Francisco-based pop/rock band who mixed rockabilly, R&B and Creole influences on eight fondly remembered US Top 10 singles between '69 and '71.

25 Def Leppard: the very definition of poodle rock.

26 SST was one of *the* US independent labels of the Eighties. Run by Black Flag's Greg Ginn, it was home to Dinosaur Jr, Minutemen, Black Flag themselves, Screaming Trees, Hüsker Dü, The Meat Puppets, Sonic Youth . . . Calvin and Tobi had the Tuesday night rock show. They'd play cassettes.

27 "Danger Mouse had clever, bent-up lyrics and a wild man lead singer [Kurt Flansberg]," colleague Steve Fisk recalls. Donna also played bass with Screaming

Trees, Dinosaur Jr and Team Dresch. One of Olympia's original Riot Grrrls, she started her own fanzine, *Chainsaw*, in 1989.

28 Seaweed were a stoner Sub Pop band from Tacoma, big with skater kids and the early emo crowd. First time I met their singer Aaron he was bouncing up and down on Calvin Johnson's knee. Stauffer, as Spook from Spook And The Zombies, was part of the same Eugene, Oregon crowd that spawned Tobi Vail, Al Larsen and Melvins/Earth bassist Joe Preston.

29 Pigeonhed were a soulful Seattle duo on Sub Pop who scored a weird early Nineties grunge-dance crossover hit. Steve also produced a couple of Nirvana sessions, and was the man behind many a Beat Happening and Screaming Trees record. Formerly, Fisk was in the riff-driven, psychedelic Pell Mell, signed to SST.

30 Jean Smith: singer with inspirational boy/girl duo, Mecca Normal – one of the original Riot Grrrl bands.

31 Talulah Gosh: another great mid-Eighties English cutie band – blessed with a bouncy Sixties girl group beat and childish songs like 'The Day I Lost My Pastels Badge'. The Pastels themselves formed in the early Eighties and are still going. The Scots band is instrumental in encouraging groups as diverse as Jesus And Mary Chain, Belle And Sebastian and The Vaselines. Frontman Stephen Pastel works in a record shop: a classic punk rock librarian.

32 X were an early Eighties Los Angeles punk band – Courtney owes a considerable debt to their singer Exene Cervenka's wired, exhilarating voice. Their 1980 debut *Los Angeles* is thoroughly recommended.

33 *Forced Exposure*, Byron Coley's excellent American fanzine, championing all forms of esoteric music in an esoteric fashion: a forerunner of the UK's *The Wire*.

34 Killdozer were a brutal Midwestern band, direct precursors of grunge: known for their ferociously heavy chords, Michael Gerald's growl and the deadpan, hilarious lyrics. Particularly fine is the cover of 'American Pie' from 1989's all-covers album *For Ladies Only*.

35 The 2005 BBC documentary *Nevermind: Classic Albums*.

# CHAPTER 5

## Here Comes Sickness

*"Here come sickness walking down my street/ Shaking her hips like she's some kind of treat/ All the neighbourhood dogs licking at her feet/ Here comes sickness/ Here comes sickness/ Here comes sickness walking down my street"*

– 'Here Comes Sickness', Mudhoney, 1988

THIS is where it all started.

People ask me what the attraction of Seattle was. The energy, the insane amount of energy rising up through the boards of that town's clubs, the musicians with their long greasy hair and unflagging sick humour, the thrill of loud music. Bodies tumbling on top of bodies, faces smiling and grinning and lapping up the pain, any number of grunge bands merging into one sweat-soaked, glorious whole. The parties where I'd be barricaded into bathrooms by junkie models looking to get laid: later I'd race through streets in cars high on delirium and alcohol and the thrill of the chill night air. The skyscrapers, towering into the night like a symphony of neon and rich promise, ringed by an almost mythical circle of mountains, some of them unseen for years behind the dense cloud and rain. The cheap Mexican beer and endless supply of coffee. The top floor of the Terminal Sales Building where Sub Pop had its offices, world domination promised ridiculously in literature and on the phone, glorious views of the Puget Sound (an inland sea) and the city through every window. The warehouse, wandering through a collector's delight of coloured vinyl, knowing you could take anything you wanted and that you wanted everything you took.

What was there to be excited about? Oh, so much, so much . . .

The numerous late night transatlantic phone calls, enthusing about this or that, not checking facts – never checking facts – only on the lookout for more outrageous lies, more tales of glory. The live shows filled with noise and surprise and the hum of amplifiers feeding back, the bass too loud, the crowd a hive of wanton activity. Overnight drives spent chatting to friendly dominatrices, strip bars that doubled as discos with the mirror ball turning and Tad's band thudding, scuzzy joints that threw you on to the street when your drinking slowed down too much. Train rides that lasted for days and ended with me taking Sub Pop's bosses for all they owned at poker. Soundgarden boasted of lighting farts; Mudhoney talked of ancient scriptures; The Walkabouts[1] swung with gentle grace; Nirvana acted young and mischievous.

What was the attraction of Seattle? It was the lilt in Mark Arm's smile, that knowing smirk as he took another swing at the microphone stand. It was the insane number of friendly faces all looking to make sure your good time was your only time; dorky girls who dragged you to ridiculous places and made up songs when sleep deprivation became too much; conversations that lasted for years.

"I remember coming back from a month-long tour with Skin Yard in November of '87 and discovering the Melvins had broken up," begins Seattle producer Jack Endino. "Or so we thought. Green River had broken up. Feast had broken up. Those were three of the biggest bands in the Northwest. We were like, whoa, there's us, there's Soundgarden and . . . who else? There was Bundle Of Hiss. Tad hadn't really gotten going yet."

Formed in 1985, Skin Yard played a molten psychedelic grind that later became known as grunge. They appeared on the same mid-Eighties *Deep Six* C/Z compilation as Melvins, Soundgarden, Malfunkshun and Green River. Jack played guitar and Sub Pop sales manager (later C/Z owner) Daniel House played bass. Matt Cameron – later to join Soundgarden and Pearl Jam – was the original drummer.

Future Mudhoney drummer Dan Peters was only 15 when he joined Bundle Of Hiss in 1984: the band also boasted two future members of Tad – guitarist Kurt Danielson and singer Tad Doyle (who actually only joined as second guitarist for the last few months). Bundle Of Hiss were another prototypical grunge outfit, for the way they merged post-punk attitude with classic Black Sabbath riffs. Tad themselves played fierce relentless hard rock, fuelled by a fascination for serial killers, similar to Midwest bands like Killdozer. 'Wood Goblins' is an absolute classic of the genre.

"And then in January," Jack continues, "I found myself in the studio with Mother Love Bone, doing their first demos, with Mudhoney *and* with Nirvana, all within days of each other. Also, I met my wife-to-be a month before that. So January of '88 was a very interesting time for me. My band was starting to move upward, Sub Pop was getting their thing together and we'd recorded Soundgarden's *Screaming Life* EP a few months earlier."

Mother Love Bone was Stone Gossard and Jeff Ament's glam metal post-Green River outfit – widely expected to be the first Seattle band to cross over to the mainstream, leastways until their frontman, the flamboyant Andrew Wood (formerly with Malfunkshun), overdosed on heroin on March 16, 1990. Gossard and Ament briefly formed Temple Of The Dog with Soundgarden's Chris Cornell and Matt Cameron before reconvening in Pearl Jam. The hipper sections of the Sub Pop crowd always – rightly – ridiculed these bands.

Would you say those three bands (Mother Love Bone, Mudhoney, Nirvana) had something in common?

"*No*," the producer states emphatically. "They didn't have *anything* in common."

They had Jack Endino in common.

". . . And the fact they were all from here, played the same clubs, went to the same Black Flag concerts . . ."

They were part of the same crowd, right?

"Exactly. There was a similar aesthetic. They weren't playing the same style of music, but there was no one from the bar band scene. They were coming from a 'write your own songs' ethos. During the Eighties, the biggest bands in town were the cover bands and the blues bands – the Pioneer Square scene in the tourist/college student part of town. Bands writing their own music didn't get much support. The only people that had gotten away with that approach were Queensryche and the east side metal bands. The scene was very, very small.

"You had The Vogue on Tuesdays and Wednesdays, and [University Of Washington radio station] KCMU would sponsor these weird Tuesday night indie shows at The Rainbow, promoted by Jonathan Poneman. [Future Soundgarden manager] Susan Silver would set some up too. I have a poster that typifies the sort of thing. It reads, 'Green River + Room 9 + Soundgarden + Skin Yard + Bundle Of Hiss', all on a Tuesday at The Rainbow for a buck.

"Those three bands were coming from the same place but they were all going somewhere different. It was less obvious back then. Then, they were just guys with noisy guitars and not exactly a surplus of musical skill. None of them were great players. The focus was more about being raw and crazy and putting out emotion and sheer noise. That's the thing I enjoyed. I have a fondness for bands that are able to create huge sheets of noise. I get impatient with people doing the typewriter thing on the guitar. Music has to be good *in spite* of the technique, almost.

"Players that were too good back then were viewed with suspicion. Some people say there may have been an anti-intellectual bias to the scene, which I blame on Bruce Pavitt. Bruce is an anti-intellectual intellectual. To him, the more brainless the music the better. Maybe it filled something he needed in his own personality. At the time, however, all this analysis was not happening. We were just making the records . . ."

Back at Krist's place in Tacoma, Kurt Cobain was stepping up rehearsals: anathema to Burckhard who was there mostly for the beer. "They wanted to practise every night," he complained to Michael Azerrad. "*Every* night. I'm like, give me a break." Aaron was still living in Grays Harbour and unwilling to commit to the band. He felt he had a good chance of becoming a full manager at Burger King.

Frustrated by his drummer's attitude, Kurt placed an advert in the October 1987 issue of *The Rocket*: "SERIOUS DRUMMER WANTED. Underground attitude, Black Flag, Melvins, Zeppelin, Scratch Acid, Ethel Merman. Versatile as heck. Kurdt 351-0992." There were no immediate applicants, so Kurt and Krist practised with Dale Crover over the course of three weekends with a view to making a demo. Kurt picked out Reciprocal Studios in Seattle because he loved the sound on *Screaming Life*.

"They were excited to work with Jack because he'd done stuff for Soundgarden and Green River," recalls Slim. "It was cheap and he agreed to do it for lower than his usual fee."

The studio, in Seattle's unfashionable Ballard district, was in a brownstone building dating from the Thirties, previously known as the Triangle Grocery. From the mid-Seventies it was known as Triangle Recording – the studio where the punk/New Wave *Seattle Syndrome* LPs were recorded.[2] Reciprocal opened for business on July 1, 1986; a wedge-shaped triangle with the control room at the narrow point, the bathroom at another point and the entrance door at the other. Around the bathroom was a small isolation room, like a cupboard, where you could put one amplifier. And that was it. Doorframes hung loose and it reeked of stale beer and drummers. There was no air conditioning; when it got hot, bands would have to leave the door open and let the exhaust fumes from passing trucks come in.

"It's a terrible studio!" exclaims Jack. "It's a terrible room, completely dead, it's carpet and plasterboard, the control room is horrible and I can't believe I ever made a good record there. When I go back there now I walk in and my body starts getting creeped out like, 'I can't believe I spent *fiiiiiive yeeeeears* in this *buiiiilding*!' "

Jack is an easy-going, unassuming, former navy engineer – longhaired with big, deliberate hands and plenty of bracelets. "There was only one person to record with back then," says Dan Peters. "Jack Endino. If you wanted to get on his good side you'd bring him something sweet, a box of sugary cereal like Cap'n Crunch."

" 'Michael Grungelo' was our nickname for him, because his whole name is Michael Jack Endino," laughs Gas Huffer[3] drummer Joe Newton. "He's got these long, spidery arms and this hair hanging down. He would mix those records so fucking loud that you would go into the control room and be like, 'I'm going back out there.' Nobody mixes that loud any more. It changes the way a record sounds."

On January 23, Krist's friend Dwight Covey drove Nirvana and their equipment to Seattle in his Chevy camper heated by a woodstove. The group recorded and mixed nine-and-a-half songs in six hours: the vocals were recorded in one take while Krist went outside with Covey and got stoned. The tape ran out during 'Pen Cap Chew', but the band didn't want to stump up the extra $40 for another reel so Jack faded the song out. The entire session cost $152.44, which Kurt paid for out of his janitorial earnings. The songs were 'If You Must', 'Downer', 'Floyd The Barber', 'Paper Cuts', 'Spank Thru', 'Hairspray Queen', 'Aero Zeppelin', 'Beeswax', 'Mexican Seafood' and 'Pen Cap Chew'[4] – later played in the exact same order that night at Community World Theater under the name Ted Ed Fred.[5]

"I'm a sucker for riff rock," Jack states. "I grew up on Deep Purple and Zeppelin and all that English heavy metal stuff. The music I got into when I was in high school – earlier Blue Cheer and Cream and Hendrix – was as close to indie rock as it got in 1971 over here, the 'scary, heavy' stuff that wasn't played on the radio. That demo was Seventies riff rock with a slightly weird post-punk angularity; Dale was fundamentally a heavy metal drummer, and Kurt wrote songs around interesting guitar riffs. The thing that separated it from anything else was the singing. His voice had a lot of character and he had a weird ear for melody, he wouldn't be following the guitar riffs like typical idiot riff rock. Right off, I thought Kurt's got a cool scream. I think that's what caught Jonathan [Poneman]'s attention too."

Why did you pass the tape on to Sub Pop?

"I thought it was great."

Were you in the habit of passing on tapes to Sub Pop?

"Well, Sub Pop hadn't existed for very long at that point, and I was in daily contact with them. This was literally days after I recorded [Mudhoney single] 'Touch Me I'm Sick' . . ."

Does Dale really hit the drums harder than anybody else?

"No, not harder than anyone else," smiles Jack. "He's just a unique player and has a very good self-taught, oddball style. It's like he grew up with the stick as his limbs. Anyways, the band went to leave and I said, 'I really like this, can I make a copy?' so as they drove off I made my own copy of the mix. They came in at noon, left at six, drove to Tacoma, played a show and then Dale was out of there, off to join Buzz in San Francisco and re-form the Melvins."

"Seattle, like the other extreme corners of America, is a magnet for transients and the dispossessed," says Jonathan Poneman. "A lot of them move here and become serial killers or right-wing militia extremists. So you have this very progressive city that's got a tradition of socialist activism and academics, and these crazy backwoods radicals. It makes for a very combustible and unique environment."

Originally from Toledo, Ohio, former musician Poneman moved to Seattle in the mid-Eighties. He got a job as the DJ on the local scene show at KCMU. In 1986, Jonathan joined forces with Bruce Pavitt to start Sub Pop records after a mutual friend, Kim Thayil of Soundgarden, introduced them.

"The first time I heard of Bruce was when I bought one of his cassettes," Jon recalls. "It was amazing. He had an elegant and brilliant way of being able to give context to the American independent rock music being made in small cities – bands like The Embarrassment from Lawrence, Kansas, or Pylon from Athens, GA . . . to say nothing of The U-Men. We later became buddies. We were different in most ways, but we shared a similar gallows humour."

Seattle in 1988 had little to distinguish it from the outside world: rain, good coffee, Boeing, a fish market and a beautiful skyline, at the centre of which was the Space Needle built for the 1962 World Fair. It was a remote big city with a small-town attitude, sheltered by the Olympics and the Pacific Ocean on one side, the Puget Sound on another, Canada on a third, and cut off from the rest of America by the Cascades and 2,000 miles of badlands, cornfields and the Rocky Mountains.

Like any metropolis it had its hangers-on and a handful of cool places: Capitol Hill, 1st Avenue's red-light district, home of the OK Hotel and

The Vogue where Pavitt would spin muscle car rock against hip hop DJ sets. The first vinyl release on Sub Pop was the 1986 compilation *Sub Pop 100*. It featured only a couple of Northwest artists (Wipers, The U-Men, Steve Fisk). It wasn't until the following summer, with the release of Green River's *Dry As A Bone* EP, that Bruce became excited about the potential of local bands.

How is it that Bruce Pavitt got so rich?

"He's got dumb luck," sighs Fisk. "Really, really dumb luck. He's not that smart. He's not stupid, but he's not that smart."

Who had the business sense?

"No one," the musician/producer replies. "Bruce had great ideas. He was willing to take chances, but he's Tony fucking Wilson. Bruce wanted to create this giant monstrosity with no paperwork. Sub Pop was a clone of Factory records.[6] Bruce is an entrepreneur, but he's not Donald Trump smart. Bruce is a communist. Back then it was like a really fucked-up rock family."

The factor that differentiated Seattle from a dozen other American cities was its self-belief. Being so distant from the rest of America, musicians in the Pacific Northwest didn't feel such a need to follow the fashions of LA or New York, so they were free to develop on their own terms. Literally, they thought no one was paying attention, outside their own immediate peers – a feeling exacerbated by the dismissive attitude towards local music propagated by editors such as Charles Cross at *The Rocket*. Seattle groups listened to the same records: Iggy Pop, The Sonics[7] and The Wipers, Led Zeppelin, Black Sabbath and Flipper. Few of these artists had much time for punk's brevity or holier-than-thou elitism.

"Mostly, these musicians had been in jokey hardcore punk bands," explains Rich Jensen. "After a few years they reacted against the lazy pseudo-rebellious posing of their peers – too many Mohawks and too many leather jackets covered with shallow political slogans, no guitar solos allowed – and started riffing out, growing their hair and acting like pre-punk gods of rock."

Unlike metal, which had degenerated into a lame LA 'hair' parody of itself, this music had an impassioned urgency. Seattle musicians learned well the lessons of US punk pioneers like Black Flag, Minutemen and San Francisco's female-led The Avengers. The Northwest already had a sound of its own: "Hard music played to a slow tempo," was how Kurt Cobain described it to me in February 1989. It was a sound that took equally from hard rock, punk rock and psychedelic rock, infused with a freshness that made it sound unique. A word was needed to describe what was happening: self-deprecating, steeped in garage lore and disposable. You didn't need to look far to find something that matched the dirty, abrasive sound of Mudhoney: grunge.

Looking to discover who invented the word? Rock critic Lester Bangs described The Groundhogs as "good run-of-the-racks heavy grunge" in the April 1972 issue of *Rolling Stone*. Mudhoney guitarist Steve Turner says he's seen it used much earlier than that, on the back of an album released by rockabilly pioneer Johnny Burnette, and also in connection with Link Wray.[8] Even as early as *Dry As A Bone*, Sub Pop were promoting their label's sound as, "Gritty vocals, roaring Marshall amps, ultra-loose GRUNGE that destroyed the morals of a generation."

"Yes, people did use the word 'grunge' in 1988," confirms Dawn Anderson. "It's only when people outside Seattle started saying it that the term became a joke."

"Grunge happened because Seattle had a perfect confluence of good bands, good indie-marketing efforts, camaraderie and people making good recordings and taking good photos, all working for very little money," believes Endino. "It was the right time. Commercial rock had become so pathetic and formulaic."

"Usually something like Seattle kicks open because there are a lot of influences converging," Amphetamine Reptile records boss and ex-marine Tom Hazelmyer explains. "Seattle had a good mix of hardcore people and metalheads, with indie folk more into Gang Of Four[9] and The Birthday Party.[10] Seattle was a small city, not like LA or NYC where the kids could go off into their own clubs. They had to converge. [Jeff] Ament from Green River was a straight up metal kid. Steve Turner was a straight up hardcore kid. Also, no one had even heard of Seattle. I'm not completely ignorant and I had to look at a map to see where it was when I heard I was being stationed there.

"Seattle was not big on the tour circuit," he continues. "It was too out of the way. The city itself was a weird mix. It was big enough to have metropolitan stuff – antique stores, cool furniture houses, best record shopping I ever saw in my life – but it was also backwards, blue collar, redneck: a convergence of more cultured types and the old port city. Since then, it's turned into big yuppie-ville. Back then, a lot of bands would work on shipping vessels, take that three-month tour up to Alaska and have enough money to live off for the rest of the year."

"People who go to these centres like London or LA or New York to make it big, they want to play ball," explains Mark Arm. "They want a career as a rock musician. No one in the late Eighties, with maybe the exception of the guys in Mother Love Bone, thought you could get anywhere by being in Seattle. It wasn't about being a rock star – it was about being in a band and having fun."

"We were determined not to take ourselves too seriously," agrees photographer Charles Peterson. "Otherwise music becomes sport."

Before he returned to California, Dale recommended Kurt and Krist try out another Aberdeen kid, Dave Foster: Foster was a metal kid with a moustache and a pick-up truck, another working-class dude who liked his alcohol; he studied jazz drums at high school. Kurt told him to forget his tutorage and just hit the drums. Hard.

Kurt also insisted Dave pare his kit down from a 12-piece to a six-piece.

"Dave was a lot closer to what they wanted," insists Slim, "because he was a Dale Crover wannabe. But he had ridiculously huge drums and used two kick drums instead of a double pedal. We used to make fun of drummers who used two different kick drums because the only reason they have the second one is so that the audience can see it. All his friends wore Coca-Cola clothes. They were very preppy, that white middle-class girl-next-door kind of thing. We thought they were just awful. Me and Dylan referred to him as Anger Problem Dave because he would blow up and scream at Kurt or Krist or at the audience or grab you and throw you against the wall. Then he got into some kind of legal trouble and had to go to anger management workshop."

The first gig the new line-up played was a party at Olympia's Caddyshack house: the place was full of Evergreen students. Kurt dressed in a ripped jean jacket with his toy plastic monkey (Chim Chim, from the cartoon *Speed Racer*) on one shoulder, with a Woolworth's tapestry of *The Last Supper* sewn on to his back. Foster was in typical metal attire: stonewashed jeans and a wife-beater. Before the set even began, an Olympian 'punk' with a Mohawk[11] grabbed the mic and shouted, "Gosh, drummers from Aberdeen are sure weird-looking."

Nikki McClure saw them play in the library at Evergreen: "The first time I saw them," she says, "I immediately saw the King Dome[12] and the lighters. They had 'it'. I knew they'd be totally huge."

Soon afterwards, the trio played another Community World Theater show – for the first time billed as "Nirvana: also known as Skid Row, Ted Ed Fred, Pen Cap Chew and Bliss". The name was Kurt's: he told Dave Foster he'd drawn upon the principles of Buddhism to come up with it. "It means attainment of perfection," Kurt said when Foster noticed a flyer for the show at Kurt's house. He later explained to Azerrad: "I wanted a name that was beautiful or nice instead of a mean, raunchy punk name like The Angry Samoans."[13]

"I always thought it was a dumb name," says Slim Moon. "It didn't fit with how they sounded at all. Maybe that's what Kurt thought was cool about it. At the time they were asking all their friends for names, trying them on for size. If Sub Pop hadn't offered them a seven-inch, they'd have had a different name a week later."

Foster's aggressive attitude and attire proved a problem: he thought the other two had a downer on him because they perceived him and his friends as rednecks – they didn't like the way he'd get into fights. On one occasion, someone spat on his truck so Foster kicked him in the head; more seriously, when Foster discovered that his girlfriend was cheating on him, he beat the crap out of her lover, who turned out to be the son of the mayor of neighbouring Cosmopolis. Foster spent two weeks in jail and got his licence revoked: consequently, he was no longer able to drive to Tacoma for rehearsals.

Fed up with 'Anger Problem', Krist and Kurt had started rehearsing with Burckhard again. He didn't last long either. There was an incident wherein Aaron and Kurt were drinking together after practice. Aaron borrowed Kurt's car to get more beer, and hit the bars instead. A black cop called Springsteen pulled him over for driving under the influence; Aaron made fun of the cop's name and allegedly called him 'a fucking nigger'. Kurt's car was impounded and Krist had to go bail Aaron out, embarrassed.

Next day, Burckhard was out of the band after refusing to come over to practise because he was too hungover.

"Aaron was terrible," grimaces Slim. "They kicked him out because he ended up in jail one weekend when they had a show. I remember Kurt being really grumpy about that, but Aaron always felt like a fill-in. It felt like they were constantly talking about how Aaron sucked, but Aaron had a car. That was big because Aaron could move equipment around and get them all to the practice space."

Let's take a momentary diversion.

Mudhoney fail virtually every criteria of the Ramones Rule. Keep your songs brief. Keep the solos to a minimum. Don't revel in showmanship. Stick to the instruments you know. Root your sound in the girl group lore of the Sixties. Image is vital. Image is all. Don't overstep the 1.15 minutes mark. Don't overstep the 2.15 minutes mark. Don't overstep the 3.15 minutes mark. Keep the same haircut. When founder members leave, replace them with fans. Argue with each other constantly for 23 years and stonewall anyone who dares publicise the fact. Run off with one another's partners. Don't play lead on your own records. Never abuse a guitar. Never resort to spontaneity. Punctuality is next to cleanliness.

Matt Lukin retired from Mudhoney in 2000 after 12 years of service – they don't give out gold watches in rock, just the illusion of a pleasant house in the suburbs. Mudhoney have always been about indulgence, showmanship, spontaneity and great rock'n'roll. Oddly, they never seemed to give a damn for that most motivating of factors when it came to people who chose to live and breathe and queue up for that golden carrot in Seattle – fame.

Steve Turner is the American equivalent of Blur guitarist Graham Coxon. That's not to say he falls about drunk at the front of Billy Childish shows while trying to cop off with members of Huggy Bear.[14] It's more that, through Mudhoney's career, he's exhibited a willingness to experiment that goes far beyond the expected boundaries of his music. Plus, he's been known to fall down drunk at the front of Billy Childish shows.[15] Mark Arm, meanwhile, has an English degree and works in the Fantagraphics Comics warehouse.

Kurt idolised Mark Arm. Before Courtney Love met Kurt Cobain in 1991 – not 1990, as has been extensively and wrongly reported[16] – she tried to get it on with Mark. Back then, the Mudhoney singer was the star of Seattle, no question. What didn't he have? Fearsome stage presence, incredible songs, energy, deadpan caustic humour, lashings of rock knowledge, a drug habit, a massive nose . . . He was Seattle personified. Courtney even told me she'd been driven to name her band Hole after Mark Arm – "The hole at the centre of his being" or something.

"When Mark and I broke up, Kurt was devastated," says Mark Arm's former girlfriend Carrie Montgomery. "I saw him out one night and he was like, 'But you're going to get back together, right?' I found it so interesting that he had such a sensitive reaction. He bet me a fifth of tequila that I'd get back together with Mark. We'd lived together, so I had some boxes with Mark's stuff in, some notebooks where he had started to write songs. One night Kurt was like, 'Hey, would you be comfortable letting me look at Mark's notebooks?' There's one part of a Nirvana song I always thought was about that. I'm not telling which one," she laughs. "I might be wrong."

Did Kurt look up to you and Mark as surrogate parents?

"A little bit," replies Carrie, "but we were the same age! Plus, there were already people around like that – like Kim Gordon [Sonic Youth], who was very maternal towards Mark and Kurt. One time, Kurt came over to our apartment and I was colouring my hair dark red. Somehow it had formed a little bit of a 'V' on my eyebrows so I looked like Eddie Munster. And he's nervous coming over, like it's going to be really hip and cool. When he sees me answer the door, he's so scared he literally jumps right back. I laughed for two weeks after that. It's hard when you're a person in a new environment trying to fit in."

"Mark was a funny, goofy guy that grew into his persona – him and Steve were *nerds*!" exclaims Cat Butt's James Burdyshaw. "They were ultra-nerds! We toured with Mudhoney, and Steve thought we were the biggest group of assholes. We fucked with him. Hard. There was a party going on and Steve rolled out his sleeping bag . . . but he wasn't getting to sleep. All he did was encourage us so we danced on his bed and stuck beer in his face. He was eating pizza so I grabbed it out of his hand and ate it."

Mudhoney formed Halloween 1987. Their sound was – as I wrote back in 1989 – Motörhead meet Spacemen 3[17] meet Blue Cheer meet Iggy on a stroll back from an MC5 concert. The first practice took place on January 1, 1988. Mark Arm was 29 years old. The first Seattle show took place on April 19, five days before Nirvana's debut at The Vogue.

"I didn't even know our name until there was a picture of us in *The Rocket*," Dan laughs. "I called up Mark and was like, 'So, we're called Mudhoney?' "

Mudhoney's debut single 'Touch Me I'm Sick' is the record that encapsulates . . .

"It *is* grunge, isn't it?" interrupts Jack Endino. "It was their first session. We did five or six songs and they ended up using two of them for the single. On the first song they played, 'Twenty Four', the two guitars were wildly out of tune so I politely made them tune up. It took all of one afternoon to record those five songs."

When you recorded the song were you aware of how powerful it was?

"No. I knew it was a cool song, but it's basically 'The Witch' [by The Sonics] . . . not that I knew that at the time. I was young and not far into my career so I had not yet become jaded to the idea of somebody singing through a guitar amp."

*Superfuzz Bigmuff* (Sub Pop, 1988) and *Mudhoney* (Sub Pop, 1989) followed. I'm sure I don't need to tell you how to headbang or crowd-surf or drink kegs of beer or have yourself a damn good time. I first met Mudhoney at the Virginia Inn opposite Sub Pop World Headquarters, February 1989. In retrospect, they gave me a warped view of what all American bands were like – it was my first visit to America, and already it seemed like everyone had a brilliantly developed, evil sense of humour and endless stores of energy. Mudhoney spent the majority of their first overseas interview making shit up, and I loved it.

"The streets over here are paved with grunge," Arm joked in a remark he later grew to regret.

It would be Mudhoney that would go on to introduce grunge to an unsuspecting world via the UK. Their shows were mayhem; sweat, stamina, stagediving, sex and spontaneity. There couldn't have been a student union during the early Nineties that didn't explode into a riot of moshing at the sound of the opening chords to 'Touch Me I'm Sick'. At their laconic best, Mudhoney were untouchable.

Jack passed the Nirvana demo to a few friends; among others, Dawn Anderson, Shirley Carlson and Jonathan Poneman – their first press, first Seattle radio play and first record contract respectively.

"I loved it," says Dawn Anderson. "I was just starting [rock fanzine] *Backlash* and looking for bands to write about. I was really into Malfunkshun, Green River, Melvins, Soundgarden, Skin Yard . . . all those bands. I remember the first of the many times that scene was pronounced dead. It was early 1988, when Green River broke up and the Melvins ditched Matt and moved to San Francisco. Feast had also hung it up. Then of course, Mudhoney, Mother Love Bone, Tad and Nirvana came along, so it was a great time to put out a zine."

*Backlash* had a 10,000 circulation and was pretty close behind *The Rocket* in sales, despite always being on the verge of bankruptcy. It got a reputation among the city's commercial music establishment and at *The Rocket* of being 'that zine that always writes about bad garage bands' (like Soundgarden and Nirvana!).

"Jack was sitting in my room when he called Sub Pop to ask if they'd heard the tape yet," Dawn continues. "Jonathan told Jack he loved it but that Bruce thought it was 'too arty', causing Jack to explode, 'He's into mediocrity!!' It seems weird to think of that early stuff as 'arty', but it wasn't entirely off the mark. It was more inventive than a lot of the other grunge bands."

"I was enamoured of the idea of there being a musical insurgency from this part of the world," explains Jonathan. "I knew how many great bands were out there because I was booking these shows. I'd ask Jack regularly whether he'd heard anything new. And then he says, 'Dale Crover came in with this guy from Aberdeen. It's awesome. But I've never heard anything like it before.' So he made me a tape. I remember listening to the first song, 'If You Must', and going, 'This is kind of cool, nice guitar riff, mumbly Tom Petty-like vocals' . . . and then I came to that crescendo, that 'RAAAA' . . .! It was the first time I heard Kurt's roar. I sat there looking at the tape deck going, 'Oh my God.' I literally popped the tape out of the deck and rushed down to the Yesco offices where Bruce was working: 'You have got to listen to this tape.'"

Yesco was a Seattle company that had bought out Muzak, the company that makes synthetic elevator and shopping centre music. "The worst job you could get there was the one I had when I started," says Mark Arm. "We would get these dirty, gross, old tapes and scrape off the labels so they could recycle the cartridges. It was in this tiny place where dust was flying around and you couldn't hear shit because sanders were going on all day. It was horrible. But it was fun. Chris [Pugh] from Swallow worked there, Grant from The Walkabouts, Tad, Ron from Love Battery[18] . . ."

When Sub Pop moved to the Terminal Sales a few months later almost everyone who worked there came from Muzak. So of course Bruce played the tape during the lunch break when all the musicians were sitting around . . .

"Mark said something about how it sounded like a fifth-rate Skin Yard," recalls Jonathan. "To which I was like, 'Boo! Man!' Mark has impeccable taste, but that was the one time. He has since denied ever saying that. It could be Bruce was attributing to Mark something he felt himself."

Originally, Sub Pop wasn't part of Kurt's plans. And even while they were engaged in early discussions he continued to look elsewhere. Sub Pop was new, with no track record. During 1988, Kurt sent the demo with lengthy handwritten letters to various US labels that housed his favourite bands – Chicago's Touch And Go (Scratch Acid, Big Black, Butthole Surfers), SST and San Francisco's Alternative Tentacles (Dead Kennedys). In fact, he even referred to the tape as 'the Touch And Go demos' in his journal: he estimated that he sent 20 copies to the Chicago label, enclosing with each copy a gift, ranging from small toys to confetti to paper towels encrusted with snot. He never received a reply.

"We are willing to pay for the majority of pressing of 1,000 copies of our LP, and all of the recording costs," he wrote. "We basically just want to be on your label. Do you think you could PLEASE! send a reply of Fuck off, or not interested so we don't have to waste more money sending more tapes? Thanks. Nirvana."

Impressed by the demo, Jonathan booked the trio to play in Seattle.

Both Jon and Bruce separately insist that there was a show in early '88 that happened prior to The Vogue on April 24 (long held to be Nirvana's debut Seattle performance). It took place in Pioneer Square, at the Central Tavern: a long brick tunnel with a stage at one end and a bar at one side. The Central was known for its liberal booking policy. Sonic Youth played there. Butthole Surfers played there.

"At the first [Seattle] show there were three people present: Jon, me and the bartender," recalls Pavitt. "And their songs were bad. And Kurt had a good voice. And they played one good song, and it was by Shocking Blue. None of their original material was outstanding in the least. I thought we could probably get away with putting out the cover. That was my initial impression. And that the drummer had a moustache, and that was problematic."

Was that Aaron?

"Yeah. And to see this band and think, 'This is going to be the biggest band in the world in three years' – no way. I'd put that at about a billion to one. But we were singles-orientated, and I felt that they had enough material for a good single, and that their vibe complemented what we were doing. And that was most important because Sub Pop was cultivating a certain vibe, *à la* Blue Note[19] or Factory. They fit in."

"There was a Central show that was cancelled," says Jonathan, "but there's a second show that happened. It was Aaron Burckhard who was playing drums. And yeah, it was Bruce, Tracy, myself, and one or two other people, at the Central Tavern. Kurt threw up, as later became his custom. Bruce was standing there with a 'prove it to me' vibe. He was getting into it a bit, but when they played 'Love Buzz' he leans over and goes, 'That's the single.' It was that moment, coupled with Nirvana getting props from his friends in Olympia, that Bruce was won over."

He said there was a problem with the drummer's moustache.

"That's true," laughs Jonathan. "I can't express it any better than that. That's succinctly put."

So the second show that Nirvana played in Seattle was at The Vogue, a small alternative dance club owned by cross-dressing Monty and his stripper girlfriend. The Vogue mostly played industrial dance music, but it also featured live music, including Sub Pop Sunday once a month. It was small, not overly disgusting. There weren't too many people present: the usual enthusiasts and a handful of Seattle musicians. The burgeoning Sub Pop crowd, in other words.

Nirvana had to wait outside before playing, since Foster was under age: when they took the stage they played 14 songs, no encore, with 'Love Buzz' as the opening number. By all accounts, it was ordinary.

"I wasn't overly impressed," recalls Dawn. "I thought Kurt acted a little self-conscious, albeit cute, and hadn't quite gotten the knack of playing lead guitar and singing at the same time. There were maybe 20 people there: Tracy, Shirley and . . . were the Sub Pop guys even there? I talked to Kurt afterwards and he said his stomach hurt and that he had puked that day. Then a *Backlash* photographer took some pictures."

In the Rich Hansen photos – Nirvana's first shoot – Kurt looks unshaven, with shoulder-length blond hair and a dark cardigan: he's sitting on Krist's knee, the bassist dwarfing the other two members: Dave has his baseball cap on backwards and wears a white sports T-shirt. His moustache really doesn't fit.

"Nirvana were playing after Blood Circus, not favourites of mine, but they had the big hair grunge moves down and were exciting to watch," says Charles Peterson. "Nirvana were anything but exciting to watch. It was three mopey guys, the definition of downer rock. I was not impressed at all and didn't take any photographs. I figured, why bother photographing a band's first and last gig? I remember saying to Jonathan, 'Are you sure you want to sign these guys?' They had a pot of 'Floyd The Barber' at KCMU [a pot is like an eight-track cassette on a loop] that Shirley had been playing occasionally, usually late at night when I was at work. I found it somewhat interesting, but grating. That, on top of seeing them live, I thought, 'This band is just a snooze.'

"That's why I was photographing for the record label, not running it," he adds, laughing.

"There was a representative from every Seattle band there just watching," Kurt complained in a letter to Dale Crover, somewhat exaggerating the crowd size. "We felt like they should have had score cards. So after the set Bruce excitedly shakes our hands and says, 'Wow, good job, let's do a record'[20] . . . Now we're expected to be total socialites, meeting people, introducing etc. FUCK I'M IN HIGH SCHOOL AGAIN!"

"We were uptight," Cobain told Anderson. "It didn't seem like a real show. We felt like we were being judged."

"Kurt was fairly shy," Dawn explains, "but I was used to that. Most of the Seattle bands I wrote about weren't exactly studs, and whenever I interviewed one, they had to get past the fact that an actual female was speaking to them. I thought Kurt was nice, maybe a little baffled by the attention, since they'd only had one show in Seattle. He did act more comfortable later. I didn't get the impression Kurt was the bandleader, even though he was obviously the main creative force. Krist definitely came across as more confident. I didn't interview their drummer. I don't even remember his name. He was 'that guy with the moustache'. When that issue of *Backlash* went to press they'd just kicked him out of the band, so we cut him out of the photo at the last minute."

The show might not have been that good, but it was enough for Jonathan to call a few days later and suggest that Sub Pop put out a Nirvana single. He arranged a meeting at Café Roma up on Broadway.

It wasn't an auspicious encounter: Krist got hammered on 40-ouncers beforehand, and belched and insulted Poneman throughout their chat. He also yelled at the other customers, "What the fuck are you people looking at? Hey! *Hey!*" (Kurt told Michael Azerrad it was "one of the funniest things I've ever seen".) Tracy didn't like Jonathan's long trench coat. Kurt liked the fact that Jon had some money squirrelled away[21] that he was planning on putting into the label's initial output of limited edition singles and EPs – mostly from local bands. But he didn't like the fact that Sub Pop was unwilling to commit to anything beyond one single, and not even one featuring their own song as the A-side – or that they seemed to have zero business acumen.

"Sub Pop is always broke," Kurt wrote in a letter to Mark Lanegan. "So we're openly looking for any other offer. They mean well but we don't think it's fair for Mudhoney to be favoured and catered to on a higher level than the other bands."

Still. It was a start.

"The meeting at Café Roma was just Kurt, Tracy and I initially," explains Jonathan. "Krist came trundling in later. He was wicked pissed but a lot more gracious than has been portrayed. He was definitely suspicious and said as much but he was intrigued. We all were."

"They were disappointed that Sub Pop didn't like them enough to put out a seven-inch of their songs," comments Slim. "'Love Buzz' was a compromise because Bruce didn't like them so much. Sub Pop went back and forth. Kurt got frustrated. I couldn't believe it when they hired my friend Alice [Wheeler] to shoot the cover and it had to be black and white. Hearing all their stories about Sub Pop really brought the label down a peg in my estimation."

"The thing that Slim and all of them seem not to consider is that I was nervous as fuck," Jon says. "I was in awe of Kurt's talents. I knew he was going to have an impact. It's a fun but awkward part of being a fan. Also, I had to lure my Sub Pop crew to seeing the light about Nirvana. So any reluctance was just the art of hem-and-haw until folks felt comfortable. The cliquey shit was a bummer but it also made our scene congeal."

"Here's a classic Nirvana story," says Candice Pedersen. "Tracy gave me a tape of some stuff they recorded, and I was like, 'Hey Calvin, you should put this out.' He said, 'I'm not putting out some girlfriend's boyfriend's band.' And it sat on the windowsill for years. He wouldn't even listen to it. I was like, 'But they're fun, I go see them every weekend in Tacoma.' Oops. But you know, 'oops' moments often save you. Who knows what would have happened?"

What made them so fun?

"They were bad and stupid," she replies. "Silly and outrageous and fucked-up all the time. Not like fucked-up people, they just fucked up every song. Krist might have been a little loopy, but everyone else was sober. It was pure stupidity, how rock'n'roll should be, stupid and fun."

Gradually accepted into the Sub Pop clique, Nirvana started playing other shows in Seattle – usually with other nascent grunge bands. It took them a while to impress the locals, however.

"The first time I saw Nirvana was at the Central," recalls James Burdyshaw. "They were just another loud, bad band. It was obvious they were trying to sound like the Melvins. All Kurt did was scream. Second time I saw them, they opened up for The Obituaries at Squid Row, summer of '88. I was still drunk but this time they were better. Just. My memory of Kurt was of him going, 'WaaaaaAAAAAAGGGGHHHH!!!!!!' and the band being 'Chung-chung-chung-CHUNG!!!' I mean, Melvins Jr, completely."[22]

"They opened for Bundle Of Hiss," says Dan Peters. "Nirvana start playing and everybody is sitting around like, 'What are they doing?' The PA isn't even turned on. We were all like, 'Hey you guys, you might want to wait until the PA gets turned on.'"

It wasn't until the Squid Row gig on July 30 – where Nirvana were supporting Skin Yard – that Dave Foster realised he was no longer in Nirvana. He'd actually been out of the band for a couple of months by that point, but he was never officially sacked. That wasn't Kurt and Krist's style. He found out via *The Rocket*: he picked up a copy to check out the gig guide, and noticed Nirvana was playing the same night.

Kurt wrote him a dismissal letter but never sent it, perhaps fearing Dave's response: "Dave," he wrote, "A band needs to practise, in our opinion, at least five times a week. We're tired of total uncertainty every time we play a show. The two main reasons are Chris and his work, and you and your location. Instead of lying to you by saying we're breaking up, we have to admit that we've got another drummer. His name is Chad and he's from Tacoma and he can make it to practice every night. Most importantly, we can relate to him."

**Addenda 1: Grunge**

So it's all your fault, right?

Jack Endino: "Well, I invented grunge, didn't I? No, that's your line [laughs]."

No, I gave that up years ago.

Jack: "Oh, did you? Well, thank God for that. Good for you."

So it's your fault . . .

Jack: "Oh no, not entirely. You could blame Mark Arm."

I could, but I'm going to blame you because you're sitting right here in front of me.

Jack: "All right, all right, that's fair. You know, Steve's been doing this longer than I have, Steve Fisk . . ."

Steve's got nothing to do with it.

Jack: "You could blame Bruce Pavitt. You could make a pretty good case there."

Yeah, you could. Well, in terms of the music, then . . .

Jack: "No one cares about the music! [laughs] I'm just kidding. I'm feeling so testy . . . the grunge thing became such a huge tragicomedy after awhile it's hard to even speak about it with any degree of seriousness at this late remove. You just want to throw your hands up and . . . giggle. 'What the hell was that? How did *that* all happen?' "

Well, it was your fault. I'm sticking with that.

Jack: "OK, but only to the extent that if the records had sounded *really* shitty instead of just *sort of* shitty then maybe none of it would have happened because it would have just been like every other indie scene in the US making shitty sounding indie records for no money."

You were using shitty instruments but making them sound good.

Jack: "Yeah. And shitty recording equipment and making it sound good. That was my contribution: I made sure the records were listenable, which meant people would actually take these bands seriously . . . sort of. Seriously on the level they were trying to be taken seriously. Such as that was. If it wasn't for that, probably a lot of these bands would have stayed obscure, and there wouldn't have been anything for Sub Pop to have a label with. I get demo tapes every day that are god-awful sounding and I think, 'Thank goodness *Bleach* sounds as good as it actually does.' Because look how many people ended up hearing it. Even 'Touch Me I'm Sick' is a wonderful sounding record. It sounds exactly like it's supposed to sound. But you know what I said to Mark and Steve at the time? I said, 'Are you sure you want that much distortion on your guitars, guys?' "

★ ★ ★

Tell us about grunge. Aren't you the Godfather of Grunge, one of the many?

"There's a phrase," laughs Leighton Beezer, former 'guitarist' with Thrown-Ups.[23] " 'The Godfather of Grunge.' No. I never claimed that one. Jack Endino probably claimed it, although I've heard it applied to Neil Young. That's way after the fact though, [Young] just kind of came in and said, 'I like this!' So Jack's the Godfather of Grunge, and I'm the Leon Trotsky of Grunge. It wouldn't have happened without me, but I was way too extreme to ever make it in the real world."

You have a moment in 1996's *Hype!* film where you describe grunge. Could you recreate that?

"OK. [Imitates a Sex Pistols-ish/Chuck Berry power-chord slide up a guitar neck thing, making the noise] . . . Well, that was punk. And then one day everybody started going . . . [imitates a down-the-neck grunge power chord slide thing. Punk backwards] . . . And that was grunge. It was funnier in the film because immediately after I said that, they cut to a guy with a hose spraying barf off the sidewalk. It's the rim shot. For those who don't know, those riffs were the Ramones, and 'Come On Down' on Green River's first record. I remember watching Jeff [Ament] play that and thinking, 'That's just the Ramones backwards! Huh. Sounds cool!' There were always these great insights, Einstein or Da Vinci or whatever. It's like, 'Why don't we do that backwards?' "

**Addenda 2: Green River**

". . . So Mark Arm comes out with this big Styrofoam cooler and gets out a baseball bat and smashes that cooler," begins Seattle promoter Julianne Anderson.[24] "The cooler was full of green Jell-O and that green Jell-O went *everywhere*. Everyone was covered in it. It was the grossest thing.

"Another time, Green River played with The Mentors. The Mentors were from Seattle originally – the progenitors of shock rock, pre-G.G. Allin.[25] Their lyrics were offensive to the nth degree, they had songs about locking their women up in closets and beating them. The Mentors also performed in Ku Klux Klan outfits, so when Mark agreed to play with them, he called me up: 'Do you still have your sewing machine?' So he comes over to my house with this gigantic, flowered sheet, a magic marker and some lace eyelet trim. So we ended up making five big KKK hoods . . . and then he painted these huge, super-happy smiley faces on. It was hilarious. Everyone was always so serious or disaffected or angry, but Green River were a hilarious band *and* musically brilliant. I mean, c'mon . . . flowered KKK hoods? That's brilliant!"

"Green River was epic," exclaims Leighton Beezer. "I saw their first show, at 12th and Yessler. I was on LSD – just a coincidence. Mark and Steve were dressed like preppies gone bad. They had short hair, but it had grown out a little and they were wearing Oxford shirts with the tails out; pretty harmless looking guys. Jeff [Ament] had some weird shtick going on where he had three or four scarves tied to his bass, around the neck. He couldn't make up his mind whether he was Steven Tyler or Gene Simmons. So he had his face painted white, with the star-child thing going on, and he was probably wearing spandex, with a Destroyer bass. I was totally on board with Mark and Steve. I too was a preppie gone bad. My people! And the second they started playing, it was Mudhoney. So there I was, having a good laugh at Jeff when they blew me to the back of the room. And probably changed my life.

"Green River had been through punk rock," he continues. "They'd taken that about as far as they could, so they said, 'We're going to pretend we're Aerosmith and it's going to be really funny.' And then, to their *total* amazement, it got them laid. 'HOLY CRAP . . . IT WORKS!' Some of them went, 'This is horrible! I'm going to go back where I came from and be more intense than ever before.' And the other half went, 'Aw man. I'm calling the record labels!' So they factionalised and there was this war, but it was not a war – they were still friends – more like, 'You guys are so lame!' There came a point where you just had to laugh at Pearl Jam for being so commercial. But eventually the laughter stopped and it was like, 'Shit. They're rich!' "

## NOTES

1 The Walkabouts were an early Sub Pop signing – sometimes overlooked because their powerful windswept country rock didn't fit in with 'grunge'.

2 The line-up on the *Seattle Syndrome* records included The Fastbacks, The Fartz and The Beakers.

3 Gas Huffer were a cartoon-like Seattle garage band – more Mod than grunge.

4 Three ended up on their first album *Bleach*, four on *Incesticide* and two on 2004's box set *With The Lights Out*. The version of 'Spank Thru' that appeared on *Sub Pop 200* was recorded at the 'Love Buzz' sessions in June 1988, with Chad on drums – not from the Dale demo, as is often assumed.

5 Ted Ed Fred were named after a friend's mum's boyfriend.

6 When Atlantic Records went to sign New Order from Manchester's legendary post-punk label, they discovered that label boss Tony Wilson had never bothered tying the band to a contract so they got them for free. It was a fair exchange: New

Order had financed Factory and its loss-leading Haçienda nightclub for many years.

7 From Tacoma, WA: The Sonics were prime Sixties garage rock exponents – rough, crude and wild. Standout songs included 'Strychnine', 'The Witch' and 'Psycho'.

8 Link Wray: Fifties rock'n'roll star, king of the fuzz-tone. The Who's Pete Townshend once stated, "If it hadn't been for Link Wray and [1958 instrumental hit] 'Rumble', I would have never picked up a guitar."

9 Pioneering UK post-punk group, Gang Of Four mixed stripped-back punk, intellectualism and political outrage with asexual funk and jagged guitar. Their first album, 1979's brilliant *Entertainment!*, exerts too strong an influence on too many a weak band.

10 The Birthday Party were a late Seventies Australian band, influenced by punk, rockabilly, Iggy Pop and the blues.

11 Of course, all true punks know that Mohawk haircuts have *nothing* to do with music, being an invention of the English Tourist Board in the late Seventies.

12 The King Dome is Tacoma's monstrous bowl-shaped arena, clearly visible from Interstate 5 every time you drive down to Olympia from Seattle.

13 The Angry Samoans were a politically incorrect LA punk band.

14 Huggy Bear were early Nineties insurrectionary UK Riot Grrrls, drawing equal inspiration from Sonic Youth, Bikini Kill and San Diego hardcore.

15 England's Billy Childish is a true renaissance man: poet, musician and artist. His simple, three-chord garage howl favours antique instruments, on-stage uniform and attitude. He is a major favourite in Seattle and Olympia.

16 The source of this confusion is Courtney herself.

17 Spacemen 3 were a psychedelic, hypnotic English band from the Eighties – 1989's 'Revolution' single is their finest moment: menace and repetition used to startling effect.

18 All early Sub Pop bands.

19 Blue Note was a late Fifties jazz label, notable for its almost art deco sleeve design.

20 This happened in essence, but not then – and not via Bruce. It was Jonathan who made the offer to Nirvana in a phone call a few days later.

21 Not inheritance money as has been erroneously assumed, but a US government savings bond of around $15,000 to $19,000.

22 James is exactly describing 'Sifting' here – which is *very* Melvins.

23 Thrown-Ups were a legendary chaotic Seattle 'fuck' band who refused to practise. Both Mudhoney's Steve and Mark were members. Endino reckons Thrown-Ups to be the best Seattle band ever: "Grunge in pure pharmaceutical grade form, 99.9 per cent," he explains, "with all the bothersome impurities – like 'songs' – removed."

24 The Alpha Female Booking proprietor Julianne Anderson had a Supersuckers song written about her, 'The 19th Most Powerful Woman In Rock'.

25 Cult punk artist G.G. Allin took Iggy's famed 'rolling in glass' approach to performance to deranged extremes: frequently hurling excrement at the audience and promising to kill himself live on stage – he OD'd on heroin before he could carry out his threat.

## CHAPTER 6

# Sub Pop Rock City

FORMER Soundgarden bassist/Hater frontman Ben Shepherd is slow moving, intense. He has a keen, skewed sense of humour, but man, can he get dark. I recall sleep deprivation nights with him in Japan, shortly before Kurt died, where he seemed rooted to the spot, such was the depth of his despair. He reminds me of Kurt, and Screaming Trees singer Mark Lanegan, these super-serious, kind of grouchy Pacific Northwest musicians. They showed me a lot of respect, but I never quite figured out why. Maybe it was because, like them, I was introverted, intense, but would *explode* when I got wasted, become a total goofball, drunk on anticipation and life and desire because, fuck, it didn't really matter whether you woke up the next morning or not. Ben rarely speaks to journalists. Doesn't trust them. Prefers to have a beer with his buddies, folk like his childhood friend and former bandmate, Chad Channing.

"I first met Kurt Cobain at this party in Olympia," he says. "We were sitting on the ends of the couch alone, watching everyone else party. So we started talking and there was an acoustic guitar we kept swapping back and forth. We both admitted that this was where we usually wound up at parties, sitting alone with a guitar. Didn't really know anybody and didn't really want to. Not in the mood for it."

Ben was one of the Melvins' gang in the early Eighties. He lived in Chad's adopted hometown of Bainbridge Island for a while – it's supposed to be the first place to go if a tsunami ever hit the area, which it probably will, the way Americans are heating up the atmosphere. Bainbridge is almost heart-stoppingly beautiful: hilly winding roads lined with pine trees, a cosy village main street and marketplace, corn dogs on the ferry, sprawling mansions and homely shacks backing on to forest land. Kurt should have lived there: he'd have felt at ease with its laidback vibe, free of Olympia's elitism, Seattle's competitiveness and Aberdeen's rednecks. He might have got a little bored – the pace is kind of slow – but Bainbridge has its own scene. Chad and Ben can attest to that.

"I'd met Krist via the Melvins," says Ben in a dimly lit 15th Avenue Seattle bar, cigarette smoke filling the air. "I didn't know he was in a band until I was playing with Chad's band The Magnet Men[1] at the Community Theater in Tacoma. Those famous photos of Kurt, dressed up in the blue satin pants, were from that show. They were called Bliss that night. Krist asked me if I thought our drummer would let them use his drum set. I was like, 'Wow! You're in a band? Cool man!' They wound up borrowing Chad's funky set. I think Mike Dillard was playing drums for them. We broke up soon after and they snagged Chad.

"Chad was the power drummer in our group," the singer adds. "In Nirvana he didn't really get to play in his natural style. He's nimble. Chad can play the hell out of a guitar too. People totally underestimated him. They still do."

It's a couple of weeks later. We're seated in the living room of Chad's Bainbridge home that he shares with his wife and daughter. The house is cluttered but comfortable, open plan, low ceilings: the sort of home you go barefoot in, school drawings tacked on the fridge, signed photograph of *Peanuts* creator Charles Schulz on the wall, comfy battered sofa. The coffee is astonishingly strong, more Turkish than American: "Sorry if it tastes a little weak," Chad exclaims. "I haven't drunk coffee for years."

It's been 15 years since I last saw Chad. I used to get him and Kurt confused – both were tiny, sensitive and kind of goofy with long hair and Puget Sound accents: super-considerate, if shy.

"That's funny!" the drummer laughs. "Me, I've always been bad with numbers and names. I'm good with sounds and I've a pretty good photographic memory."

Chad looks remarkably unchanged by time. I recognise him instantly, leaning out of his car to pick me up from the ferry port (Bainbridge Island is a pleasant 30-minute ride away from Seattle), apologising for missing me on first trawl. He still dresses 'grunge' – lumberjack shirt and trainers, long hair and sideburns – but that's how he's always dressed. He's friendly, enthusiastic about music. He talks about his current band, old groups that we share a common love of (Talulah Gosh, The Shaggs, Marine Girls) and his plans to build a recording studio on the island.

As we drive through Bainbridge's snaking lanes, he points out a few landmarks: "I used to climb up that tower when I was younger and eat my lunch at the top. The platform was small and there was no railing, and it would sway in the wind. It's only about 30 yards from that to where Charles Peterson took that early picture of Nirvana in the field with all the flowers . . ."

"I'm from Bainbridge," comments Jack Endino, "earlier than those guys, and I used to climb that tower in high school. It was a leftover WWII radio tower from the defunct Fort Ward military base, overgrown with weeds and bushes. The very top was 212 feet. The place where Charles took the photos was the fort's former airstrip, now a field, which during the Seventies was one of the best places on the island to pick psilocybin mushrooms. The indigenous psych mushrooms, present nowhere else in the US as far as I know, have never gotten their proper credit for grunge."

Chad was born to Burnyce and Wayne Channing on January 31, 1967 in Santa Rosa, California. Wayne was a radio DJ – rumoured to have known Elvis Presley – whose job took him across the country, from Hawaii to Alaska to Anacortes to Minnesota. His family was constantly relocating, leaving their son unsettled and unable to make friends: "I always knew that whomever I met, it was temporary," he says. "It puts you off meeting people." He had hoped to be a soccer player but – in a similar twist of fate to Mark Lanegan, who leapt off a moving truck when he was 16, broke both his legs and thus ruined a promising basketball career – he shattered his thigh bone in a freak gym accident. It took him seven years to recover. Like Lanegan, he turned to music for solace, learning both drums and guitar.

"The first band I played drums in was with some school friends in 1982, in Anacortes," he begins. "We were totally a punk rock band. No covers. I never wanted to play covers because I had too much coming out of my own head. In Yakima for a time, I was in a band that played messed up, dark New Age stuff. Then I was in Mind Circus – me on drums, Ben Shepherd on guitar, very Melvins-ish. When I was 17, I was in Stone Crow, who were a speed metal band that played with hardcore [punk] bands like DRI and COC."[2]

Like Kurt and Krist, Chad's parents were separated and he took odd jobs to make a few dollars here and there. When he met the pair he was a sauté chef in a Bainbridge Island seafood restaurant. His interests were similar: pot, acid, hanging out, punk rock and the burgeoning Olympia scene:

"Kurt liked checking out local bands like Beat Happening. Krist was more into old-time Seventies music. Those guys turned each other on to different kinds of music. I turned them on to Shonen Knife. In '85 I found this cassette tape, *Burning Farm*.[3] I kind of turned them on to David Bowie. I found a copy of *The Man Who Sold The World* in perfect vinyl condition that I recorded on to tape and played in the car. Kurt was like, 'Who's this?' They turned me on to The Vaselines. I was familiar with Shocking

Blue. The Smithereens had an album in particular I thought was pretty cool.[4] Kurt appreciated what Calvin was doing. We all did. Olympia, man. A lot of cool stuff was going on."

First, though, came the discovery of several Seattle bands through contact with the irrepressible Mark Arm (who was then fronting the fucked-up Mr Epp): "Later on, I'd go out and see Soundgarden, Melvins and The U-Men, stuff like that," Chad recalls. "I saw Soundgarden's second show. They were really cool: not so much full metal as way more weirded-out guitar. It was much trippier. We ended up getting a case of beer and going down to the railroad tracks on 5th and Jackson."

Chad met Kurt and Krist at Malfunkshun's last show, at the Community World Theater, May 6, 1988 – Lush[5] and headliners Skin Yard also played. A mutual friend who was studying at Evergreen, Damon Romero [Lush, Treehouse[6]] made the introductions. Kurt remembered seeing Chad's band from the show they played with Bliss: he'd been impressed by the fibreglass drum kit, the way its flared shells towered over the drummer. "It was heinous looking," Chad comments, "but it was loud." Plus, The Magnet Men – who only existed for that one gig – had recorded a radio session with John Goodmanson that Kurt taped. So Krist and Kurt told Chad to check out their next show at Evergreen.

"They were like, 'Hey, want to get together with us?'" recalls Chad. "I was like, 'That'd be cool.' I hit it off with those guys. They seemed bubbly and excited. We hung out afterwards by their white stub-nosed Dodge van. It was one we ended up using for touring in the early days.

"I thought their show was pretty cool," he adds. "I recognised a lot of the songs, because they were still playing stuff like 'Mexican Seafood'. I was watching Dave, figuring out why they were interested in getting a different drummer. He was doing pretty well. Maybe he had a personality that didn't correlate."

"Chad they liked because he had the cool drums with the scoop[7]," comments Slim Moon. "He was the first guy that fit. There were problems because he wanted to write songs: kind of poppy and kind of prog. They didn't want that. Plus, his timing was suspect. He wasn't perfect, but he was good enough for them to take it out on the road."

"The first time I played with them was in Krist's basement in Tacoma," Chad says. "It was probably about the size of this room here, maybe a little smaller. There was a bunch of foam rubber for soundproofing, and some of it was hanging off the ceiling. I think they had a four-track in there. It was kind of dank – totally dank, but then again, those rooms always get that way. We had my drums, and we might have had some old beat-up drums in the corner, like a snare. And we had Krist's big red amp. I think Kurt had his Randall head, but he wasn't playing off the 212 sound techs that he had."

Although it was the giant drums that attracted their attention, Kurt and Krist made Chad strip his kit down – just like they had with Dave. The three musicians began practising in earnest: songs from the original demo, plus newer material such as 'School' (a very Olympian song) and 'Big Cheese', a Melvins-esque dirge, the title character of which was based on Jonathan Poneman: "I was explaining all the pressures I felt from him at the time because he was being so judgemental about what we were recording," Kurt told Michael Azerrad.

"We found a drummer and began playing constantly in that little house," Krist wrote in *Of Grunge And Government*. "We had the most intense jams. We'd orbit inner and outer space. It was so serious, if we felt we sucked at rehearsal we were disappointed and we'd sit around bummed out after."

Chad never officially joined. "They kept asking me to go over and jam with them," he says. "They never actually said I was in. Our first show was either at The Vogue [July 3] or at the Central Tavern [July 23, opening for Leaving Trains[8] and Blood Circus]. There weren't very many people at either place."

Before Chad joined, there were a couple of shows in early May: one at The Vogue, and a friend's 18th birthday party at Evergreen on the 14th, where Kurt played a cover of Scratch Acid's 'The Greatest Gift'. There was also a gig at The Central Tavern in Seattle on June 5, booked by Poneman again. "That show was with Doll Squad and Zoomorphics," recalls Jack Endino. "They were terrible bands, with no draw at all." Once more, it was a KCMU benefit: just before the gig, Poneman asked Nirvana to go on first, rather than in the middle, so he and Bruce could get an early night. Maybe half-a-dozen people showed up, but no one was impressed, apart from the Sub Pop pair. In fact, none of Nirvana's early Seattle shows were particularly auspicious. Feedback and bad sound all but obliterated Kurt's vocals: the trio were disheartened by the lack of an audience.

What were the early shows like?

"There was nobody there."

Was there destruction going on?

"Not really. We started raging and destroying our gear a lot, but we didn't do that right off the bat. That was probably about the third show. It started pretty quickly. I didn't do it on purpose or anything. I just joined in with what was already going on. But it is fun. It wasn't like we said, 'OK Krist, you jump really high and throw your bass in the air and have it knock you out, and Kurt, you get down on the floor and do the worm.' It was that we were so sick and tired of the big rock – all the arena rock and special effects and all that that entailed wasn't what we were about."

Were you ever drunk when you were playing?

"Never! Krist was. Everybody knew that. I could never drink while playing a show. I would drink afterwards, but I rarely got drunk."

On June 11, Nirvana returned to Reciprocal, with the express intention of recording a single for Sub Pop. The session began with 'Blandest', and continued with first takes of 'Love Buzz' and 'Big Cheese', early versions of 'Mr Moustache' and 'Blew', plus an instrumental version of 'Sifting' that used a wah-wah pedal. It was harder going than the demo session, probably because they knew it was for a finished product, but also because Chad didn't hit the drums quite as hard as Kurt liked.

In fact, Nirvana were attempting to change their sound substantially as they struggled to form their own identity separate to that of their favourite bands; incorporating the rock machismo of Black Flag and Led Zeppelin, and the more subtle approach of pop bands such as R.E.M. and The Beatles.

The trio returned twice to finish off the sessions, on June 30 and July 16. Songs were recorded over previous takes so they didn't have to fork out the extra 50 bucks needed for another reel. Take two of 'Love Buzz' was the single, with a 10-second sound collage intro lifted from Kurt's 'Montage Of Heck' tape of audio samples. Kurt wanted the song to start with 45 seconds of his sampling but was talked out of it.

"I'm not sure Kurt was entirely happy with doing a cover for the A-side but he thought it's a single, what the hell," says Jack Endino. "And they were going to put 'Blandest' on the B-side . . . the song is called 'Blandest' for a reason [laughs]. The band wasn't that enthusiastic about it and Chad didn't know how to play it. They'd only shown it to him the day before. Afterwards, they did 'Big Cheese' and some other songs and I thought, whoa, these are way livelier. They were easily convinced to put 'Big Cheese' on the B-side: you need to have something that people will notice as your first original recorded song, rather than a drone-y, mid-tempo thing. They were going to redo 'Blandest' later but never got around to it."

Was there anything to be read into the actual choice of cover?

"No," the producer replies. "It was the only cover in their set at the time[9] and Jonathan liked it. It was his idea. Using a cover for the first single can be to the detriment of the band – often it means the end of their career. They were smart not to continue with that."

Sub Pop paid for this session – legend has it that later on, with grunge in full swing and their finances in turmoil (cash flow is the biggest single cause of small business insolvency), they kept bouncing cheques on Reciprocal. "It was actually only one or two," admits Jack, "but a reputation like that is difficult to lose." The label's notorious inability to grapple with financial realities didn't inspire confidence in their artists. One time, shortly after agreeing to release a single, Bruce called up Kurt to ask if he could borrow $200.

In August, Jon and Bruce had the bright idea of combating their cash flow problems with a subscribers-only Singles Club – whereby interested fans would sign up for a one-year fixed period, paying $35, and receive a single through the mail every month. They decided that the Nirvana single would have the honour of being the first in the series, with a limited edition pressing of a thousand copies. Kurt was dismayed by the news – he wanted his band's debut single to have a 'proper' release – but undaunted: after all, most bands never even get to the stage of releasing a record.

"Yeah, 'Love Buzz'," Chad sighs. "When we were getting my snare sound set up I had this crazy idea of hooking two snares together. I took the bottom off of one and the top off another and put them together. It was all about trying to get a beefy drum sound."

Were you aware while you were recording those songs that you were doing something special?

"No! That would be like predicting the future. The only feeling I had when I first started getting involved with them, was that the band was going to go somewhere. Exactly how far, I wasn't sure. It was always a matter of, 'Is the public ready for this?' "

Things were starting to happen, in and around Seattle.

Soundgarden found themselves with the dubious distinction of being 'signed' to three labels at once: Sub Pop, SST (for the patchily astounding *Ultramega OK* album[10]) and A&M – a major label, which they ended up with. Metal band Alice In Chains[11] would follow soon after, but it was Chris Cornell's mob that was the big news in town in '88. SST had long ago picked up on Screaming Trees, issuing three albums – including 1989's claustrophobic, Endino-produced *Buzz Factory* – plus an EP of outtakes, *Other Worlds*, before the Trees briefly joined Sub Pop to release the awesome double seven-inch 'Change Has Come', and left to sign to a major, Epic. New York's Homestead records[12] was getting in on the act, putting out a joint Screaming Trees/Beat Happening 12-inch[13] (Calvin promoted the Trees' earliest out-of-Ellensburg shows).

"By the summer of '88, something had changed significantly in town," says Mudhoney guitarist Steve Turner. "After the first couple of shows, if a group of us were playing someplace, suddenly it'd be packed. We did the downstairs from the Comet Tavern – us and The Walkabouts and maybe Blood Circus – and it was packed out. It changed really fast. We'd never had people coming to see our bands before! We figured it was some weird anomaly so we were milking it for all the fun we could get out of it: a lot of beer and craziness. We played The Vogue so many times within a nine-month period that all the gigs blurred into one."

Towards the end of 1988, Mudhoney released *Superfuzz Bigmuff* and went on their first US tour. Shows were frantic, insane: a mass of sweaty bodies and long hair flailing; Mark Arm sardonically inviting kids up on stage and hurling himself straight into the fray, Matt Lukin as likely to swig from a beer bottle as pummel his bass. People from the outside – Sonic Youth, Tom Hazelmyer from hardcore Midwest band Halo Of Flies, and influential British DJ John Peel – began to take an interest.

Sonic Youth released a split 12-inch single with Mudhoney on UK label Blast First, each band covering one another's songs ('Halloween' and 'Touch Me I'm Sick'): the two bands toured the UK together the following year for Britain's first taste of live grunge. I introduced Mudhoney on the opening night, at Newcastle's Riverside, dressed in a Mod suit. The idea was that I would scream a few words then leap into the throng – the crowd was so packed I balked at the challenge and ran backstage, only to be confronted by Sonic Youth bassist Kim Gordon. "Where do you think you're going?" she barked. So I leapt off the stage *seven times*, only to be thrown back on stage each time.

I made the record UK Single Of The Week in *Melody Maker*, writing, "Instinctive, primal rock as it should be. Sub Pop's coming at ya, and you better watch out."

It felt like Bruce and Jon were starting to release singles every week – Blood Circus, Tad, Swallow, The Fluid, Screaming Trees . . . the list was never-ending. There were other labels – C/Z, Pop Llama, T/K from Portland – but it was Sub Pop, fuelled by Jon's drive and Bruce's vision, that led the pack. Band photography by Charles Peterson, production by Jack Endino . . . Sub Pop was on a roll, a home-made production line.

"Technically, the bands all had the same approach in the studio," Jack says. "Which was like, show up, stick the guitars and everything in the same room as the drums, turn the distortion up as high as it'll go, and play live. We had an eight-track machine between 1987 and 1988, and so people weren't driven to overproduce. They didn't try to get me to do crazy stuff. There wasn't a lot of architecture going on."

"'Touch Me I'm Sick' was recorded for what, $100?" asks Pavitt rhetorically. "*Bleach* was recorded for $600, and went on to sell a million and a half copies. It's possibly the best return on investment of any recording since the Elvis Sun Sessions.[14] Endino's amazing. It takes somebody to recognise the talent and maintain consistent vision, and I think that's what I brought to the situation."

"Jack is really low-key and meticulous," says Mark Arm. "At some point he was working like 60 hours a week and it was then, I think, he lost some of his spontaneity."

"For about a year, it seemed like every single band was coming to me," comments Endino. "Maybe they trusted me because I was a musician. Aside from Skin Yard, I played drums in Crypt Kicker Five, and bass in The Ones with [Sub Pop recording artist] Terry Lee Hale – I was in three bands in 1988. Plus, we were dirt-cheap. Whatever the reason, somehow I wound up right in the centre of it. Sub Pop started sending me stuff all the time. Whenever Jon or Bruce would do a one-off single for the Singles Club, they'd send them down to me.

"The seven-inches were a huge part of it," the producer continues. "During the grunge period I did over a hundred seven-inch records. Nobody cares about them any more, but they were a big deal then. It got your collectable blood flowing. 'Ah, it's a collector's item, they only made 500 of these.' I really enjoyed the seven-inch thing. It was instant gratification. Get in the studio in a day, record a couple of songs, they come out a few months later and you can say you've made a record. So we got to do all these one-offs for other bands that weren't from Seattle – [LA all-girl band] L7, Babes In Toyland, Helios Creed."[15]

I loved Babes In Toyland *the most.* Everything I understood to be important about rock was tied up with these three Minneapolis women. Kat Bjelland would stand on stage, face contorted with fury, spitting out her love-hate lyrics over a battered guitar lick. In her flat heels and chiffon she had an odd girlishness: pseudo kindergarten curls, crudely bleached, tattered baby doll dress, red lipstick and wide eyes. Courtney Love later claimed to have invented the 'kinderwhore' look (she'd been in bands with Bjelland and L7 bassist Jennifer Finch) – but she didn't. It was pure Kat. Her legs would be covered in bruises by the end of each show from contact with the guitar, pain dulled by a constant stream of whiskey.

There was nothing 'girlie' or childish about her performances. Her screams sounded ghastly and cleansing, an exorcism of her past and a recent succession of bastard boyfriends. At her side stood Michelle Leon, able to hit her bass with a demonic force that belied her size. Behind them, Lori Barbero, the brash, loud one, everyone's favourite sister, would be kicking up a major league racket on the drums, occasionally singing in her operatic, drawn-out voice. At the set's end, she'd jump up and take a photo of the audience, like we'd all been invited to a private party. It was Kat that your attention was always drawn back to, though, her eyes rolled back wide to the sky, stamping her foot and grinding her sticker-covered guitar against her hips. Kat was the *electricity*.

"[Babes In Toyland's] *Spanking Machine* [1989] is one of the most genius records ever made," Courtney raved to me in '92. "It's all truth and coolness and acid trips, bad acid trips, and lies, lame ass Minnesota boys and cut open sores and cheap wine and Valentine's Day and old stinky nighties with no boyfriends and loving Nick Cave and loving Butthole Surfers and harsh winter and cool kitty-cats and feeling like the only fucked-up girl in the world, oh and a few of my lyrics, but no big deal, it just makes it better."

"At first, we had no idea that we were creating this supposedly singularly unique aesthetic," explains Charles Peterson. "We were way more impressed with Touch And Go, Homestead, SST and Dischord. Bruce and Jon had this joke about 'Sub Pop World Domination', that we were somehow going to be huge. We were like, 'Yeah, whatever.' We just wanted an easy way to pay cheap rent. And musically it was exciting and fun and the bands were making some good records . . . but, shit, we weren't The Replacements, we weren't Sonic Youth, we weren't Black Flag or the Butthole Surfers. That was the real thing."

"Any scene explosion always has an incubation period," says Hazelmyer. "One thing that's never been written up is the influence Minneapolis bands like Soul Asylum, Hüsker Dü and The Replacements had on Seattle. Have a look at the pictures of those Minneapolis guys from '81, they're dressed like grunge guys – flannel shirts, torn jeans, long hair. I remember The Replacements showing up on television while I was at a party, and the whole room stopped and was glued to the set. To me they were just a band from back home, but to a party that hosted many of the future Seattle heavyweights, the 'ments were idols. I've read Cobain citing [Replacements singer] Paul Westerberg. There was definitely an influence."

What were the audiences like at the early Seattle Sub Pop shows?

"Small," replies Peterson. "No more than a hundred people. The Central Tavern held 250 at most."

How did the audience dress?

"Terribly," laughs the photographer. "Dress was not a big concern in Seattle. It still isn't. There's a picture of an early audience in '83 that I call the 'stray dogs from every village'. There is no uniform sense of style at all. There's a little bit of hippie, some glam, there's the trench coat, the flannel coat. One boy's got the leather jacket with the Sid Vicious pin on it, a little bit of punk. We just liked thrift store clothes. It was an amalgamation of stuff. It started to split up into camps. I was more with the Mudhoney camp where we were into peg trousers and some old school penguin shirts. A little more garage rock."

I always maintained that Mudhoney had a strong Mod feel.

"Except for Matt Lukin, you wouldn't have caught any of them dead in a flannel shirt," nods Charles. "It comes back to the old school punk aesthetic. That's what we all were inspired by and grew up with. I was more of an anglophile than them. Mark was more into weird US hardcore like The Angry Samoans. That we were all the godchildren of punk rock has been downplayed. What Soundgarden did was entirely different from what Mudhoney and Nirvana did. You'd go to an Alice In Chains gig and there'd be nobody there who would go to a Mudhoney gig. I didn't go to a Pearl Jam gig for years."

"The crowd would be anywhere in age from 18 to 29," recounts former Nirvana soundman Craig Montgomery, "dressed in old jeans and rock T-shirts, leather jackets were big, plenty of flannel, long underwear . . . People here grew up wearing flannel shirts. They were warm and cheap – not necessarily the heavy-duty lined ones – you could get them off the rack in any department store. Lots of people had long hair, Doc Martens boots or Converse shoes. The audience was college kids and slackers – certainly not mainstream rock'n'roll fans or the Goth crowd or hardcore punks. I hate to use the word grunge, but . . ."

"I came from the Eastside, so it seemed like we'd co-opted some of the bondage stuff you still had to buy in weird underground sex stores back then. It was all just black jeans," says Julianne Anderson. "No one gave a flying fuck. Everyone wore hand-screened T-shirts. Some of the girls, myself included, got very involved with thrift store clothes, like the Fifties house dresses and the vintage stuff. There was no continuity, there was no trend, all that nonsense with the flannel, that was a media invention right there. Yes, some people wore flannel shirts, but . . ."

What about Tad?

"He was from Boise!" Anderson exclaims. "Flannel shirts, those heavy wool, plaid shirts? It's cold and wet here, people, please! None of it was thoughtful or intentional. People stand in rock clubs every day and wear whatever they found at the thrift store and thought was funny at the time. It's happening across the country as we speak. Whether or not there's going to be books written about it – that's where the whole magical uncertainty of life comes up . . ."

"Everybody had long hair and they were pretty dirty," recalls Carrie Montgomery. "People wore long cut-off Levi's and band T-shirts – that was the uniform. It was very liberating as a girl because you didn't have to put together a special outfit every night you went out. One time Mark [Arm] and I cut our hair really short, and it was a big deal. But then everyone did after that, of course."

In August, a photo-shoot was organised for the cover of 'Love Buzz' – black and white, to save on costs – with Seattle photographer Alice Wheeler. The photographer was paid $25 for the session. Wheeler had met Pavitt when she was living in Olympia, attending Evergreen: "He was always around talking about taking over the world and stuff," she told Gillian G. Gaar. Wheeler also helped run GESCCO in Olympia, and was a friend of Tracy Marander.

Krist drove everyone to Tacoma where the band posed in front of local landmarks, including Point Defiance Park and the Tacoma Narrows Bridge. "I was having technical difficulties," Wheeler told Gaar. "I didn't have a very good camera. The pictures are infrared so they're kind of fuzzy."

Dawn Anderson's *Backlash* article appeared around this time: "I knew them only as friends of the Melvins," she laughs. "Fortunately, they also kicked ass."

In the interview, Kurt admitted his biggest fear at the beginning was that, "People might think we were a Melvins rip-off". The Melvins got mentioned *a lot*. Dawn suggested that, with enough practice, Nirvana could perhaps be "better than the Melvins".

"Most of the stuff that was written about us, and every other band early on, was just corny phrases," smiles Chad. "'Nirvana is a flurry of sweaty, tangled, messy hair with lash brash grash blash splashy music, swampy gooey gumby.' Get to the freaking point! It was always positive, they were just hyping up their own deal."

In September, Shelli split with Krist – the strain of their separate lifestyles telling. Shelli worked at night; Krist had just quit his job. The pair decided to live apart. Shelli was 21, and had never been by herself. The separation didn't last long – the couple missed each other too much – but it did have several knock-on effects.

Krist was forced to move back in with his mum in Aberdeen after blowing $400 in two weeks on beer and partying – "Once, I gave out a case of beer in two minutes," he commented. "Next thing I knew, I was broke" – and hence was able to practise full-time with the band. Rehearsals moved from the Tacoma basement to a space above Maria's Hair Design (Krist's mum's shop).

It also placed a strain on Kurt and Tracy's relationship: Tracy loved Kurt and was looking for some token of commitment from him, especially now her best friends had split up. Kurt didn't respond, so she decided to call his bluff – threatening to throw him out of the house. Instead, Kurt called *her* bluff, telling her that he'd go live in his car if she acted like that. "You don't have to do that," she replied. He won the argument – and continued to live with her, spending his days rising late and watching TV while Tracy continued vainly to write lists of chores for him to do while she went out to work at Boeing.

"I went over there to ask if Nirvana would contribute a song to this tape compilation me and Donna [Dresch] were putting together," recalls John Goodmanson, "and he was painting in the living room in his underwear. I used to see Kurt driving around in her car and think, 'Man, that guy is totally taking advantage. She has a really good job and he stays home and paints.' "

Tracy complained that Kurt never wrote a song about her, even though he'd written a paean to masturbation ('Spank Thru'[16]), so the following week he began to write 'About A Girl', never admitting that it was about Tracy – even though the chorus, *"I can't see you every night for free"*, was a clear reminder of their argument. It's a stunning song, plaintive, melodic – Kurt told a friend he'd played *Meet The Beatles* for three hours straight the day he wrote the song, to get himself in the right frame of mind. The title came after Kurt played the song for his bandmates and Chad asked what the song was about. "It's about a girl," Kurt told him, and the phrase stuck.

All the while, Nirvana continued to gig across Washington State – in Tacoma, at dorm parties in Evergreen, in Bellingham and in Seattle. "Those early shows were crazy and that's why they were so fun," recalls Sub Pop employee Megan Jasper. "It ruled, the way Kurt would smash up his guitars at every opportunity – we all knew he didn't have any money, but he'd do it anyway."

"That's what I heard – that this guy was so crazy he smashed up a brand new amp," confirms former Sub Pop general manager Rich Jensen. "Jimi Hendrix would do that. The Who would do that.[17] So Nirvana carried on that tradition, which was pretty impressive because these guys didn't have much money. One of the first Nirvana shows I saw was at The Vogue, either with Pussy Galore or Tad, at a Sub Pop showcase. At the end, they smashed up all of their gear. Apparently, that was something Kurt would prepare for. Ian Dickson told me his amps were all pre-broken so he could jump into them and smash them, and do it again and again."

The first commonly agreed occurrence of a totally smashed guitar happened at Evergreen State College on October 30 (two days after a support slot to Butthole Surfers at Union Station). After a storming live performance from Lush – during which the drummer punched Slim Moon in the face, and the campus cops got called – Nirvana covered themselves in fake blood and went for it.

"My band was middling but when we were in sync, we could be pretty good," says Slim. "We put on our best show ever that night and then they had to go and fucking smash their instruments. I felt that they only did that because otherwise we'd have upstaged them. It hurt my feelings because we were close friends and they still wouldn't let us upstage them just once."

Nirvana weren't adverse to showmanship when it was called for: "Someone once told me about a Halloween fundraiser," remembers Jensen, "maybe for the GESCCO space in Olympia, really early, like '87 or '88. Where Kurt imitated a rock star by having fake syringes, either hanging off his arm or drawn on. The point being, it was so laughable that he could turn into a degenerate, junkie rock star."

'Love Buzz' came out in November 1988 – Sub Pop single number 23 – packaged in a hand-numbered sleeve. The sleeve was the first time Kurt used the alternative spelling of his name in public, 'Kurdt Kobain'.[18] As it was near Christmas, Kurt gave copies as gifts to members of his immediate family: "I was really excited and proud of him," Mari Earl recalled. "As I was putting it back into the jacket, I laughed as I read, 'Why don't you trade those guitars for shovels?' etched in the vinyl on the 'Love Buzz' side." The line was a reference to a favourite expression of Krist's father.

It was accompanied by a press release, drafted by Kurt:

> GREETINGS,
>
> NIRVANA is a three piece spawned from the bowels of a redneck logger town called Aberdeen, WA, and a hippie commune on Bainbridge Island. Although only together for seven months Kurdt –

guitar/voc, Chris – bass and Chad – drums have acquired a single on Sub Pop records, one cut on the *Sub Pop 200* compilation, a demo, an LP in April, success, fame and a following of millions.

Selling their bottled sweat and locks of hair have proven to be the biggest money makers so far, but in the future: dolls, pee chees, lunch boxes and bed sheets are in the works.

From the wonderful offices of Sub Pop world headquarters our talent agents Bruce Pavitt and Johnathan [sic] Poneman have treated the boys good.

NIRVANA hope to work on more projects with them in the future.

NIRVANA sounds like: Black Sabbath playing The Knack, Black Flag, Led ZEP, the Stooges and a pinch of Bay City Rollers. Their personal musical influences include: H.R Puffnstuff[19], Marine Boy[20], divorces, drugs, sound effects records, The Beatles, Young Marble Giants[21], Slayer, Leadbelly and Iggy.

NIRVANA sees the underground music SEEN as becoming stagnant and more accessible towards commercialised major label interests.

Does NIRVANA feel a moral duty to change this cancerous evil?

No way! We want to cash in and suck butt of the big wigs in hopes that we too can GET HIGH and FUCK. GET HIGH and FUCK. GET HIGH and FUCK.

Soon we'll need chick repellent spray. Soon we will be coming to your town asking if we can stay over at your house and use your stove.

Soon we will do encores of 'Gloria' and 'Louie Louie' at benefit concerts with all our celebrity friends.

NIRVANA c/o SUB POP, 1932 1st Ave . . . #1103 . . . Seattle, WA 98101

Thank you for your time.

The song itself was repetitive, stripped-back. Over an insistent seven-note bass, Kurt kept screaming, pleading the same refrain again and again, *"Can you feel my love buzz/ Can you feel my love buzz"*. The atmosphere was restrained, claustrophobic – the guitar only occasionally being let off the leash to let rip with some wah-wah fuelled feedback. Controlled power, that's what mattered.

Reaction to the single was immediately favourable.

"In the fall of '88, we put out the single, and they played a couple of dates with Mudhoney," recalls Bruce Pavitt. "And the two people whose opinions mattered most to me at the time were Charles Peterson and Steve Turner. Charles came up to me a few days after the single came out and said, 'I had a party last night, and we put on "Love Buzz", and then we flipped it over, and then we just flipped it over all night, and that was the party.' Steve Turner came up to me and said, 'We toured with this band and they are amazing. Kurt Cobain played guitar standing on his head' [February 11, 1989, San Jose, California]. And I wouldn't have believed him except Charles took a picture of it. Look at that picture! It's unbelievable.

"And so things started to pick up and kept accelerating," Bruce continues. "We put out *Bleach* and the response was overwhelming, especially considering *Bleach* is fundamentally an OK record with a couple of great songs – 'About A Girl', 'Blew'. It's not brilliant but it had a special alchemy that people related to. Between '88 and '90, the songwriting just transformed. That level of growth was magical to see."

Initially, it wasn't Kurt Cobain who attracted the audience's attention – but his gregarious giant of a bass-player, Krist Novoselic.

"Krist is remarkably intuitive," Jonathan Poneman says. "His contribution to Nirvana is underrated. He was the only bass-player who could have filled that position. Kurt is a really good songwriter, but to the extent that those songs became full and alive, that was Krist. It wasn't like Krist was Kurt's sideman, which is what the assumption became."

Did anything stand out the first time you saw Nirvana?

"Krist," responds Nirvana's former guitar tech Earnie Bailey: "Krist was the focal point. He was hilarious. He'd mimic Sixties TV shows, doing impersonations of *Beverly Hillbillies* characters. I'd just laugh my ass off. Nirvana were easily as funny as Mudhoney – as much as I like to catch a good rock band, one that's equally good at stand-up comedy is a big plus. The first few times, I don't recall much about Kurt, other than this guitar-player with an incredible voice who had this long blond hair in his face all the time. His guitar sound really stood out, there was a lot of that screechy and shrill solid state feedback going on, but rather than trying to avoid it, Kurt was going after it and getting new sounds. But it was Krist who stood out."

"Krist was very outgoing," recalls Bruce. "He liked to party. He and Matt Lukin from Mudhoney, those guys could rage. A lot of what touring is about is networking and meeting people and building contacts. And Kurt by nature was fairly reserved and shy. So Krist was the guy forging a lot of social connections, the fun guy to hang out with. Specifically, I remember him being way into the first Jane's Addiction[22] record. He was very progressive. It's not like he was the metal guy and Kurt was the sensitive punk guy. But the social dynamic was key."

And Chad?

"Chad was, I think, a little bit more like Kurt," Pavitt replies. "He was a very sensitive guy, kind of soft-spoken, creative."

In December, Nirvana's 'Spank Thru' appeared on the *Sub Pop 200* box set. The song had been remixed on September 27 at Reciprocal, recorded over the original take of 'Blandest'. It's an odd number, almost laidback: a mishmash of Sixties pop sensibilities, spoken word segments and topped off by Kurt's mighty roar. The 'grunge' quotient is to the fore – the scuzzy-sounding guitars, thumping drums, distortion. In truth, it's one of the weaker songs on the collection.

The set, issued in a run of 5,000, was made up of 19 songs over three 12-inch EPs and a booklet, packaged in a plain black box; although the compilation was focused on the Northwest, the breadth of musical style was astonishing, giving the lie to the idea of Sub Pop being a 'one sound' label. Freewheeling beat poet Steven Jesse Bernstein nestled next to Beat Happening's stark pop and Soundgarden's rip-roaring pisstake of Seattle 'attitude' on their inspired tribute to Kiss, 'Sub Pop Rock City'. Mudhoney covered Bette Midler's 'The Rose' with enthusiastic panache; The Walkabouts and Terry Lee Hale ploughed a bittersweet country groove; Tad *crushed* with his grinding distillation of the rage and frustration and hurt inherent in a thousand dead-end lives. Screaming Trees played acid blues. Nights And Days were similar to early White Stripes influence, The Gories.[23] Fastbacks played pop, pure and simple. Girl Trouble *rocked*.

"My philosophy of Sub Pop is this," Pavitt told me at the time. "I worked at Muzak for three years with a lot of these guys. It was a classic corporate set-up. It started off by being easy-going but soon, like most businesses, it was curtailing our freedom of expression. And when, for eight to 10 hours a day, your personal freedom is being restricted, when you're being punished for being creative, then you're not living in a free, democratic country. You're living in a fascist dictatorship. Sub Pop is a business set up to *encourage* freedom of thought."

"As far as A&R goes,' Jonathan added. "You go to see one of your friend's bands and you think, 'Yeah that sounds cool.' It's only occasionally we go out on a limb. I did with Nirvana."

Inside the booklet, there were 14 pages of black and white Charles Peterson photographs, no words (save identification of artist): indelibly stamping a visual style upon the longhaired musicians of Seattle and its surrounding areas, circa 1988. Blurred movement lines, arms flailing, mostly live captures with guitars in musicians' hands, immediately exciting, immediately enticing.

Pavitt and Poneman had been smart: by giving all their artists to one photographer to document, they'd stamped an identity upon their nascent scene far greater than any number of words could ever do.

There was a time when it seemed mandatory for Sub Pop bands to have recorded with Jack Endino and been photographed by Charles Peterson. How deliberate was that?

"Extremely," replies Bruce Pavitt. "First of all, they are both brilliant. I was extremely interested in creating a label identity, looking at Blue Note or 4AD[24] as models. Factory[25] was the perfect example with the design and the production being so focused. I wanted to transpose that. The punk scene seemed fairly scattered and unfocused, with the exception of SST.

"It was Charles Peterson's photos that inspired me to step into doing regional recordings, even more so than the music," Pavitt continues. "I was at a party at the [early Seattle band] Room 9 house, and Charles had just finished printing up the 3′ × 9′ photos of his work. The house was like an art gallery. I remember feeling the energy of those photos and being completely taken in by the aesthetic. I said, 'If we can translate the energy that I am feeling from these photos, people will be moved.' He offered a vision of unification. It totally captured the essence of the music. The aesthetics of how things are presented visually is absolutely key."

"As far as graphic identity went, it was mostly Bruce's vision – and also Jeff Ament and Linda Owens, our original graphic designer," says Jonathan. "Bruce could articulate in a very simple way. He isolated immediately what he liked and didn't like about album art."

Bruce refers to a specific incident when he went around to Charles' house for the first time and saw all the massive photos up on his walls.

"That's absolutely right," Jon agrees. "Charles was the most essential ingredient, particularly early on. I had never seen anything like the shots that Charles had been taking. It was a visual signature that defined the whole scene. There was this colossal quality to everything. Everything was exaggerated and just heavier than heavy, and sexy as can be. In many ways it was the antithesis of everything that was popular at the time."

The photo of Nirvana in the *Sub Pop 200* booklet came from Peterson's first formal session with the group – taken earlier that summer on Bainbridge. "We drove all over the countryside with Shocking Blue playing on the cassette," Peterson recalls, "and did the standard 'find a location'. I had no fucking clue as to what to do for a photo shoot. It was awkward because Krist was a head and a half taller than the rest of them. They were super-nice and a bit hippie-ish. Kurt was kind of unwashed, very shy – very frail. At the end of the day, we ended up in this field of dried flowers. We were all self-conscious about it. In the end, because we knew it was stupid, the pictures are quite sweet."

"Six months after I saw them, they started to become really good," recalls Pavitt. "The turning point was at the Annex Theatre on Fourth where they played an all-ages show. Even though they spent five minutes tuning up between each song, there was definitely something there. A friend from Olympia, Dave Todd, came up and said, 'They are the next Beatles.' It was an interesting reaction because I couldn't tell if he was kidding or being sincere, and I found that my own feelings were wavering the same way – even though they were still really young, immature and barely able to tune up. And that was pretty outrageous, because there was something going on in that room that was magical, and I couldn't put my finger on it."

"What really got me into Nirvana was when Cat Butt played the *Sub Pop 200* record release party," says James Burdyshaw. To help promote the album's launch, Jon and Bruce threw a two-night party at The Underground, featuring eight of their bands, on December 28–29. Nirvana opened the first night. "There were about 40 people there. I remember standing with my mouth open – because that's when Kurt started pulling out those melodies. I was not expecting that. I did not see that craft in the same guy who just a few months earlier was doing nothing but screaming in Squid Row. The rest of the night I couldn't give a fuck about any of the other bands, all I could think about was how good Nirvana was.

"Nirvana understood the power of dynamics better than any other Seattle band," the former Cat Butt guitarist continues. "Kurt knew when to turn his pedal on and when to turn it off and just sing. Melvins could be dynamic in that they were into playing super-slow and kind of stopping and letting the drums fill up the space and Buzz would just hit a chord, but I think Kurt got that from listening to The Beatles and Creedence and Beat Happening and the K bands and those minimalist bands he was into . . ."

"The first thing that jumped out was Kurt's voice," recalls Craig. "It was big. We all thought he sounded like Creedence Clearwater Revival."

"They had a real small-town feel to them," says Gas Huffer's Joe Newton. "They didn't look like big city guys, the way they dressed and the way they carried themselves and they were kind of nervous. I remember seeing them loading in from their van and they had these little funky amplifiers – making do with what they had. But on stage, Kurt had an intensity that you could feel. For whatever that was worth."

Encouraged by the response to 'Love Buzz', Jon and Bruce started talking about releasing an album. There was just one catch, though: Nirvana had to stump up the recording costs – upfront. Kurt realised he needed someone to represent his band's interests, and started to look around his friends for a suitable contender as manager. He picked on Tam Orhmund, making her a mix-tape of his favourite music – Bay City Rollers, The Velvet Underground, The Knack, Soundgarden, Blondie, Metallica, AC/DC, Redd Kross[26] – and suggested that she could manage the band, despite having no previous experience. Orhmund was given a handful of 'Love Buzz' singles and told to send them out to potentially interested parties. In the meantime, Nirvana returned to Reciprocal Studios at the end of December to start recording what would become their debut album *Bleach*.

Kurt borrowed Donald Passman's *All You Need To Know About The Music Business* from the library and, after reading it, became suspicious of Pavitt's bohemian attitude to making records. So, one night, Krist dropped by Pavitt's place on Capitol Hill and drunkenly demanded that Sub Pop give Nirvana a contract. On January 1, 1989, Sub Pop signed a three-album, three-year deal with Nirvana. It was agreed the label would pay the band $6,000 for the first year, $12,000 for the next and $18,000 for the third.

"It was, 'Do we pay for the recording or do we pay for an attorney?'" recalls Jonathan. "Trying to put it off as long as possible because we wanted to do everything at once. We had to pay off Reciprocal but I didn't want to write a contract myself because I didn't know what the fuck I was doing. So I took a music-business book and copied out some stuff that sounded important, put it in a copy machine and said, 'Here's your contract!' And those guys, probably being equally confused by it as I was, saw some numbers that I had scribbled in which at the time were, like, $30,000 or thereabouts! All right! That was for like, LP three or something."

Was that the first contract you signed with a band?

"Um . . . well, there was a contract for Soundgarden, but that remained not fully negotiated. So for all intents and purposes I think it was."[27]

Is the whole story about the contract true? Krist got drunk, and hammered on your door and said, "We need a contract."

"Yes," replies Bruce. "That is true. And in retrospect, it was divinely orchestrated, because that gesture saved Sub Pop. We didn't have contracts back then. For one thing, back in the day, the way of doing business was with a handshake, but over and above that, we did not have the money to hire an attorney. It would have been a while before we signed them. Poneman was very interested in getting bands on contracts. We'd been talking to some majors because Jon liked to work that – you know, 'Let's go have a free lunch and listen to what they have to say.' And they always said, 'You have to have a contract.'

"I reflect back on that incident sometimes, and when I say divinely orchestrated I mean that, because the timing was perfect in every way. For one thing, I wasn't at my house. I was at my neighbour's. I had been partying a little at my house, and then I went next door. And for some reason, I decided, 'I need to step out of the house.' And the moment I stepped outside, Krist was walking up to my front door. If I had stepped out of the house a minute later I would have missed him, and he would have woken up sober the next day and probably not threatened to beat me up over the contract. So it's like one of those little things. Little things add up to big things. But he demanded a contract, and he was intimidating. He was drunk, and he was big, and he was very aggressive. So I called up Jon and said, 'You've got to get this guy signed, cos he is pissed. This is something that has to happen.' Krist was in the room when I was talking to him. 'Get the contract. This guy is gonna kick my ass, OK?'

"So Jon went to the library, and Xeroxed a contract out of some book, and used some whiteout and filled in some names – it was a 10-cent contract with no lawyer. And I remember thinking when they signed it in the office, 'This could be a significant moment.' This was the first time we had signed a group."

**Addenda 1: Thrown-Ups**

"Thrown-Ups just weren't ever going to practise, but we were going to have all the fun of a band," explains 'guitarist' Leighton Beezer. "We never practised, we went around acting like we thought we were really cool and people fell for it. Gave us shows. Always regretted it. And . . . uhhh . . . put out records [laughs]. But then the guys in Mudhoney wanted to get a little more serious and write songs, so I kicked them out of Thrown-Ups . . .

"You *play* music, you don't work music, right? It's probably anti-careerism at its heart, but the idea is the same as jazz. It's not strictly that you can't practise, it's like, just don't get it into your head that you *need* to practise. And once you get it out of your head that you need to practise, there's really hardly a good reason to do it. It's fun to play music, so every now and then you turn on a tape recorder and you're not practising, you're recording . . .

"So we were playing Scoundrel's Lair. Most of us were dressed in polyester housecoats, like your mom would wear, but Ed [Fotheringham, singer] had rigged up The Bloody Pooper. Which was a family sized jug of ketchup duct-taped to his stomach upside down with a tube attached to it connected to a hole in the back of his pants so that he could go up to the edge of the stage, hang his butt off and go, 'Pppllllbbbbpppp!!!!!!' Which was appalling . . .

"We were playing one night right around Christmas and Ed says, 'Well, this is gonna be really ironic, but I'm gonna be the baby Jesus and you guys can be the three wise men. Simple.' So Ed got too drunk and procrastinated and when I go over to his house to load up equipment he's barely got anything done. He has a sawhorse, which he's going to use to make a sheep. He's spraying it with spray glue and dropping cotton balls on it. So I'm like, 'Ed! The show is in an hour! Where's everything else?' So he goes into the laundry room and pulls out a sheet and rips it so that I can put it over myself and then he grabs some butcher paper and makes this big cone hat and he's like, 'OK, You're a wise man!' So we grab his sheep and two more wise man costumes and head off.

"And the show is a total drunken spectacle and Ed is so blotto that he can't stand up so he's leaning on the sawhorse the whole time. And the audience is *reeeaaallly* appalled. At the end I went up to a friend and said, 'You know, we really didn't get a very good reaction from that.' And he says, 'Well, I don't think you should go on stage as Klansmen and expect to get a good response! And Ed was butt-fucking a sheep!'

"The punchline is: we tried to do a manger scene and ended up with a Saturday night in Alabama."

**Addenda 2: Seattle vs Olympia**

Ian Dickson: "Have you talked to Calvin about Kurt?"

Are you kidding? Calvin's not going to talk about Kurt.

"He's not? Why not? Is there a jealousy thing going on?"

I have no idea. The only thing Calvin said to me about this book was this: in February 1989, Nirvana got made Single Of The Week in *Melody Maker*, and everyone was going around Olympia saying, "Oh, Nirvana's single of the week, isn't that cool?" and he was like, "Yeah, that is cool. But Some Velvet Sidewalk was single of the week as well. Isn't that cool?" and everybody was like, "Well, yeah, that's OK, but . . . Nirvana's single of the week!"

"He was jealous about Nirvana's success. The first time I ever listened to 'Smells Like Teen Spirit' was in Calvin's apartment. I'm sure of it. It might have been my tape, actually. And I remember both of us being like, 'This is going to be huge.' He told me, 'This will sell a million copies.' I can't imagine he was blind to the fact of how colossally talented Kurt was. Nobody could miss it. I don't know, Some Velvet Sidewalk and Nirvana? Sorry, I love Al [Larsen, Sidewalk singer], and I think Some Velvet Sidewalk is a great little jazz-art-noise project, but Nirvana's like The Beatles . . ."

I don't want to disagree with you here . . .

"Go ahead! Disagree with me . . ."

. . . but I can see where Calvin's coming from. They're both talented artists. Just because one happens to sell millions of records and the other doesn't, it doesn't make one more or less talented. It's down to the criteria you judge talent on.

"Agreed. I'm just saying it's naïve to think that, 'Why isn't everybody excited about Some Velvet Sidewalk?' Because some people like them, most people don't – and Nirvana, everybody loves! Tell me I'm wrong."

I guess I must be the one person in the world who never thought Kurt was any more talented than anyone else then. I'm not denigrating his talent, but . . . from my and Calvin's perspective, maybe we feel Kurt wasn't any more or less talented than Al.

"Right. OK. Here's a great example from my perspective. I won't agree with the Al Larsen case but the Melvins . . . as far as I'm concerned you can go the rest of your life and never find two such colossally talented people as Buzz and Dale."

That's a great parallel.

## NOTES

1 The Magnet Men became Tic-Dolly-Row once Ben became their singer. Tic-Dolly-Row is a sailor's term for a vagrant.

2 The acronyms are short for Dirty Rotten Imbeciles and Corrosion Of Conformity.

3 Shonen Knife are a cutsie Japanese all-girl group, utterly charming and kitsch. Formed in Osaka, 1983 and still creating naïve Sixties garage pop, bright and colourful. *Burning Farm* was the K cassette reissue of their debut album. "When I finally got to see them live," Kurt commented, "I was transformed into a hysterical nine-year-old girl at a Beatles concert."

4 It was probably 1986's melancholy, grungy, powerpop tour de force *Especially For You*. The Smithereens were contemporaries of The Replacements and R.E.M.

5 Lush were Slim Moon's band – not to be confused with the naval-gazing UK femme group of the same name.

6 Treehouse: naïve, happy-ish, semi-acoustic grunge-pop.
7 Krist and Kurt had also considered asking Tad Doyle to drum for them.
8 Leaving Trains' singer was the cross-dressing Falling James – Courtney Love's first husband. Courtney once told me that she'd married him only because he was dating her best friend Kat Bjelland at the time.
9 Not strictly true – both Led Zeppelin and Scratch Acid had been covered by the trio.
10 "The title means absolutely, unbelievably not bad," singer Chris Cornell told me in February '89. "I model my singing on my mom screaming at me to hide the pot plants when the police come round." Despite their deserved reputation for being heavy doom merchants, there was always a strong streak of humour behind Soundgarden's music.
11 Alice In Chains were sometimes erroneously called grunge, but they were suburban metal-heads, not punks. They only discovered the 'grunge sound' – alongside thousands of other bands – after Nirvana broke big.
12 Homestead was managed by Gerard Cosloy – before he left in the mid-Nineties to dominate the US independent sector with Matador records. Home to Big Black, Dinosaur Jr, Butthole Surfers, G.G. Allin . . .
13 The split 12-inch was issued in the UK on 53rd And 3rd, also home to The Vaselines.
14 The Beatles' debut album *Please Please Me* was recorded in 10 hours on February 11, 1963. They came down from Liverpool the night before, stayed in a B&B, were set up at Abbey Road by 10 a.m., had a lunch break and a tea break, and finished off with two takes of 'Twist And Shout', John hoarse and stripped to the waist, at around 10.30 the same night. Then drove back to Liverpool.

Fierce soul-influenced rockers The Animals played in Liverpool on May 17, 1964, drove straight to London, where producer Mickie Most had booked an hour's studio time. They recorded 'House Of The Rising Sun' in 14 minutes, two takes, of which the first was better, then did a B-side in the remaining 45 minutes, then went off to do a gig at the Southampton Gaumont. They then went back to Newcastle. Six weeks later 'Rising Sun' was number one in the UK and 10 weeks later number one in the US.

The Who recorded 'Anyway Anywhere Anyhow' between a soundcheck and a gig at the Marquee on April 13, 1965. They rehearsed the song during the afternoon soundcheck, headed off to IBC for an hour to lay it down around 5 p.m., spent an hour in a pub and returned to the club for the evening show.

15 Helios Creed played mentalist acid-fried rock.
16 It was one of Nirvana's oldest songs – on the *Fecal Matter* demo.
17 The Who actually smashed their instruments long before Hendrix – and when they didn't have any money either. Early Who had the same abandon as early Nirvana. They too were a bit scary, edgy, fearless, anything could happen . . .
18 Kurt continued to use this spelling up to the release of *Nevermind*, and occasionally afterwards. It's a nod to Kurdt Vanderhoof, guitarist from Aberdeen thrash metal band Metal Church.
19 Actually spelt Pufnstuf – a Sixties US children's TV programme, noted for its

psychedelic imagery and metaphors.

20 Marine Boy was a Sixties anime cartoon centred round the adventures of a boy able to breathe under water by chewing 'oxy-gum'.

21 Young Marble Giants were a minimal Welsh trio, who released one album, 1980's spooked *Colossal Youth.* Alison Statton whispered alienation in a curiously disconnected, melodic way – you could almost hear the emptying pits of Wales' mining villages as she sang about a girl painting her nails. Guitarist Stuart Moxham later produced Beat Happening. In 1992 Kurt listed *Colossal Youth* in his Top 10 favourite records ever: "I first heard *Colossal Youth* a year before I put out *Bleach*," Kurt told me. "I had a crush on their singer for a while – didn't everyone?" Hole later covered the Giants' 'Credit In The Straight World' – a song that Kurt had originally earmarked for Nirvana.

22 Jane's Addiction: Perry Farrell's arty, Gothic, LA rock band – they released two studio albums, including 1990's theatrical *Ritual de lo Habitual*, before drug-associated problems tore them apart.

23 Like many of the Olympia bands, Mick Collins' raw-assed Detroit garage/Mod trio, The Gories, never bothered to enlist a bassist.

24 4AD was the UK label home to Boston bands, Pixies and Throwing Muses. Highly stylised, artistic, Gothic in origin.

25 Design genius Peter Saville was responsible for the Manchester, UK label's vision.

26 Redd Kross were Sixties bubblegum pop-loving brothers from LA with a whacked sense of humour.

27 Jesse Bernstein was actually the first Sub Pop artist to demand a contract.

## CHAPTER 7

# No Intellectual Perspective

IN late '88, Sub Pop co-founders Bruce Pavitt and Jonathan Poneman realised they were nearly out of funds. In a last-ditch attempt to stir up industry interest, they decided to fly out a UK music journalist to cover their label. So at the start of 1989, it was arranged that I would travel to Seattle to do a two-part story on Sub Pop for *Melody Maker*. First week, a cover feature on Mudhoney was promised; second week, a follow-up feature on the label.

I wasn't Sub Pop's British PR Anton Brookes' original choice. He'd wanted my fellow writers, the Stud Brothers, as their musical tastes (rock) seemed more in tune with the Seattle vibe, but there were two of them – and Sub Pop couldn't stretch to that. So he sent me over a bunch of records, *Sub Pop 200*, Mudhoney (the split 12-inch with Sonic Youth) and 'Love Buzz' foremost among them. The call came at a good time. I'd started writing for *Melody Maker* a few months before, and was fed up of 'the Godfather of Cutie' tag I'd gained through championing bands like The Pastels, Shop Assistants[1] and Beat Happening at *NME*. Unknown to Anton, I'd already been turned on to Green River. My friends and I hadn't understood all the (Iron Maiden guitarist) Steve Harris triplets the Seattle band played, but we could relate on a primal level to Mark Arm's howl.

"Someone from SRD [Southern Records Distribution] came down, and said we've got this new label Sub Pop and one of their bands is touring with Sonic Youth," recalls Anton, who was working for Southern records at the time. "I knew who Nirvana, Nevada . . . whatever they were called . . . were, Tad and Mudhoney, because Peel had been playing *Sub Pop 200*. Peel liked them – so they had to be pop stars! 'Touch Me I'm Sick' was brilliant: that big farty guitar sound. So I started doing press for Mudhoney and Sub Pop."

I recall opening the package of records in the *Maker*'s reviews room, on the 26th floor of King's Reach Tower, on London's South Bank – placing the singles on to the turntable and leaping up on to the table in my excitement, dancing deranged high above the ground, as astonished editors walked by. I played them over and over, scarcely believing my ears. Before Seattle, I'd never been exposed to rock, avoided its clothing and deceits. Punk in 1977 had seen to that. It's unlikely I would have been half as enthusiastic about Seattle and its music if I, like my American counterparts, had grown up on a diet of Led Zeppelin and hardcore. But I hadn't, and neither had most of my British contemporaries. Reared on a constantly changing musical culture where the press determined that bands grew old very quickly, we were always on the lookout for the thrill of the new. Consequently, I was able to write about what was essentially traditional rock music with real enthusiasm. The Sub Pop rock bands, both in spirit and in sound, were new to this naïve English boy.

I reviewed three unknown Pacific Northwest singles together: The U-Men's 'Solid Action', 'Love Buzz' and Some Velvet Sidewalk's 'I Know', making them US Singles Of The Week. I wrote:

> *Some more serious disorder from Seattle. Singles of the . . . fuck it! Whatever time-period you want, babe! These shit-kicking muthas make ANYTHING released previously sound positively lightweight in comparison.*
>
> *The U-Men single keeps grinding on in there like a DEMENTED cat force-fed Motörhead at 78rpm, or Dinosaur Jr stuck in a time field of Green River shaking down The Stooges.* "SOLID ACTION! IF I EVER FIND BILL WE'RE GONNA RIDE A BUS! ACTION! SOLID ACTION!'" *That's how the lyrics go; sometimes frenzied, other times highly frenzied. But they always have warm red POP tunes coerced in underneath. Blistering.*
>
> *Nirvana are beauty incarnate. A relentless two-chord garage beat which lays down some serious foundations for a sheer monster of a guitar force to howl over. The volume control ain't been built yet which can do justice to this three-piece! WHAT IS GOING DOWN OVER THERE? Someone pass me a gun. Limited edition of a thousand; love songs for the psychotically disturbed.*
>
> *'I Know' has marginally less structure, but oodles more trebly feedback. There are only two members in this group? HUH? So why are my fucking ears bleeding?! Dementia personified; especially the songs on the flip. Steve Fisk and Calvin Johnson were present at the recording. That might go some way towards explaining some of all this . . . The International Pop Underground marches on.*

Here were bands that achieved what I had thought hitherto impossible: they made metal sound cool. During the mid-Eighties, pop music was anti-guitar. You couldn't pick up a music paper in the UK without reading someone telling you guitars were old and dead and phallic symbols of repression. Jon and Bruce's stroke of marketing genius was to push rock'n'roll as rebellion – an ancient credo – while allowing people to listen to big dumb rock and retain their hipster credibility. Up until grunge, there had always been a line drawn between popular and underground music; Journey on one side, Dead Kennedys on the other. People got beat up for being punk rock, especially in the US.

Sub Pop confused that line once and for all.

"There were very few people that understood all the references that I and Calvin knew," explains Pavitt. "When you came over there was an instant bond. Here there was this heavy primal music coming out of Seattle that could have been picked up by metal magazines, but wasn't. And because it was funnelled through your perspective, it took on a different flavour. It was filtered through a deeper understanding of independent music and punk rock. It was our connection that helped – you talking to me, me talking to Mark Arm, Mark talking to Matt Lukin, and all of a sudden there is this hook-up between someone who is very literate, such as yourself, hanging out with Matt Lukin, who is a metal rocker dude. If you'd just showed up and started hanging out with Matt Lukin, there would have been cultural dissonance and it wouldn't have happened."

Arriving at Bruce's place in Seattle, I found myself expected to share a mattress with my photographer Andy Catlin. Our companions were a borrowed record store rack filled with rare – even then – Sub Pop singles and a couple of beanbags. Above our heads loomed the twin radio towers of Capitol Hill. I stayed. Sleeping on floors was nothing unusual for me, and I relished the idea of staying with the guy who ran the whole operation. Andy checked into a hotel the next morning.

I can still picture Bruce and me wandering along Pine across the Interstate 5 bridge in the freezing winter air, on our way past the big department store downtown. He was explaining how 95 per cent of all body heat is lost through the head. "Excuse me Legend!" he said to me, "but do you mind if I borrow your hood?" So I unzipped the detachable hood from my parka, and he pulled it over his shaved head. We must have made an odd couple: me, all strained and bubbling with excitement; him, wearing a weird hood to match his epic beard, filling in my noise with the odd hesitant silence.

We hooked up with Calvin and Olympian friends for an all-night dance party, no alcohol involved. We danced to the cool sounds of Sixties soul and Mod, all of us comfortable in our own steps. It felt like the norm for Seattle, these fun and frantic and innocent celebrations of music.

I loved the little roundabouts in the centre of each meticulously laid out street around the Capitol Hill area, flowers and trees growing on each one. We'd rise early and walk down to Bruce's place of work, on the 11th floor of the Terminal Sales Building on 1st and Virginia, stopping off for a coffee. There we met ace radio PR Erica Hunter, whose task it was to amuse the eager Limey; sales people Daniel House and Mark Pickerel; musicians like Swallow's Chris Pugh, and Tad Doyle. People like Jonathan Poneman, a man who always reminded me of a big loveable shaggy dog, and photographer Charles Peterson.

"I was given the task of entertaining the English journalist until they could get you a band to interview," recalls Charles. "I took you to the Starbucks at Pike Place Market. At the time, Starbucks was still a novelty. You ordered two coffees, grabbed a couple of cookies and a bag of chocolate-covered espresso beans. I was like, 'Oh my god, he's just gonna lose it if he ingests all of this.'"

It wasn't until about four visits in that I got to recognise anywhere in Seattle apart from the tiny strip along 1st outside Sub Pop: all the necessary bars were downtown, either in Belltown or near the Showbox, the opposite way.

Nirvana began work on their debut album, Christmas Eve 1988. "We had nothing else to do," commented Krist. Lyrics were finalised at the last minute: some written the night before and others in transit. Chad remembers Kurt scribbling the words to 'Swap Meet' on the drive down to Seattle, resting a piece of paper on the dashboard. The basis for about 10 songs was laid down with Jack Endino in five hours. Kurt wasn't satisfied with his vocals, except for the one on 'Blew', which happened only because he'd accidentally tuned to 'drop-D' – much lower than standard. That explains the track's almost giddy, leaden, drunken tone.

Songs recorded included 'About A Girl', 'School', 'Negative Creep', 'Scoff', 'Swap Meet' (a very Aberdeen song concerning a man and a woman who meet up at Sunday swap meets to sell bric-a-brac and handicrafts and general household junk), 'Mr Moustache' (a possible reference to 'rednecks' like Dave Foster) and 'Sifting'.

"Our songs are about changing yourself, frustration," Kurt told me in 1990. "'School' was some surreal idea I had about being in school and being in social cliques all the time, and then you grow up, having to deal with exactly the same things with your friends at parties and in clubs as you did in high school."

More specifically, 'School' was written about Kurt's feelings of irritation on finding himself "back in school again" after Nirvana's first couple of Sub Pop-promoted Seattle shows. "If I could have thrown Soundgarden's name [into the song], I would have," he dryly commented.

'Paper Cuts' was far more horrific, based on the true story of an Aberdeen family who kept their children locked up in a single room – entering only to feed them and remove the soiled newspapers the children had been forced to relieve themselves on.

"They were mostly songs about lower life society and stuff like that," says Chad, "and there were some campy things like 'Floyd The Barber', taken from *The Andy Griffith Show*.[2] There was nothing particularly that stood out for me. I just went in and recorded my parts, you know? I didn't have much of a say in band decisions. 'Swap Meet' was one of my favourites – that, and 'Negative Creep'. 'About A Girl' was a good song. I always liked 'Mr Moustache', just because it was so fricking funny. I liked them all. 'Big Cheese' is probably one of my favourite Nirvana songs of all time."

"'Swap Meet' was originally spelt 'Swap Meat', which would've been funnier," comments Endino.

"You know about 'Negative Creep', don't you?" asks Steve Fisk. "I got told it was about the guy who lived across the street from the duplex and would come over while Kurt was gone to try to smoke Tracy out."

"That sounds positively Pear Street, Olympia," suggests John Goodmanson.

I thought it was a tribute song to Mudhoney, its heavy thunderous music and hook line of *"Daddy's little girl/ Ain't a girl no more"* echoing Mudhoney's *"Sweet young thing/ Ain't sweet no more"* (from 'Sweet Young Thing'). After all, as Kurt explained to *Flipside* in 1989, he didn't care too much for lyrics: "I don't consider [them] a big deal at all," he said. "As long as it has a good melody line; a hook and live energy is far more important . . ."

Or perhaps the song is about Kurt himself, with its scowling refrain, *"I'm a negative creep and I'm stoned"*. Whatever. It's hardly *Blood On The Tracks* or William S. Burroughs. It's fucking rock'n'roll. There to be hurled shimmering into the air alongside Mr Novoselic's bass for a few brief glorious seconds, and then discarded. It's not that important what the songs are about.

Nirvana were always more about the intonation, the energy, the emphasis Kurt placed on certain syllables and guitar riffs than actual words. And don't trust anyone who tells you any different.

The trio returned to Jack's studio on five occasions to finish off the album – December 29 (five hours), December 30 (five hours), December 31 (four and a half hours), January 14 (five hours) and January 24 (five and a half hours). Krist would drive as far as 400 miles on the days off in between in his white stub-nosed Dodge; from Aberdeen to Olympia to collect Kurt for rehearsal, then on to Seattle to pick up Chad who'd taken the ferry in from Bainbridge . . . and all the way back to Aberdeen.

"They were professional," says Jack. "It was just show up, plug in, tune up, 'OK, you know the songs? Good. We can record then.' Most of the Sub Pop bands were professional. Mudhoney, they were rehearsed, they knew how to play, everybody knew their songs . . ."

If you've got no money you're not going to waste time fucking around.

"No, exactly," replies the engineer. "You don't have time to spend two months in the studio 'writing the songs' and working out whether you should have two chords before the verse or three. I love indie rock because it's right now. This is it. We have to mix tomorrow. There's instant gratification."

It allows for spontaneity.

"*Absolutely*. I've done a lot of records that have taken weeks – months even – and I don't look back that fondly on many of those. The ones I still enjoy listening to are the weird indie records, strange bands that came in and recorded in a day and had a spark."

I was going to ask about recording budgets . . .

"*Bleach*, $600. It's true. OK, next question." Jack looks bemused, then realises why I'm asking the question. "Oh, that's right," he sighs. "You and me were on the same panel about grunge as Jonathan in 1998.[3] He was arguing that it cost more, and I was like, 'No, I've got the studio log sheets.' He thinks he wrote a cheque for more money than that. And yet the Nirvana contract is at the EMP[4], behind glass, and it says $600 on it. I know what we spent. It was $606.17. Now that leaves out the fact 'Love Buzz' and 'Big Cheese' were recorded at an earlier session, along with 'Spank Thru' which went on *Sub Pop 200* and 'Blandest' which is on the box set [*With The Lights Out*, 2004]. Those four songs were recorded during the 'Love Buzz' sessions for $150 or something, so you could maybe add another $75 for that portion of it – but I may have even taken that into account. In any case, it wasn't much over $600."

*Bleach* was recorded in a haze of cough medicine and alcohol. "We were all sick by then," Krist told Michael Azerrad. The band was drinking codeine syrup on prescription from the Pierce County Health Department. Money was still at a premium: if a song wasn't good enough to be used it would be recorded over.

Heard in the context of 2006, *Bleach* sounds remarkably tuneful – maybe familiarity blurs the senses because back then the general feeling was that it sounded too metal. But this is because metal, and our perception of it, has since changed. It's got more extreme. Led Zeppelin were once considered metal. Now people just think of them as hard rock.

Kurt himself felt the album had shortcomings: "*Bleach* seemed to be really one-dimensional," he complained in 1992. "It has the same format throughout – there were a few guitar overdubs, but that's it. All the songs are slow and grungy and they're tuned down to really low notes. And I screamed a lot." There again, Kurt was never satisfied with anything.

Now, *Bleach* sounds vibrant and buzzing with melody: it's an album that's matured well. Back then only the jangling love song, 'About A Girl', with its plaintive acoustic guitar intro, stood out – and perhaps 'Blew'. There was a little too much Melvins-esque torpor: not enough Olympian underground pop fervour. Not all critics agreed: Simon Reynolds, reviewing *Sub Pop 200* in *Melody Maker*, called Nirvana, "Too complex for their own good."

But that was when everyone expected anything associated with Sub Pop to be heads-down, no-nonsense, hair flailing, three-chord thrash.

"I think Kurt felt nervous about putting 'About A Girl' on there," Endino told Gillian G. Gaar. "But he was very insistent on it. He said, 'I've got a song that's totally different from the others, Jack, you've gotta just humour me here, because we're gonna do this real pop tune.' The question was raised at some point, gee, I wonder if Sub Pop's going to like this, and we decided, 'Who cares?' Sub Pop said nothing. In fact, I think they liked it a lot. Jonathan is a total pop head. And Bruce didn't like *Bleach* that much anyway, because I think he thought it was a little too heavy metal."

Kurt had already written a few other pop songs similar to 'About A Girl' – most notably the disquieting tale of rape, 'Polly' – but held back from using them. He realised the time wasn't right.

"We purposely made *Bleach* one-dimensional, more 'rock' than it should have been," Kurt told Michael Azerrad. "There was this pressure from Sub Pop and the scene to play 'rock music', strip it down and make it sound like Aerosmith."

Three remixed songs from the Crover demo ended up being used on the final version of the album, 'Floyd The Barber', 'Downer' and 'Paper Cuts'. "They weren't happy with the way Chad was playing," Endino comments. "Dale had written the drum part for those three songs; he played them the best. And Chad was good on the stuff that they had written with him. That's the way it is with drummers."

The night before the first recording session, the band stayed in Seattle at a friend of Dylan Carlson's, Jason Everman. He too was the product of a broken home and an ex-Aberdeen resident. Everman had also spent a few summers working as a commercial fisherman in Alaska, which came in handy when Nirvana asked him for a loan to meet the album's recording costs.

Jason willingly stumped up the money.

The band set off on their first tour of the US in high spirits. It was just a two-week West Coast tour, supporting Mudhoney and Melvins – down to California and back – but it did wonders for their confidence, even if Sub Pop's logo appeared on the flyers more prominently than Nirvana's name.

"We went out in Krist's white van," recalls Chad. "Before we left, he built a bunk across the back, just below the back windows. And he sawed off the top of the knob on the inside so the only way you could get into our gear was by opening the door with the key. Even if you broke the windows, you couldn't get in to our gear. I remember sliding in the amps sideways and they just fit. To this day, bands use those bunks. They're basically impregnable unless you have a welding torch."

"I booked the first couple of Nirvana tours," says Seattle musician Danny Bland. "Sub Pop was passionate and people from Seattle were too, but outside of the immediate area no one cared. We had our stops along the West Coast. All the Sub Pop bands stopped in the same places. Raji's was a stop, the Pyramid in New York, the Chatterbox in San Francisco, Jabberjaw in LA, Satyricon in Portland[5], Santa Barbara and UC Davis at the school."

"I did a fanzine in Boston," recounts independent promoter Debbi Shane. "At that time indie labels were little hype machines, and then Sub Pop released the first Soundgarden single and their little hype machine began to spin rapidly, increasing the attention to all of their bands. Mudhoney were great. I got their single on brown vinyl. Next was Nirvana. I bought 'Love Buzz' in Eugene, Oregon and was blown away. I was so excited. I was a huge fan. Candice [Pedersen, K co-boss] came and lived with us [in San Francisco] for a summer. She knew Nirvana. They wanted her to manage them, and she didn't feel like she was qualified. We went to a show and I had read so much into Kurt's lyrics because I thought he was a genius.

"It was at the Covered Wagon in San Francisco [February 10]; they played with the Melvins," Debbi continues. "They were amazing. What stood out was the embarrassment afterwards backstage when I asked Kurt what 'Spank Thru' was about. I had read so much into it that I thought Kurt had come up with this really cool metaphor. But it's basically about what it's about. They kind of laughed at me, but because I was with Candice they were sweet."

How did Kurt strike you when you first met him?

"He was sweet, quiet and almost as painfully shy as I was. We didn't have a lot of interaction. I don't remember thinking, 'This guy is a jerk.'"

It was in San Francisco, on their way to the Haight-Ashbury free clinic to pick up more drugs to combat the flu, that the band noticed a major AIDS prevention poster campaign. Billboards encouraged drug users to 'Bleach your works' (clean needles with bleach to kill the virus). Kurt had been thinking of calling the album *Too Many Humans*, but after joking around with the phrase with Jon and Bruce who were in the van at the time, the idea that bleach could – as Bruce Pavitt put it – "become such a valuable substance" stuck in his head.

The Covered Wagon show was, according to one account, a miserable experience. There was almost no one there: the band, reduced by circumstance and cancelled gigs and the necessity to find money for petrol, were driven to eating out afterwards at a free soup kitchen run by the Hare Krishna sect. Afterwards, seven people shared an apartment floor: a miserable time – or the reality of being in an up-and-coming band still being played out countless times the world over? It can be exhilarating to share your nights and drugs and friends in such close proximity, especially when you're starting out.

The night after the San Francisco show, Nirvana played Palo Alto, supporting Mudhoney. It was Mudhoney guitarist Steve Turner's favourite ever Nirvana performance.

"We played a small show with them in this place that was like a storefront with a big plate glass window and a tiny stage," he recalls. "And Kurt was rolling around on the stage and he kind of rolled backwards and somehow managed to be balancing on his head and still playing his guitar – it was the weirdest thing because he was like magically balancing on his head without using his hands. There was not a big crowd in there, maybe 50 people, and the guys were cracking up at the absurdity of it. Nirvana were a wreck but in a really great, chaotic way."

The band returned to Seattle on February 25 to play the HUB Ballroom at the University of Washington – an all-ages show, four bands for four bucks.

Kurt didn't have much experience of singing and playing guitar at the same time: a second guitarist was needed. Jason Everman seemed to fit the bill. "We were ready to take anyone if they could play guitar OK," Kurt said. "He seemed like a nice guy and he had the Sub Pop hair." So Jason joined, and even though he didn't play on the album, he was credited on the sleeve. "We just wanted to make him feel more at home," explained Krist.

The first show that Jason played with Nirvana was a drunken Evergreen dorm party. Problems began to arise immediately. Although Jason was into punk rock, he was more interested in speed metal – not the 'cool' punk of Olympia, but testosterone-fuelled exercises in seeing how fast and loud one could play the guitar. His guitar sound was much more 'metal' than Kurt's.

"What you heard on record was pretty much what the band sounded like," says soundman Craig Montgomery. "More chaotic live. Noisier. When they had Jason in the band, I would listen to each guitar-player in the headphones, trying to figure out who was doing what, and only Kurt's guitar made any sense. What was coming out of Everman's amp was just a bunch of noise. It wasn't that it made no sense, more that it didn't sound good. I'm sure he was playing the right chords, but he didn't have a good sound. To make the mix work I needed to lean on Kurt's guitar."

"Jason worked out fine in the beginning," says Chad loyally. "He was really into his speed metal. He turned me on to some of the more obscure metal bands, like Testament, and Celtic Frost before they went glam. We knew each other already, because he'd played in my old band Stone Crow – who were speed metal. Destruction and Possessed and Slayer, all that stuff, influenced us.

"Jason was a working type of guy," the drummer adds. "He was almost on the music scene more than into the actual music. We'd go record shopping, and anything new he'd pick it up. He was the fan that got a chance to play with bands he was a fan of. The dynamic of Nirvana didn't change much when he joined. Essentially, Kurt always wanted somebody to play the parts he was playing so that he didn't have to concentrate so hard. So Jason hung back and kept the rhythm parts going."

"The first show I saw them play with Jason was in San Francisco," recalls Jonathan Poneman. This runs contrary to accepted Nirvana history, which has the HUB Ballroom as Jason's first major show, but recent documents unearthed support Jonathan's claim. Melvins' new bassist Joe Preston interviewed Nirvana at the Covered Wagon for his *Matt Lukin's Legs* fanzine – and Jason was present.[6]

"I can't confirm the soup kitchen thing," Poneman continues, "but I can confirm that Bruce and I rode with Nirvana to Palo Alto the following night. That was the first time that I heard NWA[7], in the Nirvana van. You remember the first time you hear [NWA debut album] *Straight Outta Compton*. You just do. Personalities aside, Jason made Nirvana much more powerful. That Nirvana eventually took on another auxiliary player must mean that Kurt appreciated the results as well . . .

"So I get to the gig, and there's another guy on stage!" Poneman goes on. "Kurt says, 'It's my surprise for you' – because I'd been saying he needed another guitar-player. I don't know whether it was because of a lack of volume pedals or whatever but when they used to play it would be this monster roar of a sound and Kurt would go to do a solo and suddenly it would get very thin sounding. That was the first show they did as a quartet, and it was fucking great."

You always were more into the metal than me . . .

"I was," he agrees. "Not metal, but it was more Soundgarden-like. They were the big band at the time. He or Courtney later wrote Soundgarden off as being meat-headed rock, but Kurt loved Soundgarden early on."

What were you doing 15 years ago?

"I had just got out of high school," replies Nirvana fan Rob Kader. "I was working at my uncle's deli on Eastlake alongside some punk guys from Tennessee. After work, I'd go over to their house in the University District and drink, do psychedelics and listen to music. They had a roommate, Jason Everman . . ."

Can you describe Jason?

"Jason was a very sweet guy. He's portrayed as having anger management problems, but he was a pretty good friend. He was the one that was sober in the whole household – and, at the time, acted as a big brother to me. He played me the 'Love Buzz' single when it came out, and its beauty floored me. I was like, 'Fuck, you've gotta get into this band!' The HUB Ballroom show was my first taste of Sub Pop in general. I went into the bathroom after a great set from The Fluid[8] – and in walks Krist, a big bouncy funny guy yelling and being like he always is with his running commentary. I thought, 'Wow, this is so cool.'"

What was the band like as people?

"They were very down-to-earth guys. We went to Jason's house afterwards, and Kurt was smoking a bowl, attempting to mellow out after a fierce performance. Everyone was pretty quiet until they ended up in Jason's room and started to scrutinise his record collection. Jason had a whole range of tastes, but he did get some ribbing for his extensive, obscure, metal collection. Ha ha."

Does anything stand out about their performance that night?

"Just the intensity. The whole band, and Kurt in particular, played until they had nothing left. It was brutal, the way he put his body through so much. I would go up to Kurt sometimes after shows, and he'd be so exhausted he couldn't even carry on a conversation. Some people might think it was drugs, but he was sober every show I knew of."

What did you think Jason brought to the band?

"He brought a lot of hair," laughs Rob. "And he brought some money. I think . . . a little extra crunch. And I'm sure it was nice for Kurt, as he was flailing around, to have a second guitarist. Having a second guitarist added a security blanket to Kurt's psyche, allowing him to play and move more freely."

The HUB Ballroom show was my first experience of Nirvana live.

I was disappointed. I loved their single, but what was this mess of noise and hair and alcohol-fuelled banter? I'd thought of their sound as Mod – a definition crucial to this English boy[9] – but this was anything but. This was just another Blood Circus or Cat Butt; another formless compendium of noise for noise's sake, no pop tunes or spark or anything. Sure, they seemed like fun, mischievous folk: Krist in particular was determined to make an impression, whatever it took. Placed next to characters such as Tad Doyle and his gross, evil humour, though, this Aberdeen quartet paled into insignificance. Despite reports years later from people who weren't present, the crowd wasn't much impressed either: the slam-dancing and frantic stagediving[10] that were reported as taking place during Nirvana's set mostly happened while The Fluid were playing – there's a damn fine Peterson photograph taken then that adorns a reissued *Sub Pop 200*, the crowd a blur of emotion and sweat. Nirvana took too long between songs to inspire such movement.

They did destroy their instruments, though – after the show, the management suspended live bookings for a short while, due to damage incurred during Nirvana's set.

Standing at the side during The Fluid, I indicated that I fancied performing myself. You could almost picture the thought processes going through Jon and Bruce's heads, like, "Who the fuck is this guy? We've paid for him to come over here and write a big article on our label and now he wants to get on stage? We better humour him . . ." So the singer from Tacoma's garage kings (and queen) Girl Trouble offered to lend me a guitar – a fancy piece of Sixties work. "You're not going to be rough with this, are you?" he asked, catching the gleam in my eye. Jesus yes. Er, I mean no. So I took the stage just before Girl Trouble (Skin Yard headlined), drunkenly essaying my way through The Beatles' 'I'm Down' and 13th Floor Elevators' 'You're Gonna Miss Me' in front of the Seattle rock cognoscenti, before exhorting the audience to sing along with my *a cappella* take on 'Sweet Soul Music' . . .

"Do you like good music?" I chanted, and 800 voices chanted back, "YEAH, YEAH!" I segued it into a new cover, of The Inkspots' 'Do Nuts'.[11] The crowd fucking loved it. I liked this city.

That night, as far as I was concerned, Nirvana were trounced on every front. All week long, Jonathan had been pumping the band to me over Mexican beer. On course for world domination was the gist of it. I began to think it was the deluded wanderings of a fevered mind. But it seemed I was in the minority, even then . . .

"The first time I photographed Nirvana live was at the HUB Ballroom," recalls Charles Peterson. "They totally blew me away. They blew everybody away. The buzz was on. Were you at that show?"

Yes. You liked them? I thought they sucked.

"That's because you hadn't seen them *really* suck," he laughs. "I liked them because visually they were night and day compared to what I had seen before. They tore up the stage. I don't know if that was Jason's influence because he was very active. He had the 'grunge' thing nailed down."

"It was the first time I'd seen stagediving," recalls Craig Montgomery. "I was never a big fan of it because it would fuck up the sound. I just wanted to hear the music. I hated it when some yahoo was up there, bumping into the mic stand and kicking the guitar-player's pedals around. It didn't have anything to do with the music. It was like a thrill ride or a football game. I don't think Nirvana cared either way. I'd guess that Kurt would rather have been listened to than stagedived to. Especially later when it got to be dick jocks venting their testosterone."

In an interview conducted that day with the University of Washington paper *The Daily*, Krist and Chad admitted to earning money from dishwashing, Jason was living off his earnings, while Kurt was living off his girlfriend Tracy.

"I'd like to live off the band," Kurt told journalist Phil West, "but if not, I'll just retire to Mexico or Yugoslavia with a few hundred dollars, grow potatoes and learn the history of rock'n'roll through back issues of *Creem* magazine."

Kurt turned 22 in February 1989.

He was to spend most of the year touring with Nirvana – over 100 shows compared to a scant two dozen in the previous two years – and creating art at Tracy's Pear Street apartment in Olympia. He'd paint with whatever medium came to hand: acrylic paints, magic marker, spray cans, blood, pen, pencil – and on whatever improvised canvas he could scarf up at local thrift stores: often the back of board games. On rare occasions, he'd even paint using his own semen. He'd paint aliens, diseased children, grossly distorted childhood images utilising pop iconographic figures such as Batman and Barbie – his paintings increasingly folding into three dimensions. Driven by a lust for expression, he began to collect junk and general ephemera: toy cars, action figures, headless dolls – most of which would later be broken down or melted in the backyard to become part of his artistic endeavours. Everything was dark and distorted and disturbing: sexual organs would be changed between male and female and given fresh layers of meaning. He'd paint in his underpants, in home-made band T-shirts, in his striped sweaters – that is, in between lounging around and watching TV, rehearsals, jotting down ideas for songs in his journal, and looking for cheap equipment in charity shops.

"There were lots of thrift stores in Aberdeen," laughs Ian Dickson. "We'd take road trips down from Olympia and meet in Tacoma a lot. Kurt knew where every pawnshop was too because he was always looking for musical equipment. He would just drive around . . ."

What kind of stuff would he get?

"Effects pedals," Dickson replies. "Mudhoney and Nirvana and the grunge guys changed the industry for effects pedals. Before Nirvana's success, Kurt went to huge lengths to get the pedals he wanted because they didn't manufacture them any more. They were all manufactured in the Seventies by MXR, and MXR had gone out of business. Kurt and Dylan would constantly be looking for them – Tacoma was a goldmine because it was off the map. This stuff was highly technical. Kurt was an artist and he had all these crazy ideas, but he also knew what he wanted and he'd go to any lengths to get it, pretty much."

* * *

I can recall the broad brush-strokes of my first meeting with Nirvana if not the fine details. It was a sunny winter's day in Seattle along the lake front about two blocks down from Sub Pop's penthouse apartment on 1st Avenue, and a two-minute walk from Pike Place Fish Market. A little patch of green much favoured by tramps and passing hawkers on bicycles served as the venue for Nirvana's first major press interview. I remember it well because on the day of Kurt's memorial service in 1994, the preacher instructed us to all go seek out the place where Nirvana were most special to us, and remember them that way. I thought he was full of bullshit, but walked down there anyway, mainly because I felt that the other speakers that day were even more full of bullshit.

Jonathan took me down the steep hillside to meet the four chaps who comprised Nirvana: Kurdt Kobain (as he spelled his name back then), Chris Novoselic (also the original spelling), Chad Channing and temporary extra guitarist Jason Everman. Already Poneman, a master of hyperbole, was pumping me full of half-truths and promises about Nirvana's potential.

"This is the real thing," he told me in a quote I later took as my own, which then, to my undying shame, got repeated the world over. "No rock star contrivance, no intellectual perspective, no master plan for world domination. You're talking about four guys in their early twenties from rural Washington who want to rock. You're talking about four guys who, if they weren't doing this, would be working in a supermarket or lumber yard, or fixing cars."[12]

Jonathan always did have a great way with words. I'd swear he'd missed his true vocation if he wasn't like a thousand times richer than me.

"Kurdt Kobain is a great tunesmith,' he continued, "although still a relatively young songwriter. He wields a riff with passion. He's your archetypal small guy: wiry, defiantly working class and fiery. His provincial and witty lyrics bring to mind an American Mark E. Smith.[13] Nirvana deals a lot with Calvin Johnson type themes: innocence and the repression of innocence. Nirvana songs treat the banal and pedestrian with a unique slant."

The band themselves were lively, excited to meet a music critic from England, eager to distort the truth, not for any sinister purposes but because it was fun. Jason said he'd worked as a commercial fisherman in Alaska for three years – true! Chris, the lanky friendly bassist, informed me he'd once been a competitive tree-climber – false! Kurdt said his pet rat had once bit Bruce Pavitt – true![14] The singer also admitted to a love of the Pixies, told me how the band had been branded as Satan-worshippers back home and got into a momentary argument with a passing salesman, flaunting tapes.

"How much are those?" he asked.

One dollar, came the reply.

"Shit," said Kurdt. "One dollar for a Van Morrison cassette? There are pawn shops around here that will give you 20 bucks for them."

The guy disappeared, after trying to sell us some hash.

"We set that one up," Chris claimed. "To give you a taste of weird Americana. He's the fifth member of Nirvana."

Jonathan stopped by to see how the interview was going and gee us up into creating more ridiculous quotes. A cat walked by on a leash. I had a five-minute coughing fit and nearly asphyxiated.

It wasn't the most auspicious of starts to my relationship with Nirvana, although the band partly revealed their musical preferences: "Aerosmith, Tuxedomoon[15], NWA, [Sixties pop group] Herman's Hermits, Leadbelly, hard rock, punk rock, power pop, hip hop, Sub Pop . . ." When the interview finally appeared in *Melody Maker* several months later, Everman had left the band. So, in time-honoured music press fashion, I doctored the conversation – to make it appear I'd only been speaking to three people. It hardly mattered. I couldn't tell one speaker from another anyway.

In truth, Nirvana barely registered with me. There was plenty else happening at that time, during my first two weeks in America – a trip to my own personal Mecca, Olympia, for one – to divert my attention away from this group of youngsters who seemed somehow separate from everyone else. Sure, I'd made 'Love Buzz' single of the week but I knew plenty of bands that had flamed just as briefly and then flickered out.

*Bleach* hit the streets on June 15, 1989. Sub Pop's press release boasted, "Hypnotic and righteous heaviness from these Olympia pop stars. They're young, they own their own van, and they're going to make us rich!" The first thousand copies appeared on white vinyl. The next 2,000 came with an awesome Charles Peterson poster.

Choosing a cover was a problem. Alice Wheeler did a session, but the results weren't good: "Nirvana came over to my house in the afternoon," she told Gillian G. Gaar. "We went up the street and took some pictures and they weren't that great. Jason was like Mr Glam Boy compared to Kurt; Kurt looks pretty washed out in most of those pictures. I don't like them very much. And the band didn't like them. Bruce loved 'em, though. But of course he liked the idea of the scary hick from Aberdeen."

One of Tracy Marander's pictures appeared on the cover instead – a live shot of Nirvana performing at the Reko Muse art gallery in Olympia. It was a fun night: Ben Shepherd led friends in 'the worm' (a dance wherein participants wriggle around the floor, trying to make unwary members of the audience fall over) and Shelli and Krist got back together.

The Sub Pop hype machine started to swing into full effect. My two-part *Melody Maker* profile appeared on March 18 and 25 – the first stages in generating an explosion of interest in the music, both outside the city and within. Almost overnight, Seattle became the place to namedrop. Of course, it helped that Mudhoney began their debut UK tour supporting Sonic Youth the week after the first article appeared, and that they were so incredible. But Nirvana were fast catching up . . .

"Kurt had a brown wood Fender Mustang guitar with a Soundgarden sticker on it," recalled Jason Troutman, former roommate of Jason Everman. "And he just smashed the shit out of it at the Annex Theatre in Seattle [April 7, 1989]."

"They were going crazy at that show," confirms Poneman. "It was the first time Kurt had been lifted up into the air by the crowd, which was like a rite of passage that only Mark Arm had previously been privy to. There was a real tribal quality to it. It was that night Bruce finally accepted how great Nirvana was."

A week later, Nirvana played Screaming Trees' home town of Ellensburg – a show truncated brutally by an unsympathetic soundman, but one that created an instant fan out of the Trees' frontman Mark Lanegan.

"They completely blew me away," he told *Spin* magazine in 1995. "It was like seeing The Who in their prime. After two songs some jerk who worked there stopped the show – they'd gone over their time limit. So they stood there for a second and then Krist started throwing his bass up in the air, up to the top of this 20-foot ceiling, and catching it with one hand. Meanwhile Kurt was letting his amp go loud as hell, and their road manager got in a fist-fight with the jerk guy. And this was in Ellensburg!"

Not everyone was convinced. Future Nirvana producer Steve Fisk saw the same show: "They were terrible. They couldn't even get it together to play a song. Kurt broke a string, ran in the corner and started throwing a fit. He started throwing his guitar around in the case. The two songs I stayed for didn't go anywhere, like the most aimless kind of SST jam. When Jason started moving his hair and it had nothing to do with the beat, I said, 'Posers,' and walked out. If you had hair like that, you had to move it on the beat or not at all. The PA sucked bad. I had work to do, so I left."

"I was excited to see Nirvana at the Reko Muse Gallery," says Goodmanson of another early '89 show. (Nirvana played at the Gallery twice: the place was co-run by Kathleen Hanna, future singer of Bikini Kill.) "The flyer said, 'Industrial Nirvana'. It was a gag show. Nirvana had got so sick of playing benefits they'd decided to take the piss out of the whole concept. They played a noise set . . . a really terrible noise set."

"I think Tobi Vail joined them for a little that night, and borrowed my drum machine and played repetitive beats," adds Slim Moon.

"It was a noise jam thing," Vail admits. "It was fun. Everyone knew everyone. Nirvana played with a bunch of mates. I have no idea how it sounded. I do remember I had blisters all over my hands afterwards."

Whatever. There's no stopping the hype machine once started.

> *"Britain is currently held in thrall by a* rock *explosion emanating from one small insignificant West Coast American city, Seattle," I wrote in* Melody Maker. *"Seattle, home of Quincy Jones, Bobby Sherman, Heart, Bruce Lee and the Space Needle (as featured in the 1962 Elvis Presley movie* It Happened At The World's Fair*). Now it has a new claim to fame – the Sub Pop recording emporium, residing on the penthouse suite of the Terminal Sales Building . . .*
>
> *"As if from nowhere, hordes of shit-kicking, life-defying, grungy, gory, guitar bands, with one foot in the early Seventies and the other on punk rock's grave, are springing up. Names such as Tad, 'the Meatloaf of the New Wave' and his spine-crushing band, and the incredible Nirvana, barely alive, yet already one of the finest exponents anywhere in the art of marring a simple instinctive two-chord song to oceans of speakers . . ."*

My use of the word 'grunge' in the above paragraph wasn't the first use of the word in a UK music paper – I'd even used it myself a year before to describe the sound of Manchester's fucked-up baggy kings Happy Mondays – but it was the first use in the context it became infamous for.[16]

When Nirvana came to play Lamefest '89 on June 9, the Moore Theatre was heaving with expectation. It was the largest place Nirvana had played, and they didn't disappoint. By now, they were in full swing – instruments being smashed, the lot.

"Kurt was swinging his guitar by its strap, hula-ing it around his neck," remembers Gas Huffer drummer Joe Newton. "I was like, 'He's gonna get hurt!' They had this abandon that rock'n'roll is supposed to have, this 'rolling in glass' kind of thing. Just the ability to let go of your mortality . . . to not fear getting injured. I couldn't do that. It always made me mad, like: 'I can't afford that stuff either, what are they doing smashing that? I'll take it!' "

"That was really fun," comments Chad. "The show was advertised for weeks in advance. I still have a flyer for that show. It's the largest flyer I have ever been on. It was Mudhoney, Tad and Nirvana. It was crazy. A year ago, those three bands would have never been able to pull off a show at the Moore – and a large majority of the people in the world still didn't know any of those bands! Unless you were living in Seattle, you'd wonder what the heck was going on."

"That was the show where they first released copies of *Bleach*," recalls Rob Kader. "I picked up four white vinyl copies: I was so excited to have it. As I would get to go to more Nirvana shows, I was always impressed with how inclusive and ego-free the guys were. I remember hanging out with Nirvana in the van afterwards and pondering what to do next. There was a big party at the Annex Theatre and people were urging us to go and join the festivities. Everyone from Sub Pop was there. Kurt just shrugged the whole thing off and decided to go home."

The following night, Nirvana got asked by Sub Pop to step in for Cat Butt in Portland. Kader picks up the story.

"We get to this tiny club, unload, go for some pizza, get back and are like, 'Fuck, there's nobody here.' The club's hilarious. It's set up like a war zone. It has these sandbags and fake barbed wire, but there are only about 12 people there. The band starts compiling a set list and look at me laughingly: 'Fuck it, we'll play whatever song you want.' Tracy is buying me beer after beer, so I'm all lit, and deep in their set I ask for 'Sifting' for a second time and Kurt says, 'What the fuck, we already played that one!' So Jason's like, 'Dude, ask for "Big Long Now".' So I do, since it's one of my favourites. Krist exclaims, 'We don't play that one any more.' Instead of waiting for another request from me they decide to close the show with their rendition of 'Do You Love Me?' they had just recorded for that Kiss tribute album.[17] That was pretty much it."

**Addenda 1: Olympia vs Seattle**

"We didn't make the single to be Single Of The Week," replies Al Larsen. "We put out that single and we got a bunch of pictures taken, walking around town pushing our bikes. Really dull pictures, on purpose. If you try to break everything down at once, it's not going to be popular . . . but if you just break one little thing, you know? People are like, they have a weird name, dumb pictures, the guy can't sing. Yeah, it's brilliant, but they're not going anywhere."

When I made those three records Single Of The Week it's because I thought all three records were great. I didn't differentiate, but other people did.

"Early November 1991, working at Sub Pop. Looks like we're going to stay in business," recounts Rich Jensen. "About that time, *Nevermind* is demonstrating that it's a popular record. And the local TV news station, who of course ignored anything any of the artists my age were doing, is coming to Sub Pop asking, 'What's the deal with this record? Where's it coming from?' And I addressed the camera and said anybody who liked The Beatles would like Nirvana. That wasn't a good story, but maybe there's a point to it. Nirvana's success wasn't a surprise to me."

It was a surprise to me. Why would one band be favoured over the other?

"Do you ever listen to Guns N' Roses?" asks Al. "Do you know the song 'Sweet Child O' Mine'? That's a really sweet song. Formerly they were a hard rock band, but this song just cut across a full range of things. That's what happened with Nirvana. There was this heavy, ironic and appropriate Seattle sound going on, and there was this band that fit that description, but were also having real poetry that cuts across . . ."

"The single you're talking about is 'Big Cheese' [B-side of 'Love Buzz']," comments Rich. "For me, it was the sound of the bass, that clobbering sound. It seemed it was a logical extension of other rock'n'roll sounds. That was a primal man sound, whereas with Some Velvet Sidewalk the approach was more poetic and abstract."

I remember being in Olympia at Nikki's house and all of a sudden you turned to me and said . . .

"I really liked you, and I wanted to come clean about it," explains Al. "In the spring of 1989, I was on a tour and our car broke down in Pittsburgh for two days, missing shows. And we were stuck at someone's house and their roommate came home and he was really nice to us, we went up to his room to hang out, he had a *Melody Maker* open on his desk to this double-page spread about Sub Pop and the grunge scene – by Everett True. And here we are in Pittsburgh missing our shows and we're reading about how all the long hair bands in Seattle are the coolest thing happening. I was like, how could he do this to us? He's fucking everything up. Taking the camera and turning it in the wrong direction and taking a whole bunch of pictures."

I wasn't seeking to promote a certain type of band, but a diversity of bands. It wasn't my fault if people picked up on just one sort of music.

**Addenda 2: hype**

The single most quoted paragraph I've ever written was that description of Nirvana in the original Sub Pop article. And it was, word-for-word, what you told me. I was up against a hard deadline, and we were on the phone a lot . . .

Jonathan Poneman: "I remember those conversations. I know I'm going to sound like a complete bumpkin, but as someone who's a devotee to all kinds of rock, to have a real live British music journalist in our midst, particularly one from *Melody Maker*. Seriously! I was in awe. So when I looked at that article . . . I always set out to read it word-for-word but I was so impressed that our little scene got written up in *Melody Maker* I could only take it in as a whole. I was like, 'Wow, there's Chris Pugh [Swallow singer]. Who'd'a thunk Chris Pugh would end up in the *Melody Maker*!' No offence to Chris. The whole event was really so amazing to me on a very fan-boy level and it continues to be one of my most cherished memories."

When I got back after leaving Seattle I had maybe 48 hours to write the Mudhoney story up. It was a big deal. So I got home and I must've got food poisoning because I was throwing up the entire time. Not only that, but I lost the entire story when my computer crashed. I had to travel across London to the *Melody Maker* offices about midnight to rewrite that story, vomiting the entire way.

Jonathan: "Now that's grunge!"

One of the things that first attracted me to Seattle bands was the fact that everyone blatantly lied to me. I thought that was awesome. No one in the UK did that; everyone was so earnest in their attitude towards the press – people took us way too seriously. I know why musicians did it in Seattle. It was because no one thought that they were going any place. But that attitude was instrumental to Sub Pop's – and Nirvana's – early notoriety.

Jonathan: "I think it's retarded to talk about [Sex Pistols manager] Malcolm McLaren or [Monkees manager] Don Kirshner or [Seventies *Hit Parade/Creem* critic] Lisa Robinson, the people who in their respective ways were manipulators and hype-masters, but so much of this shit isn't true. The fact of the matter is that the fantastic is so much more interesting than the pedestrian, normal truth. Maybe a lot of people did bullshit you because they didn't think that they were going anywhere, but I'd like to say I bullshat you because I thought we *were* going somewhere."

Megan Jasper (Sub Pop president): "Also, you have to remember that the Sub Pop offices were small and the people who worked there were funny. So when someone lied, even about the smallest, most retarded thing, it made all of us laugh. You weren't the only person who was lied to, but you were certainly one of the most fun people to lie to."

Jonathan: "I would regularly lie to Bruce about how much money we had in the bank."

And I certainly made up my share of lies.

Jonathan: "That's what it's about, you know? You need to make the gullible think they're reading the truth, but the idea that they actually *are* reading the truth is, to me, ridiculous."

I used to say that the only goal I ever had with my writing was to make people jealous of me.

Jonathan: "And you know what? I think you are a brilliant writer for that very reason. Don't quote me on that."

## NOTES

1 Shop Assistants were an Eighties female-fronted Scots pop band – the exact mid-point of Ramones, The Velvet Underground and Jesus And Mary Chain, with a little Blondie thrown in. Sadly only released one album, 1986's poignant *Shop Assistants*.

2 *The Andy Griffith Show* was a hit Sixties American TV comedy show; the names Floyd, Opie, Aunt Bee, Andy and Barney in the song all come from the series.

3 It was part of a symposium held in a Capitol Hill bar, and filmed. I forget why.

4 Experience Music Project – the rock music museum in Seattle.

5 Nirvana actually played their first out of state gig at the Satyricon on January 6, 1989.

6 Kurt revealed a hitherto forgotten band name during this interview: Ying Yang Valvestem.

7 NWA were Dr Dre, Ice Cube and Eazy-E's incendiary gangsta rap group from Compton, CA.

8 The Fluid: explosive early Sub Pop band from Denver whose live fury – think MC5, Minor Threat – never quite translated to vinyl.

9 Think of the compressed fury of The Who, The Kinks, The Jam . . .

10 I recall being particularly impressed when both Jon and Bruce were passed over the crowd's heads.

11 'Do Nuts' was later recorded in NYC with Sonic Youth's engineer Wharton Tiers, and issued as a Sub Pop single. I recall showing up at Wharton's studio in the meatpacking district, no instruments, nothing. "Is that it?" he asked, surprised. "Yep," I replied. "Switch the mic on, and let's roll!"

12 Either consciously or not, Jonathan listed two jobs that Kurt's dad had held.

13 Mark E. Smith is the singer with The Fall – perhaps the single most bloody-minded English band to have been thrown up by punk in the late Seventies.

14 It happened on Bruce's first visit to Kurt and Tracy's apartment in Olympia, the same visit where Bruce brought down copies of The Shaggs and Daniel Johnston albums in an attempt to woo Nirvana.

15 Tuxedomoon: an experimental avant-garde New Wave group from San Francisco.

16 When the EMP started up in the mid-Nineties, I had an idea that I could present them with a typewriter, claiming it was the implement I wrote the original story on. It would have paper hanging out of it, and where the story said 'grungy', I was going to have it say 'sludgy', scribbled out and changed to 'grunty' and . . . finally . . . 'grungy' – with three exclamations next to the word.

17 This was the only session Everman did with the band, recorded at Evergreen. The *Hard To Believe* compilation was later released by Seattle label C/Z.

## CHAPTER 8

# $50 And A Case Of Beer

*"In the summer of 1989, I flew to New York to cover Tad and Nirvana for* Sounds. *The American underground rock scene was in a boom period, having just gone through SST and Homestead. It was the tail end of post-punk – and Sub Pop was the next step on.*

*"We stayed on the Lower East Side. It was really hot, steaming New York midsummer heat. The flat was small, and there were two tired and smelly touring bands holed up at the end of a long tour waiting to play one last gig at the New Music Seminar. Tad were immediately friendly – older and more worldly wise than Nirvana. Behemoth frontman Tad Doyle would hold court while Nirvana sat around looking spaced out on the floor. He and his band were like older brothers to Nirvana, making sure they didn't fuck up too much. In many ways Krist Novoselic was like a mini-version of Tad, because Kurt was the kind of guy who couldn't look after himself, even to make a cup of tea.*

*"The flat was so damn hot. The air conditioning was broken and there were about 20 of us crammed into a tiny room. Even the cockroaches had bailed, appalled by the heat and the grimy man stink of touring rock bands. It was a fair old squeeze in there – me, my photographer Ian Tilton, a press agent, some people who never said who they were, plus the exhausted Nirvana and Tad, who are big, big guys. We didn't even have any sleeping bags. We slept as we were on the kitchen floor. Kurt was wiped out and spent most of the time curled up asleep.*

*"There was a lot of snoring, a lot of sweaty socks and a lot of exhausted rockers. Nirvana had the burned-out look of a young band at the end of its first toilet tour, playing to five people every night in some clapped-out venue. Those weeks on the road with no food, no audience and to little acclaim, this is the stuff that gives the greatest bands a galvanising inner strength.*

*"The night before the Seminar, Nirvana played Maxwell's to about 10 people. No one was too impressed, apart from a girl from their French record label who thought they were going to be massive. I thought they were fantastic. I loved Kurt's voice – it reminded me of John Lennon and*

*Noddy Holder.*[1] *It sounded old and weary, yet wild and free, a cracked rough gnarl of a voice, a voice that sounded like it had screamed hard down the mic many times – it cut right through. I dug the band's primal, feral bestiality and the way on their first single they'd taken Shocking Blue's original and turned it into a fierce blast of teen alienation.*

*"At the end of the show, they smashed the drum kit, and stuck the guitars through the roof. It wasn't contrived. There's no way you would bother in front of so few people. It was Krist who instigated it. He had a longer reach than everyone else. He could knock everything to pieces on the stage just standing there with his bass.*

*"We did the interviews beforehand. Bruce and Jon from Sub Pop were 100 per cent into the band. Their belief was incredible – I thought they were good, but they said they'd be enormous. When they said that, I thought of Sonic Youth, that they might end up selling 50,000 records! Krist talked about Serbia and the Balkans – he was quite political. Kurt was tired, so I spoke to him the next day. He was shy and exhausted in the heat of the flat, rubbing his eyes and lighting up to talk about rock'n'roll. His intensity was stunning. He started neatly with a rant about the sea of fakes. He had a tough work ethic and a burning creativity that needed to be sated. Kurt was unfazed by the burgeoning hype. 'We were a band before we were on Sub Pop, so being on a hip label means nothing to us,' he told me. 'There's been a lot of hype and that's fair enough – there are some great bands on the label. But that hype doesn't affect us.'*

*"A couple of hours later Nirvana started the long drive back home. We helped them pack their gear into their battered van. Small time cult status seemed assured but they were too intense and exciting for the dull, grey world of the mainstream. MTV was hardly likely to embrace this wild and soulful cacophony – to them Michael Jackson was revolutionary! They wearily started the drive back across America, a five-day haul in all. It was a tough journey and one that underlined their guerrilla mentality. I pondered their fate sadly. Anyone who says that crawling out of the cesspit of rock'n'roll is easy is a damn liar."*

(Interview with musician and journalist John Robb, November 2005)

IN June 1989, Nirvana set out on their first proper US tour.

"Sub Pop hooked us up with a company from LA called Bulging Eye," recalls Chad. "They set up our tour, and it went down to California, all the way to New York and back and every place in between. It was the first time we played the Blind Pig show in Ann Arbor. We played that place a couple times. Those were big shows!"

It was a "total hungry punk rock tour", as Krist put it – 26 dates in just under a month, starting on June 22 at the Covered Wagon in San Francisco. Rob Kader and pals bought them a farewell 24-pack of Mountain Dew; Jason printed up box loads of a new band T-shirt, the infamous 'Fudge Packin' Crack Smokin' Satan Worshipin' Motherfuckers' one[2], and for once Shelli and Tracy weren't going with them. Space – and money – was too tight, so Krist took on the role of band mother, making sure the van only stopped at certain petrol stations, refusing to allow the air conditioning to be turned on and insisting no one drove over 70 mph. The bassist collected what little money they got from clubs (100 bucks maximum, plus a case of beer) and handed out the PDs (*per diems* – band currency the world over). Nirvana blew what little they had left over after fuel and food on records.

"We ate a lot of crap," Chad laughs. "A lot of fast food stuff. It would be like a 7/11 or whatever – the worst possible food on earth. Kurt ate corn dogs. It was funny because Krist was pretty much a vegetarian, so he'd always be trying to find a Safeway's and get a salad – and I'd go with him, try and find a deli sandwich to get away from the fried food. Jason was into McDonald's."

For accommodation, local promoters were expected to find floors to crash on – often those of other musicians, such as Lori Barbero (Babes In Toyland, Minneapolis – where a drunken Krist fell backwards into a cabinet of plates) or John Robinson (The Fluid, Denver). Sometimes, the job would fall to people affiliated with the record company, like Joyce Linehan in Boston or Janet Billig in New York. "I was friendly," explains Billig, "so I had a lot of bands stay at my place because no one could afford a hotel."

Janet first got involved with Nirvana after Caroline Records signed a distribution deal with Sub Pop. Part of the deal was that when bands came to New York, her company would handle East Coast publicity and promotion. Billig's apartment soon became known as the punk rock Motel 6. "Mudhoney, Tad, Nirvana . . ." she continues. "That's how I met them." Janet bonded with the Seattle musicians over a shared love for Minneapolis bands like Hüsker Dü and Soul Asylum. Indeed, she'd graduated from high school early in order to follow The Replacements on tour.

"My flat was on 7th between Avenues B and C," she recalls. "It wasn't even 400ft, very small – of course it was New York City. One strange thing was it didn't even have a regular bathroom door, but a swinging saloon kind of door instead. There was a loft bed, with a mattress underneath. People would pile up in the loft and on the couch. And it's not like today. Avenue B was not a safe neighbourhood back then. When L7 stayed there, [singer] Donita got stabbed just outside. Another time, a box of Mudhoney's T-shirts got stolen when they were loading out. Rumour had it that for a few months the homeless people in the area were wearing Mudhoney shirts.

"I met Nirvana on their first trip to New York. Chad was sweet. Kurt was quiet. I don't remember having any conversations with Krist. The thing I recall is Kurt sitting in my bed eating bags of Chips Ahoy. Another time, they showed up and I had a girlfriend who was moving to Queens in a taxi, and she needed a van to move her bed. And they did it for her, and after driving 15 hours to get to New York, which was really sweet."

The night before the Covered Wagon, Nirvana played a packed show at The Vogue. "It was full of people from the other bands – Cat Butt and Coffin Break and Swallow," Chad recalls. "Everyone was out in full force. It felt like folk were throwing a going-away party for us. The feeling I had that night was unique."

There was a bigger crowd in San Francisco than previously, but Sub Pop was having trouble convincing stores to take *Bleach*. An in-store at Rhino Records in LA two days later saw the shop with only five copies – but more important to Kurt was the interview he conducted with *Flipside*, the local cool punk fanzine, wherein the band discussed cockroaches, the heat and an 'Elvis Cooper' poster the band carried with them on tour, bastardised from an Elvis backdrop.

"I fucking hate Elvis Presley," commented Krist. "But Alice Cooper is cool."[3]

The tour continued on through Long Beach and Santa Fe, New Mexico and on into Texas, where the heat became so overwhelming the band would pull over on to garage forecourts and wait until the day had cooled down. The attendances weren't high – maybe a couple of dozen people, often musicians connected with Sub Pop there to check out the new guys – but Nirvana were beginning to make an impression.

"Usually, Nirvana ended up opening the shows," recalls tour booker Danny Bland. "Being from Arizona, I begged them to put this band on. I said you'll love them; they ended up playing second of four bands and their guarantee was $50 and a case of beer and the club didn't even give them the $50. It was a place called the Sun Club in Tempe, Arizona. I remember going back years later and they had a framed picture of Nirvana. Fuck you: you didn't even give them 50 bucks. Probably made them pay for the beer, too. That was what the deals were in a lot of places. People hadn't heard of them.

"The only person I really talked to was Krist," Bland continues. "Kurt was real quiet. This is how minimal our operation was: their itineraries weren't even typed, they were handwritten itineraries that I made copies of and gave to everybody, and I had a meeting with them where I was on a chair and they were all sitting around on the floor like I was reading them a children's story. That would be when Chad and Kurt and Jason showed up for the first time. I wasn't even aware of Jason going on the tour until we were loading their crap in the van."

On the van's tape player were artists like Talulah Gosh, The Vaselines, Shonen Knife, Leadbelly and Shocking Blue – and sometimes Krist's choices of Led Zeppelin or Soft Machine.[4] And, in between, Nirvana would listen to Seattle bands like Mudhoney and Soundgarden. "It's weird," comments Chad, "because everyone was into it. It wasn't like the LA scene where it was like battle of the bands, and you'd put the other bands down.

"Me and Krist would do the driving, so we'd choose the music," he continues. "And then when Jason joined us on that one tour, he did a lot of the driving. Kurt never drove. I think he drove once, for like an hour." Reputedly, he wasn't that good a driver: travelling slowly, like an over-cautious old man.

In Texas, the band stayed near a national park – essentially a swamp – in the middle of some woods. There were signs everywhere saying, "Beware of the alligators". That night Nirvana slept with baseball bats by their sides.

Krist was the livewire of the bunch: almost every night he'd get wasted, out of his head on alcohol. "First, he'd tell everyone how much he loved them, then the next thing you know he's picked up a chair and is hurling it across the room," recalls Chad. "Ranting about how none of us understood shit about love, or telling us how he doesn't want to deal with us. But then he'd get this awesome puppy-dog face. I've always loved that about that guy. Everyone knows when he gets drunk he can get completely crazy and out of hand. But at the same time he's like the biggest fricking teddy bear in the world."

"I couldn't help confusing Krist with Latka [Andy Kaufman] from *Taxi*," comments Craig Montgomery. "Very smart, very left wing, he sounded like a hippie sometimes. He had that laidback, laconic way of speaking. He could drink a lot and get really, really drunk before he passed out. Really out of control."

He was a fun drunk, though?

"It could get negative," replies the soundman. "Not that he was mean to you, it's just that he would make a big scene and make it uncomfortable. Making a big mess that some poor person is going to have to clean up. But you know they were young, and drunk, and had never been anywhere before they were in this rock band. Well, Krist had."

It didn't bother Kurt. "Everyone gets drunk," he told Michael Azerrad. "It wasn't every single night. It was just every other night. [Krist] drinks to the point of oblivion and literally turns into a retard, unable to speak, gesturing and knocking things over. I've known so many people who drink it seems quite ordinary." Kurt was still suffering from stomach complaints, but was the cleanest living of the band (next to Everman, who drank only Mountain Dew), having temporarily given up smoking.

Although the drives were gruelling and the pay was bad, the band stayed enthusiastic – they were getting to see America *and* play rock'n'roll! What could be better? By the time they hit the Midwest, Sub Pop were getting the record into shops and attendances had started to pick up – college radios were finally playing songs from *Bleach* like 'Blew' or 'About A Girl'.

The day after Nirvana played the Uptown Bar in Minneapolis, Kurt bought a large crucifix at a garage sale in Chicago. To relieve the tedium on the road, he'd sit in the passenger seat with the crucifix in his hand, wind down the van window and stick it in some poor sap's face – just to see their reaction. "We were passing this limousine and he shows the crucifix like that," recalls Chad. "And he filmed it with his Pixel Vision camera. It was pretty funny."

It was around this time that Jason started to withdraw more into himself, feeling left out by Krist and Kurt's camaraderie – meanwhile, the pair were becoming concerned at Jason's penchant for showmanship, and the fact that with him in the band Nirvana were too 'rock'. Jason was into strutting round the stage, whereas Kurt and Krist and Chad were much goofier. "He was like a peacock on amphetamines," recalled Kurt. "It was embarrassing." Neither Krist nor Kurt approved of the old-fashioned male rock attitude towards women – there to be used and then discarded – and didn't appreciate the couple of times Jason brought girls back to his room after shows.

"When Jason was in the band it stood out because they sucked," laughs Candice Pedersen. "When they played in San Francisco and he wore that Mickey Mouse outfit with buttons and suspenders, I was like, 'What are you thinking?' "

"The worst part was when they had the four-piece line-up," comments Steve Turner. "That was useless. Jason was so unfocused."

Everman wasn't too pleased with Kurt and Krist's disregard for their instruments, especially as the band was mostly broke. "Chad lost all his clothes at some point," says Rob Kader. "Somebody stole them or he left them at somebody's house, so he had one shirt that he wore for the last two or three weeks. He was a stinky nightmare by the time they got back."

On July 9, Nirvana played a show at the Sonic Temple in Wilkinsburg near Pittsburgh. It went well, so well in fact that Kurt smashed an old Fender Mustang because all 20 people present started rocking out and grooving. Jason may well have been pissed off because he was part-financing the tour with his T-shirt money – but Krist and Kurt saw him as far too uptight, too concerned with image.

How on earth did Nirvana afford it?

"We get good deals," Krist told me in 1990. "You see, we live in Tacoma and things aren't so expensive there. In Seattle, people are really into old guitars but in Tacoma they couldn't care less."

"Why do I do it?" Kurt asked rhetorically during the same interview. "Why not? It feels good. Somebody already cut down a nice old tree to make that fucking guitar. Smash it! We only ever do it if the feeling's right, it doesn't matter where we are."

"We'd get in trouble with club owners from time to time," smiles Chad. "Mostly due to after-shows. There were a couple places where people would be like, 'You're done playing, get out, beat it.' Surprisingly, it didn't happen that much."

On July 12, Nirvana played a sparsely attended JC Dobbs – a small Philadelphia venue that they would return to a few times. A couple of days later, the band played a couple of shows in Massachusetts – one at the Green Street Station in Jamaica Plain, and the other a fraternity party – the 'Eating Club' – at MIT in Northampton.

"At the Green Street show, Kurt had smashed his guitar the previous night, and didn't have one to play," recalls Debbi Shane. "He sang and Jason played the guitar. We were a little disappointed, but in the end it didn't matter because they were really great."

"They were impactful shows," says Billig, who was present at both. "It was like watching a rolling ball of fire that kept getting stronger and stronger. No matter how cool Mark Arm was, or how wild it was to watch Tad, there was something magical about Kurt. You didn't want to take your eyes off him when he had a guitar, and wanted to listen to whatever he said. They'd either implode at the end, break all their stuff, or walk off stage and go and have some beers."

The following night, the band hit the legendary Maxwell's in Hoboken, just across the water from Manhattan.

"The first time I met Nirvana was at the New Music Seminar, at a show with Tad at Maxwell's," reveals Anton Brookes. "Two vans went down from NYC, full of Sub Pop people. There must have been 50 people there. Nirvana were amazing. Kurt smashed his guitar up and kicked over his amps and marched off. We all stood and watched Tad and then went back to New York.

"After Kurt smashed his guitar, it was sat on the dancefloor for ages and I remember thinking, 'I should take that,'" Anton continues. "And I thought, 'How am I going to explain a broken guitar at Customs?' Kurt had long hair and wore a plaid shirt . . . Sub Pop was the plaid shirt brigade. Krist was dressed in skintight jeans and a jumper. He had hair back then, too – straggly hair. Krist was the joker of the pack, Mr Funny Guy, the unofficial band spokesman. He was the one meeting and greeting, kissing the babies. He was about 8′ 2″, while if Chad had been any smaller he'd have been classified as a dwarf. There's a famous picture in *Sounds* where Krist is on his knees, and he's got his shoes underneath his knees and he's still taller than Chad – and Kurt is just a little taller than Chad."

"Maxwell's was an amazing show," recalls Dan Peters. "They were totally on fire. That night Krist took his bass and was beating the shit out of Chad's kick drum, but these guys are in New York and probably midway through a tour, and they don't have any money, and I'm like, 'What the fuck is going on?' He just split that bass drum in half, and they duct taped the drum back together. I'm sure that drum kit sounded like fucking hell anyway, but it must've *really* sounded like shit after that. That boy, that Chad, he put up with a lot."

A couple of nights later, on July 18, Nirvana played at the Pyramid opposite Tompkins Square Park in NYC.

"I saw them at the Pyramid with Jason and the numb energy and the big hair," recalls City Slang[5] boss Christof Ellinghaus. "My first impression was that the band was unbelievably powerful. After the show, Kurt was selling T-shirts, and I laid into him: 'Give me a T-shirt right now! I'm your German agent, I'm booking your dates in November!' and he was completely intimidated by this drunk, obnoxious German who got away with a T-shirt."

"I had the same feeling again," enthuses Anton. "I was blown away – I remember Jonathan saying that if ever Mudhoney and Nirvana played the same night in Seattle more people would go to see Nirvana and a bigger percentage would be female. Everyone thought Kurt was cute. Whereas Mark Arm had that massive . . .

"It wasn't until I saw them live I understood Jonathan's words," he explains. "Because within this rage, this tornado, there was a subtlety and a tenderness. Nirvana's songs were ugly-beautiful. It was the same with Kurt's lyrics – one beautiful letter to one ugly, let alone words, or verse to verse. 'I've got a really good riff! Let's fuck this up!' 'I've got a great couple of lyrics that are really nice. Let's make them offensive and fuck with people's minds!' When they played live, one minute it would be this huge monstrous noise and the next, these beautiful, almost soft, swirly songs. And then the next minute, the whole place would be going mental because they'd be playing 'Negative Creep' or something. They had such an intensity."

The band was supposed to continue up to Canada, but after the Pyramid Club, Kurt no longer wanted Jason involved. Despite Christof and Anton's enthusiasm, most people present remember the show differently. It was a dud. One day while staying at Billig's, Krist and Kurt scored some cocaine while Jason and Chad were out sightseeing with the British journalists. Later that night they got drunk, snorted it and decided to sack Jason. Only thing was, no one bothered *telling* Jason. He later claimed that he quit. Either way, he couldn't have been too bothered when a few weeks afterwards, he was asked to join Soundgarden as bassist.[6]

"I saw the show at the Pyramid," says Danny Bland. "They were awful. Cows stole the show, as they do. I remember [Cows singer] Shannon had two broken arms. Supposedly he had fallen through a glass roof in New York. One arm was tied up with some sort of metal and the other one was taped to his chest while he walked up to the microphone. He had pants on. Nirvana didn't play well that night. They were getting ready to toss Jason out of the band, so they decided to cancel the remaining four dates and drive back to Seattle [which they did, in near-total silence]."

"They left him at my apartment," recalls Janet. "They were like 'blurgh blurgh blurgh' and left him there. They drove him home but they were going to leave him. I don't think he had any idea. He was a really weird guy in a good way. He's very uncommunicative, and he was with people who were uncommunicative. He was a stranger. Kurt told me before, the Jason thing's not working. Maybe that was my conversation with them: 'Can we leave him?' 'No, you can't leave him here.'"

★ ★ ★

Kurt returned home to Olympia but Tracy's apartment was feeling more cramped by the day, what with their menagerie of animals and their litter, and Kurt's collection of busted-up amplifiers and guitars and found art . . . and the mould growing on the walls in the middle of summer. "I once caught Kurt defrosting the freezer with a kitchen knife," Slim Moon recalls. "He was rushing the animals outside in their cages because he'd poked a hole in it, and didn't want them to die from the fumes." The pair later moved to a slightly more expensive, bigger apartment in the same house.

Kurt's stomach continued to trouble him. Tracy made a couple of appointments for him with a specialist in Tacoma, but he took off after the first, claiming he was scared of needles. Kurt would frequently vomit during the night: his bandmates urged him to change his junk food diet but he refused to listen.

In July, while Nirvana was still on tour, a Go Team single, 'Scratch It Out'/'Bikini Twilight', came out on K. The band – centred round the core of drummer Tobi Vail and guitarist Calvin Johnson – started 1989 with the intention of releasing a single a month, featuring various guest musicians.[7] They got most of the way through the year before parting ways. Nine singles eventually came out. The July single featured Kurt on guest vocals.

"It was a grand idea, but we fell behind," explained Candice Pedersen. "We were going to package them in a bag, with a label on top, like cheap candy. But after the first month – I mean, my God, we were hand-stapling them, and stuffing them and pressing the bags – I was like, 'This is a nice concept but it's not going to work!' "

"The Go Team was about process," explains Tobi. "I liked to go make stuff, partially as an excuse to hang out with people – that is where the collaboration came from – but then the tapes would be rolling; and the result would turn into a K release. The documentation was Calvin's thing. He's always been into that. Sometimes we'd leave stuff out deliberately to incite participation in the listener. *Donna Parker Pop*, our first K release, featured all instrumentals but included the statement 'Make up your own words and sing along' – and people did. We recorded with some of those people later.

"The Go Team played together from 1985–89. I played my first show with The Go Team shortly after I turned 16. For the first three years we played around Olympia and released cassettes. Some people, most people probably, thought we sucked because we'd often improvise or play stuff that was unfinished sounding. That this was deliberate – an aesthetic/

conceptual choice – really confused a lot of people. We got a reputation for being arty, so a lot of interesting people got into us. Dylan Carlson and Slim Moon were huge Go Team fans. We'd sometimes play cocktail parties where people would perform songs in a cabaret style – we'd be the band that played background music while people talked. Sometimes we'd project films over ourselves, usually Super 8 movies that Calvin found at garage sales. We often didn't have vocals. I doubt that Kurt was a big fan, although he was interested in K and drawn to anything different to the college rock or generic hardcore bands of the era.

"On the West Coast around this time," continues Vail, "there were a lot of boring metal-ish punk bands and he wasn't too into that – there were also a lot of math-y 'tight' bands influenced by nomeansno[8], The Rhythm Pigs, Beastie Boys and Red Hot Chili Peppers. This was a funky jam-band skater thing that was super male-dominated. Sub Pop was different, they were arty and more into darker, weirder stuff like Big Black. K was pretty much the opposite of that kind of macho wankery, and The Go Team was the most extreme example of this – we were minimal, deliberately amateurish and didn't have songs in the conventional sense.

"On the one hand we were trying to demystify music and encourage all people to play songs in public – if they wanted to. On the other hand, we actually liked what we sounded like, and we hated most of the pro-sounding jam bands/shredding metal-punk bands that played parties in Olympia. We were interested in ideas, quiet sounds and driving beats. We embraced chaos and rejected mastery. We challenged conventional notions of 'the pop song' or punk music. We wanted to disrupt the audience/performer dichotomy – we were punk kids in a loose collective, experimenting with music and documenting our work.

"Kurt approached Calvin with a demo of some mellower songs he'd been working on, and Calvin was like, 'Hey, this is great, why don't you come down and record with The Go Team?' At that time, Kurt was into playing music as much as possible, so any chance to record or play was welcome. We did a version of [early Iggy Pop signature song] 'Loose' because Kurt really wanted to hear Calvin sing those twisted lyrics.[9] He taught Calvin to play the bass line – so there is a bass on it. It kind of sucked so it didn't come out.

"In my mind it was kind of like [beat generation author] Jack Kerouac's idea of writing on a roll of paper; we were focused in on the rhythm of making stuff up. The Go Team idea/aesthetic was very beat. Kurt was more of a mastery type guy – even though his performances embraced elements of chaos head on, his songwriting was extremely structured. I'm not sure he really saw what we were doing as songwriting. He probably thought of it more as jamming, that later there would be a time to revise and finish the songs/weed out the 'mistakes'. So in that sense the tapes are incomplete. But as a document of a creative moment of three people in a room together they are pretty great. I'd say it was one of the more invigorating Go Team sessions."

In the first week of August, Nirvana returned to the studio – to Music Source, a 24-track studio on Capitol Hill[10] that specialised in movie soundtracks and commercials – with producer Steve Fisk, to record two new songs for the *Blew* EP timed to tie in with an upcoming European tour.[11] Fisk was surprised when only three people showed up to record. "I had heard later that Jason was in the Sub Pop office that day, telling folk he was still in the band," he explains.

"It happened over two nights," Steve recalls. "Krist had spent all day trying to get his bass amp together because it was all trashed from touring. There were two speakers and only one of them worked, and that didn't work that well. The bass was also fucked up. Chad Channing had the big black plastic drum kit. It also was held together with tape. Kurt was the only guy who had gear that was working. The Music Source had little booths that opened up on to a big room. The ideal is you put everybody's amps off into the ISO booths with the doors wide open so you wouldn't need headphones. We recorded five songs, and we did some overdubs that night on two of them. We came back the next week and mixed two songs. And we all got paid."

How was the band?

"Very nice, very serious about what they were doing. They weren't exactly professional, but they wanted to get it right. I was excited that a good band, and not a stupid band, was coming in. I recorded a lot of stupid bands back then and I really liked Nirvana. I had gone from gagging at how ugly it was to really digging what they had going, and how it fit into Jack [Endino]'s little pantheon of what he had going. They all had similar approaches, but inside that there were big differences."

"I've always liked working with Steve," comments Chad. "I was a fan of [Steve's SST band] Pell Mell. It was obscure, really bizarre stuff. I don't know why we switched producers. They'd just say, 'Hey, we're recording at so and so with Steve Fisk.' Maybe Jack was busy. The business end, I was way out of the loop."

The songs were noticeably poppier and lighter than on previous recordings. "We want a big Top 40 drum sound," Kurt announced, conveniently overlooking the fact that Chad's drums were held together with duct tape. Indeed, the *Blew* sessions were to be the last appearance of Chad's old drums.

The two songs that appeared on the single were fine: 'Been A Son', with its unwieldy bass solo and *Rubber Soul*-style double-tracked vocals, a number inspired by Don Cobain's statement that he would've preferred Kurt's sister Kim to have been born a boy; and 'Stain', another song dealing with feelings of familial rejection and inferiority, a pile-driving bass-driven number with its twin guitar solos – "on equal volume, like squabbling hens," as Fisk memorably remarked. And the three unfinished songs[12] were even more exciting: 'Token Eastern Song' was an old-fashioned floor churner in the tradition of 'Negative Creep'; an absolutely storming version of 'Even In His Youth' that just ground away into eternity, a worthy follow-up to 'Love Buzz' and in much the same vein; and an electric version of 'Polly' (originally called 'Hitchhiker').

"We had a hard time getting the feel right to 'Polly' at the beginning," recalls Fisk. "They started it three times. They couldn't hold the tempo together with Chad playing the pulse on the cymbal. Chad was slipping and Kurt was finger picking. It was the first time Nirvana had recorded on the industry standard, two-inch, 24-track format. If they sounded lo-fi with Jack you figured it was the cheap gear. Once you're on the 24-track, what it plays back is theoretically what you've got. Maybe that's why Krist was trying so hard to get his bass together.

"When it was all over with, we played 'Been A Son' really loud on the big stupid speakers three times and stood up on the client tables in the back room and danced. I don't ever dance, but I danced because Nirvana wanted to dance."

So this was after they'd started to get bigger?

"Yeah, you'd written your nice little article in *Melody Maker*. Mother Love Bone was still together when I recorded Nirvana."

Did they say anything about how things were going with Sub Pop?

"Yeah. Bruce and Jonathan were giving them a bunch of money to make a second record, maybe $10,000–$12,000. They were talking about doing it with me, and coming back to the Music Source. It was during that strange time period where Andy [Andrew Wood, Mother Love Bone singer] was still alive, Chad was still in the band and Soundgarden was still the biggest band in Seattle."

Did you get the impression that these songs had massive potential?

"No. As a matter of fact, we were joking about how stupid we wanted to make the drums on 'Been A Son'."

Were they freaked out being in a big studio?

"They understood that they had x amount of time to get it right. Sub Pop was broke. It was recorded on some used tape we had lying around. And Sub Pop wanted to do everything as cheap as possible, so any corner we could cut we would cut."

Later that same month – August 20 and 28 – Kurt and Krist joined Mark Lanegan and Mark Pickerel from Screaming Trees to record some Leadbelly songs at Reciprocal. It was a casual, off-the-cuff session, but the recorded results were startling: emotional and ponderous with some stunning vocals from both Mark and Kurt. The version of 'Where Did You Sleep Last Night' ended up on Lanegan's debut solo album, 1990's *The Winding Sheet* – Nirvana later covered the song, in partial tribute to Mark himself. 'They Hung Him On The Cross' was brief, but sweltering with emotion. 'Grey Goose' was a heavy blues jam, while 'Ain't It A Shame' boasted a quite terrifyingly deep vocal from Kurt.

"Mark and Kurt got drunk together, or really stoned," Endino told Gillian G. Gaar, "and wrote a bunch of songs, and got all excited and told Jonathan, 'Hey we want to do an album together! And we've got a name for it – The Jury.' And so Jonathan said, 'OK, OK, get in with Jack and record.' And then finally they show up at the studio, and Kurt goes, 'Well, we forgot all the songs, because we didn't tape any of them! And I lost my lyric book. So we're going to do some Leadbelly songs instead.'"

"It's a misnomer to call those Nirvana songs," comments Slim Moon about the fact that they have since resurfaced as such. "They weren't intended to be. It was a different drummer, a step up – or a step sideways. Every time a step up happened, it was a shock, like when they started rehearsing in Alice In Chains' rehearsal space. It's not that Alice In Chains were big yet, but Alice In Chains was a band that had aspirations to be big, so we were like, 'That's so official and pro.'"

Kurt wanted to hear Leadbelly after reading a William S. Burroughs article on the black folk singer, so Slim lent him his copy of *Leadbelly's Last Sessions*. Kurt felt a connection to Leadbelly's almost physical expressions of longing and desire.

"It's so raw and sincere," Kurt explained to me in 1992. "It's something I hold sacred. The songs are amazingly heartfelt. Leadbelly was this poor black man in the early 1900s who went to jail a few times for wife beating and robbery and getting into fights and bootlegging liquor. While he was in prison, he started playing the guitar, and he sang so well that the governor started to like him and let him out of jail. Leadbelly became an apprentice with Blind Lemon Jefferson and started recording songs, but none of the commercial recordings he made ever captured his true essence, except for his last sessions.

"I'd hope that my songs approximate that honesty," he continued. "That's what I strive for. I think of his life as like a party with balloons, you know? But this was a unique mixture of balloons and folk music and storytelling all at once, it's something that had never happened before. He was like the first punk rocker, because he was such a hardened person. He'd get into town, walk into an all white bar, try to have a drink, get beat up and then go to jail because of it. So it's really cool to hear this music, especially the air of the recordings themselves, because it's so eerie to hear it on this crackly two-track. He'll start off with a little introduction on what the song is about, play a little and [dive] in."

The same month, Kurt helped Dylan Carlson record his first EP.

"Lush broke up, and Dylan had decided he was going to play guitar again, despite how good the Melvins were," explains Slim. "So we formed Earth. Kurt played bass for us for a bit while we were living in Olympia, but his instrument was strung for a right-hander so he was trying to play it upside-down. We were like, 'You need to restring that so it works for you.' He was like, 'I can't do that. Other people want to borrow it.' So we kicked him out.

"I quit Earth after Dylan and I got in an argument of how I should sing in the band," Moon continues. "He wanted me to sing in a high Ozzy-like voice, and I wanted to sing in a low Michael Gira[13]-like voice. His argument was that voices had spoken to him from across the universe and declared that the reason our band existed was to cause the end of the universe, but it would only be achieved if I sang in a high voice."

So, bereft of Slim, and with Dave Harwell and Joe Preston both playing bass, plus a couple of guest vocalists, Dylan travelled down to Portland to record the immensely dense *Extra-Capsular Extraction* EP for Sub Pop, released in 1991.

"I remember doing that Earth record," smiles ex-Dickless/Teen Angels singer Kelly Canary, "only because I wasn't drunk for that whole time because we were in the middle of nowhere. Kurt and me were the backup singers. It was five days in Portland and my vocal part took 20 minutes, so it was literally four and a half days of sitting around, during which Kurt slept on the couch constantly. I was dope-sick, trying to find dope on the street, Kurt was sleeping and they were in the basement recording. I'd hang out at Fred Myers for fun because there was nothing to fucking do. That's when Kurt started teaching me how to play the guitar."

How did he teach you? When he got me to play his guitar on stage, he put it on upside down.

"Oh yeah, because he was a lefty," the singer laughs. "He just taught me a few power chords. They were really easy – and then he taught me a 13th Floor Elevators song, 'You're Gonna Miss Me'. It's the same chords as 'About A Girl'. I wrote a whole Teen Angels album round those chords – Kurt told me they were all I needed to know."

In September, Nirvana set out on a short tour of the Midwest, partly to make up the gigs they'd bailed on the previous time.[14] The Midwest dates lasted from September 9–22, and then October 3–8. This time they had a U-Haul truck to carry their equipment, a promise of between $100–$200 a night, and soundman Craig Montgomery and friend Ben Shepherd in tow. The tour was reasonably successful – 200 fans showing up at some shows, encouraged by the growing buzz around both band and label. Nirvana returned to Seattle with $300 each, after expenses had been subtracted. It felt like a fortune to Kurt.

The opening date was in Chicago, at Cabaret Metro, supporting mentors Sonic Youth. It wasn't an auspicious start: "Kurt fell into my kit, and then the bottles started," recalls Chad. "We looked at each other, and ran underneath the stage. I had to leave my drum riser behind." Dates in Louisville, Denver and Toledo followed – and a return to The Blind Pig in Ann Arbor, on October 3, in between Steel Pole Bathtub[15] and The Flaming Lips.[16] Kurt's mic didn't work during the opening 'School' so the band played through it twice, oblivious to crowd reaction.

"I remember talking to the club owner. He was so pissed off because The Flaming Lips played with so much smoke," chuckles Chad. "It was so thick that I could barely see his face. He was like, 'Goddammit! They have these fucking smoke machines and I can't fucking see my beer!' It was hilarious."

Driving through mid-America, especially its long flat hinterlands, could be a tedious business. "When I got bored I would drive with my teeth," Chad says. "One time we were going through Montana, which is a big flat stretch of beautiful nothing. Kurt and Krist were sleeping. Krist woke up and he saw me and went, 'Oh, No! No! What are you doing? Drive with your hands!' And I didn't have the heart to tell him that I had been driving that way for over two hours."

Shepherd acted as surrogate tour manager, not because that was his role but because he'd been invited along as a friend and took it upon himself to act that role. There was also a chance he might replace Everman as second guitarist.

"After Jason left, Nirvana said, 'Hey, you want to try out?'" Ben recalls. "Kurt told me, 'Shit, I would have asked you to play first if I'd have known that you play guitar.' The next day Soundgarden asked me to try out as bassist.[17] And I said, 'Well, Nirvana asked me to try out first so I have to do that.'"

What made Nirvana and Soundgarden ask you to join them at the same time?

"Both Kim [Thayil, Soundgarden guitarist] and Chad knew me," the soft-spoken musician replies. "I wound up playing just one soundcheck with them because we only did *Nevermind* stuff when we rehearsed, but on that tour they only played *Bleach* stuff. There was a point when we were in Ann Arbor and Kurt asked me, 'How would you feel about not doing any of your songs?' and I said, 'That's fine, this is your band' . . . the whole time I was thinking they should stay a three-piece anyway."

Other Seattle musicians agreed. Both Mudhoney and Tad urged Kurt to keep Nirvana as a trio, concerned with how much Jason's presence had affected the sound. Kurt later regretted his decision not to have Ben in Nirvana: "He would've added to the band, definitely," he said. "He's kind of crazy sometimes – but that's OK."[18]

"I got to play one soundcheck while Kurt was out back puking in Minneapolis," the guitarist laughs. "That was the same day that they said, 'Sorry, you missed your brother's wedding and you're not in the band.'"

Did you think they were going to be big at that point?

"I knew they would. I didn't know they were gong to be that big, but yeah. I knew they were going to have a musical career."

Why did you think that?

"You could tell by the way the fans acted. Even though some of the shows would be to 20 people – because they'd cancelled the tour before – those 20 people went back. Omaha [October 8] was the only time I've ever seen a real motherfucking encore, besides one time for Soundgarden in Belgium. Nirvana got one, and they never did encores. We were all packing up and Chad's drums were still mostly set up and Kurt was undoing his guitar case, and the whole crowd was like, 'You guys didn't play all your songs, man. You skipped out on us last time, come on! Play the rest of 'em.' They came back on rather sheepishly and blew the fucking doors off the place. It was at a fake chateau called The Lift Ticket.

"A lot of times in the van, Kurt and I would be the only ones awake, driving late at night," says Shepherd. "We'd play Screamin' Jay Hawkins[19],

The Sonics, [Brian] Eno[20] . . . We all had our little cassette collections with us. I remember feelings and scenery more than actual conversations. We'd talk books sometimes. Mostly it was just Kurt and Krist, and me and Chad. During that time I was into big band music and I was like, 'Guys, this is what we should open the shows with.' I would always joke about Johnny Cash playing with Motörhead or someone. After a while, that wasn't even a joke any more.

"That was right when the underground kids started realising that Nirvana was going to be the thing, not Mudhoney," he adds. "I was always astounded that people liked Mudhoney as much as they did because I'm from the [Mark Arm's first band] Mr Epp generation. For me, there were two sides of Seattle: there's Malfunkshun, Mr Epp and [hardcore band] The Fartz, and everything else seemed too light. When the Melvins moved out, I was like, 'Ah, Seattle's blowing it again.' I was more into the heavy, tripped out shit."

Back in Seattle, not everyone was happy with the way the scene was going . . .

"In 1989, Sub Pop threw this concert called Nine For The Nineties," recalls Slim. "They had nine bands on. One was Beat Happening and another was Cat Butt. This person I knew watched Cat Butt and was dancing around and having a great time. Then Beat Happening came on and within a few songs the person came to me and was like, 'This is the worst band I've ever seen – they can't play their instruments.' I looked at her and I said, 'They are playing their instruments as well or better than Cat Butt, they just don't have distortion hiding how poorly they are playing.' That, in essence, is the Seattle versus Olympia argument. Seattleites always wanted it big and loud and in leather pants. Olympia always wanted it minimal and naked.

"She was like, 'The songs are dumb,'" the label boss adds. "I was like, 'Both bands play three chord rock songs. What's the difference except that the one has distortion and a cool shtick?' Yes, we are elitists, but Seattle was so elitist and had the world on its side that we remained the underdog. We used elitism as self-defence."

There again, the Seattle musicians were having a ball . . .

"We played with Nirvana and Mudhoney at the COCA [Center of Contemporary Art, Seattle – August 26, 1989] for this big Sub Pop showcase," recalls Cat Butt's James Burdyshaw. "There was no air conditioning and it was absolutely packed. The first night was Dickless in the small room, and then Dwarves[21], Tad and GWAR.[22] That was something.

"There was this big tub backstage filled with ice and Black Label," the guitarist continues. "It was so hot that all the ice had melted into water and I was flinging the ice water in people's faces as they came in, just to test their reaction. Matt Lukin came off stage and he was like, 'Eeagh! What the fuck you doing?' Kurt was behind him, and I asked him if he wanted to be splashed.

"He goes, 'No, can you dunk me in there instead?' and I was like, 'Really?' and he was like, 'Yeah! Dunk me in that water.'" James laughs. "So I took his head and went 'Sploosh!' into this tub of ice cold water. He kept his head under there for a long time and I was like, 'Whoa. This is weird. He's not coming up.' After about a minute he came up and was like, 'Yeah!'

"The innocence and playfulness, and the incredibly unpretentious nice guy that Kurt Cobain was, came across heavy that night," Burdyshaw finishes. "When people bad-talk weird things about him, like how depressed he was, I say I didn't know him as that person. I knew this sweet, cool, fun, weird, unpredictable human being that wrote great songs. And the dark guy unfortunately took a hold of his soul but that was only one part of this person. There was another part that was really fucking cool. That's somebody who doesn't get written about enough. The person that I knew, he was one of us. He was a brother. He wasn't a rock star. He was a weird, freaky, goofy, punk rock kid."

**Addenda: the girls and Kurt**

"My unique perspective on Nirvana is that I wasn't paying attention," explains Julianne Anderson. "Green River and Sub Pop started percolating at the same time, so there was like, 'Crazy Olympia Bruce Pavitt! And His Crazy Radio Show! And His Crazy Singles thing!' Bruce was always this fabulous disaster of a kook, while Poneman was another one of these Ohio music intellectual geeks. I referred to Kurt Cobain as 'that blond kid' because to me, he was 'that blond kid'. All my girlfriends had crushes on him, they thought he was the cutest thing in the world, so they would all drag me out to see this Nirvana band play – and, again, it was the little short guy, that big tall guy and the revolving drummer . . . We'd go out to the shows and I'd sit at the bar and drink myself stupid because I was always so happy to get in because I wasn't old enough . . .

"It was just a social thing. We didn't think about it as this great artistic revolution, it was just those kids from Aberdeen are coming to play. I took one look at Kurt and decided he was too short and he was trouble. He was so withdrawn and introspective, but so explosive on stage, you could tell he was battling a bunch of demons. Frankly, Kurt lived 10 years longer than I ever expected."

Why do you think all the girls loved him?

"He was an attractive kid. He was a very handsome guy. He had those blue eyes that were super-penetrating, but for me it was more like, 'Wow, that guy's really mad about something.'"

"My band [the all-girl Dickless] were all so in love with Kurt," sighs Kelly Canary. "We practised in the same building. Every single one of us was either in love with Kurt or Jason. It was embarrassing getting ready to go to practice, putting our make-up on. I'll be totally honest. Kurt intimidated me from the first time I met him. He was so talented."

When did you first see him?

"It was at The Vogue. Nirvana opened up for The Flaming Lips, but The Flaming Lips said they were probably the worst band they'd ever seen. And it was probably no shorter than a year after that that they took over the world. One time we went to see Nirvana and Melvins in Olympia, and this guy comes over to yell at me. So I blow my rape whistle, and when he's walking up to me I scream out, 'Somebody here has date-raped a woman.' In Olympia! Girl's gotta party."

## NOTES

1 Noddy Holder: much loved frontman with England's Seventies glam stompers, Slade.

2 Sub Pop bands always did have a way with a slogan: I preferred Soundgarden's 'Total Fucking Godhead' T-shirt, and the label's 'Fuck Me I'm Rich' but this wasn't bad at all.

3 Maybe not so much now that Alice Cooper appears on 'Top 100 . . .' TV shows the world over, like a low rent version of Ozzy – but certainly back then, if only for 'School's Out'.

4 Robert Wyatt's late Sixties' outfit, Soft Machine, straddled the divide between soul-based psychedelia and free jazz-influenced avant rock better than most.

5 City Slang later became Hole's European record label.

6 Jason lasted only a few months in Soundgarden before being replaced by Ben Shepherd. Jason then joined Mindfunk as guitarist.

7 The series included The Legend! as vocalist on 'Breakfast In Bed'/'Safe Little Circles'.

8 Best avoided. Funk-punk from Vancouver – nomeansno were early precursors of the Red Hot Chili Peppers' style.

9 The cover of 'Loose' was also ironic, because what Calvin did was in so many ways anathema to Iggy's spirited, histrionic approach to rock'n'roll.

10 The studio is now a flower shop on the corner of Summit and Pike. Other artists recorded there include Screaming Trees, Soundgarden, Love Battery, Some Velvet Sidewalk, Beat Happening and Kenny G.

11 The EP eventually came out in December on Tupelo, after the tour finished: 'Blew', plus the two Music Source songs, plus two songs culled from *Bleach*.

12 They're now available on *With The Lights Out* (2004) with the original guide vocals.

13 Michael Gira was the Swans singer – Swans were similar to Melvins or Earth, heavy, slow and very loud, a decade earlier.

14 They also played Iguana's in Tijuana, Mexico on September 1 – and spent most of the summer playing home state shows.

15 Steel Pole Bathtub were a slow and psychedelic rock band – but not too slow or psychedelic.

16 Now they're the new R.E.M. or something – but back then, Wayne Coyne's acid-deranged psychedelic punk rockers, The Flaming Lips, were one of the most jarring bands around.

17 Shepherd eventually joined Soundgarden in 1991: "I went straight from the garage to playing Copenhagen at the Rosskilde Festival," he says.

18 I can concur: I well remember being out drinking with Ben in Japan in 1994, when he was hurling glasses left right and centre out on the street.

19 Screamin' Jay Hawkins was a stylish, theatrical, bluesy rock'n'roll singer, known for leaping out of coffins and his deep, guttural grunts and moans – exemplified on the chilling 1956 hit 'I Put A Spell On You'.

20 It was probably the former Roxy Music keyboard-player's angular and artful 1973 album *Here Come The Warm Jets*, rather than his later ambient work.

21 Dwarves were notorious: infamous for the graphically explicit cover to 1990's *Blood Guts And Pussy*, and for faking their own bassist's death. Oh, and for singer Blag Jesus' habit of pissing on the audience.

22 GWAR are like a low-budget Kiss – dressed up in monster costumes and splattered the audience with fake blood while playing hard rock.

## CHAPTER 9

# Corndogs And Candy

*I don't know if this is fun so much as exhilarating: being crushed under 3,200 pounds of writhing flesh – one foot in your crutch, another rammed up your nose, a body stretched tight across your legs, another pinioned across an arm – wondering why your bones aren't broken yet. And people do this for enjoyment?*

*Mudhoney and Dickless*[1] *in Seattle – you could write the fucking review yourself, couldn't you? Just grab a handful of words, chuck 'em in the air, and see where they fall; pub rock for the Nineties, primal noise therapy for people scared of the eternity of silence; one-dimensional flailing hardcore for people with not enough imagination to be seduced by music which causes them to lose themselves – although, right now, I can't think of any better way to attain a transcendental state than through the mindless metallic time-warp of a Motörhead or a Mudhoney, say. Let's call it repetitious, deranged, riotous, pulsating,* grungy *and relentless, and move on, shall we? No.*

*Dickless take to the stage like oysters on acid and have people stagediving into silence, whether they're playing or not. An all-girl, indigenous quartet, the standard Dickless song (a) lasts under two minutes, (b) lifts the riff from 'Smoke On The Water', (c) is lucky if it finds itself with the bass and guitar playing simultaneously, and (d) is the funniest thing I've experienced since Laibach*[2] *covered 'Sympathy For The Devil'. Or the Rocky Mountain ride at Disneyland. Pandemonium, I suspect, is the Everett Truism to use here.*

(Live review, *Melody Maker*, 1989)

ON October 20, 1989, Nirvana left Seattle for their first European tour.

They were to spend the majority of the next seven weeks squashed into a nine-seat Fiat van with their gear, merchandise, Tad Doyle and his band, a soundman and a tour manager: 11 people belching and smoking and making crude jokes all the way across the continent. The shows were

promoted as being part of the *Heavier Than Heaven* co-headlining reference to the two bands' dense, sometimes lethargic, sound an 300-pound Tad Doyle himself.[3] Kurt was ill when he arrived in L while his fellow travellers sampled Britain's frankly superior beer, valesced, suffering from bronchitis, at the band's hotel.

"They were staying at this little B&B in Shepherd's Bush ca Dalmacia," says Anton Brookes, "just round the corner from Russell [Warby, Nirvana's UK booking agent] worked at The A They should have a plaque. "Right," the press agent nods. "The got in, and we went out for a Chinese takeaway. Kurt was curled u bed all night."

He had a very particular diet: pizza, corndogs and candy.

"He had a very white trash mentality when it came to food," Anton, a vegetarian. "He couldn't eat a lot of stuff because it affe stomach."

"Every time you went to London, you had to stay in the Dal confirms Craig Montgomery. What? Even though it used to lock out if they got back too late? "I don't know about that," the easy Seattleite shrugs. "It must have been pretty tolerant, since there steady stream of grungers and rockers."

The tour called for the bands to play 37 dates in 42 days across countries, sometimes necessitating overnight drives after the show. of this, the Dutch tour manager Edwin Heath – supplied by th agency that booked the tour, Paperclip – often insisted the band direct to soundcheck without checking in at the hotel first.

"The first European tour was gruelling and long and cold," recalls "We were staying in little bed and breakfasts. Often, a family ran th one, we go to knock on the front door and these two schnauze yapping, and Tad goes, 'Oh, this place comes with complimentary sc zers.' So the rest of the tour, we wanted our complimentary schnauze

"We listened to The Vaselines[4], Leadbelly and The Beatles, engineer adds. "I think we had Shonen Knife. Pixies, oh yeah, the [Many critics – and Kurt himself – have commented on the debt N owe to the Boston band's inspired opening brace of albums, partic 1988's offbeat and furious *Surfer Rosa*, with its quiet/loud dynami surf music-warped take on Americana. Kurt's progression in his m tastes from Melvins' primordial sludge to Pixies' ferocious college ro major contributing factor to Nirvana's success.]

"You wouldn't believe how much we listened to Abba," Craig tinues. "It's good travelling music, and somehow when you're d

around Europe, the vibe is right. We listened to some Seventies rock, maybe Queen or Badfinger.[5] I don't think there was a lot of super-abrasive punk rock-y stuff. We didn't listen to Black Sabbath or anything. Edwin did all the driving so we were all in the back, drinking. Is that legal in Europe?"

Oh probably.

"It's hard," Craig explains, "because you're up late every night, and you're sleeping somewhere that's probably cold and there is a shared bathroom down the hall. And in the van you have to sit up, the seats don't recline and every seat is occupied. One of the places we stayed in Austria was a college dorm. Budapest [November 21] was bizarre, because no one knew who the bands were – they just knew they were American rock bands and that was it."

Not everyone remembers the tour as a downer. Chad Channing, for one, has fond memories (it must be said that most of the others recall Chad as being almost insanely stoical) – "Europe was fun," the drummer reminisces. "Some people would complain about the food, 'I'm sick of eating this bologna and salami spread' . . . that kind of stuff.[6] Not me. Some people were so used to being around their own home that after a while they got irritable. Never happened to me. I'd make a point to wake up an hour before we had to leave, and walk around whatever city we were in. Try to pick up some language."

The bands loved to hold food fights in the dressing room: one of Kurt's favourite tricks was to empty an ashtray over a couple of slices of bread, to create a dirt sandwich. Other times, he'd be seen wandering around with flowers sticking out of his trouser fly.

Kurt often roomed with Kurt Danielson, guitarist with the Tad band. He was missing his mother, and Tracy – to whom he sent postcards, sometimes with the words 'I Love You' scrawled over and over again, other times a sketch of an Italian toilet with no water but plenty of excrement. Nights were spent discussing the turn of events that had led both musicians to lead such squalid lives in pursuit of a rock'n'roll dream neither had thought through. Novoselic would escape reality through alcohol, Channing was used to constant change because of his childhood, and he'd often talk to himself – "In weird voices," claimed Cobain – while Kurt's way of coping was to fall asleep. He relished it, and developed a knack of falling asleep during soundchecks. Often, he'd be sleeping right up until the moment he had to be on stage. It was the easiest way to deal with the situation.

"Tad was a very loud snorer," reveals Craig. "We were sharing rooms,

always two to a room, if not more, and you did not want to be the guy sharing a room with Tad, because you were not going to sleep. He couldn't do anything about it, and he would apologise. There'd always be someone who was sleep deprived, more than ordinary."

Tad had his own problems: every morning before the van departed, he would vomit. Kurt Danielson told an apocryphal story about how Kurt Cobain used to stand in front of the van with a plastic basin, waiting for Tad to throw up into it so he could examine its multi-coloured contents. Only Kurt was allowed to hold the basin: no one else.

It is true that Kurt was fascinated by bodily functions; witness the diseased carnal display on his fridge door back in Olympia. Tad's dietary problems helped to inspire the Nirvana song 'Breed' – its original title, 'Immodium', was taken from Doyle's diarrhoea medicine. Whether Danielson was guilty of exaggeration or not, shit and vomit are regular sources of amusement for travelling musicians. And Nirvana and Tad certainly weren't above such humour.

"There's a certain frequency, 27 Hertz or something, that's been proven to make people shit their pants," Tad told me when we first met. "We're searching for that frequency. Our guitarist almost manages it, so people kind of shit their pants when they see us."

It was in the UK that Nirvana and Tad made the biggest impression. The country was primed. Mudhoney were in the middle of a very successful tour. Soundgarden and Screaming Trees had already been over. In the wake of my *Melody Maker* articles (another one appeared on October 24, a straight Nirvana interview entitled *Bleached Wails*) and John Peel's continuing support, plus write-ups from sympathetic journalists such as John Robb, Keith Cameron, Roy Wilkinson, Push and Edwin Pouncey, the kids wanted a piece of the Sub Pop action. Even if not all the critics were convinced . . .

"First, *Bleach* came out," says Anton. "The reaction was scant. Back then it was all metal magazines like *Metal Forces* and *Kerrang!* and they were like, 'It's not poodle enough for us,' even though Nirvana rocked harder than a lot of their rock bands. *NME* were patronising: 'Nevada, from where?' Until Keith Cameron went there, there was no one. *Sounds* and *Melody Maker* were supportive – but there were two camps at the *Maker*. There seemed to be a lot of pettiness and even envy towards your involvement with the Sub Pop camp, because of the way bands would call you up when they came to town. If a band was perceived as an Everett band then they'd never sell more than 200 copies or get beyond doing a Peel session.

When Nirvana became popular, there were a lot of people unwilling to put them on the cover . . ."

Still. The buzz was on. All the bands needed to do was deliver the goods – and that wasn't a problem. Tad looked demented on stage, his entire bulk shivering and wobbling, his lumberjack shirt pouring with sweat, as he thrashed out another fudge-packing riff and roared into the microphone: and what Krist and Kurt lacked in grace they more than made up for in energy, mayhem and drunken unpredictability.

You never knew what was going to happen next. This, at a time when the critical bands of choice – (the awesome) My Bloody Valentine, Ride, Chapterhouse – were lumped together under the sobriquet 'shoe-gazing' because all they'd do on stage was stand there and gaze at their shoes.

"Nirvana are very much a band that would like to say, 'Hi, this is us and we're having fun, too!'" I wrote, "But the band are also a little bit weird. They're a little bit gross and a little bit awesome. And a bit too determined to be content with just messing around. What else could you be if you grew up in the redneck hell town of Aberdeen, a zillion miles away from the isolated capital of the Northwest, Seattle?"

The opening night was at a packed Newcastle Riverside on October 23. Someone threw a beer bottle and hit Krist on the side of his head. In retaliation, Novoselic smashed his new bass straight through a couple of amps – rental amps that were supposed to last the entire tour.

"They didn't really break anything on that tour because they didn't have a lot of spare guitars," says Craig, "except at that first show, where they had this wimpy bass amp that wasn't loud enough. Here's poor Edwin, who doesn't know these people at all, and he's like, 'What the hell is this?' We had to go back down to London and get a good amp."

The following night at Manchester Polytechnic was better: desirous of full-on rock, the crowd went crazy. There had long been a tradition of crazed slam-dancing and stagediving in the UK, part-fuelled by the Minneapolis bands of the mid-Eighties and also British psychobilly and garage outfits such as The Meteors and Billy Childish's Thee Mighty Caesars. It didn't take much to set the kids off again. European fans were much more appreciative of Sub Pop than their US counterparts. There again it's easy to take for granted what's on your doorstep.

Witness Seattle's own music paper, *The Rocket*'s attitude towards Sub Pop. Contrary to revisionist reportage since, *The Rocket* was not the first magazine to feature Nirvana on their cover. Even the British music press beat them to it, with John Robb's article in *Sounds*. *The Rocket* followed three months later, with a cursory 750-word story. You'd have thought a local publication might have been faster to react, for news value alone.

"I went up to Leeds to see them, at a two-thirds full Duchess Of York," recalls Anton. The Duchess was a classic perennial on the UK 'toilet circuit' – backstage was up a steep, cold flight of stairs, pub dance floor capacity around 200; vibe was friendly. "I remember Krist walking off the stage and saying to him, flippantly, 'Krist, you haven't thrown your bass.' He went, 'Oh yeah,' and just threw it behind him without looking. You could see everybody looking down to where the moshpit was, and then every one of the dancers moving their heads back as the bass came flying down. Upstairs afterwards, everyone was getting stoned. It was winter: freezing, wet and cold – a load of labels had gone up there to see Nirvana and Tad."

The next day, Nirvana travelled to the BBC's studios in Maida Vale to partake in the time-honoured tradition of recording a John Peel Session – four songs; 'Love Buzz', 'About A Girl', 'Polly' and 'Spank Thru'. On October 27, Nirvana played their debut London show at the School of Oriental and African Studies (SOAS) – home to a kick-ass Mudhoney/ Soundgarden double headliner a few weeks earlier where the stage collapsed and a handful of UK music journalists had to physically hold up the trestle tables it was resting on while the mess was sorted out. Security had walked a long time before.

"The thing that struck me most about playing SOAS was that the crowd was 100 per cent white," comments Mark Arm. "People were falling over the stage, and we were getting pushed back. So I made this crack like, 'Hey, let's everybody get on stage!' which the crowd took at face value. At once everyone tried to get on stage and security got really mad. You and Anton and Keith Cameron were trying to keep things under control. Things got underway again and I was thinking, 'This is so absurd. How can I show the absurdity of it all?' So during the next song I told the crowd – to illustrate a point of how dumb they are – to climb the PA stacks. At which point people did and one of the security guys started charging me, and Anton had to take him out. That's where our version of sarcasm didn't translate at all. I remember it being considered a riot, but it was hardly a riot. It was just overenthusiasm."

None of the newly converted Sub Pop fans were going to miss a chance to have fun like that at the Tad/Nirvana show. "Kids were jumping off the speaker stacks," exclaims Craig. "I'd never seen anything like it. People were losing control of their bodies entirely, both the band and the audience. It was a temporary set-up in a school cafeteria, not a concert venue at all, so there was very little security and the room was packed."

"Kurt came off stage at SOAS, and he's looking for something, and I'm like, 'What are you doing?'" Anton smiles. "He was like, 'I need to do something and I don't know what.' I asked, 'Why don't you let off a fire extinguisher?' You could see his face light up like a naughty child. And so off he goes to let one off . . ."

To be honest, it's hard to remember most of these concerts. Everything folds into a blur. Even though I'm the commentator most Nirvana historians quote when it comes to the early shows – credited or not – I'm fucked if I can recall what happened from one show to the next. Was it at the Astoria that Tad leapt off stage during Nirvana's set, straight on to Matt Lukin, knocking him cold for 15 minutes – or did I imagine that? All I can recollect is long hair and faces insane on alcohol and heat, body aching from constant dancing, head spinning from resting it within the bass bins . . .

Some mornings, I would wake on the stairs outside my flat, cassettes smashed at my feet. Other days, I can recall physically shaking from lack of alcohol, walking across Blackfriars Bridge at 10 in the morning. I hung out with Mudhoney and Tad way more than Nirvana back then – preferred their music, and the guys drank more too. (Well, except Krist Novoselic.) There must have come a time when Nirvana went from being a second-rate Soundgarden to an incredible, emotionally charged live act and it must have happened on this tour, but what made me change my opinion?

I'm not the only one confused.

"I've played so many shows, hardly anything significant stands out," says Chad. "Like that time in New York when the bass cracked, or the time at the Chicago Metro when everybody started throwing bottles at us – but they weren't throwing bottles at us because they were angry at us but as encouragement. They have that over in England. I remember when we first played over there, in Manchester, people showed their appreciation by spitting and throwing bottles. That happened at a number of shows. We were like, 'Oh this again! Quick, duck!' "

"I thought Nirvana were one of the good Seattle bands, but didn't see their potential," says Ruud Berends, ex-Paperclip. "I thought Tad was a little better and Mudhoney were a lot better. I thought the Tad/Nirvana tour was four or five months too early. We had 50 people a night, on average."

The band travelled from the UK to Hilversum, Holland, where they recorded 'About A Girl' and 'Dive' for radio station VPRO on November 1. The Dutch dates were in bigger places – nicer, but more reserved. The shows included nights at the communal Vera venue in Groningen with its excellent hippie food and table-tennis table and end-of-year charts rating the staff's favourite bands[7], and Melkweg in Amsterdam. The Melkweg gig ended with Kurt smashing his guitar and then screaming into a mic as the band jammed on some noise number (later to spawn the closing 'Endless, Nameless' on *Nevermind*) – and afterwards, the pot-smokers headed off to the red-light district, to the Bulldog bar and all that.

Not everyone was impressed by Nirvana's behaviour.

"Krist bought a bottle of whiskey on the boat and finished it alone," Edwin Heath told a Dutch magazine *Oor* in 1994. "Drunk as a donkey, completely wasted. At one point, we're waiting for a traffic light in Den Haag, next to a police car without lights. All of a sudden Krist opens the side door and shouts, 'Turn on the lights, motherfuckers!' The cops stayed behind us for another 15 minutes."

The band stayed at the Quentin Hotel in Amsterdam, a regular Paperclip spot for small bands: "Krist, still completely drunk, went to lie down in the hallway," Heath continued. "The hotel is run by two cool guys, one of whom, Philip, looks like Freddie Mercury. He goes to Krist to put him on a chair and when Krist sees him coming he shouts, 'Fuck you, Freddie Mercury fag!' and we're told to leave. Later, Krist got on top of the van to curse to the whole world. He apologised later . . ."

After Holland, it was off to West Germany.

"The first show we played in Germany was in a tiny little place," recalls Craig. "Sound-wise, the show was an abortion. You remember the times that were exceptional – when they smashed up some equipment, or got in a fight with a bouncer – but Nirvana was actually very consistent. Their shows weren't always a shambolic wreck. They were well rehearsed, and they had good songs, and they played them."

Understand this: I used to go to concerts to dance. There was no other reason. If I liked a band, I'd be flailing wildly, often by myself, at the front. If I didn't, then I wouldn't watch them and I'd hide in a corner. It was as simple as that. Attending concerts wasn't a social event for me – I had few friends – and it certainly wasn't an excuse to get drunk and behave obnoxiously. That came later. I wanted bands whose energy I could feed off, and to whom I could give some energy back.

That's why I loved Nick Cave's Birthday Party in the early Eighties: the man made an effort. We screamed our approval when he'd fall back into the crowd, arms akimbo, trusting us to bear him up. We'd punch, kick, scratch to get hold of the microphone and yell a few words down it while Nick's back was turned. "Express yourself," he would scream possessed, to his adoring faithful, and a few of us did. If you listen closely to the start of the 1982 Lydia Lunch/Birthday Party live 12-inch you'll hear a deep bass voice singing *"Danger zone in the heart of the city/ Danger zone in the heart of the town"*. My first recorded performance, thank you.

Likewise, Half Japanese singer Jad Fair – the epitome of a geek with his big glasses, ordinary clothes and battered guitar that he sometimes forgot to plug in. Faced with abuse as he often was, he'd jump into the crowd and face off his oppressor who would invariably bottle it. Likewise, The Slits. Conventional rock wisdom ran in the face of these girls' unequivocal glee at being allowed on stage and given a chance to scream and show off and wear their knickers on the outside of their clothes, and create a wonderful, bass-led dub sound ripe for dancing to.

So it was with Nirvana in 1989 and 1990. After the initial shock of seeing them pretend to be a heavy metal band had worn off and they'd lost Jason, they turned out to be super fine. Hey, the heavy metal tag is fair enough. Would Nirvana have been signed to Sub Pop without the hard rock connections? I doubt it. I don't know what fucked-up shit the kids in small-town America have to suffer and lose before they can express their feelings, but I suspect that back in Nirvana's day it included mandatory exposure to Aerosmith and Kiss. Remember: punk rock didn't break till the year 1991 in America when *Nevermind* charted. Before then, and before the Internet, Edge City kids had no access to the cool shit which us big city kids took for granted.

Indeed, Nirvana turned out not just to be super fine, but rather special. That much was apparent from the first time I saw Kurt trying to destroy his amp with the aid of a much-abused guitar and fists. In this, Nirvana reminded me of the glory days of 1985 when John Robb's Membranes would clear college stages of all obstacles within a few seconds. Well I remember the look on the faces of London's famed Marquee bouncers when they saw us beating the crap out of their stage with 10-foot metal bars, and realised they were powerless to stop us.

Nirvana felt frustration. I could relate to that. After all, what had my frantic dancing been if not a manifestation of my sexual frustration? Nirvana felt frustration with shit club engineers and the life that had dealt them such a crap hand and everyone who didn't immediately cotton on to their genius. Not to mention the fact it was almost impossible to express sensitivity within their chosen medium of punk rock/grunge.

Years later, Courtney Love explained to me that "punk rock is a Marxist rite of passage, one that has nothing to do with women". Unfortunately, by the time bands like Black Flag and Dead Kennedys began to exert a stranglehold on US counterculture in the mid-Eighties, this was true. Initially, punk in NYC and the UK had sought out fresh ways of communication, a way to channel conflicting emotions, and a way in for women previously excluded by rock's patriarchal set of rules. It soon solidified into another, even stricter, set of male-centred rules from which you could not veer if you wanted to belong.

This frustration at their surroundings was why Nirvana's early songs – from the nerve-shredding Shocking Blue cover to Jack Endino's inspired grunge production on 'Negative Creep' – sound so brutal and alive. Nirvana had so much angst to get out of their scrawny systems.

That's also why Kurt started leaping backwards into the drum kit, forwards into the crowd, like Nick Cave and Iggy Pop before him. And that's why I loved Nirvana so much initially. They made a goddamn effort – by leaping around and gurning and groaning and screaming so much on stage, it was obvious that they were merely doing what any half-awake fan would have done in their stead. Get up on stage and have a good time! Put your heart and soul and body into it, because you know what? Outside of tonight, nothing exists. Nothing. What, you want to go back to that crap job as a railway engineer, as a printer, as a nobody? Make some noise! Not along preordained lines, but in your own time and in your own space and inspired by your own emotions.

So . . . did any of this stuff even happen? You begin to wonder; you read so many accounts that fail to capture the excitement, the sheer thrill, that block off whole tours and unique shows. Did I even get up on stage with Nirvana to scream the encore on several occasions? Not according to any of the books I've read. Was Nirvana an exhilarating, mind-bending band with an appetite for destruction or was Kurt just a sad junkie with a big mate who looked after him? I know which version I experienced, but you do start to question your own memory . . .

"The first time we toured all we had was that single and that's it," explains Chad. "Audiences were random. We'd play at some club in LA and pack the place. And then we'd play in Tucson, Arizona to 30 people at best, and leave with just 50 bucks in our pockets. The next time we went out, it was a different story. Every place we played was packed. And when we went over to Europe, every place we played was from 500 to 850 – and we played the Astoria. What does that seat – 7,000?[8] Nothing was ever enormous, but every place was packed. The people that were into the music scene, those were the ones that knew about Nirvana. Your average public didn't know about Nirvana until Geffen pushed them. Or pushed and pulled them, I should say."

Something happened between 1989 and 1990. I'm not sure I know what it was. I was too busy enjoying myself to take notes. *Bleach* came out halfway through '89 – an album I listened to about two-and-a-half times before realising that, as ever, with this sort of music, records can never compare to the live experience. I concentrated instead on going out.

On November 9, 1989, the Berlin Wall came down – and Tad and Nirvana were in Hanover, preparing to travel to Berlin.

"The band was on their first European tour," states their German booking agent Christof Ellinghaus. "They played in this little village in the middle of Germany and were scheduled to play Berlin on Saturday night. It would have been a guaranteed sell-out, there was such a buzz on that first record. We had a really good feeling. And you know what happened? On Thursday night, the bloody wall came down. So these guys were stuck in transit traffic of little cars going each way into Berlin or West Germany. You can imagine how done they were when they finally got there.

"There was an atmosphere in Berlin I have never seen again. It was a love-fest for some reason," he jokes sarcastically. "Thousands of East Germans in their stonewashed jeans arriving in capitalist Germany – welcomed by money and bananas. The party was in the streets. It was huge. People were out and about, so there goes our 600-capacity Nirvana show. When the bands got there they were so pissed off, they didn't even realise. 'Why are we stuck in traffic? What are all these funny cars?' The theme of the tour was a porn movie called *Barnyard Fun*, which had a fascinatingly cheesy soundtrack. First, they were pissed off because it took them 20 hours to get there, but then we explained, 'Hey, come on, you are witnessing history in the making!' There was a lot of drinking going on. They played, Tad opened, Nirvana finished, and gosh . . ."

The venue was half-full: "227 people," remarks Ellinghaus in precise Teutonic fashion. "Kurt smashed his guitar during 'Breed' and walked off." The band had nowhere to stay, so they slept upstairs at the venue, the Ecstasy Club, no beds, with their jackets rolled up under their heads – or stayed up all night smoking hash.

"We were driving there in mid-afternoon, and I was talking to Edwin," recalls Chad. "I was like, 'What is up with all these cars?' because there were DDR cars lined up forever over there. We had a great show that night. If we'd played the night before, we would've had West Germans at our show not East Germans. We had both. The club we played was only four or five blocks from the wall, so we walked over and there were still a lot of people there. It was cool."

"That fall, we toured Europe with our label-mates Tad," Krist wrote in *Of Grunge And Government*. "We found ourselves in Berlin the day after the wall fell.[9] We counted a column of little Trabant cars, 27 kilometres long, on the Eastern side, waiting to enter the West. The emotion of history in the making was in the air. The West had much to offer and this wasn't lost on me when I noticed all of the Trabants parked on the Reeperbahn, Hamburg's notorious avenue of booze and sex."

After a fairly extensive German tour came four dates in Austria – including "the troll village up in the mountains," as Kurt described one place – and then on to the heavy metal club in Budapest, and Switzerland.

In Mezzago, Italy, Kurt joined Tad to sing Tad's songs 'High On The Hog' and 'Loser'.

"Tad had passed out from the heat, so Kurt jumped up on stage," recalls Craig. "At the end, some kid reached over the barricade for Krist's shoes. And I knew that Krist couldn't be shoeless in Europe. That would be bad. So I jumped over the barricade, and I must have scared the crap out of this kid, because he just gave them up to me.

"Maybe I had my cycling cap on," he laughs.

Nirvana played Rome on November 27. It was a disaster.

In a typically extravagant and somewhat thoughtless gesture, Jon and Bruce had flown out to see how the tour was going – much to the resentment of the bands being forced to get by on sleep deprivation in cramped surroundings, barely breaking even. "It was a gruelling schedule," comments Craig. "If the bands did have a day off it was a travel day, or they were doing a session." Rome would prove to be the beginning of the end of Sub Pop's relationship with both bands: the musicians viewed their appearance – intended as emotional support, a pair of friendly faces to help prop up flagging spirits – as sheer arrogance, the act of record company moguls out of touch with their roster.

"This was the tour where they were still destroying their back line every night," says Christof. "They flew into their drum kits, specially made drum kits too. It was one of the most powerful rock shows I've seen by a three-piece. Tad was really amazing, but Nirvana had the songs. Kurt was an impulsive little fucker, so if a microphone wasn't working, he'd throw it down and walk away. Kurt was passive/aggressive and full of drama. It was a danger element when Krist would swing his bass towards the end of the show."

"Rome was a bad show for Nirvana," remembers Craig. "There was a bad attitude and Kurt quit early. He walked off the stage. He wasn't happy with the sound. I think he was just unhappy in general. There was a big blow-up between Kurt and Edwin. Kurt quit, and then Edwin quit, and Kurt threw a fit about bad monitors . . ."

Kurt smashed his guitar during 'Spank Thru' and clambered up on to the PA stack, threatening to jump off: "The bouncers were freaked out," recalls Bruce Pavitt, "as were the crowd. Everyone was begging him to come down. He had reached his limit. If he'd dived he would have broken his neck." Kurt clambered up into the rafters, and from there, into the balcony – where he threatened to hurl chairs at the audience.[10]

"Afterwards, the venue's sound guy was peeved with Nirvana over breaking some mics," adds Craig. "He came up to Edwin and Kurt and showed them the broken mics, which looked fine, so Kurt took them and threw them on the ground and said, 'Now they're broken.' Edwin did not take kindly to that: 'From this point on, I am not going to tour manage Nirvana!' I'm not sure how it got patched up."

Poneman took Kurt outside to cool off: "He was ranting, saying, 'I don't want to play for these morons, I just want to go home,'" the label boss recalls. "He was like, 'I want to go home to my girlfriend and never have to play music again.'" Jon promised to buy Kurt a new guitar when the tour got to Geneva in Switzerland, and a train ticket to the next city. His concern was to get Kurt out of the pressure-cooker conditions of touring in a van so he could make it to the final England show in a few days time.

Krist and Chad also momentarily quit Nirvana that night.

The next day was a rare day off: Nirvana visited the Coliseum and matters cooled down – but only briefly. During a border crossing on the train between Rome and Geneva, Kurt fell asleep and his wallet and passport and shoes were stolen. "That," Jonathan comments wryly, "was the perfect picture of unhappiness, Kurt sitting there with his hood pulled up over his head, not speaking to anyone, drinking a cup of hot chocolate."

"Yeah, we had to go to the consulate in Berne, Switzerland, which was not a city on our tour," sighs Craig, "and sit there for six hours, while the paperwork got done. It was at least a day lost."

It was when the tour returned to England on December 3, for the opening night of Lamefest at London's Astoria[11], that Nirvana totally tore up the rulebook. This, in many respects, was the show that changed everything.

Going on first, it seemed that the trio would be faced with an uphill struggle to impress those who'd arrived especially early to catch them. What were we thinking? Nirvana had driven all the way from Dover to London in freezing fog, arriving 20 minutes before they were due to go on: no soundcheck, no rest period, nothing. It didn't matter. After 30 minutes, they'd pulverised their way through four guitars and left the stage for dead. I'm not saying Nirvana bettered Mudhoney – who were at the peak of their considerable power – but that night they unsettled and bewildered any number of people with the force of their performance.

"Remember Lamefest?" laughs Christof. "The show scarred me. There was a lot of stagediving, Mudhoney headlined, but Nirvana stole the show. They were a menace, amazing."

"It stunk," Krist flatly stated. "On a scale of one to 10 it was a zero."

Opinion of this show is all over the place. I have a vivid memory of Tad Doyle lurching towards the front of the stage, about to dive off . . . but did he? I can recall the stage battered and laid bare, amplifiers and guitars and mic stands all swept to one side as Nirvana exited . . . but was it that show? I can't recall the songs, but I can still feel the emotion, the anger manifesting itself as Kurt hurled his guitar towards Krist only for the bassist to casually bat it away with his instrument, splintering it into several shards. I have a feeling they tried several times before Krist connected but . . . who knows?

Some friends feel the show was one of the greatest they witnessed. Others are equally vehement it was the absolute pits. Yet I'm sure this is the night that I first really connected with the power and rage and frustration and sheer devilment of Kurt Cobain.

"Kurt was in turn full of terror and gentleness," recalled *MM* photographer Stephen Sweet. "He threw himself around like nothing existed outside of each moment he played and sang."

Simon Price slagged off Nirvana in *Melody Maker* the next week, singling out Krist for most of his vitriol, claiming that, "It all falls apart when the lanky, rubber-legged, frog-like bassist starts making a fool of himself." Others were similarly unimpressed.

"It was our tour," growls Mudhoney drummer Dan Peters. "We had been over for nine weeks. My recollection was that Nirvana was fucking horrible and they were fucking shitty. They could barely get through a song, let alone 10 songs. They were breaking strings left and right. At one point Krist was swinging his bass around and I was standing on the side of the stage. All of a sudden it got loose and I fucking had to put my hand up and the butt of his bass hit me. If I'd been any slower, it would've totally gotten me."

My recollection is that it was the first time I ever liked them live. I might be confused . . .

"You talk to anyone in Mudhoney," replies Dan, "and we all remember that show. I was sitting there going, 'This sucks.' I wasn't saying that they sucked, but I was saying, 'This sucks that this is the big London show and this is happening.' Ever since then I've been reading stuff like, 'If you weren't there, you missed out. Nirvana blew all the other bands away.' History has definitely changed that show in a lot of ways."

Maybe I enjoyed it because there was a lot of stagediving going on.

"They pulled up, and there was Tad and Nirvana," recalls Anton, "and their crew all crammed into this small van. Standing outside, they tossed a coin to see who would go on first and it was heads, so Nirvana did – which they were pleased about cos it meant they could have rest of the time off. That night was the turning point. There were a lot of hipsters there, the cool bands – Kurt came off stage and his knees were all cut up and grazed because he'd jump four or five foot in the air off something and land on his knees. We used to joke how we'd have to get him sponsorship with a kneepad firm . . . he was constantly covered in bruises or abrasions."

Do you remember everyone lining up at the side of the stage to jump off?

"Yeah, from the label," nods Anton. "Everyone, Tad, publicists, promoters, journalists, other musicians, catering."

Do you remember their set being good?

"I thought it was really good," he replies. "The following week all the reviews made Nirvana out to be the band. I felt sorry for Mudhoney because I thought they were amazing those nights, but it was Nirvana getting the accolades."

"I still have it, never worn but once, that pullover from the show," brags Chad. "Yeah, that was a cool show. It was cool because we were hanging out with Mudhoney. Mark Arm and Matt [Lukin] stagedived during our set. Kurt stagedived during Mudhoney's set. I don't think Krist ever stagedived too much. You would be pretty wary of some guy like Krist coming down on you, he's a pretty big dude, but then Tad . . . He laid himself down on the crowd that night. If he'd dived he would've killed somebody."

I remember Nirvana being amazing at Lamefest.

"I don't remember if I even watched them," Steve Turner sighs.

Other people told me that they sucked.

"I know they were in bad shape," Steve agrees. "Both those bands were exhausted. There was some question of whether they could even make it there. I'm sure I watched some of it. Some of those big shows were still freaking me out a little. So I was kind of . . . hiding." He laughs. "Drinking and hiding . . ."

Steve starts reading from his journal: " 'At Lamefest, The Legend! came with Tad and Nirvana . . . very party-like. Tad and Nirvana break all their guitars and Tad borrows mine to do his Peel Session the next day. They look ready to go home . . .

" 'Second night at The Astoria. Didn't sell out but it was really crowded. Tad and others were there and tossed us off the stage except me. Bill from Cosmic Psychos couldn't get me. We met Jason [Pierce] from Spacemen 3 whose new band, Darkside, opened. Total chumps. Darkside were doing coke backstage and shit. I let Mark deal with them . . .' "

While Nirvana were in Europe, their first non-Sub Pop track appeared: 'Mexican Seafood', released on the compilation seven-inch EP *Teriyaki Asthma Vol 1* (C/Z). Daniel House, C/Z's boss, worked for Sub Pop for a while. He would've offered Nirvana a deal, "but Jonathan jumped on them so fast," House explained. The other artists on the record were Coffin Break, Helios Creed, and Yeast.

**Addenda: project bands**

So tell me about your jam with Kurt Cobain.

"It's splendid because it's something I can tell my grandkids," smiles Rich Jensen.

"One day, I was messing around with Dylan and Slim at the practice space they had at the back of their house. A weird hippie guy with stringy hair is playing a broken bass with two strings – the neck is broken and only just hanging on. He's bending the head and thwacking it. It's turned up really loud, going 'Phwam phwam' – this big booming sound. We go into the room and, because everybody's friends with everybody, I start playing with a little drum sampler and Slim's doing something, and we continue to put noises on top of his thwacking. I don't remember exactly, except there was this really peculiar fellow thumping at this broken thing – not musical, just horrendous thwacks and thwamps. He did it the whole time we were messing around – for, like, an hour. We leave, and as we're walking away, half a block away, we hear him continuing to thwamp and thwamp. I always imagined he thwamped like that for days."

## NOTES

1 Put together by The Supersuckers' Danny Bland, the concept of Dickless was based round the Redd Kross teen exploitation movie, 1984's *Desperate Teenage Lovedolls*. "They were great – terrifying, actually," says Jack Endino. "The guitarist

Kerry was completely unschooled, but she'd figured a way round it. She tuned the whole guitar to a chord, so all she had to do was use one finger to play punk rock guitar. Kelly Canary's voice was like the secret weapon. You could stop armies with that voice."

2 Laibach are a sinister Slovenian experimental metal group, with guttural voices, thunderous instrumentation and a warped, warped sense of humour.

3 Sub Pop claimed the Idaho heavyweight was a former butcher and deranged woodsman.

4 Nirvana had started covering The Vaselines' simple, riff-driven 'Molly's Lips'. I still have the fax somewhere from Bruce Pavitt asking if I could contact singer Eugene Kelly on Kurt's behalf to ask if it was OK for Nirvana to cover the song.

5 Badfinger were a melodic pop band signed to Beatle's Apple label, best known for writing Nilsson's mega-hit 'Without You' and two members committing suicide.

6 Most Seattle bands had a problem with English cuisine: Mudhoney even named an album after it, *Boiled Beef And Rotting Teeth*.

7 One year, The Legend! came about number 44, four places above the band I supported, Soundgarden.

8 More like a couple of thousand.

9 It was actually two days afterwards.

10 The description of this concert has spooky parallels with a Hole show in Amsterdam I saw in 1995, where Courtney used the PA system to climb up into the balcony to pursue a heckler. Her guitarist Eric Erlandson and myself engaged in a furious chase through the crowd, trying our damnedest to stop Courtney from braining her tormentor.

11 Mudhoney headlined both nights, with the hard drinking, wah-wah wielding, Australian punk band Cosmic Psychos supporting the second night.

# CHAPTER 10

# Duct Tape And Splinters

*You know what it's like, touring with a band. Time seems to stretch into infinity – an endless procession of highways, byways, houses, factories and the odd traffic jam. You eat a little. You sleep a little. You pray that your van doesn't break down or end up in a crash. If you've got a little dope, you light that up too, anything to relieve the boredom.*

*We're in a van with the Tad band, travelling the 160 miles between Seattle and Portland along the west coast of America. It is early evening and it's sheeting it down with rain outside, visibility zero, with clouds of cigarette smoke fogging up the inside. We're fighting a losing battle against time for the soundcheck for tonight's show with Screaming Trees and Nirvana at Portland's Pine Street Theatre, but we're doing OK, stoked up on tapes of the new Boss Hog*[1]*, Bastro*[2] *and Melvins' albums, M&Ms and crackers. It's just another night on the road.*

. . .

*Tad. Hell. You know what this lard-ass dude is all about by now, don't you? He's a gross, near-mythical figure, responsible for some of the most uncompromising music around; music that rocks, hard and heavy and relentless, but music that also contains elements of disquiet, of bitterness at being the perpetual outsider, of anger at never quite achieving.*

*He and his band have just released a new mini-LP* Salt Lick *and are out touring the west coast with Nirvana to promote it; Portland through San Francisco, Long Beach and Phoenix. The usual. It's a tour that will take them through February and the best part of March.*

*Portland was great: 500 suburban punks dancing, Nirvana trashing a few guitars through frustration, Tad thrashing with his usual aplomb, and the whole place like a Palm Springs pinball machine that no one could touch me on. Everyone got plied with dope; the bar downstairs served tofu and falafel only, beer was limited to over-21s. The video crew that turned up got rewarded with a show of blistering proportions – metal twisted and distorted so out-of-shape its origins are barely recognisable.*

. . .

*Every night on tour, Kurdt smashes up at least one guitar, often two.*

*In Portland, it was because he was enjoying himself. In San Jose, it was through sheer apathy. While making for an entertaining spectacle, one can't help feeling that if Nirvana continue this way they'll either degenerate into the realms of self-parody, run out of money – or both.*

*Right now, though, Nirvana are awesome live. The San Francisco show with Tad and Dickless is stunning: the Washington trio blow every other fucking band in existence off-centre with their potency and ferocious intent. 'Love Buzz' and 'Stain' spiral and shatter, leaving precious shards of the purest manic pop thrill in their wake. Chris trashes his bass out of petulance, Kurdt – not to be left out – smashes his guitar and then trashes the drums. Meanwhile, our man Tad is standing left of the stage looking worried. It's his bass that Chris is now using.*

*They encore, exploding with malice and annoyance at a crap PA system, leaving San Francisco's Gavin Report new music seminar in no doubt whatsoever as to quite who is happening where.*

*. . .*

*I wonder what Kurdt's idea of beauty is. I don't think I've ever wondered that before.*

*"Antique craftsmanship," the singer replies. "Something that is built well, built to last, something solid. Values that my grandparents had – pretty much the opposite of the way things are going now. It's the same with music – sincerity, craftsmanship. If you do a job you should do it well – that's just good business sense. Same thing my grandfather used to bitch at me about when I was a kid, and I never understood him."*

(Excerpts from *The Larder They Come*, author's report of Tad/Nirvana US tour, *Melody Maker*, March 17, 1990)

IN December 1989, Krist and Shelli flew to Yugoslavia to visit Krist's dad. On their return, the couple announced their engagement. They got married on December 30, in a private ceremony at their Tacoma apartment conducted by an acquaintance of Shelli's – the flat was packed with family and friends, including Krist's mum, Shelli's mother and step-father, most of Tad, Kurt and Tracy, and Dan Peters and Matt Lukin from Mudhoney, the latter being a suitably inebriated best man. A drunk wrestling match between Tad, his guitarist Kurt Danielson and Krist marked the happy occasion.

The drive down to Tacoma from Olympia was particularly fraught for Tracy – about to witness two of her closest friends exchanging vows, she pressed Kurt for signs of commitment. He refused to give any, telling her instead, "I'd still like to have sex with you because I really like it." The sad fact for Tracy was that Kurt wasn't ready to settle down. Their relationship was starting to draw to its natural end, despite Tracy's comforting arms after Kurt's frequent nightmares (vampires, thugs with baseball bats or knives coming for him), and despite the fact she was able to help him pursue his rock'n'roll dream by being financially supportive. Kurt wrote weird entries in his journal about lactating, or being unable to masturbate because he'd imagine, "My father, little girls, German shepherds, TV news commentators but no voluptuous pouty-lipped naked female sex kittens . . ." – a standard worry for most healthy young male adults, but one also guaranteed to freak out most girlfriends.

On January 2–3, Nirvana returned to Reciprocal Studios to work on another song, 'Sappy'. It took them 10 hours in total, and they weren't happy with the results. "Part of that was getting a Steve Albini drum sound," recalls engineer Jack Endino. "Kurt was very specific. That was the first time he seemed fallible to me. Everything up till then had been amazing. 'Sappy' just wasn't very good. He ended up re-recording it several times." Nirvana spent around $500 on the session – just $100 short of what it took to record their entire debut album.

"I told him he should just write some more songs," Jack laughs.

So Kurt did. One of them, 'Lithium', was previewed later that spring when the group shot four videos on March 20 in an Evergreen State College classroom with a couple of friends. Payment was "$40 and some pizza," according to cameraman Alex Kostelnik. The band played live while snippets of TV footage drawn from the numerous hours of meshed-up video montage Kurt had taped in Olympia was projected behind them: shots of Seventies teen idol Shaun Cassidy, *Star Search* with Donny and Marie Osmond tap-dancing, *Fantasy Island*. For 'Big Cheese', a silent film about witches was projected, interspersed with some of Kurt's childhood Super 8 footage – "Broken dolls, dolls on fire, dolls put together all wrong," as Kostelnik remembers it. Videos for 'School' and 'Floyd The Barber' were also recorded.

Picture the scene. We're at the Squid Row on Pike St on Capitol Hill, just down the road from the Comet Tavern. It's Seattle, 1990 and the venue is heaving with people; everywhere, the smell of human perspiration and hum of overloaded amplifiers.

On stage, Mudhoney are finishing their final encore. Mark Arm is lying heedless to the world, a sea of bodies on top, beside and underneath him. Around are the scenes of pandemonium: scattered amplifiers, stagedivers nursing bruised tendons, a bouncer at his wit's end attempting to retain control over the constant stream of people on and off stage. Steve Turner's guitar is howling with sexual frustration. Dan Peters has thumped his way into oblivion. Matt Lukin, meanwhile, has been drinking vodka for 14 hours straight, and he isn't going to stop now.

"Anyone want more?" he yells to tired cheers.

Loud harsh music pumps out from the speakers. A 50-year-old in diapers wanders up to me and asks to be chastised. Toilet walls are covered in piss-stains and graffiti from local musicians boasting of their sexual prowess, plus diatribes against Sub Pop's inner sanctum.

Throughout 1990, Sub Pop was continually on the verge of going under. Tad, Nirvana and Mudhoney sold well – but not enough to support Jon and Bruce's grandiose plans. The label offered share options to musicians in place of royalties – which in the long term would have made the artists extremely rich, but wasn't particularly helpful back then. Sub Pop even asked Mudhoney if they could borrow half of their European advance. It wasn't until Mudhoney's album *Every Good Boy Deserves Fudge* shipped 50,000 copies in June 1991, through word-of-mouth alone, that Sub Pop started to become financially solvent. This was several months before the Nirvana royalties started to roll in.

"That period from May to September '91, when the distributor was obliged to pay for the records they shipped in May, was particularly dicey," recalls former Sub Pop general manager, Rich Jensen. "The bookkeeper, my boss, quit coming in to the office and got real hard to reach on the phone. Eventually I took over and worked a couple of months without pay. There was a particular afternoon in early August where a potential investor finally came through on a $6,000 loan he'd been promising for weeks. The next day the phones were due to be shut off, the van was to be repossessed and the county tax authorities intended to barricade the premises. I think it was August 7. Anyway, I got the cheque from him about 4.45, shook his hand pleasantly, smiled as I showed him out the door and then sprinted several blocks to the bank before it closed at 5 p.m."

Enthusiasm oozes from every adrenalin-charged pore. Arm goes over to where Charles Peterson, the man who defined Seattle's look with his hyper-focused highlights stolen from the music's blurry sea of chaos, is standing vaguely shell-shocked. He checks to see if he's all right, then laughs and rushes backstage to throw up from the heat. Ed [Fotheringham] from the Thrown-Ups tries to balance a few beers on his head, not very adroitly. The beer goes everywhere, splattering a couple of Californian wannabe hipsters. In one corner, Sub Pop's human press dynamo Jenny Boddy[3] chats with Seattle's Queen of Blarney Megan Jasper about the latest outrage perpetuated by Mudhoney manager Bob Whittaker. Tad Doyle is surrounded by a phalanx of admirers a quarter his size, cracking open a fresh Mexican bottled beer every five minutes.

Similar scenes were happening almost nightly in the Pacific Northwest at shows by bands like supercharged punk-powerpop trio Fastbacks, The Walkabouts, Swallow and a hundred lesser hopefuls. Heads thrust in bass bins, T-shirts soaked with beer and perspiration, coloured strobes flashed in a dizzying symphony of light.

"I was at the Crescent Ballroom in downtown Tacoma where for the first and only time I thought Nirvana was better than Melvins," says former Seaweed singer Aaron Stauffer. "The Crescent was a really down and out place that was once a cool dancehall. The Sonics and The Wailers played 'Louie Louie' there in the Sixties. In downtown T-town in the late Eighties only cops, junkies, whores, gangsters, the homeless and random punk fans would be found at night. At this show, the Crescent was called Legends – and Nirvana were the best I'd ever seen."

"Because Nirvana weren't from Seattle they'd get people from round here to ham it up a whole lot more," explains Megan Jasper. "They'd get the Mudhoney guys to lose their minds in the most fun way imaginable. The Fluid played in Tacoma, and after the show Kurt and Krist found these huge wooden spools and tipped them sideways. Krist pushed the spool and Kurt's in the middle, spinning like in a washing machine. It was the funniest thing you'd ever seen. And then he'd get out and be super-wobbly and goofy and Krist somehow managed to get his lanky weird body in, and everyone was pushing him . . ."

"That's one of the things that made Nirvana so great," agrees Jonathan Poneman, "and by Nirvana I mean Chad and Krist and Kurt. There was this whimsical, childlike, silly thing that they had going on. They managed to have that and still be incredibly cool; it wasn't like this fey, contrived thing. It was who they were that informed what they were and how they projected themselves, but they were total rock studs at the same time."

"My favourite Nirvana shows were the ones at Evergreen," says Candice Pedersen. A couple more happened in early 1990. Students and friends would cram themselves into the tiny dormitory rooms and drink wine until campus security came by. "They were like Judy Garland, Mickey Rooney, 'Let's put on a show.' They were more organic. I didn't like drinking or smoking, so that was good to me. They'd break a lot of instruments, but it wasn't intentional – more from people tripping over because space was so tight."

★ ★ ★

On February 9, Nirvana set out for another West Coast tour with Tad; Portland, San Jose, Sacramento, San Francisco, Long Beach, across the Mexican border to Tijuana and back again to Phoenix, Arizona. It was a welcome break for Kurt and Krist from life in Washington – they'd briefly started up their own office cleaning business, Pine Tree Janitorial, advertised with the slogan, "We purposely limit our number of commercial offices in order to personally clean while taking our time." Oddly enough, they didn't get any bookings.

"I know he worked for one day as a dishwasher," laughs Ian Dickson. "I know he worked for a week as a janitor."

"I don't know if we told many jokes," Chad says of the February tour. "Reality was the funniest. We always thought it was funny to make jokes of white trailer trash type stuff. We bought all these redneck type hats. 'I'd Rather Be Hunting'. I think mine said CBS Sports or something about fishing. And Kurt got this Day-Glo orange hunting hat. It's because we figured we were going towards the south and didn't want to look like grungy rockers and get frowned at. We were afraid that some rednecks would gang up on us and beat us up while we were on tour. And we fit right in! We'd try to eat at all the truck stops we could."

There's a classic Peterson sequence of Kurt falling backwards into the drums – originally taken for *Melody Maker* – that was shot at Raji's in Hollywood, in a venue designed for 200 people, but host to easily double that number that night. Robert Fisher, former art director of Geffen Records, told journalist Carrie Borzillo-Vrenna that, "Kurt was tearing the place up. I couldn't believe he didn't walk away from that without a broken back or anything."

Nirvana stayed that night with L7 bassist Jennifer Finch. Out of the people interviewed for this book, she's easily my favourite. She's the only one who still cares enough to lie to me.

"I was always the one who would be like, 'Everett, put Kurt down,'" she says, swigging a mineral water with Danny Bland, Charles Peterson and myself in a Pioneer Square bar. "'We don't want an accident; someone's going to lose an eye.' I was the child of the adult alcoholics. I was like, 'Do you have to do heroin before the show? Can you wait? Do you need me to hold it for you, I'll put it somewhere safe.' I was that guy. That's why I look so good and own a house now."

"We played with Tad and Nirvana in San Francisco[4]," says Kelly Canary. "Tim and me stagedived straight into the ground, and Kurt stopped right in the middle of a song to ask if we were OK."

This was the same show where I got up on stage, and lasted precisely one-and-a-half songs before the power got turned off. "OK," I rashly stated, parka hood pulled up tight over my head, ensconced in the heart of San Francisco's gay district, "Last night in Portland I made $1.71 from coins thrown at me on stage. Let's see how much you faggots can manage tonight . . ." Dwarves were also planning on playing, but after one look at the mayhem caused by my appearance, singer Blag Jesus declined. He was too busy laughing his ass off.

"We went out for Thai food and Kurt just sat there," Kelly continues. "He was the funniest guy ever but so weird and shy and quiet. He actually had a bit of a cold so all the ladies of Dickless who wanted to sleep with him – each one of us brought him our sleeping bags and our leftovers. He just had that look, 'Take care of me.' The ladies go crazy for it."

March was spent practising at The Dutchman, a rehearsal space in south Seattle sometimes referred to as 'the birthplace of grunge'.[5] A recording session had been booked at Smart Studios in Madison, Wisconsin with Tad (*Eight Way Santa*) producer Butch Vig. Nowadays, Vig is best known for his work on *Nevermind* and as the drummer with mainstream Goth band Garbage, but back then he was renowned as the man behind albums from hard-ass underground rock bands like Killdozer and The Fluid.

On April 1, Nirvana played Chicago's Cabaret Metro as support to Eleventh Dream Day.[6] "Kurt was screaming his guts out the entire night," *Chicago Tribune*'s Greg Kot told Carrie Borzillo-Vrenna in *Kurt Cobain: The Nirvana Years*. "He looked like he was in the jaws of this giant invisible Rottweiler and the Rottweiler was shaking him back and forth. At the end, he did the whole set-thrashing, drum-trashing routine. Every instrument on stage was in splinters. The drummer was still pounding away and Cobain had completely destroyed his drum kit and was lying splayed across it. People looked at each other, like, 'God, how do you follow that?' "

After the show, the band drove overnight to be at the studios on time.

"I wasn't crazy about *Bleach* the first time I heard it, except 'About A Girl'," Vig told Gillian G. Gaar. "The funniest thing was I remember Jonathan Poneman saying, 'If you saw Nirvana here in Seattle, it's like Beatlemania. And they're going to be as big as The Beatles!' And I'm thinking to myself, 'Yeah, right.' Now all I hear is, 'This band's going to be the next Nirvana!' "

The April 2–6 sessions were intended for Nirvana's second Sub Pop album, provisionally entitled *Sheep*. The title was a dig at the doubtless countless hordes of music fans that would be buying a copy, driven by fashion. In the event, they ended up being used as demos for *Nevermind*.

"May women rule the world," Kurt wrote in his journal, in a spoof ad for the album. "Abort Christ. Assassinate the greater and lesser of two evils. Steal *Sheep*. At a store near you. Nirvana. Flowers. Perfume. Candy. Puppies. Love. Generational Solidarity. And Killing Your Parents. *Sheep*."

"My studio was right next to Sub Pop on 2nd Ave," says Charles Peterson. "One day I get a knock on the door and it's Kurt and Krist and they have this little kitten with them. They're like, 'Take a picture. We do this thing where you pull the kitten's face back and it looks really weird.' They wanted to use it for a single or album cover. Of course as soon as I got the camera they couldn't get it, and I was like, 'OK. Cuckoo. Go back to Aberdeen.'"

When Nirvana arrived at Smart, the sum total of their instructions to Butch was that they wanted to "sound heavy, very heavy". "They were actually very funny and charming, particularly Krist," Butch told Gaar. So Vig – as much a pop freak as he was an underground rock nerd – obliged with a sound that was both thunderous, particularly on Chad's drums, and surprisingly tuneful.

"Kurt was an enigma," Vig says. "He'd get moody and sit in the corner and not talk for 45 minutes. I didn't have to do too much fine-tuning to the actual sound. Kurt wasn't too pleased with Chad's drumming. He kept getting behind the kit showing him how to play things."

Although Chad was still very much part of Nirvana, he was becoming dissatisfied with his place in the band – he considered himself a songwriter, and could play guitar, bass and violin. "I started to feel like a drum machine," he says. "Kurt had promised me more input, but it became clear that wasn't going to happen." It certainly wasn't. Kurt referred to Chad's Bainbridge Island-influenced music as, "Elfin music. You just kind of shudder, because it's so stupid and dorky." He liked Chad as a person, but was looking for something very different in a drummer.

Nirvana raced through several songs – 'In Bloom', another version of 'Polly' recorded on a 'really shitty' five-string acoustic guitar that sounded like a ukulele, 'Dive', 'Pay To Play' (a diatribe against small venues' policy of demanding money from bands upfront in exchange for a booking, later renamed as 'Stay Away'), 'Lithium', 'Immodium' and 'Sappy' again – plus a straightforward version of 'Here She Comes Now', a *White Light/White Heat* Velvet Underground song (eventually released as a split seven-inch single with Melvins). Five of the songs ended up being used on *Nevermind*. "Kurt was having problems with his voice," Vig recalls. "Except for 'Polly', which was soft, he'd get through one or two takes and wouldn't be able to sing any more. We had to take a day off in the middle."

"I liked working with Butch," says Chad. "I got the idea he was a fairly healthy guy, vegetarian and everything. He was soft-spoken. The idea was to record for a new album. They weren't meant as demos. It would've been the first time we recorded demos, and I don't know what their use would have been. We already had an album out."

Many Seattle musicians I've interviewed feel you don't get enough credit for *Nevermind*.

"It's weird because on the songs they pulled off the Madison sessions, all of the drum parts that I wrote are on *Nevermind*," he replies. "There are minor little differences, like on 'In Bloom' – I wanted a more structural kind of thing. But that's it. It's a hard thing to think about because when you're in a band, you put everyone's collaboration together and everyone should get an equal share. But the only share I got off that was 'Polly' because I actually play four cymbal heads on it. Nobody ever wrote my parts for me. Kurt wrote the lyrics and the guitar and that's it. He couldn't even play drums, just in a makeshift sort of way. So yeah," Chad says, shaking his head. "I don't know. It's confusing."

"I noticed right off the bat that Kurt wrote amazing songs and Krist wrote super hooky bass lines," Vig says in the sleeve notes to *With The Lights Out*. "The bass lines are really melodic, and the hook under the song was in the bass, at least musically. And that works so well with Kurt's vocal melody. They have a cool, interweaving, quality."

The sessions took place right at the start of another US tour – after Chicago, it was the Underground in Madison with Tad and local band Victim's Family; and on April 9, with Tad at the 7th Street Entry in down-town Minneapolis.

"It was through Steve Turner I encountered Nirvana," recalls Tom Hazelmyer.[7] "He was sending me boxes of free shit from Sub Pop on the side. I was at a party at [U-Men singer] Tom Price's where I heard Nirvana's first single. I wasn't the biggest fan, but I was a fan of Tad's definitely. The 7th Street Entry was like the Minneapolis equivalent of CBGBs.[8] It was sparsely attended and they weren't impressive. Tad asked me what I thought and I was like, 'Man. That "Love Buzz" song just drove me nuts and not in a good way.'

"But meeting Kurt afterwards," Haze continues, "there was this insane amount of . . . charisma, impact, I don't know what you'd call it, a guy sitting backstage, not even talking. I could never put my finger on it. Even after years of being round shit-loads of bands I've never sensed that level of charismatic presence again."

After Minneapolis, it was on to the Blind Pig in Ann Arbor[9] (where Krist destroyed Chad's drums), Cincinnati, two dates in Canada on April 16–17 where Krist climbed up on some speaker cabinets and bottles were thrown . . .

On April 18, in Cambridge, MA, Kurt threw a pitcher of water at Chad that missed his ear by inches.

"Nirvana was really mean to Chad," sighs Carrie Montgomery. "Kurt would break his drums every night and he didn't have any money. His drums were duct-taped together and it was funny to watch, but I always felt bad for him. He didn't look like he was having fun. He knew he'd have to piece his drum set back together every night.

"When me and Mark caught up with Nirvana, they had been on tour for a long time and Chad didn't have any socks, so I literally took the socks off my feet and gave them to little Chad," she adds. "And I felt so bad about how Kurt was to him. It seemed like Kurt was pissed at Chad, and this is from the perspective of, 'Why is that guy picking on that little drummer guy? He doesn't have any duct tape left even!' "

The tour reached New York's Pyramid Club on April 26. Among other attendees at what was fast becoming an almost clichéd nightly feast of destruction[10] was the godfather of punk Iggy Pop, plus Sonic Youth, Helmet and Geffen's head of A&R, Gary Gersh.

"I would shoot all of Sub Pop's bands for them in New York," says photographer Michael Lavine, a former Evergreen College student. "Bruce [Pavitt] phoned up and said, 'I've got this band. They're going to be huge.' I was like, 'Right. You say that about all your bands.' I photographed Nirvana in my loft at 2 Bleecker St, right across from CBGBs. They showed up at my door in their white van, and handed me the excellent Butch Vig demo. Kurt was sickly and mellow, but sweet. The running theme was, 'Where's Kurt? Oh, he's asleep in the van.'

"I was shooting Iggy Pop that day, and played him the Sub Pop stuff," the photographer continues. "Nirvana was the band he liked best – so I took him to see them. I introduced Iggy to Kurt. The meeting was very cordial and funny, and they shook hands." Afterwards, Nirvana were depressed because they thought they'd fucked up big time in front of a crowd of such prominent hipsters. But of course they hadn't . . .

"That was the night Chad was really late," Lavine recalls. "Kurt was pissed, and they trashed the drum kit."

"At the Pyramid, they came out and took over NYC," enthuses Janet Billig. "They were amazing, but didn't realise it themselves. Second show, at Maxwell's [with The Jesus Lizard[11]]: I remember Krist shaving his head because, he told me, it was penance for their blowing the previous show with Iggy Pop in the audience. The next day they shot the first 'In Bloom' video in downtown NYC walking around the seaport.[12] Krist's bald head made shooting the video a bit problematic as he has hair in some shots but not others. At Maxwell's, Kurt destroyed his guitar, and I still have the remnants of it, packed away somewhere. Just the head and the back, the part you play with the strings, and if you touch it, it would splinter."

"I think Kurt had made guitars," says Chad. "He had the necks made, and cut out the bodies. There were three different guitars that were all handmade and spray-painted different colours, like powder blue. So when a guitar got destroyed, we'd just take the guts out and put it in another one."

Krist went on record as saying the Pyramid was one of the worst shows Nirvana ever played, and – for the band anyway – the second night was just as bad. Not least because on the day off in between, Kurt called up Tracy from Amherst, Massachusetts and told her he no longer wanted to live with her. The date was April 27, Tracy's birthday. Kurt wanted to let Tracy down easily but didn't know how, so he suggested they could still 'go out' together even after they moved apart. That was obviously not going to work.

"Kurt was in one of those moods where shit was going bad and he was going to make everyone else suffer," says Carrie Montgomery of the Maxwell's show. "It was really traumatic for me to see that. I just couldn't understand that kind of aggression, depression, anger, but they'd been on tour for a long time. It almost seemed like they weren't going to last. It was really volatile. As I got to know him more later, he was the exact opposite, just so gentle and sensitive."

Carrie laughs: "He liked babies and animals."

The tour progressed through the 9.30 Club in Washington, DC, JC Dobbs in Philadelphia, North Carolina and Tampa Bay, Florida on May 4 – where the band stayed the night at a fan's dad's luxury condo. Krist and Kurt took the opportunity to take some acid and thoroughly abuse their host's hospitality, especially the next morning when they woke and found no one was home.

"They took out all the food, and destroyed the kitchen," recalls Craig Montgomery. "They were frying mayonnaise in the pan, stuff like that. And then Krist starts wandering around naked in the cul-de-sac, shouting at the top of his voice. I was just embarrassed, but I couldn't say anything. No one likes the guy who plays dad. Krist left a $100 bill on the counter as we departed."

Over the next dozen days the tour took in Georgia, Ohio, Oklahoma, Texas and Nebraska – but Chad was nearing the end of his tenure. On May 17, Chad Channing played his final show with Nirvana, in Tad's hometown of Boise, Idaho. A couple of weeks after the band returned home, Kurt and Krist showed up at Chad's house in Bainbridge Island, unannounced, and told him he was out of the band.

"I felt like I'd just killed someone," remarked Kurt.

Before he left, however, there was one last Charles Peterson photo-shoot.

"It took place in my studio, which I was sharing with a screenprinter, Jeff Ross, who was doing all the Sub Pop tour posters and T-shirts," says Peterson. "I had no idea what to do, so I had a white piece of seamless paper and strobe lights. The band came in, and Kurt was like, 'White piece of paper, that's boring. Is there anything we can do, do you think?' I looked around and there was a can of black spray paint sitting there so I said, 'Let's paint something on it.' He's like, 'Cool, cool.' He walks up to it and does a big plus and a minus, and I was like, 'That works.' The interesting thing is, the way they posed for the entire session was Kurt and Krist under the plus and Chad under the minus."

"Chad was great," comments Craig. "I was sad when they fired him. Super-nice, always cheerful . . . Kurt and Krist could be downers sometimes, but Chad would try to keep a positive attitude. They liked Chad personally. They were frustrated with him as a drummer. I think he'd be the first to tell you he wasn't the strongest drummer. He'd drop beats, make mistakes and when the drummer makes a mistake it's kind of glaring."

Did Kurt actually pick on Chad other than the drum kit thing?

"Well, I mean, he *fired* him," Carrie laughs. "No, but he always made Chad feel like he wasn't good enough at his drumming . . ."

He could be really perfectionist. Towards the end of Nirvana, I saw him pick on Krist . . .

"When you're a miserable, unhappy person you're not going to be supportive to anybody else around you," Carrie suggests. "Kurt wanted Chad to play hard and loud, and Chad wouldn't do it. He was like a hippie jazz drummer. I was sad when Chad got fired. He was just a nice little hippie, you know? It was like, just when it looked like something might happen, they kick the guy out who was there through the crappy van tour in New York . . ."

"Those guys were back from tour," Ben Shepherd recalls. "Krist pulled me aside and told me they were booting Chad out of the band. He goes, 'What do you think?' and I go, 'Damn. I don't know, man.'"

It seems like that's when they decided to get serious.

"Mm-hmm," the former Soundgarden bassist agrees. "That's pretty much when I saw the ambition change. I talked to Chad about it and he said it was amiable. Chad's got more spirit than just about anybody you'll ever fucking meet."

"Here's the way I've always looked at it," Chad says now. "Had I somehow changed things, yeah, I'd probably have a few more bucks in my pocket, but I don't know if I'd have been that satisfied. It was cool playing the songs and stuff, but all my life I've never been a drummer's drummer. I've never been single-minded about one particular instrument. I can't be – I'm a songwriter first and foremost. I've always seen music as a whole. And Nirvana was the first band I had ever been in where I didn't have any contribution.

"One time I talked to Krist after Kurt's death, and he said, 'You know, you didn't miss out on that much. The best times were what we had before everything got big, because things got crazy and out of hand.' Back then we had a lot more control over ourselves. Everyone knows when you get hooked up with a major label a good part of the majority of the decision-making in your life goes to them, and you can either deal with it or you can't. A lot of bands and people can't."

The same week Chad parted ways with Nirvana, Kurt broke up with Tracy.

Unbeknown to her, he was already in love with one of her friends, Tobi Vail.

## NOTES

1 Boss Hog were another Pussy Galore spin-off – their 1989 *Drinkin', Lechin' And Lyin'* album on Amphetamine Reptile was a glam sleaze garage classic, notorious for the cover shot of singer Cristina Martinez, naked except for thigh-length boots and arm-length leather gloves.

2 Bastro: art-thrash trio.

3 Jenny Boddy was later the subject of a particularly vitriolic Hole song, 'Jennifer's Body' – written after Courtney wrongly assumed that I was sleeping with her. There's a line in it that goes *"Sleeping with my enemy . . ."*

4 This was one of Kelly's last shows with Dickless. Megan Jasper was her replacement: "It was super-fun and super-goofy and super-retarded," Megan comments. "But I don't think about it a whole lot, to be honest. I'm glad I did it. But I'm also

glad I don't have to dress up like a mermaid any more and scream like I'm being stabbed in the bladder. The good days, right?"

5 Screaming Trees, Tad and the psychedelic grunge band Love Battery also rehearsed there.

6 Eleventh Dream Day were a Neil Young-influenced Chicago rock band.

7 The ex-marine kept a semi-automatic rifle in his AmRep office just in case the world turned *Mad Max* or Minneapolis had its own version of the Rodney King LA riots – the offices were in a 'bad' part of town.

8 CBGBs is the legendary New York home of Seventies punk bands like Ramones, Television and Talking Heads.

9 Birthplace of Seventies rock insurrectionists The Stooges.

10 Not un-coincidentally, the show was being videoed.

11 The Jesus Lizard singer David Yow and bassist David Wm Sims had been in Scratch Acid. The Jesus Lizard played deranged, powerful rock music reminiscent of Nick Cave's The Birthday Party: it was all about the performance – Yow was frequently cited for indecency due to his habit of exposing his penis on stage. The first time I interviewed the Chicago band was in a bar populated by 50-year-old (plus) strippers. 1991's *Goat* is a particular favourite.

12 For the *Sub Pop Video Network Program 1* compilation – 'In Bloom' appeared alongside clips from Beat Happening, Mudhoney, Afghan Whigs and Mark Lanegan, among others.

## CHAPTER 11

# We Take Baths, Not Showers

TOBI Vail first met Kurt Cobain when he was one of the Melvins' entourage. She saw a couple of the early Nirvana shows – Pen Cap Chew, Skid Row – but didn't become good friends with Kurt and Tracy until the spring of '88, when she started visiting because he had ID to buy beer.

"I wasn't into drugs," explains Tobi. "I drank beer a few times a month at parties, but that was it. The Melvins thought I was innocent. I think they liked having me around because it made them feel more corrupt. Dylan [Carlson] used to tell me that I was like a member of the Manson Family. Michelle Phillips[1] was another one I used to get. I had really long, natural brown hair, didn't wear make-up, etc."

The couple started dating officially a week before Tobi's 21st birthday, July 1990 – when Tracy moved out of the Pear St apartment, to go back to Tacoma. Tobi seeing Kurt was problematic at the start – not only was her friend living with him, but Tobi was allergic to cats. And after Tracy left, the flat became even more squalid . . . Piles of washing-up mounted up in the sink, dirty clothes spread across the floor, empty pizza cartons and beer bottles lay discarded all over. Sounds like a typical student house.

So he stayed on in the apartment? How did he afford to keep it?

"He would get cheques," Ian Dickson replies. "They'd get delivered to our [Ian and Nikki's] apartment so we'd see them occasionally. They'd be for a few hundred bucks – but they were working on deals with DGC, and there was some money coming in from touring. They made money selling T-shirts and stuff. The rent wasn't exactly exorbitant – $150 a month probably."

Kurt continued to live at Pear Street for a year after he broke up with Tracy, so someone must have been paying the rent. "Maybe Sub Pop?" queries Tobi. "There was graffiti all over the house after Tracy moved out," she adds. "I was in school and working and in three bands. So I didn't see him much, just sometimes. He would disappear and then come back."

"It was hard," says Ian. "Kurt lived off Tracy. She'd make him little lists of things to do . . ."

Tobi did that. I know because Courtney used to show me them.

"Are you sure they weren't Tracy's lists – that doesn't sound like Tobi to me. I bet Courtney was . . ." Ian breaks off. "I bet it was Tracy."

Tobi and Kurt were in love with one another: Kurt was so nervous the first time he spent an evening with her, he threw up. He admired her, both for her creativity and feminist polemic. Also, Tobi was a total music buff, exhibiting an obsessiveness more commonly associated with male fans. Influenced by Calvin Johnson and Olympian female artists such as Stella Marrs and Lois Maffeo, Tobi started a fanzine, *Jigsaw*, coining the phrase Riot Grrrl in its pages to describe a sense of female empowerment that she saw naturally occurring in people around her, that she also felt was lacking from most independent music of the time. In 1990, punk rock was a very white male, testosterone-led movement – with cool ideals, and some fun music, but exclusionary. It mostly still is.

Tobi wanted to counter that sense of exclusion. With a few like-minded friends, she formed the inspirational punk band Bikini Kill.

"Kurt's taste in women was curious to me," comments Carrie Montgomery. "There didn't seem to be any common denominator except for being creative and smart. Tracy Marander was really nice, easy-going. He'd talk to me about how bad he felt about breaking up with her, because he cared about her a lot, even after he felt it wasn't going to work any more. He just felt she deserved somebody that was around and knew what their future was going to be. It wasn't that she wasn't supportive of his music or his career, but he needed to be free to do what he wanted to do . . . not to sleep around or anything. He worried about her being at home and him being away, just feeling like it wasn't the best time to be in a relationship. He was torn."

Tobi was different from Tracy in terms of how she viewed relationships: where Tracy was nurturing, Tobi considered herself an equal, not to be taken advantage of. It was quite an eye-opener for Kurt, who up to that point had undeniably been influenced by society's insidious belief that it's man who is the leader, woman the comforter.

There isn't a shadow of a doubt that Kurt thrived on Tobi's attitude – even if it did later lead to feelings of inadequacy (which, truth be told, the singer felt towards anyone he considered an equal – it's that very insecurity that fed his artistry). Indeed, he soon found himself in difficulties trying to keep up with her enlightened attitude towards 'dating' – which, in Olympia, didn't really exist as a concept. You hung out with someone if you liked them – and slept with them if you found them attractive.

No one owns anyone.

Not everyone saw it so straightforwardly.

"The way Kurt talked about Tobi," Carrie says, "it seemed like she had him wrapped around her little finger. He thought that she was really cool. He looked up to her and thought she was too good for him. She made him feel he wasn't very important. So I didn't like that. I didn't see what he saw in her. I thought she was bratty. But there again, I didn't really know her . . ."

"Some of us played the Nirvana demo for Calvin [Johnson] early on, and he was not impressed," comments Slim Moon. "Somewhere along the line, Calvin realised that Nirvana was a great band. The Go Team was happening, and him or Tobi pulled Kurt into their orbit. Kurt also had this project with Tobi called The Bathtub Is Real.[2] I have a tape somewhere of one or two songs."

What's it like?

"It sounded like the minimal quiet pop songs that Olympia is known for. Both of them sang; it was really good," Slim replies. "Kurt was still telling Tobi he was going to make a Bathtub Is Real record six months or a year down the road, even though we all knew there was no way that Courtney would allow that to happen. He would get drunk and call her on the phone and say, 'We need to make that Bathtub Is Real record!' "

"Our 'band' was pretty much just us playing music together," Tobi explains. "He would play the songs he was writing, I would play the songs I was writing and we'd record them on my dad's four-track. Sometimes I'd sing on the songs he was writing and play drums on them. Some of the riffs and lyrical ideas turned into Nirvana songs later on. I never got him to sing on any of the songs I was writing, but that was OK, they were my throwaway songs! He did play drums on some of my guitar songs and help me figure out which ones were good. He was really into the fact that I was creative and into music. I don't think he'd ever played music with a girl before. He was super-inspiring and fun to play with.

"Kurt had a lot of cool ideas about how to approach songwriting," she continues. "He told me the first thing you have to do is decide a singing style. This was a big revelation. I realised that you could use your voice as an instrument and that you weren't just stuck with the sound that came out naturally or whatever. I was listening to Yoko Ono[3], Frightwig, early B-52's[4] and The Slits, so my punk singing style came out of this idea. Before that I just sounded like an out-of-tune Heather from Beat

Happening. I didn't have the idea that you could shape the sound of your voice like it was a guitar. We were also listening to The Shaggs, The Marine Girls, The Breeders[5], Pixies, The Beatles, The Raincoats, etc. Sometimes people would try to get me to join Nirvana – and I was like, 'I'd rather not.' We talked about it, and my drumming style was not heavy. Kurt had songs that weren't heavy too, so we'd work on that kind of stuff. Eventually, he figured out a way to work that into Nirvana – the pop element – The Velvet Underground, The Vaselines, Beat Happening, etc.

"We learned a lot playing together," Tobi adds.[6] "I had mostly played with people who didn't know how to play their instruments up to that point, in The Go Team and Doris [Tobi's teen punk band with Tam Orhmund] – which was cool – but I was learning how to manipulate sounds, developing a punk aesthetic with a female sensibility. He was really inspired by that and encouraged me to play with girls. Of course, we both were into The Stooges and Black Flag, too.

"We wrote 'The Bathtub Is Real' on a demo and it got misunderstood as the band's name," she comments. " 'Israeli Donkey', as well . . . I don't know why! This got repeated a lot. I think it was Bathtub, then we realised there already was Steel Pole Bathtub. At the time most people who lived downtown didn't have showers in their apartment, and [The Go Team] had this thing where we'd say, 'In Olympia we take baths, not showers,' as a kind of silly thing. That might be where it came from."

> *Who moved you to thoughts of hatred this year?*
> *"Men I see in the street. I don't know their names"*
>
> – Jon, Huggy Bear

Here's what I hate about '77 punk, and The Sex Pistols in particular: commentators stuck in time, stunting the development of those they're supposed to be informing by their constant referral back to that one moment when everything was still vivid *for them*. Critics speak of how The Sex Pistols were a one-off, something special beyond everything that came after. "It was incredible the impact they had, considering how short a time they were around," reads the standard line. No. What's incredible is how much space has been devoted to one moment that was great, sure, but which would never have taken on such shades of importance if the media weren't composed of such dullards. Likewise, Nirvana and the 'last great revolution of rock'.

Life is about perception. People are often defined by the moment they are first exposed to the outside world and never move on, least of all in their own minds. Twenty years ago, it was the Sixties kids, all going on about the Paris riots and how incredible, never to be repeated, the hippies and *Sgt Pepper* were. (1985 was the exact date critical opinion turned. You could see the new hipsters turning to one another and saying, "*Sgt Pepper*? I don't think so.") Now, it's the turn of Stuart Maconie, Julie Burchill and their forty-something British media chums to relive their youth while stifling everyone else's.

How did the definition 'independent' crystallise and become sterilised into one form of music, one that basically means white boys playing guitars that jangle? Blame the perpetually frightened breed of A&R men stumbling over one another to sign Last Year's Sound. Blame the media. Critics who pride themselves on their impartiality are deluded. Every objective decision made is based round a subjective core judgement, usually informed by others, that there are 'right' and 'wrong' ways to play guitar, or paint a picture, or to read a book. There is no such thing as good art, only good and bad participators. You don't ever have to be ashamed of liking crap like The Strokes and The Doors. If something touches you, it touches you. It doesn't matter how facile or ordinary or manufactured it is.

That phrase from Huggy Bear's[7] classic 1993 single 'Her Jazz' – *"This is happening without your permission"* – I swear that's what rankled their detractors the most. *"Face it,"* screamed Niki with a searing fervour. *"You're old and out of touch."* No one likes being told that. It confused critics no end. Before Riot Grrrl they had been above suspicion. Riot Grrrl formed immediate divisions, refusing to indulge passive consumers trying to figure out what is 'good' and what is 'bad'. The Riot Grrrls just got on with having a glorious good time while simultaneously challenging notions of sexual stereotypes. If you weren't with them, then you were against them and, yes, that *did* make you old and out of touch.

As gender-confusing punk Jayne County once sang, *"If you don't want to fuck me baby, fuck off!"*

Bikini Kill only had one idea – Inspire! Inspire! Empower all females, at least the ones we like! – but they carried it out with such venom, humour and fervour, it didn't matter. Live, they were equal parts intimidation and inspiration. Male dancers were instructed to keep to the sides and the back, leading to charges of (inverse, presumably) sexism. Bikini Kill wanted to even up the odds facing women at shows for once; this was a girl-centric band, make no mistake. Female fans were encouraged to take the microphone and detail when they'd felt abused and/or used by men. The music was storming, driven by the heavy repetition of Tobi's drumming and Kathi Wilcox's bare bass. The token male, Billy (he kept changing his second name), filled in on purposeful, abrasive guitar; but the main focus was singer Kathleen Hanna – her voice resonant of youthful Day-Glo '77 punk, Poly Styrene of X-Ray Spex – cajoling and tormenting, teasing and pleading, in control and always demanding respect.

I never invested Riot Grrrls with sexuality. I don't know why, especially as it was one of their most potent weapons. Early press about Bikini Kill harped on about the fact that Kathleen was a stripper, something she shared in common with Courtney Love. I knew I was doing the women involved a disservice by thinking of them so cerebrally, but perhaps it was the only way I could cope with my own inherent sexism . . . or so I thought back then.

Bikini Kill were hardcore, not punk. That is, their music was formulated along a rigid series of rules and ideologies that didn't brook dissent. It was only later that Kathleen came into her own with the brilliant improvisational low-cost dub-pop of Julie Ruin. Confusion always arises at this point: is Olympia hardcore or punk? It's hardcore, through and through. That's where its sympathies lie. Beat Happening may have been a confrontational – and thus punk – band, but those who followed were already preaching to the converted. Olympia provided a blueprint to live by. Hardcore is about providing an alternative to society's norms, a counterculture. Punk is far more contradictory: it's where the underground meets the mainstream – The Sex Pistols on Bill Grundy, Nirvana on *Saturday Night Live*.

Jack Endino disagrees with some of this interpretation, however. "*Nevermind* was no more of a punk album than [Seventies stadium rock band] Boston's first album," the producer says, "and *Bleach* was no more of a punk album than Deep Purple's *Fireball*. Nirvana's lyrics, pre-*In Utero*, are no more punk than Don McLean's 'American Pie'. They were a classic rock band. I never heard any punk in them whatsoever. I think this is a convenient myth. If their music had actually been punk then it would *not* have broken.[8] The only punk record they made, sorta, was *In Utero*, which was punk in the same way John Lennon's 'Cold Turkey' was punk.[9] Nirvana's live show was no more punk than The Who's – which was sorta punk, admittedly. Did punk break in America with *Who's Next* in 1971 then? It did not. Punk 'broke', sadly, with The Offspring and Green Day."

Kurt may have fallen under Tobi's influence, but that didn't mean he shared her ideas. Disillusioned with Sub Pop – and especially Jon and Bruce's continual brinkmanship, which meant that bands frequently didn't get paid and studio cheques got bounced – he and Krist began looking round for another label. They didn't want to sign to an independent like Touch And Go or SST any more. They couldn't see the point. Instead, inspired by the examples of peers like Soundgarden and Sonic Youth (who had just signed to Geffen), they began looking towards 'the majors'.

Sub Pop was also in the process of looking for a major label distribution deal.

In May 1990, in anticipation of the second album, Sub Pop gave Nirvana a new contract – it was 30 pages long, and tightened up the label's rights considerably. Kurt didn't want to sign it: he and Krist asked Soundgarden's manager Susan Silver for advice. Shocked by the band's antipathy towards the label – among other complaints, the pair mentioned bad promotion for *Bleach*[10], no accounts and bad distribution – she told them they should find themselves a lawyer.

"Kurt was well read," comments Nirvana's former UK PR Anton Brookes. "He read a lot of rock'n'roll books. It's almost like he educated himself how to be a rock star. I remember going with him to a few meetings – it was when they were looking for managers and I'd kind of fallen out with Sub Pop because I'd taken Nirvana's side – and we'd seen a few labels and a particular publisher, and they'd been completely patronising towards him.

"I remember standing outside with Kurt," Anton continues, "and he was smoking, and he said, 'I've got songs on the next record that will be number one. These songs are very poppy and very accessible in a Nirvana way.' He *knew*. When people ask me, 'So Nirvana, did you think they were going to be big?' I'm like, 'Yeah, as big as Sonic Youth at least, as big as the Pixies. Hopefully, they'll sell out the [4,500-capacity] Brixton Academy, and maybe in a few years' time even headline the Reading Festival. They'll be able to stay in Seattle with a good standard of living, with houses and be able to have families, but they'll have to constantly supplement their income by touring.' And anyone who says they said any different is a fucking liar."

Via Susan, Nirvana met up with music business attorney Alan Mintz in LA, a lawyer who specialised in finding deals for new bands. Impressed by their music, if not their attire – Mintz called Nirvana the scruffiest band who ever walked through his door – he started sending out the Butch Vig 'demo' to major labels, looking for deals.

They weren't difficult to find. Sub Pop by this point was generating massive media interest (even the US press was starting to write about the label): "Almost every record company with an A&R man wanted Nirvana for the same reason we did," former Gold Mountain management boss

Danny Goldberg comments, "because Sub Pop were a trendy new company and *Bleach* was one of Sub Pop's most successful records. There were five or six labels clamouring for them – Columbia, a division of Virgin (Charisma), MCA and Atlantic."

"Things got exciting when Nirvana started getting label interest," says Debbi Shane, who by this point was dating Dale Crover. "The bidding war had begun and for them it was fun – free food, free drinks and they could bring their friends. Kurt invited us [Dale and Debbi] out on an A&R dinner once. We went to this Thai restaurant and got really drunk. The A&R guy, to me, was pathetic because he didn't know much about music and didn't get where Nirvana were coming from, but wanted to sign them anyway."

"I was extremely upset and hurt when they started talking to major labels," says Bruce Pavitt, "because I was the last person to hear about it. Everyone was telling me, 'Hey, I was down in Olympia. Nirvana are driving around in a limo and everything.' Which you have to realise, pre-*Nevermind* and in Olympia, you just didn't do.

"In retrospect, everything makes sense," the former Sub Pop boss continues, "but at the time, very few bands had signed to major labels. It was a shock. The label was taking every ounce of energy that we had to keep it together. So I felt that even though we were constantly broke, and in some ways dysfunctional, the least we deserved was to have some honest communication with the group. I would reflect back on memories like being in Rome with Kurt on Nirvana's first tour there, when he had his nervous breakdown and he smashed his only guitar. Jon and I then took some of the last bit of money that we had to buy him a new guitar! Then he got his passport stolen and we helped him get a new passport. Remembering those little things, where you give everything you have to help someone out . . . so for them to do all this shopping and not even tell us – it didn't feel good. It really sucked."

Clearly, you modelled Sub Pop to some degree on lessons learnt in Olympia. And you would have tried to engender a sense of community as part of that.

"Exactly," Bruce nods. "My view was not, 'This is a business and we are going to funnel bands up to major labels and make money.' The label turned into that, but it was a different sensibility that I was bringing to the table. However, I had a business partner that saw things differently, and it was the synergy of our two philosophies that made Sub Pop what it was. My sensibility was much more family oriented: it was about community building, about provoking the system and helping each other out. So, bailing for major labels . . . I was really upset. After that happened, my whole relationship with artists changed. I started to distance myself from the bands."

"I was a little freaked out," comments Jonathan Poneman, "because when we started hearing about this, Bruce and I were in England on a business trip, talking to our distributor about late payment. It seemed much more underhand because it was going on when we were out of the country. I've been asked this question a few times about Nirvana, and the thing that hurts is that people never seem to understand that it wasn't about the business side of things. Business gets worked out. The thing that hurts is the sentimental side: the fact that you are working together for a common goal. You talk to these people regularly, your lives are integrated . . . and suddenly it's like a divorce. Suddenly your life partner comes in, and they're marrying up. It was emotionally traumatic on that level.

"I remember Susan Silver telling me one time, 'Jonathan, Soundgarden's got to move on. I'm sorry that they're not going to be recording with you.'" The label boss bangs on the table for emphasis. "I don't give a shit about that stuff! She was talking to me like, 'Your meal ticket is going away,' and it's like . . . as long as there are talented people in the world, and people who want to hear what talented people have to say, there's a place for me to do what I do. For me, the most essential part of what we do is building relationships. The times when Sub Pop has failed as a label it's because we have not adequately built those relationships, or when it has been more about business than the holistic depth and breadth of what relationships are supposed to be about.

"So that's the thing that stung about Nirvana talking to other people," Poneman finishes. "It wasn't so much . . . even if the business of things had not worked out in the manner in which they did, Sub Pop would have survived, albeit in a completely different way."

So Nirvana was without a drummer. Again.

Wild rumours started to fly round the British music press as to who could fill the slot – the laconic singer of Dinosaur Jr, J. Mascis (J. originally started out as a drummer), Tad Doyle, Dale Crover and Mudhoney's Dan Peters. Dale was asked to stand in for an eight-date tour of the West Coast in August, supporting Sonic Youth, but there was no way Kurt could have convinced Crover to leave the Melvins, even if he'd wanted to.

Just as he had with the demo, Crover agreed to help out[11], under one condition: they were not allowed, under any circumstances, to touch his drums. "He was like, 'You can't ruin my drum kit,'" recalls Debbi. "It was off limits, Dale made that clear to Kurt. More for the fact that Dale couldn't afford to buy a new drum kit."

Dale himself put it more strongly to Michael Azerrad in *Come As You Are*: "Not only did they comply with that request, but they also did not smash one guitar on the tour. I'm glad they didn't do that stuff. It's anti-climactic. Kurt trying to break a guitar – it takes him 15 minutes. By the time it's over, it's like, big deal. I think that's guitar murder. I think guitars have souls. I don't think any of that stuff is cool at all."

"So anyway," continues Debbi, "Nirvana is starting to get big. Chad is out of the band, and Dale toured with them. Everybody knew it was temporary. It was a favour. I went to the Sacramento show. Nirvana was really excited to be opening for Sonic Youth."

The tour's first stop was in Long Beach, California on August 13. Before the tour started, the band stayed a few days in San Francisco at Melvins' singer Buzz Osborne's house where – on Buzz's recommendation – Nirvana checked out Washington, DC band Scream. Scream played solid, catchy songs, like an old school hardcore punk band. "They wanted a heavier drummer than Chad," says Carrie. "I can remember Kurt telling me after the Scream show, 'I wish we could get a drummer like that.'"

The next night, Nirvana and Sonic Youth played at a former brothel in Las Vegas – Youth bassist and tastemaker Kim Gordon was so excited by Nirvana's set she danced down the front. Not everyone was impressed, however: "At the end of the set, there were more people in the parking lot than inside the venue," sniffed one radio person. Three nights later, the bands played at the Casbah in San Diego – a tiny venue built to take about 75 people, but sold out twice over. Drunk Ted from *Flipside* fanzine was in attendance: "It was really weird," he told Carrie Borzillo-Vrenna, "because when Nirvana showed up, Krist and Kurt had totally short hair, and Sub Pop was known for having long hair and playing punk-ish garage music that was authentic. Watching these guys play this totally twisted, hard music with short hair was strange. It was cool, though. They pulled it off."

"On their days off they played little shows to make money, like in San Diego," notes Anton Brookes. "At the party afterwards, I remember Kurt got laid, because we were waiting for him to drive back up to Los Angeles. Krist tried to kidnap a pig. We stopped off at a service station with a farm next to it. Krist was worried the pig was going to be bacon. He tried to catch it with his jumper. He said, 'He can travel with us, life on the road! He'll have stories to tell his piglets! I'm liberating it.'"

The bands then travelled to San Francisco – where past appearances guaranteed an enthusiastic crowd – and Portland, before Nirvana returned to Seattle on August 24, where they played the Moore Theatre, with Julie Cafritz's wired post-Pussy Galore band STP opening.

"I remember going to the Melvins house in San Francisco," recalls Anton. "It was freezing. Buzz and his girlfriend had this big house, like a tiny version of *The Addams Family*, loads of dolls and weird stuff. We sat watching *The Simpsons*. Dale played in his underwear, drum sticks stuffed down his pants. With his black hair he looked really pasty white. We watched *The Simpsons* for hours and hours . . ."

It was while on tour with Dale that Kurt and Krist were introduced to Sonic Youth's manager, the wise-cracking, devilish John Silva[12] – and, through Silva, Danny Goldberg, best known for having gone from being Led Zeppelin's publicist to running their Swansong label in the US.[13]

"I had a management company called Gold Mountain," Goldberg says. "At some point I realised I was out of touch with the next generation of rock'n'roll – I had [bluesy, politically active Seventies singer] Bonnie Raitt, Rickie Lee Jones.[14] I liked [Southern folk blues band] House Of Freaks. Silva was their manager. He was a smart guy who needed a place to work out of. He came with Redd Kross. After six months, we signed Sonic Youth as a client, just before they released *Goo*. That put us on the map. Sonic Youth were held in highest regard. Thurston, in particular, had the most comprehensive awareness of new bands. In essence, he was the greatest A&R person of the moment.

"Sometime during the cycle of touring, Sonic Youth took Nirvana out on some shows," Goldberg continues. "Silva came back enthusing about Nirvana, and Thurston called me saying how great Nirvana was. I had 100 per cent trust in Thurston. If he was excited, I was excited. So I called a lawyer and Nirvana came down to LA and had a meeting with us. Kurt didn't do so much talking, Krist did. I knew we wanted them and they wanted to be with us because they similarly trusted Sonic Youth. It was not a difficult courtship.

"Nirvana didn't like Sub Pop very much," Danny points out. "On one hand Kurt felt he hadn't been paid correctly, and secondly he wanted to reach a big audience. There was no ambiguity. At the first meeting I indicated Sub Pop were OK by us, but they were like, 'We don't want to be on Sub Pop, we want to be on a major. If Sub Pop have to be paid something, fine.' Kurt Cobain wanted to be who he became. He was a fan not only of the Melvins but also of Kiss and AC/DC. They wanted the challenge of reaching the biggest possible audience, no question."

Before Nirvana left to tour with Sonic Youth, however, Sub Pop wanted them to record another single – and Dale was still in San Francisco. And Mudhoney were on the verge of splitting up . . .

"We didn't split up," Dan Peters states. "Steve [Turner, guitarist] wanted to go back to school. I don't know if we ever shot ourselves in the foot, but we definitely whacked ourselves in the foot a few times by not taking advantage of things while we could – but that was Mudhoney all over. It was never our intention to be successful."

In the summer of 1990, Dan bumped into Shelli at The Vogue – and suggested he could fill the vacant Nirvana drum stool. "I had fought my whole life to get to do the stuff I was doing in Mudhoney; I wasn't ready to give it up," he explains. "I was like, 'What the fuck?' I'm 22, 23 years old and I have no skills as far as I don't know how to do anything other than play drums." Surprised and complimented by his proposal, Nirvana agreed. Dan immediately started rehearsing with Kurt and Krist at The Dutchman. Kurt and Krist bought Dan a huge, battered kit to play on, concerned that his compact set wouldn't be able to compete with the sheer volume of their guitars. Dan rejected it all, except for the bass drum.

"It was a big hunk of shit," he succinctly puts it. "If I'd known they were that serious I would have pursued another kit somehow."

From the British perspective, we were pretty pissed off that Dan Peters was leaving Mudhoney to go join Nirvana.

"It was a choice that Steve made," Peters replies curtly.

"By that point I was totally into Nirvana," he continues. "[Matt] Lukin had a copy of the *Blew* EP while we were on tour in Eugene, Oregon. We were supposed to be staying in these people's house, but Matt and me said, 'Fuck that, we'll sleep in the van.' So we sat out there and smoked pot and drank beer and listened to Nirvana. I remember hearing 'Been A Son' and being like, 'Man, that's a fucking great song.' We played it over and over."

How many shows did you do with Nirvana?

"One. One show – and one recording session," the drummer grimaces.

Did you seriously think you were going to be joining Nirvana full-time?

"Yeah. At that point it was up in the air as far as what Mudhoney was doing. If it had worked out, I think I would have stuck with it. They'd come down from Tacoma, hang out, or Krist would come to my house, knock on the door, I'd hop in the van and we'd go down to the practice space. Kurt would be in the back, sleeping. We'd get there, Kurt would wake up, walk into the practice space, plug in his guitar and go, 'I can't hear your drums.' 'Neither can I!' He'd just crank the amp. There was no real hanging out. I think we went out for beers once after a practice. I said, 'Look, what do you guys want? If you're looking for another drummer, let me know, I'll step aside – I don't want to be auditioning.' They were like, 'No, no, no, you're going to be the guy.' "

Did you rehearse 'Teen Spirit' with them?

"No. 'Pay To Play' I played with them. 'In Bloom' I played with them. After I stopped playing with Nirvana I joined Screaming Trees for at least a good full tour. I had a great time with Mark Lanegan. He hadn't drunk for five years and I did a big trip with him and he started drinking again. Unfortunately the drugs came into play with Mark."

'Sliver' was written in a couple of minutes at one of The Dutchman practices with Dan. It was Kurt's poppiest song yet, autobiographical, oddly naïve and Olympia-influenced with its repeated chorus of *"Grandma take me home"* howled over and over again with increasing anguish. It starts off innocuously enough, like The Sonics in a down mood, before exploding in frustration and a welter of electric guitars and feedback. The chorus is as climactic as the verses are sensitive and considered. The kid doesn't want to be left with his grandparents, not eating, not playing – not doing anything. He's not having fun, not at all. He's lonely. He wants to go home. What part of that sentence don't they understand?

"Mom and dad go off somewhere and leave the kid with his grandparents and he gets confused and frightened, he doesn't understand what's happening to him," Kurt explained to *MM* journalist Push in December 1990. "But hey, you mustn't get too worried about him – grandpa doesn't abuse him or anything like that. And in the last verse he wakes up back in his mother's arms."

The single was recorded over the space of 90 minutes during a lunch break in a Tad recording session, at Reciprocal, on July 11: "We called Tad up and asked if we could come over and record the song," Kurt told Push. "We used their instruments while they sat around eating. But that's nothing new. We approached the recording of *Bleach* like it was a radio session. The key to a successful album is to get the fuck out of the studio before you're sick of the songs."

"I don't know why the session was such a rush," recalls Peters. "Jack stuck around and we hopped in behind their instruments. I used Tad's drummer Steve's kit, and the sounds were already up."

'Sliver' was eventually released in the UK in December, thereby once again missing the tour it was supposed to help to promote. It weighed in at a fraction over two minutes and was, as Push suggested, "a hell of a pop song", halfway between two of the poppier numbers on *Bleach*, 'About A Girl' and 'Swap Meet'. For the B-side, the far more ponderous 'Dive' was lifted from the Vig sessions – rounded off on the seven-inch by a sliver of conversation between Jonathan Poneman and a hungover Krist Novoselic.[15]

How was that one gig you played with them?

"It was fun, kind of chaotic, lots of people on stage," Dan replies. It took place at Seattle's Motor Sports Arena on September 22, Nirvana's largest headlining gig yet – in front of 1,500 people, with Melvins, Dwarves and punk band The Derelicts in support. "There was a lot of stagediving. There was a complete lack of security."

One Nirvana biography says that show was the turning point.

"It probably was. It was a huge show. Mudhoney had done a show there before and it was one of the first times that this big old shed area was opened up to random fuck-offs. I was talking to the woman who put the show on about what I thought was my first show – not my only show – and she's like, 'How many backstage passes do you need?' Kurt and Krist were like, 'I need two.' I'm like, 'I need 40.' I got all my friends to the backstage area. Not that there was much going on, but we could bring all the booze we wanted through the back gate. I just wish they'd told me what was up. So my memory of that night is kind of tainted."

Dan Peters thought he was Nirvana's new drummer, especially when, on September 23, he sat in with the band for a photo-shoot for UK music paper *Sounds*. But, unbeknown to Dan, Nirvana already had someone else lined up – Scream's 21-year-old drummer Dave Grohl.

"Kurt called me up to tell me a new drummer was coming to try out," recalls Anton Brookes, "coming up from Washington or LA, I can't remember which."

"There was a lot of shifty stuff I found out about afterwards," Dan says. "I went down to a party the day after I played that show, doing all those pictures for *Sounds*, sitting in on an interview and making an idiot of myself. Dave's in the background sitting there, all like, 'doo be doo'. None of those fucking guys had the balls to tell me. That's what pisses me off. I don't need to feel like an idiot. I'm in fucking Mudhoney. Fuck you guys."

"It wasn't that we were unhappy with Dan's drumming," Kurt told Push. "It was just that Dave has qualities that match our needs a little closer. He takes care of the backing vocals for a start. We were blown away when we saw him playing with Scream, and we agreed that we'd ask him to join Nirvana if we had the chance. Ironically, that chance came a week after we got Danny in. It was a stressful situation, but it now looks like Dan will rejoin Mudhoney and they'll carry on as before. The idea of that band stopping because of Dan coming over to us had caused us considerable distress."

"It never reached the stage of me leaving Mudhoney," Dan states. "We [Nirvana] were supposed to do a tour of England with L7 after Kurt and Krist got back checking out record labels. Kurt called me up and said, 'Looks like we're going to sign with Geffen.' I'm like, 'Well, what's up with this trip to England?' He's like, 'That's what I'm calling about. I just want to let you know that we got another drummer, we've got Dave.' I was like, 'Well, talk to you later,' and hung up. I was more relieved than anything – it didn't exactly feel like I'd been having a bonding session with those guys."

On September 25, a few hours after Dave Grohl auditioned for Nirvana, Kurt travelled down to Olympia to record four songs for Calvin Johnson's *Boy Meets Girl* KAOS radio show. His performance was so impromptu that even Tobi Vail was caught unawares: "I have a tape," she says, "but it cuts off halfway through and you have to change it over and start listening again. It sounds really good, though." It was just Kurt and his acoustic guitar, playing live in the studio: 'Lithium' (sounding remarkably similar in both tone and structure to the recorded version that ended up on *Nevermind*), 'Dumb', 'Been A Son' and a caustic, punk rock-influenced rarity, 'Opinion', the direct lyrics castigating the self-appointed tastemakers and hipsters of Seattle.

Kurt used the opportunity to announce the identity of Nirvana's new drummer: "He's a baby Dale Crover," Kurt told the handful of Calvinists[16] listening. "His name is Dave Grohl and he plays almost as good as Dale. And with a few years' practice, he may even give him a run for his money."

**Addenda 1: Sonic Youth**

Kurt idolised Sonic Youth – how did he act when he met you? Were Nirvana nervous about opening for you on the West Coast?

Lee Ranaldo (Sonic Youth guitarist): "Kurt was shy. He was obviously pleased to be opening for us, but he was 'cool'. It was more fraternal and peer-like than anything else. Our fans reacted very positively to Nirvana from the very first."

Sonic Youth were signed to Gold Mountain management and DGC. Nirvana later signed with both companies. Did Sonic Youth recommend

Nirvana to both companies? Did you have any idea of how popular Nirvana were going to be?

Lee: "It was hard to predict the level of popularity they would achieve – I don't think anyone saw that coming. They saw us in a relatively good situation with both DGC and Gold Mountain – and that was the most important recommendation to them, coming upon all this 'big business' stuff as suddenly as they were. I'd say Dave and Krist were probably more business-minded than Kurt, but I'd never discount him having had strong opinions about all their dealings."

How did you yourself view Nirvana?

Lee: "I thought they were incredibly exciting and, like everyone else, relished their great combination of raw power energy and pop Beatles-esque sensibility."

Where do you see Sonic Youth's influence on Nirvana and the 'Seattle scene'? Did you feel you had certain aspects in common with Nirvana and bands like Mudhoney?

Lee: "If anything, our influence on them, and the Seattle scene, was less musically than about how a band survives in the climate that existed then – few labels, little money, little or no press recognition. What we took from those Pacific Northwest bands – and others like [raw and bluesy Ann Arbor garage-punk band] The Laughing Hyenas, [innovative, metallic Milwaukee band] Die Kreuzen, Dinosaur Jr, etc – was a more 'rockist' approach to the music, which we had all grown up on but which got subsumed in the nature of the NYC music scene, which was at least as interested in experiment and boundary-pushing as it was in blasts of rock'n'roll nostalgia. The 'grunge movement' opened us back up to all the things we loved about such ferocious thrashing music. We were energised by it – and had to compete with it live, which meant raising our music to that task."

**Addenda 2: managers**

"Kurt asked me to manage Nirvana," reveals Candice Pedersen. "We had talked about it before I went to San Francisco in 1990. I think I would have been good at it, but I liked what I was doing at K."

What were they looking for in a manager?

"They were looking for someone who was pragmatic, and who liked them," Pedersen replies. "One of the reasons Kurt and I got along well is that America wants to think there aren't class differences, but there are. And I have life experiences that I shared with Kurt. We just understood each other better. Also, I was fun, and I was sober: that had to help.

"We're all blue collar and below, and that wasn't the case for some of the other people we interacted with. I had quite a long argument with Ian MacKaye about this because he was saying it shouldn't be about money. People who grow up with money always say that because they have safety nets. We don't have safety nets. I don't even know why I thought I could go to college, nobody in my family ever had. I didn't have a dime, my parents didn't have a dime and they actively discouraged me. Both Kurt and me grew up in really white trash ways. My family wasn't quite so trailer trashy because we were hicks. Ian will say how they played word games at the dinner table, or Calvin will talk about how they read certain books, but we ate macaroni and cheese out of the pan. Also, I wasn't the kind of person any of them were going to be attracted to, so there wasn't going to be any confusion in that regard.

"It wasn't like it was well thought out. It wasn't like the band sat down and built up a business plan and realised where they needed to plug in a manager."

## NOTES

1 Impossibly beautiful Michelle is the female Mamas And The Papas singer who wasn't Mama Cass (and also was mother to one of the dreadful whimsical Nineties female trio Wilson Phillips).

2 Dylan Carlson, Tobi and Kurt also grouped together for a Gang Of Four-inspired project featuring Tobi on guitar and vocals, Dylan on bass and Kurt on drums.

3 Yoko Ono's body of experimental Seventies work remains unsurpassed – look no further than the flipside of 'Happy Xmas (War Is Over)' for proof of her extraordinarily moving muse.

4 Athens, Georgia band best known for their monster 1989 hit 'Love Shack' – The B-52's matched Sixties pop ephemera to a dance floor beat and stacked beehive wigs.

5 For the longest time, The Breeders' singer Kim Deal was my definition of rock. She was casual about her genius it was genius. The Breeders' first album, the sparse, Steve Albini-produced *Pod*, appeared in 1990 while Deal's main band, the Pixies, were turning into a lame surf rock parody of themselves.

6 Tobi now sings with righteous Riot Grrrl band Spider And The Webs.

7 Huggy Bear were the British boy/girl counterparts to Bikini Kill – the link came about after I passed along a copy of Bikini Kill's *Revolution Girl Style Now* cassette and fanzine to Huggy members Jon and Jo.

8 Reference to Dave Markey's excellent Sonic Youth tour video documentary, *1991: The Year Punk Broke* – its title itself a reference to the success of Nirvana. Markey was also the man behind *Desperate Teenage Lovedolls*.

9 In other words, Nirvana's third and final album was an exorcism and cry of frustration, partway inspired by success. John Lennon's 'Cold Turkey' is, famously, a reference to the state junkies experience trying to kick heroin.

10 Perhaps a little harsh – as promotion was something that Sub Pop clearly excelled at.

11 Someone should get that man some royalties!

12 John later became manager of The Beastie Boys. Charles Peterson tells a great story about how I once managed to browbeat Silva into clearing a space at the side of the stage during a major Beasties festival appearance for Charles, and Charles alone.

13 In this capacity Danny Goldberg learned the trade from Zeppelin's pugnacious manager Peter Grant who was both feared and respected in equal measure.

14 Rickie Lee Jones is a left wing singer-songwriter best known for the excellent, playful 1979 hit 'Chuck E's In Love'. Went on to host a talk show on Olympia's KAOS radio station.

15 In using recorded conversation, Nirvana – probably unintentionally – paid tribute to Soundgarden, who used a similar device on the outro to their version of 'Sub Pop Rock City' on *Sub Pop 200*.

16 'Calvinist' was a derogatory term devised by either Kurt or Courtney Love to describe all those who'd fallen under the charismatic K records' founder's influence: certainly, Calvin Johnson can inspire almost religious devotion. "The Calvinists are a handful of Olympia residents between the ages of 16 and 50 who wear *Leave It To Beaver* hats and sweaters, worship Calvin and follow him around," Kurt told me sarcastically in 1992. "They leave him gifts, and they have Calvin altars, and candles and effigies of Calvin. There's some weird sex thing going on."

# CHAPTER 12

## Monster Of Rock

*It surprises me that lesser critics are taken in by the seeming slothfulness of bands like Nirvana and Teenage Fanclub*[1] *and mistake it for some kind of attitude problem, or laziness. Sure, that on its own isn't an excuse for anything, but both bands have so many fucking tunes lurking underneath their outer shell it's damn near impossible not to trip over them as they flood out the speakers.*

*Take 'Sliver', for example. Sure, the vocals are lazily throat splitting, the guitars belligerently grungy, the bass up and out of the place . . . but check the melodies, damn fools, check the melodies. The only reason this isn't Single Of The Week is because three even mightier singles were released this week.*[2]

*Got it?*

(Author's review of 'Sliver', *Melody Maker*, December 1, 1990)

DAVE Grohl was born in Warren, Ohio on January 14, 1969.

Dave's father James worked for the Scripps-Howard newspaper franchise. His mother Virginia was a high school English teacher. Dad was an accomplished flautist. Mom had been in singing groups when she was a teen. When he was three, Dave's family – including sister Lisa, three years older – moved to Springfield, North Virginia, a middle-class suburb of the resolutely working-class US capital, Washington, DC, just six miles up the Interstate 95. His parents divorced when he was six, and his mother was left to raise the two kids on her own, schooling them in her liberal world view. Great store was placed on creativity.

"When I was about two years old," Dave recalls, "my parents took me to the Ohio State Fair. My father had a press pass, so we got to sit in the press pit, and I watched The Jackson Five." The drummer laughs. "I have no recollection of it at all."

When Dave was 11, he formed a duo with his friend Larry Hinkle.

Larry would bang kitchenware together while Dave strummed a one-string guitar, recording songs about friends or his dog on a Fairfax County public-issue cassette player. For Christmas 1981, Dave was given a Sixties Silvertone guitar with an inbuilt amp – to be replaced by a black Gibson Les Paul later that spring.

"I played with neighbourhood friends," Grohl says. "I was jamming in garages and basements, playing blues songs and Stones songs, simple shit. And I'd play guitar alone in my room along to this Beatles anthology book my mother gave me for Christmas." He even took lessons for a year or so, before deciding – like Krist and Kurt before him – they didn't really teach him anything about the music itself.

"I was told to [take lessons], because everyone was so sick of hearing 'Smoke On The Water'," he comments wryly.

Dave started playing drums from an early age, but he didn't own a drum kit until he was 17, by which point he'd already been playing drums in bands for three or four years. "The house I grew up in was small," he says, "and I couldn't fit a drum set in it. I'd much rather wait until the drummer in my band went home after practice and I'd sit down and play the drums.

"I didn't really notice the drums until I heard Edgar Winter's [1973 number one bluesy instrumental hit] 'Frankenstein'," Grohl continues. "Up until that point I'd just listen to whatever my parents or my sister were listening to, which was mainly pop music and things like *West Side Story*, Carly Simon[3] and The Beatles. But when I heard 'Frankenstein', I thought, '*Wow*, these musicians are really playing, everything about this song stands out, the riffs, the keyboards, the drums,' and as it was an instrumental, it was all about music.

"That summer, one of my cousins gave me Rush's *2112*.[4] I didn't know how, but when I listened to *2112*, I could tell what each piece of the drum kit was doing. I knew *this* sound was a hi-hat, and this was a ride cymbal, and this was the crash, and these were the small toms, and these were the large toms. I learned about drums through that record: setting my pillows up on my bed and on the floor, and beating along with these big fucking marching sticks I stole from a friend."

It was through another cousin – Tracey Bradford from Evanston, Illinois – that Dave was introduced to punk in the summer of '82. It happened on a family visit. "Tracey was two or three years older than me," Dave explained in a biography for his post-Nirvana band, Foo Fighters. "We showed up at the door, and my aunt called her downstairs. But this wasn't the Tracey I had grown to love. This was punk rock Tracey. Bondage pants, spiked hair, chains, the whole nine yards. It was the most fucking awesome thing I'd ever seen. Those few weeks in Evanston changed my life forever.

"From then on, we were totally punk," he told Michael Azerrad. "We went home and bought [Xeroxed punk bible] *Maximumrocknroll* and tried to figure it all out."

Through Tracey, Dave discovered an entire underground network of punk bands, records and magazines – a far remove from his only other previous experience of the genre, The B-52's on *Saturday Night Live*, and Devo's first album *Q: Are We Not Men? A: We Are Devo!* It was the difference between punk rock and hardcore, fashion over a blueprint for living.

"Before Tracey, the only punk rockers I'd seen were on *Quincy*," Grohl says, referring to the primetime US TV show centred round LA County Medical Examiner Dr Quincy. Dave must have his dates mixed up somehow, because the one-off *Quincy* episode that 'examined' the LA punk subculture came out in December '82. It was essentially a cheesy TV rip-off of Penelope Spheeris' *Decline Of Western Civilization* punk documentary released the previous year.

"Pat Smear [Germs guitarist] did a lot of those type of shows," laughs Dave, "because the punk rock kids in LA, once they realised they could get extra work for money, fucking went for it. I think Courtney [Love] did some too. I think that's how Pat and Courtney met. But that was all I knew about punk rock. When I found out that some of the most legendary hardcore bands were right in my backyard, I flipped out. It took me a while to work out how to find that scene, because it wasn't in nightclubs, it was in community centres and Knights Of Columbus halls."[5]

There were many similarities and connections between the hardcore punks of DC – led by the influential 'straight edge' practitioner, Minor Threat/Fugazi singer Ian MacKaye and his Dischord label – and the punk rock librarians of Olympia. Both sets of musicians were principled and motivated, saw music as a natural extension of their day-to-day lives and vice versa. Both sets eschewed rock's more libidinous excesses and believed in the idea of creating their own culture separate to that of their parents, and the mainstream. The main difference was that while Olympia was rooted in a more liberal, female culture, DC was much more male – apart from the occasional DIY entrepreneur, such as Simple Machines' founder Jenny Toomey.[6]

"I didn't grow up going to rock concerts," Dave explains. "The first live performance of a band on stage that I saw was Naked Raygun[7] back in 1982, in a place called the Cubby Bear in Chicago. I was 13. That was the first show, and I loved it, the intimacy of it, that it seemed so simple, and human and exciting. I talked to the singer and I jumped on someone's head and I felt completely at ease with the band and the audience. It was just a bunch of people having a good time.

"Then I got into punk and hardcore, and that's how I learned how to play drums, from listening to Bad Brains[8] and Minor Threat and nomeansno, mostly all punk rock bands.

"The first time I went to a 'big' concert, was the fucking Monsters of Rock at a stadium in DC," Dave grimaces. "It was Kingdom Come, Metallica, Dokken, Scorpions and Van Halen. And it seemed so unreal to me. This was five or six years after the Naked Raygun gig, five years of going to see Corrosion Of Conformity[9], Bad Brains, MDC, all smaller club gigs, DC hardcore bands, punk bands, metal bands like Trouble and Slayer – a 'big' show to me was 2,500 people. And then seeing this stadium gig, it was taking four seconds for the sound of the snare drum to hit me . . . It made no sense at all."

Ironically enough, this arena rock is the music that Grohl now so successfully plunders in Foo Fighters. Whereas Nirvana always were uneasy playing venues over a certain capacity, Foo Fighters right from the off embraced the corporate, the 'lighters and the King Dome'.

Be that as it may, the young Grohl was well suited to punk: a bratty, hyperactive kid, he started running round town, and smoking dope – "Like a little punk shit," he smiles. Indeed, Dave once estimated that between the ages of 15 and 20 he smoked dope four or five times a day, every single day.

"I'd sit there with a bong in my hand and listen to [Led Zeppelin's] 'Rain Song', figuring out the song structure," he says. "We'd congregate at my friend Barrett [Jones]'s house, and rehearse our band every Friday. Play music and sell pot to one another. But I was a weird, intellectual kind of stoner because I was still vice president of my freshman class." Dave attended Thomas Jefferson High School in Alexandria, Virginia – where his mother taught, and his sister was a senior. Laidback, fun loving, up for the craic, Dave has always been popular.

"Dave was the most hyperactive kid you've ever met," comments Barrett. "Bouncing off the walls, really skinny. Total maniac. He was always breaking stuff of mine. The first time I saw him sleeping, I was amazed."

In the summer of 1984, Dave joined local punks Freak Baby as their guitarist: "Nobody knew who we were," he laughs. "We had a demo tape we sold at a local [punk] record store [Smash]. We'd play shows every now and then." The demo was recorded at Barrett Jones' original Laundry Room studios, in Barrett's parents' house in Arlington. The main control room was in the actual laundry room, while the band played live in Barrett's bedroom, seven feet away.

"The next band was called Mission Impossible," continues Grohl. Mission Impossible played supercharged hardcore: all pent-up teen energy and a welter of drums. "We even did the theme music, it was fucking ridiculous. I was about 15. Dave Smith, our drummer, wasn't so good – so he gave me the sticks, we did a little switcheroo and I started playing the drums.

His new band gathered quite a few plaudits: Ian MacKaye publicly declared his love for them, they supported Trouble Funk[10] at a high school prom, even released a split single with local heroes Lunchmeat[11], distributed by Dischord.

"Mission Impossible broke up and Dave joined Dain Bramage with my housemate and the same bass-player [Dave Smith]," reveals Barrett. The appallingly named Dain Bramage recorded one album, *I Scream Not Coming Down* for LA label Fartblossom. "I recorded a few demos with Dain Bramage in my new house. Bands would play and record in our living room.[12] I had a little walk-in closet that was the control room. That's where I did the first Pussy Galore records [*Groovy Hate Fuck*[13]] and Flat Duo Jets."[14]

"At that point we'd started taking acid and listening to *Houses Of The Holy* [Led Zeppelin's righteous 1973 album, from which 'Rain Song' is taken] every day," explains Dave. "Our singer/guitarist Reuben Radding introduced us to [singer with Seventies NYC art-punks Television] Tom Verlaine, the New York No Wave scene and the post-punk stuff like Mission Of Burma[15] and R.E.M. We didn't fit in with DC bands like Rites Of Spring, Embrace, Beefeater, the whole Revolution Summer thing[16], because we were a rock band with a hardcore rhythm section. That's when I got into the dynamic of a delicate melody over a thunderous rhythm section. Hüsker Dü was the band we got compared to the most."

"Dave had a part-mullet when I first met him," laughs Barrett, "with long hair at the back. The first time he ever picked up drumsticks, he was amazing. He was really rough, but he could play so loose. Dale Crover was Dave's favourite drummer."

Crover, and also Led Zeppelin's wild man thumper John Bonham[17]: "I used to rip him off like crazy," Grohl told Azerrad. Dave drew Bonham's three-circle logo on his drum kit – later, he'd get variations of it tattooed on his arms. "I was just amazed by Bonham's sense of *feel*," Grohl says.

"He's still the best rock drummer in the world. He was such an inspiration. Before that, when I was 13, I gave myself a Black Flag tattoo, prison style, with a needle and pen ink.

"Most of the rock music I enjoyed was kind of aggressive, like early AC/DC," Dave explains. "Really, my first punk rock moment was going to see [AC/DC's] *Let There Be Rock*, the movie. It was the first time I'd felt that energy, like I just wanted to *break* something. Hardcore and punk rock and thrash metal was like a dream come true, taking all of that energy to an extreme. The thing I didn't like about a lot of rock music was the superhuman pretension. I had a Kiss poster, but I didn't think they were a 'good' band. I liked them as comic book characters. But I had an AC/DC poster, and when I looked up at [rhythm guitarist] Malcolm Young, I was like, I wanna be *that* guy, fucking jeans and a T-shirt, he hasn't taken a shower all week, he's drunk and he just plays music for the sake of it."

Who cares if Nirvana could rock and wrote catchy refrains? Anyone can rock and write catchy refrains. Fuck. Give me five minutes and the fingerings to three chords, and I'll write you a song to set the world ablaze. There's nothing smart or clever about having the ability to plug your amplifier into the wall and flick the switch to 'on'. The chords in 'Smells Like Teen Spirit', that famous guitar riff that helped launch a thousand MTV executives' bank balances, are basically Boston's 'More Than A Feeling' updated.

But the reinforcement of rock stereotypes wasn't on Nirvana's agenda, even if it did help shift the units. Nirvana had far more to offer the public than that. Nirvana played punk rock as preached by UK bands like The Raincoats and Slits and The Pastels, not the hardcore of Henry Rollins' Black Flag and Minor Threat. At their finest, at Kurt's finest, Nirvana's music recalled the hurt, overly sensitive soul of punk outcasts like Half Japanese's Jad Fair and Austin idiot savant poet/singer Daniel Johnston.

Nirvana's soulful force came from the female side of Kurt's nature – nourished and fed by Olympian people like Calvin Johnson and Bikini Kill and, yes, even Courtney Love. This wasn't rock in the classic sense, far from it. Kurt might have loved the heavy metal riffs that helped free him from a life of small-town drudgery in Aberdeen but he was also aware that there was a better way than simply to emulate the people creating those riffs.

* * *

In 1986, Dave Grohl joined Scream. The band had started off on Dischord, but by the time Grohl joined, they'd moved to reggae label Ras, and recorded their fourth LP, the Bad Brains-influenced *No More Censorship*. Dave recorded two live albums, and one studio album with the hardcore outfit. "I did one American tour with them in October 1987 as soundman/roadie," states Barrett Jones. "It was really fun. Most of the shows were set up by kids, but the venues were pretty big, like 300–500. One show, at an old casket company in Texas, there was no PA. Some kid tried to bring his own PA – a little guitar amp and a mic. After the show, the promoter didn't want to pay the band, and pulled a gun. Texas is crazy."

"Scream are legendary," explains Grohl. "Most of the DC hardcore scene came from DC and Maryland. In Virginia, you're right there on the Mason/Dixon line. If you go south of DC, you're considered to be in 'the South'. Though I wasn't raised a redneck, I grew up with duck-hunting and pick-up trucks. Virginians were considered a little more bum-fuck than others. The DC hardcore scene was almost impenetrable – it was hard to get into that scene as an outsider.

"But Scream were badass. The first time I saw them was in '83; I was still a kid, and they were so fucking good. They played rock music, but they also played hardcore, influenced by Bad Brains. They'd slip into reggae. They were fucking musical. And they were from Virginia! When I learnt that, I almost lost my fucking mind. They were my idols.

"One day in '86 I walked into our local music store in Fall's Church, Virginia to buy some drumsticks, and on the bulletin board it said, 'Scream: Looking for drummer, call Franz'. Ho-ly shit! I called Franz [Stahl, guitars] up, lied about my age – I was 17 at the time and told him I was 22. He never called back. Eventually, I convinced him to let me audition. He asked me if I wanted to play some covers, some Zeppelin or AC/DC. I said, 'No, let's play some Scream.' I'd seen these guys play a hundred times. We ran through their whole fucking catalogue, note for note. And they asked me to join. I freaked out, because this was a band that had toured Europe and the States several times. I'd never been past Ohio. I had to drop out of high school. It was a little nerve-wracking, but I did it.

"One of the reasons I fell in love with the scene," Grohl continues, "was because it was such a strong community. It was totally independent: all fanzines and tape trading and independent booking agents, stuffing your own sleeves, making your own singles, screening your own T-shirts, stuffing your equipment in a van and sleeping on people's floors, going to Europe and playing squats where you walk in with your equipment in your hand and they're still trying to rig the equipment to the electricity from the building next door. And it was so great, because the motive was so pure. I didn't even care if I ate. I just wanted to play.

"We had a rough ride in Scream, though. We toured America I don't know how many fucking times. We stayed on the road, so we didn't have to work at home. We'd never come home with any money, but while we were out there, we'd get somewhere to sleep, people would feed us, we'd maybe get a couple of beers at every show. And that was fine. But then things started happening in the band, where people would quit because they couldn't take it any more, and then there'd be a replacement, and then they would come back, and then they'd quit again, and back and forth. Some people got fucked up on drugs. I started thinking working at the Furniture Warehouse wasn't so bad. That maybe the seven dollar *per diem* wasn't enough; you can only eat so much Taco Bell. I was smoking more and more cigarettes, and those aren't cheap either. It all came to a head when we were in Los Angeles on our last tour in 1990, and our bass-player split without telling anyone.

"So I called Buzz from the Melvins and said, 'Uh, Skeeter [Thompson, bass] quit again, we're stuck here.' He said, 'What are you gonna do?' I said, 'I have no idea, nobody wants to release a record, and I don't have any money.' I was tiling floors in Costa Mesa coffee shops just to get enough to eat. And he said, 'Have you ever heard of Nirvana? Those guys came to see you play at the I Beam in San Francisco a couple of weeks ago, and they're looking for a drummer, and they commented to me how impressed they were with your drumming. Maybe you should call them.'"

Dave had actually noticed Kurt and Krist after the Scream gig, but he didn't say hi: "I was talking to Buzz and Dale in San Francisco," Grohl told *Vox* journalist Shaun Phillips in 1992. "And there was this real huge, tall guy going, 'Wuh-uh, wuh-uh,' waving his arms like Shaggy imitating Robbie The Robot. And there was another guy sitting in a corner like he was taking a shit."

"Chris, who was 6′ 8″," Grohl told *Mojo* journalist Stevie Chick in 2005, "was all over the room, drinking and laughing, and Kurt, who was 5′ 5″, was so quiet. [Dave still refers to his old bandmate by the name he first knew him, Chris – not Krist.] I remember asking someone, 'Who are those guys? That's Nirvana? You're kidding me, no shit!'"

The three musicians nearly met again shortly afterwards, at a party in Olympia thrown by Slim Moon. "Scream was playing in town and they all came to my party," Slim recalls. Neither Slim nor Kurt thought too much of Scream as people, especially when Dave started making fun of Tobi Vail who was playing on stage that night. Dave disparagingly refers to her performance in *Come As You Are* as that "sad little girl with the bad fucking songs".[18]

"They were real rocker dudes," Kurt stated bluntly. "I hated them. I thought they were assholes." Matters weren't improved when Dave tried to get his Primus[19] tape played.

"So I waited, held on to the phone number," continues Dave. "I felt lost enough as it is, and I'd never imagined moving away from Virginia. After a few more days of starving I thought, what the fuck. I called Chris, and said hello. I asked if they were looking for a drummer, and they said they'd already asked Dan Peters to join. But they said they'd give me a call when they came into town, we'd have some drinks and it would be fun. And that was it.

"They called back that night and said, maybe it's a good idea that you come up and play. I spoke to them a few times, and we talked about music. They both knew and liked Scream. We had a lot in common. We loved everything from Neil Young to Public Enemy, from Black Flag to Black Sabbath. Right off the bat, we seemed compatible. So I went to the record store and bought a copy of *Bleach*, and played it 10 times, and went to U-Haul and bought a big fucking cardboard box. I dismantled my drum kit and telescoped them into a shell, threw my duffle bag in it and duct taped it up, and flew up to Seattle.

"I didn't know what to expect. I only knew Nirvana from the cover of *Bleach*, and they looked like these dirty fucking biker children. I didn't expect them to be as sweet as they were. I'd been to Seattle about two months before I joined Nirvana. My mother was considering retiring and she wanted a report as to its suitability. After I got there I called her and said, 'Seattle's a beautiful city with good people, great food, mountains and oceans.' At that time it hadn't become the most overcrowded city in America. It was progressive, liberal. I loved Seattle, but I didn't know anyone there. So I showed up with my one box, and Chris and Kurt greeted me at the airport."

Trying to be friendly, Dave offered Kurt an apple. "No thanks," Kurt said. "It'll make my teeth bleed."

"We jumped into their old van," Dave continues, "went up to Chris' house and I started living there."

"[Back in DC] my landlady found out about the studio in the house, and flipped out," Barrett Jones recalls. "She showed up one night when I was practising with a band and went, 'AAAAAHHH!' Gave me two weeks to get out of there. That exact same time, Scream fell apart in LA. I was trying to get Dave to come back so we could do our band [Churn] for real and he mentioned this band in Seattle, Nirvana. He said he was going to blow them away. I knew it would happen. I mean, you can't deny his drumming."

"So I moved to Tacoma and lived there for a month and a half with Chris, and then I moved down to Olympia with Kurt," adds Dave. "We lived in this tiny apartment that was just fucking demolished, an absolute fucking dumpster, and I was on a sleeping schedule where I would go to sleep about 6.30 in the morning – the sun never really rises there in the winter months anyway – and wake up maybe around 4.30 in the afternoon, just as the sun was going down.

"We were doing a lot of rehearsing in this barn out in Tacoma [Nirvana's new rehearsal space with brown shag carpet and a massive PA that hissed], and we had no television. It was just a small stack of albums, a four-track, cigarette butts and corndog sticks everywhere. There were nights where it was so quiet, and Kurt was in his bedroom writing lyrics or journals or poetry or whatever, and my home was the couch, which was about four and a half feet long – I'm six feet tall – it was just a fucking nightmare!"

Dave's first show with Nirvana was at the North Shore Surf Club in Olympia on October 11, 1990. The show sold out with just one day's warning. "The Surf Club was a large, empty bar that held probably 300 people," remembers Slim Moon. "The kids were going crazy for Nirvana. Something happened once Dave Grohl joined. Suddenly, they seemed much bigger."

The power blew twice during the opening cover of The Vaselines' 'Son Of A Gun', and Dave was drumming so hard that he broke a snare drum – which Kurt picked up and took to the front of the stage, thereby announcing the arrival of the band's new, and final, drummer.

"If he ever leaves the band, we're breaking up," said Krist.

Still, Grohl's inclusion had been last minute – so last minute that when the band arrived in London for the start of a week-long UK tour with L7, their tour manager Alex Macleod was expecting to see Dan Peters walk through customs, as his name was listed on the itinerary. He wasn't a fan of Grohl's, having already met Scream. "Fuck," thought Dave, when he saw Alex waiting at the gate. "Fuck," thought Alex. Another Peel Session was recorded the day Nirvana arrived, four cover versions: The Wipers' 'D-7', Devo's 'Turnaround' and The Vaselines' 'Molly's Lips' and 'Son Of A

Gun'. The tour was sold out – drawing around 600 people every night, and, at London's Astoria on October 24, over twice that.

"That tour was when I first met Dave," comments Craig Montgomery. "It was like a big breath of fresh air. He was young and fun and funny. He gave them the sound that took them over the top. And his ability to harmonise with Kurt's vocals really improved the live show. He sounded and looked much more solid."

"Dave was a really nice geeky kid, larger than life," says Anton Brookes. "He had a mass of hair with dreadlocks. He had shorts cut down from combat trousers, with long johns underneath. His hands would be moving, doing impressions, taking the piss out of everyone. He was always smiling, very cuddly. He fitted in straight away. They became a rock band when Dave joined. He unified with Kurt and Krist – because for a long time it had just been those two, all the line down from school. He was the final piece in the jigsaw. Not only was he a powerhouse, he gave Nirvana a different dimension."

"I remember Kurt was so fucking psyched about Dave," says Janet Billig.

L7 were a hard-rocking all-female band from LA, sometimes erroneously lumped in with Riot Grrrl – much to their anger, as they viewed it as exclusionary and patronising, although that was better than being called foxcore, a term invented by Sonic Youth's Thurston Moore to describe bands like Babes In Toyland, L7, NYC's trash-loving Lunachicks, Dickless and Hole.

"Nirvana and L7 were always hanging out in the same dressing room, getting drunk and doing crazy things," recalls Craig. "Playing pranks on each other and the venue, and throwing food. Someone punched a hole in a door, or pushed out a panel, and everyone stuck their heads through it and screamed at each other. There was a lot of videotaping going on, people acting out of their heads . . . it really did feel like being at the centre of the universe."

For entertainment, Nirvana had a video recorder with two tapes, Monty Python and *This Is Spinal Tap*, mandatory viewing for any touring rock band.

"Kurt had to conserve his voice," Craig explains. "If he sang too many days in a row he would start being worried about his voice. He never went for singing lessons, not that I know of. I don't think you could sing properly, the way he sang. It ripped his vocal cords to shreds. He was always taking some kind of cough syrup. He was always sick.

"They were still doing their own soundchecks," the soundman adds. "Kurt needed a lot of vocal monitor and it was hard to get enough of him because of how loud they played. The only way to really test it was to do it with him. If you didn't get it checked, then there were going to be feedback problems. That was a continual worry for us."

"Kurt and Krist came over to the house one evening for tea," recalls Anton Brookes. "Kurt had crazy-coloured his hair blue, and was sat there like he'd gone to meet his girlfriend's parents for the first time, strait-laced, very polite. My roommates were all like, 'Oh my God! It's Kurt Cobain!' They wanted to go in, say hello and get autographs, but they were too scared. If they'd had mobile phones they'd have been taking pictures, sending messages saying, 'You won't believe who's here.' Nirvana weren't big yet, but already everyone was going round saying, 'This is the band that's going to make it.'"

It was while the band was in Edinburgh that Kurt met one of his musical heroes, Eugene Kelly of The Vaselines.

"I just have a feeling that they [Eugene and Frances McKee, the two members of The Vaselines] had a really cool relationship," he told me in 1992. "I don't know if that's true or not, but I think it's amazing when a couple can get together and write some of the most beautiful songs I've ever heard. It's like they're sharing their life with people. Eugene and Frances are the [Seventies husband and wife US pop music duo] Captain & Tennille of the underground."

"I was asked to re-form The Vaselines for a Nirvana gig at Carlton Studios," Kelly told *Q* magazine.[20] "I knew they were covering 'Molly's Lips', but I was intrigued to find out why they were so keen on us, because we were incredibly obscure. We didn't know what they'd sound like. When we arrived, their agent approached me and goes, 'Do you want to meet Kurt?' He said that Kurt was nervous about meeting *me*!"

"We all got drunk in Edinburgh on free booze from Island records," recalled their booking agent Russell Warby in the same article. "Fantastic! I slept in the same room with Krist and Craig, and we got really drunk in the Ailsa Craig hotel bar. We'd checked in five people, but in the end about 16 of us stayed. Krist was totally drunk. There was a toilet cubicle in the room, and he climbed up on the roof of it in the middle of the night. I was carrying all the money [Russell was standing in as tour manager, as Alex had a prior commitment] and I was having this dream that all the money was fluttering down on me. I woke up with a scream, covered with paper, and I was thinking, 'My God, the money!' In fact, Krist had found all these leaflets on top of the cubicle and he'd been throwing them in the air, shouting, 'Frou-frou!' That was always known as the Frou-frou Night."

The final night of the tour was in Nottingham on October 27. According to *Melody Maker* photographer Stephen Sweet, who was watching the Trent Polytechnic show from the balcony, the lights were going up and the crowd trudging off home, satiated, when Kurt rushed back on to the stage to announce, "We've got a very special guest for you." The fans raced back down the front, expecting Tad at the very least, only to hear Kurt complete the words, ". . . Everett True from *Melody Maker*."

I stumbled up to the microphone and muttered something about how I'd only play a song if Nirvana played one afterwards. Kurt strapped his left-handed guitar over my shoulder – wrongly – and he and Krist settled behind the drum kit, and started bashing away. We lasted about two minutes into my Sub Pop single 'Do Nuts' until Kurt began to comprehensively trash the drums, at which point I quit my vocal duties and turned around to watch.[21]

Afterwards, someone produced a pair of false eyeball joke sunglasses and Krist filmed everyone wearing them. Drunk as I was, and with Nirvana in support, I convinced L7 that I wasn't in fact the London journalist who'd travelled up to interview them. Man, they were mad when they found out the truth.

"That whole night reminded me of a scene from Tony Hancock's[22] 1962 film *The Rebel*," recalls Sweet. In the film, Hancock plays an office worker trying to escape the nine-to-five rat race. "There's one moment when he's in a room surrounded by these beatnik hip dudes, explaining how everyone where he comes from dresses identically . . . and then the camera pans back, showing everyone around him wearing roll-neck sweaters and dark glasses. And that's what it felt like, being surrounded by all these kids with their long hair and Mudhoney and Nirvana T-shirts."

Tell me about Dave Grohl.

"We were sitting in my bed one evening in Los Angeles and he was playing this guitar like he was somehow a songwriter," recalls Jennifer Finch. "I asked him if he thought there was anything wrong with our relationship, and he said 'No', and I said there was, and could he please leave. I saw him a year after that and he said, 'Did you get the letter I sent you?' I'd never gotten the letter. In 1996 when my father passed away, I found a pile of mail that had been unopened, and I found this letter, and I still have it today; it's unopened. It could have been my house on the hill, Everett."

You knew Dave, right? Did he have a motorbike?

"He moved to Los Angeles with his band Scream," she replies, "and I believe that he had a motorbike at that point. And then he was called to Seattle to perform the duty that he performed."

Do you remember a couple of drunken English people at your show in Nottingham?

"I quite well remember you," the musician laughs. "I didn't understand then that to be in a band you needed to conduct interviews. We were all so young. You know what I remember about that night? The theme of the venue was a dock, and it had chain link. The stage was long, and to get to the dressing room you had to walk up some steps."

Does anything else stand out about that visit to the UK?

"I had a great time staying on afterwards. What else do you want, what are you driving at? That's when Dave and I got together, that's the second time we met. I'd booked his band in Los Angeles, Scream, a couple of years prior, with [LA rock band] Bad Religion. I went to the park, the zoo. I have very cute pictures of me and Dave holding pigeons, like you English do – hold the pigeons and feed the pigeons. We were trying to blend in."

**Addenda 1: Chad vs Dave**

"You can't underestimate how much Dave Grohl brought to that band," says Ian Dickson. "Kurt told me after they toured with Dale, he was like, 'Dale's a great drummer but just won't do what I say, basically. He has no ability to play with anybody but Buzz.' Dave joining the band brought it all together. Dave is a colossal talent. His contribution to *Nevermind* is massively underrated – both in vocals and in drum tracks. And I didn't even like Dave back then!"

"To me, Dave didn't fit into the band," complains early fan Rob Kader. "Especially if they wanted to blast Jason for his heavy metal record collection and then ignore Dave's rock leanings."

"I don't like Grohl's drumming at all," comments Steve Turner. "I like things with a bit more finesse. I like Dan's drumming. I like Chad's drumming for Nirvana, a little sloppier and a little looser. It swung more. Grohl doesn't swing, he bashes."

I think that Dave joining was the crucial moment when Nirvana went from being an Olympia band to a Seattle band – or an LA band.

"LA Band!" the Mudhoney guitarist laughs. "They became pro. They were totally unpredictable with Chad. Sometimes Chad would be really *shitty*. But so would Kurt, so would Krist, you know? But with Dave's big pounding beat behind them, they could do just about anything. He connects more of that innate anger and aggression. What's weird, though, is that the songs got poppier when he joined; they were no longer as sludgy as when they used to imitate the Melvins' song structures. It's a weird dichotomy. I liked them right in the middle when they were switching over, when they did the demos with Chad on the songs from *Nevermind*. That's my favourite stuff."

How would you compare Dave Grohl to Chad Channing?

"Simpler, harder hitting," replies Jack Endino. "There wasn't a lot of difference at the end. Chad turned into a really good drummer. Dave himself has pointed out repeatedly that, on *Nevermind*, he was playing Chad's drum parts. Chad had a good musical sense. He knew what to play and how to play it. He's very underrated. The only thing he lacked was Dave's power.

"Grohl had power; nothing fancy, but very efficient," Endino adds. "The bare minimum but played really well. He always hits two cymbals at once. Everything he does is extra. You'll see his drum set shaking when he plays. Chad was a nice, pleasant, short fellow while Dave Grohl has a very animal, Neanderthal vibe. You just feel like he's smashing people's heads as he's playing. They got that violent energy from Dave."

**Addenda 2: Olympia vs Seattle (reprise)**

"If there's any one city that can claim them, it has to be Olympia," says Slim Moon. "They lived in Olympia; they left Aberdeen the instant they could. The whole career of the band from the time that they recorded their first demo to *Nevermind* breaking as a number one hit, Kurt lived in Olympia. So you could call them an Aberdeen band if you really insist, but you can't call them a Seattle band at all. Seattle has no claim to them unless [Smiths singer] Morrissey is a Los Angeles artist because he moved there at the end of his career. It's ridiculous to call Nirvana a Seattle band.

"Another way that I think you can claim Nirvana as an Olympia band is the massive transformation they underwent from the days of 'Beeswax' and the original demo," the kill rock stars boss continues. "At first it was just about having the structure of Melvins and Scratch Acid. Kurt had a pop sensibility from day one, but he didn't unleash it until it became OK to do so, when he was around people that embraced the pop sensibility. He once played me the first song he ever wrote and it sounded totally like Boston. It was a hard rock anthem. It was a pop song. It was a little heavy, but it was a pop song with really good hooks. He backed away from hooks because it wasn't cool when he was loving Scratch Acid."

So Olympia gave him the confidence to rediscover the . . .

"Yeah, he was in project bands with Tobi and he was in The Go Team, and that's where he started doing stuff that was catchy again. 'About A

Girl' came out of that experience. The first catchy songs he wrote were the acoustic, quiet, minimal songs. He snuck back into the big rock stuff after that. 'Sliver' is like the bridge between Olympia and 'Smells Like Teen Spirit': on one hand it has a totally powerful guitar line, but then the lyrics are totally Olympia – the whole *'Grandma take me home'*.

"We can't sell Seattle short, though. The opening rhythm of 'Smells Like Teen Spirit' is pure Mudhoney. To me, it's almost a Mudhoney rip-off. Kurt felt fairly comfortable being lumped in with the Sub Pop sound. He consciously wrote songs that were in the same style as Mudhoney and Tad and Swallow. And Mudhoney were by far the best of those bands."

But Olympia gave his music a more feminine aspect . . .

"If he hadn't lived in Olympia, he probably wouldn't have written 'Rape Me' and stuff like that. A lot of the bands that involved women were musically more progressive and interesting. That was a last minute influence on their music, though. That's not the whole three years they lived in Olympia. That's the last six months of what was happening in Kurt's life while the songs for *Nevermind* were being written. There's the well-known story of the title of 'Smells Like Teen Spirit' being suggested by Kathleen Hanna . . ."

## NOTES

1 Teenage Fanclub are a Scots band, influenced by Dinosaur Jr's heavy riffs and doomed Seventies country rockers Big Star, part of the same Glasgow scene that spawned The Vaselines and The Pastels. Their 1991 album *Bandwagonesque* was a massive personal favourite, recorded on to the other side of my *Nevermind* advance tape – and played back-to-back wherever I went.

2 In case you're wondering: the other three Singles Of The Week were Madonna's salacious 'Justify My Love', Afghan Whigs' anguished post-Replacements Sub Pop single 'Retarded' and a reissue of Doris Day's 'Winter Wonderland'.

3 You know . . . bleedin' 'You're So Vain' . . .

4 *2112* was the legendary 1976 concept album from the bloated Canadian rockers – it's the future, all rock music is banned, then a boy discovers a guitar underneath a waterfall . . . Eventually he commits suicide. In my original review of *Nevermind* I ironically compared Nirvana to Rush, because they were a trio.

5 Big old meeting halls owned by Fraternal and Social organisations typically associated with Labour or Political or Charitable movements in the early 20th century.

6 Simple Machines and its brother label TeenBeat were home to Toomey's Tsunami and to Mark E. Robinson's equally poppy Unrest, among plenty of other International Pop Underground/punk bands such as Superchunk, Lungfish, Eggs,

Versus and the all-girl Scrawl. Initially, Simple Machines favoured beautifully packaged seven-inch EPs, and cassette-only releases.

7 Naked Raygun: mid-Eighties melodic and art-damaged Chicago punk band.

8 Bad Brains were an extremely influential Eighties US hardcore band that played a whirlwind barrage of thrash and reggae-influenced tunes. Could make Black Flag sound like Destiny's Child.

9 Corrosion Of Conformity: a North Carolina punk band – one of the many that blurred the lines between thrash and all-out metal.

10 In the early Eighties, Trouble Funk ripped up the dance floors of their native DC with the sound of 'go-go' – full-on blend of uptempo Seventies funk and Sixties-style horns.

11 Lunchmeat became Soulside, who eventually became Touch And Go artists Girls Against Boys. Imagine if Psychedelic Furs' singer Richard Butler, instead of slumming it round art galleries all his life, had grown up hanging out with Ian MacKaye and Steve Albini.

12 Similar to Jack White's Third Man studios set-up – which was based in the front room of his house.

13 *Groovy Hate Fuck* is screeching, muffled, feedback-drenched, offensive, minimal . . . now that's what I call NYC art punk!

14 Stripped-down rockabilly. As the name suggests, a duo. Flat Duo Jets were a big influence on The White Stripes.

15 Boston, MA band Mission Of Burma ploughed some mighty riffs indeed in the early Eighties – modern classical music meets The MC5. 1981's *Signals, Calls And Marches* EP, featuring the claustrophobic, jagged 'That's When I Reach For My Revolver', is the one to buy.

16 'Revolution Summer' is a reference to an attempt made by the DC punk community in the summer of 1985 to distance themselves from their more meat-headed, violent members by slowing down the frenetic thrash into more melodic, introspective music. The three bands Dave names were prime movers in this change – Rites Of Spring, in particular, have been credited with helping invent 'emo'.

17 The White Stripes' drummer Meg White has been called a 'baby Bonham' – shades of Kurt announcing Grohl as a 'baby Crover' on KAOS radio.

18 Indicating perhaps why some Nirvana fans prefer Chad to Dave – because he understood where Krist and Kurt came from.

19 Don't even ask! Primus ploughed the lowest form of 'wacky' collegiate funk metal.

20 Eugene Kelly went on to form the more straight-ahead rock band Captain America, later to change their name to Eugenius after Captain America's comic book company, Marvel Comics, threatened legal action. That his band would be offered a record deal was put beyond all doubt once Kurt started wearing a Captain America T-shirt in photo shoots.

21 I have a recording of this show. The song is unlistenable, a deluge of feedback and off-time screaming.

22 Lachrymose British TV comedian, Tony Hancock was best known for his portrayal of the doleful yet caustic everyman. He reminds me a little of Jonathan Poneman.

## CHAPTER 13

# Angels In The Snow

"I DIDN'T meet Kurt officially until I moved to Olympia," says Seattle resident Cheryl Arnold. "I was staying in the Martin, and I went over to Kathleen [Hanna]'s apartment to bum a cigarette, and there were a couple people there, Mikey Dees, Kurt and Kathleen . . . It was snowing out and Calvin was out of town so I was staying at his apartment, but I couldn't sleep. I had really bad insomnia, so I was just going to walk to my mom's house, and Kurt came over while I was putting my shoes on and asked if he could walk me home. And I was like, 'Heh heh . . . *of course!!!*' "

He was cute?

"Oh my *god*, he was so cute. I was totally crushed out on him from the first time I met him. He had beautiful blue eyes, but there was something about him that . . . I don't know how to explain it. Like you wanted to find out what the secret was. It was December 1990; right before Christmas. I think there was a Christmas party at the Martin."

When he walked you home what did you talk about?

"I don't know, shit! You want me to remember what I talked about 15 years ago? I have no idea."

So you started hanging out after that?

"Yeah."

People thought you were going out, right?

"I don't know what people thought." Cheryl laughs. "I'm sure some people may have thought we were going out, yeah."

Did you travel with Kurt anywhere?

"No. Well, we went to Aberdeen. We never got on any planes. I'd been to Aberdeen before, just driving through to go to the ocean. Aberdeen was dead. We went to meet his mom and his little sister. They lived in a normal little house. Aberdeen's a weird, real small town."

What kind of stuff did you do with Kurt?

"Uh . . . we ate chocolate cream pie. Wrestled. I don't know . . . rented movies? *Texas Chainsaw Massacre.* He kept turtles. I'm sure he loved them at some point, but he told me they annoyed him because all they did was float up to the top and then float back down and then back up, all day long. His apartment was really messy, full of pizza boxes. He liked to eat lots of pizza."

He had a pretty particular diet, didn't he?

"Yeah. Pizza. Chocolate. Candy. He had a really fucked up stomach. He was in pain all the time. He liked cold cereal, like Fruity Pebbles . . . and pizza."

Did you see any signs of narcolepsy?

"You're kidding me. Oh, that's funny. He also had Tourettes."

Did you go to Nirvana shows with him?

"A couple. I don't know if we ever went in the same car together. Kurt and me didn't go 'out' a lot. We just hung out and stayed in: lots of craziness. We were young, you know? We did lots of crazy things. You know, Everett – what would you do on a typical crazy night?"

I can't remember.

"*Exactly*. Getting drunk and, you know, 'Woo-hoo,' shooting BB guns and dancing around in weird high-heel platform shoes. Throwing eggs at cars. All the typical stuff youngsters do . . . "

Did Kurt dress up in women's clothes?

"Doesn't everybody? I don't know if it has anything to do with them being women's clothes. People like to play dress up. I know I do!"

Me too.

"I went to see a demolition derby with Kurt and Dylan. It was somewhere north of here [Seattle]. Monroe? The night before, Kurt and I were going to drive to the ocean and spend the night there, but we didn't realise it was the night before the 4th of July and that everybody and their dog goes to the ocean for the 4th of July. So all the hotel rooms were booked, and we had to drive back into Aberdeen and got the last room in this shitty motel called The Flamingo. They'd just shampooed the carpet, so we had to jump from the couch to the bed so we didn't get our feet wet. We drove around in the car a lot. He had a Falcon or a Valiant. He didn't like to drive very much so I drove a lot. Went to the drive-in movies in between Olympia and Aberdeen."

Did you drive up to Seattle with him?

"Yeah. We were supposed to go see Hole one night and only made it to Tacoma."

Was that before Kurt met Courtney?

"I don't know. Why don't you tell me . . . *Everett*?" Cheryl places emphasis on the final word, aware that I know more than she does. "Yes, I think so."

Did you hang out with Kurt after he met Courtney?

"Maybe for a little while. Kurt and I stopped hanging out in August '91. He had this awesome painting of Iggy Pop that I wanted. I never saw him doing drawing or anything. We hung out with Ian [Dickson] a lot, Dylan a bit. Dave [Grohl] was sleeping on Kurt's floor for a while."

How was that?

"Fine." Cheryl laughs. "I wasn't the one that had to sleep on Kurt's floor. I don't know how it was for him. He might have hated it. One time, Dave dumped a jar of glitter on us . . . and glitter doesn't go away. It was in my ears, stuck to my scalp for weeks – up your nose, in your ears, not to mention various other nooks and crannies. It's like sand, only worse. It was awful."

What's the hit that you get off of heroin?

"Very warm and very euphoric and very slow," replies Frances Bean Cobain's old nanny Cali De Witt. "It's a downer. It doesn't amplify anything. It dulls all the problems and all the screaming and the yelling in your mind. It just brings you to a blissful state."

How long does it last for?

"Depending on how much you're using, it should last a few hours. It's pretty much the exact opposite of coke."

Dave moved into Pear Street, Olympia on Nirvana's return from the UK.

The same week, Kurt and Krist flew down to LA, courtesy of MCA, whose A&R man Bret Hartman was keen to sign Nirvana. One meeting with the company's president was enough to convince them it was a bad choice. He behaved with the typical arrogance of his breed[1], being both rude and dismissive – the encounter lasted seconds. So the pair took advantage of being in LA and visited Gold Mountain again. They appreciated John Silva's enthusiasm for underground rock music – he owned a large seven-inch collection and had once shared an apartment with Dead Kennedys' singer Jello Biafra – and the fact that Danny Goldberg previously worked with Led Zeppelin.

"Dave Grohl was the big Zeppelin fan," recalls Goldberg, "although I later learnt that Kurt was as well. Grohl was obsessed with [Zep drummer] John Bonham and wanted to hear stories about him. John [Silva] wanted me to talk about my activism at the ACLU [Goldberg was president of the

South California branch of the American Civil Liberties Union], which was something that resonated with the guys. I felt we needed to pitch them on why we were good managers, but in retrospect I think they'd already decided because of Sonic Youth."

Nirvana signed with Gold Mountain after Silva came down to Olympia to take the band out for dinner. It wasn't as straightforward as all that, though. While Silva and the others waited in the restaurant for what felt like hours, Kurt rode a tiny children's Swinger bicycle round in the Washington State Lottery car park. The bicycle was so small he had to hunch over it with his knees almost up to his neck. Eventually, Kurt turned up and demanded that Silva come with him to see Beat Happening play across town. Silva agreed and realised he needed to enthuse about Calvin's band in front of Kurt – even though their very presence on stage ran alien to everything the savvy businessman liked about music. (No bass!) He thus passed Kurt's inspection.

The bicycle had been bought a few days before, together with a couple of BB guns, some Pixelvision video cameras, a Nintendo games system and Evel Knievel[2] action figures from Toys 'Я' Us. The total came to nearly a thousand bucks; and was paid for out of Kurt's $3,000 share of Nirvana's advance from the Virgin publishing money, the band's first big cheque.[3] "He bought crap basically," admitted Joe Preston, who was with Kurt at the time, "junk he could destroy." The gun was used to shoot out the windows of the Washington State Lottery building across the street from Kurt's apartment.

Gold Mountain started sending Kurt a retainer of $1,000 a month. Goldberg told Nirvana that their best bet would be to sign with Geffen: "They'd just signed Sonic Youth, so I knew they had people who were tuned into the music – Mark Kates with his access to college radio, Sonic Youth's A&R person Gary Gersh, Ray Farrell who was sensitive to independent retailers . . ." the manager explains. "Culturally, Geffen had a lot of people who really understood the aesthetics of the newer generation of rock'n'roll. And they were willing to pay whatever anyone else offered.

"Krist did much of the talking initially," Goldberg continues. "Kurt only really started talking to me around the third time we met. John had told me they wanted to do a poster based round an eye chart. I thought it was hackneyed, and John must've told Kurt, because he cornered me and asked why. The level of intensity he brought to the conversation made me realise how serious he was. That was the first glimmer I got into how focused he was."

Grohl's upbeat personality was to prove a relief to Kurt – who, over the summer, had become more withdrawn, troubled by his relationship with Tobi. Before Dave's arrival, Kurt had taken to staring into space for hours, speaking only when he was spoken to – retreating behind a barrier of silence (known as J. Mascis' Fifth Amendment, after the Dinosaur Jr's singer's legendary reluctance to answer questions in interviews). He claimed to be suffering from narcolepsy. He wasn't, but it was a useful defence mechanism. In sharp contrast to his relationship with Tracy, Kurt wanted to settle down with Tobi – but Tobi was too independent, despite her love for Kurt.

"There was a time that Dale [Crover] and I went over to Kurt's house, and Tobi was there," recalls Debbi Shane. "All four of us were super-shy and uncomfortable. Kurt asked Tobi to make some macaroni and cheese. There was a bottle of whiskey in the kitchen; I took a shot because it was a really weird, awkward night. Nobody could talk. Kurt wanted to start bands with everybody[4] – and because we were all sitting looking at the floor, not saying anything, he thought that should be the photo."

"Krist and Kurt had more of a co-dependent relationship and Kurt and Dave didn't," explains Carrie Montgomery. "Dave was just Dave. He was young and cocky and didn't have anything to lose. He knew that his place was cemented in the band. Kurt was never going to get rid of Dave. He was like a young rocker dude; dirt bike on tour, get a tattoo at every show, kind of guy. Those guys had a little hip bachelor pad down there. They had a lot of people in and out. Cheryl was down at their place a lot. They were always playing video games and eating hot dogs and junk food and being gross . . ."

Dave taught Kurt how to do rudimentary home-made tattoos with India ink and a needle. This in turn inspired Kurt to go along to an Olympia tattoo parlour to have a proper tattoo done. With Candice Pedersen along as support, he had the K logo (a K inside a shield) tattooed on his arm.

The choice of tattoo surprised some of his friends.

"I think he liked the records K distributed better than the records they put out," Dylan Carlson remarked. Indeed, K's distribution – often releases from cassette-centric imprints like Simple Machines, the UK's Bi-Joopiter label and like-minded International Pop Underground labels – was exemplary, a real education for anyone looking to discover the vast undercurrent of music bubbling up in America's cities and heartlands in 1990, separate to the mainstream. Superchunk[5], Polvo, Sebadoh[6], Shonen Knife, Australian pop band The Cannanes, Gravel . . . these were all bands

I discovered via Calvin Johnson's goldmine of a storeroom just across the road from the Capital Theater, upstairs in a dilapidated building.

"We went up to Aberdeen for Christmas," says Debbi. "Krist and Shelli were there, and Kurt went because he wanted to see his little sister. In Aberdeen there's nothing to do. We piled into a car and went out for coffee and played those pull-tab things, and I won $30. The next day Kurt and I drove back to Olympia. Kurt wanted to get back to see Tobi and just to get back home. He was obsessed with Dinosaur Jr. He wanted to know everything about J. Mascis."

Rightly so – Dinosaur Jr were a huge influence on the Seattle scene. The description that was applied to grunge early on – 'hard music played to a slow tempo' – could have been designed for Dinosaur. The opening song on 1988's *Bug*, 'Freak Scene', invented the slacker generation. J. plays guitar like he skis: effortlessly and fully in control. The song slows down, catches on fire, whispers sweet harmony and then starts blowing a tornado. *"So fucked I can't believe it/ If there's a way I wish you'd see it,"* J. sings with heavy resignation, a sentiment Nirvana could only echo with their *"I found it hard/ So hard to find/ Oh well whatever, never mind"* line from 'Smells Like Teen Spirit'. *"Don't let me fuck up will you?"* J. pleads, helpless in his slumber. *"Because when I need a friend, it's still you."*

The Holy Trinity in the late Eighties was Dinosaur Jr, Steve Albini's Big Black and Sonic Youth. The second group was always too in thrall to the jagged post-punk rigours of UK 1979; the third made pure art-rock nirvana, unobtainable to all but the most gifted – it was left to the shy Amherst, Massachusetts trio to supply the necessary primeval volume for the grunge generation to come.

"I remember Kim Gordon saying that [Dinosaur's second album] *Youre Living All Over Me* [1987] could've gone huge like *Nevermind* if the production was a little cleaner," mused ex-Dinosaur Jr bassist/Sebadoh singer Lou Barlow to *Loose Lips Sink Ships* editor Stevie Chick. "People would go buy the exact same equipment J. used, the same amps and pedals. He embraced the Marshall Stack as something that could be expressive, not some bludgeoning heavy metal crap. I was reading some crappy *Rolling Stone* 100 Greatest Guitarists list a while back; Kurt Cobain was in there, Kevin Shields [My Bloody Valentine], even Frank fuckin' Black [Pixies], but not J. And he was so fucking influential. He was the progenitor of that style.

"I remember hearing 'Smells Like Teen Spirit' was influenced by the Pixies," Barlow told me. "I thought, who the hell is influenced by the

Pixies?" He laughs. "Why would anyone want to be influenced by the Pixies? It's beyond me. I thought Nirvana were like a Sub Pop singles grunge band. I didn't hear any Dinosaur. They were more like Melvins and whatever heavy metal shit they were into up in Seattle. I even thought 'Smells Like Teen Spirit' was Metallica when I first heard it. I was like, wow! This is a really good new Metallica song!"

Man, Dinosaur Jr could be loud. Walking into one of their early gigs, you could almost physically feel the waves of volume. But loudness wasn't all – Dinosaur Jr's first three albums have a base passion to match the pyrotechnics, and an inventiveness that is startling to hear 20 years on. Their debut album, 1985's *Dinosaur*, is all over the shop – but in a brilliant, spontaneous way, recorded on the cheap after Homestead boss Gerard Cosloy informed J. he'd release anything Mascis recorded. Lacerating screams fade to indie mumbles: New Wave guitar signatures melt into horrific feedback-laden guitar solos melt into self-pitying bedroom introspection. And throughout, the lyrics are shot through with a 'loser' sensibility that later proved so popular it sold a million Sub Pop records.

Grohl was like a husband to Kurt – tidying up after him, feeding him, filling the role that both Krist and Tracy had taken on earlier. "The house became boy-land," laughs Nikki McClure. "Dave and Kurt started to have this real married couple vibe to their relationship." Grohl dated Kathleen Hanna for a couple of weeks, and the Nirvana/Bikini Kill couples briefly socialised together, skateboarding and indulging in the occasional spot of vandalism. It was during one of these nights that Hanna spray-painted "Kurt smells like Teen Spirit" on his bedroom wall – referring to the brand of deodorant Tobi used to wear.

Kurt was still wracked by self-doubt, though – conflicted by his desire to sell millions of records and by the attitude of his Olympia/K records friends. In Michael Azerrad's biography, there's a telling passage where Kurt reveals that he felt signing to a label came down to a straight choice: K or Geffen. "We were really close to signing to K," Kurt told Azerrad, clearly deluding himself. It's unlikely that Calvin would've ever signed Nirvana, however much he liked them. For one, K didn't have contracts. For two, Nirvana were too traditionally rock. (They had a bassist, for Christ's sake!) For three, Calvin would've been aware of Kurt's ambition and known there was no way K could help him to realise it. Still, that didn't stop Kurt from dreaming – the idea was to follow The Sex Pistols' model, wherein they would sign to a major label for a million bucks, split up, change their name and sign to K.

Kurt was lonely. He felt excluded by Tobi's self-assurance and youth (she was 21, he was 23 but she made him feel older). He wanted something more. And as much as he felt energised by her creativity, Kurt Cobain was essentially a solo creator. The couple would help each other write songs but they weren't a songwriting team. "He was in the process of writing the whole next two albums of songs," Tobi recalls. "He'd always be revising stuff – he wouldn't have all the words, but he'd sing them anyway." Kurt and Tobi would discuss one another's songs, but not in a, "This means this, this means that, kind of way," Vail explains. "He didn't talk a lot about lyrics. He would really argue with you if you said something sucked. But he hated people who agreed with him for the sake of it. And he'd probably be secretly agreeing with you later."

Self-hating and dissatisfied with life in Olympia but not wanting to admit it, and frustrated that his relationship with Tobi wasn't progressing as he wanted, Kurt decided to split up with her. Even though the couple had agreed they were in love with one another. It was October 1990.

"He was a wreck," says Dave Grohl.

"Contrary to popular belief, he broke up with me," Tobi states firmly. "The idea that I broke his heart, and that he was helpless and fatally wounded by that, is just stupid romantic tripe. I am sick of being the girl who is blamed for his suffering. That idea doesn't come from anything that really happened. It comes from *The Sorrows Of Young Werther*."[7]

It was Kurt who split up with Tobi. Not the other way around.

"I read stuff from time to time," says Tobi. "Nothing that I've read is like anything I recognised that happened. I wasn't there for all of it but I don't recognise anything from when I was there."

What's missing?

"The way people write the story is like it was tragic from the beginning," Tobi replies. "They try and make it like a Greek myth when it was a lot more random. People say that Kurt was always suicidal – but isn't that true of a lot of people you know? It's another matter whether you do it. It can happen that if you go through a really bad time in your life you actually do it; but I know a lot of people who are crazier than Kurt was and who have lived longer. I really don't hold with the whole idea of the inevitability of it; that people are born to end up committing suicide, or even born to write certain songs."

Hurt, and plagued by insecurity, Kurt was in the perfect frame of mind to write more songs. His new numbers were self-indulgent and full of loathing – both for himself and for others, where anyone could make sense of them: angry, petulant and heartbroken. Although it was Kurt who'd broken up with Tobi, he was reacting as if it had been the other way round. The fact the split wasn't clean increased the misery on both sides.

'Aneurysm' was one of the first Nirvana songs to address the relationship, having been written before the break-up; *"Love you so much/ It makes me sick,"* Kurt pleaded, referring back to the first night he spent with Tobi, unashamed to sound neurotic. *"One baby to another/ Says I'm lucky to have met you,"* he wrote in 'Drain You', touching on the way that love can make its participants feel like they're children again, such is the feeling of wonder and awe engendered. There was 'Lithium', 'Lounge Act' – songs touched by Tobi's presence, with their references to secret understandings and pacts. And of course there was 'Smells Like Teen Spirit' with its famous *"Over-bored and self-assured"* reference to both Tobi *and* Kurt's personalities. "Boredom: the desire for desires," as Russian philosopher Leo Tolstoy once wrote. What was there to do in life, now that the adults had grabbed all the fun adolescent stuff for themselves? No point growing up, that's a crock.

"The songs were confusing," comments Tobi. "Who really knows what they are about? They sound great and some of the imagery is strong, but as far as them being about any one person or thing or situation – it's not clear, is it? I think people respond to the emotional quality of his voice and the phrasing of his words rather than to the actual meaning of the songs. They seem to be written in code. Do they make sense? On some level they do. 'Smells Like Teen Spirit' was supposed to be called 'Anthem', but Bikini Kill had a song called 'Anthem' and we got in a big argument and I won so he had to change it.[8] Our song never came out, but it was quite good."

The original draft of 'Teen Spirit' included a line later picked up on by his future wife Courtney Love, used to highlight her status as Rock Royalty with her husband – *"Who will be the king and queen of the outcast teens?"*

Clearly, it was intended for Tobi.

Now we come to one of the nastiest of Nirvana myths. Kurt Cobain started taking heroin directly as a result of his break-up with Tobi.

Never mind that in the official biography, Cobain claimed to have dabbled with hard drugs while living back in Aberdeen (this last fact is unsupported, and was probably invented by Kurt to shift some of the focus away from his future wife's involvement in his usage). Never mind that it was his decision to try the drug that may well have contributed to the breakdown of relations between himself and Tobi. Not the other way around.

The book says she broke his heart.

"So fucking what?" Slim Moon replies. "That may or may not be true. People's hearts get broken every fucking day. He was a junkie before his heart got broken, and if people try to intimate that he was a junkie because she broke his heart, that is bullshit. If you find out your boyfriend is doing heroin and he's not going to change and you break up with him, are you the bitch? I don't care how broken-hearted he is, are you the bitch, really? No, you're just someone who drew some healthy boundaries."

Kurt was unhappy, dissatisfied with his life. He was going through a traumatic break-up. Some people turn to religion, or get married on the rebound. Some lose themselves in their work, or get violently drunk for months on end. Kurt turned to his journals and drawings, self-righteous in his pain, searing and authentic in his anger, however misguided. "I purposely keep myself naïve and away from earthly information because it's the only way to avoid a jaded attitude," he wrote in his journal. "I can't speak. I can only feel. Maybe one day I'll turn myself into [inspirational deaf-blind author] Helen Keller by puncturing my ears with a knife, then cutting my voice box out.

"Thanks for the tragedy, I need it for my art," he wrote another time, bitterly aware of his main motivation.

Dave first heard about Kurt's heroin use when he was in LA in November, deputising on drums for L7 at a Rock For Choice benefit. He was on the phone to Krist when the bassist broke off in mid-sentence and said, "Wait. I have to tell you something. Kurt's doing heroin."

Kurt had phoned Krist up earlier the same month to tell him he'd tried the drug. Krist was immediately concerned. Aside from the straight edge K kids, Olympia had a reputation during the Eighties of being somewhat of a dark place, a dangerous town – a place where people died because of drug abuse. Andrew Wood, singer with Mother Love Bone, had died in March 1990 from a heroin OD. Kurt told Krist he wouldn't try it again, that the drug was lame. He lied. Soon, he and Dylan Carlson were renting cheap Olympia hotel rooms once a week so they could shoot up, undisturbed.

There was an incident where Kurt went with Tracy Marander to see Bikini Kill play in Olympia, and he was nodding off in the car – behaviour Tracy had never before experienced in Kurt. After the show, on the way to a friend's party, Kurt asked to stop at his house so he could use the bathroom. After about 15 minutes, she heard a crash and there was Kurt passed out, one sleeve rolled up, and a bottle of bleach on the floor (to clean his needle). She was shocked, and angry.

"That whole winter was the most depressing time I'd had in years,"

Kurt told Michael Azerrad. "It was so fucking small and dirty and cold and grey every fucking day. I almost went insane. I was so bored and poor. We were signed to Geffen for months and we didn't have any money. We ended up having to pawn our amps and our TV, just to get money to eat corndogs. All we did was practice. That saved us."

**Addenda: heroin**

How big an influence do you think heroin was on grunge?

Danny Bland [ex-Seattle band, The Supersuckers]: "I don't think heroin can influence a sound."

Why did Seattle have such a rep for it?

Danny: "I don't know. People theorised that it was because of the weather. It was rainy and miserable so you didn't go out and play kickball, but stayed in the basement and played music with your friends, and that's good. Also, when it's that cloudy all the time you get down and that makes people more predisposed to heroin."

What's the attraction of it? I've never done heroin.

Danny: "I was a junkie for 10 years. Heroin makes you forget about everything else going on in the world. It makes you forget about the fact your band isn't getting as much attention as another band, or that you have to go to work throwing fish around Pike Place Market. It's pure comfort. It's fucking great. And then later on, it turns on you. And yes, you steal your friend's Sub Pop 45 collection and sell it down at Cellophane Square, and take old ladies' purses, and steal from your places of employment. You sell your own stuff first, of course: you don't jump right into criminal activity. And we lost a lot of great friends and a lot of great musicians to it. I got lucky: I lived. And I stopped, eventually. The appeal is weird, and the danger involved is strange too, because it's not like we don't know what's going to happen, but when you start, you don't think it's going to affect you. We're such pompous egotistical assholes. We think it won't happen to us."

Yeah, it's always someone else . . .

Danny: "I remember when the guy from Mother Love Bone died, and the arrogance that consumed me at the time. I thought, 'What kind of guy dies from a drug overdose?' You don't know what's in that needle when you shoot it, but because I'd done it for a few years and not actually overdosed myself, I thought you were an idiot if you overdosed. What an arrogant shit-head I was."

People always paint a depressing picture of taking drugs, but they're fun, aren't they?

Danny: "That's the nature of drugs. Of course it's fun when you start or else you wouldn't do it. If you shot dope one time and all your shit was stolen and you were in jail for stealing your mom's car, you'd never do it again, but it's the nature of the beast: it's really fun for awhile."

I wasn't aware of drug use back then. Except, by 1993, I realised that at least one person in pretty much every American band I knew was doing smack.

"I wasn't," replies Megan Jasper. "The weirdest thing about moving here was that I'd never been around so many people who did such intense drugs. That's not what Boston was like."

Half the time, doing the interviews for this book feels like being at an AA meeting.

"That's so funny," Megan replies. "I said a similar thing not so long ago. I had this huge awakening that almost everyone I knew either had been a smack addict or dabbled with it. It made me feel so weird."

## NOTES

1 Record company bosses always conveniently forget they're dependent for their livelihoods on the very musicians they look down upon.

2 A favourite stoner's joke at the time was, "What if Evel Knievel had a son and he called him Ken, and he turned out to be wicked? Would he then be known as Evil Ken Evel Ken Evil?"

3 There are two pieces of copyrightable property in a song. One is the composition. The other is the master recording. Often, they are handled together but they can come apart and be handled by separate companies. Some bands that are conscious of indie record sales and distribution and who wouldn't work with a major, have no problem selling their songwriting rights because the link seems invisible. Publishing companies have their own A&R agents.

4 The idea of recording a joint single, featuring Kurt and Tobi on one side, and Dale and Debbi on the other, was floated.

5 Superchunk were a fiercely independent Chapel Hill, North Carolina band. Their self-released 1989 single 'Slack Motherfucker' (Merge) is one of its generation's mightiest roars of disaffection.

6 Sebadoh was Dinosaur Jr bassist Lou Barlow's side project. The Boston, Massachusetts trio started 'for real' after J. Mascis split Dinosaur in '89 and re-formed the band a couple of days later without telling Lou. His loss. Over several albums of varying consistency, Sebadoh have come to represent a certain strand of American underground music. This is ironic. I'm sure that was never the intention. Yet on records like 1994's biting *Bakesale*, 1996's patchy *Harmacy* and 1991's sprawling

*Sebadoh III*, Sebadoh became standard-bearers for a generation – the geeks, the punk kids who got left behind while their jock mates went off and slammed to Rollins, and their smart friends were out romancing. The beauty of Barlow's solo recordings (Sentridoh) isn't that the songs are brief, or that the tape crackles and wobbles, or that his guitar is out of tune. The beauty is that he records as he sees fit, and moves on when his mood changes. The beauty lies in his wavering voice, his direct words that he never labours over or dwells on, the awesome tunes he stumbles over because he isn't looking for permanence.

7 *The Sorrows Of Young Werther* was Goethe's vaguely autobiographical 1774 German novel of doomed love – presented as a series of letters between friends. Over 2,000 readers were supposed to have committed copycat suicides after reading it.

8 Here's a link to the lyrics to Bikini Kill's 'Anthem' and an essay Tobi wrote in the autumn of 1991: www.bumpidee.com/yokoanthem.html

# CHAPTER 14

# The Will Of Instinct

*Trios are perfect. Live, and on record. There's no refuting the fact. When they get the balance right, there's no stopping them. Think of The Jam, Young Marble Giants, Dinosaur Jr, Hüsker Dü, Cream, The Slits . . . Nirvana. Trios strip music down to its basics and then, having worked out what it is that makes it work, build it up again with the minimum of fuss and the maximum of effect. Four's unnecessary. Five is unwieldy. Three is just about perfection.*

*It's got to be. The three finest albums to come out of what could be loosely termed 'the US Collegiate Scene' have all been made by trios. First there was Hüsker Dü's* Zen Arcade. *Then, Dinosaur Jr's first,* Dinosaur. *And now* Nevermind, *Nirvana's startling follow-up to their 1989 debut* Bleach. *Forget all the prejudices you may or may not have about bands whose origins may or may not lie in Seattle's Sub Pop scene of three years back. There will not be a better straight-ahead rock album than* Nevermind *released all year.*

*A lot of this is down to the sheer melody of the songs – songs such as the outrageously plangent 'Smells Like Teen Spirit', which opens this album and blows the listener straight out of the water. Songs such as the two which follow it and make for as strong an opening sequence since that of The Jam's* Setting Sons*: the menacingly poignant 'In Bloom' with its rapture-full hook line,* "He's the one/ Who likes all our pretty songs/ And he likes to sing along/ And he likes to shoot his gun/ But he don't know what it means" *and the unfathomably wistful 'Come As You Are'. And how about the acoustic 'Polly', with Chris' gentle lead bass, which finishes side one? But we're merely talking melody and harmony and tunefulness and all those kind of things you'd more commonly associate with some band with their toes stuck deeply in the Sixties. Nirvana (produced here by Killdozer's man Butch Vig) have more going for them than that.*

*Nirvana have power, oozing out of every guitar line and ripped snare – just check side two's opener, 'Territorial Pissings', which wouldn't have been out of place on Metallica's latest, or the hyper-ventilating 'Lithium'.*

*Listen to the turbo-charged 'Stay Away', perhaps the only weak link here, or 'On A Plain', a raw blister of pain.*

*Nirvana have emotion, raw emotion, the sort where the singer bares his soul all the way down the line and with the use of but a few simple words and phrases communicates way deeper with the listener than this sort of music is meant to. Take 'Drain You' and 'Lounge Act', for example, with the words coming from Kurdt Kobain's cracked, hurt voice almost indecipherable, but dreadfully moving nonetheless. And when he starts screaming, unable to bear whatever demons he sees crushing down on top of him, it's like your worst nightmares about babies crying and buses crashing and skyscrapers falling come true all at once. Never underestimate the power of a good scream.*

*When Nirvana released* Bleach *all those years ago, the more sussed among us figured they had the potential to make an album that would blow every other contender away. My God, have they proved us right.*

(Author's review of *Nevermind, Melody Maker*, September 14, 1991)

"THE first time I saw Nirvana after I left was Dave's first show in town at the Off Ramp," says Dan Peters. "It was so great. They kept playing and the bar closed down. So they kicked everybody out on the street, put away the alcohol while the staff cleared up, let everyone back in and Nirvana played for another 30 minutes. I was sitting there going, 'Yeah, pretty good.' "

The drummer laughs.

"Dave was great," he adds. "Phenomenal. It made perfect sense to me why they chose him over me. I wasn't going, 'I'm just as good as him.' I was like, 'He's the fucking guy for the job.' "

That night – November 25, 1990 – there was a pack of A&R people present, reportedly more than at any other show in Seattle's history: MCA, Geffen, Charisma, Slash, Polydor, Columbia, Polygram, RCA . . . Nirvana played 18 songs, 12 of them as yet unrecorded, the crowd moshing so wildly that the light fixtures got smashed. "They played 'Lithium'," says Ben Shepherd. "And that's when I knew. That was their first Top 40 hit right there." Charisma came close to signing the band that night, with a $200,000 advance, Nirvana even got their lawyer Alan Mintz to call them two days later – but Gold Mountain had other ideas.

Shortly afterwards, Nirvana signed with DGC/Geffen records[1] – in return, they received $287,000 (a sizeable amount for a new band at the time), plus full merchandise rights, and full mechanical royalties if and when the album went gold. Sub Pop were given a buyout fee: two per cent of Nirvana's next two album sales (and the Sub Pop logo on the back sleeve of *Nevermind*), plus $75,000 – money that, when it finally came through[2], put an end to Sub Pop's financial worries once and for all. That is, until the next crisis came along . . .

"This whole business is full of shit," Dave Grohl commented. "Of all the labels we looked at, Geffen seemed the coolest. At least they weren't big old fat men with cigars in their mouths, looking at how much M.C. Hammer was making."

"I particularly found it was an easy decision," remarks Danny Goldberg. "We got what at that time was as good a deal as possible: afterwards, the deals got better because Nirvana had raised the bar on the commercial potential for alternative rock."

As part of their agreement, Sub Pop released one last single in January – a limited edition (4,000 print run) split single featuring The Fluid's 'Candy' and Nirvana playing The Vaselines' deadpan sexual innuendo 'Molly's Lips' live. The version is fairly throwaway. Kurt didn't even want it released. On the vinyl, Sub Pop etched a laconic one-word farewell, "later".

On New Year's Eve, Nirvana played Portland's Satyricon, another sold-out whirlwind of bruised limbs and braised emotion: "Nirvana were clearly getting bigger all the time. That was the first time I saw a really attractive girl in the front row making eyes at Kurt," comments Slim Moon. "It had reached the stage where Nirvana were getting . . . *groupies*!

"However," he adds, "Kurt didn't notice. He went home alone."

The same month, Dave Grohl recorded several songs on Barrett Jones' eight-track at the Laundry Rooms, Washington, DC – released in 1992 by Simple Machines under the pseudonym Late! as the *Pocketwatch* cassette: "I was doing a lot of local stuff," says Barrett. "Velocity Girl, Jawbox[3], TeenBeat, Simple Machines, some Dischord. Dave started playing in my band, Churn. Sometimes, he'd be like, 'I have a song, let's record it.'

"He did everything first take," the producer says. "I was surprised at how good it was. He did all the instruments. I'd play something here and there, but he had it all in his head. Jenny [Toomey] heard the stuff and asked if she could put it out. This was pre-CD. She'd have a master cassette, and if someone wanted to buy it, she'd copy the tape [five at a time] and send it [tapes cost between $3.50 and $5 to buy]. It was very low budget. Cassette was not the right way to put it out, though. It didn't do it justice."

At the start of 1991, Nirvana once again found themselves in a studio – Seattle's Music Source – recording on New Year's Day. The choice of public holiday wasn't a coincidence: "My friend Brian worked at the studio," explains Craig Montgomery, who engineered the session, "and he said that we could get in there for free on New Year's Day. We set up, recorded and mixed the songs in one day. It didn't sound good because their gear was in bad shape."

Nirvana ran through several songs including an early version of 'All Apologies', 'Aneurysm', 'Even In His Youth' and a song that later became 'On A Plain'. "They weren't interested in making the songs sound good," the engineer explains. "They just wanted to play. The only songs with a finished vocal were 'Even In His Youth' and 'Aneurysm' [both of which sound excellent now – the first, pounding and hammering away, magnificent in its alienation; the latter, impassioned and bruised violet raw in its invitational vocal]. The rest of them weren't finished yet, so for guide vocals we used Kurt's typical process of making sounds that went along with the songs in his head. The sounds were raw and noisy, and not in a good way. Recording takes time."

Nirvana played a handful of dates in early 1991 – Evergreen State College on January 16, four shows in Canada at the start of March. The most famous Nirvana show – possibly ever – took place at the OK Hotel in Seattle, on April 17. They headlined above Fitz Of Depression and Bikini Kill. According to most accounts, the gig was a benefit for Fitz Of Depression singer Mikey Dees, who was facing jail unless he paid off his fines for traffic violations.

The venue was packed out, being filmed for a future documentary featuring Seattle music and the furore surrounding it, brilliantly titled *Hype!*[4] Ironically, the show wasn't a complete sell-out, because there was a party being held the same night for the launch of *Singles*.[5] Kurt took to the stage with the words, "Hello, we're major label corporate rock sell-outs." The set included suitably excited versions of 'Wild Thing' (The Troggs), 'D-7' (The Wipers) and 'Turnaround' (Devo) . . . and an unfinished, sometimes mumbled, version of a brand new song, 'Smells Like Teen Spirit'.

"I was at soundcheck," recalls Carrie Montgomery, "with Susie [Tennant][6], of course. We were waiting for them to get done so we could go eat, and Kurt was like, 'I wanna try this new song' . . . They played it all the way through and we all looked at each other, like, 'What was *THAT*?' "

"When it started, I remember thinking, 'Wow, this is a good song,' " says Jonathan Poneman. "Like, 'Wow, this is a really catchy verse' . . . and then it came to the chorus, and it was like time had stopped still for a second. Everyone was like, 'This has got to be one of the greatest choruses I've ever heard in my life.' The reaction was instantaneous. The crowd went absolutely crazy. The first part of the song was so good, and then it goes into the chorus and the chorus left the verse in the dust."

"It was an unannounced show – we only heard about it that afternoon," remembers Rich Jensen. "I was working hard at my spreadsheets and didn't get down there till seven o'clock. It was all sold out. There were these giant dudes, older motorbike gang type guys at the door. I actually bribed one of them, I gave him 20 bucks and he let me in. That was significant. It was not a fey, Olympia-style rock crowd. It was 'in the know' people so it had to be friends and family, and somehow fans, and the vibe was 'biker gang'. It was a lowlife scene. There were 500 people there and there were all kinds of people. It was a lower, more criminal element than you'd expect at a hipster type club show. It was definitely one of the great experiences. 'Smells Like Teen Spirit' just slayed; it was incredible. The song fit the crowd really well."

Dees denies that the show was last minute, or a benefit: "The show was already booked," the Fitz singer says, "and we were leaving on a tour soon, with the Melvins. Afterwards, Kurt graciously gave us an extra $250 from their take, to help us get tabs for the van, and yes . . . pay off a few traffic tickets. But I don't recall the show being organised for the sole benefit of the Fitz, or facing prosecution."

"When Nirvana were great, they were like beauty coming out of the darkness," explains James Burdyshaw. "They were a weird, nasty, dirty metal band but they were also a sweet pop band. They were the amalgamation of the darkest sludge that the Melvins could produce with the sweetest harmonies of a John Lennon or the stuff that Kurt was really into, like The Vaselines and The Meat Puppets. In some ways, Nirvana was like a folk band too. There was a lot of depth in their simplicity. The songs hit you so hard because he had this amazing voice.

"I can't think of anybody else from our era who could write nonsense lyrics in the van on the way to the studio and have them be brilliant," Burdyshaw continues. "I heard 'Teen Spirit' was written like that. The fact he could come up with these deathly dark and eerie, psychedelic chord progressions simultaneously was really cool."

The week after the OK Hotel show, Nirvana headed down to Van Nuys, California, to begin recording their second album at Sound City Studios with Butch Vig. Vig was, by his own admission, an eleventh hour choice: "It sounded like Don Dixon[7] was going to produce and I'd engineer," he told Gillian G. Gaar. "I was very unknown at the time. It was my first major label album."

"Somebody should give Killdozer credit for the whole Butch Vig connection," comments Tom Hazelmyer. "Up till then he hadn't done shit, just a guy sitting in a teeny little studio up in Madison, but those Killdozer records blew everyone's heads off. They were the first guys who took that sound and made the drums big and meaty, and got that separation between the bass and guitar and big pounding drums. Production values were not at the top of anyone's list back then. People probably wanted them, but then hit the studio for $150."

At the end of April, Butch received a rough tape of the songs: "A really, really raw boom-box cassette recording," he related. "It distorted so badly that you could barely make out what they're playing. But I was very enthused hearing 'Teen Spirit' for the first time. I just wanted them to play that as often as possible."

Krist and Shelli took the Volkswagen van with the band's equipment; Dave and Kurt left a few days earlier, in Kurt's battered Datsun car. A hundred miles out of Olympia, however, they had to turn back because the car kept overheating – so they drove it back to Tacoma, where they dumped it in a quarry and hurled rocks at it for 30 minutes, before going over to Krist's and picking up the white Dodge.

On the way to Sound City – known for its work with Foreigner, Jackson 5 and Cheap Trick; even Evel Knievel had recorded there[8] – Dave and Kurt stopped off in San Francisco for a couple of days, to visit Dale Crover and Debbi Shane, and then in LA at the Universal Studios theme park.

"They wanted to see Flipper play live," recalls Debbi. The San Francisco proto-punks had briefly re-formed. "At the time, Kurt was into starting bands with everybody, so we went to the practice space my band Dumbhead shared with the Melvins, and formed The Retards for two days. We played some of my songs, some of Dave's, some of Dale's and some of Kurt's. The odd one out looked after the four-track. Kurt announced he had a song, which wasn't a Nirvana song because it didn't have a drum part. When Dale started playing drums, he was like, 'Wow, we have a drum part.' The next day he sat down and finished the vocals. The song eventually became 'Drain You', after it had a new middle part added – it changed from metal to a more Sonic Youth noise thing."

Nirvana moved into the Oakwood Apartments for six weeks, close to Sound City. The building was in an upmarket, suburban part of LA, all mauve and powder blue walls, framed pictures of flowers and leafy lanes. The trio quickly began 'humanising' their new lodgings, graffiti-ing the walls, rearranging the furniture and staying out all night at Venice Beach.

Nirvana were slightly overwhelmed by this plush new world: tropical weather instead of constant drizzle, and the panelled wooden corridors of Sound City were lined with gold records for Tom Petty and Fleetwood Mac's *Rumours*, a far cry from Reciprocal's peeling paint. So they acted accordingly – at one point, John Silva had to bail out Krist Novoselic who'd been arrested for drink-driving and thrown in the drunk tank.

"Krist's craziness gets overlooked a lot – and he's so frickin' big!" exclaims Carrie. "There was this one show in April 1991 where Sonic Youth was opening for Neil Young. The backstage area was a series of cement tunnels like a maze, grey and sterile. The hospitality people had this huge handcart piled high with different beverages – and here comes Krist barrelling out of Sonic Youth's room and he just lays himself out on the cart. We're like, 'Why would you want to do that to the beverage cart? We like beverages.' Everything was off the cart, Krist was laughing, rolling on the ground . . . so they kick him out of the whole venue, and rumour has it they pass his photo around to the security people. Half an hour later, he's back. He'd somehow crawled *underneath* the stage to get backstage. He's six foot seven! How could you miss this crazy mountain man from Aberdeen, drunk off his ass, shimmying under the stage to get back? But the sweetest guy, not a mean bone in his body. He was just so big. That's why it was so funny, him and Kurt together . . ."

Like a comedy team . . .

"A bit," agrees Carrie. "They were like a married couple, but they adored each other. They loved each other like almost no other male friendship I've seen. It was so endearing. But hate also, I'm sure. They could be the meanest to each other and the most protective of each other. It was surprising to me at the time – I didn't give men that much credit."

On May 2, the group rented a set of drums for Dave Grohl, including an incredibly loud brass snare nicknamed 'The Terminator', from LA's Drum Doctor – the 10-day rental cost $1,542 (over twice the total cost of *Bleach*) – and began recording. Work was slow: the budget was set at around $65,000 but came in at over $120,000, the band frequently not showing up till three in the afternoon, preferring to play pinball and sleep in while Vig sorted out the drum sound on the old Neve mixing board. By the end of the first week, only basic tracks had been recorded. By the end of the second week, 10 songs were in the can – but hardly any with Kurt's vocals.

"We downed a lot of hypodermic cough syrup and Jack Daniel's and lounged on the couch in the recreation area of the studio for days on end, writing down a few lyrics here and there," Kurt told *Melody Maker*'s Ann

Scanlon before adding jokingly, "If we hadn't met our time commitments at the end of our recording period, we would have bought our songs from Gloria Estefan or Warrant [the hair metal band had just finished recording at Sound City] or J. Mascis. J's got a shit-load of songs he's always trying to palm off on people: 'Here, you wanna buy a song for a quarter?' That's a quarter of a million dollars – that's what we mean when we say a quarter – and we can afford that cos we're on a major label now."

Nirvana settled down into a routine, working between eight and 10 hours a day, changing drum heads every other song, Butch always trying to talk Kurt into doing a second take. "There weren't any major arguments," Vig said, "but I could tell when I was pushing him a little too far. A couple of times, he just put his guitar down or walked away from the mic, and I knew I wouldn't get anything else out of him."

Krist and Dave recorded their parts fairly quickly. As ever, it was the words that caused the most problems: "Before I moved from DC to Seattle," Barrett Jones recalls, "I flew out to LA. I was there in the studio when Kurt was writing the lyrics to 'Teen Spirit'. I remember when 'Stay Away' was still 'Pay To Play'. I'm actually the one who suggested 'stay away' as a lyric. They'd take forever to do anything. Like nothing happened. They'd spend the whole day there and record one guitar part!"

Smoking a lot of weed, I bet. It goes hand in hand with being at a big studio. It seems like the more money you spend on the studio, the more time you waste. Maybe it's so nice you don't want to get out of there too fast. Maybe we need more shitty studios. I've seen the studio that The White Stripes recorded their first few albums in, and you wouldn't want to stay there any longer than you had to.

"I was blown away by how good everything sounded," retorts Barrett. "I made a bet with Kurt that they'd be on the cover of *Rolling Stone* within six months. I won that bet."

There are so many great songs on *Nevermind* it's difficult to know where to start. Perhaps with the album's closer, the cello-sweetened torch song 'Something In The Way', so breathy and intimate you feel as if you're in the studio right next to Kurt, fingers delicately plucking at guitar strings as the night closes in.

"'Something In The Way' is the quietest song on *Nevermind* and the most intense," Butch Vig told *Rolling Stone* in 1996. "We attempted to record it live, but Kurt was singing and playing the guitar so quietly, all I could hear through his microphones was the bleed from the bass and drums. I suggested we isolate him in the control room and record his performance separately. Kurt decided to use his old, beat-up five-string acoustic guitar, which he never bothered to tune. He slumped down on the couch and began strumming the guitar while I was setting up the mics, and he was pretty soon flat on his back. I unplugged the telephones, hung a Do Not Disturb sign, turned off the lights, locked the door and hit record. His performance stunned me. He had gone deep inside himself and brought out a haunting portrait of desolation, weariness and paranoia."

There's the intoxicated-crazy spontaneity of 'Territorial Pissings', the song that opens side two of the original vinyl release in a blister of indignation and a lifted Youngbloods refrain[9], screamed with cheerleading fervour by Novoselic, *"C'mon people now, smile on your brother, everybody get together and try to love one another, right now"* – the drums pounding their way into oblivion, Kurt's voice red raw and throbbing. It was loosely inspired by militant feminist Valerie Solanas' searing indictment of the male race in the late Sixties, *The SCUM Manifesto*. SCUM was an acronym: the society for cutting up men – Solanas followed her own teachings by shooting pop culture icon Andy Warhol in 1968. Kurt was moved by, and sympathetic to, her idea that women should rule the earth, by whatever means necessary.

There's 'Polly', the song referred to when critics talk about Kurt's more feminine side – but in reality a chilling evocation of the dark side of maleness, its alienated narrative refusing to take sides. 'Polly' is often held up by commentators as the most 'mature' example of Kurt's songwriting craft – as if maturity had anything to do with it. It was inspired by a newspaper story of a real-life rape wherein a young girl was tortured with a blowtorch. Kurt took the part of its perpetrators, a common literary device but one rarely used within popular song – see also Detroit rapper Eminem's astonishing 'Stan' – to explore both the horror and motivation of the act. The final line, *"It amazes me/ The will of instinct"* stands in bleak contrast to the remainder – and also to the overtly melodic feel of the song. Years later, Kurt would regret writing such a memorable, poppy song with such unsettling sentiments when Nirvana played to 20,000 fans who sang lustily along, obscuring any meaning whatsoever. But it was a typically contrary Cobain act, to match beautiful chords to such jarring words.

'In Bloom', meanwhile, was a powerhouse of a single, relentless and surging.

"I think some of Chad's drum parts on *Nevermind* are amazing, but he doesn't get credit for 'em, which kills me," comments Dan Peters. "Gotta give credit where credit is due. The crucial songs like 'In Bloom', that's a Chad song."

'Lithium' is pure genius with its Big Muff fuzz sound and dark call-to-arms about turning to religion when all else fails. "In the song, a guy's lost his girl and his friends and he's brooding," Kurt explained – clearly reflecting his own state of mind. "He's decided to find God before he kills himself. It's hard for me to understand the need for a vice like that," he added, conveniently forgetting his own fondness for heroin, "but I can appreciate it too. People need vices."

It was during a take of 'Lithium', where Kurt got so frustrated at his own inability to get his part right that he smashed his guitar on the studio floor, that Vig left the mic running and used the resulting noise as a bonus track, 'Endless, Nameless' – put on the finished version of the album, hidden at the end. It appears 13 minutes and 51 seconds after the end of 'Something In The Way'[10]: "a cool, loud prank," according to Novoselic. The methodology of the song's inclusion was partly inspired by Kurt's old friend Jesse Reed: back when the pair were sharing a flat in Aberdeen, Kurt recorded himself one time saying, "Jesse . . . Jesse . . . I'm coming to get you," towards the end of a blank 90-minute cassette. Just as Jesse was about to go to bed, Kurt put the tape into the stereo and pressed 'play' . . .

'Breed' is old school Aberdeen – it wouldn't have sounded out of place on *Bleach*. Dale Crover's influence is to the fore, as Grohl hammers his way through several skins in support of Krist and Kurt's battering rhythm. The guitar solo is twisted and atonal, and out of key. "I never practise solos," Kurt said. "For every guitar solo I've ever recorded, I've always just played what I wanted to at the time and then just picked the best takes."

'Come As You Are', meanwhile, is tricksy; a booming Eighties production masking a heartfelt plea for companionship, Kurt's voice so plaintive and hurt that even now it feels painful to hear him, 15 years on.

"[The songs] are just ideas I've had, different scenarios, stuff from television, books and characters I meet," Cobain told journalist Karen Bliss in '91. "I have a lot of notebooks that I use as reference. I take lines out of things that were written before, when I write poetry and stuff like that. But a lot of the lyrics were written minutes before we recorded the vocals. I don't like to take my time on things. I like to be as spontaneous as I can. It usually adds to a better creative force."

And then there's THAT single. Right from the opening stuttered refrain it sounds like pure adrenalin, a revolution waiting to happen. Kurt's brief guitar solo is a masterpiece of restraint, remaining note-faithful to the melody, driving it deeper into your brain.

> *"Pull up a chair, there won't be a warmer sound for years," I wrote in* Melody Maker, *November 9. "Heck, I know this is a week early and everything, but I couldn't resist. I rushed out and bought this on import like it was the very first time.*
>
> *"The part I like best for tonight occurs third time through when Kurt sings,* 'I found it hard/ So hard to find/ Oh well/ Whatever . . . never mind' *and nearly gives up, sounding all bruised and little boy hurt, like a favourite toy truck battered and chipped, hidden 'neath your brother's bed. He's this close to chucking it all in, but then the inexhaustible chorus breaks through, the bravado guitars rush in, and you start wondering if the world's turned mad, that people like Axl Rose and Perry Farrell and Mötley Crüe can dig something as poppy, as puritanical, as passionate as this. The metal world must be yearning for credibility real bad if they're willing to embrace such avowed anti-rockers.*
>
> *"Single of the year, in case you were wondering how to fill in those Readers' Polls."*

"All of us when we heard the rough mixes knew it was an incredible song," confirms Danny Goldberg. "It was not clear it would be the pop song it became. We thought it could be a massive rock song, like Nirvana's identity song, but it wouldn't be the first single off the album – it wasn't crossover enough. It was too edgy. It should be the first track, but 'Come As You Are' should be the first single. No one thought it would be a number one, but it was the one that jumped out at everyone."

"I was trying to write the ultimate pop song," Kurt admitted to *Rolling Stone* journalist David Fricke in 1994. "I was trying to rip off the Pixies. When I heard the Pixies for the first time I connected so heavily I should have been *in* that band. We used their sense of dynamics, being soft and quiet and then loud and hard. 'Teen Spirit' is such a clichéd riff. When I first came up with it, Krist looked at me and said, 'That is so ridiculous.'"

"I was completely nihilistic up until about four or five years ago," Kurt told me in 1992. "When I first heard [Pixies' second album] *Surfer Rosa*, it changed my attitude. It made me finally admit, after being into punk rock for so many years, that I liked other styles of music as well. It made me finally admit that I'm a music lover. Their music reminded me of the music that I always wanted to do – and was doing – before I got into punk rock. When I started writing songs, they were a mixture of punk rock and The Beatles, but then I abandoned that and did nothing but Black Flag rip-offs.

"It's obvious that when *Bleach* came out I was very set in one frame of mind, except for that one song 'About A Girl'," he continued. "I had a few more like that that I could've put on the album, and I wish I had because then it would've sounded more like *Nevermind* and it wouldn't have been such a drastic leap."

The album was remixed by Andy Wallace at Sound City at Gary Gersh's behest: Nirvana's A&R man had deliberately kept a low profile during recording, realising it was best to let Nirvana think Geffen's influence on the album was minimal – indeed, he was so low-key, Dave Grohl called up John Silva concerned that Gersh didn't care about his new signings.

Gersh, however, started to take charge once Vig played him the rough mixes: he wasn't happy at the way they sounded, Butch seemed a little burnt out from the recording – the band was several days behind schedule – and he decided Andy Wallace needed to come in and finish off the job, sweeten the mix. His presence doubled the budget for the album. Wallace had previously worked with Madonna and on Slayer's radio-friendly metal album *Seasons In The Abyss*. The band weren't entirely happy with his inclusion – Kurt wasn't the only person who later compared the resulting sound as being like "closer to a Mötley Crüe record than punk rock", while Grohl complained that the drums sounded "too digital" – but, as Krist admitted, they went along with his presence because they just wanted the damn thing to come out.

"It wasn't a dispute," comments Goldberg. "There were conversations. When *Nevermind* was done, Gersh called and said, 'I don't think it's a good mix, the drums don't sound so good' – so we held a band meeting and Kurt said, 'Let's try something different.' Gersh suggested Andy. As soon as Kurt heard those mixes he was fine with it."

It was the old digital versus analogue, vinyl (everything compressed, warm) versus CD (everything separated, cold) argument all over again. Butch was more in tune with the US rock underground and Nirvana's live sound, but Wallace was able to create the necessary separation between the drums and guitar to ensure radio airplay.

"*Nevermind* isn't grunge," complains Chad Channing. "It's a freaking rock album. That's what happens when you get to the major labels. They want everything crisp and clean, so perfect. And that really sucks, because it sucks the soul right out of music."

"It always felt like Kurt was making it up as he was going along," suggests Charles Peterson. "And I think they lost it with their big studio recordings. I'm not a fan of the 'dirt rock' genre, but Nirvana twisted it all around and made something special and unique with it. And they lost some of that when 'Smells Like Teen Spirit' got so crammed into our brains."

Tapes of the sessions filtered through to insiders, who – Nirvana's early Seattle peers aside – were stunned by what they were hearing: "The first time Nirvana registered with me wasn't until Susie Tennant told me that Geffen had signed them," sighs Seattle musician Kim Warnick. "She brought home a copy of *Bleach* and I realised I should've heard that album a long time before. It was obvious just from the tambourine on 'About A Girl' that someone in that band was listening to The Beatles.

"Shortly thereafter she got the advance cassette of *Nevermind*," the former Fastbacks bassist continues. "I took it to work with me in the car, and I was 45 minutes late because I played 'Teen Spirit' over and over. It was so good. I couldn't believe it. Susie was so mad at me for taking that cassette; she needed it. She was like, 'You know, there are other good songs on there.' It's like, 'I don't care! I'm sure there are, that's the best one in the world.' Every band touring at that time had a copy of that cassette – it must have been the most copied cassette ever. If advance cassettes could go gold or platinum, that would have done. Everybody I knew had it."

There weren't many outtakes: "They had about 15 songs they were working on," Vig told Gillian G. Gaar for *Goldmine*. "There were a couple that Kurt never finished the lyrics on. One was called 'Song In D'; it was really catchy. It had an R.E.M. feel to it. And one was more of a punk thing. He had one other he was playing on acoustic; it was kind of bluesy. And Kurt may have given part of the chord progression from one of the songs to Courtney for a Hole song – for 'Old Age', I think."

The cover to *Nevermind* came about after Kurt saw a documentary on underwater childbirth and sketched out the idea of a baby chasing a dollar bill on a fishhook. Geffen hired underwater photographer Kirk Weddle to shoot various babies swimming around – although the inclusion of five-month-old Spencer Elden's penis on the cover later caused controversy, it wasn't deliberate. "Some of the babies were girls," recalled Geffen's art director Robert Fisher. "We didn't particularly care if it was a boy or a girl. The penis happened to be in the shot."

The back cover featured Kurt's toy monkey Chim Chim, placed in front of the collage of diseased vaginas and meat by-products from Kurt's fridge back in Olympia. "I was in a bohemian photography stage," Kurt told US journalist Kurt St Thomas. "Everyone thinks it's a real monkey but it's just a rubber monkey I've had for years. The collage I made years ago. I got these pictures of beef from a supermarket poster and cut them out and made a mountain of beef and then put Dante's people being thrown into hell and climbing all over it. If you look real close, there's a picture of Kiss in the back, standing on a slab of beef."

Fisher thought the band should try and duplicate the cover shot in a swimming pool in Van Nuys, photographed by Weddle once more – but "Everything that could have gone wrong did go wrong," the director recalled. "The pump of the pool was broken and it was really windy, so the water was really murky and the pool was cold. Kurt was really, uh, sick. He'd sit at the top of the water and kick to try and go underwater and he couldn't do it."

So for press photographs, Kurt hired his Sub Pop contact, Michael Lavine. The New York photographer showed up at the studio on May 23. "It was very hot, the studio was very dark," Michael recalls. "Krist and Butch were there, and they were like, 'Listen to this!' – and it was 'Teen Spirit'. I was like, 'Holy shit that's a great song!' Kurt woke up from where he was sleeping on the couch and gave me a big hug, opened his mouth wide and showed me his gums. His teeth were rotting away. We walked around, ate Tacos and shot a bunch of portraits. Kurt was like, 'Hurry up before I pass out.' I was like, 'You're fucked up – have some more whiskey!' He drank an entire bottle of Jim Beam."

**Addenda 1: Peter Bagge**

It was in the pages of *Hate* in the early Nineties that Seattle-based comic book artist Peter Bagge helped to define the generation he was lampooning – grunge. In among the anarchic, dope-dulled, cigarette-fuelled concerts of fictional band Stinky And The Love Gods, slacker Buddy Bradley and his constant arguments with neurotic girlfriends Lisa and Valerie, and paranoid roommate George, Bagge managed to capture the spirit of Seattle in a way few others did – Charles Peterson, Mudhoney, *Backlash* maybe. Indeed, *Hate* is a far more accurate depiction of what it felt like to be in your early twenties in the Pacific Northwest in 1991 than any amount of scratched vinyl. You should salute Peter Bagge for this fact alone.

Like cartoonists Robert Crumb and Gilbert Shelton in the Sixties – with the hippies and San Francisco – Peter was there when he was most needed, to document the cultural fallout. Grunge wouldn't have been grunge without Bagge there to give it shape.

"It was pure serendipity," the artist says. "The comics were just about people in rock'n'roll bands. I happened to live in Seattle; it was all association. When I started doing *Hate* – that was in 1990 – I was already 32 years old. Fantagraphics Comics moved here and all of a sudden every other employee had a band going and were looking for a manager so they could make it big. Everything changed so fast. Nirvana was just a band at the time I was drawing it, but by the time those particular issues came out, they were a huge phenomenon. The characters in the comic were all named Kurt. It had nothing to do with Kurt Cobain. It was my very small, private joke about the fact that it seemed like every band that I met had a guy in it named Kurt [Bloch – Fastbacks, Danielson – Tad, Cobain]. The only Kurt's I knew back in New York all spelled their name with a C, short for 'Curtis'. Maybe it's a Scandinavian thing?"

You must have frequented some of the same parties and venues to portray them in such scathing detail: did you feel sometimes your depictions were too exaggerated?

"As long as they rang true I felt safe in what I wrote," Bagge replies. "Occasionally I would make up something outlandish strictly for entertainment's sake, but someone would always write to me and say, 'I did that once.' Thus proving once again that truth is stranger than fiction."

That reminds me of one of my favourite grunge anecdotes, from ex-Sub Pop employee Michael John:

> *"On my first week at the Off Ramp club, I show up at work early and my boss Jan takes me upstairs to an apartment of an ex-employee, a junkie who stole some money and skipped out. Jan tells me, 'Keep what you want and throw the rest away, you might want to wear gloves, I think he shoots up.' The room was bright yellow, a pigsty littered with garbage, decorated with porn under a fluorescent light. I went into the kitchen and hanging on the wall is a picture of Christ on the cross, sticking into his neck was an actual needle with blood still in the chamber and dripping off the wall. I just stood there. It was raining outside and below me in the show room a shitty band was doing a shitty version of the Mudhoney anthem 'Touch Me I'm Sick'. I was locked in a cliché."*

And here's another one: "The 'loser' is the existential hero of the Nineties . . ."

"True, yet so contradictory!" Bagge agrees. "Like saying, 'The bad guy was the good guy.' "

". . . You have nothing to lose because you're already under the minimum wage. You pay too much in taxes, you can never get your head above the ground and you live in a shitty apartment. You work overtime all week and that's still not enough. You own a credit card, but you're always in debt."

Kurt Danielson said that.

"The rest of Kurt D's quote is typical of this wilful defeatist attitude that a lot of Gen X slackers adhered to back then," Peter points out. "They didn't really believe it, though, or they wouldn't have bothered trying to make anything of themselves otherwise. They just liked to whine. But grunge didn't just happen in the Northwest. There was music that sounded like grunge coming out of everywhere. What was that record label out of Chicago? Touch And Go? Wasn't a lot of that music the same genre?"

Absolutely.

"Sub Pop weren't shy about running with it," Bagge suggests. "That's another reason why Seattle got associated with grunge. Compared to all those other labels, Bruce and Jon were the most shameless hucksters. When they were still working as a team . . . I was about to say they weren't good businessmen, but they suckered millions of bucks out of Warners. They convinced everybody that they had the mightiest touch, but they lucked out with Nirvana. Pavitt always had a good sense of what the next big thing will be. He's a very open-minded fellow."

So you felt it was a little ridiculous, all this music?

"Sure, of course," Peter replies. "Some of it I liked. Everything about it, like the way everybody dressed and the music too, it reminded me of the early Seventies. Besides obvious people like Iggy Pop, it reminded me of early Alice Cooper, Steppenwolf[11] – you know, before grunge it was called heavy metal. We used to just call it hard rock. The flannel shirts and the thermal underwear – when I was in high school [on the East Coast] we wore that all the time. It was because everyone was hanging out in the woods and it was just clothes to keep you warm when you get stoned. So it really surprised me, especially when they started having fashion spreads in magazines of people dressed the way we dressed in high school.

"Seattle was – and still is – a real provincial town," he finishes. "Back then, people were very suspicious of outsiders, and resentful and envious of New York and LA. Coming from New York, what used to always make me laugh was how getting a mention, let alone a good mention, in *The Rocket* was like life or death. I was like, '*The Rocket*? Who cares?' I almost feel bad for a lot of the local bands, that they didn't enjoy it. They didn't seem to realise or appreciate how rare it is that your town becomes this focal point, this phenomenon. It seemed to mainly threaten them and piss them off. There was all this talk about, 'Oh, there are too many journalists.' I kept thinking, 'How long is that going to last? Seattle is not going to be the centre of everybody's attention forever.' "

**Addenda 2: Steve Turner**

Seattle had a pretty parochial attitude, didn't it?

"It was not so much distrustful as that usually no one comes here," the Mudhoney guitarist points out. "It was a stopping off point. It never felt like a big city to me. It still doesn't. Now it just seems like a city that got too big and collapsed on itself."

There was certainly a point, around about 1991, when local musicians started to become resentful . . .

". . . of people moving here," agrees Turner. "Yeah, because people came with a different attitude. The people here, we weren't expecting to get anywhere. I was already over a lot of the music that my friends' bands were playing; I never even liked Soundgarden or Mother Love Bone. But seeing people move here and start dressing and sounding like Alice In Chains just made me hate that kind of music even more.

"In Mudhoney," Turner continues, "the reaction against that was *Every Good Boy Deserves Fudge* [1991], totally stripping things down, smaller amps, garage keyboards and playing a bunch of punk rock cover songs to remind us of what we actually liked about rock'n'roll in the first place. It certainly isn't bombastic, pompous, fucking 'Jesus Christ Pose' [Soundgarden single]. For me, the whole thing was over the minute it exploded – I was already over it, even with Mudhoney. I said, 'That's it. I'm taking a year off and going back to school.' In 1990, I was like, 'Yawn. Whatever. Done.'

"Then it exploded a second time with the whole Nirvana *Nevermind* thing and it really got shitty here," Steve laughs. "The first explosion, that was fun for a little while, and then I got bored with it. I never had even a secret dream to be a rock star, so other people's dreams like that soured it for me. Going to the Off Ramp or something, to me that was the end of the world. I hate all that stuff. People with [Soundgarden singer Chris] Cornell hair . . ."

## NOTES

1 Future Nirvana tour-mates Teenage Fanclub also signed to DGC around this time.

2 The actual deal wasn't cemented until April 30, 1991.

3 Jawbox were post-grunge (one of the many bands of their generation who signed to a major, and shouldn't have done), and Velocity Girl a poppy Anglophile female-fronted Sub Pop band.

4 *Hype!* (1996) is extremely viewable – featuring incandescent live performances from bands like Mudhoney and The Gits, plus acerbic commentary from local luminaries such as Steve Fisk, Jack Endino and Mark Arm. And, on the DVD section, a bonus 'grunge' cartoon from Peter Bagge.

5 *Singles* (1992) features many locations and faces familiar to Sub Pop fans (notably Pearl Jam) but it's basically standard Hollywood romantic comedy fare.
6 Susie Tennant was DGC's Seattle promotion rep, and was the label's direct point of contact with Nirvana. Always up for a good time, the Capitol Hill house she shared with Fastbacks singer Kim Warnick acquired a reputation as one of *the* party houses, alongside places rented by folk like Charles Peterson and Sub Pop PR Nils Bernstein.
7 Don Dixon co-produced R.E.M.'s debut album, 1983's *Murmur*, with Mitch Easter.
8 Kurt stole the master tapes to Knievel's album and sent them back to Olympia, phoning up Dale Crover the next day to brag.
9 Lifted from The Youngbloods' peace-loving late Sixties hit, 'Get Together'.
10 Only on the CD version – and not on initial quantities either, due to a pressing plant mix-up.
11 Steppenwolf were San Francisco rockers best known for their monster hit 'Born To Be Wild', as featured in Dennis Hopper's classic biker movie, 1969's *Easy Rider*. Sometimes credited with inventing heavy metal.

## CHAPTER 15

# Love Is The Drug

IT was during the recording of *Nevermind* that Kurt Cobain first met Courtney Love.

**Part One: Everett True**

I remember the hotel.

Stepping down from the canopy into the cool, dark lobby, a haven from the oppressive heat. Laidback, hushed. The fairy lights twinkling among the tree borders like it was Christmas time already; the soothing, pastel colours: the ground level apartments; the concierge who didn't sneer at us as we walked in.

This was the hotel where Prince was rumoured to have indulged ladies with baths full of rose petals. This was the hotel where we lounged for days by the swimming pool, sipping beer and multicoloured cocktails, basking in the LA haze, calling record companies and industry people up on our mobile phones, eager to extend our stay. Desperately, we lounged by the pool and waited for folk to call us back. Every now and then, we'd call up London, just to smirk. "How's the weather over there? It's raining? No, not really? What a shame."

This then was the hotel where I first met Courtney Love and her band Hole. It was May 1991. I can still see them now, walking across the tiles at the far side of the pool to where we were idling in our English swimming trunks, the smog-filled sunlight catching in Courtney's unkempt hair. In sharp contrast to the tanned legs and pastel clothes of our fellow guests, they looked shockingly overdressed and anaemic. Courtney's tights were ripped, drummer Caroline Rue boasted a chin stud long before they became fashionable and bassist Jill Emery was a tiny dark-haired Gothic abrasion. The shy guitarist, Eric Erlandson, meanwhile, was almost the most startling of all – with his long scraggly hair and pale skin, lanky like Thurston Moore, it looked like he hadn't seen daylight for several years. The hotel management couldn't have dreamt up a bigger collection of home-town freaks in their darkest nightmares. Courtney seemed very taken with our Englishness, laughing at our accents every opportunity she got. Or maybe it was the trunks. Eric refused to shake my hand because, he explained, then we would be friends. And it's not right, being friends with a journalist.

Nothing seemed more natural than Hole's presence there in that playground of the privileged. Nothing could've seemed more out of place. At the Sunset Marquis, even the cigarette machine is hidden away in the basement.

Later, we talked.

"There are two types of people," Courtney told me. "Those who are masochists and sadists, and those who are perfectly square who have no desire to inflict pain or get pain, and that's the majority of people. You and me, Everett, we're in the minority. But then we're a little bit more sensitive than a lot of stupid people who are happy to be in a nice relationship and live a nice life and not desire anything else. They don't desire truth and they don't desire hate. They don't desire evil or decadence or purity . . .

"That's fine," she continued. "I envy these people, those Russian farmers who live to be 120 on yoghurt with their simple lives. They don't have any stress. But it's so *fun*," she said, drawing out the word like a plea for help, "to be like we are and to me the most fun part of it all is when you show bone. I'm so full of shit that when I'm honest enough to show some bone, it's almost like a Christ thing. It feels pure when I do it, even if it's a deep emotional lie."

Courtney always was in touch with her dark side.

"Men are intimidated by me, but I'm past caring about it," she said. "They're intimidated because I wasn't raised coquettishly and don't know how to be real demure. I don't know the tricks in that realm, and I haven't taken the time to learn them because I feel I have other stuff to do. I have relationships with people who are brave enough to deal with me and I don't want to deal with people who aren't.

"I've always been hated by the pen-pushers, the people who answer telephones," she said. "The people who love me are the people behind those telephones, people with power: [cult English pop star] Julian Cope, Elvis Costello, [filmmaker] Alex Cox and . . . Everett True."

That one cracked me up, I can tell you.

We talked long, ceaselessly, with energy and a burning passion. About everything, anything – anything that Courtney thought I wanted to hear. About her flirtations with ancient British rock stars and being bullied at school, the media's expectations of women, vaginal accoutrements, love, desire and hatred.

Before we started, Courtney showered and carelessly changed into my white flannel hotel dressing gown. Her feet were uncovered, bare thighs prominently displaying their whiter-than-whiteness, laughing at Jill while the bassist grew more and more paranoid. Courtney sent all the other members away out of the room, so we were alone together, intimate.

For 30 minutes, I avoided asking the lady a direct question. I knew it would annoy her. Once she started to speak, my life didn't stand still for years, until late one summer when it ground to a juddering halt. But I'm getting ahead of myself.

> *Hi ET.*
>
> *OK, my memory is shite too, but I do remember our first interview with you and how evil you were and how you were just trying to get into Courtney's knickers. I remember getting Chinese food with you in Seattle during those sad surreal days after Kurt's death. I remember filming you push him out on stage in a wheelchair at Reading. I remember climbing fences with you to go see Elastica in the tent at Reading. I remember you getting up on stage with us in St Louis and singing some songs. I remember shooting smack with you in CBGBs. I'm joking, of course. Sorry. I remember the* Vox *interview and photo session at Olympic studios.*
>
> *Eric*

I have read so many part-truths and lies about Courtney that it becomes difficult to sort out fact from fiction, even in my own memories. Did Courtney first meet Kurt in Portland in 1990, as reported in some detail both in the semi-official Poppy Z Brite Courtney Love biography, and Charles Cross' exhaustive examination (and further creation) of the Cobain mythology *Heavier Than Heaven*?[1] Not according to Eric Erlandson, who was dating her back then – or other close friends. Not according to the couple themselves, either.

In an interview with *Sassy*[2] in January 1992, they reported that their first meeting took place at another concert altogether. "I saw him play in Portland in 1988[3]," Courtney told journalist Christina Kelly. "I thought he was passionate and cute, but I couldn't tell if he was smart, or had any integrity. And then I met him at a show about a year ago."

"Butthole Surfers," says Kurt. "And L7," adds Courtney. "I really pursued him, not too aggressive, but aggressive enough that some girls would have been embarrassed by it."

Yet each time I read the 'official' version of Kurt and Courtney's first meeting, it grows more and more detailed, a delightful little fantasy incorporating Dave Pirner (Soul Asylum singer who had tousled blond hair like Kurt's), punk rock, an impromptu wrestling match and exchange of guitar case stickers. Absolute bullshit. Oh, and let's not forget the perfumed heart-shaped box filled with "three dried roses, a tiny porcelain doll, a miniature teacup and shellac-covered seashells" that she was supposed to have sent to Kurt in Olympia in late 1990. Bullshit. She wasn't interested in Kurt back then.

Did Courtney have any influence on her friend, Babes In Toyland singer Kat Bjelland's famed 'kinderwhore' look or music – a look and music she later took for her own? Not according to Kat's Minneapolis boyfriend of the time. How long was Courtney married to her first husband, the cross-dressing Falling James of LA punk band The Leaving Trains? Surely longer than to consummate the relationship the one time she told me about.

OK. Here's what I (sort of) know. Courtney Love was born Courtney Michelle Harrison on July 9, 1964 in San Francisco: her father Hank Harrison was a Grateful Dead roadie, and was rumoured to have been responsible for booking the Hell's Angels security at the infamous Rolling Stones free concert on December 6, 1969, at Altamont Raceway near Livermore in northern California.[4] Her mother, Linda Carroll, later became a therapist – notorious in the US counterculture for convincing fugitive radical Katherine Ann Power to turn herself over to the authorities after 23 years on the run.[5]

Courtney changed her name several times, moved around at length during her teens – from Portland (in a reform school) to New Zealand to Japan, where she became a stripper, to Ireland and England in 1981, where she met Julian Cope and members of Echo & The Bunnymen. She sang in an early version of Faith No More, and in Babes In Toyland briefly, and formed the extremely gothic Sugar Baby Doll in Minneapolis with Jennifer Finch and Kat Bjelland. She auditioned for the role of Sid Vicious' girlfriend Nancy Spungen in Alex Cox's 1986 punk biopic *Sid And Nancy*, and ended up with a lead role in the same director's spoof spaghetti western *Straight To Hell*. In Portland, she plotted out her future plans for 'making it' in the music industry in her scrawled girly diaries[6] – later found by Olympia singer-songwriter Lois Maffeo, the diaries going on to inspire the formation of Lois' sweet, lo-fi Courtney Love band.

"You have to understand, Courtney was a character," comments Rich Jensen. "She was somebody who would go down to Portland's X-Ray

Café Monday night poetry readings and give screaming presentations about her anatomy. She wanted to be a recognised, powerful character on the streets of Portland. So when she leaves her diary, everyone in the house takes a great deal of pleasure in reading from it."

Back in LA, she continued her part-time work as a stripper, and in 1989 answered an ad in *The Recycler*, placed by Eric Erlandson, seeking "people into Big Black, The Stooges, Abba and Fleetwood Mac" for a new band, Hole.

"In the beginning, it was more about assault," explains Eric. "We had three guitar-players . . . one guy into speed metal, Courtney's Rickenbacker insanities, and me doing my weird tunings and voicings. Slowly, the whole mess got more and more refined. And then it was just Courtney and myself on guitar. I was always into New York bands where there would be two guitarists playing different parts off of each other. We didn't have the skills for standard rock/pop guitar playing. So, we came up with our own version of what we heard coming out of New York."

It's possible Courtney *saw* Nirvana play at the Satyricon show in Portland – but she probably wouldn't have been too impressed. (Her tastes always did run to nu metal and bad English New Wave.) Her opinion probably changed after the record store where she was working was sent the first batch of Sub Pop records.

"I wouldn't have a band at all if it wasn't for Mudhoney," Courtney told me in 1992. "After Kat kicked me out of my own band, I got really depressed and moved back to Portland and was just going to be a stripper for the rest of my life. But I heard 'Touch Me I'm Sick' one night and I was saved. I knew I could scream on key like that. So I moved to Seattle for two days because Portland was seriously a pit, trying to find someone to start a band. I figured there must be cool girls in Seattle who knew who Mudhoney and Big Black and The Fall were. But after two days I realised I had to move back to LA instead. Don't ask me why, LA's gross. I just belong there. But I sent Jennifer this record for that Christmas and it rejuvenated both of us and she talked me into moving to LA to start a side band with her. And we sat down and listened to it, over and over. It was really whole, it still is. That's how I got the name for my band, after the whole of Mudhoney."

"She sent down *Bleach* and the 'Touch Me I'm Sick' 12-inch to me in LA," confirms Jennifer, "and goes, 'Look at what is going on in the Northwest.' I put on both records and I say, 'You know, Mudhoney could really make some money.' "

After Jennifer became romantically involved with Grohl, Courtney started showing more of an interest in Nirvana; although she was by then dating the Smashing Pumpkins' singer, the rather self-centred and pompous Billy Corgan, she was attracted towards the energy emanating from Seattle and its rather geeky stars like Arm because she was a geek herself. Both grunge and Sonic Youth influenced the first Hole album, 1991's *Pretty On The Inside.* Indeed the Youth's bassist Kim Gordon co-produced the scouring, invigorating record. Pure, nasty, howling and distorted with misplaced rage it's easily the most poignant music Courtney has recorded.

But Arm had already rejected her . . .

"The first time I met Courtney Love was over the phone," recalls photographer Charles Peterson. "I went over to Mark Arm's place and Mark's like, 'Here, talk to Courtney.' I was like, 'Courtney?' He's like, 'Yeah, she's in that band Hole, you know?' She was extraordinarily abrasive. She had a certain energy or a charm about her; it's not really a charm. Maybe intriguing. It ties into the whole punk lust thing."

Hole were named after Mark Arm. It's really convoluted: something to do with the 'hole in Mark Arm's soul'.

"Courtney, the queen of spin," laughs Charles. "By the time I met her in the flesh, she was with Kurt. It's weird, because I don't really think of them together. A lot of times I would see Courtney out, or I would see Kurt out. Very rarely I would see the two of them together."

There's a lyric on 'Asking For It' from Hole's second album *Live Through This*[7] that is drawn directly from the second interview I did with Courtney in my Cricklewood flat in '91. *"Every time that I sell myself to you,"* she sings, *"I feel a little bit cheaper than I need to/ I will tear the petals off of you/ Rose red, I will make you tell the truth."* The way she phrases the lyric is a reference to topics we talked about during our first interviews. Likewise, 'Softer Softest' with its opening lines *"I tell you everything/ I hope you won't tell on me,"* is a reference to a relationship that went far beyond standard press/artist.

Sure, our relationship was . . . what? Friends and peers tell me how Courtney took advantage of me, how she used my position for her own ends and then dumped me, how she's manipulative and insanely ambitious and a bad, bad person. Others might say she's matured in recent years, grown into a fine actress and strong defender of certain rights, sometimes female. They usually agree on the relationship part, however. Sure. Except that Courtney never 'dumped' me. We drifted apart, as often happens with friends. There was a Barney Hoskyns novel, *The Lonely Planet Boy*, that came out in 1995, based around the fictionalised relationship of a naïve male, middle-class English rock critic and corrupting female rock star/diva, she leading him into a sordid lifestyle of drugs and emasculating sex. The parallels seemed uncanny. Sure. I'm prepared to believe all that. That's what attracted all of us to her initially, right? The forbidden fruit is the sweetest.

Courtney was insanely great fun to be with, had a most endearing way of turning to me for help and succour with her little girl lost eyes when she was at her most fucked-up, and could be relied upon to create a situation where none had previously existed. Is that bad? She made me feel special, like I was the most special person in the world when I was with her. Fuck all you dull nine-to-fives who can't even perform that simple trick.

On our first meeting, I found myself rubbing whiskey away from her groin. That was about as close as we ever got, and as close as I wanted to get. Whenever we'd first meet, I'd make her cry through being mean when drunk, which I always was – referring to her weight, or lack of voice or talent. I didn't want to be that way. She made me like that – and yeah, I loved it.

Oh, and listening back to some of the bootlegs of Hole shows from '91, '92 and '95 . . . who's to say I didn't encourage her to misbehave, too?

Here's the secret to why I loved Hole: the music. Those first two singles I received, unsolicited in the post, 'Retard Girl' and 'Dicknail', seemed like an entry to a darker, more turbulent world. Eric's guitars were weighed down with a claustrophobic intensity. The lyrics were spiteful and full of passion. The reason I fell for 'Retard Girl' was that all of its meanness and blackness and squirming reminded me of Lydia Lunch[8], Sonic Youth and my other Eighties passions. I liked the fact nothing was cleaned up, that this was far removed from gregarious pop. The drums and bass were heavy, relentless. The guitar seemed to chuckle with maliciousness. 'Dicknail', meanwhile, was pure Babes In Toyland, and I wasn't going to resist that. Listen to the voice. Isn't the promise of trouble seductive in itself?

You've seen those rock movies with 'groupies' in, like Cameron Crowe's *Almost Famous*. They aren't fiction. These stories actually happened, albeit without the cosy endings. It's odd. Ask me what I hate about rock music, and I'll tell you straight out. Axl Rose and those ridiculous things Steven Tyler ties round his head. Heroin and disrespect towards women. Crap situations where the people are there only for the party, the drugs – not the music. Johnny Thunders and the Velvets. The guitar used as a penis extension.

Yet I lived through all of that, and I loved most of it.

* * *

"I only ever asked Courtney Love out on a date to impress you," Kurt Cobain once confessed to me.

I never knew whether to believe him. Was he winding me up? For, troubled as Kurt was, he had a wicked sense of humour. The singer claimed the incident happened the same night that I introduced the couple to each other, at a concert by Austin's favourite retarded sons, Butthole Surfers, in LA, May 1991. It's possible, certainly. How would I know?

Years after that Surfers gig, I was still bumping into strangers who delighted in recounting how they'd helped pour me into a taxi that night, how they'd been personally insulted by me, how they'd heard all about me from other people present. Also, as Kurt liked to remind me, when he first encountered Courtney and I at that show, we were rolling around on the floor in the VIP area upstairs at the Hollywood Palladium, out of our heads.

"Afterwards, when you and me were back at the apartment," Kurt continued, "you kept going on and on about how wonderful this girl Courtney Love was, how you'd only just met her and how you were going to make her into the biggest star in the world and everything. So I decided to act like an arrogant, pissy rock star. I started boasting about how I could get a date with her if I wanted. So I did. I phoned Courtney up right there and then, at two in the morning, and arranged to meet her the following day. I never showed up, though. I only did it to impress you."[9]

Sure. Maybe it is true. Maybe Kurt did ask Courtney out that night at the Palladium because he wanted to show off in front of me. Crazier things have happened. Kurt knew me. Courtney knew me. And it's true that he wouldn't have spoken to her if I hadn't been there . . .

Certainly Kurt knew me well enough to recognise the signs of infatuation in his drunken English buddy. Infatuation? Sure. Sure, I was infatuated with Courtney. Even on our first meeting, she had this knack of making you feel you were the most important person in the world while she spoke to you. Kurt realised this. Indeed, he probably couldn't have avoided it. I was drunk. I would have been going on and on about her. So: what better way to show off in front of a friend than to ask his crush out?

Every story has to begin somewhere. Over the following years, both Kurt and Courtney would remind me that I'd introduced them. "You're the one to blame," they'd say laughing, aware of how much the critics looked down upon their marriage and saw Courtney as a gold-digger. "Don't worry, you'll get 10 per cent of all royalties."[10]

I remember the concert. It took place during my first visit to LA. How could I forget it? Butthole Surfers, Redd Kross and L7 – what a great triple bill! I wasn't on the guest list, so I turned up early during the soundcheck to blag my way in, walking straight past the queue of punks and freaks stretched out across the tarmac patrolled suspiciously by security with guns. There, I bumped into Redd Kross (and Beastie Boys) manager, John Silva. Unbeknown to me, Silva had also been managing Nirvana for several months.

I told him that I was on a mission. The evening we'd checked into our LA hotel I'd spotted an ad for a Hole show eight days away. I didn't know who the band was. I only knew what they sounded like, venom and semen and vitriol and passion all exploding over ferocious Black Sabbath-style riffs. Their two singles had blown my head apart. I was desperate to meet them. I didn't know anything about them. Indeed I figured they were from Minneapolis because Kat Bjelland had put them in contact with me. And they were playing so soon! I had to meet them.

So I asked Silva if he knew who Hole were, and how I could get in contact with their singer. Silva was that kind of guy. Knew everybody.

"I can do better than that," he told me. "I can introduce you to her right now."

So it was that I first met Courtney Love.

I can picture her now, walking across the empty dance floor to meet me: loud, bedraggled, all smudged make-up and tights full of holes, the neon light shining through her dirty yellow-blonde hair. She introduced herself, and within minutes she'd mentioned half-a-dozen famous names that she claimed to be intimately acquainted with. She bought me a whiskey and demanded that I buy her one back.

Neither of us had any money, so we raced around the room stealing and begging drinks in equal proportions, becoming increasingly lairy and drunk. Someone introduced us to the curly-haired one from *Bill & Ted's Excellent Adventure*. A member of L7 slipped acid into our drinks. The room spun around our heads as we talked and fought. We got on ferociously well. I was an English music critic, on the lookout for the Next Big Thing. She was a struggling musician/actress, desperate to become that Next Big Thing. She loved the attention she was receiving from a 'name' English journalist. I loved the affection she lavished upon me in return. Even if I was annoyed when Courtney questioned my motivation, and started flirting very heavily with me. (What did it matter to me what shape someone's nose was, when I had the purity of my passion for music to sustain me?) We scammed our way into the velvet-curtained VIP area upstairs, slipping underneath the ropes when security's back was turned. No one was going to stop us. We were untouchable.

Later, Nirvana showed up. The Aberdeen band was in town recording sessions for *Nevermind*, the album that defined an era. Kurt saw me, and his eyes lit up. It was clear that both Courtney and myself were engaged in some major misconduct. Seeing us there, loud and drunk and behaving obnoxiously, it was natural for him to make his way across to the two most drunken, wasted people in the venue and start rolling round the floor with them.

"How's it going?" Kurt asked, as I lurched around the floor with Courtney. "And who's this with you? Aren't you going to introduce us?"

"I know you," Courtney yelped. "You're Kurt Cobain and you're an asshole."

Wham! No sooner had Courtney spoken, than she punched Kurt in the stomach: it was the customary way for alternative rock sorts to greet each other back then. Kurt fell over, and wrestled me on top of him. I clutched at Courtney, and the three of us went down in a drunken heap in front of all the fancy LA cats with their wide lapels and stone-pressed jeans. Some security began to take an interest in these three drunken fools spoiling the rock'n'roll ambience – "Don't touch Kurt," Courtney yelled. "He's a fucking ROCK STAR!"

Kurt liked this idea, so he grappled Courtney round the throat. Introductions over, we decided we all needed a drink. And that was it. Kurt met Courtney.

I'd like to be able to say that there was instant chemistry, that the light of love started shining through both their eyes as soon as they met, but . . . that's a pile of bullshit. The only attraction that existed between the future married couple that night in LA was that of one drunk for another. That of two party animals looking for more alcohol, ways to get high, enjoy themselves and get fucked up. Two minor stars revelling in the feeling of freedom that excess substance abuse brings.

I remember the lights doubling back on themselves, and the way people seemed to be gazing at the three of us tumbling around the floor with a strange look in their eyes, something akin to jealousy. What? Were all these beautiful people jealous of me – a drunken English asshole? That couldn't be right.

Courtney departed back to her one-bedroom flat somewhere in Hollywood on the back of Dave Grohl's motorbike. Kurt dedicated himself to looking after what was by now his almost comatose English journalist friend and making sure he didn't end up the wrong side of security's muscle. So I was driven back to Nirvana's temporary living quarters, a plastic bag tied on over my face to catch the vomit, one handle per ear, while Krist Novoselic attempted to run over a few wayward Nazi skinheads. At one stage we stopped off in a garage so I could use the bathroom. Incapable of even the most basic of human functions, I staggered rather than walked to the back door, to the sound of the clientele pissing themselves laughing.

"It was so awesome," Kurt later told me. "Everyone was making fun of you because you were completely insensible. But you got your own back."

Why? What did I do? Piss on their rhododendrons?

"No," Kurt laughed. "You walked out of there, with the complete set of keys to the establishment dangling from your belt hook. They must have been mighty pissed when they realised."

I awoke the next morning, naked, underneath a glass-topped table in Nirvana's Oakwood apartment, a thick cloud of dope hanging in the air, the apartment a complete wreck, Krist and *Melody Maker* photographer Phil Nicholls engaged in some deep philosophical discussion (about drugs probably). My back was aching from where someone had accidentally hurled a heavy glass ashtray at it. All I could hear in my mind was Kurt Cobain boasting about how he'd asked out some girl we'd met the previous evening. I ignored my fevered imagination, checked the time – fuck, 6 a.m. – and wandered out into the street clad only in my underpants to hail a cab back into Hollywood with Mr Nichols.

We had another interview call at eight.

**Part Two: Debbi Shane**

". . . the Melvins were going on tour and so Kurt invited me down. He's like, 'Hey, they gave us these apartments to live in, come down any time you want, come down for the weekend, Shelli is down here with Krist.' They kept calling and saying, 'When are you coming, when are you coming?' Finally, one weekend I decided to go down. We planned to meet up at this Butthole Surfers/L7 show at the Hollywood Palladium, and from there we would go to the apartments. We flew in, rented a car, got lost and ended up at the club. We got there really late. We found Kurt, and Krist was super drunk. He either got a DUI [driving under the influence of alcohol] that night or almost ran someone over in the parking lot. Then I remember Courtney – someone who I had heard about and read about for years via other people I knew who knew her or were married to her . . .

"I remember being outside afterwards and Kurt wanting to get back to the apartments and asking me if we could go back. He just wanted to leave. I'm pretty sure we saw the very end of the Butthole Surfers. I know it was my friend Alex, myself, Kurt, and Barrett [Jones] may have been in our car . . . and maybe you were in our car? You were with Krist then."

Do you remember Kurt saying anything about Courtney that night?

"He was sort of mumbling stuff about her. There was some talk about her trying to get him to go with her but he didn't want to. My friend Alex kept a journal back then, and she recently emailed me a quote from Kurt from that night that might've been about Courtney: 'I want to meet a woman twice as intelligent and half as jaded as I am.' So we went back to the apartments and it was quiet for a little while and then chaos ensued. There was a drunk English guy there, I think his name was Everett True, and he was walking through the bushes. I don't remember why we were outside, I just remember this very drunk English guy yelling, 'I love Courtney Love. I love Courtney Love.' Then he'd fall into the bush and we'd have to pick him up. 'I love Courtney Love. I want to marry Courtney Love.' "

Were you awake most of that night?

"Well, Krist started throwing furniture out the window. He threw an ashtray and it hit Alex in the head on its way out. She started crying and he was so apologetic. I remember the apartment being trashed. Krist was the biggest and so he could pick up the biggest things: the coffee tables and the couches. The next day Alex and I went into Hollywood. I bought a guitar. I got an old tattoo covered that I'd wanted to get covered forever. There was a big party with Jennifer from L7, but Kurt didn't want to go, so he and I stayed home and watched TV. He wanted to finish lyrics and we watched a really cool cartoon that blew our minds, *Night Flight*. And then he wrote something down. I wondered if that had to do with the cartoon thing."

That next night did Kurt mention anything about Courtney?

"No. He was writing lyrics. He was worried because they were going into the studio and he had to write lyrics. I bought some beer and he didn't drink any beer. I just remember he and I watching TV, and nobody else was around. I don't know what happened later."

Did you have the impression that was the first time they had met?

"The night before? Oh yeah, definitely."

Why did you get that impression?

"I remember a time whenever Courtney was interviewed she would always talk about this guy named Kurt Cobain who she wanted to meet. To the best of my knowledge that night was the first night that they met. I think Kurt may have mentioned it in the car, like, 'I finally met Courtney.' "

You are aware that in the official version of Nirvana history that's not the first time they met.

"I don't think that version is correct. I think that story was fabricated because at the time people didn't like the fact that Kurt was with Courtney. So in defence of what was going on they created this story where it appeared as though they'd already known each other and she wasn't just some star-fucker."

**Part Three: Jennifer Finch**

"I've known Courtney since high school, and she's always had a tendency to destruct herself going out with men. One day she told me that she wanted to meet Kurt so bad, and I said, 'You don't want to meet Kurt, he's a terrible person, and he's going nowhere.'" Jennifer Finch shakes her head and laughs. "See. That's why I'm not a good A&R person. And she said, 'No, I really want to meet him.' It was her birthday, and we were doing this Rock For Choice show, so we put both bands on the bill, so she could see just how terrible he is in person. In my mind they never got together, so it's all OK."

Did they meet that night?

"She had told me prior that she had never met him and really wanted to meet him and that was the purpose. And she thanked me. And that's when they met. As far as I know they met that night and went home with each other, and were horribly obnoxious and I hated them every second. I feel so bad that I gave them that bottle of whiskey. I thought they'd just get drunk and she'd see how terrible he is. I didn't like him, Everett, that's why no one interviews me. That show was in Los Angeles at the Palace."

So how was Dave Grohl?

"In what capacity?" the musician laughs. "We're not together now. Am I scaring you?"

Yes, but don't worry. It's about time someone scared me. Why didn't you like Kurt?

"He just didn't give a lot, he was very self-centred, and he could be very sweet. I did like Kurt; I just didn't think he'd be appropriate for my friend. I'm really opinionated that way. I thought that it was more beneficial for him in the relationship, or on the creative side, to be with her. I think she had a lot to give, and she gave a lot."

That Rock For Choice thing, was that before you toured with Nirvana in the UK?

"See, these are not the questions to ask me."

I thought you said you were a vast repository of knowledge.

"Well, concepts, and certain memories. No, it was after we toured with Nirvana in the UK. It was not exceptionally well attended. We had a fun time. Kurt was still a joy to be around at that point, very lively . . . I first met Courtney at a New Year's Eve party in LA."

How old were you?

"I don't want to say because I don't even think it was the Eighties. And for someone who walks around saying that I was born in 1974, that could be a problem."

What attracted you to Courtney?

"Courtney is an enigma; she's wonderful, particularly back then, she was stunning. She was clever, and smart, and creative. Still is. And funny, hilarious."

There was a show in Los Angeles in 1991 that I got really seriously fucked up at. Do you remember that? It was the first night I met Courtney. We got in a fight early on and started punching each other.

"I remember wanting to wash my hands of the whole thing. Here were two rock professionals that could really do something with rock history, and here you were . . . what's it called when something turns into liquid and just kind of liquids around a room? The only place that I remember the both of you wasn't in the backstage area, it was in the balconies."

Yeah, we were fighting on the floor and we were trying to roll underneath the velvet rope. Can you furnish me with any details?

"I can only furnish you with the details on my end of it where Donita [L7 singer] was getting very upset with Courtney for always showing up and coat-tailing and being louder than anyone else. Courtney introduced me to you. Something like, 'This is my friend Everett.' "

Nirvana showed up that night.

"No, they didn't."

Yeah they did. Kurt leapt in on top of me and Courtney, and started fighting both of us.

"In '91? I'd have to go back and look at my diaries."

You have diaries?

"How do you think I remember any of this stuff? 'Tonight Everett got really drunk. Again.' Does that mean that Kurt and Courtney did not meet at the Rock For Choice show?"[11]

Yes.

"Interesting. Then why did she tell me that they'd never met?"

You should ask your friend Courtney. She also said they'd met in 1990 in Portland.

"See, I vaguely remember that. Because also there was this whole thing where Courtney was seeing Billy [Corgan], she was calling me saying that she really wanted to meet Kurt, but she had never met him. I remember that so clearly. Maybe she was just saying that she wanted to get to know him better. Should I call Courtney and ask her?"

Sure, don't tell her I'm here.

"I think it was in 1990. Donita hit me by accident, I think, with the head of her guitar and split the inside of my lip and it cut a tendon in my mouth. I'm getting it fixed this month. That's the kind of disposable income I have."

So you don't believe Kurt was at the show?

"I'm sorry to belittle the whole situation, but the only thing I remember was that over by the right-hand side of the stage you and Courtney were rolling around on the ground. I don't remember it as that show, though. You must have rolled around on the ground with her more times than that. True or false?"

I'm not answering that.

**Addenda: Sub Pop**

"I've always been a fan of troublemakers, and Courtney was a lot of fun and a load of trouble," explains Danny Bland. "To me, she was a first-rate troublemaker before she had access to all the resources she has now. She was a more hands-on troublemaker."

Why did you put out the second Hole single ('Dicknail')?

"Good question," laughs Bruce Pavitt. "Next question."

"I went down to see the Afghan Whigs open for L7 at Raji's in LA," says Jonathan Poneman. "Jennifer Finch told me, 'You've got to see my friend Courtney's band, try and get there early.' But I missed them. I remember seeing this tall, kind of dorky woman walking around, thinking she was a transvestite. It soon became clear she was the singer for Hole. She emanated madness, but she was funny. She had total attitude.

"Fast-forward a few weeks later, and Hole are playing at the Off Ramp," Jon continues. "I don't have anything to do that night so I go watch them rock. It was very much like a Nirvana-type situation, in that there were maybe 20 people in the audience and they fucking blew my head off. To this day, even. She was so commanding. It was like watching Mark Arm's twin sister. She aped a lot of his attitude and moves, but she's a good actor. She pulled it off. And particularly the fact she was doing that in an empty room was like, 'You rule!' So I walked up to Eric and Courtney afterwards and said, 'I'm Jonathan from Sub Pop,' and she was like, 'Yeah, I remember meeting you in LA.' And I said, 'I really would love to do a single with you.' I can see the movie now. I'll be played by the podgy dork actor."

"It began for me when I was the Sub Pop receptionist," says Megan Jasper. "She kept calling, and calling, and calling, and calling. You'd come in to work and it'd be, 'Gee, I wonder how many messages from Courtney we're going to have today?' . . . [whiny high voice] 'Nyah, when are you putting my single out Sub Pop, nyaah' . . . you know. 'I hate you motherfuckers nyah nyah nyah where's my single!' I was like, 'Jesus motherfucking Christ!' Erase. Erase. Erase. It was like getting beaten up every single day. There was a guy who had moved up from California, he worked at Dr Dream records, so we called him Dr Dream. Rather than sending her to Bruce or Jonathan 40 times a day I'd send her to Dr Dream and say that he was doing all the signings. Then we got this letter from Thurston Moore and it said, 'You should do a seven-inch with Hole, they fucking rule.' The next thing I knew we were doing a seven-inch with Hole. The funny thing is, at that time there were two singles you couldn't give away at Sub Pop. One was Hole and one was the Smashing Pumpkins."

"Courtney could be very charming," allows Poneman, "and she could be very, very funny. She was a larger-than-life character in a very much not larger-than-life life, if that makes any sense."

## NOTES

1 The story of the first meeting in Charles' book is astonishingly similar to what actually happened: the crucial difference is that Charles' version is 18 months too early, and thoroughly embellished.

2 Trendy US teenage girls magazine, loved among the alternative rock literati for being pro-Riot Grrrl, and for not patronising its readers. Editor Christina Kelly had a great project band, Chia Pet, whose Shimmy Disc 1992 seven-inch 'Hey Asshole' still kicks (male) ass.

3 Nirvana didn't actually play Portland until January 1989.

4 The festival where several Hell's Angels beat an innocent black man to death, right in view of Mick Jagger, and the subject of filmmakers David and Albert Mayles' inspired documentary *Gimme Shelter*.

5 And not averse to cashing in on her daughter's fame either, as Linda Carroll's shamelessly marketed memoirs *Her Mother's Daughter* (2006) proved . . . a case of 'like mother, like daughter'.

6 "Number five: befriend Michael Stipe," read one particularly prescient journal entry.

7 *Live Through This* was released the week after Kurt killed himself, in 1994. In the UK, Hole's first album, *Pretty On The Inside*, was released the same week as *Nevermind*. In *Melody Maker*, it was reviewed on the same double-page spread.

8 Where do I start? Lydia Lunch's first band Teenage Jesus And The Jerks – she was 16, and they were formed with all the anger and certainty of youth – encapsulate NYC 1978 better than any band this side of Television. She followed that up with 1980's slinky and lustful cocktail, *Queen Of Siam*, and two decades of disturbing, abrasive spoken harangues. Courtney owes her *a lot*.

9 That's one interpretation. Another version has Kurt phoning Courtney to come over and bring drugs. She declined. She wasn't into him.

10 This last quote was printed as a possible fact in *Select* magazine after Kurt's death.

11 Jennifer is getting totally confused here – the show happened on October 25. The reason for her confusion might be because it was at the Palace that Courtney arranged to fly to Chicago the following night, where it is commonly accepted the pair first 'got it on'.

PART II

# THERE

CHAPTER 16

# Excess All Areas

*It ends with a knock on my door at eight in the morning.*

*Two obscenely aggressive security men storm into my hotel room, wanting to know if I'm hiding a phone anywhere. Seems one went missing the previous night after Kurt took exception to a painting hanging in Chris' room and threw it out the window. Shelves, tables, sheets, glasses, mirrors followed – and then, a quick trip to Kurt's room for more of the same. The televisions stayed, however – have you ever tried lifting one of those fuckers? All of this culminated in a prompt departure from Washington, DC the next morning, before the journalist has even properly risen.*

*My clothes are covered in vomit, someone's using the back of my head as a pinball machine, there's a barbecue happening at the end of my bed and the rats in the back alley are so fat and complacent you can use them as footballs. It's just another day on the road with Nirvana.*[1]

*Two days earlier, tour manager Monty Lee Wilkes*[2] *was picked up for questioning in Pittsburgh at two in the morning. The show that night had ended with some harsh words spoken between band and club, and later someone attempted to set the place alight – piling up cushions, seat covers and carpets in the dressing room downstairs and dousing them in petrol – and The Man figured Nirvana might know something about it.*

*"That was a classic case of coked-out Pittsburgh Mafioso promotion," Kurt assures me. "That club was the type of place that would have John Cafferty And The Beaver Brown Band*[3]*, Huey Lewis And The News and all those other professional bar bands. What's rock'n'roll to them?"*

*Nirvana had nothing to do with it. Kurt had merely smashed some bottles in the toilet and thrown a couple of things around. But, fair do's, Nirvana have been responsible for their fair share of trouble in the past.*

*"When we were in Europe," says Kurt Cobain, backstage at DC's infamous 9:30 Club, "we nearly set the tour van alight. No one knows it, but those Sonic Youth kids, they're wild," he continues, gleefully. "They were instigating violence and terrorism throughout the entire European festival tour; their manager [John Silva], also. He antagonises people and leaves us to take the rap, beating us up, tearing our pants,*

*conking Chris over the head with a bottle, turning beetroot red when he's drunk. He's wild."*

*Kurt is one of those people for whom the words 'butter', 'melt' and 'mouth' were invented. He looks angelic. Yet last time I saw him, backstage at Reading Festival, he had one arm in a sling after leaping backwards into Dave's drum kit, and the previous time, his manager was sent a bill for God knows how much, after the band destroyed an LA apartment.*

*Yes, Nirvana like to wreck stuff: Chris usually finishes a set by throwing his bass 20 feet into the air (and occasionally catching it). In Pittsburgh, Kurt rammed his guitar straight into the snare drum out of sheer frustration; in DC, he ran off the stage 10 minutes before the end to take a breather and throw up, it was so damn hot, before rushing back on to destroy the drums. New York's Marquee was blessed with an encore that was just bass, drums and Kurt screaming melodically from somewhere within the audience, he'd fucked his guitars up so bad.*

*Nirvana have a $750 equipment allowance per week.*[4] *And Kurt hates cheap guitars! They live the classic rock'n'roll lifestyle (rampant vandalism) because it's the only life they know, and because it's fun. And, along the way, they've been responsible for some of the most invigorating rock music of the Nineties.*

*One listen to their new album* Nevermind *confirms this. I'm up to about 230 and still have the opinion there's no better record this year. Songs like the terribly open 'In Bloom', 'Drain You' and mind-numbingly fine single 'Teen Spirit' (something to do with a girl sitting alone in a room, or is that the aching lament 'Come As You Are'? Fuck knows, fuck cares) are my life. No exaggeration.*

*All I have to do is hear the opening strummed acoustic chords to 'Polly' or the all-out melodic, self-centred attack of 'On A Plain' and my mind flips. One note from Kurt's torturously twisted, magically melodious scream on 'Stay Away' and my heart beats at my chest and makes a try for the heavens. Works every time.*

*Meanwhile, back in the real world . . .*

*"Yeah, I lit the curtains in our tour van on fire while we were doing an interview," Kurt says. "This was a few hours after some other destruction. This representative from MCA*[5] *gave us a gift, a wastepaper basket full of candy and magazines, with a little note welcoming us to Germany.*

*"The gift had been lying in the dressing room for two hours, while we'd been doing our set and eating our dinner. During this time, Kim Gordon had written 'Fuck you' underneath the woman's signature on the note. So we saw this and thought, 'Gee, that's kinda peculiar, but we can make good use of the sweets.' "*

*Kurt is a candy freak. Does anyone else buy those little wax bottles you drink about one cc of pop out of?*

*"So we met the rep, thanked her and Chris proceeded to get drunker and drunker," he continues. "He shot off a fire extinguisher, ripped up the magazines, threw the candy all over the place and destroyed the whole room, Sonic Youth's dressing room, too. Classic rock'n'roll angst."*

*So the band went outside, the MCA woman came back, saw the note, assumed Nirvana had written it and threw a fit, threatening to drop them from the label. "By this time," Kurt goes on. "We'd been doing interviews in the van for about an hour and I lit the curtains on fire, and we opened the door and this bellow of smoke came into her face. She thought we'd set the van on fire. The rumours were a bit exaggerated when they finally got back to MCA to the extent that we'd assaulted the woman and destroyed the club and completely burned out our van."*

*Rock'n'roll, eh kids? There isn't nothing like the real thing.*

*"In Belgium," Kurt continues, "all the band trailers were very close together. Ours was right next to Sonic Youth's, so we were throwing our fruit and chairs back and forth through the windows at each other, having a war. We climbed on top of trailers. We stole [Pixies singer] Black Francis' nametag and stuck it on our door. We went into the cafeteria tent where there were some nicely decorated tables with flowers, very chic. We changed the nametags so the party of 12 Ramones and their friends had to sit at a four-seat table. And [Pogues singer] Shane MacGowan was sat on his own at this really huge table being spoon-fed baby food because he couldn't chew, so we gave him a plate of apples."*

*Everyone giggles.*

*"There were about 30 of us sitting at the tables with Sonic Youth," the singer adds. "Someone throws a carrot stick and someone throws a grape. Then someone else throws back some dressing and it turns into a huge food fight. We wrecked the food tent, but it was a lot of fun. If there were televisions there we would have thrown them out the windows.*

*"We snuck into Ride's*[6] *trailer and stole their champagne," he continues. "This guy who was with us, videoing the tour, peed in their champagne bucket. We stole all their flowers and candy too."*

*"We were doing a station ID for a station called Space Shower TV so Kurt goes, 'Hi, I'm Dave from Nirvana, you're watching Space Shower TV,'" recalls Chris. "And I go, 'Hi, this is Chris from Nirvana and you're watching Golden Shower TV,' and they didn't get it and said, 'Oh thank you very much,' and then the lady at MCA heard it and it got turned around that I told them to suck my dick."*

*Isn't this rather rock'n'roll? Isn't this all opposed to what Nirvana are about? I thought you were meant to "hate the average American macho male" (not my quotes). I thought you'd abhor such boorish behaviour as the province of Axl Rose and his ilk.*

*"Well, no one does this stuff any more," Kurt says. "They're too scared. But that isn't our point. We only do it cos we're bored and we want to have fun. And we do – real sincere fun!"*

*"I think the alcohol has a lot to do with it, too," Dave adds.*

*But doesn't this sort of behaviour lead meek Limey journalists like myself to assume you're just a bunch of redneck no-good delinquents?*

*"We're not boasting about it," Kurt retorts. "You asked us."*

*I asked you? Me?*

*"Yes, you did," he replies. "You started the whole fucking thing!"*

*"But at the same time, who fucking cares?" Dave asks. Dave woke up this morning on his mom's couch to the strains of 'Teen Spirit'. It was being used as background music to an advertisement for antique cars. He thought that was kind of cool. "It's all entertainment," he adds. "The people who'd call us stupid rednecks are the people who give us that champagne to pee in, are the people who put on those shows."*

*"Champagne," Chris says disgustedly. "Like if there was a fifth of whiskey there, I'm going to drink champ-agne!"*

*"Ride should have had that fucking champagne," Dave sneers. "Make them stop staring at their fucking feet the whole time, goddamn it!"*

*Do you think it's a conspiracy that all this stuff never gets written about?*

*"We want to keep it out the press so we don't turn into a third-rate Sex Pistols," explains Kurt.*

*So how much do Nirvana love rock'n'roll? Let's find out.*

*"Rock'n'roll?" asks Dave perplexed.*

*Yeah!*

*"When they asked Jesus how much he loved the world, they nailed his hands to the cross – 'This much!'" Chris comments.*

*C'mon guys. Let's talk about rock'n'roll – Sammy Hagar, Van Halen, Warrant or whatever their damn names are!*

*"They're not even worth slagging," Kurt replies, aware that I'm trying to wind him up. "Let's just say I don't want to be associated with 99 per cent of rock'n'roll bands."*

*"The Youth, the 'Honey, The Breeders, the Cross, the Knife, the Nails[7], Fugazi – they're the bands we like," explains Chris.*

*Do you provide an alternative to heavy metal? Courtney Love reckons 'Teen Spirit' is your anti-heavy metal song.*

*"Why?" asks a perplexed Dave.*

*I think she thought you were singing 'heavy metal' over and over again at the end.*

*"A girl at the* Melody Maker *interview said [puts on English accent], 'There's a line in the song that says, "A metal band we've always been and always will until the end,"' " the drummer replies.*

*"Oh, we've been called an alternative band before," Kurt sneers. "But we eat meat so I think we're disqualified: chilli dogs, corn dogs, Jimmy Dean sausage breakfast."*

*"When I first joined this band," Dave comments, "I was living on Kurt's couch and there was an AM/PM convenience store right down the street where you could get three corn dogs for 99 cents. I lived on them for a year."*

*"It kept him regular too," Kurt adds. "I knew when to avoid the bathroom, nine in the morning and 12 at night. He had to walk through my bedroom to get to the bathroom."*

*"That's right," Chris agrees. "I took a shit in your backyard once, because I didn't want to stink up your whole house. It was really pleasant: warm and wet. Sweet!"*

*I ask Kurt if he thinks he's developing a rock star complex. It seems appropriate.*

*"We talked about that," he replies evasively. "I can't remember what I said."*

*"What the hell?" Chris asks, shocked. "Where did that come from?"*

*You were saying that sometimes you couldn't work out what the matter is.*

*"What did I say? Can you remember?" he asks pitifully, sounding like Courtney Love momentarily.*[8]

*It's something to do with wanting to weed out certain elements of your audience.*

*"That's true," Kurt confirms. "The people who scream 'Negative Creep' throughout the entire show, even after we've played it, and who talk really loud during songs like 'Polly'. Like, last night, that exact type of people were the ones yelling, 'Sell out' after we played because we didn't do an encore, because we didn't sign autographs. But what could be more rock'n'roll than that?"*

*Anything else?*

*"We went to this alternative commercial station today and I'd already vowed I would never do something like that again. It frustrates me and makes me feel ashamed to be in rock'n'roll. I thought it was going to be for a college station ad. We were supposed to play an acoustic set, but they didn't provide us with the right equipment, and I stormed downstairs and had a cigarette with you and we shared a cookie."*

*We also had a conversation a few days earlier, in that weird street in Philadelphia where every other building was a witchcraft store and the queue for that night's show doubled back around the block, where you said how little making music means to you any more.*

*"That's partly true," Kurt replies. "That's because if we ever had any conscious goals, we've already gone past them. We now have guaranteed distribution, we've gone up to a pretty high level on the underground circuit and that's all we ever wanted.*

*"We're not going to be proud of the fact that there are a bunch of Guns N' Roses kids who are into our music. We don't feel comfortable progressing, playing larger venues."*

*You mentioned how people in Olympia ostracise you, for not being 'pure' enough, now that you've signed to a major label. We spoke about the bullshit this industry gives up and you even had an inspired rant against 'rockers' like Hagar and Halen in the van between NYC and Pittsburgh when there was nothing else to do but scarf junk food and flip through copies of* Sassy. *You mentioned the buzz you get from the after-effects of your troublemaking, the exhilaration of being confronted by a truckload of angry officials.*

*"I'm disgusted with having to deal with the commercial side of our band at the moment and, as a reaction, I'm becoming more uptight and complaining more. And it feels like I'm adapting a rock star attitude," Kurt explains, "but it's just a reaction of disgust."*

*So we're talking your classic white liberal guilt complex here, right?*

*"What?" Dave asks affronted.*

*"The only guilt that I have is that I'm bumming other people's fun," Kurt patiently replies. "I'm not pleasant to be around in those situations and I'm concerned that my bandmates might be having a bad time."*

*Why are you doing this right now?*

*"Because I'm under contract," the singer responds. "Because I'm in fear of having to go to court if I were to leave the band."*

*What would you be doing if you weren't doing this?*

*"I'd be a street musician, definitely. That's my goal in life."*

*"It's better than working a 9–5 job," comments Chris.*

*"All my fucking redneck friends who live around this area graduated from high school, started working gas stations or being personal shit-boys for other people, they're stuck," Kurt says. "I was lucky enough to get something done."*

(*Melody Maker*, November 2, 1991, supplemented by the original transcript)

ON May 29, two days after finishing recording *Nevermind*, Nirvana did a riotous, drunken show at Los Angeles' hip, tiny, all-ages punk rock club Jabberjaw – donating all the door money to Mikey Dees once more, whose Fitz Of Depression were also on the bill. In the audience to hear 'On A Plain' and 'Come As You Are' being played live for the first time were Courtney Love and Jennifer Finch – there's a bootleg where Courtney mock-screams, "Jennifer loves you, Kurt!" Kurt was messed up on drugs and alcohol, taking 15 minutes to change a string – not that the crowd cared. It was all part of the occasion.

On June 10, Nirvana were on the road again; a two-week West Coast trip opening for Dinosaur Jr, with The Jesus Lizard in support, taking in Denver, Salt Lake City, San Francisco and Portland, among other stops. Some new songs were incorporated into the set: 'Drain You', 'Endless, Nameless', 'Rape Me' – the latter, a disturbing gentle number with its repeated exhortation to *"Rape me/ Rape me again, my friend"* and its deliberate loud/quiet echoes of 'Teen Spirit'. Indeed, it was almost like an answer song to the soon-to-be-ubiquitous single, pre-empting the furore shortly to surround Kurt and his band. I'm sure I wasn't the only journalist close to them who felt a twinge of unease every time I heard Kurt howling those words: his antipathy towards the music press was well documented – distrustful of outsiders and latecomers by instinct, it always sat particularly hard with Kurt the way, post-*Nevermind*, people only wanted to talk to him because of his fame, not for his music.

Or so he perceived . . .

It was beginning to feel like the band was constantly on the road – existing in that weird bubble of late rising, boredom, intense exhilaration and alcohol abuse that surrounds most tours. The vans and concerts may get bigger, the destinations may spread as far as Australia and Japan, but the routine remains the same.

And all the time, Nirvana were creating fresh converts, overwhelmed by the energy and unpredictability and sheer melodic force of the live shows.

"I thought it was great when they got huge," J. Mascis told *Plan B* writer Hayley Avron. "For one moment, it seemed like the universe made sense. It seemed like something that was meant to happen, happened. Then he killed himself and it was all fucked up again."

"I had not seen them play before I managed them," recalls Danny Goldberg. "I was blown away at how good they were at the [Hollywood] Palladium [June 15]. The intimacy they created with the audience blew my mind. Just the way Kurt related to the audience, the body language, the way he talked to people – Dinosaur were a great band but there was no comparison to the emotional connection Kurt had. It was a life-changing moment. Before that, I thought they were a good signing for our company. That was when I realised what a genius he was."

Also in June, Sub Pop – never slow in seizing a marketing opportunity – released *The Grunge Years*, a killer compilation that featured Nirvana's 'Dive', Afghan Whigs, 'Retarded', Mudhoney, Babes In Toyland and a rare Dickless outing, among other highlights. The cover showed two corporate types seated in the back of a limo, clearly discussing the latest 'grunge' deal (k-ching!!!) – "Limited edition of 500,000" boasted the strap-line. I took umbrage against its packaging at the time, accusing Jon and Bruce of gross and unseemly arrogance: behaviour like that is only funny when you're on the outside, not when you're on the winning side . . . but fuck it. It's as close to the definitive document of grunge as it gets, superior even to *Sub Pop 200*.

Kurt returned to Olympia from the tour, flush (sort of) with merchandise money, and bought himself a new second-hand car – $500 for a beige 1963 Plymouth Valiant, with 140,000 miles on the clock. His friends disparagingly remarked that it looked like the kind of car an old woman would drive.

Kurt was still missing Tobi, even though the pair continued to see each other. "We hung out casually for a year or so after we split," the former Bikini Kill drummer says.

"Dating is such a weird thing when you are that age – maybe at any age," she continues. "So much confusion . . . confusion is sex[9], etc. Did we go out? Did we break up? Who knows really . . . especially at this point?"

"The only time I ever took payola was when I ran out of beer at the Central Tavern, and Kurt came up to me and asked if I'd put Nirvana on the cover of *Backlash*, and I said yes, if he gave me a dollar," reveals Dawn Anderson. "He did, and I interviewed Nirvana again, right before *Nevermind* was released.

"We met Krist in Tacoma," the writer continues. "He was ranting against the Gulf War and singing 'I'm Against It' by the Ramones. Then we went over to Kurt's house in Olympia, and Krist went into his bedroom and said, 'They're here, it's time to get up.' Kurt rolled out of bed with his clothes still on. It was about two in the afternoon. He seemed OK, though. Krist was Krist. Grohl seemed a little dazed, like he still couldn't believe he was in fucking Nirvana. I fed them 'fish beer', Schmidt."

In July, Dave Grohl moved to west Seattle – where he rented a house with Barrett Jones who'd moved up to the Northwest shortly before: "My girlfriend and I were living in her van outside of Krist and Shelli's apartment," the engineer recalls. "Their apartment was small: one bedroom and a living room, that was it. They were so kind to let us camp in front of their house, and use their bathroom in the morning. For the next month, I was driving up to Seattle every day and trying to find a place."

Kurt was left alone with his cat Quisp, and the remainder of his menagerie: the turtles and a rabbit called Stew. He dyed the white kitten's hair red, white and blue, according to one account: although this story may have become confused in the telling – Carrie Montgomery (who is a hairdresser) recalls an occasion, in December 1991, when she dyed *Kurt*'s hair red, white and blue.

"It was so strange that he wanted his hair dyed that colour," she says, "because that was when [glam metal brother combo] Nelson was on DGC and they wore flag-coloured leather coats and stuff. Maybe that's why he wanted it, because of the irony. It was literally red, white and blue, striped all around his head. I rinsed it off and was like, 'Fuck. This is horrible. He couldn't have known it was going to turn out like this.' So he runs into the bathroom to look at it and he was like, 'I love it! It's perfect!' "

Another friend takes offence at a recent portrayal of events.

"All right," begins Ian Dickson, "let's start with this, page 185 [in *Heavier Than Heaven*]. [Charles Cross, Cobain biographer] says that I said, 'Kurt said to me, "Look! You can see their little arms and pieces floating in the tank." ' Talking about the tadpoles that we had brought back from the quarry and he had in his aquarium in the apartment. And he says, 'A young man who used to save birds with broken wings was now delighting in watching tadpoles being devoured by turtles.' Kurt didn't throw the tadpoles in his tank thinking they were going to be killed by the turtles. He wanted them to grow up to be frogs. It was a mistake of reasoning on his part because he could have probably figured out that they would get devoured by the turtles and yeah, he did point out the pieces of them to me, but I wouldn't say he was delighting in it, I would say he was horrified by it. And then he dumped that stuff out in the backyard and yes he was irresponsible, but I wouldn't say . . . I mean this makes him out to be some kind of a sadist. Which is just totally wrong.

"He's using that as evidence of a change in Kurt's psychology," Dickson continues. "About how he changed from wanting to save birds to 'delighting' in killing [the tadpoles]. Maybe he had, but you can't take what I said as an example of that. Kurt was irresponsible, certainly, but he didn't put them in there to be killed. Not that I recall anyway. It's not necessarily Charles' fault. That's the difficulty of representing the past."

Shortly after Dave moved out, Kurt became homeless: on July 29 he returned to his Pear Street apartment after a promotional trip in LA to find all his belongings sitting on the pavement. He'd been evicted for non-payment of rent.

On August 15, Nirvana played the tiny Roxy Club on LA's Sunset Strip.

It was an industry showcase, designed to parade the band in front of their new record company's employees – who were suitably impressed, and exhilarated, and blown away. (Fancy that! Real! Live! Rock! Music!)

"We were all awed by the velocity of *Nevermind*'s success," recalls Goldberg. "We thought we had a spectacularly good record, and that it was going to be big within our world of alternative rock – big in terms of the Pixies or Jane's Addiction, big like the way Sonic Youth had sold 125,000. There was no history at all of anyone from the alternative world going on to the pop world. There was an incredibly exciting and shocking explosion of interest within weeks of 'Teen Spirit' being on the radio. Someone told me it was played on the PA before a big show and the whole audience cheered. The interest from MTV was immediate.

"I remember walking across the street after the Roxy show with several Geffen executives," the manager continues. "We knew the first 150,000 sales were there, which meant they'd saturate the Sonic Youth audience. We thought the maximum audience was half a million, but there was fatigue among the generation who didn't want the hair bands. They wanted a new rock'n'roll. It didn't take long to realise what was happening."

In the moshpit, Geffen's art director Robert Fisher handed out flyers, asking for extras for the 'Teen Spirit' video shoot due to take place in two days. College radio station KXLU also broadcast an announcement: the response was so great that hundreds of fans were turned away from GMT Studio, a sound stage at Culver City, CA made over as a high school gym, with wall-bars, basketball hoops, cheerleaders waving pompoms and all.

Kurt came up with the concept of the 'Teen Spirit' video, broadly based on Ramones' classic trashy 1979 film *Rock'N'Roll High School*, and also 1981's teenage delinquent punk outing *Over The Edge*. The idea was for the cheerleaders to have anarchy symbols on their chests, kids emptying their wallets on to a bonfire of the vanities, the cheerleaders to be awkward-looking geeks – a "pep rally from hell," in Dave Grohl's words. The video director Sam Bayer agreed with the concept, but not with anything else: the cheerleaders needed to be conventional 'babes', the mayhem had to be contained, and there was certainly no moshing to take place.

Kurt and Bayer got into a yelling match – partly fuelled by whiskey on Kurt's part – the singer afterwards telling everyone how the director was a "little Napoleon". The idea was for the crowd to look bored, complacent: when that didn't happen, Bayer grabbed a megaphone and yelled at everyone to shut up. "It was just like we were in school," Kurt sniggered, "and he was the mean teacher."

Still, the video did the trick. Within weeks of its release, 'Teen Spirit' had been placed into heavy rotation by MTV – at that point desperate for an identity, having failed to capitalise on its status as America's first dedicated music cable channel. In 1991, it was still a novelty to see a black face on MTV. It's undeniable that MTV 'broke' Nirvana in a way that the myriad live shows and rave reviews could never hope to have done, reaching direct into the suburban heartland of America. But it was a two-way exchange: before Nirvana and 'grunge' (which MTV quickly pulled apart and distorted out of shape until it came to represent the hair metal bands it was professing to oppose), MTV was floundering. MTV may have made Nirvana, but Nirvana equally made MTV, not least by giving the station a much-needed jolt of credibility.

The video for 'Smells Like Teen Spirit' was perfect for MTV: it's irritating and asinine – a betrayal of the music and disgust at corporate America that Nirvana lived and breathed. Not so much for the undeniable energy emanating from the band and sucker punks in the audience, but for those fucking cheerleaders posing every chance they get in front of the camera.

Or is it just me?

On August 19, Nirvana flew out of SeaTac airport for a nine-date European festival tour, as vividly documented in Dave Markey's film *1991: The Year Punk Broke*[10] (starring Sonic Youth, and also featuring Nirvana, Mudhoney, Babes In Toyland, Dinosaur Jr, Gumball[11] and Ramones).

This was a high point in the Nirvana story: the calm before the storm. The release of *Nevermind* was still a month away, but the songs were there, and the band was playing at the peak of its power and enjoyment: indulging in larks and escapades and mischief at every opportunity, relishing the rare sort of camaraderie that playing a whole series of European festivals with the same bands often throws up. "The most exciting time for a band is right before they become really popular," Kurt told *Rolling Stone* journalist David Fricke. "For us, it was right before *Nevermind* came out. It was awesome. There was so much excitement in the air you could taste it."

There was no Courtney on the scene, creating rifts within, but she was around; indeed Hole played their first UK tour in August, supporting Mudhoney and unnerving audiences with their vitriol, but she was dating Billy Corgan and getting wasted with UK rock journalists. There was no dragging weight of expectation, no lurid press stories to deny and become obsessed by. Nirvana were free to let rip, unfettered – and Krist, Dave and Kurt responded accordingly. Krist was temporarily separated from Shelli: in an attempt to calm him down, John Silva called Tacoma and asked her to have a word with her errant husband. Nothing doing. Shelli hopped on the next plane out, and joined the madness.

Glenfiddich and vodka were the drinks of choice: Krist handling the whiskey by himself, while Kurt shared the vodka with Ian Dickson, along for the craic. Dave was drinking red wine.

"It was crazy," recalls Dickson. "It was really fun. Krist had moderated his drinking enough where he wasn't blacking out every night. [This runs contrary to other reports, but doubtless Ian is speaking from experience.] Dave was having a great time, and Kurt and I were having a great time and we pretty much fucked everything up that was in our path . . . and," he adds, face lighting up, "we managed to not get arrested or kill ourselves. We lit curtains on fire. We had dressing rooms full of food and alcohol that we'd put all over somebody else's dressing room wall . . . we were 22 and completely out of control."

Dickson's inclusion on the tour came as a surprise to Nirvana's management, who suspected Kurt might be gay, especially after he volunteered to share a room with the Earth musician, to keep costs down. "Kim and Thurston specifically told me Ian Dickson was Kurt's boyfriend," recalls Dave Markey.

"Here's the deal," says Ian. "We went to Larry Flynt[12] publications, because we were being interviewed by *Rip* magazine . . . ha!"

Ian catches himself.

"'We' were being interviewed . . . I was only there because I was starstruck. I was a groupie, basically. They took us out to a Chinese restaurant, very LA, but there was a moment where we were in the editor's office and he goes, 'Well, you know, normally I'd offer you guys a big stack of pornography, but I know you're not into that sort of thing.' Like, what was the difference between a hair metal band and a grunge band? You'd offer the hair metal band the porn because they were into strippers and teasing their hair, but the grunge guys . . . ? Who knows what they're into! All the assumptions about a rock band were out the window with Nirvana. Which is a good thing."

So what did they offer? Anything?

"Nothing," he exclaims. "I was bummed. I really wanted to get some porn."

After playing two shows in Ireland[13] – Cork and Dublin's The Point – Nirvana headed over to England to play the Reading Festival. Nowadays, when every last corporate sponsor is throwing a summer festival and they merge into one squalid whole, late night bonfire after bonfire of smouldering plastic containers and endless queues for the toilets, this means little. Back in 1991, however, Reading was it.[14] Iggy Pop and Sonic Youth were two of the headliners: Nirvana went on at around 3 p.m. on the Friday, after Silverfish[15], and just before rightly forgotten Brit shoe-gazers Chapterhouse, who never recovered from the ignominy of following such a terrifying live act.

Nirvana were sensational. I have no real memory of the show, despite instructing everyone staying on the floor of my hotel room to get their ass down to the site early to see them. I could sometimes be badly behaved at Reading Festival. That year, I thought I'd take it easy. On the London train down to Brighton the night before, I bumped into Bobby Gillespie from Scots dance/rock crossover pioneers Primal Scream. I had a bottle of whiskey in my bag. One thing led to another, and we ended up playing old soul records and drinking red wine back at my place till 5 a.m. Ah well, I thought, I can get some sleep now. Fifteen minutes later, the phone rang. It was Courtney in London, wasted. She wanted to come over. Instead, we chatted on the phone for two-and-a-half hours, and then it was time to go.

Krist danced around the stage like a cumbersome angle-poise lamp on acid. The sound was typically obstructive, blustery winds whipping the noise of Nirvana's first UK festival appearance everywhere. I went off in search of solace, and found it in a bottle of Mudhoney's whiskey.

"There was a kind of cockiness to Nirvana that day," recalled tour manager Alex MacLeod. The band only played for 40 minutes – including Kurt clambering all over Krist while they were both playing their instruments; an on-stage dancer[16] covered in face-paint and dancing even worse than the MTV cheerleaders; a version of 'Teen Spirit' that the crowd roared as one, despite the fact not one of them should've known the words[17]; and Kurt's walk through the photo-pit dressed in *Sounds* T-shirt and leather jacket, seemingly oblivious to the world, before he was pulled back on stage by Thurston Moore – but they were stunning, ferocious, on fire. Eugene Kelly was invited on stage to duet on 'Molly's Lips', an honour for Kurt that he would later refer to as "the greatest moment in my life".

"Kurt was carrying around that Covonia cough mixture stuff that had codeine in it," recalls photographer Steve Gullick. "I took pictures of him basking in his codeine heaven and flaunting the product. I'd always preferred Mudhoney to Nirvana – but Nirvana were undeniable that day. It's one of the few daytime performances I've seen that was as exciting as a gig. They made that stage seem like a tiny club."

"Before Reading, the press only grudgingly acknowledged Nirvana," says Anton Brookes. "After Reading, everyone wanted to know them."

> *"The sky is grey and looks like rain as we pull into the Reading station. Trudge through the mud and make my way to the backstage. I gather there were 60,000 plus people out there. It sure looked great from the stage. Nirvana pretty much stole the show, hands down. Kurt dove into the photo-pit, and spoke right into my camera and said, 'This is known as the blues scale . . .' as he wailed away discordantly on his guitar with a Feederz[18] sticker on it. And then he dove into the crowd . . ."*
>
> (Taken from Dave Markey's online diary of 1991: *The Year Punk Broke* at www.wegotpowerfilms.com)

Not everyone was convinced by the wanton destruction: "By that point, it seemed like Nirvana *had* to smash their instruments," comments Mark Arm. "It was really dumb. A roadie would remove all of the mics from the drum kit so they wouldn't get hurt. What the fuck?"

"The official reason for smashing up their guitars was because their equipment was a bag of shite," explains Anton. "They had literally boxes of guitar bodies lying around backstage, waiting to be smashed. Part of their energy was ugly beauty, destruction. Kurt's a handsome man, but he defaced himself a lot."

Mudhoney had arrived earlier that day: "Courtney was with us," Dan Peters says.[19] Later, a few of us – Dan, myself, Mark Arm and Kurt – were walking around backstage looking for mischief. Courtney was following a few yards behind. Dan takes up the story: "We'd spent the entire day getting fucked up. After awhile, I had gotten bored and was looking for shit to fuck up. Somehow I looked into this portable and I saw this big old thing of cooking oil. Before I did anything I sprayed it around in the portable. I thought that was pretty funny. Courtney was walking on this plank above me so I gave that bottle a huge squeeze and doused her with a bunch of cooking oil. It was a joke."

Courtney ran away, mortified.

"Then somebody else came looking for me," Dan continues – referring to the owner of a car that also got deluged with the oil. "And somebody I know ratted me out. Said it was Dan Peters from Mudhoney. I'm like, 'Shit!' I'm standing there hiding. I'm like, 'You son of a bitch.' Save yourself first, Everett! Women and children first! Then you went into great detail, 'He's wearing ripped jeans, he has a red shirt on, got a chain wallet that's dangling . . .' "

There's a lovely story – reported extensively in several Nirvana books – about how Markey filmed Courtney at Reading drinking whiskey with Kat [Bjelland] and Kim Gordon, saying, "Kurt Cobain makes my heart stop. But he's a shit." Trouble is, this footage doesn't exist. It's another myth. Courtney's sole contribution to the documentary is a sequence wherein Thurston makes fun of her naked ambition.

Back in America, Shelli was hanging out with Debbi Shane in Tacoma, pooling their food stamps together in a Safeway's car park to buy food: "The next time I saw Nirvana was at the Warfield in San Francisco [October 26]," Debbi says. "We were walking downtown to meet Krist and Shelli, and people were screaming Krist's name in the street. He had no idea what was going on. We were like, 'You're famous. They play your video all the time.' He was like, 'Huh?' They didn't know."

The day after Reading, Nirvana and Sonic Youth flew to Köln, Germany for the Monsters Of Spex festival: "Nirvana were meant to go on at four in the afternoon," recalls their former agent Christof Ellinghaus. "They called up and said they'd be late. The local promoter freaked. The schedule for the other bands had to be turned upside down. Nirvana claimed they'd been held up in customs. It was a total scam. They just didn't want to go on that early. They got there for about six, and were given a 20-minute slot. So they came out, ripped through five songs, blew everybody away and were told to leave. The next act on was [former Hüsker Dü frontman] Bob Mould, and he was booed for minutes. People had just been hit! They wanted to hear more Nirvana – and this was before anyone had heard *Nevermind*.

"*Bleach* wasn't really a big record in Germany," Ellinghaus adds. "I was booking all these Sub Pop bands, so when Nirvana signed to Geffen it was like, 'Does that make sense?' I never thought of it as something that would happen. But that show was such a sign of things to come."

Then it was on to Hasselt, Belgium for Pukkelpop – which is where the incident with Black Francis' nametag happened: Kurt also sprayed a fire extinguisher at the Pixies singer while he was performing.

> *"Pukkelpop. Got there just in time to catch the last half of Nirvana's set. They are getting progressively wilder as the tour goes on, and all this at 11 in the morning! The crowd just stood there dumbfounded. The sight of Kurt straddling Chris and spinning into oblivion was priceless."*
>
> (www.wegotpowerfilms.com)

There were three shows in Germany, including one in Bremen, which is where the incident involving the lady from MCA took place. The tour ended in Rotterdam on September 1, at the Ein Abend in Wien indoor festival in de Doelen, a very clean, 3,000-capacity, performance centre with mostly seated venues.

"I had to convince my colleagues to include them in the festival," reveals Dutch promoter Carlos van Hijfte. "Most of the others thought of Nirvana as just another Paperclip band.[20] I had seen Nirvana at Maxwell's in July 1989, where they really impressed me, partly by destroying their equipment. The day before the show, [Sonic Youth guitarist] Lee Ranaldo came to my house and played me a tape of *Nevermind*, telling me, 'This will be massive.' On the day of the show, an atmosphere of chaos was never far away. Somehow Nirvana had got hold of doctors' outfits . . . When the band hit the stage they were already pretty wasted."

The festival included all kinds of art performances, and one of the installations was a hospital room including nurses and doctors. Kurt and Ian Dickson had been knocking back vodka in large quantities: the pair later dressed up in face masks and smocks, writing 'Black Francis Arkansas' on the walls, and drenching all visitors to Nirvana's dressing room with orange juice and wine. At one point, Ian was even pushing Kurt around on a hospital bed.

"The room was packed," continues Carlos. "By the end, the band got in destruction mode: first, their own gear, and then the PA. Security, who had been warned about the band's reputation, invaded the stage, stopped the band and kicked them off." Krist clambered up the PA speakers, with his trousers round his ankles, swigging from a bottle. "I'm not sure if a couple of members were kicked out the building later that night. It's very possible."

Van Hijfte – unsurprisingly – saw things differently: "I have seen so many groups that decide to close a show by tearing everything down," the promoter told Dutch magazine *Oor* in 1994. "When you assume your record company will pay for the damages, you are just another spoiled American rich kid. That I fought with Krist is bullshit. The security that night was dressed as nurses so when they came to help me get Krist out of the PA, the whole stage was full of hospital personnel. When four security guys grab you, you cannot move any more. Neither were they evicted from the venue. They simply went back to their hotel."

Courtney was also present – backstage, she introduced Billy Corgan to Sonic Youth and Nirvana. "Everyone was vastly underwhelmed," comments Markey. "After they left, Kurt scrawled on the wall in magic marker 'Courtney + Gish'[21] and smiled incessantly." Courtney hitched a ride back on the ferry back to England in Nirvana's van, where she flirted non-stop with Dave. She was definitely aware of Kurt's increasing fame, though – Steve Gullick recalls standing behind Courtney and Lori Barbero at a Smashing Pumpkins gig, where the Hole singer was bragging about how she'd got in for free by claiming to be 'Mrs Cobain'.

In England, Nirvana recorded another Peel Session – a stripped-back version of a new song 'Dumb', plus 'Drain You' and 'Endless, Nameless' – before flying home on September 4.

Kurt arrived back in Olympia to find that the place no longer felt like home: both literally – according to one report he slept that night in the back seat of his Valiant[22] – and metaphorically. In his absence, Olympia had staged the first International Pop Underground convention: a get-together for friends and like-minded bands. There were no guest lists, and its brief wasn't limited to music. "They tried to structure the IPU in a way that was counter to a lot of typical rock industry behaviour," explains Rich Jensen. "For example, there were no special privileges for 'important persons'."

There was a barbecue, a cakewalk, disco parties . . . It was Do It Yourself incarnate. It was hardcore not punk (lifestyle, not fashion). It was from the first IPU that the burgeoning Riot Grrrl movement drew much of its inspiration.

"The idea wasn't so much to bring bands together as bring people together," Candice Pedersen explains. "It wasn't about categorising bands or people. That's why we had so many non-music activities, so that you could actually spend some time socialising."

Nirvana had volunteered to play, but were rejected as unsuitable. This was a big deal to Kurt: he felt the rejection keenly and often referred to it afterwards in conversations with me (as a rare journalist who empathised with his love for Olympia). He felt betrayed, that his friends should be so exclusionary.

"I don't think they'd have played it anyway because they had committed to the tour," comments Ian Dickson. "Do you want to tour Europe with Sonic Youth or play a gig in Olympia? That's what it comes down to."

* * *

On August 20, the nascent kill rock stars label released the 18-track *kill rock stars* compilation to tie in with the convention – a stunning collection, it featured exuberant Riot Grrrls Bratmobile, the sweet acoustic stylings of Courtney Love (the band), Unwound's mighty pounding groove, maverick Seattle producer Steve Fisk, Bikini Kill's scathing 'Feels Blind', the righteous political anger of Canadian two-piece Mecca Normal, Kicking Giant's solitary jangle, Slim Moon's own 'fuck' band Witchypoo, Melvins, Some Velvet Sidewalk's towering 'Loch Ness'[23], Fitz Of Depression, Half Japanese's sweet and special singer Jad Fair, Seattle's all-girl 7 Year Bitch, the outrageously charismatic posturing of Nation Of Ulysses, and ultra-heavy Olympia metalheads Kreviss, among others. Indeed, this one record is a more accurate and challenging and entertaining document of the Pacific Northwest scene than *anything* from its time.

Just because Olympia bands and their peers didn't wear leather jackets and thrash their hair around – although some of them did – didn't mean they didn't rock. Fuck yeah they rocked! The initial print run was 1,000, with a hand silk-screened cover, and . . . oh yeah . . . one of the tracks was by Nirvana, 'Beeswax' from the original Dale demos.

Slim Moon takes up the story.

"Once me and Dylan had our parting of the ways [in Earth]," the label boss says, "I was still perfectly friendly with Nirvana, but it wasn't like, 'Hey, we should hang out.' We were still close enough that in '91 when I put out that compilation, Nirvana gave me a song for it."

Can you tell us about that?

"Calvin had never released an Olympia band on record other than Beat Happening," Slim starts. "He'd done cassette compilations with local bands, but despite all the talk of regionalism that came out of Bruce and Calvin's zine, they weren't a local label. There was this local band I thought should put out a record, but I knew neither Sub Pop nor K would do it. They had a name that was like a star with just letters and numbers.

"This was about one month before the IPU convention. I knew that a bunch of people was coming from out of town to visit our town and they were going to be at all of these shows. I thought, 'Well, what if I put them on a compilation of local bands? Maybe people would buy that, since they're coming to our town.' But I had no idea how to go about making an album.

"Somehow Calvin hears about it, so he calls me up and says, 'So, are you doing this compilation?' He had answers to everything. He was like, 'I'll record Justin's [Trosper, Unwound singer] band, you can totally get it done in a month, but you'll have to do home-made covers, I'll be your distributor so even after it's over, you'll be able to sell some more.' He recorded what became Unwound later that day. I called a bunch of Olympia bands that I knew, and I called up Kurt and asked him, and he called Krist and Krist called me back. They came down the next day and brought a tape. They didn't want to give me the original tape, so we went down to the radio station and the people there were kind enough to let us use their reel-to-reel tape decks to make a copy. So, the version that's on *Incesticide* is probably one generation better than the version that's on the *kill rock stars* compilation. We spliced it all together on reel-to-reel tape. We mailed it in and got the records back about three weeks later and it took a week to silk-screen all of the covers. We got it done for the second day of the convention.

"It ended up being a compilation of bands who were either from Olympia or played the convention. When we originally pieced it together, both Fitz Of Depression and Nirvana were on the compilation but not scheduled to play. Coincidentally, Calvin asked Fitz Of Depression after that to play. So Nirvana ended up being the only band on the compilation that didn't play, which kind of made me look bad, like I put the big band on there even though they didn't play."

Nirvana's inclusion presumably helped you cover your costs.

"Sort of," Slim replies. "We hit a bad bottleneck because there was a lot of demand, but K as our distributor was just awful. It came to a point where they owed us $20,000 and they came to us with a plan to pay us $300 dollars a month until it was paid off. We sold 25,000 copies of that, so we were able to put out Bikini Kill and Unwound with that money. Later we put out [proto-Riot Grrrl band] Heavens To Betsy and [massively loud rock band] Godheadsilo."

Back in Seattle, Kurt quickly grew tired of speaking to journalists, particularly radio DJs. He took the first few phone calls, started to lie outrageously, became bored with doing that and passed on press duties to Krist and Dave. Mostly, American journalists depressed and disgusted him: few of them were interested in the music, just the phenomenon. Sadly, most music critics are dullards.

"Kurt didn't tolerate fools," notes Anton Brookes. "He respected people's intelligence, but if you asked him arsey questions then you were going to get an arsey interview."

'Smells Like Teen Spirit' was released on September 9 in the UK, backed with 'Even In His Youth' from the Music Source sessions. Four days later, Nirvana got thrown out of their own album release party. The event took place at a packed Re-Bar in Seattle, full of music industry insiders (Sub Pop, Geffen, the odd local journalist) and friends. Someone smuggled in a load of whiskey: Washington State has the weirdest liquor laws in the country – and the Re-Bar, despite being an, erm, *bar* wasn't allowed to sell what Yanks call 'hard liquor' if they were serving food. Or something.

"I had a really cute dress that I'd just got from Basic," starts Carrie Montgomery. "It ended up with onion dip all over it . . ."

I see a pattern forming here.

"There was a whole bunch of food at the Re-Bar," Carrie continues, "and Kurt and I sat in the corner of the big main room and drank a fifth of Seagram's – out of the bottle, very classy." The band convinced DJ Bruce Pavitt to quit playing *Nevermind* – Bruce didn't take much convincing – and start spinning New Wave and disco. Kurt threw some ranch dressing at Dylan and Krist, who responded in kind. "It was Green Goddess dip for vegetables, actually," states caterer Nils Bernstein. The bouncers grabbed the offending miscreants, and threw them on to the street, unaware of the rich irony.

"It was so much fun," laughs Kim Warnick. "Empty kegs were being rolled around on the floor. Finally they got asked to leave. Maybe that should have been how you knew they were going to turn into the next Beatles. So we went to some other party at a loft and somebody set off a stink bomb [some say a fire extinguisher] so we had to leave. Then we all came back to my and Susie [Tennant]'s house. Kurt would stay at our house when Nirvana came to town – he didn't have a place to live so I'd give him my room."

How did the food fight start?

"Oh, there was always a food fight," Carrie exclaims. "It was inevitable, these guys were like children. There was egg throwing, food fighting, putting CDs in the microwave, it was just ridiculous. One time we were at [Nirvana T-shirt designer] Jeff Ross' loft and I was in the hammock and Kurt flipped me out of the hammock and so I went in Jeff's kitchen and got a bag of flour and dumped the whole bag of flour over Kurt's head. And then Susie [Tennant] went and got the vacuum cleaner and vacuumed Kurt off with the hose part . . .

"Anyway," she continues, "after we got thrown out the *Nevermind* record release party we all went over to Susie's house and dressed the Nirvana guys up in dresses and put make-up on them and danced around the house and I think that was the night that Kurt was slingshot-ing eggs off of Susie's porch at the neighbours' cars. [Fastbacks singer] Kurt Bloch made a huge mountain of Nelson CDs in the living room and people started running at them and chucking them and burning them. Susie was the Northwest promotion person for DGC so she had all these Nelson CDs . . . don't ever tell David Geffen that, but, bless her heart she couldn't stop them from doing it, it was just going to happen.

"There was a bottle of pain medication on top of the refrigerator," Carrie recalls. "Kurt and I saw it and were like, 'Oh! Those look good!' So we took the rest of the bottle, and he and I decided it would be fun to jump from Kim [Warnick]'s bedroom window on to the roof of the garage next door. He's wearing a flowered dress and red lipstick and I remember sitting in that window just laughing and laughing with part of our bodies hanging out, and Kim or Susie or somebody wouldn't let us jump and we were pissed, like really mad that somebody is not going to let us do something so ridiculous.

"The next day," Carrie adds, "Dylan came over and picked up Kurt and they said they were going to go shoot guns. They used to go buy big hunks of meat at the store, like a big ham, and go out in the woods and shoot their guns at it . . ."

Susie also had a Nelson gold disc on the wall, which Kurt defaced by rubbing lipstick into it, and then sticking it in the microwave. The party continued until dawn, Kurt falling asleep still wearing Susie's little green and white Holly Hobby dress: "He looked better in it than anyone else I knew," the rep laughed. Dave also wore a dress with big polka dots on.

Would you say Nirvana were mischievous in the early days?

"They'd have really fun parties where they'd just wreck shit," explains Warnick. "That was the funnest thing about Kurt – he liked to break stuff. I remember him sitting in Susie's chair, at her desk, just fucking around, drinking beer in her office. That night, Kurt Cobain and Kurt Bloch also set a paper bag full of beer on the burner and turned the heater on, and it started to catch fire. For as quiet and shy of a guy as he was, he liked to wreck stuff. Nothing is more fun than breaking shit."

Three days after the record release party, Nirvana played an in-store at Beehive Records in Seattle's University District. It was notable for being one of the first occasions Kurt felt publicly overwhelmed by his new fame: the band was besieged by autograph hunters, fawning over Kurt, refusing to listen when he tried telling them about Bikini Kill, not allowing him any space. A year ago, he was their peer. Now he was their idol.

Over 200 fans were lined up outside the record store built to take 50 comfortably. That was at 2 p.m. The event was scheduled for seven.

When the show started, staff had to line up racks of albums in front of the windows to protect them: it was supposed to be acoustic but someone had brought along speakers – the crowd went crazy, slamming into the front like they'd learned to do from the 'Teen Spirit' video being shown on MTV. Even Tracy and Tobi were present, dancing. A couple of Montesano kids from Kurt's old school showed up, demanding autographs – something that freaked Kurt out more than anything.

Krist has cited this show as the moment when everything started to change, for the worse: "Things started to happen after that. We weren't the same old band," he lamented. "Kurt, he just kind of withdrew."

There's a famous Charles Peterson photograph from that day, of Kurt sitting looking absolutely devastated, head held between his hands, on the brink of tears. "I was still fairly shy," says Charles, "and the idea of these bands, that were going on the road and going through these press junkets, would come back here and have me shove my camera in their face was just wrong. The funny thing is that Kurt was painfully shy as well. So you get a painfully shy rock star and a painfully shy photographer, and it just doesn't work. Kurt was sometimes a bit intimidating for me. Even more so once he became this supposed god-head, which he wasn't."

**Addenda 1: Kurt is cast out of Olympia**

Rich Jensen: "Calvin told me something about getting a call from Kurt while they were working on *Nevermind* in Los Angeles. It seemed to me it was about inquiring to be on the bill and playing. They had a conversation about the purpose of IPU, and given where Nirvana was at in terms of the rock music industry – something beyond just friends sharing things – it was agreed it wouldn't be appropriate for them to play. IPU was for other communities to have an opportunity to thrive."

But, in a weird twist, Nirvana were partly responsible for helping launch kill rock stars because they had a track on that compilation album.

"I would say it was Bikini Kill that launched kill rock stars, not a particular track on a compilation. I think kill rock stars was much more involved with an emerging social network. The Bikini Kill albums – because of what Riot Grrrl had already been in the fanzine community among young women and with the hype, particularly through *Sassy* magazine – sold 50,000 pretty darn quick. That's independent of Nirvana. Olympia is a place that is so small, if anybody is working, you're liable to be talking to each other about things and helping each other out if you're on the same side of the revolution."

So I guess that conversation that Kurt had with Calvin about the IPU was fairly important. He referred to that conversation on several occasions afterwards to me, how he felt Olympia had turned its back on him. He might have felt that they were being deliberately exclusive and elitist.

"One of the reasons why Nirvana is interesting is because, particularly in the figure of Kurt – Kurt was the most out with his personality, so we focus on Kurt – he encapsulates the problem of being a band of men engaging in this traditional macho practice while having sympathies that run completely counter to that practice. It's a very complicated situation. It's like, how far can this go? The quote should stop there, but in terms of what did Kurt think or what did Calvin think – it isn't about anybody turning their back. I think Kurt understood that complication completely. It's throughout his work and it's one of the things that makes it worth talking about even today."

It is a point I need to make in my book. That casting out from Olympia, whether it was deliberate or not, it did happen.

"It's not just Olympia. You could look at revolutionary movements in Marxism. In order to try to advance an idea of a better world you come up with some measures. Before long, you're finding some people high on the stick and some people low on the stick. Either you show that you think somebody's low and they deal with it, or you don't. It's not just Olympia. It's true that Olympia is a place where some of those formulations took place: the very idea that certain economic choices about how to go about making music could actually have importance in manifesting a better world. For 20 years that idea's been banging around, and it's generated a lot of noise. What that means is, it's not just Kurt Cobain that's been cast out. Almost anybody can find somebody that thinks they're part of the problem, not part of the solution. The point is, I think people that might be down on Olympia might be more down on the process of even trying to figure out good from bad – solution from problem – rather than having an objection to a particular formulation of that."

> *"Kurt was pure and he was also insanely ambitious," explains Courtney Love. "He wanted what he got, but because of his training, because of Olympia, he decided he didn't want it. One has only to look at old Nirvana when Jason Everman was in the band, to see him posturing like Soundgarden but beating with a pop heart. Nirvana were exposed to Olympia, though – and none of that is talent-based and that's where those people bother me the most, Everett. It's not about talent, it's about purity – it's about having a manifesto and it's bullshit."*
>
> *Hold on a moment . . .*
>
> *"No," Love replies. "I believe that Ian MacKaye had a sacred, divine*

*vision but that by the time it got to Calvin Johnson it was elitist and un-inclusive and cutie-pie – and I'm not saying that because they ostracised me, there are plenty of scenes I love that I was ostracised by. Listen. Lois Maffeo*[24] *was my roommate, and I had Marine Girls and [ace late Seventies Swiss all-girl band] Kleenex played for me about the same time Kurt was getting that shit played for him, maybe even before. For him, it was a save because Olympia provided him with some pop – as did Teenage Fanclub and The Vaselines and The Pastels and all those cute personalities I didn't care about. He was as aware as me of fame. He just couldn't handle it."*

*Listen. Mariah Carey has so missed the point – it doesn't matter how many damn notes you can hit. What the fuck is talent? The purest form of music is gospel. Mariah has nothing to do with gospel. Gospel is all about passion, purity – it's not whether you hit the note, but that you try to hit the note. It has nothing to do with talent, and everything to do with passion.*

*"You and me are absolutely in agreement on that, but that doesn't apply to Olympia and its elitism and its lack of spirituality."*

(*The Stranger*, February 25, 1999)

**Addenda 2: grunge lite**

How soon did bands start coming into Reciprocal and saying, "Can you make us sound like 'Touch Me I'm Sick'" – specifically wanting to sound like a grunge band?

"Oh, not until the early Nineties when everybody got *self-conscious* about it," laughs Jack Endino. "Nobody wanted to sound like another Seattle band, people had too much self-respect for that. The people that wanted to sound like Seattle bands were not in Seattle. Everybody in Seattle was running from it as fast as they could. Sub Pop was running from it. I was running from it. Over the mid-Nineties I ended up working in 10 other countries just because people would call me up and pay my way; France, Denmark, Portugal, Australia, England, Germany, Holland . . . and I'd get these very earnest, slightly naïve bands who would be, 'Oh, we love that *Bleach* album' . . .

"I stayed away from the ones who were obviously trying to be imitative because I don't want to be the Leonard Nimoy of engineers, stuck in this one role for the rest of my life," the producer explains. "It almost happened. It was just 'Grunge, Grunge, Grunge' for a few years until I was ready to scream. Right around '92, '93, that was everybody's meal ticket; 'Oh, we've got to sound like Nirvana, or the Melvins or Soundgarden' . . . *or, times a thousand* . . . 'We've gotta sound like Alice In Chains.' That was the easiest blueprint for the suburban metalheads to follow because Alice In Chains made the transition from metal into grunge, whereas the other bands had come from punk rock. You couldn't imitate Mudhoney convincingly. You could sort of imitate the mechanics of Nirvana but you'd end up sounding like bad Nirvana. And bands still do that today. The difference is they usually have a shittier singer, and no originality. It's hopeless. You just want to make them stop. But everybody copped to the metal side of grunge and that was where the really bad horde of imitators came from, the Soundgarden and Alice In Chains side of the grunge equation. The people who were hair metal bands a few years ago and now they're a grunge band."

Did you ever get people in the studio saying, "Wait, that sounds *too much* like a grunge album"?

"Not that often, no," laughs Endino. "Sometimes it would be *me* playing devil's advocate, going, 'You know, that sounds exactly like the second Black Sabbath record, third song, it's the same riff, you sure you wanna do that?' 'You know, that sounds exactly like that AC/DC song on *Let There Be Rock*.' I try to be a watchdog because people plagiarise more than they'd like . . ."

## NOTES

1 The first I knew about any of this was wandering out on to the landing a few minutes after convincing the security to leave: the tour manager was hiding behind a corner, finger pressed warningly to his lips. "What the . . .?" "Shh," he admonished. "Don't say anything. Get your shit together and meet us outside the hotel in five minutes. We're leaving." Later that day, we went to a barbecue thrown by Dave's cool mum: "I don't know, man," Kurt said, laughing at my dissolute state. "If I'd drunk as much as you last night I wouldn't even be alive."

2 Monty lasted as tour manager of Nirvana for just over a month, until October 29.

3 Yes they do exist!

4 Really? I think I invented this figure out of thin air.

5 MCA were Geffen's parent company.

6 Ride were a classic UK guitar band of the time: renowned for staring at their feet on stage. Cynics might remark Coldplay used to sound uncannily similar.

7 Sonic Youth, Mudhoney, The Breeders, Upside Down Cross (a spoof Satanic Boston hardcore group, that J. Mascis briefly played drums for), Shonen Knife, Nine Inch Nails (Trent Reznor's poppy industrial Cleveland rock group) . . .

8 Whom he had yet to start dating . . .

9 A reference to the title of Sonic Youth's second album.

10 The title of *1991: The Year Punk Broke* was inspired by a comment of Dave

Markey's, made when he saw Mötley Crüe struggling through 'Anarchy In The UK' live on MTV. "Wow, 1991 is the year that punk rock finally breaks," the film director caustically remarked.

11 Gumball were a demented heavy powerpop band from NYC. Singer Don Fleming also co-produced Hole's *Pretty On The Inside*, Teenage Fanclub's *Bandwagonesque*, Seattle pop band The Posies and Alice Cooper. When I caught up with the nascent Gumball, Don got me stoned and took me to a Greenwich Village chess shop where we did battle to the sound of three Greek guys screaming, 'Master Dick!' and betting openly on the players sitting at the table next to us. The only rules of the place were 'no gambling, no eating, no iced tea'. Within five minutes we'd broken every rule.

12 Famous porn broker – subject of the 1996 film *The People Versus Larry Flynt*, co-starring Courtney Love.

13 In Dublin, Kurt found a rare OG copy of William S. Burroughs' *Naked Lunch* – "He was happy as a clam," remarks Dave Markey.

14 Oddly, in 1990, Reading wasn't 'it' at all – it was stuck in a morass of bad Eighties chart bands and sub-metal. MTV wasn't the only institution to benefit from a grunge makeover.

15 Silverfish were excellent madcap and noisy Camden types: progenitors of the 'Camden Lurch'.

16 The dancer's name was Tony, the drummer from grungy Nottingham, UK band Bivouac.

17 They probably did, however, due to the volume of seven-inch bootleg singles from the *Nevermind* sessions.

18 Feederz were a situationist punk rock band from Arizona – Dave Markey is referring to the title of their 2002 album, *Vandalism: Beautiful As A Rock In A Cop's Face.*

19 Contrary to other reports, neither Mudhoney nor Hole played the 1991 Reading Festival.

20 The Paperclip agency was a telephone number in the book of every USA band in the late Eighties. They brought over dozens of great and not so great American bands for European tours.

21 A reference to the Smashing Pumpkins' appalling 1991 album.

22 Although it's much more likely he slept on a friend's floor.

23 'Loch Ness' is the best song recorded about a mythical underwater monster . . . ever!

24 Later of the band . . . er . . . Courtney Love. Not sure if this statement of Courtney's is true. Lois moved in after Courtney moved out.

CHAPTER 17

# Beautiful, Beautiful Eyes

"KURT had a straight choice. He chose. He wanted to bite that apple. He chose the darker, more interesting one, but that doesn't make it right. Courtney's position was probably that Kurt had no choice, because she had decided she wanted him – but he did. I think Kurt wanted to live out his junkie couple fantasy with her, like Sid and Nancy. That was his way out of the fame that had suddenly come crashing in on top of him. What craziness. It was Christmas Eve, 1991 and they were living in a tiny room in someone else's apartment." – Eric Erlandson, ex-guitarist with Hole

"Nirvana's success was like a validation for all the years I had worked in so many different capacities music-wise, in record stores, college radio, fanzines, setting up shows. Things back then were so different. Pussy Galore couldn't get a show in Boston because of their name. When I came to Seattle the first time, I called Bruce Pavitt. He was like, 'Mudhoney, Soundgarden and The Fluid are playing at . . .' Everything changed really quickly. Bills changed overnight from Nirvana opening for Mudhoney to Mudhoney opening for Nirvana. They changed for the better, no matter how horrible the worse was too." – Debbi Shane, ex-Dumbhead

"Someone hummed 'In Bloom' to me on the phone. It sounded so cool that I started looking high and low for it. The demos for *Nevermind* became really hard to find. I finally found it and when I heard it, um, I just started to cry. Not because it was so insanely beautiful, but because I couldn't believe it was better than anything ever written in the underground. I instantly felt sorry for Kurt. I knew immediately the nightmare that awaited the poor thing. Like everyone, I over-listened to *Nevermind* on tour and it followed me wherever we went, every song better than the last. It's also a totally depressing record because no one can top it, not even the Pixies. It's bad for your self-esteem if you're a songwriter. It makes me feel small and stupid for even trying to write a song." – Courtney Love, 1992

Four days after the Beehive Records in-store, Nirvana set out on another North American tour.

Melvins opened for them on the East Coast; New York's heavily psychedelic Das Damen[1] played the south; Chicago's sartorially elegant Urge Overkill[2] took the Midwest slot; and Sister Double Happiness[3] opened on the West Coast. The tour had been booked long before the release of *Nevermind*, and the places were ridiculously tiny for the band's new status, a riot of bruised limbs and disappointed fans.

"After *Nevermind* had broken," states Craig Montgomery, "there was some talk of booking an arena tour but we couldn't do it. We spent a lot of time overseas on that record but very little in the US."

'Teen Spirit' debuted at number 27 on *Billboard*'s Modern Rock chart on September 21: radio stations – who had initially refused to play it because they couldn't make out the words – were deluged with kids wanting to hear it. "My wife bought *Nevermind* and I was like, 'Holy fuck,'" exclaims Tom Hazelmyer. "Nirvana had taken all the balls and gristle of what the Cows and Melvins and The Jesus Lizard were doing and made it into what Tad called it – Beatles pop songs."

Events began to snowball so rapidly it was impossible to keep track. The opening two nights of the tour Nirvana played in Canada, before heading down to Boston, Massachusetts on September 22, where they had dinner with Mark Kates, DGC's head of alternative music. Almost inevitably, another food fight ensued: "They threw ribs at each other," recalls DGC radio rep Ted Volk, who was present. "It was by far the best dinner I've been at in my life."

After dinner, Nirvana decided to go see Melvins playing at The Rat. They arrived to discover their names weren't on the list and Kurt got into an altercation with the doorman. "Out of nowhere," Volk told Carrie Borzillo-Vrenna, "this blonde grabs the bouncer's hand and says, 'Don't you know who this is? This is Jesus Christ and you gotta let him in this club right now.' I turn to my girlfriend and say, 'Now that's fucked up.'"

The blonde was Mary Lou Lord, a local singer-songwriter[4] who eked out a living busking in the subways. Kurt asked what her favourite bands were, and she listed The Pastels, The Vaselines, Daniel Johnston and Teenage Fanclub. "Bullshit," Kurt replied. "They're my favourite bands in that exact order" – and he asked her to name songs by each artist to prove she wasn't having him on.

The following day Kurt went round to Lord's flat. A portrait of renowned gonzo Seventies rock journalist Lester Bangs was hanging on the wall. Bangs had long been the only acceptable face of rock journalism to musicians like Lord and Cobain – Kurt even wrote an imaginary letter to him in his journals – not that he couldn't be boorish, narcissistic and derivative like everyone else. But during the Seventies Bangs championed good bands, and forged his own unique voice and, even more importantly, he was dead – so folk could get on with worshipping him without his tiresome presence being around to remind them how ridiculous it was. Kurt told Mary Lou he still really missed Tobi, and that he'd recently become enamoured of an Eastern religion called Jainism. Jainism venerated animals, and saw the universe as an endless succession of heavens and hells.

"Every day," Kurt explained, "we pass through heaven and we pass through hell."

The following day, the pair went down to local alternative radio station WFNX's[5] birthday party at the Axis in Boston – Nirvana were headlining with Smashing Pumpkins and local rock band Bullet Lavolta in support. Before the show, MTV News filmed Krist Novoselic playing a game of Twister with the support bands using Crisco oil for extra lubrication – Krist was stripped down to his boxer shorts, and used an American flag hanging nearby to wipe some of the oil out of his butt-crack. A few locals took exception to Old Faithful being used in such a way, and Krist ended up with a bodyguard.

Kurt, meanwhile, ducked out of most of the band's promotional tasks to spend time with Mary Lou.

Mary Lou Lord has been almost written out of the Kurt Cobain story. Courtney long ago invented a scurrilous story about how Kurt was once disturbed in the middle of receiving oral sex from a Boston girl in the back of a van – and how this was the only time they met. Yet I have a strong memory from around this time of meeting a besotted Kurt going on and on about this girl called Mary Lou Lord, how in love with her he was, and how he was going to move to Boston to be with her.

Fantasy perhaps, but he believed it at the time.

*Hi Everett.*

*Sometimes you meet people and you know right away that your life is about to change. That's how it felt when I met Kurt. The intensity of the situation is enough to merit an entire lifetime of the memory of that short time – one of those 'love at first sight' affairs you read about in books. A brief but nevertheless real relationship where you learn the person's entire history in a very short time and just get so close somehow. Hope I'm not being too* Bridges Of Madison County *here . . .*

*I am well aware that my relationship with Kurt was brief and that there was so much going on in his life it seems impossible that he could have felt the same about me as I did about him, but deep in my heart, I knew he did. I also know that Courtney played a big part in changing his mind about me – not just by the fact she moved in on what I had going on with him, but also through the lies she made up about me. He wasn't the kind of guy that would take on a challenge of asking me, 'Is this information true?' Just a few weeks after I left Kurt for the last time, Courtney went to Europe, and a week or so later, in Europe, right around Thanksgiving, Courtney became pregnant.*[6]

*So, I would guess that my relationship with Kurt lasted all of about two months, but it could have been two days and it would have been just as unforgettable. It had nothing to do with sex. It was more of a chemistry between two people that really worked. It was like I had known him for years and we were just getting reacquainted. It was as special as it gets.*

*I sometimes wish I had taken more risks at that time. Like the night in Detroit: he begged me to come to Chicago with him, but I couldn't. I was fearful of losing my job and I didn't want to be a burden on the band. I had no money and I didn't want to have him think I was trying to latch on for a free ride. I think he looked at it entirely differently. I think he thought I was being 'aloof' and 'disinterested'. It was the image that I was trying to pose, even though I felt the exact opposite. I just didn't want him to get frightened away. I didn't think a boy in a rock band would want something serious. If I had only known how much he had wanted to be loved, I would have shown him exactly how I felt.*

*It was that very same night in Chicago when Courtney really made her move on Kurt: what would have happened if I had been there? Would he have introduced me to her as 'his' girlfriend? She was still sort of going out with Billy [Corgan], or had recently broken up, and she'd flown up there to get the rest of her clothes from Billy's. If I'd stayed on the tour, the whole thing would have been different. He would have been taken, and hopefully she would have respected that – but maybe not. I'm sure Courtney would have found a way. After I hooked back up with Kurt in England, she found a way to break us up . . .*

*Kurt didn't mention anything about Courtney when I met back up with him in the UK a few weeks later. The first show was in Bristol. I don't remember much about the show, but it was great to be back with Kurt again. He'd called me from the road four or five times a week – this was before everyone had cell phones – while they were touring the States. I had played in the subway 10 hours a day every day to save enough for the trip. All through October I would play until my fingers bled. I got a horrible bout of carpal tunnel syndrome*[7] *and I was in agony, but there was nothing that was going to stop me from buying a plane ticket to meet up with him again. I wanted to surprise him. I didn't know anything about Courtney, and I don't think he had any idea that they were to become as serious about each other as they did. He never mentioned her.*

*When I arrived in England, I went to the show and soundcheck, and met up with Kurt. He seemed really tired and a whole lot less enthusiastic about touring. He was having a bad time with his stomach and I feel that this was where the drugs really started to come into the picture. I was totally naïve about heroin. I had seen what it had done to some of my heroes from a very early age and wanted nothing to do with it. I let Kurt know right from the beginning how I felt about drugs. I could tell that there was tension, and that my disapproval of drugs did not sit well with the direction he was going in.*

*I hung out through a couple of shows in the UK. The Astoria in London was the last show of Nirvana's that I would see. After the London show Kurt and I went back to the hotel, went to bed, and the phone rang at about 3 a.m. It was Courtney. I had no idea that she had been in the picture. I had no idea who she was apart from the fact I owned a copy of [Hole single] 'Retard Girl'. I also owned a copy of Courtney Love's 'Motorcycle Boy' – talk about confusion . . .*

*Courtney had found out about me while being interviewed for a radio show in Boston. The radio host was a friend. Courtney pumped him for info and used it as a trap. She had enough info on me to twist stuff around and make it seem true. After the interview, she called Kurt. The phone call lasted for about 40 minutes. I tried not to pay attention. The next morning, Kurt asked me, "So how are you going to get to Wolverhampton?" I had no idea what he was trying to say, so I said, "I have things to do in London" (a lie). Although I was confused I thought I would see him some time soon. He gave me an itinerary book and a kiss, and told me he would be in touch.*

*The next afternoon, Nirvana were on a TV show called* The Word. *Kurt came out and the first thing he said was, "I just want everyone in this room to know that Courtney Love, the lead singer for the pop group Hole, is the best fuck in the world." I was crushed, and as confused as anyone could be. Just the night before, I had been with him and he never said a word about her. Well, he did, but I have always been too much of a good person to repeat what he said. I feel that he said that because she forced him to. It was vicious and mean. This is where I knew that he would be forever changed by whoever this 'Courtney Love' person was.*

*By the time I returned back to the US – November 11 – Nirvana were totally blowing up. It was really hard for me because everywhere I*

> *looked there was the music or Kurt's face or voice. Kurt looked like total shit. You could see the drugs beginning to ravage. It was so gross. By this time Courtney was pregnant. It was really quick . . .*
>
> *There was a period where Courtney was leaving messages on my answering machine non-stop. It was ridiculous. I never once tried to get through to Kurt or did anything to either of them for Courtney to have gone so far out of her way to harass me like that. I think she was bored, or they were paranoid during that phase. And I will always feel that she considered me a threat because she knew all along that he really did like me, and that she had 'artificially' broken us up through her lies . . .*
>
> *Mary Lou*

I love rock'n'roll, me.

All my life I've been looking for a purpose, a sense of belonging, the knowledge that perhaps there are others like me out there after all. All my life I've been looking for a semblance of glamour – *"The nearest thing to desperation I know of"* (The Legend!, 1983) – for a sprinkling of stardust to lift me above the mundane. You think that part of me didn't enjoy this strange new power I had in the wake of Nirvana's success? You're crazy. I relished it, revelled in it, rolled around in the dirt with it and got good and mucky. I loved how female musicians and groupies were suddenly starting to flirt with me – me! – and that notable faces across the underground rock scene wanted to hang out. I was up for it. If people wanted me to get drunk and behave outlandishly, all the better. That part was easy. I once had a fellow *Melody Maker* journalist scream at me for the entire duration of a train journey from Brighton to London, "You're just a fucking music journalist!" No, I wasn't. I was Everett True. I was untouchable. Hate me or love me . . . that didn't matter. At least someone was paying attention.

One event lifted me above the herd that was soon to follow Nirvana's every move. Shortly after the Reading Festival in September 1991, someone at *Melody Maker* complained that our rival *NME* had been offered the first major Nirvana exclusive for *Nevermind*; this, despite the fact we and the soon-to-be defunct *Sounds* had been the major supporters of grunge in the UK. *NME* was the brand leader, with the bigger circulation, even if it wasn't on the ball, and that's all that counts to management types.

"OK," I stated rashly. "Get me out to America and I'll do the rest."

Three hours later, our features editor announced he'd fixed up a trip for me to interview The Breeders, in New York. Fine, I thought, but Nirvana are on the other side of the country! No worries – the night we arrive,

Nirvana are playing at New York's Marquee Club. I go straight over and sit by the entrance during the soundcheck until Kurt notices me.

After the show, Kurt asks if I want to come on tour. He also begs for an introduction to singer Kim Deal, whose debut album *Pod* he loves. I agree to both, with some relief. So we go down to the studio where The Breeders were recording, Kurt cowering behind the partition in the control room, almost too shy to talk to one of his heroes. A few days later, I clamber up on stage at Washington, DC's 9.30 Club to scream my *a cappella* punk/soul songs in front of a sell-out crowd of 800 rabid punks who, to my surprise, all sing them back at me. I discover that my status as performing artist entitles me to free drink tickets, so I knock back doubles and triples with alacrity – later the band have to pour me into their van, where I break all rules of tour etiquette by throwing up and then rolling out on to the pavement.[8] Oddly, Nirvana seemed to enjoy my indiscretions. They still allowed me to travel with them the next day.

"Most people have this idea that the band travelled with a black cloud following us everywhere we went," Dave Grohl told Stevie Chick in 2005. "And it's absolutely not true. So many great things happened, and we had so many fucking good times, good laughs. A lot of it was dangerous. A lot of it was fucking dark – but not all of it. If I had a nickel for every time Everett True threw up in our van . . . those guys got to see a lot of great shit, and there was a lot more."

In Pittsburgh, the show was even crazier and smaller.

Rock'n'roll, however seedy or disgusting, gave me a sense of glamour. Kurt Cobain understood all about this desire for glamour, it had been his escape from teenage years filled with upheaval. He was also narcissistic in his self-loathing. Many suicidal people are. As he sang on 'On A Plain', *"I love myself, better than you/ I know it's wrong but what can I do?"* Oh, but I could relate to that.

Initially, rock music helped to define a new me far removed from the taunts of schoolmates who looked down on me because my family didn't have enough money to buy new clothes. When I started making records, records fired with anger and sexual frustration and disaffection, I became someone. I knew finally that I was unique, also that I had a place to turn to when all around rejected me. How could I not love the music that had given me The Beatles, Yoko Ono, early Ramones, The Jam, Young Marble Giants and Mudhoney? Of course I love rock'n'roll. Even now, especially now, it has the power to move me, to keep my spirits from flagging. Just flick the volume up a notch higher, and play the new CD from The Gossip or Quasi or The Concretes or Misty's Big Adventure, search out an old Dexys Midnight Runners album or Teenage Jesus And The Jerks 12-inch or SST single. How can I despise anything that has given my life such validity and direction – that has enabled me to communicate with so many others over the years? It's not rock music's fault that most people are dumb. As a US punk band once said, stupid people shouldn't breed. I love rock music, and they don't come any more rock than Nirvana.

Important qualification, though: depending on your definition of rock.

On September 24, *Nevermind* was released in the States: 46,251 copies were sent out – approximately 953,749 too few. Despite Goldberg's assertion that Geffen realised what a monster they had on their hands after the Roxy show, the company still greatly underestimated the demand for Nirvana. It was a similar story in Britain.

"When Nirvana signed to Geffen, Jo Bolsom was the product manager," says Anton Brookes. "She was used to bands like Guns N' Roses – and then Nirvana got dropped on her lap. At first, she seemed like a rich middle-class girl with no idea how to handle Nirvana, but after a few months she was 100 per cent into them. Without her, my job would have been a thousand times harder. Geffen pressed up 6,000 copies, initially. They thought they'd be lucky to sell two or three. After two days, all the albums were sold out and consequently *Nevermind* went in at number 34. Even Mudhoney's album went in higher."

The night *Nevermind* came out, Nirvana played a last-minute all-ages show at The Axis in Boston: "The excitement was palpable," remembers *MM* photographer Steve Gullick. "The club was shaking with energy. It was like being on the edge of a tornado." In the tiny cordoned-off VIP area, Krist was holding court next to Kim Gordon, talking politics and totally in his element. "We went back to the hotel," continues Gullick, "and they were playing 'Teen Spirit' on MTV. I was like, 'Fucking hell, this is going to go off.' "

The following night, Nirvana played Club Babyhead in Providence, Rhode Island – where Kurt blew his amp during the first song, and Nirvana opened with The Vaselines' disturbingly sexual 'Jesus Doesn't Want Me For A Sunbeam', before segueing into the Velvet Underground cover 'Here She Comes Now' and an edgy version of The Wipers' classic 'D-7'. Shows in New Haven and Trenton followed, before they arrived in New York on September 28, where Kurt saw himself on TV for the first time. He phoned his mother to let her know he was on *120 Minutes*, MTV's 'alternative' show. "He was really excited," recalled Mary Lou. "He would playfully tell her every time he appeared during the video."

'Teen Spirit' went US Top 20, and Nirvana played an acoustic in-store at Tower Records, Kurt pulling out a pack of Oreo cookies from a fan's bag and washing them down with a carton of milk, mid-performance.

That evening's show, at the tiny Marquee, was killer: I watched from the balcony alongside Breeders singer Kim Deal as the crowd bounced up and down in unison, Kurt and Krist and Dave a welter of emotion and movement, guitar shattering guitar, drums pounding drums, bass hurled high in the air never to return. Kurt laughed the entire show. The crowd got crazier and crazier. At the set's climax, 'Negative Creep', Kurt had no guitar left so he dived into the crowd where they bore him triumphantly aloft, still singing – with only the bass and drums in support. It still sounded like there was an orchestra of guitars playing.

"I was shocked at how good it sounded," Gullick concurs. "Normally, it would've sounded flat without the guitar but it was unbelievably full."

Pittsburgh I don't even remember, too hopped up on alcohol and the infectious excitement surrounding the tiny tour bubble. I have a vivid memory of the minuscule JC Dobbs show in Philadelphia the next evening (October 1), though: people flying feet first over the speakers wedged on to the front of the stage, sheer pandemonium reigning as Kurt struggled to make himself heard above the constant hubbub and cheering, tune after razor-sharp tune cutting through the fog of cigarette smoke and clink of glasses from the bar. I was sat by the monitors, to the right of Kurt, fuming alongside the band as folk started chatting through a quietened, devastating version of 'Polly', happy at Nirvana's refusal to come back on stage after the set's end to a chorus of boos, arms flailing wildly as they launched into 'Drain You' followed by 'Aneurysm', body a mess of sweat and emotion, laughing as the trio launched into yet another extended jam much to the bemusement of most of the punters.

As I wrote at the time:

> *In Pittsburgh, Kurt pushes guitar through drum kit at the end, snare I believe. Dave smashed up drums. Pittsburgh didn't leave much impression. Philadelphia club was really fucking small. Crammed monitors and speakers around drum kit. Nice though. More fun. Made impression. Club was down a street full of occult or voodoo shops, and the Mutter museum of human deformities. Weird town. From where I'm sitting I can see factory chimneys.*

Kurt's moods were swinging wildly. After the reaction in Philadelphia, he became depressed – his feelings probably exacerbated by a hangover and the fatigue of travelling. The following day, I accompanied Nirvana up to the top of some megalithic tower on the outskirts of DC, to conduct a commercial radio interview: Kurt and I walked out, leaving Krist and Dave to cope with the corporate beast. Years later, in the immediate aftermath of Kurt's death, my one overriding image of the band – the one I wanted as the illustrated frontispiece to a book I knew would never appear – was Kurt standing, frail and small, head down, hacking on a cigarette, dwarfed by the shiny metal tower behind him.

"Have you been in a Top 40 American radio station before?" Kurt asked me later. No. I don't think so. "Well, you can probably imagine what it's like. These guys with eye-level swooping haircuts, finely sculpted and styled moustaches talking in a professional American radio DJ voice, not having any idea who the fuck you are, or knowing who you are just enough to have heard your music and not like you, and asking the most ridiculous questions you've ever heard. And you're there for the purpose of exposing your band when at the same time I didn't really want to expose our band any more. I felt we were getting too big. I felt guilty about that and I also felt guilty we're supporting this crap radio station that has nothing to offer anyone except commercial music. And so after a while I started not showing up for these, so I got a lot of flak from my label and from other people. Chris and Dave are still going through the motions and going to these fucking radio stations because they'd committed to it. I honestly couldn't do it any more."

Shortly after this incident, Kurt refused to be interviewed by radio DJs, full stop.

The October 2 show at Washington, DC's 9.30 Club – situated in a very bad part of town, but very close to all the state capital's tourist attractions – was incredible once again, perhaps fuelled by Kurt's minor act of rebellion. It was hotter than fuck, support band Das Damen having their work cut out to divert the rabid punk audience: and it was so packed! No room to stagedive after my three-number support set, I had to crawl off the side to hefty slaps on the back from Krist and Kurt. Nirvana opened with The Vaselines cover, 'Jesus Doesn't Want Me For A Sunbeam', which is . . . let's face it . . . a pretty fucking cool way to start a show!

Beforehand, our entourage had almost been turned away from the fancy restaurant the DGC rep had found for us, for being 'too scruffy'. Not that we cared: it looked well up its own arse – we ignored the fancy food on offer, preferring instead to partake of the 9.30 Club's legendary 'pizza' rider, sharing a slice with Dave's ultra-cool mom and sister. It was at a barbecue thrown by Dave's family the following day that Kurt told me of his love for Mary Lou Lord.

After DC, it was off down to the south-east: Georgia, North Carolina and Memphis – it was while Nirvana were in Athens, Georgia, partying at R.E.M. guitarist Peter Buck's house (instead of doing more press interviews) on October 5, that 'Smells Like Teen Spirit' moved up to number five.

Mary Lou Lord rejoined the tour a few days later, in Ohio, where she found Kurt in a particularly foul mood, cursing sound problems and claiming the previous night's show had sucked. She travelled to Detroit, Michigan with the band before leaving the next morning to fly back to her job at a record shop in Boston. That day, Nirvana were playing at the Metro in Chicago, with Urge Overkill in support.

The same morning, Courtney Love flew from LA to Chicago.

Courtney wasn't there to see Kurt Cobain. She had nurtured an on-off, volatile relationship with Billy Corgan. This flight was just the latest in her long-running affair with the self-obsessed, preening Smashing Pumpkins frontman. Neither Kurt nor Courtney had indicated to me before Chicago that either felt a particular attraction towards one another – and this was during a time when I was talking to Courtney several times a week: but Kurt was becoming famous and he was cute and sensitive, while Courtney had a real sexual charge. Plus, they both had a desperate edge to their hedonism.

"She was there with Lori [Barbero]," recalls Danny Goldberg. "That was one of the first times I met Courtney. She was schmoozing me, self-effacing, charming, working her way into this group of people. I was talking to her backstage after the show one minute, then I was talking to someone else, and when I looked over again she was sitting on Kurt's lap. She was bigger than him; so sitting on his lap was memorable. From that night on they were connected."

Courtney had no idea Nirvana were playing in Chicago that night, but she'd arrived at Corgan's apartment to find his long-term girlfriend there. Shoes were thrown from the window and she was unceremoniously booted out. So she took a $10 cab ride over to the Metro. It was somewhere to go. (Courtney actually showed up 15 minutes from the end, just as Kurt was getting into his destruction routine.) Feeling scorned, she called Corgan from the club to inform him of her intentions as regards Kurt – she already knew how intensely jealous her lover was of Nirvana – and then made her move, as described by Goldberg.

"A lot of people were there," says Craig Montgomery. "The Urge Overkill guys were there, management was there, I think the non-Corgan members of Smashing Pumpkins were there, and that was the night that Dave came and slept in my room [at the Days Inn, along Lake Michigan] because Kurt and Courtney were getting it on in the room that Kurt and Dave had been sharing." The soundman pauses. "I don't know if memories I have of her from that night are from what I've read or if they're really my own," he laughs. "Chicago was my first night of the tour. The band was anxious for me to come out, if only because my soundchecks were shorter than Monty's."

The show that night was pulverising – Kurt and Dave joined forces in decimating the drum kit with the remains of a guitar. "The buzz in the air was unbelievable," Butch Vig told Gillian G. Gaar. "Kids were screaming and crying, and almost everyone already knew all the lyrics. I was thinking, 'Wow, I might eventually have a gold record,' and of course it went gold in a matter of weeks. [It debuted in the *Billboard* Top 200 the day of the Chicago show, at number 144.] A few months later, I talked to John Silva and asked if there was any chance of *Nevermind* going number one. And he said, 'No way, not a chance.' The next week it was number one."

Courtney headed back to LA the following morning . . . possibly because the next date of the tour was in Minneapolis, one of her old towns, where her reputation preceded her. As was her wont, however, she laid siege to Kurt by fax and telephone over the following weeks.

"I was Courtney's lawyer," says Rosemary Carroll. "She started calling me because she wanted me to represent [Courtney's first husband] Falling James. Then she asked me to represent Hole – the first show I went to, she was wearing the debutante dress with the perfectly pressed bow in the back. It was a breathtaking performance, electrifying. On stage, she was playing with images of male beauty and female dominance and female submissiveness in a rock'n'roll context. She seemed very brave and fearless. There were elements of Patti Smith[9] in Hole's performance, and that in itself was enough to win me over.

"I met Kurt through Danny [Goldberg]," Rosemary continues. (Danny and Rosemary are married.) "It was that night that she and he hooked up: she borrowed money from me to get a plane ticket to Chicago to follow him there.[10] Did she say, 'I have my eyes on Kurt and I want to close the deal'? No. You know what she's like. She talks a mile a minute, a stream of consciousness, but very well informed. That was why she went to Chicago, though – she had no other reason for being there that I was aware of.[11] I never lent money to her any other time, nor did she ask me."

"[Jane's Addiction manager] Tom Atencio really wanted to manage

Courtney so he paid for some of it," corrects Janet Billig. "She was going to see Billy, and Billy or the girlfriend threw her out."

"Kurt was quiet," Rosemary says. "I had heard so much about him before I met him I expected someone about seven and a half feet tall and monstrously charismatic, but he was this small undemonstrative person with beautiful, beautiful eyes."

It was in Dallas, at Trees, on October 19 – the first of three Texas shows – that one of the more notorious incidents in Nirvana's history occurred: captured for posterity on videotape, from the moment when the bouncer first pushes Kurt in the face . . .

"The place was absolutely packed, stuffed with people," recalls Craig Montgomery. "No one could move. When Nirvana would play a song they'd whip into an uncontrollable tornado frenzy and people would float up on to the top of the crowd from the sheer pressure. There was nowhere for them to go because security couldn't let them on the stage, so they would push them back out. The sound system at this club was weak, especially the monitors, and it made Kurt really angry. They might have been cutting in and out."

"I was in Dallas – I had the flu," the Nirvana singer told me in 1993. "A doctor came to my hotel room and gave me unnamed antibiotic shots in the ass. Drunk again, and feeling the results of the antibiotics and heavy booze, I stumbled on stage and played four songs. In the middle of the fourth song, I took my guitar to the monitor board, smashing it to bits as the crowd cheered, 'Bullshit, bullshit.'"

"After a while Kurt got frustrated with the monitors," explains Craig, "so he wielded his guitar like a hatchet and put a giant dent in a bunch of the channels and walked off stage, and the band went up into the dressing room. No one knew what to do. The crowd was chanting and yelling and throwing things and wanting the band to come back out, and meanwhile the local sound crew were extremely pissed off, along with security. After a while, we managed to patch into some undamaged channels of the monitor console and get the band back out."

"The bouncer, who was also the owner of the monitor board, didn't appreciate what I'd done," continued Kurt. "For the next five songs, he paced back and forth, punching me in the ribs. I jumped into the crowd with my guitar [during 'Love Buzz']. He pretended to save me from the vicious crowd, yet he grabbed my hair and punched me in the ribs a few times. I swung the butt-end of my guitar into his face. He bled, and proceeded to beat the shit out of me."

"I've read lies about what happened next from the bouncer and his friends in Texas," Craig fumes, "but I saw [the bouncer] giving cheap shots to Kurt while he was pretending to pull him back from the stage and then I saw Kurt trying to use his guitar to ward the guy off – the guitar hit the bouncer in the head and opened up a cut. When the bouncer saw his own blood he turned into a raging bull. The band ran off stage with this enraged bouncer following them."

The bouncer punched Kurt on the back of his head, and also kicked him when he was down: "Monty, the tour manager, somehow managed to get the band out of the club and into a taxi, but while they were in the taxi, the guy was pounding on the windows," continues Craig. "Meanwhile, the rest of us were back in the dressing room hoping he didn't come back. It was funny and scary. It was funny because the guy had been nice earlier in the day – he helped us load in, and I couldn't believe that he had turned into such an asshole."

Kurt later admitted that he was behaving obnoxiously at that point on the tour, and had thrown a 'star fit' that night.

"After the show, Chris and I got into a cab," he continued, "only to be greeted by the bloody bouncer and 10 of his heavy metal vomit friends with Iron Maiden and Sammy Hagar T-shirts. The bloody bouncer smashed his hand through the side of the cab and choked me senseless. We couldn't move because we were stuck in the traffic. After 20 minutes of cat and mouse, we fled away into the night."

Meanwhile, *Nevermind* climbed from number 144 to 109.

Nirvana, Hole and Sister Double Happiness played Iguana's in Tijuana, Mexico on October 24 – another scary evening. Kids leapt from 18-foot balconies on to the backs of other kids, fans got trampled underfoot in the frenzied moshpit while security stood by helpless, and the stage was swamped with fans stagediving.

"That was a scary place," recalls Craig. "Everything was made of concrete. It had all these levels, no security. Any time you played there it was a night you just wanted to get through and get the hell out. Lots of shows happened at Iguana's. It was in this sort of desolate, half-finished shopping mall and the only things open was a grocery store and an American style, sort of gringo, Mexican restaurant. It fancied itself as a nice place; so here comes Nirvana to try to eat there and Krist asks them if they have an English menu and we're told that the English menu is broken."

The following evening, Nirvana played at The Palace in Hollywood, headlining a Rock For Choice benefit over a bill that included L7, Hole and Sister Double Happiness. "Dave was friends with one of L7 [Jennifer Finch]," says Danny Goldberg. "John [Silva] said Dave wanted them to play this benefit: then the leader of the Feminist Majority organisation called, and asked for Nirvana. It was consistent with Kurt's values. He was a strong proponent of feminism."

The LA rock elite turned out in force: Mötley Crüe drummer Tommy Lee whining to anyone who'd listen that he'd had to pay, Axl Rose turning up backstage with the Geffen president. Kurt really didn't want to hang out with such obvious progenitors of cock rock, so he slipped out and stood anonymously by the dressing room door, ignored by Nirvana's new 'fans' who had no idea what he looked like. Even the then-current kings of metal Metallica sent a fax: "We really dig Nirvana. *Nevermind* is the best album of the year. Let's get together soon, Metallica. PS, Lars [Ulrich] hates the band."[12]

It seemed like the metal world was trying its hardest to bond with the new kids, claim them for their own. The same day as the Palace show, Krist and Kurt taped a segment for MTV's big-haired metal show *Headbanger's Ball*. Kurt wore a yellow prom dress for the occasion – "because it's a ball," as he explained at the time.

Courtney was present that evening: she and Kurt stayed up the entire night before the show, "drinking and fucking", in Kurt's words. "It was during our romantic period," he laughed. There's a lovely, though probably untrue, story that Courtney told a Seattle journalist about how Kurt helped her shoot up heroin back at the hotel – Courtney apparently had a phobia of needles[13] – and then later the two musicians went out for a walk, when they stumbled across a dead bird. Kurt pulled three feathers off the bird, passed one to Courtney and kept one for himself. "And this," he said, brandishing the third, "is for the baby we're going to have." How beautiful.

More prosaically, Monty Lee Wilkes recalls seeing the couple together in the back of the tour bus, surrounded by old beer cans and empty crisp packets, spread out like decaying royalty. "It was pathetic," he sneered.

Courtney's childhood was similar to Kurt's inasmuch as she'd been shunted around from relative to relative, and indulged herself in petty larceny and drugs. Kurt was more naïve, but he wanted to learn. He wanted that rock'n'roll fantasy, hating himself because his training from Olympia spoke out starkly against the way he'd chosen to direct his life, and needing to feel anger and repression to create. His success should have provided him with security, but security was the last thing he was looking for. He needed diverting. He needed challenging, even while simultaneously retreating into a heroin-made unreality and detesting strife.

Tobi's attitude had been too hardcore even for him, and Tracy hadn't provided any sort of foil, but Courtney was punk through and through, wildly argumentative and contradictory, talking a torrent of ideas, extravagantly funny and quick to anger, but even quicker to please. One of Courtney's former lovers confided in me that she was a genius in picking out her paramour's deepest fantasy, and acting on it. She had no scruples, and few morals; and could act on impulse, especially if she was bored – well I recall having to ferry her around Reading Festival 1995 in the mud, in her high heels, her screaming at security because we had no passes, leaping on stage to rugby-tackle and slap pop stars in the face, myself made helpless by the bottle of vodka I'd drunk beforehand.

Kurt wanted his own punk rock girlfriend, his own Nancy Spungen – to Courtney's later detriment. But it was a conveniently easy fantasy for her to live out. The fact of the matter is that neither Courtney (too conventionally mainstream, wannabe Hollywood blonde) nor Kurt (too hardcore, sensitive and fucked up by his myriad contradictions) was anywhere close to Sid or Nancy, but they were roles they took upon themselves because it suited them at the time.

Courtney didn't turn Kurt on to heroin, though: even Krist Novoselic, a man who has more reason to dislike Courtney than most, will tell you that. In 1989, she'd been addicted, but she was trying to break free. All she ever did was alcohol and pills. Courtney was everywhere that first Hole tour of the UK; brawling, screeching, being manhandled off stages, telephoning in the dead of night, starting fights for no apparent reason, lying comatose in a corner, barricading me in toilets so we . . . oh no, I'm not telling everything. And everywhere, a constant stream of scurrilous and outrageously entertaining gossip and questions about music and other musicians and life.

It was Kurt who encouraged Courtney to take heroin again. He wrote in his journals about how he decided to start using heroin on a daily basis following the Sonic Youth tour, to alleviate his stomach pains. "There were many times that I found myself literally incapacitated, in bed for weeks, vomiting and starving," he wrote, concerning his stomach. "So I decided, if I felt like a junkie, I may as well be one."

Courtney used heroin as a social drug – and she was able (or so she told people) to control it, not have it control *her*. For Kurt, it was much more of a private matter: a shutting away from the world.

Were you aware of Kurt's medical problems? Like his stomach . . .

"The stomach thing was so non-specific," Carrie Montgomery complains. "It was just, 'My stomach burns and I'm gonna throw up.'

Whatever. He threw up before every show, but a lot of people did. Mark [Arm] used to throw up sometimes. It didn't seem that unusual to me. One time I was talking to Kurt at a club and I was like, 'God, dude, you have bad breath, did you just throw up or what?' And then I was teasing him about being on tour: 'It's probably kinda hard to get laid on tour when you have puke breath.' He was like, 'What?!'

"He couldn't believe I said that to him," she laughs. "Because he was not that guy, he was not the 'I'm Gonna Get Laid On Tour' guy. None of them were. It felt like he had a fragile system. He was thin and sickly and he was never the picture of health and he was never the picture of happiness either, not that he was horrid to be around.

"One time we were up in Vancouver [October 30] sharing a hotel room," she continues, "and he was really complaining about his back, so I tried these chiropractic moves on him. I had him on the floor with all kinds of pillows around him and he was like, 'Oh yeah, no. I've had that done before . . .' like totally not impressed. We were in these two double beds in the same room like [*I Love Lucy* stars] Lucy and Ricky, and we had one cigarette that we were passing back and forth, and he was like, 'Shit, what are we gonna do for cigarettes?' "

On October 26, the album jumped another 44 places to number 65. According to one report, Kurt seemed disinterested at that night's show in San Francisco. The band dressed in red and black terry robes with the Nirvana logo on the back, as a mark of respect to Bill Graham, the legendary San Francisco music promoter who'd died the night before and who'd given them the robes. Kurt spent much of the evening falling over mic stands. The next night, Hole and The Wipers supported Nirvana at The Palace in LA.

On October 29, *Nevermind* went gold (US sales of 500,000 copies) – something Nirvana only found out by chance from Susie Tennant at their Fox Theatre show in Portland. "She thought they knew, and they didn't," explains Kim Warnick. "She was quite offhand about it, but she didn't mean to be. She went up to Krist and congratulated him. He wanted to know why. He was very excited when he found out."[14]

For the next three dates Nirvana were supposed to be supporting Mudhoney – but with the buzz around *Nevermind* the way it was, the headline slot clearly needed to be switched.

"When *Every Good Boy Deserves Fudge* came out and *Nevermind* was coming out, we both went off on separate tours," recalls Dan Peters. "We had this plan to come back in Portland and Seattle to do a couple of shows together. We head off on our tour and everything's great. Every fucking club we get to is like . . . [imitates 'Smells Like Teen Spirit' riff]. I mean every fucking club. We were like, 'Whoa!' It was obvious something was up."

How did you feel about that?

"It was pretty cool actually," laughs the Mudhoney drummer. "We were psyched for them. By the time we got back to Portland, we realised. Mudhoney will not be headlining."

Many regard the Seattle show – at the Paramount on October 31, with Mudhoney and Bikini Kill in support – as the end of an era. Incontrovertibly, Nirvana was now big news. The second grunge explosion was beginning. John Silva hired a video crew to film proceedings:[15] in partial retaliation, Bikini Kill scrawled words like SLUT and WHORE over their bodies with thick marker pen – and Kurt, on a whim, asked his Olympia friends Ian [Dickson] and Nikki [McClure] if they'd care to dance on stage with Nirvana.

"More evidence about Nirvana being a feminist band," comments Rich Jensen. "Ian and Nikki were just indie kids, a boy and girl, from Olympia. They danced like hell, I mean with spirit, but they weren't like strippers. Nirvana wasn't macho, so they had anti-go-go dancers."

The pair must have looked a strange sight: Ian with his dark glasses and skinny frame aping Sixties moves, Nikki lost in her own private world, dancing without fear. Nikki got Ian to wear a T-shirt with the word 'boy' written large on it, while she wore one boasting 'girl'. Gold Mountain made sure the cameras were kept away as much as possible from the pair.

"John Silva comes up to me as we were getting up to go on stage and says, 'I didn't spend a quarter of a million dollars on this video for you to fuck it up!' " exclaims Ian. "He had, like, towels around his neck and was ready to hand the guys towels when they came off stage, that whole business. I'm like, 'Fuck you John. I don't work for you. Kurt asked me to do this.' "

"The record label, unbeknown to Nirvana, had set up a big film shoot," recalls Charles Peterson. "There were six guys all clad in black running around with compact 35mm movie cameras and I was like, 'Yeah, this is the beginning of the end.' It was so unfair to their home audience because it stilted the performance. It reeked of money."

Before the show, Kurt went out for a stroll with Carrie Montgomery, to purchase some new socks and underwear[16] from Bon Marché, where the singer deposited his old shoes on the counter, trying to find enough cash to buy his purchases with. "He started unfolding the money really slowly,"

Carrie laughs, "taking forever to count it out, with great deposits of fluff next to the dollar bills. The salesman was looking at him like he's a homeless person.

"The same evening," she continues, "we walked downtown to go shopping for his Halloween costume. And there was a record store in the Westlake mall that was full of Nirvana posters. He was shocked. Then we went to the bank machine and he got out some money and he got the receipt and again he was shocked. He had no idea how much money he had. We went down to the sex store and got a blow-up doll, and he got inside of it and wore it. We stayed at Kurt's hotel downtown. Me and my girlfriend were staying there and Tobi [Vail] was there. They wanted to go talk, and got another room. So we had the MTV on all night, and it was Nirvana all night long. I kept waking up and thinking, 'This is insane.' We teased him about it. It was very surreal and very strange."

"The Portland show was fun," states Dan Peters, "but when we got to Seattle it became evident how out-of-control events were getting. There was this huge-ass film crew present, these corporate goons hanging about, and we couldn't even stand on the side of the stage and watch. I don't blame the band for that. I blame the people they let hang around them."

"I hated that Paramount show," comments Rob Kader, before adding mistakenly, "*The End*[17] fucking put these dancers on the side, and I thought, 'How cheesy is that?' That threw the whole thing off, like, 'These guys are fucking rock stars.' The tone of it disappointed me."

The following day, Tobi moved to Washington, DC.

Two days after the Paramount show, Nirvana departed for Europe. *Nevermind* was now at number 36 in the *Billboard* Top 40.

**Addenda 1: Courtney Love and Hole**

On my first trip to LA, I visited Disneyland. There's something fascinating in the sight of Americans revelling in their own excess. I was there for 18 hours and had to invent a plane crash to get to 'the happiest place on earth'. I returned at least twice afterwards, once with Hole and once with the Melvins. Taking a band as screwed up as Hole to Disneyland seemed a brilliant juxtaposition.

"I remember this whole weird thing where Courtney insisted on sitting next to you on all the rides, even though she was going out with me at the time," Eric Erlandson says. "I was convinced that she'd fucked you, too – during that first interview when she changed into your dressing gown. She told me to keep quiet about our relationship to you. We kept it quiet for a year, and then we had a huge fight during which Courtney threw a trashcan through my car window. So it was hard to keep it a secret after that.

"She moved in with me the day we fell in love, on St Patrick's Day 1990," he continues. 'It was while we were recording 'Retard Girl'. She phoned up her husband James and said she wasn't coming home. When we met you that was the beginning of the end. As soon as it became serious like that, with her sitting down and talking to journalists, there was a whole new set of rules. I remember that during the first interview, you kept asking me odd, disjointed questions, like, 'How do you feel about aeroplane flights?' and I wanted to kill you. I was really taken aback by the way she was using her womanhood on you to get what she wanted."

Eric was working at Capitol Records at the time. It was from there he posted the first two Hole singles to me.

"When I first met Courtney, I was in awe of how fucked up she was," the guitarist recalls, "and almost irresistibly embarrassed by the way she was acting. She used to pick on me for having one foot in her apartment and one in the hallway, because my car was always double-parked when I'd visit her. I was totally into hanging out with her but not fully committed, thinking of my escape the whole time. I used to think that was a great metaphor for our relationship – yours, too. Except, of course, both of us eventually put both feet irretrievably in her apartment."

I don't want to sound too cynical. Everything that involved Courtney was a raucous good time certainly up to the end of '91, and many times after. That held true even when she phoned me up to boast about punching enemies out. I shouted at her then. After all, I was a target for violence myself, with my photo in *Melody Maker* almost every week.

The memories blur into one, me drunk and her whatever. We meet outside the Dominion Theatre in London; she sends her personal manager out into the crowd at the Phoenix Festival to find me; storming off before shows to go score drugs and turning up hours late; curled up in bed on drugs; arguing and screaming at the top of our voices. Hanging out in LA, shopping in unrelenting sunshine, hours wasted in dusty vintage dress shops.

The first time Hole played England, they headlined at the Camden Underworld where the belligerent crowd, tanked up on hype and alcohol, molested Courtney. She leapt off stage after Eric had jumped in still playing his guitar, and had her dress ripped from her body. Tiny Delia kicked at the ankles of louts twice her size; Courtney screamed my real name from on stage like it was my fault; friends wandered around afterwards in tears of anger. Post-show, the two of us hid beneath the dressing room table as her friend Bill (the one with the monstrous moustache) fended off the curious. Courtney gave me a ring from her fingers as a bond. I wore it faithfully for months afterwards until it broke. It was a Crackerjack ring.

Why did I hang out with Courtney? What, are you going to resist gossip-dripping phone calls lasting three hours, five days a week, usually at 4 a.m., sometimes with songs attached? Once, the singer left a message where she was boasting to Kurt how I had made her a star and introduced the couple. So I put it on my answer machine. The first person to leave a message afterwards was, of course, Courtney. There was a stunned silence, and then she continued talking oblivious.

Are you going to resist the temptation to create mischief and upset and scandal at every turn? You're a duller person than I thought then. When I drank, I drank without fear of the consequences because I had low self-worth. I partied like it was my last evening because it could well have been.

At the Zap Club in Brighton on the first Mudhoney/Hole tour I felt frightened but irresistibly drawn towards the emotion directed straight at me from the stage. Courtney was in her usual confrontational stance; feet on speakers, dress riding over the audience. London, the same tour, and Courtney ad-libs between songs with Morrissey references that I'd instructed her to say. Backstage, she hurls a solid glass ashtray at Eric's head. It misses him by inches. This was one of many concerts where security tried to restrain us.

I hung out with Courtney because she was fun to be with. I didn't even know what she looked like when I fell in love with her music.

### Addenda 2: Kurt on The Breeders and feminism

The following is taken from the transcript of an interview conducted in Kurt's temporary LA home, 2002 – just down the street from where the Rodney King LA riots were taking place. The interview was partly structured around Kurt's favourite 10 records. The list started off with The Breeders' debut *Pod* – Kurt had meticulously written down notes in his journal about each record. His line on The Breeders read, "It's an epic that will never let you forget your ex-girlfriend" . . .

"By that, I don't necessarily mean that the record reminds me of my last girlfriend," Kurt explained. "It seems that when the girls in The Breeders get together, they give off this air of . . . their ex-boyfriends."

The Breeders are one of your favourite bands. What is it you like about them?

"The number one reason is their songs, for the way they structure them, which is totally unique, very atmospheric. I wish Kim was allowed to write more songs for the Pixies, because 'Gigantic' is the best Pixies song, and Kim wrote it. I love their attitude. 'Doe', the [Breeders] song about where a girl gives a boy head and he pats her on the head like a doe, is very funny. They're strong women, but it's not that obvious. They're not militant about it at all. You can sense they really like men at the same time."

But you're attracted more to feminine people? Is that because you've been through the phase of liking masculine . . .?

"Yeah, I went through that stage about five years ago. I went through most of my adolescent life being a male and not being aware of feminism, but I was always more of a feminine person. I always felt more inclined to hang out with girls, and I appreciated softer pop music during most of my childhood, until I became a teenager when I started smoking pot. That was the time that my hormones started swinging around in my testicles and I started getting facial hair. I had to let off my male steam somewhere so I started listening to Black Sabbath."

I often felt that the problem with early punk was that it excluded women mainly. It was meant to be right-on, but it excluded half its potential audience.

"Yeah, definitely. And that was only something I realised later because I didn't get to see the punk movement in the Seventies. Like, on that live Dead Boys record, *Night Of The Living Dead Boys*, the singer was spewing off about how some girl was sucking his cock while he was on stage – that was the common accepted thing in punk rock."

It seems now, switching on MTV, that the metal world is still stuck with the same tired values.

"It might be getting a little bit better because of bands like Soundgarden. They have a good image and a healthy feminist attitude as far as metal goes. Maybe others will follow them. Even Pearl Jam, who were obviously cock rock poseurs down on Sunset Strip last year, are preferable."

What does feminism mean to you?

"What does it mean to you?"

I asked you first!

"It's not so much of an ideal as so much of a sense I have to be politically feminist by talking about feminism structurally, supporting it. I don't want to preach about it. I don't think there's such a thing as feminism any more, not in the sense of it being a movement like it used to be during the Seventies – but there does seem to be a collective awareness nowadays, because people are taking it up individually."

What would you say the main effect of having a feminist outlook on your life is?

"Um, just everyday living, being aware of not offending women and not supporting sexist acts, you know. Just be aware of it all the time, not so wary that you become so anal, so paranoid of offending women that you can't feel comfortable. There are lots of sexist jokes that I laugh at and it's harmless, up to a point. But I know these people who pride themselves on being bohemian, who put on this act all the time, 24 hours a day, of pretending to be a macho redneck. Their excuse is that they're trying to remind you that that is the way of the redneck, but I noticed that after someone talks like that for a while they usually turn into a redneck."

I definitely agree with that. That was one of the main reasons I fell out with Sub Pop a couple of years ago.

"Absolutely. That's the main reason why I never get along with very many people at Sub Pop."

It was funny for a while, and then you started to wonder whether they meant it or not – or if it even mattered whether they meant it or not. Dwarves are a great example of that: the singer is smart, funny, but you'd never guess it from his stage act.

"That's also kind of a statement within itself, which I kind of respect. People that go out of their way to act like an asshole or an imbecile all of the time when they're really intelligent. The statement is that literally there's no point. It's a really nihilistic way of living your life. There's no point in trying to be human any more because things have gotten so out of hand. It's still a very punk rock attitude, but I just think it'd be really boring to be Johnny Rotten after all these years. I'm not saying Johnny Rotten has ever been sexist . . . I mean that negative attitude, not appreciating passion at all or not admitting that things are beautiful."

Yeah, that's the problem. You cut off so much if you cut off enthusiasm. Feminism, as far as I'm concerned, is women taking matters into their own hands and me not standing in their way. It's women controlling their own lives, not men.

"I really agree with that."

## NOTES

1 At one point, Das Damen – sweet Beatles/metal-loving SST rockers – were considered the equals of Soundgarden. 1991's *Triskaidekaphobe* is the one to buy. Das Damen also played on the Sub Pop Legend! B-side.

2 Urge Overkill played a hard, shiny kitschadelic power pop that assimilated both the bell-bottomed past and 'cool jam' present, most notably on their taut, Cheap Trick-influenced, 1993 Geffen album *Saturation*.

3 Sister Double Happiness were a very ordinary Austin, Texas rock band – presumably booked because a couple of members had been in legendary Eighties punks, The Dicks.

4 The songwriter part is questionable, as Mary Lou Lord normally covers other people's songs, singing with a babyish lisp.

5 WFNX DJ Kurt St Thomas was the first person to premiere *Nevermind* in its entirety, on August 29, 7 p.m. EST.

6 Not actually true. Frances Bean was born prematurely.

7 Carpal tunnel syndrome is a condition that occurs when there is an inflammation of the median nerve that runs through the carpal tunnel. The tunnel itself is made up of bones and ligaments in the wrist area – ie: it's a common complaint for guitarists and typists.

8 It would have been OK the other way round.

9 Patti Smith is a rightly revered NYC poet: her early work from the Seventies includes the venomous 'Piss Factory' and the seminal albums *Horses* and *Radio Ethiopia*. Kim Deal, Kim Gordon and Courtney all owe a debt to Patti's fearless live performances.

10 Courtney was good at raising money from allies: when I first met her in LA, I needed money to stay on another few days so I could catch Hole playing live with Melvins. Courtney contacted Janet Billig, then working at Caroline in NYC, and Janet wired me 200 bucks. It was probably the wisest 200 bucks Janet ever spent.

11 Of course Rosemary could be correct, but by Courtney's own recent admission she was there to continue her pursuit of Corgan.

12 Metallica were the metal band most similar (musically) to Nirvana and their Seattle peers: the 'Enter Sandman' band would later tour extensively with Soundgarden. Nirvana didn't dig their pompous attitude, however.

13 Although how this tallies with Courtney's well-documented drug use is not explained.

14 Here, the account contradicts Krist's attitude in *Come As You Are*, where the band were trying to appear cool and uncaring about success.

15 Some of the footage later ended up being used in the 'Lithium' video.

16 Boxer shorts; he'd been admonished for his tiger-print Y-fronts by Courtney.

17 *The End* is Seattle's own alternative commercial radio station.

## CHAPTER 18

# Territorial Pissings

NIRVANA were based round the very Olympian belief of spontaneity being at the heart of great rock music. Sure, Kurt could spend weeks – years even – crafting a chord change or set of lyrics, but it was only a base from which to explode. Spontaneity is something rock'n' roll frequently aspires to, or pretends to embrace, but rarely achieves. Most rock shows are as polite and pedantic as a Sunday morning Anglican Church service or sports meeting – especially when the shows are over a certain size. There are so many factors to take into consideration: ticket sales, and lighting rigs, and outside recording units, and smoke machines . . . even the encores are scripted out. Normally.

Yet why get up on stage if you're not going to present something special each time? This is a dilemma that doesn't seem to bother 99 per cent of rock musicians – who prize 'professionalism' above anything, the ability to deliver the goods in a manner so slick and glib that they're indistinguishable from a thousand other nights, a thousand other bands. All that concerns them is making sure the lighting engineer knows precisely when to flash the lights to 'strobe' during the extended drum solo, second from last number; and that the stage crew out front and side know precisely how many encores are being played, and for how long. Touring arena rock bands take a travelling entourage with them the size of a small community, and within well-oiled 'machines' like that there's very little scope for spontaneity. Why worry about that, when you're raking in £100,000 or more a show? It bothered Kurt, though. And this confusion he felt towards the constraints of success is what set his band apart.

Courtney Love was a perfect foil for Kurt, prematurely jaded with an industry he never liked in the first place. She was entirely spontaneous. There was no safety switch in her head for when things got out of hand. She took a delight in fucking shit up, didn't care whose feelings she trampled over, even her handful of friends whom she loved with a passion as fierce as hate. Kurt liked to instigate trouble, anything to shake up complacency – he'd leapt on the backs of enough bouncers, and let off enough fire extinguishers in his time – but he also liked to sit back and watch, be the voyeur. That was where Courtney came in. She didn't care. Not back then.

"Kathleen had a big influence on him too," argues Ian Dickson, referring to the equally volatile Bikini Kill singer. Between '91 and '93, while Courtney was pretending to be a feminist, she imagined Kathleen Hanna to be a rival, culminating in an infamous incident where she punched Hanna.

"Imagine if you had two superheroes, one 'good' and the other 'bad'," Ian suggests. "That's Kathleen and Courtney. Kathleen embodies all these feminist ideas and has always been very consistent. Courtney adopted a lot of her agenda and used it to become famous. Kurt was tremendously attracted to [Kathleen's ideas] because he loved the underdog. He had a belief in, and tremendous feeling for, women and gays and people that were underpowered and underprivileged. He saw that in Courtney, but it was all twisted."

The burgeoning relationship between Kurt and Courtney began to overshadow Nirvana's success. Kurt's declaration on November 8, live on crap UK youth culture programme *The Word*, that "Courtney Love is the best fuck in the world" – a rather dismal, bragging rock'n'roll statement much more suited to Mötley Crüe drummer Tommy Lee or one of his ilk – attracted enormous attention. Nirvana switched from being a rock phenomenon to front-page tabloid news: success *and* controversy is a potent combination.

Mary Lou Lord may remember Kurt still being enamoured of her when she turned up in England, and that he didn't mention Courtney's name at all[1], but there's no doubting that Courtney's wild, unfocused and dazzling barrage of phone calls and faxes over the couple of weeks he was in Europe soon worked their magic.

"I'd never met anyone so outspoken and charismatic," Kurt said, mirroring the way several of us felt. "She's like a magnet for exciting things to happen." He claimed the pair of them would fuck standing up against the walls of rock venues.

Their romance blossomed through November: Courtney sent faxes telling Kurt he smelt of "waffles and milk". He would reply with stream-of-consciousness notes that betrayed his continuing fascination for excrement, babies, needles and punk rock.

"Kurt was attracted to Courtney because she was who he wanted to be," suggests Janet Billig. "It's that Jerry Hall thing: she could be a maid in the living room and a slut in the bedroom. He loved that she was controversial. Drugs weren't a part of it. That was an activity that each liked separately before they met.

"They made a great couple . . . better than Courtney and Billy Corgan certainly!" Janet laughs.[2] "They complemented each other so well: Courtney said everything that Kurt was thinking. Kurt was quiet, but he wished he was a loudmouth. People were obsessed with him as a musician and her as a character. There was equality at one point: his was as the rock star, and hers was that she was crazy. Really, they were both crazy – but in an artistic way. She's one of the greatest poets of her generation. She said a lot of things girls needed to hear and maybe some things they didn't."

Courtney was aggressive and running rampant, now she'd been given another chance at the spotlight. Another chance? Let's backtrack a moment. She'd tried to become a film star via Alex Cox in the Eighties – *Straight To Hell, Sid And Nancy* – the maverick English filmmaker simultaneously charmed and wary of her naked, ranting ambition. But it was taking too long. She'd tried pushing her male friends into the spotlight – livewire boyfriend Rozz Rezabek-Wright in Portland, Falling James in LA – but she didn't have the patience to wait for either of them to live up to her expectations. Despite having joined Faith No More briefly as a singer, and forming Sugar Baby Doll, she lacked the necessary self-belief to push *herself* as the rock star – but thought she'd give it another try when she saw Eric Erlandson's advert for a singer in a LA paper. Through sheer annoyance factor and charm she managed to talk a couple of labels – Sympathy For The Record Industry, Sub Pop – into releasing her singles, and befriended Janet Billig over at Caroline.

She still wasn't a star, however. Then I appeared on the scene – a name journalist in a position of power. I was totally blown away, bewildered by and enamoured of her, helped by my love of her Sonic Youth/ Mudhoney-influenced music. My task was easy. All I had to do was quote what she had to say, and capture her personality in print. I came back to the UK, and turned this peripheral figure into a minor celebrity. I also introduced her to Kurt Cobain, but that was an accident.

She did the rest.

She made a mistake, though – or so her champions like myself, and Kim Gordon, and Jennifer Finch felt. We warned her against hitching herself to the Cobain bandwagon. We thought that her undoubted personality and artistic talent would become secondary, marginalised, in comparison to

Kurt – because the music industry is fundamentally sexist, and she would be viewed as a gold-digging girlfriend.

So it proved.

*How much did meeting Courtney change you?*

*"Totally," Kurt says, emphatically. "I'm not as much of a neurotic, unstable person as I was. I used to feel I was always alone, even though I had lots of friends and a band that I really enjoyed being with. Now I've found someone I'm close to, who's interested in the things I do, and I really don't have many other aspirations."*

*Did you know who she was before you met her?*

*"Not really, no," he replies. "I'd heard about her, though – some nasty rumours, that she was this perfect replica of Nancy Spungen."*

*Kurt laughs.*

*"That got my attention," he remarks, maliciously. "Like everyone else, I loved Sid [Vicious] cos he was such a likeable, dopey guy. I've often felt that many people think of me as a stupid, impressionable person, so I thought that maybe going out with someone who was meant to be like Nancy would stick a thorn in everyone's side, cos it's the exact opposite of what they would want me to do – they would want me to go out with some little troll girl."*

*I always thought you were more John and Yoko than Sid and Nancy.*[3]

*"Yeah, sure, OK. Maybe you should put that."*

*Kurt starts flicking through a Nirvana comic, and pauses, struck by a sudden thought.*

*"Courtney helped me to put Nirvana in perspective," he adds, "to realise that my reality doesn't entirely revolve around the band, that I can deal without it if I have to. Which doesn't mean I'm planning on breaking up the band or anything, but that the minimal amount of success I strived for isn't of much importance any more.*

*"I'm so far beyond thinking about the band," he continues, "that I can't let it bother me any more. It's so exhausting. I feel so raped that I have to just have fun now. I don't mean to take it so seriously. I know that that comes across in interviews but that has a lot to do with the questions that they ask of me all the time. People think I'm a moody person, and I think it's lame that there are only two kinds of male lead singer. You can either be a moody visionary like Michael Stipe, or a mindless heavy metal party guy like Sammy Hagar."*

*I tried to portray you as a mindless party animal type and you got annoyed.*

*"Oh, OK," Kurt laughs. "I guess it is better to be called a moody visionary than a mindless party animal. Alcoholism is totally acceptable, though. People just laugh about it."*

*It's because people don't feel threatened by it.*

*"I tried to become an alcoholic. Didn't you, too? It didn't work, did it?"*

*No, I kind of took it a bit far but . . .*

*"I remember that."*

*We wander through to Kurt and Courtney's bedroom, to see if Courtney's awake yet. Just. The box in the corner is still dribbling out MTV. Talk drifts on to how MTV controls the American rock world.*

*"I want to get rid of my cable," Kurt declares. "I've done that so many times in my life, where I decide I'm not going to have television, become celibate. It usually lasts for about four months."*

*I was just going to ask you about your fondness for smashing up guitars. Don't you ever get bored with that?*

*"No," replies Kurt. "I don't do it nearly as much as everyone thinks I do. I just wait for a good time to do it – like when I'm pissed off, or if I want to show off in front of Courtney. Or if I'm appearing on TV, just to piss the TV people off. I have my guitar-smashing room in the back, where I practise four hours a day."*

*Pause. Kurt's building up for a rant.*

*"You know what I hate about rock?" he asks me. "Cartoons and horns. I hate Phil Collins, all of that white male soul. I hate tie-dyed T-shirts, too. You know there are bootleg tie-dyed T-shirts of Nirvana? I hate that. I wouldn't wear a tie-dyed T-shirt unless it was dyed with the urine of Phil Collins and the blood of Jerry Garcia."*

*Courtney overhears this last comment from her bedroom.*

*"Oh God, Kurt, how long have you been thinking about that one?" she castigates him, annoyed.*

*"Well, fuck," he whines. "No one ever prints it."*

*"It's fifth grade!" Courtney yells. "It's so boy!"*

*"Well ex-ker-use me!" Kurt shouts back, sarcastically.*

(*Melody Maker*, July 18, 1992)

Ask anyone about what was happening to Nirvana around this time, and they'll all tell you a different story.

Some will focus in on *Nevermind*'s continued race up the US charts – from number 35 to number 17 to number nine through November and December. You couldn't switch on MTV for more than a couple of minutes without seeing 'Teen Spirit'. Not that the band cared by this point – matters were too out of hand for that.

Some will focus in on the ever more climactic smashing of instruments, the goofing off on European TV shows, the drunken capers and ribald excitement. A favourite tour bus tape at the time was The Jerky Boys' album of inane and downright nasty prank phone calls: the words 'jerky' and 'fuckface' soon passed into common usage. In Italy, Shelli and Ed 'King' Roeser from Urge Overkill broke into the hotel's wine cellar: a discovery that led to formation vomiting, Krist and Shelli winning hands down in the husband-and-wife stakes.

Krist got to the stage where he was downing three bottles of Bordeaux a night, plus any amount of cigarettes and hash. Kurt's stomach was playing up again, his condition made worse by the singer's insistence on smoking hand-rolled cigarettes. He'd drink cough syrup constantly and vomited before several shows. Even Dave – young, fresh and definitely up for the ride – was starting to feel claustrophobic.

"We resented the success so we turned into assholes," Kurt explained to Michael Azerrad. "We got drunk a lot and wrecked more equipment than we needed to. We just decided to be real abusive pricks. We wanted to make life miserable for people."

Some focus in on the shows: the band played extensively over this period – England (November 4–9), Germany (November 10–13), a one-off in Vienna, Austria with Jack Endino's Skin Yard, Italy with Urge Overkill – but it's so difficult to separate one show from the next, one crazed live band from another, especially in 1991 when everything was spinning so fast it felt like the only way to stand still was to party even faster.

"Corey Rusk from Touch And Go called me up," says Christof Ellinghaus, "and said, 'Nirvana have invited Urge Overkill to go on tour with them, can you help us put this together?' So I quickly got Urge a van and a back line, and they stayed on my kitchen floor and so I got to see another Nirvana show. That was at The Loft [November 10], it was sold out, 650-capacity in Berlin. I don't remember much from the show, it was so busy and you couldn't move around. To me, it was more remote. There wasn't the warmth of before."

Kids walked around London shows with T-shirts spouting lines written about me by famous rock stars[4] . . . who were queuing up to brag about how they'd punch me out next time we met. None of them ever did, except for Kat Bjelland and Jennifer Finch – and Kat could hit hard! A few poured beer over me, but I poured more back over them. Billy Corgan dressed up in a clown suit for an entire UK tour's worth of encores after I'd called him a clown in print, and came looking for me with security in tow at Reading. But I can move fast when I want. Oh, and I once had a screaming manager hold a glass to my throat for 10 minutes . . .

Kurt Cobain, September 1992. *(STEPHEN SWEET)*

Growing up in Aberdeen: Kurt, April 1969.
*(COURTESY OF EARNIE BAILY)*

The Cobain family
(Wendy, Don, Kim, Kurt) 1974.
*(TDY/REX)*

Kurt in 1982 with his high school band. *(WENN)*

Early Nirvana, with Dave Foster (left), 1988. "Dave was a lot closer to what they wanted, because he was a Dale Crover wannabe. Me and Dylan referred to him as Anger Problem Dave because he would blow up and scream at Kurt or Krist" - Slim Moon *(RICH HANSEN)*

"Kurt was schooled in Olympia. Kurt made money in Seattle. And Kurt probably partied in Tacoma" - Bruce Pavitt at the New Music Seminar, NYC *(CHARLES PETERSON)*

Slim Moon, founder of Olympia Riot Grrrl label kill rock stars. *(JOHN VANDER SLICE)*

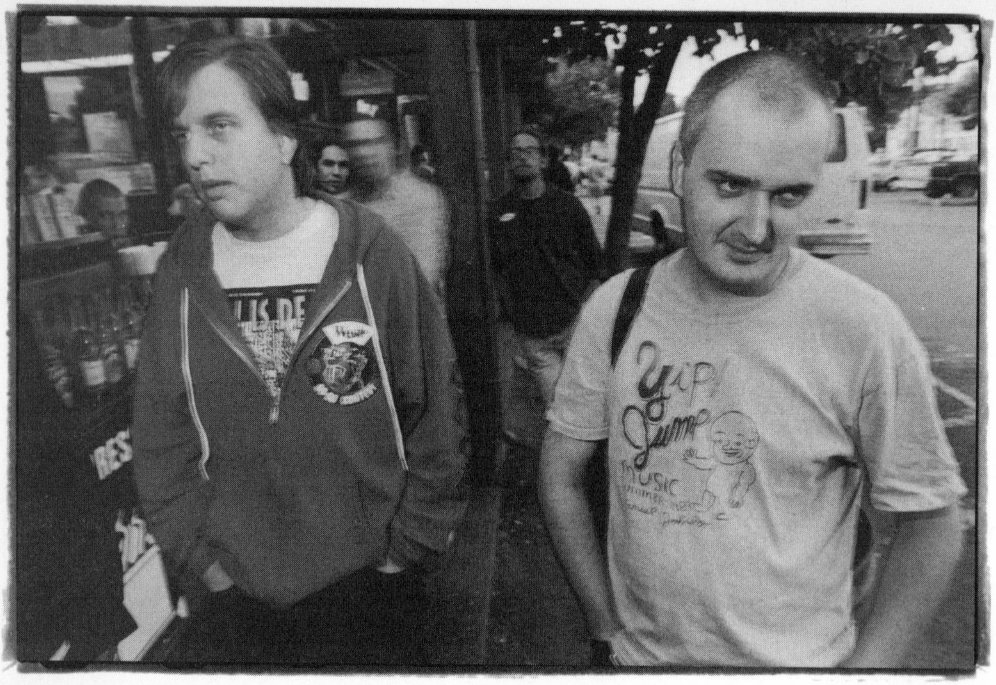

"I know I'm going to sound like a complete country bumpkin… but to have a real live British music journalist in our midst! I was in awe" - Jonathan Poneman with Everett True, Seattle, 1991 *(CHARLES PETERSON)*

Nirvana, Seattle 1989 with temporary extra guitarist Jason Everman (third left) and *Bleach* drummer Chad Channing (first left). What do you think Jason brought to the band? "He brought a lot of hair…and some money" - Rob Kader *(IAN TILTON)*

Krist Novoselic, London Astoria ('Lamefest'), December 3, 1989. "Krist was swinging his bass around, when all of a sudden it got loose and I fucking had to put my hand up. If I'd been any slower it would totally have gotten me" - Dan Peters *(STEVE DOUBLE/SIN)*

Kurt Cobain airborne at the 'Lamefest'. *(STEVE DOUBLE/RETNA)*

Nirvana, London Astoria, December 3, 1989. "Remember Lamefest? The show scarred me. Mudhoney headlined, but Nirvana stole the show. They were a menace, amazing" - Christof Ellinghaus *(STEPHEN SWEET)*

Grunge takes Seattle: "Gritty vocals, roaring Marshall amps, ultra-loose GRUNGE that destroyed the morals of a generation" - early Sub Pop press release describing pre-Mudhoney band Green River. Top: Soundgarden, Seattle, 1987 (from l-r: Kim Thayil, Hiro Yamamoto, Chris Cornell, Matt Cameron). Bottom: Mudhoney, 1987 (from l-r: Dan Peters, Steve Turner, Mark Arm, Matt Lukin). *(CHARLES PETERSON)*

Tad Doyle proudly sporting his 'Loser' T-shirt, 1989. "We discuss to this day reprinting those shirts. Such a great slogan" - Jonathan Poneman *(IAN TILTON)*

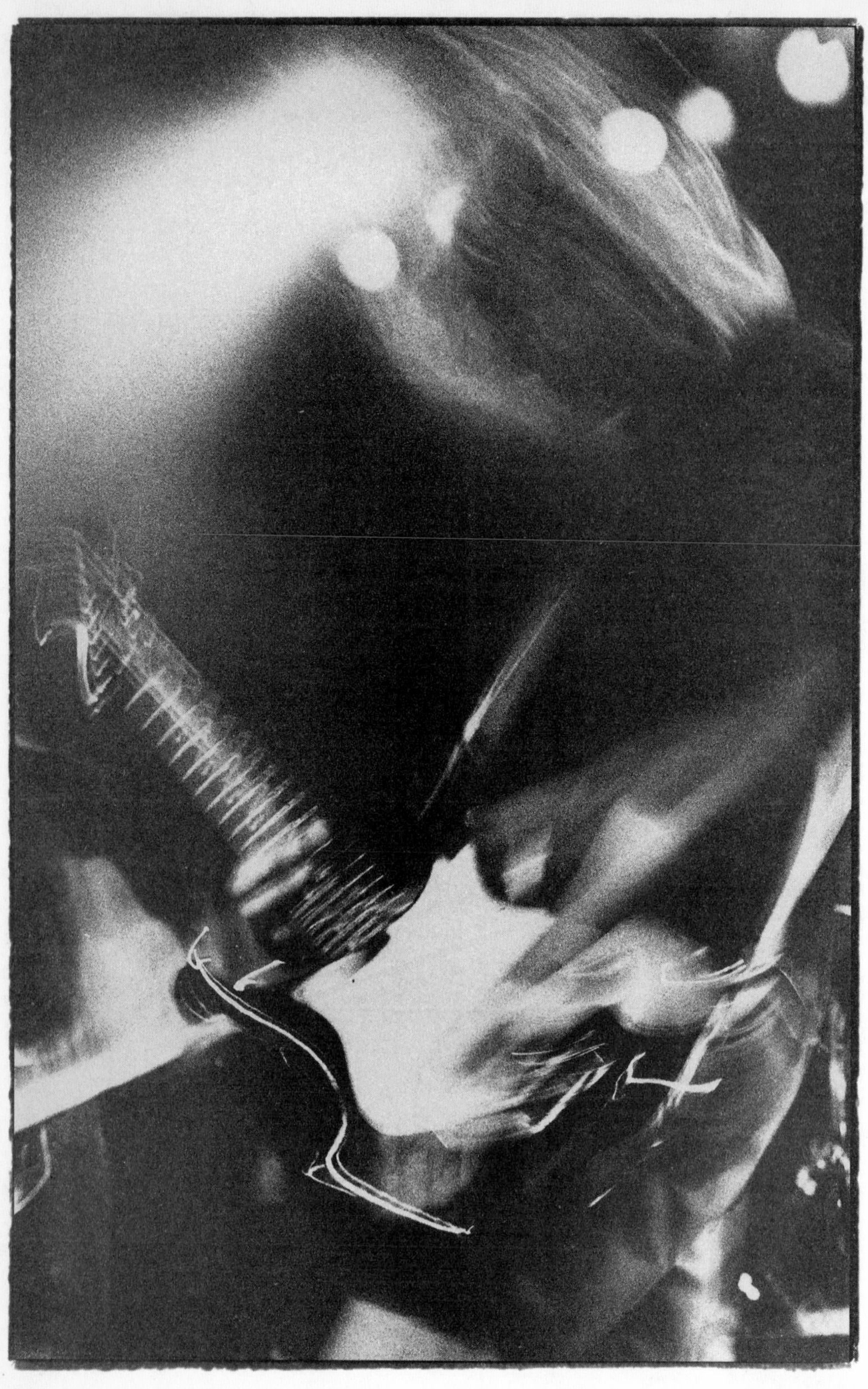

Kurt Cobain, December 3, 1989, Lamefest. *(STEPHEN SWEET)*

Kurt, Krist, Chad, New York, 1990. "Krist was the joker of the pack. He was about 8' 2", while if Chad had been any smaller he'd have been classified as a dwarf" - Anton Brookes *(STEVE DOUBLE/SIN)*

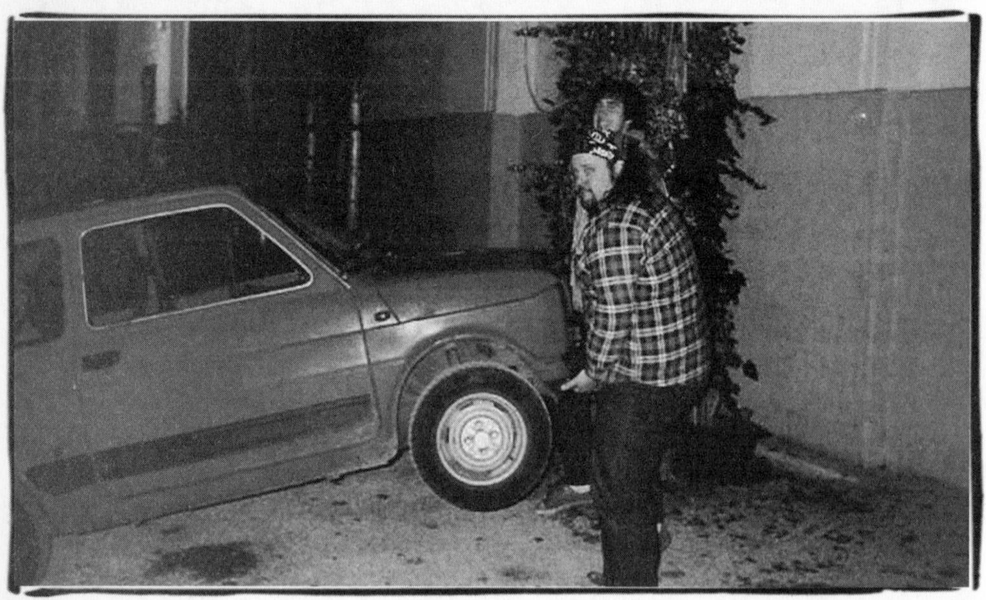

Tad and Nirvana on tour in Europe, October/November 1989. "The first European tour was gruelling and cold. You're up late every night, and you're sleeping somewhere that's probably cold and there's a shared bathroom down the hall. And in the van, the seats don't recline and every seat is occupied" - Craig Montgomery, soundman. Above: the two bands pose with some border guards - Craig is front right, next to Chad. Below: Krist and Tad work out. *(CRAIG MONTGOMERY)*

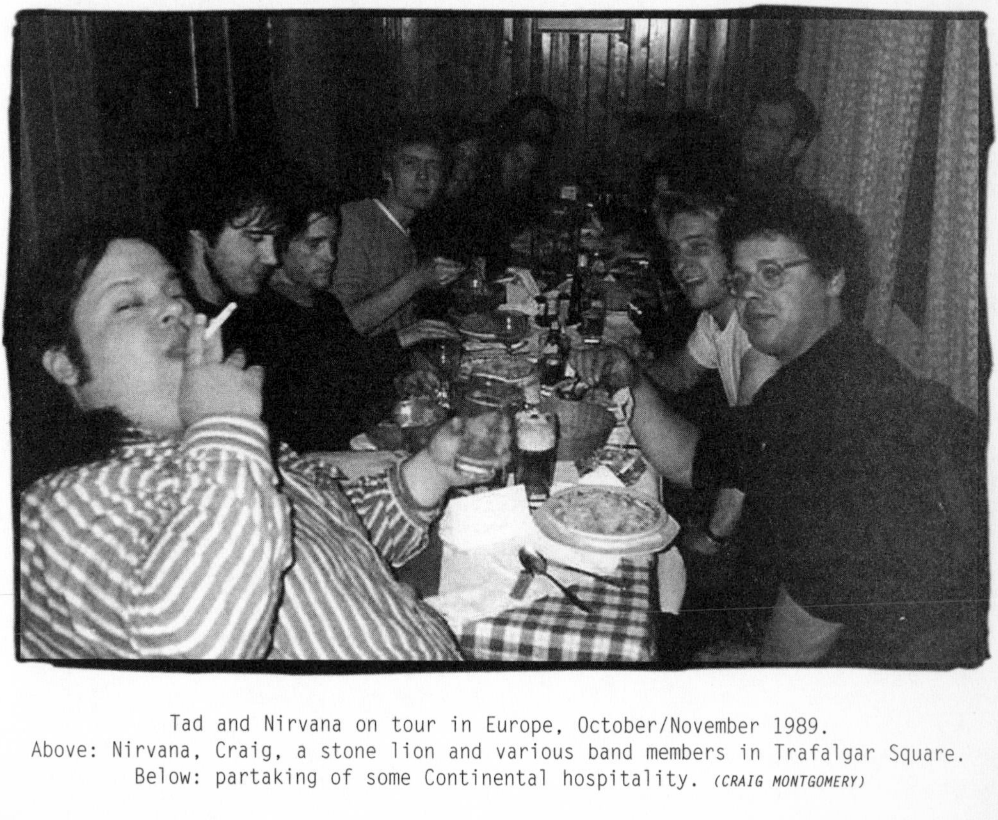

Tad and Nirvana on tour in Europe, October/November 1989.
Above: Nirvana, Craig, a stone lion and various band members in Trafalgar Square.
Below: partaking of some Continental hospitality. *(CRAIG MONTGOMERY)*

Four major influences on early Nirvana (clockwise from top left): *Bleach* producer Jack Endino outside Reciprocal Studios, Buzz Osborne and Dale Crover from Aberdeen's own Melvins, Earth founder Dylan Carlson, Beat Happening and K Records' founder, Olympia's Calvin Johnson. *(CHARLES PETERSON)*

Nirvana, post-Chad, with temporary drummer, Mudhoney's Dan Peters, Seattle September 23, 1990. "If I'd known they were that serious I'd have purchased another drum kit somehow" - Dan Peters *(IAN TILTON)*

Charles Peterson, the photographer responsible for the 'look' of Seattle grunge. "Charles was the essential ingredient, particularly early on. It was a visual signature that defined the whole scene" - Jonathan Poneman *(CHARLES PETERSON)*

Krist and Shelli Novoselic indulging in a spot of home cooking, Tacoma, autumn 1990. *(IAN TILTON)*

*"Who will be the king and queen of the outcast teens?"* Tobi Vail, inspiration behind 'Smells Like Teen Spirit'. "If you find out your boyfriend is doing heroin and he's not going to change and you break up with him, are you the bitch? I mean, really?" - Slim Moon *(CHARLES PETERSON)*

Boston singer-songwriter Mary Lou Lord: "Sometimes you meet people and you know right away that your life is about to change. That's how it felt when I met Kurt." *(HAYLEY MADDEN/SIN)*

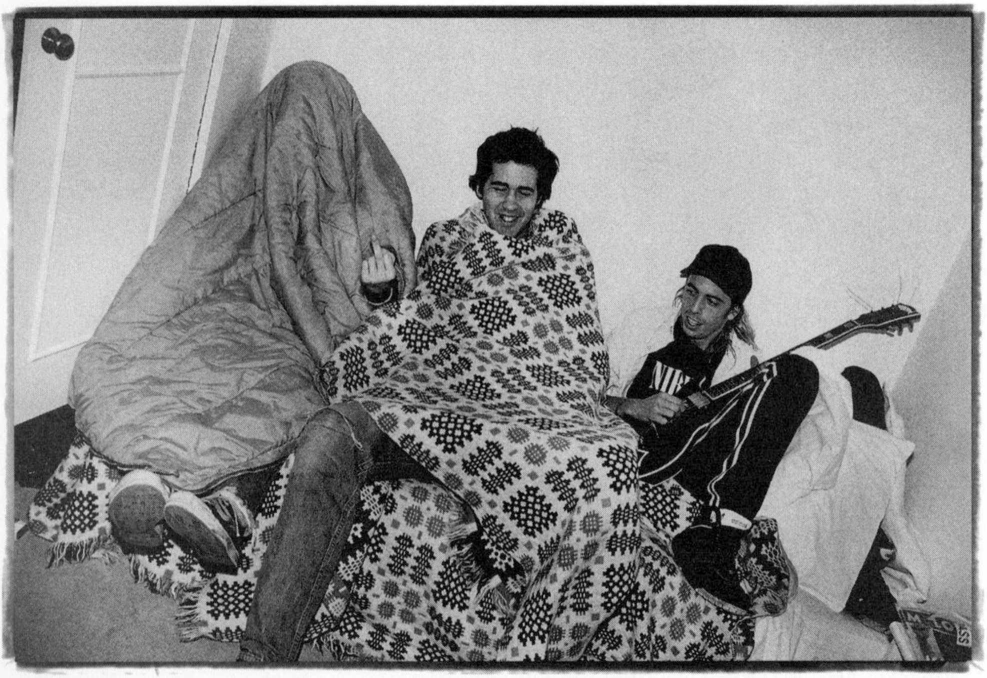

(Above, and next page) Nirvana in one of their first photo shoots with new drummer, Washington DC's Dave Grohl at London's Dalmacia Hotel, October 24, 1990. Peek…a…boo! *(STEPHEN SWEET)*

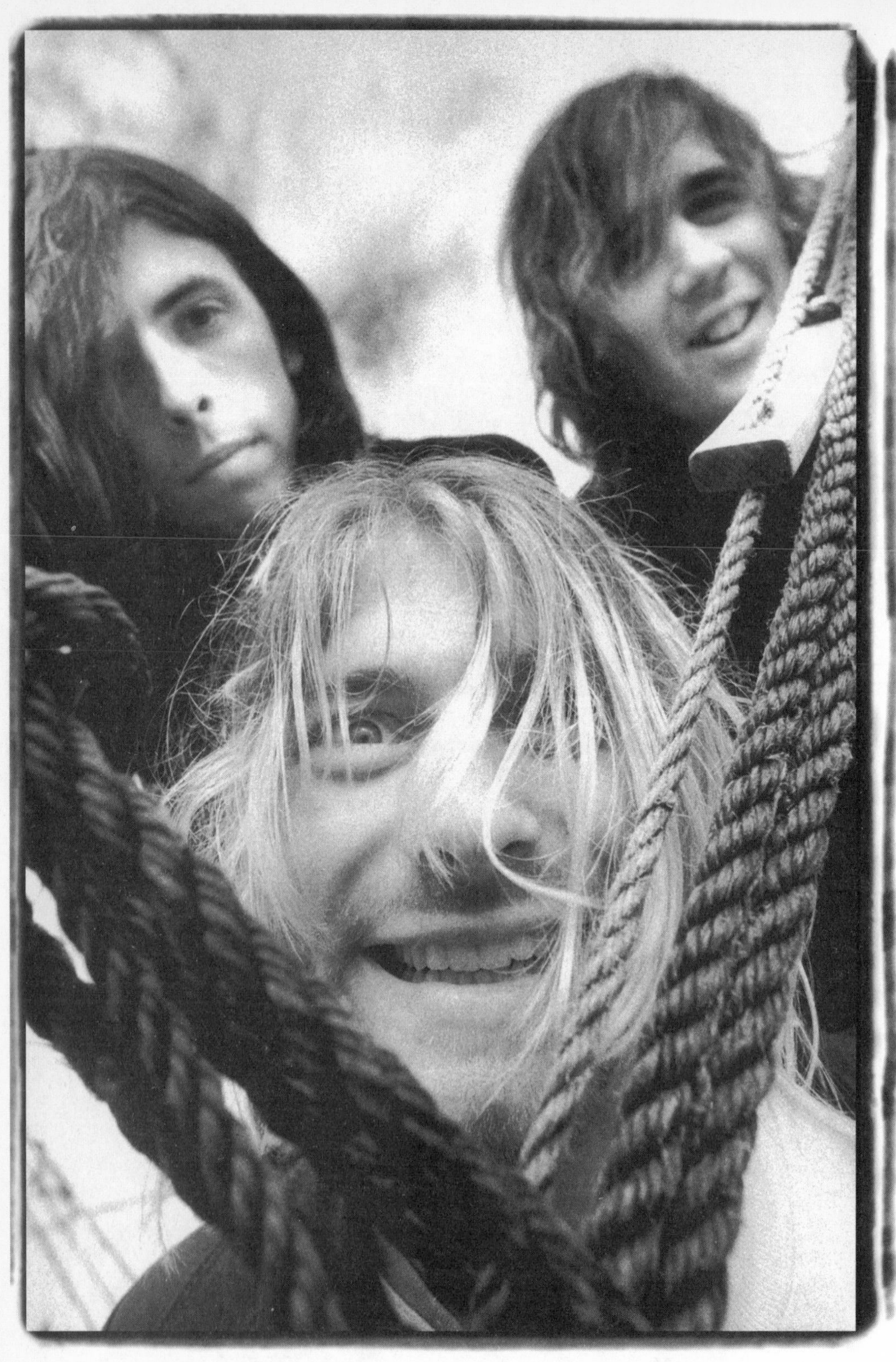

Nirvana, Reading Festival, August 23, 1991. "There was a kind of cockiness to Nirvana that day" - Alex MacLeod *(STEVE GULLICK)*

The boy'z in the hood, Kurt Cobain, Stockholm, June 30, 1992. *(STEVE GULLICK)*

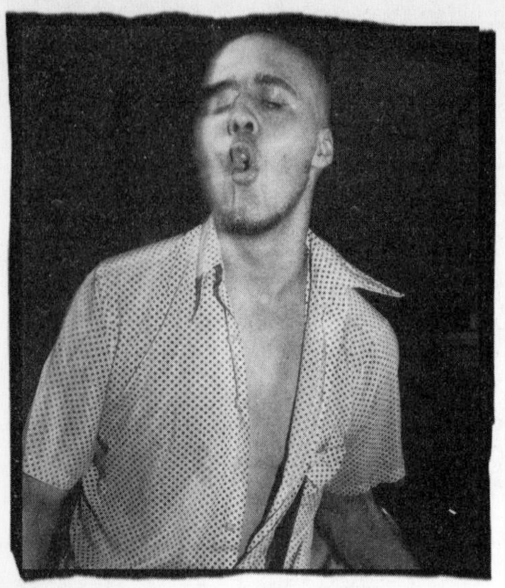

Krist Novoselic, Amherst, MA, 1990. "Krist was very outgoing. He liked to party. He and Matt Lukin, those guys could rage. A lot of what touring is about is networking and meeting people and forging contacts. So Krist was the guy forging the social connections" - Bruce Pavitt *(STEVE DOUBLE/SIN)*

Kurt Cobain and Jonathan Poneman, Seattle, 1990. "Kurt was an enigma. He'd get moody and sit in the corner and not talk for 45 minutes" - Butch Vig *(IAN TILTON)*

Kurt Cobain in full-on destruction mode, The Axis, Boston, MA, September 24, 1991 - the same day that *Nevermind* was released. "The club was shaking with energy. It was like being on the edge of a tornado" - Steve Gullick *(STEVE GULLICK)*

Backstage at Reading Festival, August 1991; a heavily bandaged Kurt Cobain with Eugene Kelly (The Vaselines) and Norman Blake (Teenage Fanclub) *(STEPHEN SWEET)*

Spot the Daniel Johnston T-shirt! Original owner Everett True with Courtney Love, slightly inebriated, backstage at Reading 1991; Kurt Cobain with Krist and Dave, 1992 – note Dave's Dickless T-shirt. *(STEPHEN SWEET, STEVE DOUBLE/SIN)*

Sonic Youth (Thurston Moore in foreground), live at Kitsap County Fairgrounds ('Endfest'), August 8, 1992. "[Sonic Youth's] *Sister* is more bad acid trips I never took, plus physics or psychics, Philip K Dick, astronomy, best bending of English and football, no boyfriends at all, lots of cigarettes and bad drugs…" - Courtney Love *(CHARLES PETERSON)*

Jennifer Finch, L7 bassist: "I told Courtney, 'You don't want to meet Kurt, he's a terrible person and he's going nowhere' …see. That's why I'm not a good A&R person." *(CHARLES PETERSON)*

Kurt Cobain with Nirvana/Sonic Youth manager John Silva and Mudhoney bassist Matt Lukin. "Those Sonic Youth kids, they're wild; their manager, also. He antagonises people and leaves us to take the rap, beating us up, tearing our pants, turning beetroot red when he's drunk" - Kurt Cobain *(CHARLES PETERSON)*

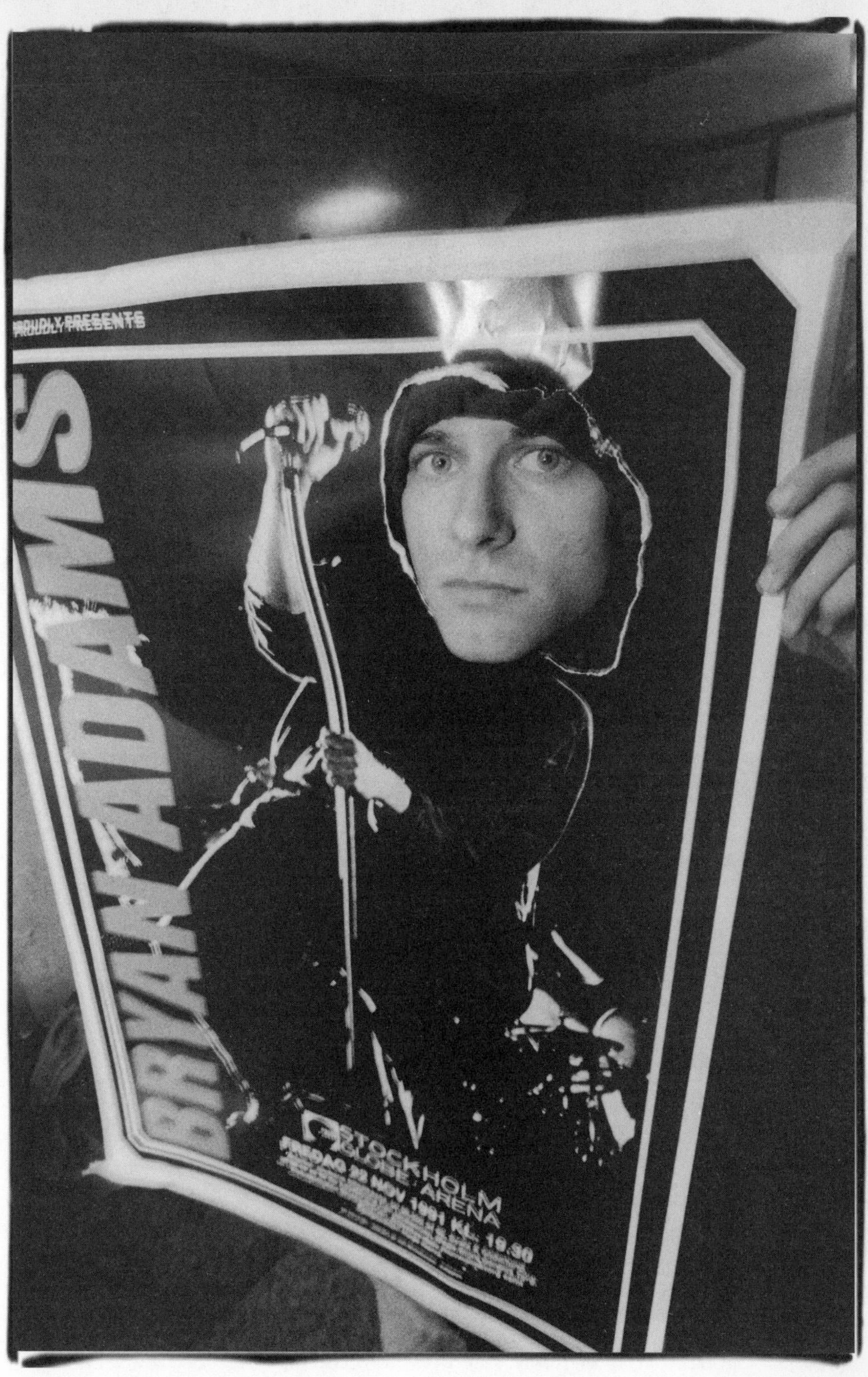


Kurt Cobain vainly attempts to disguise himself as a 'rock star', Stockholm, June 30, 1992. *(STEVE GULLICK)*

Nirvana, live and backstage with Everett True in Stockholm:
"They don't deserve any of this. Forget any reports you may have heard that rock is alive and kicking. The world's only credible arena rock band is close to cracking" - *Melody Maker,* July 25, 1992 *(STEVE GULLICK)*

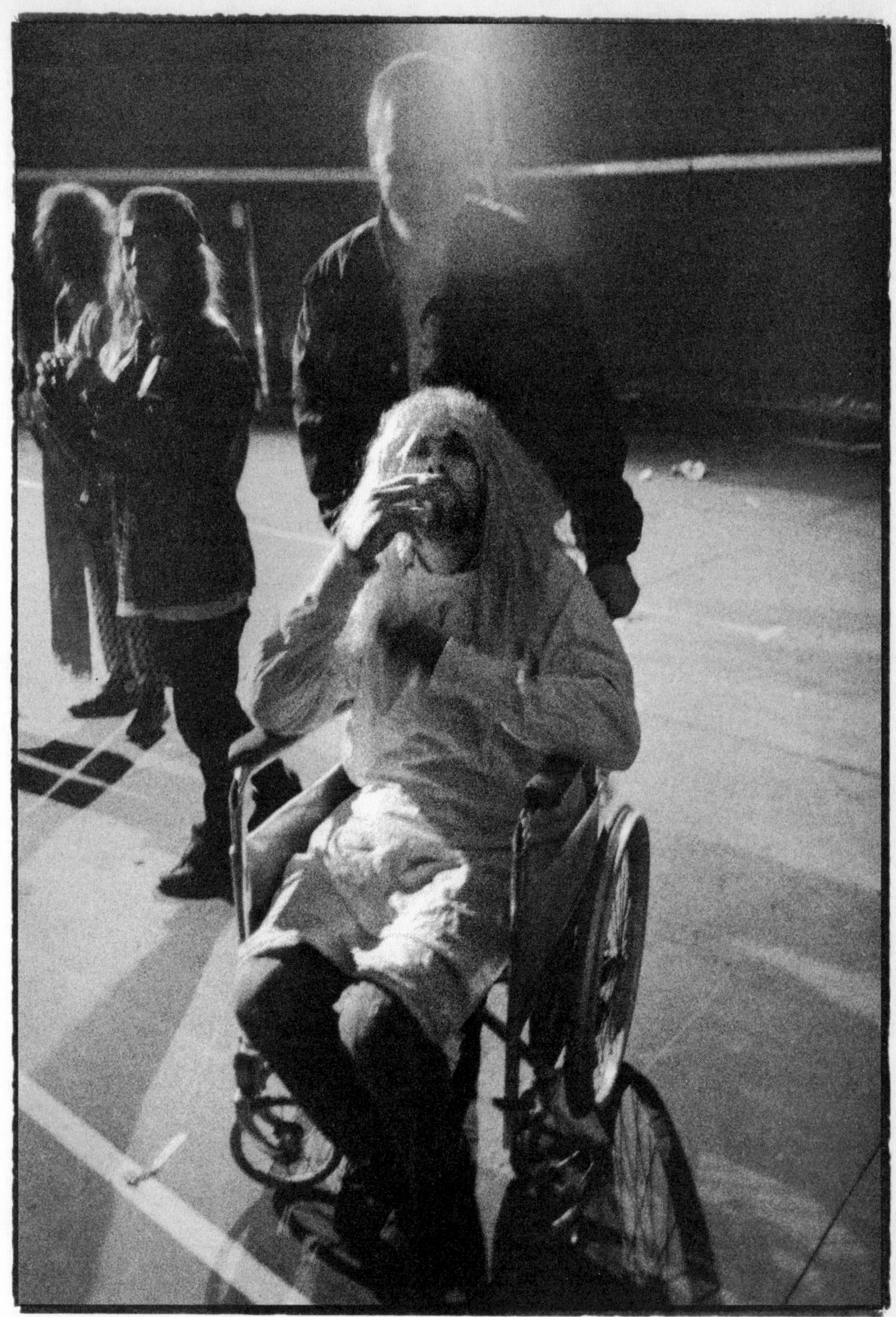

Everett True pushes Kurt Cobain on stage for Nirvana's headline slot at Reading Festival, August 30, 1992. "The lights. That's all I can remember. The lights. You can't see a single face. The crowd is invisible, and all that you feel is this incredible euphoric roar that increases every step you make towards the microphone."
*(CHARLES PETERSON)*

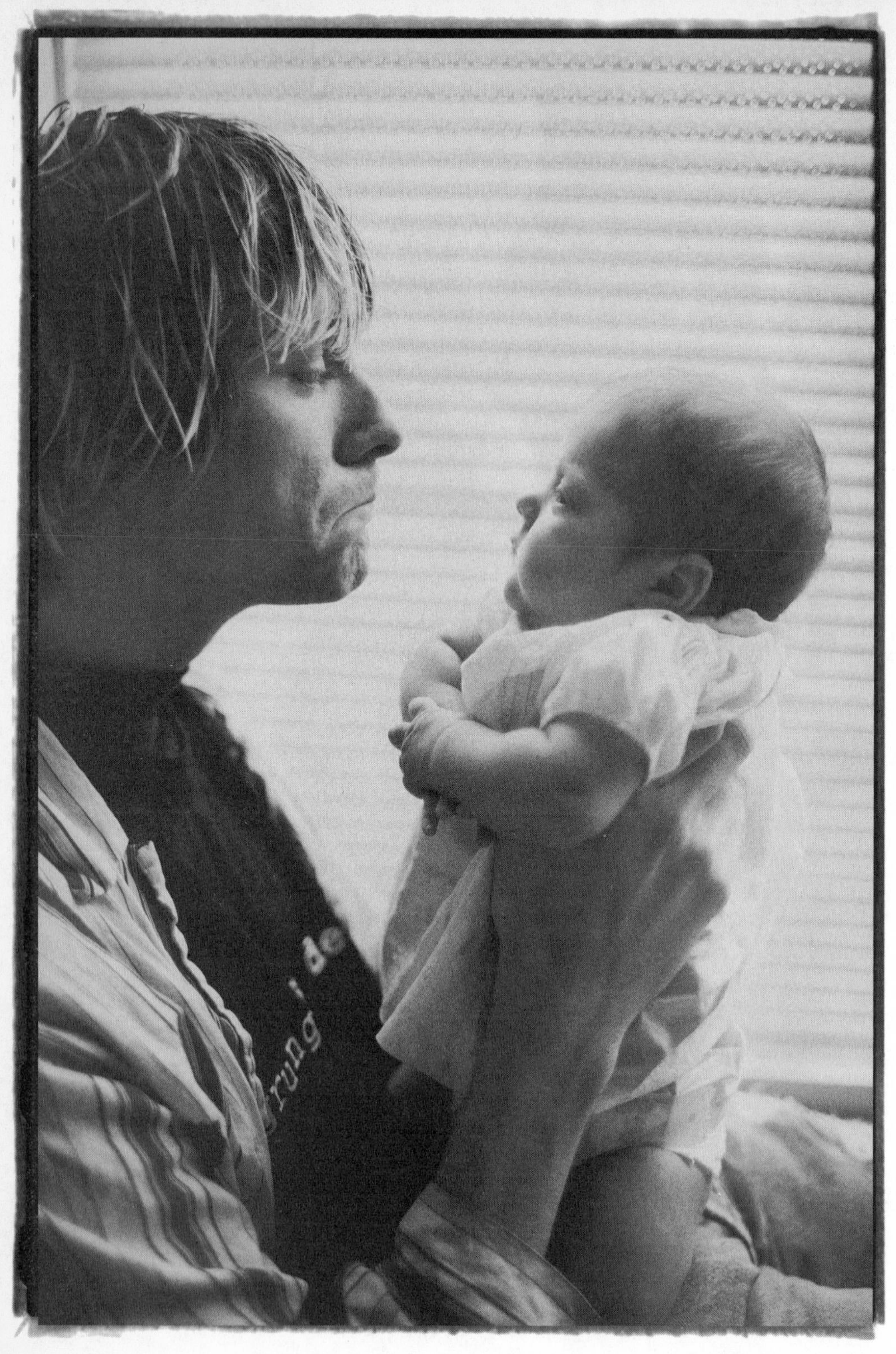

Kurt and 'Diet Grrrl' Frances Bean Cobain, Seattle, late 1992.
"I've pretty much exhausted the baby options. I mean, duh, it's fun, it's great, it's the best thing in my life" - Kurt Cobain *(STEPHEN SWEET)*

Nirvana, New York City, July 24, 1993, the day after the band unveiled their new 'acoustic' section live at Roseland, and less than 48 hours after Kurt OD'd in his Manhattan hotel room. *(STEPHEN SWEET)*

Nirvana, NYC, July 24, 1993: Kurt and Krist; Kurt reading the same *Melody Maker* live review of Neil Young and Pearl Jam that later caused Pearl Jam singer Eddie Vedder to storm out of a rival magazine cover interview and refuse to return; Dave and Kurt share an intimate moment. *(STEPHEN SWEET)*

Nirvana guitar 'doctor' Earnie Bailey, backstage; "You never really knew what was going to get it, and things got it for different reasons. I felt the destruction set should have been phased out by the *In Utero* tour." *(COURTESY OF EARNIE BAILEY)*

The Cobain family at the MTV Awards, September 2, 1993. "That was the first of Courtney's 'trying to be somebody else' dresses" - Cali DeWitt *(LFI)*

Kurt relaxing - with Frances Bean, and preparing to go hang-gliding in Rio de Janeiro, January 1993. "Kurt said he'd never done anything in his life that he'd enjoyed so much" - Earnie Bailey *(EARNIE BAILEY)*

Nirvana on the *In Utero* tour in Bethlehem, Pennsylvania and Springfield, Massachusetts, November 9/10, 1993: Krist Novoselic and second guitarist Pat Smear; Pat in typically playful mood; Kurt resting backstage before the show. "Pat's energy onstage was so different to what they were used to. Once it started he was going ape-shit like none of them ever did" - Cali DeWitt *(STEVE GULLICK)*

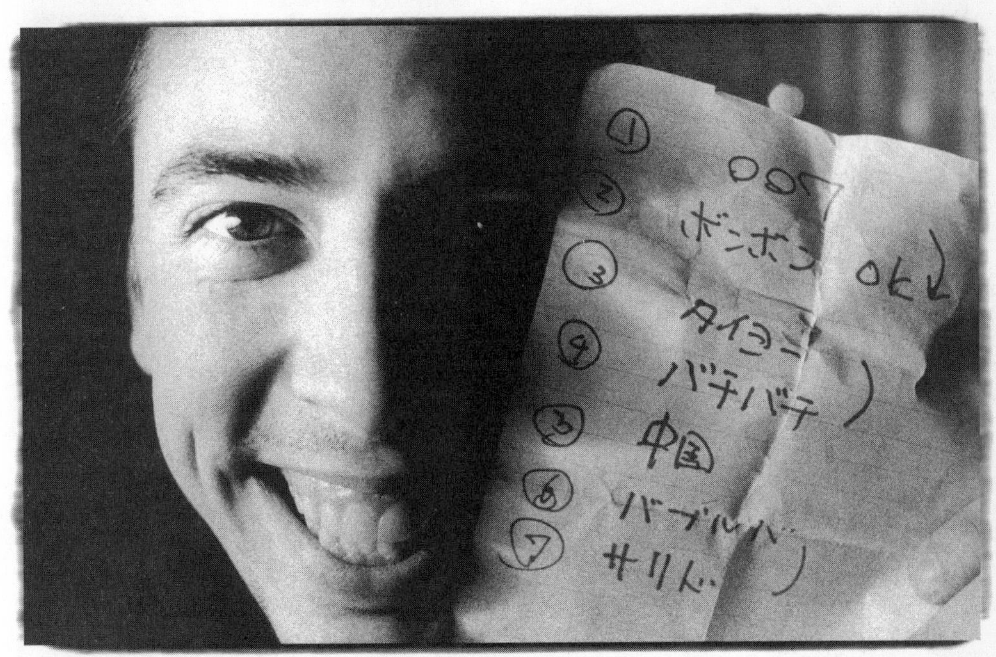


*In Utero* tour, 1993: cellist Lori Goldston, Kurt Cobain; Dave Grohl with a set list from tour support, Japan's Boredoms. "Nirvana were like Melvins but catchy. Black Sabbath meets Bay City Rollers, or whatever he said, that's how it works for me" - Lou Barlow *(STEVE GULLICK)*

Krist backstage at the taping of MTV's *Live And Loud*, Seattle Pier 48, December 13, 1993 *(STEVE GULLICK)*

Eric Erlandson and Frances Bean Cobain, St Louis. *(STEPHEN SWEET)*

*MTV Unplugged*, November 18, 1993. "That was an incredible show. Kurt was so focused and in it. He was so excited about his songs being taken seriously" - Janet Billig *(FRANK MICELOTTA/CONTRIBUTOR/GETTY IMAGES)*

Kurt Cobain in his 'Dennis The Menace' bumblebee jersey, Roseland Ballroom, NYC, July 23, 1993. *(STEPHEN SWEET)*

Backstage on the *In Utero* tour, 1993. "Why do I do it? Why not? It feels good. Somebody already cut down a nice old tree to make that fucking guitar" - Kurt Cobain *(EARNIE BAILEY)*

In London, at the Astoria gig on November 5, I watched genius beat poet group Television Personalities deliberately fuck up their last shot at fame, playing all of their achingly honest songs at half-speed as the self-consciously 'grunge' crowd looked on bemused. Eugene Kelly's fairly ordinary Captain America provided main tour support.

Dan Treacy's TV Personalities started as a post-school project in Chelsea, London around 1977, and soon gained notoriety for their portrayal of the burgeoning, media-fed punk movement in 'Part Time Punks'. The single was direct, humorously observant: *"They pay half-fare on the buses/ And they never use toothpaste/ But they've got two-fifty/ To go and see The Clash/ Tonight."* The song was representative of one side of the TVPs' oeuvre – the fun, 'light' side, one populated by characters from Swinging London, pop artists Roy Lichtenstein and Andy Warhol, Sixties beat group The Creation and David Hockney. One where Dan could dream of hanging out with his heroes of the printed page and celluloid, everything was easy and free, 'happenings' coloured in with the odd blissed-out trip and sly art . . . nostalgia as only young people can handle it: trauma heightened by inexperience, regret tempered by deep longing.

By the time Dan came to record the TVPs' fourth album, however, 1983's *The Painted Word*, he'd lost his *joie de vivre*. Nothing could've prepared fans for the complexities and tortured fevers of his dark side that were thrust into the spotlight – songs of immense longing and loneliness. Often overtly psychedelic with lashings of backwards guitars and delayed vocals, the lyrics introspective and hurting, everything drawn out and lingering, it was a 60-minute album without any waste – as record label magnate Alan McGee put it, Treacy's own *Sister Lovers*.[5]

"Kurt Cobain was sweetness on the occasions we met," wrote Treacy in his online diary. "He stood at the side of the stage watching as we finished with 'Seasons In The Sun'. Afterwards Krist went up to us and said, 'Shit, guys, you know that's Kurt's favourite-ever song?' Just then Kurt introduced himself and said, 'Hey, what was the B-side of Terry Jacks' version?' '"Put The Bone In",' I replied. He smiled and shook my hand. To this day I cannot remember a top headline act letting the support use their equipment . . . really nice guys."

Backstage, Nirvana set up a booby trap of a plate of cold cuts and assorted condiments on the top of the dressing room door, waiting for me to step through – retaliation for the *MM* cover story that ran a few weeks earlier, that they felt portrayed them unfairly as rock'n'roll animals.

I'd been banned from going backstage – until Dan's girlfriend, photographer Alison Wonderland acted as a go-between and explained to Kurt that I was truly sorry for having caused offence. "Hello guys," I blathered, opening the door. "How's . . . oh!" I stood there, dripping from head to toe, covered in sweaty ham and processed cheese.

Courtney later screamed at Kurt for an hour down the phone over the incident: hurling barrage upon barrage of invective about rock stars who think it's funny to bully sensitive writers. "Jeez, Courtney," Kurt tried to explain. "It was a joke. The Legend! doesn't mind."[6]

I have a memory of waking from a blackout backstage, to find Courtney and a female PR seated on each knee fighting for my attention, no holds barred, Mudhoney crowded round with cameras, crowing, "Look! Look! The Legend!'s scored!" – but was it that show? Who knows? Later that evening we went clubbing, and Courtney and I got into a fist fight with a magazine editor. At least . . . it was somewhere around this time.

On November 23, in Ghent (Belgium), Nirvana covered Leadbelly's 'Where Did You Sleep Last Night?' – Dave playing bass lying flat on his back, Krist on drums and Kurt with his guitar jammed into the drum kit. Bits of the instruments ended up all over the stage. "I remember *that*," Craig Montgomery exclaims, "when they smashed the bass and part of it flew out into the audience and hit this kid in the face." Krist tried to comfort the stricken fan while paramedics strapped him into a wheelchair, blood pouring on to the dressing room floor.

"By that tour," the soundman continues, "there were a lot of times where it seemed like Kurt wasn't enjoying himself, or maybe he was preoccupied with Courtney, but it felt down at times – when that kid got hit, that was a real downer. We were afraid that someone was going to get sued or arrested . . .

"We were also concerned for the kid's health," he adds hastily. "I think it knocked a tooth out. Krist felt pretty bad."

Courtney was becoming inescapable. Hole played support that night – linking up with Nirvana briefly in the middle of their own European tour – and Courtney was egging Kurt on from the side of the stage. According to *Oor* journalist Willem Jongeneelen, "Krist was playing bass naked[7], and Hole were provoking him. [Guitarist Eric Erlandson also ran on stage and rugby-tackled Kurt – a favourite sport for rock stars back then.] I do not know exactly when their child was born but it would not surprise me if it had been conceived that night. After the show, Kurt and Courtney were horsing around and playing tag like little children."

Nirvana travelled to Amsterdam, where they stayed at the Museum Hotel. Meanwhile, Hole played in Nijmegen, where Courtney stated that she'd fallen for Kurt, and asked from on stage if someone could drive her to Amsterdam. Nathalie Delisse, a local musician, took up the offer.

"It was like an auction," she told *Oor* in 1994. "She offered 150 guilders, I raised my hand: deal. Complete madness. When the show was over there were some calls made to the hotel, to announce her arrival. She had to perform in Lyon the next day, so I had my doubts, but we went to Amsterdam in my Citroën 2CV, through the fog. She was still wearing her stage dress and started talking about babe bands like Babes In Toyland, the Chili Peppers and her love for Kurt. She had a real crush on him. After the Belgium show the day before, they really seemed to hit it off. She told me that together with Kurt they smashed guitars and she found it to be a very sensational, liberating experience. She was tired, busy and chaotic. At the hotel she invited us in but I did not feel like it. The rest of Hole was not so happy with the departure of Courtney. The manager was very pissed."

The couple bought heroin, and spent the day in bed together. "That was bad news, her missing that show," comments Craig wryly. "So yeah, Courtney was riding around in our van, which was fine, she was fun to have around. Everyone was getting along with her back then."

The show the following night – at the legendary Paradiso Club – was the hottest ticket in town. "It sold out in 10 minutes," enthuses Dutch promoter Carlos van Hijfte. "It was a lot of excitement for those of us who had been supporting the American underground guitar scene. We realised that one of the bands we'd booked in clubs, put in vans, slept on our floors, had become huge in the mainstream world. Susan Sasic [Sonic Youth/Nirvana lighting director] invited me to dinner with the band and crew. We went for a nice Indonesian meal – everybody except for Kurt. In the afternoon, someone from Belgium showed up who'd been hit by a guitar. They wanted some payback maybe, for some damage."

A bailiff temporarily impounded the band's equipment. "Four minutes before the band went on stage a settlement was reached," recalls Paperclip's Ruud Berends. "Money was not an issue."

The following day, Nirvana returned to the UK for yet more dates. Shonen Knife was the opening act: "Shonen Knife were very shy," says Craig. "And they were much more mild-mannered than L7 [the previous tour's opening act]. They'd drink a beer but they weren't going to be destroying stuff. They played beautifully, and sang like angels. Shonen Knife was exactly the kind of band that Kurt liked."

"I'm sure that I was twice as nervous to meet them as they were to meet us," Kurt told me in '93. "I didn't want to offend or scare them in any way, because I know I'm a scruffy, slimy person who might scare them off . . . and that's exactly what I did. They were afraid of me. In fact, on one of our first dates together, they saw me in the backstage area walking towards them and they screamed at the top of their voices, turned around and ran away from me, and then peeked their heads out of their dressing room. I had to say, 'I promise, I won't hurt you!' The communication we had with them was deathly silence and a lot of smiling."

On November 26, Nirvana played Bradford – and then Birmingham and Sheffield, the latter town on the same day that they travelled down to Shepherds Bush in west London to make their legendary appearance on chart show *Top Of The Pops*. Kurt sang the vocals to 'Teen Spirit' live, dressed in bug-eyed sunglasses and striped top, stuffing the microphone in his mouth and lowering his voice until it was a grotesque baroque approximation of the former Smiths singer, Morrissey. Meanwhile, Krist and Dave hammed it up, not even pretending to play their instruments. At the end, a handful of grungy 14-year-olds climbed up to dance with the band in what had to be one of the lamest stage invasions ever: but still, it was nice for the kids watching on their parents' TV sets to see teenagers like themselves momentarily hogging the spotlight.

"I'd pay a lot of money to see a playback of that again," smiles Craig. "We were laughing so hard we were crying and couldn't sit up any more. They were always a hilarious band. People forget that it wasn't all drugs and angst and downers, it was the funniest thing you ever saw and if they played on a festival with serious bands they'd make the serious bands look silly. They had a great sense of humour, including Kurt, even though he was very devious about it. That *Top Of The Pops* thing might be one of the best comedy moments ever on British TV."

The performance did the trick. At the time, an appearance on *Top Of The Pops* guaranteed a rise up the charts. 'Smells Like Teen Spirit' had been hovering round the Top 10. The next week it dropped straight out.

The new UK dates were weird. It was weird that Nirvana were back in Britain, for a start. It went against all conventional industry wisdom to ignore the larger market, their home country, especially as *Nevermind* was exploding across the States – not that anyone over here was complaining. The tour travelled up to Scotland for three dates, and back down through Newcastle, Nottingham, Manchester [November 4] and London [Kilburn National, November 5]. But it was obvious the band was starting to feel burnt out from all the attention and non-stop partying – Krist and Dave were in meltdown mode, while Kurt wanted to be anywhere other than on the road. "By now, Kurt had stopped moving on stage," recalls photographer Steve Gullick. "He didn't seem as interested. They were still incredible."

It didn't stop the mayhem, though.

"We decided to hire two Manchester Mafia goons to fend off T-shirt bootleggers[8]," Kurt told me in '93. "I got very drunk during Captain America's set and exited out the side door with drink in hand to urinate. The two goons didn't recognise me as being their employer and decided to rough me up a bit for pissing. I threw a rock star fit, threw my half-empty glass of vodka in their faces, and darted back in through the exit door. They chased me round inside the hall among the dancing fans until my Scottish tour manager [Alex MacLeod] rescued me.

"Two shows later," he continued, "the same two goons were hired as bouncers to keep the unruly slam-dancers at bay. During the first half of our set, I kept noticing splashes of beer in my face, coming from one of the goon bouncers. I threw off my guitar and jumped straight on to his chest and bounced off of him. He and the other goon began to beat me up, but I was soon rescued by my Scottish tour manager again."

At the Kilburn show, I turned up late and wondered how the fuck I was going to get in past the enormous queue lined up in the street outside. Afterwards, there was a UK record release party for *Nevermind*; bored with the industry shenanigans I tried to start a food fight with Krist, throwing a stick of celery at the bassist. Krist came over to me, looking quite serious, and said, "You shouldn't do that, man. We got thrown out of our own party in Seattle for doing that."

The next morning, lying awake in their hotel bed, Kurt and Courtney decided they should get married. As was her wont, Courtney soon called me – and several other thousand friends – to impart the happy news. I wasn't totally enthused, mainly because I had a stinking hangover. I wasn't the only one worried, either: "Kim Gordon and Julie Cafritz[9] told me when me and Kurt got serious," Courtney told *Rolling Stone*'s David Fricke. "They spelled it out. 'You know what's going to happen? You'll become junkies. You'll get married. You'll OD. You'll be 35. You'll try to make a comeback.' I don't give a fuck. I love this guy."

I lied, and told her I was very pleased for both of them – even though I hated the institution of marriage back then – but I wasn't convinced they were being very punk rock. Courtney rose to the bait, and we happily got into another vitriolic one-upmanship match. But her heart wasn't really in it: she was too happy. She celebrated with an engagement ring from the 1900s, with a ruby stone.

Later that day, Nirvana were up to more mischief, launching into a coruscating last-minute version of 'Territorial Pissings', instead of the projected 'Lithium', on late-night British TV chat show *The Jonathan Ross*

*Show*. At the end, the band absolutely trashed their equipment, leaving the usually verbose Ross momentarily lost for words.

"It's so hard to play on a live television show," Kurt told me. "There's no point trying to do a good job because you can hear the missed notes so easily. There's too much attention on the guitar. I tend to just tell them to fuck off."

After a brief visit to France to play the Transmusicales festival, Nirvana cancelled the remainder of their European tour dates (six days in Ireland and Scandinavia). Kurt's stomach was troubling him again, and the stress had become too much. The band returned home. Krist and Shelli decided to buy a house in Seattle, and took out a small mortgage. Later on, they bought their $265,000 home in one go, cash.

*Nevermind* was now number four in the *Billboard* Top 40.

Do you remember Courtney meeting Kurt?

"Well, I had known of Courtney before because of Mark [Arm]," replies Carrie Montgomery. "He'd call me and be like, 'Yeah, this girl from Hole is real . . . uh . . . *interesting*. And friendly. She won't leave me alone. As a matter of fact, she's here now in my room . . .' But I didn't have any specific preconceived ideas when Kurt told me about her. I lived with my mom at that time in Madison Park and he used to stay down there with me in Seattle, and he had given her my mom's number to call him at while she was in Europe – I remember answering the phone to her, and we were lying in bed together, so I assumed she must've known about me . . . The first time I met her [on December 22], we went to that fancy French restaurant, Maximilien's, in Pike Place Market. Kurt really wanted us to be friends. When she went to the bathroom he was like, 'What do you think?' I was like, 'I don't know, she seems like a natural disaster to me but it's fun to watch, I guess.'"

What was she doing?

"Just screaming at the top of her lungs about how famous she was, and causing a commotion, crazy – but nice. We got along. I was like a deer in her headlights. I'd never ever met anyone like this before. But he liked her. I liked her. He was my best friend at that time so it was like, 'If you like her, I'll give her a chance.' We actually did get along for a long time. Courtney likes to talk, so I would sit and listen to her talk for hours and hours and hours. She's a genius. She's a very intelligent, well-rounded, educated person and very dramatic and exciting. It was a lot. Wait . . . Kurt made me go with them when Courtney met his mom for the first time. He made me go."

How was that?

"Well . . ." Carrie hesitates. "Kurt's mom wanted me and him to go out. Because we were such great friends, she didn't understand why we wouldn't be a couple. She was reluctant to . . ." She stops herself and laughs. "Can you imagine Courtney in *Aberdeen*, Everett? It just didn't go together. And we were all reckless and debauched. Probably he just wanted me to drive, and to act as a buffer between Wendy and Courtney. I tried, but there was no buffering that."

At the end of 1991, Nirvana set out for another week of dates, this time at 20,000-capacity arenas – December 27: LA Sports Arena; December 28: O'Brien Pavilion at Del Mar Fairgrounds; December 29: Arizona State University; December 31: the Cow Palace in San Francisco; January 2: the Salem Armory, Oregon. These dates were absolute proof that the music industry had got its claws firmly into the band. Nirvana were sandwiched in the middle of two bands they had little in common with, ideologically or musically: the emo-metal band Pearl Jam, formed out of the ashes of the doomed Mother Love Bone and already being tipped for major league success, and the horrendous funk rock strutters Red Hot Chili Peppers.

At that point, Nirvana were far bigger than either band.

"The Chili Peppers were headlining," recalls Barrett Jones, "but everyone was there to see Nirvana – crowds of people jumping up and down, going nuts for Nirvana. It was me, Nick [Close] the Sonic Youth tech, Alex, I don't think we had Susan [Sasic] yet. During Pearl Jam's set at midnight on New Year's Eve someone tried to jump from the balcony to the stage and missed, hit his head and got carried out. I had never seen a crowd this size be so unified with a band. Their live shows were just so powerful, but I attribute most of that to Dave."

Before the Sports Arena show, local industry 'zine *BAM* conducted an interview with Kurt that rapidly became notorious. In the article, the writer noted that the singer "kept nodding off occasionally in mid-sentence" – a trait that Kurt would later try to explain away as narcolepsy – and described his "pinned pupils, sunken cheeks and scabbed, sallow skin". The heroin rumours had begun. It was an accurate enough depiction: by his own admission, Kurt spent December 1991 in a narcotic haze, he and Courtney staying on the floor of Eric Erlandson's apartment until Eric kicked them out for doing smack.

It was also on the arena tour that Krist finally admitted to himself that Kurt was on heroin: "He looked like a ghoul," he said. "But what am I going to do? It's his fucking trip, his life, he can do whatever he wants."

Kurt announced to the *BAM* writer that he was planning on getting married, much to the surprise of most people outside what was fast becoming a very small, intimate circle of confidants – Courtney throwing out anyone she considered 'disloyal', or threatening to their relationship.

"I've always blamed Courtney for it," mentions Ian Dickson, who fell out of favour once the pair moved in together at the start of 1992, "but I don't even know if it's true any more. A lot of it was his inability to deal with his fame. She was a very intimidating person. She's so smart and so vocal. And she had this amazing x-ray emotional vision, where she could instantly size you up and cut you to the quick. She has the ability to say the shit that nobody else will say."

> *"I was a part of Jabberjaw," explains Rene Navarette. "Cali [DeWitt] and I had run away from home to work there for free, on the door, serving coffee. Courtney was a big part of the beginnings of that place. We had a secret friendship. I would score drugs for her and in return she taught me about Leonard Cohen. I remember being in Courtney's one-room apartment that she shared with Eric when she started getting calls from Kurt – listening to his messages while splitting a toasted sandwich. She'd downplay our friendship because I was a known drug connection – and she was on the way to becoming a star. She toted Cali a little more. He was the prettier, happier of the two of us.*
>
> *"I met Kurt when Nirvana played Jabberjaw [May 29, 1991]. Right after that was all that mess with her going to see Billy Pumpkin in Chicago and getting in a fight with him and seeing Nirvana instead. That's when the whole crazy circus started. I lost touch with her for a while after that.*
>
> *"The first real great conversation I had with Kurt was at the end of 1991. Kurt and Courtney were seriously together and talking about having a baby. Out of the blue, I got a call saying that she and Kurt wanted to invite me to San Diego. They said there would be a bus waiting for [Jabberjaw founder] Gary Dent and me – I guess she was sending for some of the old friends to come along. Ten minutes later, I got another call from Courtney saying, 'This is a secret between you and me, but please can you buy us $300 of drugs and we'll give you $800. Keep it real quiet, go along with everybody else, and don't steal from me.' So I went ahead and borrowed the money and scored the drugs, because I knew they were good for it.*
>
> *"I went along with the trip to San Diego, but when I got there they were looking for me already: 'Hi everybody, but where's Rene, where's the chief?' They took me backstage and got everything from me. I never saw Kurt look so healthy as he did that time – he'd been on tour forever,*

*he was so happy, they were so in love. He was real interested to know who I was because he didn't know anyone from the streets of LA, or any Mexicans. He was shy, but as forward as I ever saw him become. We hung out, used drugs and I got to see him play a big show."*

(Interview with author, February 2006)

At the Cow Palace date, Pearl Jam played the intro to 'Smells Like Teen Spirit', and stopped – a gesture that served to irritate the Nirvana camp. The two bands became rivals, certainly in the press: Nirvana sought to distance themselves from a band they saw as grunge bandwagon jumpers. The enmity between the two bands – or more specifically, Kurt and Courtney ('Kurtney') and Jeff Ament/Stone Gossard – dated back to the time of the Green River/Mudhoney split. Kurt and Courtney never missed a chance to take a pot shot at their Seattle peers, correctly seeing them as suburban metal kids who had nothing to do with the punk roots of grunge.

"So I am outspoken and I say nasty things about Pearl Jam and I get a lot of flak for it," Kurt complained to me in 1992, "and a lot of people condemn me and put me down or call me an asshole. I have so many people who hate my guts for putting down Pearl Jam and then I think, 'What value do those people have in my life?' You know? I have to speak the truth, I have to say what I feel, I'm being honest and people aren't used to that, especially in the commercial world."

Not everyone in the Nirvana camp viewed them as the enemy: Krist Novoselic has been at pains to express his admiration for them. Barrett Jones thinks it was more down to the attitude of certain journalists than anything serious.

"They never had any problems with Pearl Jam," Barrett states. "We did a lot of shows with them, the two years I was with them. There was just that one thing where Kurt said that he didn't like them following on their coat-tails. I thought it was ridiculous to take this word, grunge, and apply it to these incredibly different bands. That's your fault, you know."[10]

Nirvana played for about 35 minutes in LA, including an irreverent version of The Who's 'Baba O'Riley'. The Who fascinated Kurt, especially what he perceived as their rapid transition from being a taut Mod whirlwind of destruction and incisive pop anthems to bloated rock gods in the Seventies. "Hope I die before I turn into Pete Townshend," Kurt caustically remarked about The Who's guitarist, referencing the English band's most famous lyric.[11]

The Cow Palace show was an industry bun feast. River Phoenix and Keanu Reeves showed up, among myriad other slumming film stars. And of course the rock cognoscenti were present. Kurt was spectacularly unimpressed – a sign hung later on his and Courtney's hotel door read, "No famous people please. We're fucking."

"We jumped in the car with Kurt and Courtney and ran over to see the Melvins at the Kennel Club," recalls Debbi Shane. "We all walked into the dressing room and [Faith No More singer] Mike Patton was there. He looked up at Courtney, said something and laughed. She grabbed Kurt and they left. The next day we met up for breakfast – Kurt, Krist, everybody – and it was all so new. There was a table of guys sitting across from us, making fun of Nirvana for eating breakfast in a fancy place."

Kurt felt increasingly trapped by the attention of his new fans – famous and unknown. He hated the continuous attention, wanted some level of control back in his life, just wanted to spend his days like he had in Olympia only a few short months ago, taking drugs and fucking.

Kurt wasn't the only one having problems either – witness the following interview, conducted with Krist Novoselic halfway through 1992.

Krist, unlike Kurt, was facing up to his demons, though . . .

*I heard you quit drinking . . .*

*"I quit drinking on January 1," Krist laughs. "On New Year's Eve, I was in San Francisco. I was a raging drunk for two weeks on a tour. I was going around a hotel and bumped my head on an overhead-heating appliance. Pow! I hit my head, it was all bloody, and I woke up in the morning and thought, 'God, I gotta quit this shit.' I went to Australia, Japan and Hawaii, and I didn't drink for three months. I got home and all these bad influences like Matt Lukin [Mudhoney] and Kurt Danielson [Tad] came around and corrupted me. Now I don't drink when I play. I used to go on totally drunk, but now I go up there pretty sober. I moderate my drink more."*

*Maybe the pressure/success you were enjoying made you want to drink more?*

*"Yeah, that's what it was. I had to learn how to deal with it; either ignore it or deal with it like a mature adult instead of just running away. It's the same old story, running away into booze, all human beings are the same and have pretty much the same reactions to things."*

*People thought Nirvana would self-destruct.*

*"I was driving through Seattle listening to the radio station. They played a Nirvana song, I know I should have changed the channel, but I was listening to it," he laughs. "The DJ goes, 'Now there's a band that I don't see playing local loser clubs five years from now.' I had that feeling too. We took off in such a fury. Our record came out, we were drinking, flying up the charts, flying into the stratosphere, and I know I was a*

*really messed-up drunk. We had three months off where we chilled out, relaxed, so everything was OK."*

*Do you find success makes it much harder for your art?*

*"No, it's much easier now. I have all this time and not a lot of distractions, because other people take care of things. Managers worry about the band, accountants worry about money and I stay at home and do whatever I want. It's weird I have this sense of liberation now. Did it take money to liberate me, or was it just that I got older and had a revelation and chilled out?"*

*Maybe cutting down drinking helped.*

*"Yeah, but I've had some of my most inspiring moments being drunk. Heartfelt inspiration, good things came out of it."*

(Author's transcript of 1992 Krist Novoselic interview)

**Addenda: Earnie Bailey**

"I had a guitar repair shop in Spokane for many years, and then I got a job managing an espresso bar in Seattle. I missed working on guitars and I still had all my tools and collected guitars so I decided to get into it again.

"In January '92, I ran into all three members of Nirvana separately. I ran into Kurt first at The Vogue, because I was at a Sub Pop showcase where Earth was playing. It was like a Sunday night. There was kind of this commotion out in the parking lot, there was a gal out there with bleach-blonde hair and she was really loud and really animated, and I thought that was odd, because most people around Seattle aren't like that. She was pretty fascinating. Maybe Kat [Bjelland, Babes In Toyland] was with her, and Kurt was too, but Kurt had his hair dyed red so I didn't recognise him. They walked in right in front of me, and when they went to check his ID, I could see this picture of Kurt with blond hair and he looked healthy. And yet he looked horrible. His skin was a terrible colour and he was really rough. I said hi. I think I said congratulations for knocking Michael Jackson out of the game. [*Nevermind* went to number one in the US on January 11, 1992, deposing the self-styled King of Pop.] I told him I was a friend of Rob [Kader] and we talked about the old days a bit. I had a Seventies black Stratocaster that was left-handed that I'd just gotten in, so I said, 'Hey, if you need a Strat, I've got one.' Because I said it was Seventies he said, 'Why would I want that?' It had a maple fret board on it and he wasn't crazy about it.

"Krist and Shelli bought a home close to where we lived in Greenlake. We used to go up to this bakery called The Honey Bear for coffee in the morning. It was close to their house and we'd walk by Krist and Shelli working on their yard. We were talking one time and I asked him, 'Who fixes all the stuff that you smash up?' And he rolled his eyes and he said, 'Oh god, nobody,' and he was complaining that the local repair shops would never call him back about it. I thought that was funny because I used to go around to the guitar stores and they would be blasting Soundgarden and Pearl Jam through the speakers, but never play Nirvana. Punk was really not cool in those places. I had been doing guitar and amp repair work for a decade and couldn't understand why they wouldn't be treating this band like they were important, so I told Krist, 'If you want, I'll round up all this stuff and have it fixed by tomorrow morning.' I think he said, 'You're nuts, but OK!' So I did: I got in my car and drove around to all these places picking up their broken gear and stayed up all night doing repairs.

"I waited until what time I thought he'd be up and called him. He was surprised I'd done it all, and after that we started to hang out. They were vegetarians and new to the neighbourhood, and we ran this vegetarian café. On top of that we could talk about politics, rock groups and electric guitars until you could hear the morning commuters leaving their driveways. Krist and I fixed about everything in their house that wasn't working. At one point we were driving across the Wallingford bridge in Krist's Volkswagen bus, and he says, 'Hey man, how about it? You know, you go on the road with us and fix our stuff?' I said, 'OK,' and he said, 'Right on, we should go get some Wild Turkey.' That was the extent of my interview process."

## NOTES

1 He's hardly going to mention one girlfriend to another when they're sleeping together, is he?

2 Janet Billig has managed both Courtney and Billy Corgan.

3 Yoko Ono is held in far higher regard in the counter-culture than in the mainstream.

4 Mainly Courtney, actually – during the first round of UK press interviews, Courtney slagged me off as 'sexist' incessantly, for claiming that Hole's third single, 'Teenage Whore', was autobiographical. She soon realised she was better off with me *on* her side.

5 *Sister Lovers* was the Memphis band Big Star's legendary third album, recorded in 1974 and released four years later – darkly confessional and brimming over with gorgeous, cracked, melancholy, Beatles/Byrds-influenced melodies.

6 The ongoing minor *ménage à trois* between Courtney, Kurt and myself became a

source of fascination for my fellow *Melody Maker* writers, and was parodied hilariously in the paper's back pages.

7 This is the only report I've ever seen of Krist behaving thus, so it can perhaps be taken with a grain of salt.

8 Scalpers and bootleggers are a constant problem for any touring rock band, especially as they often come armed and belligerent. Eric Erlandson and I almost got beaten to a pulp one time outside a Hole show when we attempted to give away a couple of free tickets right in front of the touts' noses.

9 Julie Cafritz was ex-Pussy Galore, also in Kim's Sonic Youth spin-off band, the virulent free noise Free Kitten.

10 There was a famous incident where Eddie Vedder, singer with Pearl Jam, stormed out of a rival magazine's cover photo shoot, and refused to come back, after catching sight of a review I'd written of their live show in *MM* the week before – where I compared his voice to that of Phil Collins with a backache. In the movie *Singles*, the fake rock band Pearl Jam were moonlighting and shrugged off a bad review as inconsequential. Not in real life.

11 The Who were not bloated rock gods like the Stones/Led Zeppelin/Aerosmith, etc, with their own planes and six limousines in a line and drugs and groupies galore. They didn't like being remote from their fans, especially Pete Townshend. However, it was obvious why Kurt felt that way – because that's how the media portrayed all bands that played stadiums. Drummer Keith Moon's escapades didn't help, because it often seemed like he was lording it up, but he was actually quite similar to Kurt in his own way – didn't give a shit about property or propriety, drank like a fish and took loads of drugs, blew all his money, and deep down inside loved rock'n'roll and believed it should be spontaneous. He might have had a Rolls-Royce, but he'd be just as likely to smash it for fun as he would smash a bass drum.

# PART III

# DOWN

CHAPTER 19

# Dirty Linen And Brimming Ashtrays

THE grunge explosion was nothing like the way MTV later chose to portray it.

It wasn't just testosterone-driven, bare-chested rock gods, whining about how hard their life was because they had to walk 100 yards to the tour van[1], nor was it the easy-going alterno-*Friends* lifestyle as so revoltingly portrayed in films like *Singles* and *Sleepless In Seattle*. Nor was it Courtney 'Axl Rose' Love and her loser husband. No. It was loud music, and rain. It was vomit and laughter and not knowing where you'd wake up the next morning. It was countless hours of tedium, waiting for another crappy band to soundcheck down the OK Hotel and The Vogue. It was shared mattresses and Greyhound coach journeys, wired partners who'd as soon smash you over the head with a beer mug as fuck you. It was house parties and Mexican beer, sweet coffee and lumberjack shirts. And it was a healthy dose of cynicism to carry you through it all.

It's even misleading to talk of a grunge 'explosion', singular.

There were actually two.

The first happened shortly after I wrote the initial series of articles in *Melody Maker*, and lasted through 1989 into the first few months of 1991. Other critics and fanzine writers and hip radio DJs enthusiastically championed a form of music based in Seattle – firmly rooted in punk rock, not suburban metal – that in actual fact was being played in countless bars and garages and damp-infested practice rooms across America. Not just the Pacific Northwest. Local musicians complained about the attention but secretly they mostly relished it. It was exciting, fun and even helped a handful of bands to find work. Few outside groups had moved to town yet, because – as hip and cool as the writers were making Seattle sound – there was little else going on. Lovely scenery, but that isn't usually conducive to rock explosions. Microsoft hadn't broken big, neither had Amazon.

About the biggest thing happening in 1990 was the sales of Sub Pop affiliated T-shirts – but man, there were some good T-shirts! In particular, the word LOSER emblazoned across a thousand music fans' chests, a good couple of years before Bart 'proud to be an underachiever' Simpson, and the slacker lifestyle, grabbed the popular imagination. In Seattle, at least in the rock clubs frequented by Mudhoney and Nirvana and their pals, it was not good enough to aspire to being a macho sports fan or rock'n'roll dude. It was incredibly un-hip to be seen chasing success, especially as success was perceived as coming with too many strings attached. Far better to give up before you've even started: "No one likes us and we don't care," runs the chant of London's deadbeat football club Millwall. That's how grunge musicians and fans felt about the outside world: 'punk' was originally an insult, a put-down, a term of abuse towards gays. Mum and dad think you're a total waster, a disgrace? Feel rejected by those flash kids at school, with their big American cars and trust-fund degrees? Don't sweat it. Parade it.

You're a LOSER and proud of it.

The word was originally popularised by a T-shirt designed by Green River's Jeff Ament. "Sub Pop wouldn't have been Sub Pop without Jeff," remarks Julianne Anderson. "That whole 'it's cool to be un-cool' thing, the glorification of a geek – that's all Jeff Ament."

"'Loser' was more [Mudhoney manager] Bob Whittaker than Jeff," suggests Jonathan Poneman. "The idea of doing the shirts was Bruce's and mine. Jeff Ament came up with these Green River shirts that had Green River on the cover and said 'Ride the fucking six-pack', and before we did the 'Loser' shirts those were far and away our most popular shirts. We discuss to this day reprinting those shirts. Such a great slogan! The idea of doing a bald-faced 'Loser' slogan . . . if anyone looks at the fanzines that Bruce Pavitt has been involved with, you can see his stamp on that shirt. It has that elegance, that kind of in-your-face quality."

"We should give some credit to Tad," adds Megan Jasper, "because Tad would wear that shirt on tour all the time."

"Yeah, and he had a song called 'Loser' as well," Poneman agrees. "But that concept, the idea of embracing loser-dom, has been around for a long time. I think Tad wore that shirt for a long time for rather depressing reasons, actually."

Sure, Soundgarden and Alice In Chains and Screaming Trees and Pearl Jam had signed to major labels. Sure, Sub Pop was attracting undue attention – but you could find parallels happening in other cities in America; Dinosaur Jr and Pixies in Boston, Amphetamine Reptile in Minneapolis, Merge records in Chapel Hill, Touch And Go's fierce and hard rocking Chicago roster, Sonic Youth and the loft kids of Manhattan . . . The centre of the music industry was still LA and New York. The grunge 'explosion' was relatively low-level, comparatively innocent – confined to tens of thousands of music enthusiasts across Britain and Europe, and increasingly America. It would blow over. These things always do.

Not this time. The feeding frenzy around Nirvana in late 1990 precipitated an explosion of interest in the city and its bands and lifestyle that hadn't been seen on such a scale, in such a localised fashion, since the Summer Of Love hippies in San Francisco in the late Sixties. As Sonic Youth famously claimed in their documentary film title, 1991 really was the year punk rock broke . . . if by punk rock one means the disdain Olympia musicians like Calvin Johnson and Al Larsen, Kurt Cobain and Tobi Vail, Nikki McClure and Lois Maffeo felt towards 'adult' interference, their determination not to be suckered in by the same old industry tricks and their desire to follow self-made paths.

Of course, using this definition as a basis, one could argue that punk rock never broke big at all – these people are barely known outside of their immediate peer groups. But why else did people call Nirvana 'punk' if it wasn't for the influence of Olympia? For, as Jack Endino argues in chapter 11, the music Nirvana became best known for playing was in no way punk rock in its traditional form, but an update on prime Seventies hard rock with all the glossy production and radio-friendly chord changes that made it so commercial.

Still, once Nirvana via Sub Pop started to stir up industry interest – not hindered in the slightest by Kurt's devilish charm, his smouldering blue eyes, his way around a lyric of such impassioned alienation it couldn't but help appeal to millions of others like him – and especially once Nirvana via DGC released the super-polished cry of rage that was *Nevermind*, it lit the touchpaper for a thousand other labels and magazines and TV programmes to try to suck the city dry.

"I didn't let it bother me," says Chad Channing. "Someone was going to have to come up with something to call it. You couldn't just call it hard rock music. I began to think it was silly after a while, when I'd see clothing stores selling 'Grunge Wear'."

"I didn't see how it pertained to them at all," says Nirvana guitar tech Earnie Bailey. "Kurt wore flannel for a really short period of time, for a month or two maybe in 1990. You never saw him wear flannel after that, unless it was for a joke."

Almost without exception, these industry-appointed arbiters of taste ended up pushing all the bands that had little to do with Nirvana – and certainly nothing to do with their adopted home city of Olympia.

But then, they had come to the wrong place.

Or maybe they hadn't. John Silva, Nirvana's manager, loved Sonic Youth and The Beastie Boys but he didn't like Beat Happening because he didn't understand the appeal of such a deliberately childish band without a bassist and, worse, any appreciable (traditional) musical talent.[2] Would Beat Happening have broken big given the same exposure? Doubtful. Daniel Johnston's one major label album, 1995's *Fun*, sold less than 20,000 copies.[3]

In the early Nineties, the record industry wasn't geared up to sell truly alternative music. Punk rock sold and popularised by post-Nirvana bands such as Green Day and The Offspring, Rancid and Blink 182 is trad rock by another name, dumbed down even more. It is entirely misleading to call Nirvana punk – grunge is a much better description, if only because it was a term invented to describe a specific time, place and music: theirs. Grunge; as in dirty, scuzzy hard rock played slow, with the amps turned to 11. Of course, the reason people shy away from using the word is that it became devalued through familiarity. It came to mean any musician who might once have listened to a Nirvana or Soundgarden record and passed by a thrift store window: it certainly *never* meant cock rock, which is what it became synonymous with.

Post-*Nevermind*, the mainstream media – even notoriously slow US media outlets like *Rolling Stone*, *Spin* and MTV– wanted to know all about Seattle. Their interest didn't stop at the music. Thrift store shopping became the height of popular culture, fashion models falling over one another to prove how 'street' they were, TV cameras lurking outside the Comet Tavern.

"Maybe the reason people got resentful was because the hype was so all-encompassing," suggests former *Rocket* journalist Gillian G. Gaar. "The mainstream press didn't write about Seattle the way they wrote about Atlanta or Minneapolis. It wasn't just about the music. It was this whole lifestyle thing where everyone drinks coffee and microbrews, and wears flannel. It was everywhere, it was insane – K-mart ads were stamped with the word 'grunge' for their back-to-school line. Some people were horrified. I thought it was funny. There would be [US gossip columnist] Liz Smith in her brand new Converse sneakers in *Vanity Fair* . . . no one wore brand new Converse!"

"It was the best," smirks Fastbacks bassist Kim Warnick. "Finally people knew that Seattle wasn't in Alaska. I was psyched. Yeah, there were a lot of shitty bands that got started because they wanted to be signed. All these A&R guys were flying here to sign what they thought would be the next 'that' – but it didn't matter to me, and if nothing else, maybe Fastbacks could have a record deal and not have to move to LA. Before all that stuff started happening, you pretty much had to move to LA or New York to make your career. Here they were coming to my backyard and that was fine with me."

Besides you, were there any girls in Seattle playing music?

"Not really," the bassist replies. "I'm sure there were, but none who really liked rock'n'roll. They were either too arty, or . . . we liked Deep Purple, we liked butt rock. We liked The Archies and Queen, Elton John. I came from seeing rock shows like Kiss, which a lot of people might say this whole genre was a backlash to. To me, it was all the same. I liked it as much as I liked Led Zeppelin. I didn't give a shit. My theory is those people just didn't get to see their first Kiss concert, motherfuckers. I did. I got to see them the first time they came through. First Ramones, first Kiss show."

A lexicon of grunge sprung up, directly from the fevered imagination of Sub Pop receptionist Megan Jasper: 'swinging on the flippety-flop' (talking on the telephone), 'bound-and-hagged' (staying in at the weekend), 'lamestain' (an un-cool person), 'wack slacks' (old torn jeans), 'harsh realm' (bummer), 'big bag of blotation' (drunk) and 'k-ching!' (another of your mates gets signed to a major label).

"I jotted down a bunch of words while I was chatting to one of those douche bag reporters," recalls Jasper. "It was a case of, 'I drank too much coffee and I'd much rather not be doing my job right now. Sure, I'll talk to this kid on the phone!' It was beyond ridiculous. It was ridiculous in 1990 – and that was like a year and a half later. The whole thing was retarded. I remember the guys from Tad coming into the office and using the word grunge as a joke. Kurt would say, 'The next record, we got it all figured out. It's going to be grunge.' And everyone would laugh like it was the funniest thing they'd heard in their lives. I remember thinking, 'This shit has got to end. I hope this is the peak.' But it wasn't."

The second grunge 'explosion' happened the instant *Nevermind* hit *Billb*oard number one at the start of 1992. You could almost taste the sweat on a thousand 'hair metal' [soft rock] bands' brows as they feverishly packed up their brand new Converse sneakers and $100 lumberjack shirts, and hopped on a plane from LA to Seattle.

*At what point did the speed of Nirvana's success exceed your expectations?*

*"It got really crazy around January of 1992; the album was at number one, we were playing on* Saturday Night Live. *That's when I*

*knew it was nuts. We'd gone to Europe the previous year, and played the Reading Festival main stage, and I realised that was pretty crazy – but we were on the bill with Sonic Youth and Dinosaur Jr, Iggy Pop was headlining, we were on at midday. I didn't really know what any of that meant. I just thought, wow, these people are fucking insane, they must do this for every band. It wasn't until I came home and had a gold record and we were on* SNL *that I realised OK, now this is fuckin' crazy. But it still seemed somewhat natural at that point, because we weren't playing stadiums, we were still playing places that held 2,000 people. It hadn't gotten to that Monsters Of Rock, four-seconds-before-the-snare-hits-the-audience level yet. The music was the same, and the people were the same. As we played these shows, the audience didn't seem like the Monsters Of Rock audience, it just seemed like more Nirvana fans.*

*"The thing I started to notice was, people were starting to pull. People would pull you to an interview, or pull you to the dressing room, and people would push you on stage. And that's when I thought, OK, this is getting a little weird. It didn't bum me out, but there were times where I'd excuse myself from an interview to have a piss, and have an extreme anxiety attack, saying why am I so stressed, so nervous? I was really happy, I didn't feel down or depressed, I felt elated. But I was pretty overwhelmed. And if you think about it, I was only in that band for three and a half years, so everything happened over such a short period of time. A lot of it is a blur."*

*The three of you had no chance to prepare for what happened . . .*

*"That's a cop-out. Anyone can handle what I do. It's a fucking luxury. I never not wanted it. I never expected it. We never had that world domination career ambition because our kind of music made it impossible that we could be the biggest band in the world. It was the same with Scream, same with Mission Impossible, same with Dain Bramage. When I joined Nirvana, it was for the same reason I joined Scream, and that's where people get fucked up, when you have that insane ambition and expectation. If music's not enough, not its own reward, don't do it. When I worked at Furniture Warehouse and only played music at the weekends, that was my vacation; those weekends meant so much to me."*

*You still felt that way . . .?*

*"I still feel that way. It's a much different scenario now, but I do it for the same reasons. There's no way I'd let a guitar sit around and gather dust, there's no way. It's so much a part of my life. The most embarrassing question I could be asked is, what do you do other than music? I don't have any interests outside music. Nirvana was the same. Even at the height of the insanity, it was a place I'd rather be than anywhere else."*

(Interview with Dave Grohl by *Mojo* journalist Stevie Chick, 2005)

On January 9, 1992, Nirvana arrived in New York to run through rehearsals for *Saturday Night Live*. It was a big deal. The late night comedy show was – and is – an institution because of its huge influence on American popular culture, if for no other reason than for the way its stars like Eddie Murphy, Chevy Chase and Dan Ackroyd have gone on to have long and glorious (too long and glorious, in some cases) movie careers.

"Seeing Nirvana play that show felt like such an odd validation," exclaims Jonathan Poneman. "It was like, '*Hello*, Middle America!' They were already huge, but you knew there was going to be a whole bunch of people who would have a new appreciation of the band because *Saturday Night Live* had established itself as being an arbiter of hip."

"I had a crush on Keanu Reeves," laughs Carrie Montgomery. "He used to go to Nirvana shows and Kurt would call me afterwards like, 'Guess who's here?' So, as a Christmas gift for doing his laundry this one time, he flew me to New York for *Saturday Night Live* so I could meet Keanu because he was supposed to be hosting the show. I flew there with Wendy [Kurt paid for both flights]. She had never flown before, so we got on the same flight and shared a hotel room. Keanu never showed."

On January 10, Nirvana recorded a live nine-song set for MTV's *120 Minutes* alternative rock show, with Courtney, Wendy and Dave's mom and sister present; and attended to bits and pieces of press. This was the first time many of Nirvana's crew had met Wendy, and they kept complimenting Kurt on his 'hot mom' – something that irritated the singer considerably.

The hip, Riot Grrrl-associated magazine for teenage girls, *Sassy*, had asked to feature Kurt and Courtney on their cover as some sort of ideal of true love, and the pair agreed. "Kurt and Courtney sitting in a tree/ K-I-S-S-I-N-G," ran the headline on the smart Christina Kelly article. The magazine was far cooler than stuffy magazines such as *Rolling Stone* and *New York Times* – two papers that they'd rejected interview requests from, on the correct basis that they were out-of-touch. *Sassy* had sizeable music content, and featured Olympian bands like Bratmobile, Bikini Kill and Nation Of Ulysses – something that *Rolling Stone* singularly failed to do. Unlike 99 per cent of rock magazines, it was also aimed at females, something that particularly appealed to Kurt.

"*Sassy* was the first cool magazine for tweens," explains Janet Billig. "It was a cooler version of *17* or *Cosmo Girl*. It spoke to young girls like adults and approached music with the passion of a fan. I set that interview up – I was friendly with Christina, and I was a publicist at the time. It wasn't initially going to be a cover, but with everything heating up for Nirvana they made it a cover. Kurt absolutely loved the magazine. He wouldn't have done the interview and photo shoot if he hadn't. Everyone loved *Sassy*. It was snarky and smart and they were music fans."

Later, it was back to the rehearsal studio for a run-through of the planned *SNL* songs – 'Smells Like Teen Spirit' and 'Territorial Pissings'. Neither the show's producers nor Nirvana's management wanted the second song played, preferring the more radio-friendly 'Come As You Are', but Nirvana didn't care. The band also refused to rehearse their regular instrument destruction, much to the displeasure of *SNL*'s crew, who preferred to have everything worked out in advance – great for camera angles, but anathema to the idea of rock music being spur-of-the-moment.

On January 11, the day of the show, Michael Lavine took photographs of Nirvana at his apartment as Kurt nodded in and out of consciousness. The shoot took place in complete silence – Krist and Dave disgusted by their singer's behaviour, and his obvious drugged-out state. "I asked Kurt why he was doing this," Lavine says. "He told me it was the only thing that helped his stomach. I was like, 'Dude, that's the one thing that's guaranteed to make your stomach worse.'

"They hung out at my house the whole day," Lavine adds. "Kurt was so fucked up he could barely keep his eyes open or stand up. The tension in that room was so thick you could cut it with a knife. Kurt was like, 'Gimme the Flipper album, gimme the Flipper album,' so I passed him over a copy and he took out a pen and drew the cover of the album [a crudely stencilled fish] on to his T-shirt."

When the time came to go over to NBC, the band refused to get into the show's transport – a large limousine – preferring to travel in a small van. Once there, Kurt was throwing up outside and being studiously rude to the show's host Rob Morrow[4], and any corporate types in suits.

This might seem like obvious punk rock behaviour to you and me, but it is frowned upon by the elite, who like to consider themselves as 'with it' as the people they're exploiting.

It was while the band was in New York that the remainder of the Nirvana camp woke up to the fact their meal ticket was on smack. The same day the *Sassy* interview took place, the *BAM* article with its heroin innuendo appeared. Even if no one bothered to read the piece (the ads-led magazine was scorned by music fans) the evidence was there for all to see. Mysterious hour-long visits to the bathroom while everyone else was waiting to go on stage: pallid faces and unexplained blackouts.

"The dressing rooms at the *SNL* studios are not large rooms at all," states Craig Montgomery. "You're in a space about 10 by 12 feet with a bathroom off it, and there's about six or eight of us – band, wives, management, crew – in there. So Kurt and Courtney go into the bathroom and they're in there for what seemed like hours . . . I was naïve, I didn't know what they were doing there. Later it dawned on me – and by then the people that handled Kurt just handled Kurt, and the rest of us just did our jobs and tried to have a good time. Because you couldn't run the tour and the production *and* try to get Kurt from the hotel to the show, you know?"

"I'd known enough people in my life that had this glassy-eyed look and kept nodding," says Danny Goldberg. "There had been a request to find a bunch of cash. Courtney wanted to go shopping. It obviously didn't happen overnight, but it was an overnight realisation. Kurt was a nice person and incredibly considerate, so he rarely uttered a harsh word, but a lot of us became extremely worried about him and we did some sort of an intervention in LA around the time Courtney became aware she was pregnant. After that, there were times he cleaned up and times he didn't . . ."

Danny sighs.

"But he was still a genius, playing great shows, making great records, creating great art and doing great interviews," the manager continues. "He was not a junkie in terms of being constantly out of it. Inwardly he was affected, but outwardly he had great periods of clarity, lucidity and so on. Like a lot of addictive people, a large majority of the time Kurt denied he was doing drugs – and some of the time it seemed credible because of his behaviour."

"I remember Jonathan [Poneman] phoning me up one night and saying, 'Anton, I've got a serious problem,'" recalls Anton Brookes. "'A friend of yours is on heroin.' And I said, 'What, Kurt?' And he said, 'You think Kurt's on heroin?' And I'm like, 'Yeah,' and he says, 'No, Mark – Mark Arm.' I'm like . . . *fuck*. I wouldn't say Kurt was on heroin when he first came over to the UK but I'm sure he flirted with it once or twice. I got the impression that they all dropped E and smoked enough weed to knock out a whale. They drank and everything, but they were just teenagers. I always thought his stomach problems were genuine. When the heroin problem became known people started thinking that if Kurt ever cancelled a gig or an interview it wasn't because he was ill or tired, it was because he was smashed out of his tits, which was never the case. Sure, he could be late for an interview – there was rock'n'roll time, which is late, and then there was Kurt Cobain time, which was like having jetlag."

Kurt and Courtney's hotel rooms were a mess. They were too paranoid to allow anyone inside to clean up – being petty larcenists themselves they figured everyone else was the same – so everything lay where they discarded it: pizza cartons and empty make-up containers, dirty linen and brimming ashtrays, deli trays and unused room carts, clothes strewn all over the floor . . . The pair could turn a pristine five-star room into a run-down Olympia apartment in less than a minute.

Dave and Krist thought Kurt was being pathetic: "I remember walking into their hotel room," the drummer told Michael Azerrad, "and for the first time realising that these two are really fucked up. They were nodding out in bed, just wasted. It was disgusting and gross."

"The camps were starting to separate," Carrie explains. "Kurt and Courtney against everybody else. That episode of *Saturday Night Live* was not good. It was not funny and I was sitting right next to Rob Morrow's mother, the guy who ended up hosting, and I was pissed and resentful that Keanu wasn't there. So we didn't go to the after-party – me and Kurt and Courtney just went home. We weren't part of the crowd. I was in the 'bad camp'. People would get pissed at us for behaving foolishly. I couldn't understand it. Everybody participating in those extracurricular activities was a willing participant. Kurt was bankrolling the whole thing, so why was I the bad guy? But I was and that's fine. Livelihoods depended on him. The band and the management and the record label and everybody needed Kurt to be healthy, and he wasn't. I understand now. And you don't want that person to die. I mean, it's not safe to participate in those sorts of activities . . ."

For the show itself Kurt wore his home-made Flipper T-shirt and a bearded Krist wore a Melvins T-shirt. Grohl was topless, hammering metal mayhem out of his reinforced drums. Despite the singer's state, the performance of 'Teen Spirit' was riveting, inspired – although Kurt noticeably wasn't looking at the camera. His hair was dyed a disgusting red-pink, a last-minute change of colour after Courtney objected to Carrie's dye job of red, white and blue.[5] 'Territorial Pissings' finished with its ritual destruction; at the end, as the cast milled around the band, Krist pretended to make out with Dave before grabbing Kurt and French-kissing him, an obvious two-fingered salute to the more homophobic elements of the metal/Nirvana crossover audience. *SNL* refused to show the kiss on repeats.

"That was so spontaneous," Krist told me. "And on the rerun, they showed a different ending. I know why – two guys kissing on TV, that's 'offensive'. Whatever. There are so many more urgent problems than two people's sexual orientation."

In Charles Cross' biography, the Seattle journalist paints a powerful picture of Kurt OD-ing a few hours after the *SNL* performance. Courtney woke up at 7 a.m. to find the other half of the bed empty and her lover sprawled out on the floor, his skin a pallid green, not breathing. If she'd woken up minutes later, he'd have been dead. She revived him by throwing water over his face and punching him in the solar plexus. Poignancy is added to the incident by the fact that *Nevermind* was due to hit number one the very next week. By this point, the album had sold two million copies. Here Kurt was at the very pinnacle of his success, and here he was lying dead on the floor.

The writer takes great pains to describe the scene of depravity and squalor: "Half-eaten rolls and rancid slices of cheese littered the tray tops," he writes, allowing perhaps for some artistic licence. "A handful of fruit flies hovered over some wilted lettuce." How very touching and ironic – especially the timing of the incident.

The only problem is: I don't think any of this actually happened – certainly not at the point when Courtney claimed it did. The reason I think Courtney told Charles that it did occur the evening of *SNL* is partly for dramatic effect and partly for the same reason she told Michael that she and Kurt met earlier than they actually did – to remove her culpability from the situation. If Kurt really did OD that early into their relationship, then it meant it had little to do with her influence – it's just because that's the way he was.

And in the same way Courtney lifted the actual details of her first meeting with Kurt to a fake, earlier time to lend the incident authenticity, so she has with this reported OD – probably from the time of Nirvana's Roseland Ballroom appearance in 1993, where I can recall Courtney telling me, almost word-for-word, of a similar occurrence.[6]

"Technically, it's possible," says Lavine, who took the *Sassy* cover photographs later the same day, "but they seemed fine when they showed up, if a little fried. I also think the incident happened at the Roseland show."

I interviewed Kurt (by phone) the day of the *Sassy* photo shoot – he was in an excitable mood, telling me how he'd switched on MTV News, only to find them announcing his engagement to Courtney, and that Nirvana had just recorded a live version of 'Territorial Pissings', with the express intention of getting it on heavy rotation on *120 Minutes*. "How does it feel to be number one on *Billboard*?" Kurt repeated my question, laconically. "It's like being number 16, only even more people kiss your ass." He was playful, friendly. He certainly wasn't behaving like someone who'd been technically dead only a few hours before.

But who knows? Memory plays tricks on the clearest of minds.

Drug use increased the pair's paranoia. Kurtney moved to another hotel – the brand new Omni Park Central – but their distrust of outsiders wasn't helped by their own actions. I recall Courtney calling me up from the lobby of the Omni, beside herself with anger, clearly off her head[7], recounting some garbled story about how she'd been accused of being a prostitute and a thief and how she was being refused re-entry to her husband's hotel room because she'd wandered down to the gift shop in the lobby to buy cigarettes in her underwear (which was always ripped and had holes in, as was her wont). She wanted me to call up reception and talk to them on her behalf.

"They wanted to arrest her," agrees Carrie – who was present. "They thought she was a hooker. She was all like, 'Caaaarriiiiiiieeee!!!!!' And I'm like, 'Oh my God. I don't know her, I swear to God.' Kurt wouldn't go down and get her. I had to go down and get her. And she was so pissed at these hotel people, there was a little concierge stand by the elevator banks and every time she went by there she'd steal the flowers off of it."

Scenes like this were common when Courtney was around: the mayhem her lover created on stage was far outstripped by her everyday life. It's rare for people like Courtney to exist, even rarer that they're allowed to get away with such behaviour.

"Kurt was so sweet in New York, he gave us money to go shopping. 'I know you guys probably want to go buy some expensive cosmetics, so here's some money,'" Carrie says, imitating Kurt's voice. While Courtney and Carrie and Wendy shopped for clothes, Kurt went down to Avenue C to score heroin. "People wait in a line," he told Michael Azerrad. "Lawyers, business people in three-piece suits, junkies, low-lifes, all different kinds of people."

"How does he know we want expensive cosmetics?" continues Carrie. "Of course we do! But then Courtney got pissed. She didn't want him to buy me anything. She just wanted him to buy her stuff, like he was going to run out of money. The end of that New York trip was the last time I ever talked to Kurt. It's so stupid, it's embarrassing to even say it . . ."

Carrie lowers her voice.

"Kurt and Courtney started telling people in their closest circle they were pregnant, and Wendy got freaked out. It was all a bit much for her to take. So when I got back from New York I got a phone call from Courtney where she says, 'Wendy tells me that you said that I love Kurt for his money and you love him for his heart.' And I say, 'I would never say something that stupid. Can I talk to Kurt please?' 'He can't talk to you right now. He's too upset. You better call Wendy and get this straightened out.' 'I'm not playing this bullshit game, Courtney. I'm not calling Wendy and talking about some shit that didn't happen. Let me talk to Kurt.' 'No. You can't talk to Kurt.' So that was how I got kicked out of the deal, just like Ian [Dickson] and – well, maybe not Dylan so much – but most everybody else got systematically taken out of the equation."

"Kurt and Courtney's relationship was tempestuous," Goldberg says, carefully. "They definitely loved each other. At times, they definitely hated each other. He had a very romantic sense of his commitment to her, and at the same time she drove him crazy."

On their return from New York, Kurt and Courtney moved into a two-bedroom apartment in west Hollywood, LA. The city wasn't Kurt's choice: he quickly grew to loathe its legendary falseness and isolation, missing his friends in the Northwest and even the rain far more than he expected. He'd never lived outside of Olympia and Aberdeen before – not even in Seattle – and moving to such a massive city felt entirely alien. But initially he welcomed the distance from his peers; especially since all he wanted to do was 'fuck and get high'. LA was Courtney's choice. It tallied with her ambition *to succeed on society's terms*, with its surreal juxtaposition of Hollywood glam and a far seedier underbelly. People drive everywhere in LA. Courtney couldn't drive, but that didn't faze her – she could get people to drive her anywhere she liked.

"Kurt loved his sisters and he loved kids," says Carrie Montgomery. "When he started making a little money it was his little [half-]sister Brianne's birthday[8], and Kurt and I went to this art store and bought her a bunch of art supplies and an easel and a mini-drum set. It was almost the happiest I'd seen him. We went down to Aberdeen, gave her all this stuff and spent the night watching movies with her. He doted on her. And he was close to Kim [Cobain] too – Kim would come over and hang out at Susie [Tennant]'s now and again. Once, his mother and his cousins came over and they treated him like a celebrity, which was odd. Maybe she was just happy for him, but the cousins were having him sign stuff."

The couple moved into 448 North Spaulding, a fairly laidback street situated between Fairfax and Melrose. Rent was $1,000 a month. Kurt kept to pretty much the same routine as when he lived in Olympia: get up, take drugs, listen to music, paint and play guitar. Watch TV late into the night. At this point, Kurt claimed to have had a $100-a-day heroin habit.

It was while Kurtney were in New York that Courtney realised she was pregnant[9], unsurprisingly to some cynics who saw it as the fastest way for Courtney to consolidate her position in Kurt's affections. This was unfair. Kurt was besotted with Courtney, and she with him. Whether it was just the closeness they felt through being drug buddies or their joint paranoia about the outside world, or incredible sex, it hardly mattered. Kurt felt he'd found his soulmate. Courtney likewise.

Kurt became obsessed with the idea the baby might be born deformed because of the couple's drug use – he'd painted enough pictures of 'flipper babies' when he was younger to be able to visualise the full horror. Courtney visited a Beverly Hills specialist in birth defects, who gave her the necessary reassurance that the risks posed by her taking heroin during the first trimester were minimal.

"There was never any concern the baby would turn out malformed," states Rosemary Carroll firmly. "I hooked Courtney up with my gynaecologist who had delivered both of my children, and he was very clear she would have a normal child. That was a rumour started in the press."

Even so, Kurtney decided they needed to detox, especially as Nirvana were due to tour Australia and Japan. The couple checked into a Holiday Inn, with tour manager Alex MacLeod stopping by occasionally to make sure they were OK. The process wasn't pretty: withdrawal can include diarrhoea, vomiting, muscle spasms, mood swings and insomnia.

"Dave and I went to go visit Courtney after she got her first . . . I want to say sound scan," Jennifer Finch laughs, "but that's how you sell records. Ultrasound scan. They put it on a videocassette and Kurt was just sitting in front of the television looking at the little video. He won me back over, definitely – cos I hated him at that point. It was very sweet. Then I left her a pound to remind her how fun rock is and how much it was going to suck being a mom. Because I thought she'd have to stay home or cut down on the shenanigans. God, I'm so stupid. Like they'd both somehow get in touch with reality over the whole thing."

Where did the name Frances Bean come from?

"Bean came from looking at that ultrasound that day, thinking she looked like a tiny little bean," Jennifer reveals.[10] "And she really did. I think biology is scary and disgusting. I can't believe Courtney even went through that. I understand why she couldn't stop smoking. There's so much expectation when you're pregnant."

We were all disappointed it wasn't a freak.

"I think it might be," the musician laughs. "There's still a possibility; she's still young. When you're forced to be the mommy you tend to grow up quick. Thank god she's mature and well-rounded. Till she hits 19 and it's all over."

It was on January 19[11] that Krist and Dave joined their singer in LA to shoot the video for 'Come As You Are'. His bandmates were shocked by Kurt's state. "He looked bad. Grey," Dave stated. "He just looked sad." The group and management were a little nervous about the choice of single, realising the bass line's similarities to English proto-industrialists Killing Joke's 1985 song 'Eighties' – the choice was 'Come As You Are' or 'In Bloom'. Goldberg favoured the more obviously commercial song.[12] Kevin Kerslake (Hole, Iggy Pop) directed the video, shot on three locations – Wattle Garden Park in Hollywood, Kurtney's new house and the Van Nuys Airport hangar. The band's faces were filmed through plastic and running water, so as to be distorted and partly unrecognisable.

On January 23, Nirvana set out for a proposed 12-date tour of Australia.[13]

Kurt wasn't in any sort of condition to be touring, what with his stomach problems and going through the final stage of detox. And he was particularly bothered by the prospect of not being able to find any drugs in a strange country. On arriving at his hotel in Sydney, he changed the 'Do Not Disturb' sign on his door to 'Please Burn Down My Room'.

Immediately, he ran into problems with both Nirvana's entourage and the local hospital staff when he tried to find relief from his stomach – after Alex took him to one emergency room, he overheard one doctor say to another in an emergency room, "Oh, he's just a junkie, he's still coming off drugs." Kurt later bitterly complained at the way his health problems were confused with his drug use: Shelli Novoselic, in particular, coming in for vitriol when she tried to sympathise with him. "I just wanted to fucking punch her in the face because she, like everyone else, assumed that I was doing drugs," Kurt complained. (But he was!) A show in Brisbane was cut short, and another one in Fremantle[14] was cancelled. In the end, Kurt took methadone – called Physeptone in Australia – which helped with both his detox and stomach.

The first show was at Sydney's now defunct Phoenician Club, with support from local bands Tumbleweed and The Meanies.[15] "We did four gigs with them," recalls Wally Kempton, Meanies bassist. "The Phoenician was chosen well before *Nevermind* went through the roof, and the 1,400 tickets sold out in record time. The atmosphere was enormous – the fine line between fear and pure unbridled fun came close to being breached many times. The next day at the first ever Big Day Out[16], our set started 15 minutes before Nirvana's. A huge crowd watched our first few songs, and then we played to people's backs as they walked away towards Nirvana's pavilion!"

"Australia was the most fun of that whole tour, even though Kurt was having some trouble, and looked really thin," enthuses Barrett Jones, who was Dave's drum tech. "The weather was amazing and the promoter took us camping. The kangaroos were amazing! Most of the shows were tiny, like college cafeterias. We got a week off in Sydney, which was great."

"It was warm and sunny and I was excited to be there," says Craig Montgomery. "We went out boogie-boarding and bungee-jumping with Krist and Dave . . . while Kurt was trying to score dope." Craig sighs. "I guess there was some tension between Krist and Shelli and Kurt, but by then everyone was aware of what was going on and trying to have a good time despite it. Even so, the shows were *fantastic*. There was a show in Sydney [at the Big Day Out] in a great big square boxing ring-type arena, and it was as packed as the older club shows. There was way more people outside wanting to get in than you can fit in there. That show was like World War III."

In the middle of the tour, Kurt agreed to be interviewed by *Rolling Stone*. He wasn't a fan of the magazine – both Lester Bangs' Seventies magazine *Creem* and the punk bible *Maximumrocknroll* were far cooler, as was all of the British and most of the European press – but succumbed to pressure from management and bandmates. In protest, the singer showed up for the photo shoot in a handmade T-shirt, emblazoned with the slogan 'Corporate Magazines Still Suck'.

After a gig in Auckland, New Zealand, the band travelled to Singapore for a press day on February 12. A few hundred screaming fans greeted the band at the airport – the record label had placed an announcement in a local paper, specifying the exact time of the flight's arrival. The same week, preening Kate Bush wannabe Tori Amos released a piano-drenched, wailing version of 'Smells Like Teen Spirit' that was so risible that Nirvana later used it for their opening music at European festival dates.

After Singapore, it was on to Japan for several dates. In Osaka, the band hooked up with Shonen Knife again. The Japanese trio gave Kurt gifts – toy swords and a new motorised version of his toy monkey Chim Chim. Kurt loved Japan, despite his stomach cramps. Courtney had rejoined him, and the methadone was doing the trick. But who doesn't love Japan? All those incredible fashions and weird paedophilic dolls on sale next to firearms and *Hello Kitty* paraphernalia and cartoons. The weather wasn't as nice as Australia, though. It was cold and snowy, and Nirvana were also taken aback by their audiences, everyone sitting politely in 10 × 10 foot sections and trooping out after the final song – no encore because the concept wasn't understood back then.[17]

"I hated Japan, because people were so fucking polite," Dave Grohl told me later that year. "It pissed me off."

"I remember being freaked out, flying in and thinking how incredibly dirty it was," recalls Barrett. "The smog was so thick in the middle of winter. The taxi drivers had little white gloves on, and everyone was way too polite. Dave used to play Tama drums, and at one show the band was smashing up the drum kit, and the president of Tama showed up. He was like, 'Oh no, he doesn't like the drums!' Krist let off a fire extinguisher, one of those white powder kinds, and no one could breathe."

It was on February 20 – the same day 'Come As You Are' was released in the US, and Kurt's 25th birthday – on a flight to Hawaii that Kurtney decided to get married. The couple had wanted a Valentine's Day date for their betrothal, but their plans were delayed after John Silva (not Courtney, as was originally claimed) insisted on Kurt working out a pre-nuptial agreement to cover his future earnings. According to Charles Cross' *Heavier Than Heaven*, Kurt's gross income during 1991 was $29,541 (or $27,000 after deductions) – a fair whack for many of his fans (including this author, even now) – but unusually small for someone who had sold more than three million albums on which he'd written the lion's share of the songs and performed regular paying gigs.

Indeed, Courtney was using her husband's fame to negotiate herself a record deal with DGC that had both a considerably higher advance and better royalty rate than her husband's – as did many of the bands who signed to major labels, post-*Nevermind*. She would frequently boast of this fact to people like myself and Kim Gordon – like we could care one way or another – while simultaneously complaining about how insignificant her husband's massive success was making her feel. In vain we would try and tell her she should judge herself on her own terms, not on anyone else's, but the only line she took from us was to play up on the music industry's innate sexism.

"The only reason they're treating me so dismissively, Everett, is because I married a rock star," she wailed. What, like your friends warned you against doing a couple of months ago?

On February 24, Kurtney got married on Waikiki Beach. Dylan Carlson was flown in for the dual purpose of Best Man and to bolster Kurt's heroin supply – "I just did a teeny bit so I didn't get sick," the singer lamely explained. A non-denominational female minister, picked from the phone book, conducted a brief ceremony at sunset on a cliff overlooking a beach: Kurt in his green flannel pyjamas, and Courtney in an antique silk dress. The marriage caused considerable ill feeling amid Kurtney's close circles. Kurt and Courtney's paranoia towards their friends' perceived – and actual – disapproval of their drug usage was running at a new high. Dave Grohl, Alex MacLeod, Dylan and his girlfriend, and two of the road crew were present. Conspicuous by their absence were two of Kurt's oldest friends – Krist and Shelli Novoselic.

Courtney claimed it was because the pair was being "really shitty" towards Kurtney – and also Shelli disapproved of the marriage. Not surprisingly, Shelli saw it differently. She had a major objection to Courtney taking drugs while pregnant. "Maybe at that point, maybe she was," she told Michael Azerrad. "Maybe she wasn't. I don't know, but we all *assumed*."

"That day – it was just sort of sad. I attribute it all to Courtney," says Barrett. "I was concerned that she was doing drugs when she was pregnant. And I spoke to my girlfriend about that, and my girlfriend and Shelli would talk about that, and I think Courtney found out about that. The day they were married, Kurt called me and was mad about my girlfriend and Shelli talking shit about Courtney. And I said, 'I don't care what you guys do to yourselves, but there's a baby there.' I think that's wrong. Whatever. You probably know this story."

The day after the wedding, Krist and Shelli returned to Seattle devastated by Kurt's behaviour. It suddenly seemed that there was no way forward for Nirvana from here. Indeed, Krist didn't see Kurt for another two months – and barely spoke to him for around five months, including rehearsals.

Kurtney stayed on in Hawaii for their honeymoon.

**Addenda 1: Cali DeWitt**

"I'm from Los Angeles. I was born in Canada but I moved to LA when I was three. I split my time between Canada and LA, mostly LA. I was a music fan from the get-go. When [LA punk film] *Decline Of Western Civilization* came out in 1981, my dad took me to see it. I was eight."

You have a cool dad?

"Yeah, I have a cool dad. He took me to see [Ramones film] *Rock'N' Roll High School* and [The Who film] *The Kids Are Alright* all in that time. He bought me those records and I'd carry them to school. I remember bringing the Ramones to show-and-tell in second grade. We moved a lot. I switched schools like every year. Probably around sixth grade I stopped liking school that much."

Have you been in bands yourself?

"No. I sang in a punk band when I was 13 and 14. Luckily, I was friends with people who were really good musicians, even when I was very young. Even when I was 16 I felt that I wanted to be in a band for the wrong reasons. I wasn't driven to play music and I became comfortable just loving it. I started going to shows really young. I went to see [influential punk band] DOA in 1982 when I was nine. From then on I would try to go to as many shows as I could, all-ages shows and punk shows. When I was in 10th grade in LA, this place called Jabberjaw opened in 1989. I went there the weekend it opened, and dropped out of high school to work there for free."

What did you do there, bartending?

"Yeah, bartending coffee. There were no drinks. There were 40-ouncers in the backyard. That was when I felt I had arrived. It was an all-ages space downtown with people who seemed to care only about music and art and things that were interesting to me. I hung out there all the time and helped them book shows. I tried to convince them that Sub Pop was really cool. They were like, 'Whatever.' The first Sub Pop band that I could get to play there was Swallow who were pretty dreadful, but they quickly started to get into bands like Mudhoney. The history of Jabberjaw was pretty illustrious after that.

"That's where I met Courtney. I was 16 and had a great relationship with my parents, but I was in downtown LA all the time now and I was away from home. She seemed like a scary older lady to me. It was about 1990. I was a little bit frightened of her. I knew she had just started this band Hole and she was so gregarious and kind of assaulting to other people verbally that she intimidated me. For whatever reason, she took me under her wing and behaved like my 'city mom'. She started letting me roadie for her band, and I would roadie for L7 as well. She was cool."

What was Courtney like when you first met her?

"She seemed like one of the smartest people I'd ever met. She was very funny, very fun to be around. She wasn't anything like the picture they paint of her now. She was very driven. Remember, this is pre-*Nevermind*, so the idea of a punk band getting big – a real one – was not on the cards. Her idea that Hole would be a big band was laughable to me, but I liked them."

What was she like on stage?

"Self-conscious. She would ask questions like, 'How does it look when I do this? Did you see my new move?' She would talk to me like I was her confidante."

Was there anybody she was aspiring to be at the time?

"A nemesis would be like Inger Lorre from The Nymphs. As history is written, that doesn't matter now, but at the time she was a threat. Inger was like the 'bad girl' in LA.[18] She would talk about Kat [Bjelland] ripping her off, or L7 being too macho or not being feminine enough. She had a clear vision of what she wanted, and the role of women in music, and changing that. I liked being a part of it. I liked being Hole's roadie, it was fun for me and I was young enough to work for nothing. I went on the first US tour, and we all got paid $12 a day."

Can you describe the other three members of the band?

"Caroline [Rue] was the whipping boy. She didn't fit Courtney's vision of what the band should be. She was too clumsy and self-conscious. Courtney was a little threatened by Jill [Emery]. Jill began to get attention because she was mastering this [Black] Sabbath feel people liked. After a show at the Whiskey-A-Go-Go [February 11, 1992][19], a bunch of people was talking about how great Jill was. That was the end of her.[20] Eric [Erlandson] was the manager, the one who knew what was going on. Hole opened a show in 1991 [June 14] that Nirvana played at the Hollywood Palladium, with Dinosaur Jr. That was the first time I met Kurt."

Were you around when Courtney started dating Kurt?

"I was talking to her. New York had a big effect on me when we got there on tour. I came home and saved up $200 and moved there. I lived in a meat locker. But before I did that, *Nevermind* came out. The way people say they remember where they were when Kennedy was shot, I remember where I was when they played the video for 'Smells Like Teen Spirit' on MTV. I called everyone into the room and said, 'You're not going to believe this.' It was unreal. This network of people and you sleep on each other's floors and now someone has done this. I loved *Bleach*, but I couldn't believe how good *Nevermind* was. So this guy who I'd met a few times, and was friendly with, became a bit of a hero."

**Addenda 2: Nirvana's influence on Olympia**

"Unwound used to have a drinking song," recalls Slim Moon, "where they would raise their cups and sing, *'Thank you Nirvana for buying us beer, thank you Nirvana for letting us practise here.'* After *Nevermind*, instead of it being the neighbours calling the cops and banging on your practice space walls saying, 'What's that racket?' they'd say, 'Are you in a band? Do you know Kurt Cobain? Can I buy you a beer?' Regular people would see your grunge haircut and think you were cool instead of spit on you. Even though it did sometimes lead to someone buying you a beer, mostly it was embarrassing. We didn't want everyone in America to know our secret."

One of Olympia's greatest achievements is the way it managed to retain its underground culture, despite the attention it got.

"Nirvana got famous," Slim concurs, "but it never happened in a way that put a spotlight on us."

Is that because Nirvana were marketed as a Seattle band?

"Exactly. The spotlight ended up on Seattle. And all of the duo bands and bands that break all of the rules nowadays that we used to get so ridiculed for breaking . . . they owe a big debt to our scene. The Riot Grrrl thing got a ton of attention and Nirvana got a ton of attention, but neither of them in ways that ruined Olympia. Olympia has slowly dissipated, but it never got killed by being in the spotlight. A lot of the things that influenced Olympia bands in '88 – early Rough Trade singles, post-punk – are influencing bands in 2006."

So, Nirvana's influence on Olympia . . .

"In the Eighties, there were not a lot of big rock bands in Olympia. In the Nineties there were a lot of big rock bands in Olympia. Nirvana influenced that, but Melvins influenced it more. Before, it had been just Beat Happening, Some Velvet Sidewalk and Nirvana that made records and toured. Now we had Unwound and Bikini Kill and Karp[21] who were all making records and touring. Everything became plausible, from getting signed to K, to being the next Nirvana. The reason why you start your band totally affects what you do musically. If the height of what you think you could achieve is that you could play a party and 20 of your friends bounce up and down, you do a totally different thing musically than if you think you might be able to 'make it'. Nirvana was part of a change that occurred throughout the start of the Nineties. That change was not all bad. It made some people try harder and think of it as art instead of fun. In Olympia in the Eighties, Calvin Johnson was considered a visionary for believing you could put out your own seven-inch."

## NOTES

1 No disrespect to Soundgarden intended.

2 Deliberately childish . . . no bass . . . no talent . . . Hang on! Haven't I just described Beastie Boys?

3 The Daniel Johnston album was released by Atlantic. The same man responsible for the awesome Led Zeppelin remasters signed Daniel.

4 Rob Morrow was American actor and director who starred in a popular, quirky cult show of the time called *Northern Exposure*.

5 The following Monday, schools across America were witness to the sight of kids with Kool-Aid pink hairdos. Imagine the scenes if Kurt's original hair colour had survived Courtney's wrath!

6 Or possibly from the time of Nirvana's second *SNL* appearance in September 1993, when buddy Rene Navarette recalls being told Kurt had OD'd on his hotel room floor.

7 Although, being even more naïve about heroin than almost anyone featured in this book, I didn't cotton on to Kurt and Courtney's use until halfway through 1992 when Courtney told me direct. Or perhaps I didn't care, figuring it was none of my business. I drank heavily. They did drugs. Who was I to judge?

8 Brianne O'Connor was born to Wendy O'Connor and Lamont Shillinger, just before Christmas Day 1985.

9 "You were probably present in a closet when Frances Bean was conceived," Courtney remarked to Carrie Montgomery when I reintroduced the pair in Seattle in 1999.

10 Frances was after Frances McKee of The Vaselines, who by this point was a schoolteacher.

11 Five days after Dave Grohl's 23rd birthday, and a couple of days after Dave and Krist had joined Melvins on stage at the Crocodile.

12 'Come As You Are' was later threatened with litigation, but the case never came to court.

13 To tie in with the tour, the six-song *Hormoaning* EP was released in Australia and Japan – 'Even In His Youth' and 'Aneurysm' from the B-side of 'Teen Spirit', and the four covers, including The Vaselines, from the 1990 John Peel Session.

14 Fremantle is a beautiful port city next to Perth in Western Australia.

15 The Meanies are a good solid old-fashioned punk band – with tunes!

16 The Big Day Out is Australia's massive annual outdoor travelling rock festival – sort of the equivalent of America's Lollapalooza, only far cooler because it's Australian.

17 Japan was a whole other culture: I recall playing one show with Soundgarden in Osaka in the mid-Nineties that took place on the second floor of a shopping mall. People danced, but were very careful not to bash into each other.

18 There's a legendary story about when Ms Lorre dropped her knickers and pissed on the desk of a record company executive who was refusing to play ball.

19 Courtney played a drug-ravaged version of The Velvet Underground's 'Pale Blue Eyes' and dedicated it to an absent Kurt, while outside a storm-lashed sky changed colour every few minutes. It was a cracking show: Eric and Courtney pretended to swing their guitars at me, down the front. There were more industry people than paying customers. The fiercely independent Superchunk played support. Before the show Courtney walked up to the 'Chunk's singer Mac and, pointing to me, announced, "You should pay attention, because this man is going to make you a star."

20 Indeed it was. Jill and Caroline were out of the band after that show, after which Hole went on hiatus for several months.

21 Karp were a full-on Olympia rock band that – as one critic put it – "Possess the kind of energy that most metal bands have wet dreams about."

## CHAPTER 20

# Adult-oriented Grunge

*"I have to hear rumours about me all the time," the singer growls. "I'm totally sick of it. If I'm going to take drugs that's my own fucking prerogative, and if I don't take drugs it's my own fucking prerogative. It's nobody's business, and I don't care if people take drugs and I don't care if people don't take drugs.*

*"It all started with just one article in one of the shittiest, cock rock-orientated LA magazines," he continues, "where this guy assumed I was on heroin because he noticed that I was tired. Since then, the rumours have spread like wildfire. I can't deny that I have taken drugs and I still do, every once in a while. But I'm not a fucking heroin addict, and I'm not going to . . ."*

*He trails off, momentarily wordless.*

*"It's impossible to be on tour and to be on heroin," he begins again. "I don't know any band that could do it, unless you're Keith Richards and you're being given blood transfusions every three days, and you have runners going out and scoring drugs for you."*

*Kurt glowers with anger.*

*"I never realised that mainstream audiences react towards mainstream rock stars in this manner, because I've never paid attention before," he rails. "I don't mean to complain as much as I do, but it's a load of shit. I've had days where I've considered this to be a job, and I never thought that would happen. It makes me question the point of it all. I'm only gonna bitch about it for another year and, if I can't handle it after that, we're gonna have to make some drastic changes."*

(*Melody Maker*, July 18, 1992)

SO Kurt returned to LA at the start of March 1992 and took a bunch of heroin. He tried to hide his usage from Courtney by shooting up in a locked cupboard where he kept his supplies: the heroin, the needles, the spoons and the rubbing alcohol. Courtney got mad at Kurt when she discovered what he was doing – going as far as to break his syringes. Or so she claimed: mindful perhaps of the later controversy that engulfed the couple when she admitted to doing heroin during the first weeks of pregnancy (i.e.: before she actually knew she was pregnant).

Kurt wrote several of the songs that appeared on *In Utero* during these months, but he later admitted in a 1992 interview with *The Advocate* that during 1991, "I haven't been very prolific at all." He also painted, Goya-influenced paintings of strange angels and skeletal torsos, scarlet splurges and distended aliens, and wallowed in his hatred for the outside world and his inability to come to terms with it. The working title for Nirvana's next album was *I Hate Myself And I Want To Die*.

I recall Kurt showing me a bootleg video of the Pennsylvania State Official who'd blown his brains out live on air during an otherwise innocuous political news segment after inserting a gun into his mouth. Someone had put the 20-second clip on repeat, simultaneously desensitising the viewer and making the act even grosser. Kurt watched it with me a couple of times.

Meanwhile, Krist was back in Seattle, fuming over his singer's self-immolation and distressed by the apparent ease with which he'd shrugged aside years of friendship for the sake of a girl and some drugs.

"Kurt's a fucking junkie asshole and I hate him!" he complained.

"I needed time to readjust," Kurt told *Rolling Stone*'s David Fricke in October 1993. "[The fame] hit me so hard, and I was under the impression I didn't need to go on tour because I was making a whole bunch of money. Eight to 10 million records sold – that sounded like a lot of money to me. [Also] my stomach ailment stopped us from touring. After a person experiences chronic pain for five years, you're literally insane."[1]

Even Gold Mountain were scared of their star's volatile temper and mood swings: a projected US tour in the spring was shelved when it became overwhelmingly apparent that the entire band – not just Kurt – was suffering from tour burnout. Instead, Kurt's management attempted their first intervention: Kurt checked into a rehab programme at the Exodus Recovery Center, at the Cedars-Sinai hospital in LA. Trouble was, his counsellor was star-struck and hence Kurt didn't have any respect for him, ending the treatment after four days.

Dave wasn't so bothered by his singer's behaviour, having known him for a comparatively short time. He used the down time from Nirvana to write his own songs, which he'd record on Barrett Jones' eight-track Laundry Room studio in their shared West Seattle house. These songs later materialised on Foo Fighters' debut album, 1995's *Foo Fighters*.

*Nevermind* remained in the *Billboard* Top Three through March and early April. On March 1, 'Come As You Are' was released in the US – it entered the UK charts at number nine, the same week as the reissued *Bleach* entered the British albums chart at number 33.

Nirvana mania continued to surge across America. *Los Angeles Times* reported that a British band called Nirvana from the Sixties was taking the newer version to court over name rights. Gold Mountain ended up paying them $100,000 in an out-of-court settlement.[2] A record store in Ventura, CA received a complaint for featuring a baby's penis on the cover of *Nevermind* in a window display: it never became an issue, although Geffen did have a contingency plan to airbrush the offending appendage out, or cover it up with a sticker if one of the big chains complained.

Bootlegs were rife: both of live shows and the ubiquitous demos. Kurtney took it upon themselves to confiscate any copies they saw: bootlegging is a harmless enough pursuit on the whole, but musicians and record companies are obsessed with tracking down miscreants. Courtney claimed it took food directly out of her baby's mouth, a somewhat distorted view for a woman who was clearly about to become a millionaire many, many times over.

After a bidding war, Hole signed to Geffen for a reputed one million dollars, despite Courtney's pregnancy meaning the band had to drop out of playing a projected Reading Festival slot, and despite the fact Hole only consisted of herself and Eric Erlandson at the time. As one record company executive remarked: "Sleeping with Kurt Cobain is worth half a million."

"Courtney used to get a lot of flak for going after the famous guy," says Michael Lavine, "but people forget – or perhaps didn't know in the first place. She was obsessed with him before he was famous, months and months before. I hung out with Nirvana in LA at the Raji's show [February 15, 1990]: that was the day I met Courtney. She was in line to see that show. When I photographed Courtney in July 1991, round the time of *Nevermind*, she was like, 'Let me see the Kurt pictures. Let me see the Kurt pictures.' She was crazy for him – and he was crazy for her. Kurt once told me, 'I like Courtney because she's the kind of girl who'll stand up in the middle of the room and smash a glass and then knock the table over for no reason at all.'

"Great," Michael laughs. "That's a great reason to like someone!"

"In one version of 'Teen Spirit', Kurt sang the line *'Who will be the king and queen of the outcast teens?'*" Courtney told me in 1999.[3] "Glamour aside, there could be no more perfect couple at the time. We were so right for each other because we were the most antisocial people in our entire area. I was the adventuress who'd gone out, and he was the one who stayed under the bridge, literally. It was great . . . and it was horrible because of all the drugs and the pain and the fear. Kurt was a sweet, sweet guy. People think I look upon that relationship as dysfunctional, and I am a bit disdainful in public because it's not my job to hold that goddamn flame. I will honour and adore that person because I loved him, but he was grumpy and I am grumpy. It wasn't a big surprise us getting together, anyone around Seattle knows it was the most normal coupling. It was almost like the Captain and the Cheerleader, in the converse.

"The mainstream British press was like, 'She got herself a really good deal,'" Courtney continued. "That's so absurd that I can't even get defensive about it. It's like, 'Huh?' and it's been a shock ever since."

Kurtney were so private during 1992 that most of Kurt's Olympia friends were excluded from his life – Ian Dickson, Calvin Johnson, Nikki McClure, Slim Moon, Tobi Vail . . . Most of the people Kurtney would communicate with as a couple would either be management (Janet Billig, Danny Goldberg), musician friends (Eric Erlandson, Mark Lanegan[4]), drug buddies (Dylan Carlson, Cali DeWitt) and his family occasionally. On one visit to Aberdeen in April '92, Kurt's sister Kim admitted she was gay: something Kurt had already guessed. It still came as a shock to their mother Wendy, though.

Kurt composed letters to some of his former friends that he never posted. He'd even call them up on the odd occasion. But by choosing to marry Courtney and move to LA, he'd crossed the line.

"One time Kurt and Mark Lanegan and Courtney came to Olympia and hung out at Nikki [McClure]'s house for a day," remembers Slim Moon. "Me and Lanegan walked around and talked, and that was when I met Courtney. It was all very weird. Bratmobile was all down the hall trying to decide whether to do some sabotage or something. There had been this whole thing about *Sassy*[5] where they said that Kurt and Courtney were junkies and Courtney accused Bratmobile of planting that, because Erin [Smith] from Bratmobile was an intern there – like it wasn't common public knowledge already!"

I can't even imagine Courtney meeting Nikki. They seem such disparate personalities: one all artifice and confusion, the other all naïve joy. It'd be like the universe imploding.

"Kurt didn't talk," Slim recalls. "If you directly addressed him, he'd give you a one or two word answer. But when Courtney wasn't in the bathroom – which she was most of the time – she talked a fucking hundred miles an hour. She was really stuck on this thing how girl bands only write songs in the key of E. She kept repeating the same theory over and over for hours, and then they left. There was really no interaction between the two of them."

At the start of April, 'Smells Like Teen Spirit' was officially declared platinum (sales of one million) in the US, and Nirvana returned to the studio – well, Barrett's eight-track – to record a couple more songs.

"I had my studio sent out, and set it up in the basement, which was kind of inadequate, but that's where I recorded the King Buzzo record[6], and the three Nirvana songs," reveals Barrett Jones. "One was slated for The Wipers' tribute record ['Return Of The Rat'], one was slated for The Jesus Lizard split single on Touch And Go ['Oh, The Guilt'], and one ended up on the B-side of 'Lithium' ['Curmudgeon']. We did them all in one or two takes. They hadn't even played the songs before."

The songs were devastatingly heavy: it was Grohl's first opportunity to show what he could really contribute to Nirvana in the studio[7], and it seemed like the recording was centred around his churning animal force. 'Oh, The Guilt' threatened to disintegrate under a slew of feedback and wrenched guitar strings, Kurt howling out the chorus over and over again, incisive. It was far closer to the Soundgarden-influenced sludge of *Bleach* than any tuneful Sixties inflexions from *Nevermind*. Indeed, the recordings were clearly a reaction to the cleaned-up sound on the latter. 'Curmudgeon', likewise: although it was nearly ruined by a Hawkwind-esque tunnel effect. This was relentless, heads flailing music. "I think they were trying to be a little more punk rock about the whole thing," Jones confirms. "They wanted to be as low budget as possible."

'Return Of The Rat' was more obviously early Eighties, post-punk influenced – unsurprising, bearing in mind the song's origin. It was released on June 20 by Portland's T/K Records, as part of the seven-inch box set *Eight Songs For Greg Sage And The Wipers*.

"We'd talked about it," says Barrett about the session. "Kurt was like, 'You have a studio. We should record with you.' It was quick and easy, even though my studio was the worst possible set-up, no separation between the equipment and the small room. Everything was live except for the vocals, which took a second take."

Despite the recordings, relations between the band members were at an all-time low – so low, in fact, that Nirvana briefly split up around this point. The split was brought about by Kurt's insistence that the publishing royalties needed to be renegotiated. Prior to this, they'd been divided evenly, but Kurt – brooding alone in LA – began to resent his bandmates their good fortune, figuring that if he did the majority of the songwriting, he should get the majority of the money: 75/25 of the music, and 100 per cent of the lyrics. Worse, he wanted the percentage retroactively.

Dave and Krist were livid – they felt he was taking money out of their pockets – but Kurt thought the other two were being greedy, and told the band's lawyer Rosemary Carroll he'd split the band up if his bandmates didn't agree to his demands.

"Everybody blames Courtney but it was really Kurt," explains Carroll. "That was one of the reasons he wanted a different lawyer to Nirvana's old lawyer. Alan Mintz was perfectly good but he'd been present when they'd decided to split the publishing money equally. Kurt decided afterwards that he wrote all the songs – the music, the lyrics, everything. Once it became clear to him how significant the publishing money was, he wanted what was his. He thought it would be easier to get that through a different lawyer. Whether to split your publishing money equally is entirely down to the band: R.E.M. do, Sonic Youth do, Billy Corgan doesn't. Not only did Kurt want it going forward but he also wanted it retroactively. Krist and Dave still have an interest in 'Teen Spirit', but all the other songs are Kurt's. That did lead to Krist and Dave having to pay back some money.

"Did he say he'd 'break up the band' if he didn't get his way?" she queries. "I don't think he ever said those words, but that was certainly the implication."

The situation certainly wasn't helped by the fact Kurt was taking heroin again by the end of May – the same month that *Nevermind* finally dropped out of the *Billboard* Top 10. He told a friend he was now on a $400 a day habit.

Not the best time to start a new European tour.

> *For logistical reasons, the Kurt Cobain interview takes place in his LA apartment, second week of June, a couple of weeks before Nirvana's short tour of Europe. The day's cloudy, the room dim and slightly messy. Scraps of diaries containing lyrics and ideas from Kurt and his wife plus a couple of guitars and amplifiers litter the main room. A few weird-looking stick dolls, made by Kurt for use in a future video, nestle next to multicoloured bird feathers and jars full of flowers. In the front room, where Kurt lounges in an armchair, looking studious in his 'geek' glasses and short, bleached hair, a Patti Smith record plays quietly in the background. A small kitten darts about, tiger-ish. Courtney, several months pregnant, is asleep in the bedroom with her TV tuned quietly to daytime MTV.*

*Earlier, Kurt had shown me the video to Nirvana's new single, 'Lithium', on the same TV set. Compiled by director Kevin Kerslake from live footage of the band at last year's Reading Festival, a Halloween gig in Seattle and a show in Rotterdam where he first romanced Courtney*[8]*, it's breathtakingly ferocious. Live videos usually suck, this one doesn't. Work it out for yourself.*

*The phone rings. It's someone from a radio station, wanting to know what type of music Kurt listens to. He tells them Adult-oriented Grunge. It rings again. It's Corey Rusk from Touch And Go, seeking Kurt's advice over a problem that has arisen with Kurt's management over a projected joint Nirvana/Jesus Lizard single. Kurt listens carefully and promises he'll resolve the situation with his manager.*

*Despite reports to the contrary, Kurt looks a lot healthier than the previous times I've met him. I wouldn't say that he glows, but he definitely radiates something – happiness in his new-found stability of marriage, perhaps.*

*I suggest to him, when he eventually comes off the phone, that he seems much more relaxed. "Oh yeah," he replies. "But that's because when we last met [in October 1991], I'd been on tour for five months, and I haven't played for a while now. Plus, I was getting pissed off doing commercial radio station interviews with all these DJ voices not having any idea who the fuck we were. How much exposure does one band need?"*

(*Melody Maker*, July 18, 1992)

The tour wasn't a success.

Nirvana played at Dublin's Point Theatre on June 21, with The Breeders supporting – but already Kurt was complaining of stomach pains, caused by his reliance on methadone. The next night, in Belfast, a security man punched Kurt repeatedly in the stomach after the singer tried to break up an altercation between security and a fan. The following morning, he collapsed at breakfast and was taken to hospital. Nirvana's British PR Anton Brookes found himself in the slightly surreal situation of trying to shift journalists waiting to conduct interviews from the lobby of Nirvana's hotel while simultaneously orchestrating Kurt's departure to hospital.

Someone spotted Kurt, and despite Anton's best denials – "It's a weeping ulcer, I've known him for three years and he's always had it. It's because he eats a lot of junk food" – by the end of the day CNN News was on the phone asking whether the rumours of an overdose were true.

In Paris on June 24, Gold Mountain hired a couple of security guards to keep an eye on Kurtney and make sure the pair didn't leave their hotel room to score drugs. Kurt was indignant: "I was being treated like a fucking baby," he complained to Michael Azerrad. Kurtney immediately changed hotels, purposely forgetting to tell management, checking in under their favourite false names, 'Mr and Mrs Simon Ritchie' (Sid Vicious' real name). Krist and Dave hung out with the crew, rather than become embroiled in the subterfuge and innuendo and distrust that was beginning to follow Kurtney wherever they went.

The live shows became secondary to the media circus. Page Hamilton, singer with Helmet, may remember the band being extraordinary at the Roskilde Festival in Denmark – where Nirvana headlined the 60,000-capacity stage – but if it's true, it was a one-off. None of Nirvana was happy with their status as an arena rock band, and their performances reflected it – no hurling the bass in the air, no spontaneous demonstrations of improvised destruction, just tired rituals and cursory run-throughs of the more famous numbers and the odd flash of humour. Kurt would announce, "And I would now like to play a guitar solo," and then play a mock 10-second distorted anti-solo – or start up the opening chords to 'Teen Spirit' before turning the song round into the bitter 'Rape Me'. Meanwhile, frenzied clapping drowned out 'Polly', adding to his frustration.

"In that summer of '92, when Courtney was pregnant, at Roskilde, they were at their most drugged out," says Christof Ellinghaus. "That was the saddest moment of my knowing them. Jesus Christ they were so clearly fucked, it was sad, really sad."

In Oslo (June 28), I walked along outside the arena's fenced-off perimeter with Kurtney as the pair hurled abuse at bootleggers, trying their damnedest to spark fights. Courtney told me that I reminded her of her first husband, Falling James, a sensitive man who wore tights to bed. When I came to interview the band, it was pretty much the first time they'd spoken to each other since the Laundry Room sessions. I watched TV with Kurt and Courtney, the only visitor allowed within the Holy Couple's room.

The next day, on a day off, several of us went down by the river and up a hilltop to smoke some weed, while Kurt and Courtney traversed the town looking for Nirvana bootlegs to liberate and give to kids wearing official Nirvana T-shirts. Yes, you could say they were obsessed. Back at the hotel, everyone except Kurtney – Krist, Dave, Nirvana's road crew including the near-legendary Big John, and support act Teenage Fanclub – stayed up until 6 a.m. performing karaoke favourites.

"Janet, Kurt and Courtney were in bed together when I went up to Kurt's room to talk about using some pictures," recalls *Melody Maker* photographer Steve Gullick. "At one point Kurt came downstairs and was standing at the back just watching us. He picked up a big ornate rock and threw it on the floor, seeking attention – it was like he really wanted to be there with us, but had to go back to his bedroom. The rest of the night was fantastic because it was a continuation of the stroll – that tour was the lowest point I saw them at, which is probably why those couple of days were such fun. They were a release."

While in a hotel room in Stockholm on June 30, Courtney produced Kurt's lyric book – a scrappy, lined A5 ring-binder affair, full of crossing-outs and amendments, written in blue biro. "Here, I thought you might want to take this, Everett," she cried blithely, seemingly oblivious to Kurt's annoyance. "What about the lyrics to *that song*, for starters." Like many songwriters, Kurt hated his most famous song with a passion, and often refused to play it live.

There were so many questions behind these shows that I never thought to ask at the time, the most important one being: who was forcing Kurt to go on tour and play festivals to audiences of metal kids he transparently despised? He didn't need the money.

Why were Pearl Jam able to quit, not Nirvana?

> ***Nirvana***
> ***Isle Of Calf Festival, Oslo/Sjohistoriska Museum, Stockholm***
> *They don't deserve this. Forget any reports you may have heard that rock is alive and kicking. The world's only credible arena rock band is close to cracking. Kurt Cobain is barely able to cope with the restraints of his position, the kids who are out there watching his band because Guns N' Roses aren't in town till next week and Bryan Adams was on yesterday. His band are afraid to play any new songs knowing that, if they do, bootlegs will hit the streets running. So, numbed by the intensity of their unlooked-for role as some kind of spokesmen, Nirvana attempt to inject meaning into the old as best they can.*
>
> *Which means: no emotion shown, if that's the only way they can retain self-respect.*
>
> *First night in Stockholm, I'm watching MTV with Kurt and Courtney in their hotel suite, waiting for the new Nirvana video to come on. Eddie Murphy flashes by, typically unfunny. "He used to be funny once, didn't he?" Kurt remarks. "Back before he became famous and complacent, back when he was still struggling to be heard, back when he had to try." There's no need for Kurt to elaborate. We know whom he's talking about.*
>
> *But Kurt still tries. Otherwise, why is he in so much pain? Not for the first time this year, I begin to realise why Bono and Axl and Bruce and*

*all those other would-be rock Messiahs are so crap. The market forces, the record-buyers, are that powerful – you either succumb or you go insane. Is there a third choice? Nirvana are struggling against it – they're struggling real hard and they're struggling real strong – but it's impossible to make sense of much of this confusion.*

*In Oslo, Kurt stands immobile as 20,000 kids go berserk, uncaring as to what reactions his band may or may not be getting. And the audience, with their ritualised clapping and banners and shoes tossed in the air and bare chests, couldn't give a damn about how good or otherwise the band on stage are. Why should they? This is corporate entertainment, however much the band decries it. To most of these serenely beautiful, sun-kissed Scandinavians, it doesn't matter that it's Nirvana up there. It could be anyone. It's a festival, see. They couldn't give a damn about Flipper or Shonen Knife or punk or Courtney Love or any of the things so close to Nirvana's heart. Why should they? What matters is size.*

*Festival crowds know what to expect, or so they think. They had the parameters of how they choose to spend their leisure time mapped out long ago. On this scale, art counts for virtually nothing. Rebellion? How can anyone be rebellious once they've conquered the American market? By throwing it all away again? Then you're just termed a failure, or worse, a one-hit wonder.*

*In Oslo, for all it matters, Kurt could be rampaging drunk and breaking equipment, Chris could be throwing his bass 10 feet in the air, and Dave moshing hard, like they used to. But they aren't (OK, Dave is). Sometimes, Kurt flicks his floor switch from reverb to normal, sometimes Kurt looks across to see if Chris is playing the correct bass part, sometimes Kurt will try and make a self-deprecating remark and fail. There's precious little emotion, humour, angst here – a bunch of incredible songs turned to shimmering dust, some brutally beautifully evocative lyrics which now mean less than shit, now that the whole world has learnt its part and reduced them to the everyday, the mundane.*

*Yet Nirvana still sounds glorious.*

*Yet 'Polly' and 'Stay Away' and 'On A Plain' still evoke, chastise, berate, uplift. Fuck knows why. Maybe familiarity doesn't always blunt. Maybe we're talking love.*

*In Stockholm, Kurt at least tries, buoyed by the news shouted to him across the stage by his wife that the concert has been undersold by 6,000. "Hey! We're on our way out," he gleefully shouts at me, stumbling across stage to change guitars. But then, Stockholm isn't part of a two-day festival like Oslo – it's a Nirvana show, for fans solely. So Kurt changes the set-list seconds before taking the stage, starting with a classic American punk number, 'The Money Roll Right In' (irony!), playing an impromptu 'D-7' upon request and 'Molly's Lips', even making a few jokes. Dave and Chris look happier as well. For the encore (a searing, purposeful 'Teen Spirit' and a rampant 'Territorial Pissings'), the band drag 50 kids waiting to get in by the back gate on stage – and, hell, spontaneous bonhomie can work on this level, even if it does recall something off* The Arsenio Hall Show.

*But the main set is still as bad as I've seen Nirvana play, in terms of spirit, excitement and inspiration (everything that Nirvana used to have in spades) – even if I am almost crying during 'Lithium'. It seems so appropriate, somehow. And Oslo was way, way worse.*

*Contrast the difference between Nirvana and their support band Teenage Fanclub at the Stockholm soundcheck. First, Nirvana: a roadie stands in for Kurt as the band run through a lacklustre 'In Bloom' and a flat 'Teen Spirit', sounding oddly like Weird 'Al' Yankovic*[9] *himself. Then, Teenage Fanclub – all the band present and visibly enjoying themselves, running carefree through a Todd Rundgren number, Sixties bubblegum pop, Big Star singer Alex Chilton, anything they've loved. Once, Nirvana delighted in their togetherness, forged through years of constant touring through the cesspits of America. Now, it seems, Kurt would rather be anywhere than hangin' with Chris and Dave.*

*Pressures, dude. But Nirvana still sound life-affirming.*

*How could they otherwise? Especially when* Nevermind *never did justice to the excitement and genuine power of their live sound.*

*So, Oslo is a mess of contradictions and contrary emotions. The day's so glorious, the babes are so beautiful, the sound is so exemplary, Teenage Fanclub's support slot so buoyant and inspirational, it'd take some kinda churlish fool or pining Aberdeen type not to enjoy themselves. Yet, even with the inspired choice of Tori Amos' version of 'Teen Spirit' as an intro tape, it's apparent that Kurt is torn – torn between his loyalty to the kids who genuinely appreciate and love his music, and those who are into them as a fad, as a cuter, punkier Ugly Kid Joe*[10] *alternative.*

*His voice is still inexhaustibly expressive, emotive, his guitar still bleeds angst, but his demeanour . . . remember, this is the band who built a career out of being rampant on stage, whose new video ('Lithium') mythologises the whole guitar-smashing ethos with a grandiose finality. Kurt won't even admit that he has any frustrations left. Not in public. But he has. Oh man.*

*Second night in Stockholm, the assembled Nirvana and Fanclub crews are watching an MTV clip of [Pearl Jam singer] Eddie Vedder going off the rails in Denmark. There's no appreciable glee at a well-publicised rival losing it, just a sad empathy, a feeling of genuine pity that perhaps here is another singer who is unable to cope with the lies and pressures and trauma of fame, who loathes and despises the distance forced between him and his audience, who can't see any way out of the trap, the role forced upon him simply because he's written lyrics that reach people (it's not his fault his band sucks). Pearl Jam cancelled the remainder of their European tour the same day. Bet Kurt was jealous.*

*The way people talk it right now suggests that, even if Nirvana aren't going to split up, Reading Festival will be their last show for a very long time. (On the phone the next week, the singer flatly denies this. "We'll be touring in November," he tells me, "but no festivals this time. Definitely no festivals. And, if Chris wasn't in Greece, we'd be in the recording studio laying down tracks for the new album right now.")*

*Let's hope to fuck that Nirvana learn how to adapt and survive. We desperately need people like them up there to give people like us down here hope, hope that you don't need to be an Extreme*[11] *or an INXS or a Bryan Adams to succeed.*

(*Melody Maker*, July 25, 1992)

Only one other British journalist interviewed the band during this period: *NME*'s Keith Cameron. He travelled all the way out to Spain, only to be confronted by a far more recalcitrant Cobain, unwilling to say more than a few words to someone he had previously considered a friend.

"I wonder what Keith's going to write, Jerry[12]," Kurt confided to me on the phone shortly afterwards. "I didn't tell him anything."

Keith wrote the only possible piece he could in the circumstances – one that showed up the splits and confusion surrounding the band in far greater detail than my interview. Keith mentioned the heroin rumours. He called Courtney's manager Janet Billig "a cross between a wet nurse and a human sponge" – a phrase that caused more anger within the Kurtney inner circle than any other – and asked whether it was possible for the band to go from being "nobodies to superstars to fuck-ups in the space of six months". Dave told him he didn't even know all the names of the crew. Keith was seriously disillusioned: "Everything had changed beyond recognition," he said. "All the talk was of heroin; the gigs almost seemed a diversion. They seemed static and distant from each other. I imagined that selling a lot of records might empower them. Success seemed to make Nirvana powerless. It was all doom and gloom."

The *NME* article led to Cameron being reviled by the band, a band he loved dearly. Eric Erlandson, with Kurt by his side, poured a glass of vodka and lime juice over his head at the Reading Festival at the end of August. The Cobain camp claimed Keith was being vocally disrespectful towards Courtney: this, days after Frances Bean was born. Kurt even named one of his six guns after him. "One for every person I want to kill," he told me in a stormy mood from his final Seattle home, while I argued with him not to be so stupid. "Keith Cameron, [*Vanity Fair* writer] Lynn Hirschberg, [British would-be Nirvana biographers] Britt [Collins] and Victoria [Clarke] . . ."

I can't remember the others.

Nirvana played in a bull-fighting ring in the Plaza de Toros de Valencia in Spain on July 2 – a day later, in Madrid, Courtney started getting contractions right before show time. Kurt, not familiar with the birth process[13], played the gig panicking that his wife was either about to give birth or die at any moment. On the advice of Courtney's physician, Nirvana cancelled the two remaining Spanish dates and Kurtney flew back to LA first class, booking two seats for Courtney so she could lie down during the flight.[14]

On July 9, 'Lithium' was released in the UK. The same day Courtney posed for a series of photographs for a forthcoming interview conducted by Lynn Hirschberg for upmarket tattle magazine *Vanity Fair*. Never mindful of others' opinions, she posed with a cigarette – which the editor Tina Brown later airbrushed out – while several months pregnant.

The couple arrived back in LA to discover that a pipe had burst in the apartment above their bathroom and their shower was flooded. No big deal, except that Kurt had placed several of his most precious belongings there – a blue Mosrite guitar[15], poetry books and writings and two tapes with guitar parts intended for the next album – for safe-keeping, because they figured it was the last place a burglar would look. All were ruined.

Fed up, they called John Silva and demanded he find them another place. With his help, they moved into 6881 Alta Loma Terrace in late July, set in the hills of west Hollywood – a quite surreal, intensely private, location that had been used in the Robert Altman film *The Long Goodbye*. To access the hill it was set in, you needed to use a private Victorian-style crate elevator, with its own key.

"They would always be forgetting the key and having to walk up the stairs," laughs Janet Billig. "I walked up those stairs what seemed like a hundred million times with Courtney when she was pregnant. Tons of windows, great views – but they didn't have much stuff with the exception of all the gold records that were coming in. Like a punk rock MacGyver[16], Kurt would break them open and try to use the gold records as plates because they didn't have any."

Kurt began producing Melvins' debut major label album *Houdini* at Razor's Edge in San Francisco, but quit halfway when the band refused to take his advice on how to make their songs sound more commercial. "These guys don't understand *anything*," he complained to me. On the finished version, he produced seven songs and played guitar on 'Sky Pup'.[17]

Meanwhile, Krist Novoselic was becoming engaged in politics: taking an active interest in the troubles going on back in his homeland, and fighting (successfully) alongside Soundgarden and Pearl Jam and Danny Goldberg to get Washington State's repressive 'Erotic' Music Bill thrown out – the one that stated record store employees could be held liable, and be arrested, for selling music that the state deemed offensive to minors.

Kurt started taking heroin again. On August 4, he checked into Cedars-Sinai for a 60-day detox. Three days later, Courtney checked into a different wing of the hospital under a false name, suffering from exhaustion and complications arising from her pregnancy. The *Los Angeles Reporter* stated that she was receiving daily doses of prenatal vitamins and methadone. Kurt, as husband, was her first contact. Eric Erlandson was her second.

"Eric was like the heartbeat of Courtney," comments Billig. "He understood Courtney in a really deep way. The thing about Eric is that he's a great hang, easy to be around, smart and able to talk about all sorts of different topics. Kurt really liked hanging out with him and in a way Eric was a pseudo big brother to Kurt. Most importantly, he could relate to him musically. Kurt and Courtney stayed with him some of the time as they were often moving apartments and Eric's house was empty as he was staying with Drew [Barrymore]."[18]

The Hole guitarist was the only person to visit Kurt and Courtney during the first weeks of August: "He totally saved our lives," Kurt told Michael Azerrad. "He was the only piece of reality, the only calm person who was there as an example of what life could be like afterwards."

It was only a couple of weeks until Frances Bean's due date – but before that an event took place that overshadowed her birth.

On August 11, the September issue of *Vanity Fair* hit the news-stands.

## Addenda: *Melody Maker*, July 25, 1992

> *The interview with Nirvana takes place in a dressing room on the edge of a river in Stockholm. The day is cloudy, with flashes of sunshine. People are drinking Coca-Cola and, in Chris' case, wine. Chris and Dave are sitting on one couch, Kurt on another. A bowl of chilli-roasted peanuts and some fruit nestles on the table. Someone's smoking.*
>
> *The band seems awkward in each other's presence, wary of one another. When Chris speaks, his eyes are looking anywhere but in Kurt's direction. When Kurt speaks, he does so almost defensively, as if he feels a need to justify himself in front of Chris. When Dave speaks, you know he can feel the uneasiness, but he's trying to ignore it.*

*Apart from a brief spot on Swedish TV earlier today, this is the first interview Nirvana have given as a band for a long while. This might account for the subdued atmosphere – although many people have pointed to Nirvana's success as creating friction within the band. Certainly, Kurt seems warier than when I last met him – Steve Gullick has to go through a ridiculous rigmarole of hoods and bleached hair and agreements later on before he's allowed to take any shots.*

*When I saw your performance in Oslo two days ago, I kept thinking back to what Kurt told me last year: "We're not going to be proud of the fact there are a bunch of Guns N' Roses kids who are into our music. We don't feel comfortable progressing, playing larger venues."*

*"We can't," Chris agrees. "We've always treated people with that mentality with a little bit of contempt and cynicism, and to have them screaming for us . . . Why are they screaming? What do they see in us? They're exactly the same kind of people who wanted to kick our arse in high school."*

*"It's just boring to play outdoors," explains his singer. "I've only just gotten used to playing large venues because the sound is at least tolerable. But, outside, the wind blows the music around so much that it doesn't feel like you're playing music. It feels like you're lip-synching to a boom box recording. Plus, these festivals are very mainstream – we're playing with Extreme and Pearl Jam, you know? Ninety per cent of the kids out there are probably just as much into Extreme as they are into us.*

*"I try every night," he continues, "but I just can't fool myself. I'm not going to smile and pose like Eddie Van Halen, even though he's a miserable drunk. That doesn't mean it'll be that way next month [at Reading], but that's how it is, right now."*

*Do you feel any responsibility?*

*"For what?" Kurt asks.*

*The masses. The people who bought your record.*

*"To me," Dave begins, tentatively, "our main responsibility is to not pretend to be something we're not. I don't think pretending to be a professional rock unit really works. If we're going to have a shitty show, then let's have a shitty show. I can see there's a lot of responsibility playing massive shows, but other kinds? I don't know."*

*"It's rock'n'roll to be irresponsible," Chris adds.*

*I know.*

*"Once you start considering this to be a responsibility, it becomes a burden," muses the drummer.*

*Dave starts telling me about the interview that they've just done for Swedish TV: "They thanked us for saving rock'n'roll," he laughs. "For throwing a bomb into the rock'n'roll establishment."*

*Do you feel you've done that?*

*"Maybe we blew a paper bag up and popped it," sneers Chris.*

*From where I'm standing, a great record sold a lot of copies but I don't see that it's changed that much.*

*"There's still going to be shitty heavy metal bands," the bassist agrees.*

*What do you hate most about being famous?*

*"Kids with Bryan Adams and Bruce Springsteen T-shirts coming up to me and asking for autographs," Kurt says. "When people in the audience hold up a sign that says 'Even Flow' [a Pearl Jam song] on one side and 'Negative Creep' [a Nirvana song] on the other."*[19]

*What's the best thing about being famous?*

*"You know, that's a really good question," answers Kurt, ironically.*

*"I don't even really consider this being famous," adds Dave. "I mean, is Ian MacKaye famous because he's in Fugazi and people in DC want to bear his children? When you're a kid you consider someone in a magazine famous, or someone on the news famous, but it's just a magazine, or some news show."*

*"We might get some perks here and there," Chris ventures. "A free drink or two, maybe."*

*Do you get many groupies?*

*"People are under the impression that because I'm the only non-married member of the band I'm the swinger, that I'm the womaniser," replies Dave. "It's just stupid. I'd love to find someone that I could fall in love with and spend the rest of my life with but you're definitely not going to find anyone that you'll appreciate at a rock show. Maybe it's flattering to all these heavy metal bands, but we find it kind of disgusting."*

*How about drink?*

*"I came into this tour with a fresh perspective," Chris muses. "I used to get stressed out, drink a whole lot and react to everything. Now I just go with the flow."*

*"I've always loved the spontaneity of being frustrated and pissed off . . ." Kurt challenges him.*

*". . . and drunk," finishes Chris. "Oh yeah! I've had some of my best inspirations intoxicated – it's a different reality. It's like living in a movie or a cartoon, where your subconscious takes off. That's where all the good stories come from. But it's such hell on your body."*

*Has the sudden fame appreciably changed your lifestyles?*

*"Definitely," responds Kurt, vehemently.*

*"It hasn't changed mine," his bassist disagrees. "I can still go down to Safeway, buy fruit and vegetables, walk around town. I don't care if people stare at me, or whisper, or point."*

*"You don't?" Kurt asks him. "At all?"*

*"No," replies Chris. "I just walk on. And the more they see me,*

*especially in Seattle, the more . . ."*

*"Oh yeah, eventually they'll get tired of sniggering at you and talking behind your back." Kurt finishes the sentence for him. "Well, I've been confronted by people wanting to beat me up, by people heckling me and being so drunk and obnoxious because they think I'm this pissy rock star bastard who can't come to grips with his fame."*

*"It's easy for me," interrupts Dave diplomatically, "because there's no such thing as a famous drummer anyway."*

*Ringo?*

*"Well . . ."*

*"I was in a rock club the other night," Kurt continues, "and one guy comes up, pats me on the back and says, 'You've got a really good thing going, you know? Your band members are cool, you write great songs, you affected a lot of people, but, man, you've really got to get your personal shit together!' Then another person comes up and says, 'I hope you overcome your drug problems.' All this happens within an hour while I'm trying to watch the Melvins, minding my own business.*

*"There were about five or six kids sifting around, very drunk, screaming 'Rock star! Rock star! Oh, look, he's going to freak out any minute! He's going to have a tantrum! He's going to start crying!' Then this other guy comes up, puts his arm around me and says, 'You know, my girlfriend broke up with me and took my Nirvana album, so you should give me $14 to buy a new CD, cos you can afford that now you're a big rock star.' And I said, 'Gee. That's a clever thing to say. Why don't you fuck off?' "*

*"I was really drunk with my mother," Chris tells him, "and these guys were driving round the block shouting, 'Nirvana sucks!' and yelling all this shit at me."*

*"Was that in Aberdeen?" Kurt asks.*

*"Yeah, but you have to ignore them," Chris warns him, "or it becomes an obsession. I have dreams about being nude in public, and I interpret them as worrying about sticking out. Forget it! It can become a preoccupation. I was like that, too, when I used to see someone famous . . ."*

*"Yeah, but did you pitch them shit?" Kurt interrupts him.*

*"No," Chris replies. "I didn't, but that incident you mentioned seems to be pretty isolated."*

*"It's not isolated," snarls Kurt. "It happens to me all the time – every time I go out, every fucking time. It's stupid. And, if it bothers me that much, I'm going to do something about it. Fuck it, rock doesn't mean that much to me. I still love to be in a band and play music with Chris and Dave, but if it means that we have to resort to playing in a practice room and never touring again, then so be it."*

## NOTES

1 Oddly, in all the interviews Kurt did with me he didn't mention his stomach problems once.
2 Kurt and Krist were already aware of the other Nirvana, but figured it wasn't important.
3 Thus appropriating for herself the line written for Tobi Vail.
4 Mark Lanegan's influence on Kurt has never been properly acknowledged, partly because Mark is such an intensely private and loyal and intimidating person. But the fact that the pair were intensely close friends is indicated by Mark being one of two people asked to read a eulogy at his funeral. He refused.
5 *Sassy*'s cover story on Kurt and Courtney appeared in April.
6 1992 Buzz Osborne concept album – Boner released solo albums by the three Melvins musicians, Buzz, Dale and Joe Preston, in tribute to Kiss who had worked a similar device in 1978.
7 Grohl's drum parts on *Nevermind* had mostly been already worked out.
8 Inside information: one of the couple must have told me this direct.
9 The moustached comedian Weird 'Al' Yankovic famously did a parody of 'Teen Spirit' around this time, lampooning the way no one could understand Kurt's words: "*Now I'm mumbling and I'm screaming/ And I don't know what I'm singing.*" Weird Al even used some of the same cheerleaders and actors from Nirvana's video for his video.
10 Ugly Kid Joe were a horrible pseudo-grunge corporate outfit.
11 Extreme? This Van Halen-influenced Boston, MA funk/glam metal band was anything but.
12 Courtney had always insisted on calling me by my real name, and after their marriage Kurt picked up the habit: although he sometimes slipped back into Sub Pop's favourite form of address, The Legend!
13 Contractions can happen up to several hours – or indeed days (weeks, even in Courtney's case) – before actual birth.
14 Not two rows of seats as has been reported!
15 The blue Mosrite was the same make that Johnny Ramone played – certainly the reason Kurt would have bought it.
16 "Using science and his wits, rather than violence, MacGyver could solve almost any problem . . ."
17 The non-Cobain B-side of the Melvins' album is genius: it sounds like one long drawn-out episode wherein a drum kit is thrown down the stairs. Kurt didn't see the funny side.
18 Eric started dating the former *ET* child star after she threw up on his shoes outside an LA nightclub. He phoned me the same night to tell me about it – I refused to believe him, ridiculing his story. The couple dated for two years. Drew Barrymore was quite charming.
19 This incident took place at the Ruisrock Festival in Finland and, by sheer misfortune, the Pearl Jam side was facing Nirvana for most of 'Teen Spirit', leading Kurt to change the chorus to *"Even flow/ Even flow/ Even flow/ Even flow"*.

## CHAPTER 21

# Where's The Mud, Honey?

FRANCES Bean Cobain was born on August 18, 1992.

She arrived at 7.48 a.m., a healthy seven pounds and one ounce, blue eyes and everything functioning normally. Courtney – never one to miss an opportunity for drama – grabbed her intravenous drip stand at four in the morning, and wheeled it down the corridors to where Kurt was staying. "You get out of this bed and come down now!" she screamed. "You are not leaving me to do this by myself, fuck you!" Her husband followed her to the delivery room – weakened from his treatment, and hooked up to an IV-stand himself – and passed out moments before Frances was born. It was quite the scene. "I'm having the baby, it's coming out, he's puking, he's passing out, and I'm holding his hand and rubbing his stomach while the baby's coming out," Courtney told Michael Azerrad.

Kurt recovered sufficiently to hold his newborn baby shortly afterwards.

Frances wasn't a flipper baby at all: not that you'd have known it from all the attention she was receiving. Tabloid reporters from *The Enquirer* and *The Globe* were hounding Courtney's hospital room at the Cedars-Sinai Medical Center, and reporters were going through her garbage and faxes. According to a 1994 interview Courtney gave to *Rolling Stone* after Kurt's death, Kurt went out the following day, bought heroin and returned with a loaded .38 revolver, handing it to Courtney where she sat holding Frances Bean as a reminder of a pledge they'd made to commit joint suicide if anything should ever happen to their baby.

Myth becomes difficult to separate from reality again: is this one more example of Courtney's fondness for embellishment? I only ask because Courtney mentioned the idea of a 'joint suicide pact' to me in the dismal months after Kurt's death. It makes for a lurid tale, but perhaps Courtney had confused facts – which she had a tenuous grasp on, at best, in late '94 – with emotion. "I can't remember," comments Eric Erlandson, who was also present at the birth. "I was delirious from looking after both of them in the hospital, and witnessing a live birth which was pretty intense. Not sleeping. Trying to keep two troubled souls in their hospital rooms long enough for a baby to get born."

"I've never heard that story about the gun," comments Rosemary Carroll. "In all the confusion and unhappiness that was going on, the focus was not, 'How do we get ourselves out of this mess?' It was, 'How do we get Frances out of this mess?'"

Of course, it's possible it happened – Kurt had a fondness for drugs and guns. And there was no denying his fearsome anger.

"We were totally suicidal. I just decided that, 'Fuck it, I don't want to be in a band any more,'" the singer told Michael Azerrad for *Musician*. "'I want to kill her [Hirschberg]. As soon as I get out of this fucking hospital I'm going to kill this woman with my bare hands: I'm going to stab her to death. First, I'm going to take her dog and slit its guts out in front of her and then shit all over her and stab her to death.'"

There was undoubtedly hysteria surrounding Frances Bean's birth; two days on, a social worker turned up at the bedside, brandishing a copy of the *Vanity Fair* article that appeared on August 11 with references to Courtney constantly smoking, Kurt and Courtney being the Nineties version of Sid and Nancy, and Courtney being, "A train-wreck personality: she may be awful, but you can't take your eyes off her." Among other exaggerations, Courtney told Hirschberg that she first met Kurt eight years previously in Portland – an obvious lie, as that would have made Kurt about 16.[1]

Lynn made damning references to Courtney's drug taking, reporting 'close friends' as saying, "It is appalling to think that she would be taking drugs when she knew she was pregnant. We're all worried about that baby." Even worse, Courtney told Lynn the couple had been on a binge while they were in New York for *Saturday Night Live*. "We did a lot of drugs. We got pills, and then we went down to Alphabet City and we copped some dope. Then we got high and went to *SNL*. After that, I did heroin for a couple of months."

Courtney later vehemently denied saying any of this. But would Lynn have made the quotes up? She may have got several fundamental details wrong – for instance, the prevalent belief that Courtney turned Kurt on to heroin, and that the UK music press had been interested in Courtney only because of her husband – but misquoting an artist is pretty serious, and Hirschberg was a pro. Whatever the truth, the Los Angeles County Department of Children's Services chose to believe the Hirschberg version and successfully petitioned on August 24 to have

Frances Bean turned over to the custody of Courtney's half-sister Jamie Rodriguez until Kurt completed a 30-day detox. Courtney wasn't even allowed to take Frances Bean with her when she returned home after three days.

"The *Vanity Fair* article was devastating to Courtney," says Carroll. "Courtney spent a lot of time with Lynn Hirschberg and believed she'd won her over – that Lynn liked her and spent a lot of time with Courtney because she enjoyed being in her company. That she would write a glowing piece. Of course, she did what many journalists do, wormed her way into her inner circle and then eviscerated her in print in the worst possible way. Many things were true, but many weren't or were terribly exaggerated, and the whole thing was so bitter and jealous and sarcastic. It was a hateful piece. Hole was still punk rock at that time – and punk rock doesn't do the front cover of *Vanity Fair*. I thought the very idea of doing the interview was ridiculous but Courtney was ambitious. She always saw herself moving into mainstream, like Madonna. She wanted to be Madonna basically."

Danny Goldberg rented Jamie a place to live right next door to the couple – before the hearing she'd barely even spoken to Courtney – and the pair hired their first nanny – tour manager and friend of Janet Billig – Jackie Farry. Jackie looked after Frances for the next eight months, moving into the Oakwood Apartments complex that Nirvana had stayed in while they were recording *Nevermind*.

"Jackie wanted to make a change in her life," reveals Janet Billig. "She was working in the promotion department at Epic and she was one of my best friends. Things just worked. They had to have a nanny and Jackie was someone everyone could trust, because everyone knew her and she was great with babies."

Courtney argued that she'd been clean ever since she discovered she'd been pregnant – but her pleas fell on deaf ears. The authorities were on a roll, able to take the higher moral ground and proselytise about the dangers of drug use. Kurt and Courtney were high profile – they didn't come much higher profile – and the state was determined to make an example of them, despite having little evidence to go on beyond the *Vanity Fair* piece, and a couple of scummy tabloid articles that appeared a few weeks later (sample: "Rock Star's Baby Is Born A Junkie," as published by *The Globe* on September 8).

There was a voice of reason in the *Vanity Fair* article, but unfortunately no one chose to listen to it. "Only about a quarter of what Courtney says is true," Kat Bjelland told Hirschberg. "But nobody usually bothers to decipher which are the lies. She's all about image. And that's interesting. Irritating, but interesting."

The pair attempted damage limitation – authorising joint interviews to run with trusted friends in the music press – but it was far too little, too late.

"We went to Steve Fisk's apartment in the Scud building," remembers Jonathan Poneman. "The idea was that they wanted a puff piece. I didn't go in there with a particular agenda. It was just, 'Hey, I'm psyched, these are my friends, what's going on, tell me your side of the story,' and that was it. *Spin* published it. In retrospect, I was played for a fool."

I had a similar experience. Poneman did the second joint interview (after *Sassy* earlier in the year, which was nothing to do with *Vanity Fair*). I did the third. Both were damage limitation. I wasn't aware of what was going on with regards to the kid. I knew that most of the *Vanity Fair* article was true because Courtney would call me up straight after she had spoken to Lynn Hirschberg and tell me what she'd just said, laughing, saying what a great person Lynn was, how understanding she was, how this article would help with her acceptance into mainstream America. And then she'd be telling me how she'd posed semi-naked smoking a cigarette, how candid she'd been over her drug use and emotional problems, how she'd basically opened her heart to her and how much Lynn appreciated it.

And I'd be like, "You know, you probably shouldn't be saying that stuff to a professional journalist. It's one thing to tell me – I totally get your sense of humour, the sarcasm, the self-deprecation, the goofiness and aggressiveness, and I also have an inbuilt switch where I won't repeat some of the stuff you tell me, I understand it's said in confidence and not meant for popular consumption, between friends – but you shouldn't judge all journalists by me, or even by my colleagues at the UK music press. We're amateurs, enthusiasts, fans: we aren't hard-nosed, there to get the story at any cost. How do you know you can trust this woman? You don't know her, she isn't from Olympia or Portland or Minneapolis, she didn't grow up loving punk rock and freaked out by the outside world – she's mainstream. It's one thing to tell me all your scurrilous, hilarious, outrageous stories. It's another to tell a total stranger, however ingratiating she is."

Courtney would simply brush away my objections – indeed, view them as so insignificant as to not even notice them, just race on to the next ribald anecdote she'd told Lynn.[2]

At the height of all this madness, four days after the court hearing to decide Frances Bean's fate, Nirvana flew into England to headline the 1992

Reading Festival. It was the largest show they ever played in the UK, and also the last.

**Reading Festival, Part One: Everett True**
First, let me tell you about the wig.

It was a present from my sister Alison. The previous year at Reading I'd been threatened several times by *Melody Maker* readers: two with knives. I had a very visible presence, the most visible of the UK music press at the time. A pair had wandered up to where I was chatting with John Silva, and asked in a threatening fashion if he was Everett True. He reassured them that he wasn't. "Well, how can we find him then?" the dastardly duo demanded. "Oh, he's ugly; very, very ugly," said John, laughing. "In fact, he's the ugliest person on the site. In fact, I have a feeling I just saw him go into that backstage area over there." With a gruff thank you, the pair went over to stalk the exit that John had pointed to. I told my sister the story, and a week before the 1992 Reading I received the wig in the post: "So you can dance unrecognised," she wrote. So I took it along, danced in the rain to Teenage Fanclub and got recognised anyway. Whatever.

Later on, I was hanging around backstage in Nirvana's dressing room. It was Sunday, August 30. All day long the rumours had been flying around the site that Nirvana wouldn't show. Kurt had OD'd on the heroin he was rumoured to be taking. Kurt was with his wife and proud new mother back in the States. Kurt was pissed off with the security arrangements. It didn't look that way to me where I was slumped against a wall, but who knows? Someone had passed me a bottle of vodka – Mudhoney, perhaps – and I'd drunk it. Willingly, and with an alacrity that indicated there would be trouble to come. The rumours keep increasing, wilder and wilder. Maybe Kurt was refusing to show up because of the caustic reception his wife Courtney Love was receiving in certain sections of the British press? I knew that one wasn't true, because I'd spoken to Courtney the previous night in America – where she was resting with the newly born Frances Bean. There were also stories that it was to be Nirvana's final show: something the band strenuously denied on stage.

The mud. That's all anyone remembers of that Reading. The mud. There were great seeping pools of it, making entire areas of the site unpassable to all but the most foolhardy. When inspirational political rap outfit Public Enemy headlined the Saturday night, the skies opened and drenched the entire crowd with the contents of a minor-sized ocean. Kids slithered around the grounds, bodies and faces and legs and trousers and New Model Army[3] T-shirts absolutely saturated by mud: the few desultory fires flickering in sheltered spots, fuelled by plastic cups and Kurt Cobain posters, not helping the cold one jot. During the Sunday, bands got pelted with tons of the stuff. Artists reacted in different ways. Mudhoney downed their instruments and started pelting the audience back. "You guys can't throw," taunted Mark Arm. "You're used to playing soccer and kicking balls with your feet." Just then a sizeable lump of Berkshire hit him smack in the face. "That'll learn me," he remarked afterwards. "Never taunt an armed audience." Baggy Labour cheerleaders The Farm tried to chin offenders. L7's singer Donita Sparks topped everyone, however, by reaching into her shorts and lobbing her tampon at the worst offenders.[4]

You could have heard a used tampon drop.

Backstage, it seemed unreal. The rain and mud had managed to keep the usual teeming array of liggers down to a bare dedicated minimum, certainly early on[5] – plus there was a ban on any non-personal friends of Nirvana wandering around backstage proper. This suited me fine. It meant I was one of the very few with access to decent toilet facilities that day – mega-important at any festival – and upped the availability of alcohol.

Nick Cave was on shortly before Nirvana, and I can remember a handful of us – Fannies (Teenage Fanclub), roadies, the odd tour manager – all stepping outside Nirvana's Portacabin to listen to the Aussie singer serenade the battered, splattered crowd with 'The Weeping Song' and 'Deanna', and thinking how hugely inappropriate it was. This was Grunge Day – Nirvana had cherry-picked the artists (ace Abba tribute band Bjorn Again, L7, Mudhoney, Screaming Trees, Melvins, Pavement[6], Beastie Boys and Teenage Fanclub), and Cave seemed so out-of-place, so cerebral. Up went the cry: where's the Mud, honey?

Nirvana showed up late: maybe they'd just flown in from another festival in Europe. I can't recall. I don't think they'd been hanging around the Ramada, though – notorious hotel haunt of bands, post-festival time. Suddenly, the tiny dressing room was all hustle and bustle and managers and promoters running every which way: in one corner, Tony, the band's personal *idiot savant* dancer, was slapping on layers of make-up, checking his reflection in the mirror. Plates of curling cheese and ham lay untouched on the side among the peanuts and Smarties, the bottles of beer under the tables in their coolers. It was hard to know what was going on. Kurt came over and made sure I had enough to drink: checked the name of my girlfriend. Someone was shouting something about a wheelchair: "Where did you put that fucking wheelchair?" they roared. Someone – Nirvana's tour manager, Alex MacLeod probably – poured me whiskey as someone else started to unfold the seat. Hey, what gives? My confusion turned to befuddlement.

"They're going to wheel me on stage in that," Kurt explained. "It's like a joke on all the people who've been having a go at us, saying that I'm in hospital, OD'd. Do you like my smock?"

"Oh, I see," I said, not understanding one bit. "Well, why don't you wear this wig my sister sent me as well, it will make you look a little bit more like Courtney and confuse everyone further." Kurt tried the wig on (he already had hair extensions) and approved. Alex fed me more whiskey in a futile attempt to make me unconscious. Fat chance. It was almost time to go on stage: someone dimly asked someone else whether Kurt should wheel himself on stage or . . . "Hey!" I shouted, pissed off my head. "Let me push that! I can push that! Let me push Kurt on to the stage. It'd be way funnier."

No one could think of a good enough excuse to stop me.

Thus we found ourselves hurried along up the side of the stage while in the distance a mighty crowd clapped and cheered. I have little memory of what happened next. There was a drunken wheelchair chase where I pushed Kurt round in ever-increasing circles in hot pursuit of the L7 girls on the side of the stage, while 20-foot drops waited invitingly and managerial types muttered among themselves about how they were going to, "Kill this fucking drunken English asshole journalist." Neither of us knew where the stage's edge was: we could easily have gone over. Charles Peterson, the photographer who defined the look of Seattle grunge, snapped us while we spun around laughing, framed in the spotlight. We waited a few minutes in the wings while Krist did his whole introduction thing – and then came the moment . . .

The lights. That's all I can remember. The lights. You can't see a single face. The crowd is invisible, and all that you feel is this incredible euphoric roar that increases every step you make towards the microphone.

"He'll be OK," Krist Novoselic reassured the crowd, pointing out to the wings, where we slowly materialised: "With the help of his friends and his family, he'll survive." We started walking up to the right hand microphone and halfway across the stage Kurt reached up and grappled my neck. "Great," I thought to myself in my drunken stupor. "Kurt wants to start a mock-fight like we used to have on stage with Nirvana." I started to wrestle him back. "No, you asshole," he whispered furiously. "You're wheeling me to the wrong mic."

It was a goof, a cocked pair of fingers at all the press reports of the singer being sick, unable to play with his band. Kurt climbed out of the wheelchair, unsteadily, dressed in hospital smock and wig, sang one line of a song . . . and collapsed. The crowd laughed and cheered, relieved. It was obvious the band were out to have a good time. And fuck, so they did – in fact, the show was so superior to any others they played during 1992, it was like another band altogether. It was like it was 1990 again, and the Olympia trio didn't have a care in the world.

Twelve songs in, the band deliberately cocked up the intro to 'Teen Spirit', Dave Grohl bellowing out the words to Boston's 'More Than A Feeling' over a false start. Kurt wrecked all the guitar breaks too, but it hardly mattered – the entire world had gone ballistic. With the exception of 'Something In The Way', *Nevermind* was played in its entirety: including a typically over-the-top encore of the traditional instrument-baiting 'Territorial Pissings' – Dave Grohl hurled a cymbal at a bass drum he'd carefully balanced on top of some speakers, seeing the entire stack collapse very pleasingly. Guitars got trashed, and the audience's throats went raw singing along with 'Negative Creep', 'Aneurysm' *et al.* It was like Nirvana were mocking their own importance up there and reaffirming their own mortality – not rock Gods, but three ordinary dudes out to have a fucking blast. This was the last truly great show I saw them play as a trio. We might have had mud on our soles (and in our hair, and on our faces and trousers and underwear) but fuck we were happy.

"Courtney's had some bad things written about her in the press recently," her doting hubby announced. "And now she thinks everybody hates her. I know this concert is being recorded, so I'd like to send a message to her. I'd like you all to say, 'Courtney, we love you . . .' "

The audience shouted the fucking site down.

"I remember Kurt calling Courtney on the cell phone from on stage," laughs Jennifer Finch. "I'd never seen a cell phone before. Yes, there were many people yelling, 'We love you Courtney,' yet I was sitting there transfixed on this cell phone. She'd just given birth, right? That was when I got to take back the pound I'd given her [see chapter 19]."

So I pushed Kurt Cobain on stage in a wheelchair for what turned out to be his final UK concert. Big deal. He'd have done the same for me.

After the furore from Reading had died down, *Melody Maker* ran a competition to, "Win the wig that Kurt Cobain wore at Reading". (I ran on after the show's end, and grabbed the wig as a keepsake. I thought that perhaps my sister might need it back. I wasn't sure how much wigs cost.) No one wrote in. They didn't believe it. So we trailed the competition even bigger the following week, writing something like, "Listen you dunderheads! This is for real! The first person to write in with the best reason why they couldn't actually get to Reading to see Nirvana wins the wig, and we'll print the winning entry."

This time, we were deluged with entries. We printed the winning one: it was a pithy, witty, beautifully structured and reasoned piece of writing. We congratulated the winner, commiserated with them for missing Nirvana and informed them that they were by far and away the finest entry we received.

Trouble was, by this point I'd decided I wanted to keep the wig for myself.

**Part Two: Charles Peterson**

"I'd seen Kurt earlier in the day, but I hadn't been in on the joke. Just for a minute there, when I saw the wheelchair, I thought, 'Fuck, what's wrong with Kurt?' Then I realised what you guys were up to. So I took the picture of Kurt in the wheelchair, smoking, and you standing behind him. You pushed him out on to the stage and left him there. He got up to grab the microphone and fell over, and I think the wheelchair fell over. It was eerie because there were like 60,000 people present, and they were deathly quiet. You could hear a pin drop. Nobody had any idea what was going on.

"Anton got me out to the side of the stage – the only two photographers allowed there were me and [*Melody Maker* photographer] Kevin Westenberg on the other side. Eric Erlandson sat next to me for a while doing some videotaping, but for the most part I was sitting there alone; Nirvana in front of me, and a fucking 20-foot drop to the other side, and then 60,000 people. It was epic, to say the least.

"I was mostly used to being in a club where one minute you're drinking at the bar with the band and the next they're on stage. I recall going to the press tent and seeing a list of photographers, just unbelievable: 70 or 80 photographers. I went out to photograph Mudhoney, and because the women running the press tent knew how far I'd come, they let me out there longer than everyone else. I was there with Kevin – whom I'd known from when he lived in Seattle. Kevin's really tall and he was wearing all white for some reason. During Mudhoney this huge mud fight started. I turned around to my side and I'm kind of watching Kevin and he's hunkered down a little, his shoulders are lowered, he's looking over his shoulder. All of a sudden this, boom, boom, boom, he gets hit three or four times – his white jean jacket and pants. He's done for.

"I walked backstage at the bar to get a drink with Mark Lanegan, and Mark's walking along and talking as he does, and not paying attention. All of a sudden his foot caught one of those guide wires for a tent. He didn't even put out his arms, he just went, face first into the mud. His whole body was horizontal with the ground. He got up and there's this one long mud stripe covering the entire front of his body."

**Part Three: Mudhoney**

Do you remember the mud fight in '92?

"Oh yeah," laughs Steve Turner. "We have footage of that. That was pretty funny. It was muddy. We knew we were in for it. We were like, 'Geez, man. Our name's Mudhoney. We're doomed.' It was fun. Whatever."

"I knew we were in trouble because L7 played early on, and mud was being slung up at them . . . and we were then, as we are now, known as Mudhoney," comments Mark Arm laconically. "I had this brand new white SG shaped Les Paul – it got totally pelted with mud. Pretty sad. We didn't handle it very well. Donita threw a tampon at the crowd, so we couldn't top that. I know we started flinging mud back at a certain point. The mud kept coming on stage and it wasn't really hitting us. So I said, 'You know, in America, we have this game called baseball, and we know how to aim!' Right as I was saying that, this fucking mud-ball hit me in the face! That hurt – that mud had rocks in it! I lost my cool a little bit after that."

"Every time we played Reading was nothing but a pure gas," enthuses Dan Peters. "It was so much fun because it was like you were hanging out with a bunch of your friends. We all would look around at each other and go like, "What the fuck are we doing here, how did this happen?" My favourite Reading Festival was the one with Sonic Youth, the Bad Seeds, The Cramps . . . All the bands were cool and they were all hanging out. Nobody was playing the rock star."

**Part Four: Earnie Bailey**

So you didn't see the Reading show?

"No, there was a lot of argument about that," replies Kurt's former guitar tech. "How the fuck can Nirvana play Reading with one tech? Festivals typically are stressful because you don't have all day to soundcheck and make sure everything is tops. In 1992, Big John would work the European shows, and I would work the US shows. And we'd be doing these shows single-handedly, which was difficult because they were a huge band and gear-wise they were very high maintenance. When they returned [from Reading] they said that Krist's bass had been stolen off the stage after that show, as Big John could only be on one side at a time. Essentially, he had to set up his guitar station and tune a spare bass for Krist and set it over by his amp – and nobody was watching it. I was always puzzled with that. Was there no security around? It was a big festival! How could somebody walk off with Krist's bass and nobody find it? It was the Gibson RD he'd played throughout the *Nevermind* tour, a heavy favourite. I think he was a little bit broken-hearted about it, but . . .

"Dave apologised to me because they smashed a lot of guitars. Dave was grabbing them off the rack and just throwing them. One of them had videotaped it, and as soon as they got back to Seattle we watched it on Krist's television. Dave looked over to me and said, 'I'm really sorry for what you're about to see,' as he ran over to Kurt's rack, took a guitar off and gratuitously smashed it. Meanwhile, Kurt was up there smashing his drums. It was actually hilarious – oh, if you're going to smash my drums, I'm going to smash your guitar. But Dave knew that I worked hard on those guitars, getting them right.

"I thought Krist's leather jacket looked odd. It was an unusual outfit for him. I think he had leather pants on as well. I could be wrong. When we were down in Argentina, he and Big John set out to buy some leather pants, and that was odd because Krist was heavy on the vegetarian cause. I think the story they got down there was that cattle was such a big industry that leather was really not a consequential part. It wasn't why the cows are killed, it's a leftover thing."

**Addenda: Everett True (reprise)**

Understand this: I've always despised rock music. For me, it's the language of the braggarts, the fools – those boys at public school who liked to go around sneering at others for no reason except it gave their own pathetic lives some purpose. It's the music of the playground bullies, the fake revolutionaries, the kids whose idea of rebellion is sneaking out at lunchtime to have a quick fag behind the bike shed, the conformists. It's music for people who admire James Dean's vacant, clueless rebel stance and leather jacket, desiring style over content. It's music for the thugs, the beer-boys, the ones who were good at gym and on the sports field, the ones who weren't but always dreamed of being macho somehow. It's music for the proles, the hopeless, hapless masses who like to pretend they're different and daring for a couple of years before growing up to be precisely the same, precisely as conservative as the generation before them and the generation before that.

For me, rock music is about rules, peer pressure, conformity, misogyny, sexism, ageism, hatred of outsiders, mob rule, anti-style as fascism. It's dictated to and ruled by people like Guns N' Roses, Slipknot and Jim Morrison, eternally re-treading the path of those who came before. It's about looking backwards, never to the future. It's retrogressive, searching out the lowest common denominator. Rock music leads to exploitation, degradation, segregation of any freethinking, revolutionary outsiders. Always.

Understand this: not only do I not believe in utopian ideals (the concept of paradise seems to cancel out that most basic of human instincts – the need to struggle), I don't even believe in rock music . . . if that doesn't sound too stupid. In terms of vibrancy or potency or potential for change or anything, rock was supplanted at the end of the Eighties by acid house, rave, dance, electronica and their kin. One of the best ways to judge the effectiveness of an artistic medium to alter or help shape popular opinion is to observe the establishment's reaction to it. In the UK, the government has been trying to bring dance music under its control for an eternity now. Contrast this with pop and rock music where members of the ruling elite hobnob with the rock hierarchy, primetime TV programmes are devoted to rock musical knowledge, and rock awards ceremonies take on absurd levels of pomposity. Rock sometimes proudly boasts that it can bridge generations: it should not be so proud of that claim, not at all. The vital music, or art, has always been that which creates sociological divides.

Rock music was founded on a lie: white men usurping the black man's heritage, pretty boy Elvis setting all the teenage kids a-squealing with a wiggle of his white boy hips. It was also exclusively male, created for and by men with a compulsive need to strut their cocks once they were no longer in the army. Gold help you if you were female, wanting in: rock's attitudes towards what it perceives as 'the opposite sex' are still mainly stuck in the decade it sprang from – the Fifties. Rock revels in its lack of options – unless you think stars like Perry Farrell and Canadian singer-songwriter Sarah McLachlan with their merciless selling of US 'counter-culture' events such as Lollapalooza and the all-female Lilith Fair during the Nineties were providing alternatives. Sure, they were. It's always alternative to be compartmentalised.

Nirvana knew all this. But it sometimes seemed like the sheer weight of rock history threatened to outweigh any small advances they might have made in trying to disturb the status quo. Very quickly, whether Kurt liked it or not, Nirvana became co-opted by the very art form they were trying to subvert and came to represent the entire pantheon of rock music – at least in the eyes of thousands of stupid boys going on in school playgrounds about how 'Kurt is God' and that girls (still!) couldn't play music.

In the sleeve notes to *Incesticide*, the Nirvana 'rarities' collection released in December 1992, Kurt sent a 'fuck you' to those he felt thought he was naïve and stupid enough to be manipulated by his wife. He ended up by writing: "I don't feel the least bit guilty for commercially exploiting a completely exhausted Rock youth Culture because, at this point in rock history, Punk Rock (while still sacred to some) is, to me, dead and gone. We just wanted to pay tribute to something that helped us to feel as though we had crawled out of the dung heap of conformity, to pay tribute like an Elvis or Jimi Hendrix impersonator in the tradition of a bar band. I'll be the first to admit that we're the Nineties version of Cheap Trick or The Knack, but the last to admit that it hasn't been rewarding – Kurdt (the blond one)."

Well, he said it.

## NOTES

1 But one that has since been extensively reported as fact, with only the year date changed.

2 The interaction between myself and Courtney over the *Vanity Fair* article got reported in Melissa Rossi's entertainingly trashy book *Courtney Love: Queen Of Noise*: "Before the interview sessions with reporter Lynn Hirschberg, who was known for well-crafted fluff pieces, Courtney ran into *Melody Maker*'s Everett True; as always, he fawned over her. She asked him how she should act for the interview, and he told her she should be herself. The next time Courtney saw Everett, she said, 'You gave me bad advice.'"

3 New Model Army were a mid-Eighties British agit-punk band, popular with 'the kids'.

4 Donita was also notorious for pulling down her trousers and exposing herself live on British youth TV programme *The Word*.

5 It might also have been the year that the Mean Fiddler tent struggled free of its moorings and flew off into the sunset.

6 I initially compared NYC band Pavement to abrasive, caustic post-punks The Fall, but that was like comparing mountain streams to icebergs. Like every great rock band since The Sex Pistols, Pavement sought to destroy rock while reinvesting the form with meaning. They wrote great *pop* songs, songs that drew heavily from the mid-Seventies (Cheap Trick, Steely Dan, Badfinger), yet retained enough of a twist and overflowing love for music to keep them away from the

traps of their forebears. You could draw parallels between singer Stephen Malkmus' smart, sassy music and that of arch chameleon David Bowie, but Steve never struck me as cynical. Disturbed, maybe, but cynical, no. Pavement's 1992 debut album, the still-glistening *Slanted And Enchanted*, rocked with an urbane freshness reminiscent of Jonathan Richman's Modern Lovers.

## CHAPTER 22

# Shut Your Bitch Up

IT happened too fast.

Somewhere along the line, our dreams came true and we never had a chance to reconcile them with our ideals. Nothing untoward happened for Nirvana that hadn't happened to a thousand other bands, so what was it that felt so bad? Perhaps we were too naïve. We didn't realise that people could take and twist our words and actions into any shapes they desired. The demonising of Courtney was a symptom, not the cause, of all that followed. It's very likely that no one twisted her words in any high-falutin' publication, all that was different was the focus applied.

Life is all about context and perception. We were used to existing in our own tiny insular worlds where everyone knew everyone and everyone behaved in a roughly similar fashion on roughly the same level. In rock, there's nothing unusual or odd about taking drugs, being outspoken or having opinions that fluctuate from day to day. Indeed, it's expected. The world of musicians and the music press is different to the world of the mainstream press. Music critics have no real power. There's far more hypocrisy in the 'real' press than in what to all intents and purposes is still a 'fan' press: celebrities go to extraordinary lengths to make sure their actual characters are never exposed. This was a lesson that Courtney, for one, learned too late.

Nirvana's 1992 Reading performance was an aberration, chronologically speaking. It was obvious the trio were enjoying themselves, but as a creative unit Nirvana were almost spent. Krist and Dave – and later, extra musicians such as Pat Smear – were still an incredible musical force to be reckoned with, and without them, Kurt would have had real trouble fulfilling his visions. By the end of 1992, though, he seemed intent on reducing their role to that of backing musicians.

Some time between the end of '91 and summer '92, everything changed. Kurt's paranoia and drug taking became more intense; he became separated from his close friends and in particular Krist when he moved down to LA; Courtney became pregnant. The one focus in Kurt's life became his love for Courtney. Look at the lyrics to *In Utero*; almost every song deals with his wife and/or her vilification in the press. It's possible, too, that after having been on almost constant tour for over 18 months, Kurt was never given a chance to return to normality. For him, the old normality didn't exist any more. Contrast this with his bandmates who both had a chance to readjust to life. Krist returned to Shelli in Seattle, and immersed himself in good causes, trying to make use of his fame. And Dave?

Dave was saving for the future, enjoying the ride.

By the time the echoes from *Nevermind* had died down, Nirvana barely meant anything to Kurt any more: certainly not within the context of being a 'radio friendly unit shifter'.[1] Even worse than that, the group found themselves unable to play the small clubs they and their punk heroes cherished. You create music because you feel a primal urge – right? If you want to make money, there are far easier ways than to prostitute your soul.

I stayed in contact with Kurt and Courtney over this period. I was probably one of the few who spoke to both sides of the marriage. Yes, it was sudden, so sudden that when the idea was first suggested, Courtney realised she hadn't actually *divorced* Falling James. I was told that Kurtney had tried to get married secretly a few months earlier in Seattle, only for Courtney to realise she needed an annulment first.

> *I know what I haven't asked any of you. When are you going back into the studio?*
>
> *"Next month, as soon as we get home," replies Kurt. "When I move into my tree house we'll become a band again because we'll all be in the same place. I live in a tree house."*
>
> *So you're planning to record on an eight-track.*
>
> *"I think that's what we'd like to do," the singer nods. "I've mentioned it to Chris and Dave a couple of times but we haven't decided on anything concrete. The idea is to go into Reciprocal with Jack Endino and rent exactly the same equipment as was there when we recorded* Bleach. *We record all the songs there with Jack on an eight-track, record them somewhere else again on a 24-track with Steve Albini*[2]*, and then pick the best."*
>
> *So you're aiming for a raw sound on the next album?*
>
> *"Definitely less produced," says Chris.*
>
> *"As long as it doesn't sound like* Nevermind,*" adds Kurt.*
>
> *Why? Are you fed up with* Nevermind*?*

*"No, I really like that album," Kurt replies. "And it doesn't matter what kind of production it has because the songs are good. But it would have been better rawer."*

*"We don't want to find ourselves in [thrash metal band] Slayer's situation," Dave explains, "where the same people produced their last three records and they all sound identical. That's stupid."*

*"I'd love to record a record that has production as original as* Surfer Rosa *[Pixies]," continues Kurt. "We came close to achieving that with* Bleach, *but* Nevermind *isn't that original sounding. There's no fucking way that we're going to make this into a career; our record label's going to be real surprised when we start putting out exactly what music we want to. It's time for a change. I think we all agree with that. I mean, would you guys want to be writing 'In Bloom' for the next five years?"*

*"Maybe the next record will be the one where we can judge how much impact we've actually made," Chris wonders aloud.*

*"Yeah, but we know that at least 40 per cent of people who like us now aren't going to like our next record if it has a lot of abrasive, inaccessible songs on it," replies Kurt, scornfully. "If they do . . . man, that proves our theory that you can shove anything down the mainstream's throat and they'll eat it up."*

*"But that's what I always thought of our second record as being," interrupts Dave. "Something way less produced, where we can push the sound even further and see if we can get a noisy LP on the charts."*

*You mean third record, surely?*

*"No, second major label . . ."*

*"But do you think that would happen?" Kurt asks him. "Let's pretend we haven't released 'Endless, Nameless' yet, and it's our first single off the next album – if people bought it, wouldn't it prove that they like us just cos it's cool to?"*

*"No," Chris replies. "That argument doesn't hold any water. They wouldn't be that mindless. They would not go for 'Endless, Nameless'. They just wouldn't."*

*Do you think you'll have another single as big as 'Teen Spirit'?*

*"No," states Kurt firmly. "We haven't written any songs as good . . . as poppy and anthemic as 'Teen Spirit'. We might write one right before we finish recording the album, because 'Teen Spirit' was written just weeks before* Nevermind, *but we're not going to try."*

(*Melody Maker*, July 25, 1992)

After Reading, Nirvana returned to the US – Kurt to detox, this time at Exodus at Marina Del Ray – and Kurtney agreed to submit urine samples for drug testing as part of their ongoing battle to have Frances Bean returned. Kurt wrote Courtney several rambling, self-hating letters from hospital, despising himself for being so stupid as to become an addict, denying that he ever was an addict, blaming everything on his stomach, covering his letters with candle wax and blood. Sometimes, he was poetic – "I'm speechless, I'm toothless. You pull wisdom from my tooth. You give me girth and dentures and fangs" – and sometimes, he was pleading. The treatment worked, albeit temporarily – Kurt shifted his dependency on to other drugs, barbiturates. It wouldn't last long.

On September 8, Kurt was talked into signing a waiver releasing him from hospital for MTV's Video Music Awards. No one who was cool gave a shit for them, but Nirvana's management were concerned there'd be a knock-on effect if this band that MTV had so slavishly championed over the past year didn't show up – Nirvana were nominated for four awards[3] – so Kurt reluctantly agreed to attend.

Some people felt Kurt was being hypocritical in his public distaste for MTV – Danny Goldberg, for one. "Kurt had a strong sense of achievement," his former manager says. "He kept careful track of how many times Nirvana videos were played on MTV compared with Pearl Jam when there was that rivalry going on, for example. MTV wanted him to do an awards show but he hated the whole idea of MTV – but if he'd wanted to say no, no one could've made him do it. He hated having to suck up to MTV but didn't want to pay the price for not sucking up to them. It's not like he accidentally became famous. He carefully planned it out. But the self-imposed pressure to maintain success didn't make him happy. A lot of artists find the baggage accompanying fame weird and uncomfortable."

Even at the rehearsals for the awards, controversy engulfed Nirvana. Kurt wanted to play the haunting 'Rape Me'. MTV were outraged – the station wasn't about innovation or spontaneity, but consolidation. They wanted a hit, nothing less. Plus, the executives felt the song was somehow directed at them, even though it was written in late 1990.

MTV refused point blank to let Nirvana perform the song. Nirvana refused point blank to perform. So MTV started getting heavy with the band: first, they threatened to boycott Gold Mountain's other acts such as Sonic Youth and Beastie Boys. Next, they threatened to fire Amy Finnerty, an employee that Nirvana liked.

"There was this weird stand-off where, all of a sudden, they realised MTV might have them in a headlock," explains Earnie Bailey. "My feeling was, 'Do you really think that they would blacklist you like that?

Are you convinced that they would try to take out the biggest non-industry band in the world?' "

In the event, a totally scouring version of 'Lithium' was played, Kurt choirboy cute in his cropped blond hair, cardigan and Daniel Johnston T-shirt, kids tentatively stagediving off the stage (probably prompted by an MTV exec, ever mindful of the need for the *illusion* of rebellion and chaos). First, though, Kurt nearly gave MTV kittens as he sung the opening lines of 'Rape Me' accompanied by desultory strumming, Krist flashing the devil sign. As engineers raced across to the control truck to switch to a commercial, Kurt launched into the new single, feverish and mischievous. MTV might have got their way but Nirvana had scored a tiny moral victory. It was a great performance.

At the song's end, Krist hurled his bass into the air and it hit him square on the forehead, concussing him as he staggered off stage. Kurt clambered over the drums while Dave, almost demented, grabbed the mic and shouted, "Hi Axl, where's Axl, hi Axl?"

Dave's improvised speech was a reference to an incident that had happened minutes before, involving the pompous Guns N' Roses singer and his LA hair rock band. Bad blood had been simmering for months, ever since Axl Rose had requested Nirvana play his 30th birthday party in the wake of *Nevermind*, and Nirvana had treated the request with the scorn it deserved. Next, Guns N' Roses tried to get Nirvana as their opening band for their 1992 spring tour – what were they thinking? Guns N' Roses were a trad rock band that stood for everything Kurt – and more particularly his adopted hometown of Olympia – despised. Why the fuck would Nirvana be interested in associating with them? As Kurt later explained to gay magazine, *The Advocate*, "Ever since the beginning of rock'n'roll there's been an Axl Rose. And it's just boring, it's totally boring to me."

Still, Axl was a fan; and, rebuffed, decided to take the high moral ground, publicly dismissing Kurt from on stage in Florida a week before the Music Awards as a "fucking junkie with a junkie wife. If the baby's been born deformed," he ranted, "I think they both ought to go to prison." The fact that Axl had clear feelings of inferiority towards Kurt and Nirvana was betrayed by his very next sentence: "He's too good and too cool to bring his rock'n'roll to you, because the majority of you he doesn't like or want to play to . . ."

So when Axl and his girlfriend, model Stephanie Seymour, bumped into Kurt and Courtney backstage, fireworks followed – "Hey Axl," Courtney called out, spotting the pair. "Will you be the godfather of our child?" Rose ignored her and turned to Kurt, who was cuddling Frances:

"You shut your bitch up or I'm going to knock you to the pavement." Deadpan, Kurt turned to Courtney and said, "Shut the fuck up, bitch." There was momentary silence as people figured out what he was doing and then sniggers of laughter could be heard. Trying to save her partner's face Seymour turned to Love and asked, "Are you a model?" Courtney immediately fired back, "No. Are you a brain surgeon?" Axl and Stephanie stormed off, humiliated.

"That Axl throw-down was one of the funniest things I ever saw," chuckles Janet Billig. "Axl had no comeback at all."

"My first US show with Nirvana was the MTV Music Awards," states Earnie Bailey. "I was in the food tent in the middle of a football field, right before their performance. Right in front of me is [mawkish female trio] Wilson Phillips, behind me is Elton John, and we're all holding paper plates. Everyone's sporting the big hairdos and shoulder pads and then there's us, Nirvana, and we look like the ones emptying the trash: T-shirts and tennis shoes. People were looking at us almost frightened, like we were people to watch out for.

"I sat down on a plastic cooler because most of the seats were filled up," the guitar tech continues, "and a woman came in and asked if she could sit down next to me. It was Annie Lennox. And I thought, 'Wow, I'm sitting on a cooler with Annie Lennox, eating my lunch.' And that's when the whole scene with Axl and his girlfriend played out in front of us. It was nuts.

"At the actual taping, Krist near knocked himself out and we couldn't find him afterwards. We were worried he'd done himself harm. So I went looking for him out at our trailer – I figured he was probably there duct taping his head back together – when Kurt came in, laughing his ass off. He told me he'd spit across the keys of Axl's piano as he left the stage. So we're laughing about that, watching the ceremony on TV, when these two pianos come up and Kurt goes, 'Oh fuck, I spit on Elton's piano by accident.'"

Guns N' Roses behaviour helped put Kurt's simmering feud with Pearl Jam (who were also present) into some perspective. Later that evening, Kurt grabbed hold of Eddie Vedder and slow-danced with the Pearl Jam singer to the strains of Eric Clapton singing 'Tears In Heaven'. "You're a respectable human even if your band does suck," Kurt told him. For, as Kurt explained afterwards, "There are plenty of other more evil people out there in the world."

"I think that was the show where [Courtney's half-sister] Jamie was pretty focused on having Danny [Goldberg] introduce her to Whitney

Houston," laughs Rosemary Carroll. "She was very excited at Whitney's presence. To her, that was a real star."

For their Best Alternative Music Video Award, Nirvana sent up a Michael Jackson impersonator to accept the plaudits, relinquishing his 'King of Pop' nomenclature for the 'King of Grunge'. A nonplussed audience failed to applaud. "A lot of it had to do with the fact they'd taken Michael Jackson off the top of the charts [with *Nevermind*]," explains Billig. "But no one got Kurt's joke."

Guns N' Roses weren't quite finished, however: "At one point Krist and I were walking out from the main building to our trailer and [Guns N' Roses bassist] Duff McKagan[4] approaches us," recalls Bailey. "He's got several bodyguards with him, and one person in his entourage was videotaping, like he's making a Guns N' Roses movie. Duff comes up to Krist and announces, 'I hear you've been talking shit about my band,' and Krist tells him that he hadn't said anything about his band. But Duff keeps going on about it and so Krist says flat out to him, 'Obviously, you're trying to provoke me into a fight so you can film it for your Guns N' Roses fan movie, and I could easily kick your ass but then you'd have four of your bodyguards kick the shit out of me – so let's walk over behind these two buses there and it'll be you and me. I'll be more than happy to take you on.' And Duff was like, 'No, right here, right now.' And there's no way . . . I mean Krist is like Paul fucking Bunyan [legendary giant lumberjack], and Duff was very thin and smelled like he was liquored up. So nothing happened. We walked on, laughing at how absurd it was."

"During the MTV Awards, we stayed at the Hyatt House on Sunset," reveals Earnie. "It was wild. [Legendary Fifties wild man rocker/preacher dude] Little Richard lived on the top floor – and Dave ran into him at the bar. We were up at the pool that Zeppelin had haunted. Barrett [Jones, drum tech] and I flew out immediately afterwards. He and I took a taxi straight to the airport and headed for Portland to set up for the 'No on 9' benefit."

The show was a protest against Oregon State's Initiative 9, an attempt by conservatives to limit homosexual rights. Helmet, megalithic punks Poison Idea and spiky all-female Portland group Calamity Jane were also on the bill, with Dead Kennedys singer Jello Biafra MC-ing. But even in Portland, Nirvana couldn't escape Guns N' Roses fans: "I said something about Guns N' Roses from on stage," Kurt told *The Advocate*. "Nothing nasty – I think I said, 'And now, for our next song, 'Sweet Child O' Mine' [Guns N' Roses' phenomenally successful ballad]. But some kid jumped on stage and said, 'Hey, man, Guns N' Roses plays awesome music, and Nirvana plays awesome music. Let's just get along and work things out, man!'

"And I couldn't help but say, 'No, kid, you're wrong. Those people are total sexist jerks, and the reason we're playing this show is to fight homophobia in a real small way. The guy is a fucking sexist and a racist and a homophobe, and you can't be on his side and be on our side. I'm sorry that I have to divide this up like this, but it's something you can't ignore. And besides they can't write good music.' "

The next night, Nirvana played the 16,000-seater Seattle Center Coliseum with Helmet and Fitz Of Depression – the same venue that Krist had been thrown out of, April 1991. It was another benefit, this time to fight a Washington State music censorship bill: an innocuous enough cause, but Kurt started to receive death threats for his pro-gay and pro-choice stances. The management brought a metal detector in, and he was warned he'd be shot if he stepped on stage.

"It was a great show," says *Rocket* journalist Gillian G. Gaar. "The entire floor was a big moshpit and the fans were just leaping around, leaping around, leaping around. I was thrilled to be a part of it. It was the first time since [female-fronted AOR chart group] Heart that I'd seen a Seattle band that was that popular."

"I recall them smashing up their instruments at early Vogue shows when they couldn't afford to, and I was in such awe," says Rob Kader. "You could tell that it was unplanned and spontaneous – and it felt right. Later on, it felt like they were going through the motions. They'd always switch to a cheap Mexican or Japanese strat beforehand. That Coliseum show was the last time I saw them smash up their gear where it felt true and spontaneous."

Kurt's dad showed up, alongside Kurt's half-brother Chad: Don bluffed his way past security by showing his driver's licence, and there was an awkward moment backstage where Don confronted the son he hadn't seen for seven years. Also present was Wendy, Kurt's mom, and Kim, Kurt's sister, plus Courtney and Frances Bean – neither of whom Don had met before. Eighteen years had elapsed since Wendy and Don had divorced, and the reunion wasn't friendly – both sides sniped at each other about their age. Kurt told his dad to shut up, and Kim and Wendy soon left. Many folk suspected that Don was only making contact because he was after money, but Kurt was cool about it – or so he told British journalist Jon Savage in 1994.

"I was happy to see him because I always wanted him to know that I didn't hate him any more," he said – echoing a line from 'Serve The Servants', the first song on *In Utero*: *"I just want you to know that I/ Don't hate you any more."*

"On the other hand, I didn't want to encourage our relationship because I didn't have anything to say to him. My father is incapable of showing much affection, or even of carrying on a conversation. I didn't want to have a relationship just because he was my blood relative. It would bore me."

"That show had an incredible destruction scene at the end," smiles Earnie. "It began when Kurt approached the amp cabinets that were in front of my work station, so I cleaned up all my stuff, and sure enough he toppled these two top cabinets over on to what would have been my area, and then he went over to a second bank of amps and tipped them over front ways on top of the guitar and then climbed back on top of the cabinet and rocked the cabinet on top of the guitar and got it to make these amazing sounds by squishing the cabinet on the strings . . . and just when you think the guitar is finished, it's not, he's got a long way to go with it. He dismantled it slowly, over the course of what seemed like about 15, 20 minutes – and it was still plugged in. It was awesome. They systematically threw every drum at Kurt, and Kurt was handling his guitar like a baseball bat."

It was time for Kurtney to return to Seattle. They kept their LA apartment for a while, but purchased a house in the country, in Carnation, 30 miles outside Seattle, for $300,000. The house needed a lot of work done to it – "I don't think anyone spent a whole lot of time there," comments Rosemary Carroll – so the couple spent the last few months of 1992 moving from one four-star Seattle hotel to the next, with their entourage in tow. Wherever they went, they left cigarette burns in the sheets and the carpets.

"I went to that house once," comments Michael Lavine. "He was there, and Kevin Kerslake and Courtney. Nothing was there. It was empty, with a Hotwheels circuit in the middle of the floor, boxes of stuff from Europe, pictures and underwear, and the kitchen covered with junk food. That was it."

"I saw Star Pimp[5] at the Colour Box in October 1992," recalls James Burdyshaw. "Kurt and Courtney were there, trying to look inconspicuous . . . well, he was trying to look inconspicuous. I was in line for a beer and she was right in front of me, checking out the crowd, like, 'Oh, nobody I really care about is here.' I said hello to Kurt – 'Remember me? James? I was in Cat Butt,' and he was like, 'Oh yeah! How are you?' All of a sudden, the nice guy came back. We talked for a good 15 minutes, and I said that I'd heard he had a farm, and he goes, 'Well, we don't have any sheep or cows or anything like that, but we own some property.' He was real soft-spoken and then Courtney gives him a dirty look and he says, 'I gotta go now.' I shook his hand, and that was it."

Everywhere the couple turned, it seemed they were under attack.

Minor Liverpool pop star Julian Cope – famous for his vegetarianism, his vanities and his dedication to Krautrock – took out an ad in the British music press to vent his spleen on his former fan: "Free us," he wrote, "(the rock'n'roll fans) from Nancy Spungen-fixated heroin a holes who cling to our greatest rock groups and suck out their brains." This was risible; sexist, and a charge that had been equally as wrongly made at Yoko Ono 20 years earlier when she started dating John Lennon. Cope fell into the same trap as Axl Rose: assuming that because he'd read about Kurt Cobain a couple of times, it gave him the right to pontificate about his private life.

Victoria Clarke and Britt Collins, two British-based writers, started work on a semi-authorised biography of Nirvana, *Nirvana: Flower Sniffin', Kitty Pettin', Baby Kissin' Corporate Rock Whores* – a book named after one of Nirvana's early T-shirt slogans that quickly became unauthorised after Kurtney learnt they were planning on speaking to Lynn Hirschberg and had already spoken to Falling James. They suspected a stitch-up.

This assumption led to one of the nastiest incidents of Kurt Cobain's life, where he – and Courtney, and Dave – left a series of messages on Victoria and Britt's home phones, threatening to kill them (some from Jack Endino's studio). They might have got Gold Mountain to deny it and later claimed it was a joke – but it didn't sound very funny at the time. Kurtney were in a powerful position and quite able to carry out threats if they wanted to: and from the way Kurt talked about it afterwards, it certainly seemed they wanted to. Sure, the two writers were opportunist, but that hasn't stopped scores of journalists since.

One night, Kurt called Victoria's answer machine nine times, his invective ranging from, "If anything comes out in this book which hurts my wife, I'll fucking hurt you," to calling the pair "parasitic little cunts" and claiming that, "I could throw out a few hundred thousand dollars to have you snuffed out, but maybe I'll try the legal way first." His anger, verging on the misogynistic, was creepy and depressing. Victoria and Britt were being made scapegoats for all the anger and confusion Kurt felt about his life – but he confirmed to his biographer Michael Azerrad in 1993 that he was justified in his actions: "I'm a firm believer in revenge," he growled.

Courtney's messages were just as vitriolic. A couple of months later, there was an incident in an LA club where Courtney was alleged to have hit Clarke with a glass. Victoria filed a complaint with the LA Police Department. Courtney filed a counter-complaint the following day, claiming it was self-defence.

"I ended up covered in beer on the ground," Clarke told one Nirvana documentary maker, "and she pulled me along the floor by my hair and tried to get me outside. It was quite scary."

Well, I remember the scene at *Melody Maker* when the story broke: my news department yelling at me to get a statement – while in my other ear, Courtney is excitedly talking down the telephone, howling with laughter about the event, as I try to tell her: first, this really isn't the time or the place to talk about this, and second, I can't condone this sort of behaviour *ever*, especially considering how many threats had been made against me.

Gold Mountain filed a suit against the pair if they ever published the book, after having obtained an advance copy of part of the manuscript. An Irish magazine published Gold Mountain's complaints in full: I can't remember the other 29 or so, but I do recall that one of them was that, "Courtney Love does not believe Everett True is an asshole." Well . . . it was nice to know!

"Courtney used to call me up all the time," comments Slim Moon. "She'd send me and Mary Lou faxes. There was one fax that was reportedly from Kurt, but seemed to be from Courtney about how, 'I never liked you and I'd rather see your head stuck in an oven.' Time passed and she took on this whole new tactic where she would say, 'Kurt needs friends who are a better influence. Your friends all suck, but I like you, so you should come have dinner with us.' I didn't feel comfortable doing that. If the invitation had come from Kurt, I'd have gone, but it didn't."

That autumn, Nirvana made a handful of secret appearances.

Kurt joined Sonic Youth and Mudhoney on stage in Valencia, California on September 26, where he performed the harrowing Leadbelly song, 'Where Did You Sleep Last Night?' and played guitar on Mudhoney's cover of 'The Money Will Roll Right In'.

On October 3–4, Nirvana opened for Mudhoney. The first show was at Western Washington University in Bellingham, two hours drive from Seattle. "That was a lot of fun," says Earnie, "because it was genuinely a surprise. At the end of Mudhoney's set Matt Lukin brought these kids up out of the crowd, and one wound up with Krist's bass, and he was going to smash it. I thought it was pretty funny, but Krist was looking at me like, 'No, don't let him smash that bass,' but he didn't want to be the one to stop it . . ."

Charles Peterson attended both shows – the final shows at which he'd photograph Nirvana. "Bellingham was really good," he told *Goldmine*. "There were all these student photographers down in the pit, and there was this one guy, he's got his camera, and he's dancing around, but he's right in front of where Kurt is. I'm like, 'If you're not going to take pictures, get out of the way.' And he was like, 'I've only got one shot left and I'm waiting for the destruction!'

"And the brilliant thing was, that night they didn't destroy their instruments," Peterson added. "These two kids came on stage and Kurt draped his guitar around one of them, and Krist draped his guitar around the other kid's neck. And everyone was like 'Smash it! Smash it!' And somehow this kid hauled Krist's bass over his head and smashed it on to the stage. Alex, their tour manager, is back there with his head in his hands, cos Krist never smashed his basses. It was the perfect ending."

"That was the show I gave Kurt that sunburst Univox guitar," Earnie continues. "I felt like he was in this weird frame of mind, and wanted to give him a guitar like he used to play. He really liked it, and played the Univox on the 1993 *Saturday Night Live* show and *In Utero*. It was a pretty important instrument."

The next night, Nirvana played support to Mudhoney once more – this time at Seattle's Crocodile Café: Kurt's happiness at being in a small club again was infectious. He stagedived during Mudhoney's set, and jammed on a few punk rock numbers. Gillian G. Gaar, who was interviewing Courtney for *The Rocket* the same day, picks up the story: "The phone rings, and it's Patti [Schemel, ex-Seattle band Kill Sybil and Hole's new drummer]," says Gillian. "She says, can you meet and talk with Courtney in an hour's time? So I go down to the Four Seasons [the fancy five-star downtown hotel where the Kurtney camp stayed for two months] and Courtney comes down – on time. She brings Frances with her. I really liked her. I'd ask her a question and she'd go off on this long spiel and eventually circle in and answer the question. She just had a huge amount of context to set up her answer. But she was funny and had a lot of great anecdotes. She'd been in Hollywood and the music scene. She was self-deprecating, too. I came away thinking she had been given a bad rep.

"Later, I saw the Crocodile show and it was great," the journalist continues. "Word got out, so it was full. They did a lot of unfamiliar material and were having a good time. During the set Kurt asked if there were any requests, so Krist leant over and in a funny voice goes, 'Play "Teen Spirit". Play "Teen Spirit".' But they didn't.

"Then I got word that Courtney's management had said she didn't want to do the interview – which was my first clue to how there was a disconnection between Kurt and Courtney and her management."

Why do you think Courtney got a bad rep?

"She doesn't hold back, does she?" Gillian laughs. "She has no idea what self-censorship means. She doesn't restrain herself, like if she's mad at someone she'll just blurt it out and attack him or her. It's like she doesn't care, so that rubs people the wrong way. Maybe part of it was there were a lot of rumours going on about Nirvana, and no one knew what the true story was. And whenever Kurt was in the hospital, it was always, oh, the stomach thing.

"Oh yeah, she was going to break up Nirvana, when it fact it was her band that fell apart in that period. She put everything on hold to be with Kurt, and have Frances. So she's not only a bad mother, she's ruining Nirvana."

On October 15, Nirvana filmed a video for the new British single, 'In Bloom'. It was the fourth track to be released off *Nevermind* as a single in the UK, and it seemed that Geffen were milking the album a little too much – even for the most diehard Nirvana fans.

> *"Nirvana have a new single out,"* I wrote in *Melody Maker*, relegating the single to an also-ran the same week I made Christina Kelly's caustic, feminist Chia Pet Single Of The Week. *"Pop those corks. Hang high your washing. Feed the cat, and don't stint on the servings. Whoop whoop bloody whoop. Forgive me if I don't sound too thrilled. This release is stretching even my credulity beyond repair. Like, milking a still-breathing (sacred) cow, or what? Badly inferior live versions of 'Polly' and 'Sliver' on the flip don't help matters either. I know 'In Bloom' is an awesome double-edged terrace anthem and the video's cool, but . . . Save your money for the* Incesticide, *kids. Now, that's worth buying."*

The video for 'In Bloom' certainly was cool. Directed by Kevin Kerslake, three versions were made – all shot on Kinescope, parodying the classic US Sixties variety programme, *The Ed Sullivan Show*. One featured the band in dresses, one in Beach Boys-style suits and dresses, and the other in the suits alone. Imagine Ritchie Cunningham's achingly square band in *Happy Days*, or The Monkees on prime-time kids' TV, and you'll get a good idea of the feel: Nirvana appear un-hip with their short hair and geeky glasses next to all the manic grunge kids watching them in the video audience – a smart satire of the manufactured, carefully marketed bands they were competing alongside for MTV's attention – but I knew which side I'd rather be on.

"Let's hear it for these three nice, decent, clean-cut young men," the announcer says at the video's end, as the band suddenly appeared into drag and started destroying their equipment. "I really can't say enough nice things about them!"

> *ET: Why did you wear a dress in the new video for 'In Bloom'?*
>
> *KC: "I don't know. I like to wear dresses because they're comfortable. If I could wear a sheet, I would. I don't know what to say . . . If I said we do it to be subversive then that would be a load of shit because men in bands wearing dresses aren't controversial any more. Basically we wanted to make the video with as little fuss as possible, in as short a time as possible, for a few thousand dollars. There was no hidden agenda. The dresses only came about at the last minute. We wanted to be like The Beatles – no, The Dave Clark Five, I was wearing glasses – we would never make fun of The Beatles. There's nothing more comfortable than a cosy flower pattern."*
>
> *ET: In your particular context, an MTV hard rock band that sells millions of records, surely it's a subversive act?*
>
> *KC: "It may be subversive as far as a very small amount of people go, who've never seen men in dresses before or who aren't comfortable with the concept, but I don't give a shit about those people anyway. It's not subversive. There's no point in being subversive in rock any more. There's no way you can be, unless you ram a stick of dynamite up your ass. Queen dressed in drag. Male bands do it all the time. It just feels comfortable, sexy and free wearing a dress. It's fun."*
>
> *ET: How do you feel about the suggestion some of your fans are called 'fags' for liking such a presumably effeminate hard rock band?*
>
> *KC: "I love it. Knowing that gives me as much pleasure as when I used to dress up as a punk at high school, and rednecks driving by in trucks would yell 'Devo!' at me. It's good to have a nice, healthy battle going on in high school between the Guns N' Roses jocks and the Nirvana fans. It vibes up the kids who are more intelligent, and at least it brings the whole subject of homosexuality into debate. It's very flattering our fans are thought of as 'fags'. I've heard stories about kids being beaten up for wearing Nirvana T-shirts. It reminds me of when I used to support strange or weird bands who were that little bit more dangerous because they weren't accepted by the mainstream. Devo were a great example – a*

*Top 10 act that were far more off-the-wall than us."*

*ET: Do you approve of cross-dressing?*

*KC: "Of course. Men shouldn't wear a dress because it's feminist, but because it's comfortable. Sometimes my penis will literally fall asleep or feel like it's dropped right off because it's been constricted by tight Levi's, and I'll have to wear baggy pants or a dress instead."*

*ET: How about men wearing make-up?*

*KC: "Sure. If it's applied in a real gaudy fashion, really thick and makes you look like a TV evangelist's wife. I go through an eyeliner phase about one month every year. Pete Townshend did too, but it didn't last very long. I know all about rock stars who use eyeliner. It never lasts very long. Supposedly it burns into the eyes during shows under the bright lights. Maybe you should tattoo it on. Cross-dressing is cool. I'm sorry I can't come up with any better reasons for why we wore dresses for our video shoot, it's just that I wear them all the time, round the house, wherever. I'd just as soon wear a bathrobe or sheet with a hole in it. It's not particularly because I want to wear a woman's dress."*

(*Melody Maker* 'Sex' issue, December 12, 1992)

On October 24, Nirvana returned to Reciprocal – now called Word Of Mouth – to record demos for their next album. The trio didn't have many songs worked out, and certainly no lyrics. It wasn't a good session.

"For the *In Utero* demos, I brought a bunch of oddball pedals around and some odd sound effect devices," remembers Earnie Bailey. "Kurt plugged in everything – all 12 pedals – and I told him his guitar would sound a lot better if he took the ones he wasn't using out of the effect chain, because they were bogging down his signal and making his guitar sound terrible, and he said, 'Well, that's what I want.' I thought, 'Well, your ideas have gotten us this far, so you're either fucking with me, or . . .' "

He could have been serious. There's supposed to be a frequency that blows out speakers: I remember Kurt telling me he wanted it at the start of *In Utero*, but preferably one that only worked on really expensive hi-fi systems.

"Dave was the loudest drummer I've ever recorded," Jack Endino comments. "While we were doing the demos, the cops came by. It was the only noise complaint we'd had at that studio in five years. It's an old building, with triple walls. It's soundproofed. And yet Dave was so loud there was a noise complaint from a house three doors away. I was out in front talking to the police. The cops said, 'You guys need to turn it down.' I was telling them, 'You guys know who Nirvana is?' I'm trying to explain to the cops that I've got Nirvana in here, and I'm trying to explain to Nirvana that I've got the cops outside. I'm going, 'What a time for the cops to show up, I'm doing demos for Nirvana, Jesus Christ, I'm going crazy!' What am I going to tell the band? We have to stop? It's a studio! The studio's been there since the Seventies.

"Nirvana called up and said they wanted to do some quick recordings on the old eight-track," the producer recalls. "They booked the time and cancelled it because that was the weekend Frances appeared in the world. They cancelled a couple of times. Finally, the band showed up. We set up the drums and amps, and waited for Kurt. He never showed. The next day he showed up, and they did six songs, exactly the same as they are on *In Utero*. It was very tense. There was something dark in the air. Just the idea of Kurt showing up 12 hours late – it wasn't like a band. People were not communicating with each other. Kurt was in a different reality from everybody else."

I know from conversations I had with Kurt at the time, he was concerned that *Nevermind* had gone way too far in the production, and he wanted to get back to basics.

"Right," agrees Jack. "They wanted to feel like they were doing something opposite again, go in and record in one day. At no time did I think I was doing the next Nirvana album. In fact, while they were there they said, 'Oh yeah, we're probably going to go and do the next record with Steve Albini.' I was sitting there thinking, 'OK, thank you very much!'

"The closest you get to my version of *Nevermind 2* is that version of 'Rape Me', because that's the only song we finished," he continues. "It's not a bad version. It's all right. Having Frances on there was a little weird. Courtney came down with the baby and they held her up to the microphone – 'Hey, let's record Frances here and put her on the song!' It wasn't a sample we dropped in. She was like a week old or something, two weeks old."

None of the songs had any vocals, except for 'Rape Me', but Kurt's singing lacks the cynical venom that characterises the song. "No one ever called back to finish them," sighs Jack. "It was like someone had talked them into doing 'demos'. The band had no interest in it, and Kurt acted like he didn't even want to be there." All the other numbers were instrumental tracks: run-throughs of songs that appeared on the third album proper, the helpless and affecting 'Dumb', the all-out frenzied metal attack of 'tourette's', 'Pennyroyal Tea' . . .

"Courtney came down at the end of the sessions, right when Kurt was doing vocals for 'Rape Me'," continues Jack. "The song dated all the way back to '90, '91, but it didn't have a bridge, so he had to come up with some words. I think Courtney helped Kurt with his lyrics, because after he met Courtney his lyrics all changed."

They became understandable.

"Yeah, exactly," the producer nods. 'On *In Utero*, the lyrics are much more concrete. He was literally writing the words in the studio, and running them by Courtney – he'd read her a line and she'd be like, 'That's cool, but what about that other line you used to sing?' I thought, 'Ah, the verbal one and the introspective one are bouncing off each other.' Courtney may not be able to carry a tune, but she's an explosion of words. She's a crazy lyricist. I'm sure she helped him focus on his lyrics. I don't think she wrote any of them, but she raised the bar as far as what he made himself try to do."

Presumably if Courtney was at the studio, the dynamics of the band were very different to before.

"The other members left about then," replies Jack. "Once the bass and drums were done, everybody else went home and it was just Kurt and Courtney in the studio with me finishing it up. The dynamics were all right. It seemed like Krist was a little uneasy around Courtney; Dave and Courtney were getting along fine. They were horsing around and being goofy. I remember them making these weird calls from the studio phone and then coming out and laughing hysterically. They were making threatening phone calls to these journalists, but in a jocular way. It was Dave and Kurt and Courtney. The three of them were egging each other on. I'm not sure how seriously they were taking these phone calls while they were doing them. I think maybe they were taken very seriously by some of the recipients."

On October 30, Nirvana played another sub-standard show – this time in front of one of the largest crowds of their career: nearly 50,000 at the Velez Sarsfield Stadium in Buenos Aires, Argentina. The band hadn't bothered rehearsing, their spirits were low, and when the partisan crowd started heckling Calamity Jane – simply because they were female (or so Nirvana surmised) – everything really went downhill.

"The entire crowd were throwing mud and rocks, just pelting them," Kurt told *Request* in November '93. "Eventually, the girls stormed off crying. It was terrible, just a mass of sexism all at once."

"That's my most vivid memory of while we were there," recalls Earnie Bailey. "There was some profanity towards the fact they were women, which was not the right thing to do with Nirvana headlining. They didn't play 'Teen Spirit'. Kurt started playing the intro at the beginning of almost every song, and stopped. You could tell he was really pissed off. But there was an amazing destruction sequence at the end [where the band played 'Endless, Nameless']. Dave and Krist got into a great spontaneous jam and Kurt was pulling down some incredible sounds, so that kind of saved that show." Nirvana started the 40-minute set with a noise jam, and played mostly songs from *Incesticide* – much to the annoyance of the audience.

"It's funny," Earnie comments, "because I'd had little interaction with Courtney up until that point, and somebody came backstage and announced that Calamity Jane were having a terrible time out front. Courtney blew up at me, saying, 'Why aren't you out there taking care of their stuff?' I can't remember what I said, but I lashed back viciously. The whole room was silent. Nobody could believe I did that, because people were kind of afraid of her. Even Kurt was like, 'Holy shit!' People were looking at me like, 'There goes your job.' But she seemed to respect the fact I was nasty back to her. After that, we got along fine.

"My other main memory was looking out of the hotel window and seeing people camped on the grass, day and night," the guitar tech continues. "We landed in the airport and had to go past this checkpoint where they had soldiers with rifles. It was this strange feeling of, where the hell are we? And then once you roll into traffic, you notice these 1963 Ford Falcons everywhere. The taxis and the police cars were all Falcons and yet they had modern hubcaps on them and digital dashboards. Dave and Krist and I were into Ford Falcons . . . I know Kurt liked Darts, but we thought this was hilarious. Were they pimping out these Falcons here? So we asked our bus driver, why are there so many Falcons? He told us, after the body style went out of production they sent the stamps down there and they've been producing them ever since. So either Dave or Krist was hot to buy one of those Falcons and get it shipped back to Seattle, but it was too expensive considering the cost to ship and then modify to suit US emissions."

By mid-November, Kurtney and their management finally convinced the Los Angeles court to allow them guardianship of Frances Bean – so Jamie left the travelling entourage. Jackie Farry stayed, and kept up Jamie's strict tutorage, not allowing Kurtney to go near their daughter when they were high and taking care of all the usual humdrum parental duties, such as changing nappies and bottle-feeding.

She reported, however, that both parents doted on their daughter.

"Kurt always loved children," confirms Rosemary Carroll. "He told me that his favourite job he'd ever held was helping kids learn to swim. My daughter was born in 1990 and he was always very sweet and playful to her – and he sure loved Frances. He was delighted to have a child."

"I think fatherhood suited Kurt," says Danny Goldberg. "He doted on his daughter. He was a great father when he was alive, and I think he would have continued to be one. It wasn't enough to overcome his inner demons, but it gave him a great deal of joy."

Kurt returned to Word Of Mouth on November 8–10 – this time to help his wife record a new single for European label City Slang, as Hole were still missing a bass-player. The three songs recorded were 'Beautiful Son', '20 Years In The Dakota'[6] and 'Old Age'.

"I actually played bass on 'Beautiful Son'," reveals Endino. "Their new drummer Patti [Schemel] was very, very good. She rocked. She was like the female Keith Moon. That was my first experience of being in the studio with Courtney as a recording artist, and my last. It was quite negative. She was very civil to me, but she was shouting at the other members of the band. 'You're fucking up my song!' And then she'd be on the phone, right behind the control room, calling up and screaming at people and slamming the phone down. It was really strange, cognitive dissonance."

She would have been aware that you could make her sound awful.

"Yeah, she's not stupid." Jack laughs. "I always respected that she treated me civilly, but I didn't enjoy being around her. It was like fingernails on a blackboard."

Did she actually play guitar on the single?

"Yes, a little bit. It was mostly Eric and Patti, and Courtney directing. She played bass on one of the songs. Supposedly Kurt was going to come down and do the bass, but it got around to 11 p.m. and Kurt still hadn't shown. I said, 'Look, I still have to mix all three of these songs and I'm getting tired. Just give me the bass. I don't want to stay here till 5 a.m. mixing these three songs.' When Kurt finally showed up, he just said, 'Oh, you played bass, cool' [Jack played bass on 'Beautiful Son'; Courtney on 'Dakota']. He didn't give a shit. He was fine, hanging out.

"Once Kurt was there things were mellow. The two of them together were always relaxed. Kurt was very funny with her, because she sort of bossed him around, but he would have a smirk on his face like, 'Yeah, whatever.' He was playing along. The weird thing about 'Beautiful Son' is that the riff on it sounds exactly like 'Smells Like Teen Spirit'. Eric [Erlandson] pointed it out, because he was trying to strum it a different way, but Courtney was like, 'No, this is how it should sound.' There was no indication that Kurt might have written the song. I'm sure he didn't have anything to do with it."

I love rock'n'roll.

When you're at your lowest, when everything comes crashing through on top of you, when gloom has overpowered your life and it seems there's no way out . . . hey! Slap on that stereo and turn the volume up a notch even higher. Doesn't matter what it is, virtually anything will do the trick . . . Buzzcocks' 'Something's Gone Wrong Again', Dexys Midnight Runners' 'Plan B', The Raincoats' 'In Love', The Records' 'Starry Eyes', The Ronettes' 'I Wish I Never Saw The Sunshine' . . . Nina Simone's 'Trouble In Mind' – Love's 'Alone Again Or', even. When I was in my twenties, I used to put Hüsker Dü's desperate, guitar-saturated version of The Byrds' 'Eight Miles High' on my Dansette portable mono record player, turn the volume up full, turn all the lights off and set the dial to 'repeat'. It was either that or Otis Redding's 'I've Been Loving You Too Long'. When I was sent a copy of Nirvana's 'Love Buzz', I played it on that same Dansette, carving a groove into the floor with my head for hours on end. There's nothing to be ashamed of in having a passion for music, although for years after Kurt's death I tried to convince myself otherwise.

So Nirvana in concert during 1992, aside from the Reading Festival headline slot, weren't much cop. You think that was an end to it? Of course it wasn't. As Kurt reassured me several times afterwards, he still loved to make music with Krist and Dave. Forget the rumours and speculation and whatever may have been happening in their private lives. All the band needed was to return to the studio. They did so, with Steve Albini at the start of '93, in Chicago. The resultant sessions may not have set the world alight like *Nevermind*, but the band never intended them to. All they wanted to create was great music, and they did so with *In Utero*, the album that proved to be their epitaph.

Is that such a crime: creating music with no concern for sales?

Rock'n'roll won't save your mortal soul, but fuck me. I can't help thinking that yes, Neil Young and Kurt Cobain are right: it *is* better to burn out than to fade away.

**Addenda 1: Cali DeWitt**

"I moved to New York after that first Hole tour. I had romanticised drugs and alcohol from as far back as I can remember, but New York was the first time where I got strung out. I remember thinking, 'Ooh, I'm in another town, I know where to get drugs, I can do this every day and I'm not going to feel any guilt.' I was gone for less than a year. *Vanity Fair* was right around the time I left LA. I remember her venom over that."

The problem was that the journalist didn't understand Courtney's humour. She printed it straight.

"Courtney's humour is viciously sarcastic and very, very funny. I was raised on that kind of humour, so I thought she was funny right away, but I wasn't surprised when other people didn't. She could lash out just as hard as she could do anything, obviously."

Did you encounter Nirvana while you were in New York?

"No. I was a little bit ashamed of what was going on with me. The closest I had was talking to Courtney a lot, especially when she was furious about this Lynn Hirschberg situation, and she started to ask me to come and help with the baby. Which, if I was 18, turning 19 soon, sounded not good to me. Taking care of a baby and I'm having this trouble with drugs and everything, so . . ."

Did choosing you to be the nanny strike you as a good decision?

"I kind of understood it, because she felt really close to me and I'm someone she can trust. I hadn't hung out with Kurt nearly as much as her, but he liked me and she had a problem getting people around who he liked. So, it didn't strike me as that weird. Now, I think they lied to themselves, even on their own. Just because I'm their friend, and because they trust me, and they know that I'm not going to run to the *Enquirer* every time there's some drama. They're denying the fact that I'm a 19-, 20-, 21-year-old kid who is an addict or an alcoholic.

"That's the thing about drugs and alcohol; if you're doing them, you deny they have any lasting effect. For years I was like, 'Drink has no effect on me.' Now I'm just like, what? I can't remember most of four years, and I'm saying it didn't have any effect on me!

"Also, when I was younger, it was a lot more fun. It didn't really start to get dark – it got dark fast for me – but it got dark in New York, so I left New York. So, to me, the problem was solved. Again, I said, 'Why can't Jackie do it?' They said, 'Why don't you come do it?' I said, 'I don't think so.' This was while they were in LA."

Was that the house with the elevator?

"Yes."

Can you describe it?

"It's an old, high ceiling-ed house with a view in the Hollywood Hills. There was a kind of a mezzanine area – the front room was really big with windows overlooking the Hollywood freeway and Capitol Records. You go up the stairs and there's a hallway that overlooks the living room, and behind that there's two bathrooms and two bedrooms."

What kind of stuff was around? Were there records or posters?

"There were records, the current crop of indie records at the time. There were Vaselines singles, Sebadoh singles, anything on AmRep. At this point *Nevermind* was huge, huge and I'm sure any cool label was sending them their whole catalogue to check out. You know, 'Take my bands on tour'. 'What do you think of this?' "

Which posters?

"There weren't many posters, but there were paintings that Kurt was doing. One of them was the *Incesticide* record cover. There was a steel-floored kitchen by the entrance. It was also the house where I think Victoria Clarke and them had been coming up to and going through the garbage or something. At least that's what Courtney told me. Again, I was young and naïve to a few things, and I was still doing drugs and drinking. It wasn't as habitual as it became later, but at any given moment, if I was offered anything, I would do it. There was a rock doctor in LA named Dr Mark and he was giving out this drug called Buprenex in these glass vials. It was a synthetic opiate to stave off heroin withdrawal. They [Kurt and Courtney] had a lot of that around. I just remember these bottles of this clear liquid, and you'd inject it and you wouldn't be sick from heroin withdrawal. They weren't there for long [in LA] when I got there. I got there with my best friend who was with me through most of this, Rene Navarette. We didn't come and do drugs or party or anything, I came to see the baby, I came to hang out."

From what I remember, they were pretty lonely. Kurt especially was lonely because he'd just moved away from the region he'd spent his whole life in. Six months earlier hardly anyone had heard of them, then all of a sudden, they're the most famous couple in the world, and they were lonely. They were looking for people to hang out with.

"That was more of what it was, just hanging out. They were planning on moving out of that house soon."

Kurt hated it in LA.

"Yeah, he did not like it in LA. That's why that house was good, because you had to take an elevator up the side of the mountain to get to it."

It was hard to find as well.

"So it was a nice hiding place, but it was miserable. It was where we did the photo shoot that wound up being that picture of me on the actual CD for *In Utero* [Cali is in drag]. It was just us fucking around with Polaroids and markers."

So how old was Frances at the time?

"Four, five, six months . . ."

**Addenda 2: Jessica Hopper**

"Someone in Huggy Bear got a copy of my fanzine *Hit It Or Quit It* and passed it on to you. Courtney came to know about me through you, but I'd also sent her a copy. There was a Hole review in there and it was really positive. It was the first issue. I was 15, in Minneapolis and just started working at a record store. I'd discovered punk rock and I wanted to write and no one would let me, so I started my own fanzine.

"A few weeks later I got this oversized package with a Hole T-shirt and stickers. Then Courtney sent me a 16-page letter she wrote the day after she had Frances, whacked out on birthing drugs. The letter was all about Minneapolis, and how I should start a band with Michelle Leon [original Babes In Toyland bassist], and how her life had got so weird, and how all she ever wanted in Minneapolis was to work at [record store] Northern Lights. She wanted to know how I was so young and cool – I was totally making fun of the Minneapolis cognoscenti, saying sarky things about [bad local rock band] Run Westy Run and Soul Asylum, all these older dudes.

"I insinuated myself into the cool people circle, in a tangential way. It was such an anomaly. I was alienated from most girls my own age, and most guys were intimidated by me. I was pretty sharp. I wasn't into getting high and getting laid like most people in high school. I was into feminism and bands Don Fleming produced [Gumball, Hole, Sonic Youth, B.A.L.L.[7]], and into Riot Grrrl, all at the same time. There was overlap between me getting to know Courtney and discovering kill rock stars, that was when they were putting out the Wordcore singles [Kathleen Hanna of Bikini Kill was the first to contribute to the spoken word series].

"I got the letter and was like, whoa. She really craved a certain amount of attention and notoriety. She'd started to become notorious. There was not a person in town that had a kind word to say about her, and I identified with her over that. Opinions were divided about me. However badly behaved she had been while she lived here, I knew how Minneapolis could be; it was a real boys town, and so I suspected there was really something to her – that she wasn't just this crazy bitch who was fucked up on drugs, like people said. Any woman who is that demonised, there has to be more to her than people just being angry that she had supposedly introduced people to drugs.

"Her letter was funny and strange and encouraging. She wrote about how becoming a mum was impacting on her and her life. It was clear she was struggling with how gross and bloated and disgusting everything had become – the *Vanity Fair* story had just come out. She was talking about not having an identity of her own and just being this signifier. Shortly after she sent the letter she tried calling me. I called her back, and I think we talked every day for about a year and a half.

"Her and Kurt had paid for the printing for my fanzine, cos I'd run out of money. So they sent me 300 bucks to have as many fanzines as I could. Also, Courtney had given me this box of the first two issues of *Pretty On The Inside* to put out in *Hit It Or Quit It*. Her fanzine within my fanzine: I was also given a photo of Kurt, Mark Lanegan and Dylan dressed like Babes In Toyland for Halloween and I put them on 50 copies but it was a weird thing to put even in the fanzine, cos people wanted to know how I was connected with Nirvana. I was going through all this Riot Grrrl stuff and had a falling out with all these Riot Grrrl people, and she'd had a similar thing – it was the beginning of her falling out with Tobi and Kathleen who'd written her fan letters and then written letters behind her back to Kurt.[8]

"Sometimes she'd talk about her problems with being famous, and my problems being this weird teenage enigma in Minneapolis. I'd have people throw bottles at me and heckle me when my band would play. She'd talk to me about what songs Kurt was writing and what she was trying to do."

## NOTES

1 'Radio Friendly Unit Shifter' was another proposed title for the third album.

2 Steve Albini, the man behind Big Black and Rapeman, was a mainstay of both Touch And Go records and the US independent rock scene. In the studio, Albini was – and is – renowned for the 'live' feel he achieves with bands, with particular attention paid to the drums, and the microphone set-up. He prefers to be called a 'recording engineer' rather than 'record producer', seeing his job to capture the band's sound, not dictate it. He refuses royalties, and charges a flat daily rate. Kurt was attracted to Albini for his work on the Pixies' *Surfer Rosa*, and more particularly, The Breeders' debut *Pod*. Albini has also worked closely with The Jesus Lizard, the romantic, guitar-led English band The Wedding Present, and abrasive English singer Polly Harvey.

3 The four awards were Viewer's Choice, Best Music Video, Best Alternative Music Video and Best New Artist.

4 Surreally, Duff McKagan played in ace Seattle powerpop trio The Fastbacks early on.

5 Star Pimp were a geeky, fuzz-box laden, female-fronted San Francisco punk band.

6 '20 Years In The Dakota' that drew parallels between the press' vilification of John and Yoko, and Kurt and Courtney.

7 B.A.L.L. were a seriously awesome, whacked-out, heavy rock band from NYC, starring Don Fleming, Shimmydisc label boss Kramer and The Rummager. 1989's 'difficult' third album, *Trouble Doll*, is the one to hear. Kramer's other band, formed with actress Ann Magnuson – the sexually charged, humorous and trippy Bongwater – was even finer. Their incredible fourth album, 1991's *The Power Of Pussy*, has an undeniable sadness, as well as a rampant carnality, obscenity and pornography. New York's Shimmydisc records – Dogbowl, King Missile, B.A.L.L., Bongwater, The Tinklers, Daniel Johnston, Boredoms – kicked *butt*.

8 Or so Courtney claimed at the time . . .

## CHAPTER 23

# The Royal Couple

LA,'92: *MM* photographer Stephen Sweet and me are on an hour-long taxi ride into the Valley, searching for a warehouse where hordes of old film outfits are kept so we can kit Kurt and Courtney out as devil and angel for the 1992 *Melody Maker* Christmas cover. It's an oppressively hot day, and we arrive there only to find all the costumes are vile, musty and old, and that the couple don't want to go through with our idea anyway. We return to the house: Courtney has copper-red hair and Kurt suggests painting 'Diet Grrrl' on Frances Bean's stomach when Stephen takes her photo. They refuse to be photographed together, a random decision that probably cost Stephen a new house. Ah, the vagaries of the music business!

The following is drawn from my two-part interview with Kurt and Courtney that ran in *Melody Maker* over the Christmas period, '92–'93. The interview itself took place before the couple moved back to Seattle.

***Part One***

*"This is the hardest job I've ever had," the reluctant star begins. "I can't believe it . . ."*

*He pauses.*

*"I like it, though!" he exclaims. "I'm thoroughly enjoying myself. It's just a lot more demanding than I expected."*

*He pauses again.*

*"You know, she can fart as loud as I can . . ."*

*"Oh, Kurt!" his wife interrupts, offended.*

*"And burp as loud as I can," he finishes unabashed, smiling his mischievous little smile.*

*"Keep it down," his wife scolds him. "It's not feminine."*

*But she's a baby. Babies are allowed to fart.*

*"Oh, OK," the protective mother says, mollified, looking proudly at the wide-eyed sproglet by her side.*

*Does having a baby make you see life in a different way?*

*"Definitely," replies Courtney. "Yeah . . ."*

*She stops, distracted by the look in her husband's eyes. He's rolling 'em.*

*"Stop it! Why do you do this?" she shouts.*

*"Do what?" he asks, innocently, as Frances reaches out for his hand.*

*"Switch off when the tape recorder switches on."*

*"I've pretty much exhausted the baby opinions," Kurt Cobain – America's most successful 'punk rock' star – says, defensively. "I just don't have anything important to say. I mean, duh, it's fun, it's great, it's the best thing in my life."*

*Silence falls over the bedroom. We go back to watching the latest* Ren And Stimpy *cartoon, the new cult favourites of young America. Frances Bean Cobain's nanny appears, ready to take the little one – a bouncing, almost nauseatingly healthy, blue-eyed child (Kurt's eyes, Courtney's nose) – downstairs for her nap.*

*Silence. Courtney takes a sip of lukewarm strawberry tea. I take a gulp of vodka. Kurt belches.*

*We all have appearances to keep up.*

*Kurt and Courtney's apartment is prime LA, surrounded by palm trees and winding pathways lined with foliage and security fences.*

*Inside, one room is set aside for Kurt's paintings – strange, disturbing collages and images (he used to paint headless babies when his wife was pregnant, now he paints angels and dolls). There's a large, old-fashioned kitchen with a mirror running along the length of its outside wall, sundry guest rooms up top. Upstairs, Courtney's wardrobe is crammed with antique 'baby doll' dresses. It's larger than some flats I've lived in. Well, almost.*

*Pizza crusts and half-full doughnut containers litter the spacious main room. There's a telescope, guitars, old rock books, clipped photos, baby things scattered everywhere – prime space is given over to a tasteful pink crib, bedecked in ribbons. A stereo in one corner blares out Mavis Staples.*[1] *The place has an air of being only half lived in, as do most LA residences. As I arrive, the couple are lying on the double bed in the master bedroom with Frances Bean ("Frances! Say hello to your Uncle Everett!" – Courtney). She: wearing a nightie. He: in pyjama bottoms and the ubiquitous scruffy cardigan and T-shirt. On the TV screen, three male rock musicians wearing dresses surreally smash instruments, regardless of the backing track. It's the new Nirvana video for 'In Bloom'. Courtney's sifting through a coloured box-load of Nirvana letters, sent to Kurt by just one girl. There are about 30 or 40 of them, all painstakingly hand-coloured, hand-lettered, with audiotape accompaniment.*

*"Look, Kurt!" Courtney picks on one particularly lurid specimen.*

*"She's spelt out your name over these envelopes . . . oh, here's a picture of her . . . [pause] . . . oh, she's got a muscular wasting disease . . . we have to write back. We've got to! She's an outsider, just like me!"*

*Kurt grunts affirmation. We pore over her scribbling with renewed interest, grateful that we've never been thus afflicted. Someone puts her name down on the Christmas card list. Kurt decides he wants to tell us about his high school days, but then dries up.*

*"That's because you're a stoned retard," Courtney teases him. It's well known that Kurt spent many hours at school partaking of the demon weed.*

*"Go on!" Courtney urges her husband. "I always talk! I'm sick of it."*

*Another pause. Frances gurgles slightly, a happy thought obviously striking the Bean. There's no sign of the 'Diet Grrrl' graffiti her father had drawn on her stomach earlier. Kurt sighs.*

*Kurt 'n' Courtney (or Kurtney, as they're collectively known) have only given two joint interviews before – both to American publications. They wanted to speak to* Melody Maker *to clear up certain matters mostly arising from a profile of Courtney that appeared in the September issue of* Vanity Fair, *an up-market fashion magazine.*

*Clearly, we'll have to tread carefully.*

*Courtney mumbles something from where she's sitting, behind the bed by the ghetto blaster. Sorry?*

*"You were wrong," she says. "I should have been sullen and demure."*

*What?*

*"When I asked you that question a couple of years ago," she explains. "In a bar. In LA."*

*You can't hide your personality – well, maybe you can.*

*"I wouldn't have minded," she whimpers. "I used to be sullen and demure."*

*She's referring to when she first met me, last year, when she asked me how she should behave in relation to the press.*

*"I used to be really loud and obnoxious," Kurt interrupts. "And then I stopped hanging out with people."*

*Why?*

*The singer shifts from where he's lying, sprawled out on the mattress. Courtney moves to switch the TV off.*

*"Because I was tired of pretending that I was someone else just to get along with people, just for the sake of having friendships," he replies. "I was tired of wearing flannel shirts and chewing tobacco, and so I became a monk in my room for years. And I forgot what it was like to socialise."*

*But didn't you drink?*

*"Yeah, I drank," he agrees. "And I was obnoxious when I drank too much. Then there was a period during the last two years of high school when I didn't have any friends, and I didn't drink or do any drugs at all, and I sat in my room and played guitar."*

*Then, when you formed Nirvana, you started drinking and hanging out with people, and you were back to where you were a few years before.*

*"Not really," responds Kurt, stretching. "I still have the same best friends I had a few years ago. The scale of social activity that I have is so fucking minimal – nothing, my entire life – so the little bit of socialising I did at parties when I was loud wasn't much more than when I started socialising again in Seattle.*

*"I started hanging round with people like Mudhoney," he continues. "Mainly they were just other people in bands. I wasn't really part of a thriving Seattle social scene. Both Chris and I thought of ourselves as outsiders – we wrote that song, 'School', about the crazy Seattle scene, how it reminded us of high school.*

*"It hasn't got any different. I just . . ."*

*He pauses, choosing his words carefully.*

*"I guess living in LA makes me more reclusive," he says, "because I don't like LA at all. I can't find anything to do here. It's pointless going out and trying to make friends, because I don't have these tattoos and I don't like death rock."*

*"Axl wants to be your friend," Courtney reminds him, sitting back down again. "Axl thinks that if I wasn't around, you and him could be backstage at arena rock shows fucking self-hating little girls."*

*"Well, that was always my goal," replies Kurt, sarcastically. "To come down to Hollywood and ride motorcycles with Axl on the Strip – and then you came along and ruined it all."*

*"That's what Axl says," Courtney explains. "Did you hear about that show where he got on stage and started saying something like, 'Nirvana's too good to play with us. Kurt would rather be home with his ugly bitch . . .'"*

*Well, it's true, isn't it? Not the 'ugly' part. Kurt would rather be home with you, bathing Frances Bean, wandering around in your nightie, than out bonding with Axl and the boys. Why should he act any differently? It's weird how some famous people want to hang out with other famous people, just cos they're all famous.*

*Do you like it here in Hollywood, Courtney, or are you fed up with running? From what I know of your life, it seems you've been running for a very long time.*

*"I just always ended up back here," she muses. "Jennifer [Finch, L7]*

*lives here, and she's always been a pretty good friend. I'd call her and say, 'This town didn't work out!' and she'd go, 'Oh, come back to LA!' It's so big it can just absorb you. People here are so . . ."*

*She pauses, struggling to find the right words.*

*"We thought it might be easy to live here because people are trained to deal with fame," she says. "The thing is, however, it's not really like that. They don't stare, but they know who you are and the second you leave the store, they're on the phone to their friends . . ."*

*She pauses again.*

*"It's not even that," she corrects herself. "I wouldn't have got nearly as much trouble if I hadn't chosen to live here. I just thought it would be interesting to go into the mainstream and fuck things up because people always say they're going to, but no one ever does – and I didn't have any choice, really. It's weird here: nurses calling Cowboy Capers [a Hollywood delivery firm] for their Valium prescriptions. It's scary, because everybody wants the fame. They all want fame."*

*"Fame is more of a reality here," her husband agrees.*

*"See, here's where it started, too," she adds, "before I became the poisoner of my husband, before I occupied this position I'm now in. But until we started going out, I never realised that's how the people in LA really are."*

*Do you feel poisoned by Courtney, Kurt?*

*"By Courtney, or by Courtney's stigma?" he asks. "Poisoned by . . . the whole fucked-up misconception of our relationship. Everyone seems to think that we couldn't possibly love each other, because we're thought of as cartoon characters, because we're public domain. So the feelings that we have for each other are thought of as superficial."*

*"It's not everybody who thinks that, though," Courtney adds. "It's a couple of has-been, pontificating, male rock stars and, mostly, women who work in the American music industry. I think that's because, in the early Eighties, if you were a woman and you wanted to play music, there was a real slim chance you would succeed. So a lot of women who wanted to empower themselves within rock without being self-loathing joined the music industry – and these are some of the most vicious women I know.*

*"I've heard industry women talking about how horrible L7 are, I've heard industry women talking about how unattractive P.J. Harvey is, which is ridiculous . . . I just think these powerful women have this real competitive, jealous nature that manifests itself like this. And when I married Kurt, they went into overload.*

*"It's insane, this real complex issue . . . it's an attempt to create something out of nothing – the whole superstar thing. They at least try to take away my intellect, and take away my ethics, and create . . ."*

*She pauses again, jumbled.*

*The thoughts are pouring out too fast for coherent speech. Spend even five minutes in Courtney's company, and you'll be overwhelmed by the torrent of words and ideas that pour from her. Courtney is rumoured to spend up to 12 hours a day on the phone. To her, to think is to be.*

*You must find it annoying, Kurt, that people perceive you to be this stupid henpecked husband, because that's implied in the whole image of Courtney Love's devious and evil nature.*

*"Yeah, there've been quite a few articles like that," he growls. "I don't know how to explain what happens to me when I do an interview, because I usually shut myself off. It's really hard to explain. I just don't like to get intimate. I don't want anyone to know what I feel and what I think, and if they can't get some kind of idea of what sort of person I am through my music, then that's too bad.*

*"I don't see how people can get the idea I'm stupid," he continues. "I know my music's semi-intelligent. I know it takes a bit of creativity to write the kind of music I do, it's not just a wall of noise. I know there's a formula to it, and I've worked really hard at it.*

*"I've always been the kind of person that if I think someone thinks of me a certain way, like I'm stupid – then I'll act stupid in front of them. I've never felt the need to prove myself. If someone already has a misconception about me, then fine, let them have it all the more. I'll be happy to massage that."*

*Jackie, Frances Bean's nanny, shouts from downstairs that Kurt is wanted on the phone. Kurt tells her to tell whomever it is to call back later. I take another gulp of vodka and continue.*

*Here's a question that's been bothering me for a while. How subversive are Nirvana? For a number of reasons, not least of which is her sassiness and the way she gets up the establishment's noses, Courtney is subversive.*

*But Nirvana?*

*"We aren't," replies Kurt, tartly. "It's impossible to be subversive in the commercial world because they'll crucify you for it. You can't get away with it. We've tried, and we've been almost ruined by it."*

*"There have been things that have happened to us that are so . . ." Courtney trails off, momentarily wordless.*

*"Like, after the baby was born," she continues, "a social worker walked into my room with a picture from* Vanity Fair, *trying to take our baby away. Having to get lawyers to the hospital, just having crazy, crazy shit. Having friends' mothers horrified, because one person lied! It's OK to say that I'm obnoxious, because I am . . ."*

*Her anger overcomes her.*

*"It's amazing what damage that one article has done," Kurt snarls.*

*It certainly painted Courtney in a very bad light, as the 'bad girl' of American rock – a gold-digging parasite, a mother who took drugs while she was pregnant, a 'Yoko' who tried to break up Nirvana, a malcontent who argued bitterly with her 'best friend' Kat Bjelland, a fraud, an obsessive, a heroin addict. It conveniently overlooked the fact that she used to be – and presumably will continue to be in the future – a highly respected artist in her own right, especially if the new single ('Beautiful Son') is anything to go by.*

*"Kurt didn't want to play the [MTV] video awards, for instance," his wife continues. "Never mind that if he didn't play the video awards, they'd never show clips of his or my band again. That wasn't it . . ."*

*"Also," says Kurt, "they wouldn't have played any Gold Mountain acts, like Sonic Youth, Beastie Boys . . ."*

*Yeah, I heard about that from Thurston Moore. They threatened your management with a boycott of all their acts if Nirvana didn't toe the line. You can be as subversive and radical as you like, but they only really bother with you once you're big enough to be a threat.*

*"So all the political nastiness that I've heard of for years from independent record people is true," Kurt snarls. "A lot of people, especially people like Bruce Pavitt and Calvin Johnson – people who have been pretty successful throughout the years with introducing underground, independent music and creating a community feel within their environment and just exercising the whole DIY ethic – have known a lot of people who have experienced the major label fuck-overs . . ."*

*Calvin Johnson runs Olympia's fiercely partisan, independent K records, Olympia being where Kurt moved to after leaving Aberdeen and forming Nirvana. Calvin used to help Bruce (Sub Pop) Pavitt run a fanzine in the early Eighties.*

*Olympia is a small liberal college town an hour's drive away from Seattle, which, in 1991, housed the International Pop Underground Convention, thus providing part of the initial stimulus for Riot Grrrl. Nirvana even contributed a track to the convention's* kill rock stars *compilation LP, before being (apparently) ostracised for signing to a major label.*

*Kurt continues with his rant.*

*"I know that some of these people I used to look up to – people who have put out magazines or who've had a record label for years – these people had the real inside dirt on what a major label is like, but they never told me . . ."*

*He sounds oddly betrayed.*

*"I never paid any attention to mainstream press, either," Kurt continues. "I never understood the mechanics of it, how it works. I never read a major label rock'n'roll interview, except when I was a kid in*

Creem *magazine and that was always so tongue-in-cheek. I've never read a* Rolling Stone *article that I can think of – just skimmed through a couple of the political ones."*

*From below, we can hear the sound of Frances Bean crying. Kurt half rises to go downstairs, but changes his mind. "Now that it's happened, I still can't help laughing at it," he adds. "But it went overboard. It went just a little bit too far to take in good humour . . ."*

*"A little bit?" Courtney interrupts him, angrier than ever. "Social workers coming to take your baby because of something you didn't do and you didn't say is not judicial, and it's not justice . . .*

*"That article," she spits. "The whole drug thing . . ."*

*She's floundering because she's so riled.*

*"We did drugs and it was really fun, and now it's over. Anybody who knows me knows I'm way too paranoid to get wasted all the time . . ."*

*She pauses again, searching for the right words.*

*"It's just so insane," she cries, "what it's done and who it's hurt because of one woman's vendetta. When you look at it, Everett, I think the end of rock is pretty near when Madonna is trying to buy Pavement for a million dollars and put out Xerox fanzines.*[2] *When Madonna thinks that I am the cutting edge – that's how you can judge how out of it she is."*[3]

*The* Vanity Fair *article dwelt fairly and harshly on Courtney's claim that Madonna was vampiric, ready to take from Courtney what she wanted, and leave the rest for dead.*

*"Who," Madonna was quoted as saying, "is Courtney Love?"*

*She should know. It was Madonna who asked her manager to sign Courtney's band to her label last year. It was Madonna herself who phoned Courtney to arrange a meeting. Want to know why I'm so sure? I spoke to Courtney immediately after the call, and nobody makes shit like that up.*

*"I wish I'd never come in her eye-line," Courtney cries. "Isn't there any punk rock value in the fact I turned her down?"*

*"It's twice as bad for Courtney," explains Kurt, "because she hasn't even had the chance to prove herself like I did. It's one thing for me to be subversive at this point, because I can afford to be. I can pretty much get away with ripping up a picture of the Pope on television and it wouldn't create so much of a stink as someone commercial like Sinéad [O'Connor] – or Courtney, who doesn't have the security of having sold lots of records . . ."*

*The baby cries. Courtney interrupts her husband, excited.*

*"How did it go so fast," she asks, sounding genuinely bewildered, "from having a record of the year in* Village Voice *and being perceived as an artist, to being Nancy Spungen in three months?"*

* * *

*There's something I'd like to get down on tape now. I'd forgotten that Hole were one of the inspirations behind Riot Grrrl. Seeing Hole play live was pretty much what motivated Kathi Wilcox, bassist of Bikini Kill, to form a band.*

*"Kathi wrote me a letter saying she wanted to start a band and what should she do," recalls Courtney. "And I wrote her back and said she should find the biggest slut-bitches in her town that everybody hates. I thought if there were three people who were like the town bitch in one band that would be fucking amazing. I don't know if that really happened, but it turned out to be . . ."*

*Kathi recounted this event in her fanzine,* Bikini Kill, *about the formation of her band, adding that, when she saw Courtney, it was like "The guitar went into flames, almost a religious experience."*

*"I'm very supportive of them, on a personal level," Courtney adds.*

*She then moves on to talking about Julian Cope, stung by the recent adverts for his tour running in the music press that personally attacked her.*

*"He's one of these people who actually knows me," she says, hurt. "Not well, but he does know me, and who was somebody – for all his horns and back-up singers – when I was younger, really affected me and charmed me and made me feel, 'Wow, for an English person he's pretty original and cool.'*

*"And for him to be slagging me in his poem in his ad, it's like . . ."*

*She pauses, struck by another thought.*

*"Wait, where do people get this fucking Nancy Spungen thing from?" she demands. "I'm sorry I dyed my hair. Is it that superficial? Is it just because I'm blonde?"*

*Well, it's partly because you joked about it in a couple of interviews.*

*"It's this Nirvana/Sex Pistols thing, too," she corrects me.*

*But Your Jo(e) Average Person On The Street never seems to realise that people in power can joke about what are perceived to be serious matters. Perhaps they aren't allowed to. Maybe it's just because Your Jo(e) Average Punter is obtuse, but I doubt if it's even that. It's probably more that it's always been the case that people take whatever they want from what they read.*

*"Right," Courtney agrees. "But the fact of this, too, is how women, unless they totally desexualise themselves, have no intellect subscribed to them . . ."*

*"That's totally true," murmurs Kurt.*

*"If I were subscribed intellect, nobody would ever think that I was Nancy Spungen, because Nancy Spungen is not intellectual," she finishes. "It's because I've chosen to negotiate the world on the world's terms – I've said, 'OK, I'm going to have this experiment,' after having*

*spent most of my life being plain and un-decorative. So I decided to lose some weight and wear some lipstick and see what fucking happens – be a little dangerous, more subversive."*

*"It's a lot fucking easier," her husband says.*

*"It was for me," she agrees, "but, at the same time, now what's happened is that we are married and these people are trying to take away my livelihood and they're trying to take away the thing that matters the most to me, other than my family. And now they're even trying to take away my family.*

*"So me and Kurt get married and we're peers – his band were always ahead, but they started before us – then, suddenly, his band get real successful and we're not peers any more. He's involved in free trade in America and I'm not making much of a dent. It's just amazing to see."*

*She pauses.*

***Part Two***

*"One thing that's pleased me," Courtney says, drawing on a cigarette, "that I've been really surprised by and learnt a lot from, is the psychic protection I've got from so many girls and women . . ."*

*She pauses. I'm not sure what point she's trying to make.*

*"I mean, it's really fucking obvious, unless you're stupid," she goes on. "Like, I walk around and say, 'Oh, he should have married a model, but he married me,' with a straight face."*

*This is more familiar territory. This is, in fact, the line Courtney usually takes when she's trying to wind up the people who think Kurt's marriage to her was ill-advised. Her argument is something like, well, whom should he have married? A model? The point being, Kurt's not like that.*

*"There were like 60 sarcastic things I told* Vanity Fair*," she goes on, "that they quoted straight because they're so stupid. Their whole attitude was like, 'Let's go and be condescending to these wacky punk rock kids and make allusions to how, in their world, success is bad. Aren't they cute?' "*

*But Kurt, you never said success was bad, did you?*

*"What kind of success?" He sighs. "Success in general? Financial success? Popularity in a rock band? Most people think success is being extremely popular on a commercial level, selling a lot of records and making a whole bunch of money. Being in the public eye.*

*"I think of myself as a success because I still haven't compromised my music," he continues, "but that's just speaking on an artistic level. Obviously, all the other parts that belong with success are driving me insane – God! I want to kill myself half the time."*

*But people still don't get it. Nirvana catch a lot of flak from people I know because (a) Kurt Cobain whines a lot, and (b) Nirvana slag off corporate rock bands, even though they're one themselves.*

*"Oh, take it back from him, the ungrateful little brat!" mocks Courtney.*

*"What I really can't stand about being successful is when people confront me and say, 'Oh, you should just mellow out and enjoy it,'" explains her husband, interrupting her. "I don't know how many times I have to fucking say this. I never wanted it in the first place.*

*"But I guess I do enjoy the money," he relents. "It's at least a sense of security. I know that my child's going to grow up and be able to eat. That's a really nice feeling, that's fine, but you know . . ."*

*But Frances will only be treated nice to her face: people will kiss her butt and stab her in the back at the same time.*

*"Yeah, but she'll know about it, because she'll come from us and she'll be cynical by kindergarten," Courtney answers, looking fondly at the empty crib. "She's already cynical."*

*"I don't mean to whine so much," continues Kurt. "There are just so many things that I'm not capable of explaining in detail."*

*"I am," Courtney interjects.*

*"But people have no idea of what is going on," her husband complains. "The sickening politics that are involved with being a successful, commercial rock band are real aggravating. No one has any idea."*

*"It doesn't matter though," Courtney almost shouts. "The whole thing with you is that you've got your success and been victimised by it and I still haven't proven myself to myself.*

*"I remember last year Kat came up to Chicago and we went to this bar and they started playing* Nevermind *– this was just when it was starting to get really big. So we sat there and drank and drank, and got really mad. Because we realised that no girl could have done that. I want to write a really good record and I haven't done it yet."*

*This is where I disagree with you, Courtney.* Nevermind *was a great record. But so was [Hole single] 'Teenage Whore'.* Nevermind *was made by a bunch of blokes. Why should it have been made by a bunch of girls?*

*"No girl could have come from the underground and done that," she argues. "It's just the fact that somebody did it. It happened."*

*But Hole were an astonishing band, particularly live. I can't think of many artists who come across so powerfully and fatally magnetic on stage as you. I mean it.*

*"Yeah, but Everett, not many people remember that," whispers Courtney.*

*What I'm saying is that you're judging yourself on your husband's terms, and that's ridiculous. You don't write songs like Kurt writes songs – why should you? You're different people. If the commercial market refuses to accept your music, then it's a failing of the market, not your music.*

*Another couple of things: your marriage and pregnancy means that your own career has been put on hold this past year. You haven't written many new songs, you haven't had a record out, you haven't played live. Which means that people who only know about you through Kurt have nothing to judge you on but your public 'bad girl' image.*

*The bottom line is, you have to get back out there and perform if you want to regain the respect for your music you once had. No amount of hedging will alter that.*

*"The fact I judge myself on Kurt's terms is part of me subscribing to the whole male rock ethic, too," Courtney explains. "You know, Kim Gordon – like every woman I respected – told me this marriage was going to be a disaster for me. They told me that I'm more important than Kurt because I have this lyric thing going and I'm more culturally significant, and they all predicted exactly what was going to happen.*

*"I said, 'No, that's not going to happen,'" she recalls, bitterly. "Everyone knows I have a band, everybody knows about my band, I can do this – my marriage is not going to be more important than my band."*

*She pauses and then explodes.*

*"But not only has my marriage become more important than my fucking band, but our relationship has been violated," she cries. "If we weren't doing this interview together, no male rock journalist would dare ask Kurt if he loved his wife. 'Do you love your wife? Do you guys fuck? Who's on top?' I'm not saying you would, Everett.*

*"They wouldn't ask him to explain his relationship with me, because he's a man and men are men and they're not responsible for any emotional decisions they make."*

*She's shaking with emotion now.*

*"Men are men!" she exclaims. "They do the work of men! They do men's things! If they have bad taste in women . . . whatever! All of a sudden, Axl and Julian Cope and Madonna decide I'm bad taste in women and it's the curse of my life and tough shit. What can I say?*

*"I never experienced sexism before," she says, excited. "I really didn't experience it in any major way in connection with my band until this year, and now I have. The attitude is that Kurt's more important than me, because he sells more records. Well, fuck you. Suck my dick!"*

*There's a brief silence. Courtney's just taking a breather before going for the kill.*

*"You wouldn't look good in leather," Courtney says to Kurt, looking fondly at him. "Kurt and Julian Cope and Axl Rose and Danny Partridge riding around in a limousine, fucking women that are idiotic*

*and self-hating that want to fuck them to get some attention for themselves, instead of grabbing their guitars and going, 'Fuck you, I could do this better, with integrity and with more ethics than you, and with revolution and – fuck you!' I created this rock thing in the first place for my own amusement and I'm going to take it back.*

*"I always have lofty ideals about it and yet I deserve it." She's resorting to sarcasm now she's so worked up. "I deserve to get raped by a crowd if I stagedive in a dress, I deserve to get raped if I go to a bar and I'm wearing a bikini, I deserve to get raped because I did all these things I said before – nipping a hot young rock star in the bud, having a baby, having been a stripper, having used drugs . . .*

*"And then to be perceived as a child abuser!" she exclaims, anguished, off on another exclamatory track. "Two of the last people on earth that would ever hurt a child or a harmless person. Ever. I've never picked on harmless people. I've always picked on people that I felt were corrupt or more corrupt than me."*

*Silence.*

*"All right," she adds, gently. "I'm done now."*

*From far off comes the sound of a baby crying.*

*"I didn't think in those terms when I was doing my record," Kurt says, stirring. "Although, at the end, I did allow the record to be produced cleaner and more commercial than I wanted it to be. I don't know what the reasoning for that was, besides just being dead tired of hearing the same songs. We'd tried remixing it three times and we rang this professional mixologist [Andy Wallace] to do it and, by that point, I was so tired of hearing the songs, I said, 'Go ahead, do whatever you want.' "*

*"You say you didn't think in those terms, cos you're more punk than me?" Courtney asks him, affronted.*

*"No, I'm not saying I'm more punk than you," snaps Kurt. "Actually, I'm wondering right now if I wasn't subconsciously thinking that I did want success, because I did . . ."*

*"Is it such a sin to say that you wanted to be in* Billboard*?" she asks him. "That you knew you were going to be popular, or that you were going to be rock stars?"*

*"I knew we were going to be popular, but I didn't know we were going to be this popular," he says. "I'm so tired of saying this. I'm so tired of saying, 'Oh, we thought we were going to be as big as Sonic Youth,' and all that shit. It's so fucking boring at this point."*

*"But isn't there another part of you, that personality who wrote 'Aero Zeppelin' that . . .?" starts Courtney.*

*"Right!" her husband exclaims. "There is! And maybe, because I allowed the record to be mixed commercially enough that any song could*

*get on the radio, maybe I was thinking it would be kinda funny, really hilarious to see how far we could push it, how popular we could get."*

*"Well, that was my excuse until this marriage thing happened," Courtney shrugs, "that it would be really funny and kinda hilarious, and now I don't think it's either of those things. Yet the desire is still there. And I'm not the Yoko Ono of Nirvana – I'm the one who lost two band members, not Kurt."*

*"You didn't lose any band members over this," Kurt shoots back, annoyed.*

*"Not over this," Courtney replies. "But my band lost two members. You can make what you want out of it, and say that you were ruining my life. Where's the theory that you're the one wearing the pants? That you're running me into the ground? Nobody's come up with that theory. You haven't been victimised with the whole macho guy persona."*

*"I'd rather be in your position than to be thought of as a fucking idiot," complains Kurt, "a puppet on a string, being manipulated 24 hours a day. You didn't lose your band members over anything connected with this marriage, or by being associated with me at all . . ."*

*"I'm not saying I did . . ."*

*"I've lost more drummers than you have," Kurt points out.*

*It's interesting that Courtney should raise this point about the imbalance in your relationship. Someone remarked to me recently that they think Kurt Cobain is one of the biggest sexists in America.*

*Kurt becomes seriously upset.*

*"That's not true," Courtney says, leaping to his defence. "No. I've looked for it, but not at all."*

*"A comment like that is just such a pathetic last attempt at having some kind of opinion . . ." starts a riled Kurt, before I cut him off.*

*No, hold on. I think what they're referring to is your relationship – the way it's so effectively castrated Courtney's art (especially when Courtney was such a strong female role model before her marriage). The comment wasn't meant to be a reflection on you – just on the way people perceive your marriage.*

*"Right," says Kurt. "I don't understand why that happens."*

*"The whole thing of the media theorising on two people's relationships," says Courtney, "is my fault for allowing journalists into my home. I see now why people say, 'I'm not going to talk about my famous husband.' I understand now. We've become these two cartoon characters you can theorise about . . ."*

*She stops, and starts on a different tack.*

*"You can't please everybody," she says. "I don't care if I get criticised. I don't give a shit if I get a bad review. I don't care if people say I'm a*

*bitch or I'm obnoxious, cos I am those things. Or that thing of being a witch, or that [*Melody Maker *features editor] Paul Lester guy saying I'm ugly and [minor US chart star] Debbie Gibson's pretty . . . I fucking think that shit's funny. It's this crazy lying. Do you understand?"*

*She's starting to rail again now.*

*"It's my life," she says, almost spelling the words out.*

*"A social worker coming into my hospital trying to take my baby away from me, trying to take my baby away from me. Spending hundreds of thousand of dollars on lawyers . . . Whatever. I know it sounds crazy . . ."*

*She pauses, takes another breath.*

*"The* Vanity Fair *article put quotes in my mouth, there were things I was supposed to have said about Madonna that I never said," she continues. "They twisted things around.*

*"I didn't do heroin during pregnancy. And even if I did, even if I shot coke every night and took acid every day, it's my own motherfucking business. If I'm immoral, I'm immoral. It's not your goddamn business if I'm immoral or not."*

*She pauses, trying to sort her words out.*

*"A photographer for* Vanity Fair *caught me smoking a cigarette. It was on my birthday. I smoked something like four cigarettes in six hours. I was smoking a cigarette in one of the pictures. And the lines around the block for magazines that wants that picture is so big that this motherfucker has charged me $50,000 to get the pictures back. It's blackmail, pure and simple blackmail. And if I don't get them, they'll keep after her [Frances Bean]."*

*In some states in America, these photographs would be enough to prove that Courtney is 'unfit to mother', thus giving the State legal rights to remove the child into their custody.*

*"They filed a legal report on me based on* Vanity Fair *and nothing else, no other fucking evidence, that I was an unfit mother," she continues. "That I smoked during my pregnancy. Fuck you. Everybody smokes during their pregnancy – who gives a shit? And it's all because I married Kurt, because he's hot, young and cute.*

*"And I certainly don't buy people worrying about the baby," she adds. "If you want to ask about my drug problem, go ask my big fat smart 10-pound daughter, she'll answer any questions you have about it."*

*"I just want to get back to the Kurt-complaining-about-his-success thing," says Kurt, interrupting his wife's flow of invective. "How many questions in every article are placed on my success? People are so obsessed with it, that's all I ever get a chance to talk about. Ten different variations on the same question every interview."*

*"You funny little boy!" Courtney squeals, mocking his tormenters. "You didn't set out to be successful! What an angle! Cinderella!"*

*"It's a fine scam, it's a fine image," he says, sarcastically. "I'm getting really fucking bored with it."*

*"Why don't we switch?" Courtney says, bringing the interview full circle. "I'll be demure and sullen and you'll be loud and obnoxious."*

*Then you'd be Axl Rose.*

*"No, then I'd be his codpiece," she corrects me. "Fuck me Kurt, fuck me Julian, fuck me Julian's drum tech, make me feel my worth! It's ridiculous. And, for $50,000, I have to buy this image of a really pregnant woman with a garland in her hair smoking a cigarette, this whole fertility image with a cigarette. As if I did it deliberately, as if I did it to provoke!"*

*She's off again.*

*"Someone called up my manager after the* Vanity Fair *article, saying, 'Does Courtney think she's being that whole Seventies cool shock rock thing?' – as if I had planted this whole drug, cigarette sensationalism!*

*"Ask Kurt," she continues. "I didn't want to talk to* Vanity Fair, *because I knew it was based on the Madonna thing and our marriage. They don't even do rock people – I sell 60,000 records, what the fuck do they want with me? But I did it anyway, because I was so sick of industry women talking and saying terrible things about me.*

*"I thought, if I was in* Vanity Fair, *it would shut their fucking mouths and they'd leave me in peace," she laments. "But that was my mistake and I just shouldn't have done it. I should have known more about the mainstream press and how they operate.*

*"Also, the whole thing where it made me seem to be so competitive with Kat [Bjelland] is just like . . . I was totally provoked. I was mad with Kat about something, and I got provoked into gossiping about something off the record."*

*According to* Vanity Fair, *Kat and Courtney are embroiled in a bitter argument over who started wearing the 'baby doll' kinderwhore dress both are famous for. Kat was quoted as saying, "Last night I had a dream that I killed her. I was really happy."*

*"And then she provoked Kat into saying things about me, by telling her what I said," Courtney continues. "If you notice, Kat hasn't gone on record as saying anything shitty about me, and I certainly didn't mean to go on record saying anything shitty about her. We're not best friends any more, but we don't hate each other. It's ridiculous that it's been turned into something where you have to choose between one of us. We're different. We write differently.*

*"But that's why it's so competitive," she adds. "That's why this whole foxcore/Riot Grrl thing is so competitive. It's like rap music.*

*There's a void, and there's only room for one of you in the void."*

*The tape switches off. Courtney decides she's said enough. Kurt nods in agreement. Time to view the new Nirvana video once more, and discuss whether to go out tonight. Irish rock band Therapy? are playing the Whisky-A-Go-Go.*

*Courtney decides to accompany me – the first time she's been out in LA since giving birth.*

*Kurt prefers to stay in, and mind the baby.*

## NOTES

1 Lead singer of The Staple Singers, Mavis had a soulful gospel contralto. The album Kurt was playing was the Steve Cropper-produced *Mavis Staples* (1969).

2 "'I really do not like myself much and feel guilty for even expressing myself,'" said Pavement singer Stephen Malkmus to me once, quoting. "That's the classic line everyone comes out with. I feel like that and I'm sure the Kurt Cobains of this world also do. What are you supposed to say? *I Hate Myself And I Want To Die* is a great title for a Nirvana album. It's a shame he didn't use it. What can you do? Love yourself and start to live."

3 Madonna's record label Maverick is best known for signing multi-million-selling whiny Canadian pop star Alanis Morissette.

# CHAPTER 24

## Foetuses And Seahorses

"KURT's a vampire," states Jennifer Finch.

He's a what?

"I think that Kurt was a great melody writer," explains the former L7 bassist, "but he lacked a lot of real life experience and the ability to really tell a story and communicate a specific solidarity of what he was thinking. Courtney is a master at that. She's a great songwriter; she's a great lyricist; she's a great writer. At a certain point, it became mutually beneficial. I think so many people think that Kurt elevated her as an artist, or as a personality. I tend to question that. What do you think?"

"That's interesting," comments Seattle photographer Charles Peterson, "because Kurt has the emotion, but for the most part his lyrics are nonsensical. I remember telling Jonathan [Poneman] that Sub Pop should print the lyrics to *Bleach* because no one could understand what Kurt was on about. He replied, 'No. The lyrics are nonsense, so that would backfire.'"

I've got a Nirvana songbook for piano and it's like . . .

"*'I'm a mosquito/My libido'*," laughs Jennifer. "I see what you're saying."

"Courtney's a real storyteller," agrees Charles. "She takes you into an environment and creates it in a very solid imagery that is mixed with what can be interpretive and what isn't. Like, 'The lamp is blue'."

He pauses: "Do you think that translated into Kurt's personal life of being unable to talk about things?"

"There would be times where Kurt would be very specific and communicative," replies Jennifer, "and other times where he couldn't communicate anything about what his needs were. He was very much a veil of chaos, of non-specific emotion. Courtney would be like, 'I need this to happen. I need this to feel comfortable.'"

How would you describe Courtney? Imagine I've never met her.

"There's not a single sentence that can engulf it," she says. "The wind blows and it changes, it becomes different people. I still think she never should have gone out with Kurt."

On December 15, DGC released *Incesticide* – a collection of BBC sessions, demos, outtakes and unreleased songs. The record company had been hoping to put out a new album, but Kurt hadn't even started writing the lyrics for his latest songs. Plus, Nirvana wanted to sort out the 'real fans' among their audience, testing their loyalty by releasing material that wasn't as immediately accessible as *Nevermind*. The fans weren't found wanting. Even with little promotion, the album sold 500,000 copies within two months and went on to sell 3.2 million copies worldwide. But, as one might expect, the quality of the songs varied.

"Christ," Kurt wrote in the original press release about 'Aero Zeppelin'. "Let's just throw together some heavy metal riffs in no particular order and give it a quirky name in homage to a couple of our favourite masturbatory Seventies rock acts."[1] The track does indeed sound heavy, dated, a throwback to another time when Kurt and Krist were greatly influenced by their immediate peers, specifically Soundgarden. Likewise 'Mexican Seafood' and 'Hairspray Queen', both also lifted from the Dale demo – although here, the main touch point is Scratch Acid.

"Their inclusion griped me for a while because I wish I'd had a chance to remix them," Jack Endino comments about the songs.[2] "They literally took the tape from the first day I recorded them, when we mixed 10 songs in one hour, and put it on *Incesticide*. They didn't give me a chance to clean them up at all."

Far better are the tracks culled from UK singles such as 'Sliver' and 'Dive', the former blistering with angst, the latter one of the finest songs Nirvana recorded with its naïve Olympian imagery and churning bass line.[3] 'Stain', too, is a relentless catalogue of disturbance and alienation, worthy of an early Ramones lyric. The next handful of songs I can take or leave: 'Turnaround' barely varies from the Devo blueprint, and I always preferred The Vaselines' originals of 'Molly's Lips' and 'Son Of A Gun' to Nirvana's straight ahead tributes. The sped-up, almost throwaway '(New Wave) Polly', drawn from the Mark Goodier sessions, pales next to the *Nevermind* version, a studio experiment that probably shouldn't have been allowed to see the light of day. 'Beeswax' and 'Downer' are fine, but didn't need reviving. 'Big Long Now' failed to make it on to *Bleach* – and with good reason. It's a mournful, sub-Melvins slow grind.

Pretty much the finest song is the final one, 'Aneurysm' – also from the Mark Goodier session – a manic, impassioned start gives way to a heavy drumbeat and Kurt screaming out his feelings of love for Tobi Vail. You don't need to understand the words to relate to the emotion. Kurt's voice connects on a fundamental, gut level.

The sleeve featured Kurt Cobain artwork: a troubling painting of a skeletal figure and distorted baby-like creature with a masked face – the larger of the apparitions is holding a couple of red poppies. The mood is sombre, hints at betrayal – both familial (hence the album's 'joke' title) and general. There's precious little emotion, more a feeling of cold rejection.

The back cover, meanwhile, is a close-up of a yellow rubber duck.

In the sleeve notes, Kurt recounts the story of a trip he took to the Rough Trade record shop off Portobello Road in west London in search of the first Raincoats album. It wasn't in stock, but the shop assistant knew The Raincoats' former violin-player Ana de Silva – and told him that Ana worked at an antique shop nearby. So she drew Kurt a map, and off he set.

"Sometime later," he wrote, "I arrived at this elfin shop filled with something else I've compulsively searched for over the past few years – really old, fucked up, marionette-like wood-carved dolls. I've fantasised about finding a shop filled with so many. They wouldn't accept my credit card but the dolls were way too expensive anyway. Ana was there, however, so I politely introduced myself with a fever-red face and explained the reason for my intrusion. I can remember her boss almost setting me on fire with his glares. She said, 'Well, I may have a few lying around so, if I find one, I'll send it to you' (very polite, very English). I left feeling like a dork, like I had violated her space, like she probably thought my band was tacky."

A few weeks later, Kurt received a vinyl copy of The Raincoats album through the post, complete with Xeroxed lyrics, pictures and signatures. "It made me happier," he wrote, "than playing in front of thousands of people each night, rock-god idolisation from fans, music industry plankton kissing my ass and the million dollars I made last year."

Kurt went on to detail all the other small instances where he felt his fame had been a blessing – the drawings he'd been sent by Daniel Johnston[4], The Stinky Puffs[5] single Jad Fair's stepson Simon had posted to him, playing on the same bill as Wipers' singer Greg Sage in LA, being asked to produce the new Melvins record, being given a signed first edition of revered junkie beat poet William S. Burroughs' *Naked Lunch*, being sent a Mazzy Star LP[6], playing 'The Money Will Roll Right In' with Mudhoney, kissing Krist and Dave on *Saturday Night Live* "just to spite homophobes", meeting Iggy Pop, playing with bands like The

Breeders, Urge Overkill, TV Personalities, the ever-riotous Jesus Lizard, Hole, Dinosaur Jr . . .

"While all these things are very special," he explained, "none were half as rewarding as having a baby with a person who is the supreme example of dignity, ethics and honesty. My wife challenges injustice and the reason her character has been so severely attacked is because she chooses not to function the way the white corporate man insists. His rules for women involve her being submissive, quiet and non-challenging. When she doesn't follow his rules, the threatened man gets scared."

On January 1, 1993 Kurt did a photo shoot dressed in his pyjamas, at the Four Seasons Hotel in Seattle, for a cover story for *The Advocate*. "It was nice," remembers Charles Peterson. "There were no publicity people, I didn't have an assistant. There was no hair and make-up. That was in the hotel they were staying in downtown, at Pike Place Market." Kurt was noticeably open in the article, flattered to be interviewed by a gay magazine[7]: talking freely about his wife, his band, his drug use, the hatred he felt towards Lynn Hirschberg and his business dealings.

"Courtney comes across in the press as the Nancy Reagan of this relationship," journalist Keith Allman commented. "It's just sick," Kurt replied. "God! I don't want to say something like, 'Well, if anything, I wear the pants in the house.' We have influence on each other. It's totally 50-50. Courtney insists on this: she has a tab when she borrows money from me that she has to pay back [this wasn't strictly true]. She's only up to $6,000. We're millionaires, and she goes to Jet Rag [an LA vintage clothing shop] and buys clothes – $5 dresses. Big deal! I'll gladly buy her some $5 dresses."

Kurt revealed that he and Courtney spent a million dollars the previous year: $80,000 on personal expenses, $380,000 to the taxman, $300,000 on the house in Carnation, and the rest on doctors and lawyers. "That's including car rentals, food, everything," he said. "That's not very much; that's definitely not what Axl [Rose] spends a year."

Krist started 1993 by visiting his ancestral home of Bosnia and Herzegovina – then caught up in the middle of a terrible civil war, as the former country of Yugoslavia ripped itself into several different sections following the break-up of the Soviet Union. He met up with members of the Tresnjevka Women's Group, a volunteer organisation offering support to female refugees, and learnt of the horrific torment suffered by numerous women – Bosnian, Muslim, Croatian – who'd been raped by the marauding Serbian army. On his return, he started organising a benefit concert to take place in San Francisco in April 1993. The bassist also wrote an article for the US music press, highlighting the troubles.

Back in Seattle, the post-Nirvana hype machine was still going crazy: Gap and Next started featuring 'grunge' sections in their clothes shops, *LA Times* ran a ridiculous feature entitled 'Grunge-A-Go-Go', the highfalutin *Vogue* topped even that with its 10-page fashion spread on 'grunge-wear'. The gist of all these articles seemed to be an emaciated, anorexic, childlike look as typified by models such as Kate Moss, draped in $500 silk flannel shirts and carefully ripped jeans, often smoking a cigarette, with editorials pontificating about how the young people of the day were growing tired of 'high' fashion and wanted a return to something more organic, more 'street' . . .

Oh, and 'layering' was in – the style first invented out of necessity by impoverished 20-year-olds purely as a means to counter the cold. The fact that this style wasn't unique to Seattle – and that its most visible practitioners, Nirvana, weren't even from that city – seemed to pass most of the writers and fashion editors by.

'Grunge' films were released – some excellent (the lo-fi, laconic *Clerks*, Richard Linklater's self-fulfilling *Slacker*), some downright crap (*Singles*, *Sleepless In Seattle*). TV stations decamped to Seattle and started making sitcoms based in the city – most notably, the evergreen *Cheers* spin-off, *Frasier*.[8] And still the recording industry signing frenzy went on – anyone in a band from Seattle, anyone sporting long unkempt hair and ill-fitting flannel, anyone who vaguely used Nirvana and the Pixies' loud/soft dynamics and screamed in a certain 'soulful' way, anyone connected with Sub Pop in any way at all . . . Stone Temple Plagiarists, Alice In Chains, Spin Doctors, Helmet, Crackerbash, The Posies . . . a thousand mediocre bands.

Then there were all the acts championed by Nirvana – Pavement, Sebadoh, Melvins, Daniel Johnston, Mudhoney, L7, Babes In Toyland, Hole, Tad, *et al.* Some retained their independence. Some got swallowed whole. Heedless, they all got lumped together and cast as one – and dropped the second that 'grunge' was deemed out of fashion.

Crazy as it seemed on the outside, on the inside it was even crazier. Halfway through January, Nirvana played two 'Hollywood Rocks' shows in Brazil, alongside L7, Red Hot Chili Peppers and Alice In Chains.

"L7 brought along this guitar tech named Ian," recalls Earnie Bailey, "and he and I became friends. Kurt kept asking me questions about him and I couldn't figure out why. Then I discovered it was [Fugazi/Minor

Threat singer, and founder of Dischord records] Ian MacKaye . . .!"

The first concert was at the massive Morumbi Stadium in São Paulo on January 16. Estimates of the arena's size vary, from 80,000 to 110,000. Either way, it was the largest gig Nirvana ever played – in a place that most of them had barely heard of, despite it being the world's fifth largest city. Before the show, some of the band and crew went out walking through the shanty town communities that surrounded the venue: "São Paulo is a little bit like Pacific Rim," explains Earnie. "It goes on and on forever. The dividing line between rich and poor is very thin. They had food stands set up in villages of plywood and corrugated tin houses."

Unsurprisingly, the band had a minor nervous breakdown on stage. Beforehand, they decided to play a 'secret set', where they'd switch instruments and cover Terry Jacks' lightweight, yet strangely affecting tear-jerker, 1974 smash 'Seasons In The Sun' – the song that Krist had told Dan Treacy was one of Kurt's favourites ever (listen to the lyrics: it's scarily prescient) – and play snippets of other cheesy pop hits, including Kim Wilde's 'Kids In America', a brief burst of Queen's 'We Will Rock You' and the horrendous Duran Duran single 'Rio', with Kurt on drums and Dave on vocals.

"That had to be the worst show Nirvana ever played," comments Earnie. "The secret set was a reaction to the slick TV the kids have to endure down there, where the shows are all like *Donny And Marie*. They kicked into that set, and there were 90,000 people – silent. It felt like a drunken party, something you would see in the basement. Certainly not an arena rock show." Forty minutes in, Krist hurled his bass at Kurt and walked off . . . but the band were under contract to play for 90 minutes, so off went Alex MacLeod and Earnie in search of the errant bassist.

"Krist walked back on stage, grabbing the tossed bass from the floor and didn't retune it or swap it out. So I grabbed a cantaloupe and rolled it on stage like a bowling ball," the tech laughs. "Kurt picks it up and starts smashing it on his strings, playing his Jaguar with the cantaloupe, and the juice and seeds ran all the way down inside his pickup cavities."

The following month, Kurt designed a guitar for Fender, half-Jaguar, half-Mustang. "I think he literally cut a photo of a Jaguar and a Mustang in half and stuck the two pieces together, and they produced that with little refinement," recalls Earnie. "The first time they sent it over, it looked like a wood shop project.

"That show, they destroyed everything in sight," he continues. "We had a lot of trashed speakers. But where were we going to find more of these British-made speakers? We had to overnight them from Los Angeles, and that cost us a bundle. I remember being stressed out about it. Krist pulled me aside and said, 'You don't need to worry about that stuff any more. We can afford it. You should relax and come to the beach with us.' "

The tension on stage was mirrored by the tension off: both Kurt and Courtney's moods were swinging wildly. After a particularly violent argument with his wife, Kurt threatened to jump out of his high-rise hotel room window. So the two tour managers – Jeff Mason and Alex MacLeod – wandered the streets of São Paulo, trying to find another hotel for Kurt to stay in, one without any balconies.

"I've actually got a funny memory of that hotel," says Earnie. "All the balconies overhung the interior – so if you looked down, you could see 20 floors down to the bar. I was awakened at 3 a.m. by someone playing the trumpet just outside my door. It turned out to be Flea [Red Hot Chili Peppers bassist], wearing a pork pie hat and playing to the stragglers at the bar. I looked down and saw hotel security looking up trying to count what floor we were on. So I yelled to Flea and he had this look of 'Oh fuck' and dashed into his room. The security guards never found him."

The following day, Nirvana and entourage flew into Rio de Janeiro: "We were all on it – the Chili Peppers, L7, Nirvana, Ian MacKaye, maybe even Alice In Chains," recalls Earnie. "When we came in for the landing, the plane suddenly flipped up and stalled in the air, then came back down and veered off the runway. The pilot slammed it down hard and hard and hard and finally got all the wheels on the ground. It was brutal. Flea was sitting next to me, and was in a trance after the plane stopped. As we were walking off the plane, he put a hole in the cockpit door, he kicked it so hard."

In Rio, the band stayed for a week at the Intercontinental Hotel on the Atlantic Ocean: "We went a few miles down to the beach, and there was a little shack selling home-made liquor," remarks the ubiquitous guitar tech. "It was powerful stuff." The following day, everyone went hang-gliding. "Kurt went first," Earnie continues. "You fly way out, over these trees and a freeway, then you fly over our hotel and the tops of the city buildings, then you fly over the ocean, come back in and land on the sand. Dave said it was the best experience of his life. Kurt said the same thing; he said he'd never done anything that he enjoyed so much."

On January 23, Nirvana performed in front of 70,000 people at Rio's Apotoese Stadium. Flea played trumpet during 'Teen Spirit', tackling the guitar solo with considerable aplomb, and the band played an *ad hoc* 17-minute version of a new song, the full-on scream-fest of 'Scentless Apprentice'[9] – both, much to the crowd's growing mystification. For the encore Kurt wore one of Courtney's black, low-cut, lacy dresses – "I think he had lemons in his bra," says Earnie – while Dave sported a Jennifer Finch bra. According to some accounts, this show was even more lacklustre than São Paulo.

"They didn't even break a string," comments the guitar tech, sounding oddly cheated. "I was expecting everything to be wiped out, because we were leaving the next day and had all the time in the world to fix stuff when we got home. They weren't horrible. They were just bad. Oh, I take it back. Kurt smashed his blue 'Courtney' Telecaster at the end, and she ran out and tried to stop him, but Jennifer Finch helped him drop a Marshall cabinet on top of it. I think they'd had a fight."

The band looks tired on the video.

"The problem might have been that everybody stayed out too late the night before," suggests Earnie. "The promoter took us out to a club where they had this entire section roped off for us, with food and drinks and a private bartender. It felt like we were being over-accommodated, plus the music was not to our liking, so we asked if we could go somewhere else. So they hustled us into the van and raced us across town to another place. By the time we got there, everything had been set up exactly the same. It was like, 'Yikes, they're going to do this all night.' So we decided we might as well hang out: there was an alternative rock band playing, and Krist and Courtney got up and played. Kurt wasn't there.

"On the way home, we went by this area with something that looked like a scaled-down version of the Washington Monument in it. Someone screamed, 'Pull over,' and we all jumped out to check this thing out, and there was a wrestling match on the lawn. It might have been Courtney and me. I'm not sure. Somebody threw a drink and it hit the monument and we all started laughing hysterically.

"Within moments, we had Brazilian police pull up and surround us. It was very sobering – we had no idea what they'd do. It wasn't like we were in Seattle any more. Our driver scuttled us back into the van, and he was shouting at the police officers through the windows and we couldn't understand a word of it, and it went on and on and on. We were all completely silent. Eventually, we were driving again – and we could see the driver was rattled. He looked back at us and said, 'Don't ever do anything like that again. You're lucky tomorrow night is the concert. If they were to arrest you now, a lot of revenue would be lost. But if the concert had already happened, you wouldn't have been let off this way.' That was scary."

* * *

On January 19–22, halfway through their stay in Brazil, the band recorded some songs at BMG's Ariola Studios with Craig Montgomery producing: "We went into this very major studio in Rio that was owned by the Brazilian division of their record company," recalls Craig. "Their A-room was very modern and slick, but the B-room looked like it hadn't been touched since about 1976. It had this great sounding old Neve desk, a beautiful Studer tape machine and all these big old vintage tube Neumann microphones. I knew a little more about recording than I had in '91, but again it was just a situation where the band wanted to throw down ideas on tape so they'd have something for Steve Albini to listen to."

Among other songs recorded was a warped distortion fest entitled 'I Hate Myself And I Want To Die' that had an extended intro of noise plus suitably jaded, disinterested vocals from Kurt. It showed up on *The Beavis And Butt-head Experience* compilation of the two MTV cartoon couch potato critics' favourite rock bands[10], a slightly pointless jam. Far better was the recording of 'Milk It' – also a song that seemed to be made up as it went along, but with a good meaty guitar sound and inspired use of the loud/soft dynamic, the lyric itself a depressed look at cohabitation and Kurt's stomach problems. *"I have my own pet virus,"* Kurt sang, bitter-wise. *"Her milk is my shit, my shit is her milk."* Also totally excellent was 'MV' (Moist Vagina), a future B-side and a song that revelled in its own anguish and Kurt's unmatchable scream.

Then there was the equally engaging and mischievous 'Gallons Of Rubbing Alcohol Flow Through The Strip', an improvised number that owed more than a passing nod to the Melvins' more reflective moments, Kurt spewing out seemingly random lyrics lifted from his journal: *"Even though we haven't had sex for a week"* . . . *"She is tied up in chains"* . . . *"I haven't had a date forever"*. The mood is playful, the instruments engaging in a game of cat and mouse, almost daring one another to explode in fury. Kurt laughs evilly a few minutes before the end, before asking, "One more solo?" The band responded accordingly.

"They wanted to goof around," Craig explains. "They did a song that Kurt had written in his head and they did a cover of 'Seasons In The Sun', and a full version of 'Heart-Shaped Box' with vocals. Everything else was guide-vocals. By this point, the band weren't having much fun together as people at all, but the mood in the studio was light."

This was evinced by the video of 'Seasons In The Sun' that showed up on the DVD part of *With The Lights Out*. Although the band didn't treat the song too seriously – something that's obvious from Krist's goofy expression while he plucks out the guitar line – it still retained a certain pathos in Kurt's warbled vocals and tentative drumming. You could tell it was a song he really liked.

'Heart-Shaped Box' (or, as it was then called, 'Heart-Shaped Coffin') was the standout: brimming over with rasping guitars and despair, and Kurt's own realisation of the situation he had placed himself in with Courtney. The title was inspired by Courtney's habit of laying out her collection of heart-shaped candy boxes in the living room of the couple's apartment on North Spaulding in LA: and was, in part, a love song – although clearly lines such as *"I am buried in a heart-shaped coffin for weeks"* indicated a bleakness that isn't present in most relationships. The stop-start chorus of *"Hey wait/ I got a new complaint"* is an obvious reference to the fact Kurt was all too aware that sections of the press saw him as a whiny, spoilt rock star – and also sent a passing nod in tribute to the Ramones' famed chant *"Hey ho/ Let's go"*.

To temper its dark sentiments, Kurtney made up a story about Courtney sending Kurt a heart-shaped box while she was courting him, but of course this was as much a part of the homespun Nirvana myth as the bridge in Aberdeen, referenced in 'Something In The Way'.

"As long as they were making music they were OK," comments Craig. "As unhappy as Kurt was, he had a lot of respect for the other guys in the band."

The day after the Rio concert, they all flew back to Seattle.

". . . so we messed around the house in LA, and then they [Kurt and Courtney] decided they were definitely moving back to Seattle," recalls Cali DeWitt. "They hired movers to pack everything up. It was like the third or something, and the rent was paid until the end of the month. Courtney said, 'Why don't you and Rene stay here because all our furniture is here and they're not packing it up until the end of the month and then you guys will have a place to stay for the next few weeks.' This was because I still didn't want to go and be the nanny. So this sounded good to us. We were like, 'Oh, we have a swanky place to stay for three weeks.'"

"We'd been pretty much destitute in LA, living hand-to-mouth, before the call came from Kurt and Courtney," says Rene Navarette. "They called us because they were having trust issues with some people. They needed to get out of LA quick. When I walked into the house I saw Kurt on the floor with brand new Frances in his lap, playing the advance of the new Butthole Surfers record for her. He was so excited about it. There was some goofy conspiracy stuff going on. There was a Chihuahua, an enemy *Vanity Fair* writer, and a few trash cans full of syringes they wanted to get rid of – they gave me a BB gun and told me to shoot any photographers I saw lurking round the house. Cali and I were real excited to help them move: two teenagers helping pack up two rock stars and a baby and getting them sent off to Seattle."

What date are we up to right now?

"Let's say January or February. [It was probably February: Courtney was in an LA court on February 1, giving evidence about the incident involving Victoria Clarke and the cocktail glass. The case was later dropped.] I wasn't in LA much longer after that," Cali replies. "Rene and I stayed on, and acted like it was our house. We had a fine time. I remember the day the movers came. Rene was directing them. I didn't want to wake up, so I was sleeping on the couch, waiting for it to be the last thing in the whole house for them to move. When they moved the bed in the master bedroom, one of the movers pricked himself on a needle that was stuck in the mattress. He freaked out. He's like, 'I'm going to the police and I'm going to go to the newspaper. What if I get a disease and what if I get AIDS from that needle?' Rene talked him out of it by giving him my Nirvana 12-inch and telling him it was very rare. I remember listening to Rene go into this long spiel about how much the [not rare at all] 'Come As You Are' 12-inch was worth."

On February 14, Nirvana checked in as the Simon Ritchie Group[11] at Pachyderm Studios, in the tiny township of Cannon Falls, Minnesota, 40 miles south-east of Minneapolis, to begin recording their third album with Steve Albini. The trio spent a total of 14 days in the studio, laying down the basic tracks in six days (they completed recording on Kurt's 26th birthday) – at a total cost of $24,000 for the studio and a one-off $100,000 fee for Albini. The entire album was done live.

"When we went in," Kurt told Dutch magazine *Oor*, "only half the compositions were ready. The rest originated from messing around in the studio. We restricted ourselves to a deadline and a recording budget. I like to work that way." Kurt later remarked that he'd wanted Nirvana to sound like *In Utero* ever since the group began: understandably so. *In Utero* is an *amazing* album, easily Nirvana's finest moment in the studio: the production suits the band suits the songs suits the sentiments suits the melodies suits the noise segments suits the time it appeared in. And it still sounds fresh even today – long after the production on *Nevermind* fades into early Nineties territory. Nirvana sound totally on top of their game: fuelled by all the controversy and rumours and hype, *burning* in their desire to cleanse themselves of everything, everything except the music itself.

Right from the opening line of the album, *"Teenage angst has paid off well/ Now I'm bored and old"* ('Serve The Servants'), it was clear that Kurt had grown as a lyricist and songwriter. Marrying Courtney had clearly helped him. Witness the powerful, moving couplet from the same song: *"I tried hard to have a father/ But instead I had a dad"* – sentiments that echoed John Lennon's exorcism, *"Mother, you had me but I never had you"* on his first post-Beatles solo album, 1970's *John Lennon/Plastic Ono Band*.

"Initially, the song was about coming of age during a time where you're old enough to support yourself without the aid of your parents," Kurt wrote in an early version of his unused sleeve notes. "I've always felt that a person doesn't necessarily have to force themselves to love their parents simply because of blood."

"Oh lord," he wrote in another version, "the guilt of success. During the past two years I have slowly come to the conclusion that I do not want to die. I am now no more of a recluse than I used to be. I lived in the K [circled with a shield, in the style of the label's logo] kingdom for a few years hiding in a little apartment. And now I stand in my room without a sandbox."

One major way that the album differed from the previous two was in how the drums were recorded. Kurt wanted live ambience, something he felt could only be achieved by placing microphones around the drum kit. Albini felt the same way. Thirty mics were used for the drums alone.

Albini had a certain *reputation* among the indie rock cognoscenti – a reputation the former Big Black frontman partly encouraged. He was known as a straight talker, possibly misanthropic – verging on misogynistic – an incredibly hard worker, but one who didn't tolerate either the music industry's bullshit or fools lightly. The misogyny charge was a little dubious: Albini just liked to wind other folk up big time – especially people he perceived as being too far up their own ass. Hence the name of his post-Big Black hardcore band, Rapeman: a name that brought any amount of controversy with it.

He was dubious about working with Geffen, but intrigued by the idea of recording Nirvana, and by Kurt's reassurance that the last thing he was looking for was another hit single. Albini even claimed he wasn't a fan: "This will sound stupid," he said shortly afterwards, "but I felt sorry for them. The position they were in, there was a bunch of bigwig music industry scum whose fortunes depended on Nirvana making hit records. It seemed obvious to me that fundamentally they were the same sort of people as all the small-fry bands I deal with."

The studio complex itself was situated at a big, modern house filled with Sixties kitsch. In the centre of the house, where the band all stayed, was a big, sunken living room: "Mike Brady [fictional architect dad of TV's *The Brady Bunch*] meets Frank Lloyd Wright [famous American architect, noted for his innovative use of light and space]," as Krist put it to *Impact*. The recording studio was situated 100 yards away, through the woods: it was spacious, wood-panelled and in immaculate condition. The room where the drums were set up looked out on to a picturesque Minnesota winter scene.

Although the band wanted to make a do-it-yourself punk rock record, they had difficulty readjusting: the first three days were mostly wasted after it was discovered they hadn't bothered to bring their equipment with them, and had to have it shipped out. Albini was appalled at the waste of money: "They wanted to Fed Ex a boom box in," he remarked disgusted, "instead of buying a new one. They wanted to fly their guitar tech in just because Kurt was having difficulty tuning his guitar."

"There was some debate about whether they should have taken me along," confirms Earnie. "The first day they were there, I got a phone call saying, 'Pack your bags, we can't get anything in tune.' Then Krist called, like a day later, and told me not to bother because the record was finished."

If Kurt and Nirvana had been allowed to release the original version of *In Utero* as mixed by Albini – the engineer claimed he had a spoken agreement with the band that no one was allowed to touch the recording after him – then rock would have been revolutionised. I swear it. Primal screaming was matched only in intensity by Dave Grohl's drumming. Tunes were partly subverted to Kurt's need to release the anguish he felt at his role as Spokesman for Generation X. All his hatred, all his drug-fuelled paranoia and disgust – it poured out with a bleak fury that was unnerving to listen to. Fuck *Unplugged* being the way forward for Nirvana. *In Utero* was the real shit, the one where they paid homage to the underground.

I can still remember Courtney's anguished phone call now.

"Jerry!" she cried. (Courtney frequently used my real name.) "What's your address? I need to send you a copy of Kurt's new album. His record company, his management, everyone is telling him there aren't any tunes on it. They want him to re-record it. You have to defend him, he's totally depressed about it all."

A few days later I received the tape: it sounded great. More importantly, it sounded like a more honest representation of Nirvana than anything since 'Sliver'. So there weren't any tunes present? Christ! What about the traumatic, almost bruised-beaten 'Rape Me'? Kurt started writing its caustic lyrics while the band were still mixing *Nevermind* – the sweet guitar motif merely served to add poignancy to the song's dark message to all the fans, the record industry people, the media who Kurt perceived as wanting a part of him. "I was trying to write an anti-rape song in a very bold way," he told *Melody Maker*'s Stud Brothers. "What I've realised is that in order to get your point across, you have to be obvious. That's how most people want songs to be. They need it thrown right in their face."

No tunes? Christ! What about the album's first single, the cancerous 'Heart-Shaped Box'? The song starts slow, menacingly; Kurt's voice rarely sounding so powerful, in control, reminiscent of his friend Mark Lanegan in the way it cracks over certain consonants – before it suddenly explodes into a frenzy of contrition, guitar buzzing plaintive and pleading. This was pure, primetime Nirvana, as commercial as they ever got. Or, as Kurt put it in his journals: "[Feminist author] Camille [Paglia]'s vagina/flower theory bleeding and spreading into the fabric that Leonardo [da Vinci] would have used to improve his hang-glider, but he died before he could change the course of history."

"It can't be coincidental that *In Utero* is full of images relating to babies and childbirth from the title onwards?" the *MM* journalists asked. "This must be an album about Kurt Cobain becoming a father."

"No, it is coincidental," the singer replied. "I've always been fascinated by reproduction and birth. I've been painting foetuses for years and making foetus dolls out of clay. There's just something glorious about pregnancy. I've got so much respect for women because they bear children. They seem the more sacred humans to me. Sea horses interest me. The female carries the babies first then transfers them to the male who actually gives birth. Shared pregnancy."

No tunes? The album didn't get changed *that* much.

Listen to the plaintive, gentle 'Dumb', a tune busting all over with plangent guitar chords. When I first met Kurt, he told me that he acted according to how people treated him. So if they thought of him as a dumb-ass punk rocker, he was more than willing to act like a dumb-ass punk rocker. "That [song] is just about people who're easily amused," he told the Studs, "people who not only aren't capable of progressing their intelligence but are totally happy watching 10 hours of television. I've met a lot of dumb people. They have a shitty job, they may be totally lonely, they don't have a girlfriend, they don't have much of a social life, and yet, for some reason, they're happy."

Listen to the moving sorry note 'All Apologies' and try denying its effect all these years down the line. *"I wish I was like you,"* sings a jaded Kurt, wanting nothing more than an end to all the shit. *"Easily amused. Everything is my fault. I'll take all the blame."* God, he tried so desperately to believe in Love.

Even now, I sit here and listen to 'Pennyroyal Tea'[12] and my glasses cloud over with tears again. Is this the effect that music that is supposed to have no resonance has on me? *Is this what music means to you?*

"Sometimes," Kurt remarked, "I wish I could take a pill that would allow me to be amused by television and enjoy the simple things instead of being so judgmental and expecting real good quality instead of shit."

There were songs that rocked out, hard and long – 'Very Ape' (originally known as 'Perky Or Punky New Wave Number'), 'Radio Friendly Unit Shifter' (previously entitled 'Nine Month Media Blackout', in response to the *Vanity Fair* article) – with squalls of feedback and grungy guitars, but these were more than offset by Kurt's tendency to shove in an aching melody when you least expected it. Plus, the band's fondness for mischief was still apparent. On the European version of the album, 'Rubbing Alcohol' repeats the same trick as 'Endless, Nameless' on *Nevermind*, coming in after several minutes of silence.

The brilliantly titled 'Frances Farmer Will Have Her Revenge On Seattle' – inspired by the celebrated story of the Thirties film star, institutionalised after she rebelled against her studio's star system, and subjected to electroshock treatment – boasts an opening bass line that unconsciously echoed the minimal, spooked sound of Young Marble Giants. It's an uncomfortable song. Kurt saw parallels between the way the actress was demonised by the mainstream press[13], and the media's treatment of his wife. "The conspirators are still alive and well in their comfortable, safe homes," Kurt wrote in his journal. "Gag on her ashes. Jag on her gash. Uh, God is a woman and she's Back in Black."[14]

"[Frances Farmer] was institutionalised numerous times and, in the place in Washington where she ended up, the custodians had people lining up all the way through the halls, waiting to rape her," Kurt told the Stud Brothers, quoting the popular version of the actress' story.[15] "She'd been beaten up and brutally raped for years, every day. She didn't even have clothes most of the time.

"[It] was a massive conspiracy involving the bourgeois and powerful people in Seattle, especially this one judge who still lives in Seattle to this day. He led this crusade to so humiliate her that she would go insane. In the beginning, she was hospitalised – totally against her will – and she wasn't even crazy. She got picked up on a drunk driving charge and got committed. It was a very scary time to be confrontational."

Courtney's call to me in the middle of March confirmed a story that was shortly to break in the *Chicago Tribune*. Two days before the album was mastered (on April 21, at Gateway Studios by Bob Ludwig), the paper published an interview with Albini in which he stated, "Geffen and the band's management hate the record. They considered it an indulgence when Nirvana asked to record with me. I have no faith the record will be released." Dave Grohl later reported that Gary Gersh, the band's A&R man, was 'freaking out' at the prospect of the band recording such an important album (for DGC, leastways) in such a punk rock fashion. "It was like, go ahead, have your fun – and then we'll find you another producer," he told *Q* in September '93.

At the time, though, the band and management strongly denied Albini's statement, even going so far as to take out a full-page ad in *Billboard* on May 17 to rubbish some of the claims made in follow-up stories in *Billboard*, *Newsweek*, *Rolling Stone* and elsewhere.

"There has been no pressure from our record label to change the tracks we did with Albini," stated Kurt in a DGC press release – directly contradicting what Courtney told me. "We have 100 per cent control of our music. We – the band – felt the vocals were not loud enough on a few of the tracks. We want to change that." Geffen also issued bland assurances that they had no intention of messing with their cash cow.

Later, Kurt even claimed that he realised as soon as he got back to Seattle that there were problems with the mix: "The whole first week I wasn't interested in listening to it and that usually doesn't happen," he told *Circus*. Again, this directly contradicts Courtney's phone call, where she was attempting to get friends and industry allies of Kurt's to rally round the recording to place pressure back on to DGC so they would realise it was a great record.

Whatever. Seemed like a storm in a teacup, really. I wasn't going to deny that overall the album made for heavy listening, but wasn't that the thrill? The album wasn't revamped that much, actually. Nirvana ended up dropping several of the noisier tracks from the finished version, the vocals got brought forward a little more in the mix during mastering, and the management brought in R.E.M. producer Scott Litt to 'tidy up' a couple of songs for US radio. A sell-out? Not really. If you want to view it that way, Nirvana 'sold out' the day they signed to Geffen . . . and they wouldn't have sold millions of records, and you wouldn't be reading this book either.

"Krist was really excited about it," recalls Earnie Bailey. "We listened to the album on his boom box the second he got back. It was cool, yet I remember thinking, 'Are you going to release it like this, because it sounds like a practise tape?' It was really raw, it sounded like it had been recorded in 45 minutes – and Kurt's vocal tracks were very dry. It just wasn't as clean as *Nevermind*. But they knew it was the perfect follow-up. It was a really bitchin' 'fuck you' to all the pressure they were facing. But then it really got strange: all of a sudden they were getting beat up [by the record company], and it became stressful, with talk about Kurt quitting."

"I saw the whole thing before it happened," sighs Jack Endino. "I said Steve is going to get all this crap because he's not going to turn the vocals up loud enough or something – and you know how Steve is, he doesn't give a shit about major labels. I didn't want to be in Steve Albini's shoes, being the guy with all those expectations piled on him to make *Nevermind 2* – because that's what the rest of the world wanted. Meaning all the fans, the record company, the managers, the lawyers, all the slime and the business people – the people writing the cheques."

"Kurt wanted to do something different," comments Carrie Montgomery. "He wanted to write different types of songs but I think that he didn't think he knew how. He only knew how to write Nirvana songs. How do you teach yourself how to write a different type of song? Listen to a different Beatles record for a month and figure out a different pattern?"

Kurt wanted to destroy the monster he'd created, that was obvious. Somewhere along the line – the constant press attention, having to deal with crap like MTV and tabloid and *Rolling Stone* journalists, Olympia and the punk rock kids turning their back on him – it turned sour. When Kurt formed Nirvana, he and Krist had been as close as brothers. By the time 1993 was over, he would be travelling in a different van to the rest of the band. What's the point of that? Why be in a band when you don't even want to speak to your fellow members? Are contractual obligations that powerful?

I kept the tape safe the only way I knew how. I threw it unmarked into a pile of thousands and tried to forget I even knew the band existed after Kurt died. It remains there to this day, but I have a feeling someone else released the original version to a bootlegger, figuring something that awesome shouldn't stay hidden forever.

Courtney flew in to Pachyderm, a week into the recording. Steve Albini wasn't impressed by her belligerent attitude, calling her with a "psycho hose-beast." Courtney, in return, added further fuel to the 'Albini is a misogynist' faction by coming up with a great line about how, "The only way Steve Albini would think I was a perfect girlfriend would be if I was from the East Coast, played the cello, had big tits and small hoop earrings, wore black turtlenecks, had all matching luggage and never said a word."

"Courtney called me and said they were making *In Utero*, 40 minutes outside of Minneapolis," recalls Jessica Hopper. "I was old enough to drive but I didn't, so I had to find someone safe enough to the Nirvana camp to bring me – and that was Pat Whalen who was Hole's booking agent.[16] They were mixing the record, and we were all having dinner. Steve's girlfriend was cooking. Steve was making jokes the whole time we were eating, much to everyone's discomfort, about how Dave was going to wake up in the middle of the night with Steve's cock down Dave's throat. Everyone was chewing in silence, laughing nervously. Pat was like, 'So, how's . . .?', trying to make some sort of conversation. Steve was making these real macho, homophobe jokes – dude locker room jokes. Afterwards, they were mixing and played stuff for us in the studio, and Courtney surreptitiously, but not quite, made a tape of the P.J. Harvey record that Steve had just done, and some of the rough mixes of Nirvana tracks."

Was Steve wearing his hat?[17]

"I don't remember," Jessica laughs. "I remember his girlfriend didn't talk. She just cooked. I don't know if she even ate with us. It was more like she served us. Steve Albini seemed like what you'd think Steve Albini would be like – cracking all these weird jokes and making people feel vaguely uncomfortable. [According to Kurt, Steve also had a habit of pouring rubbing alcohol on his ass, and setting it on fire – but one once again suspects a certain liberty with the truth.] We sat on the coach and listened to 'Heart-Shaped Box', and a song that Dave had done, 'Marigold' [originally recorded back in DC with Barrett Jones] – it sounded like R.E.M. to me."

While the band were in the studio, they helped fill the downtime by watching David Attenborough nature videos and making prank phone calls – Albini called Eddie Vedder, pretending to be legendary David Bowie/Marc Bolan producer Tony Visconti and telling him he'd be happy to work with him, if only he ditched the band. The engineer also called up dopey Lemonheads singer Evan Dando[18], pretending to be Madonna's assistant – and then shoved him on hold when Dando started salivating at the prospect of speaking to the megastar. Dave Grohl phoned John Silva, pretending to be in a state of panic, claiming that Krist had been throwing up blood the night before. It was the usual hi-jinx of a rock band in a studio.

"Everyone was friendly, but maybe a little studio stir-crazy," comments Hopper. "I remember thinking 'Heart-Shaped Box' was the best song they'd ever done. It was really dark and there was part of me that wondered if it would be as big as 'Teen Spirit'. There seemed so much more depth to it. It was really, really beautiful.

"One night, Nirvana wanted to go out and see a show," Jessica continues. "So they went to see [local all-female band] The Blue Up. It was an ID show at the 7th St Entry, and I was under age, but they let me in because I was with Nirvana. Kurt sat at the back and tried not to have people look at him. We were only there a little bit. Another time, we went to some weird medical supply store in the Mall Of America [reputed to be the world's largest covered shopping mall]. Kurt dressed up a little so he wouldn't be recognised – not that anyone noticed him anyway.

"Once word had gotten around that I'd gone to the studio and taken Nirvana to a show . . ." She laughs. "Well, people already treated me weird but after that they *really* treated me weird. Everyone's favourite band was hanging out with someone who was 16 – it was so comical."

The same month that Nirvana was in the studio, the split Nirvana/Jesus Lizard single, 'Oh, The Guilt' was released – and *Incesticide* was certified gold (500,000 copies) in the US. The band were also awarded a whole bunch of music awards, or at least nominated for same – Grammys, Brits, NARMs, what-have-you's – but punk rock kids like Jessica knew such industry backslapping exercises were a crock of shit. Maybe that's why Kurtney liked hanging out with her, and not her 'cooler', older, male record-collecting peers.

On March 19, Hole played a secret show at the Crocodile Café where they premiered songs from their forthcoming album *Live Through This*. It was their first concert with bassist Kristen Pfaff, then playing in the unrelenting Amphetamine Reptile three-piece, Janitor Joe. Kristen was dark and intelligent, and a knowledgeable champion of independent music. Winona Ryder, as she acted in *Night On Earth*, would have been perfect to play her. Many from the Minneapolis hardcore scene held Courtney as the Devil, and were aghast when Kristen left her home town for Seattle.

"Hole still needed a bass-player," says Rene Navarette. "The previous year, they'd tried out this girl, Leslie Hardy, but she couldn't play – so they moved her up to Seattle [from LA] and I was trying to teach her, all the while hoping they'd ask me. She didn't work out. That's when they got Kristen. She was amazing."

"Courtney wanted me to play bass in Hole but of course my parents wouldn't let me," Jessica laments. It was actually me who suggested Jessica to Courtney: a sassy 16-year-old with an unusual fixation on underground rock – who could be better? Jessica had also appeared in national US magazines as a typical Riot Grrrl, an act that led to the Olympia and DC Riot Grrrls disassociating themselves from her, as the movement was anti-assimilation.

Jessica continues: "She was like, 'You, me and Kurt have to get together and record a demo and [LA punk fanzine] *Flipside* will be all over it,' but of course it never happened. At the time, it was just her and Eric. My parents were totally frightened by the prospect but in my head it was awesome: I'm glad now I didn't. So Courtney was asking me who she could get, and I told her about Kristen.

"But I got to visit Courtney in LA," the fanzine writer continues. "This was when they were in the middle of a fax war with Albini. The house was a total mess and there were magazines everywhere. We went shopping and Patti [Schemel, Hole drummer] was around some, she ended up driving us. Courtney was shopping for clothes. She was trying to teach me about what cuts and styles of dresses would be cute on me. Things were pretty whacked out but it was really nice. Kurt was withdrawn. It was a lot of chaos. She was very smart, very funny, always entertaining – totally a mile a minute.

"She wanted me to help her clip articles about her and Kurt out of magazines. I remember her dropping them over the balcony into the living room to Patti. I'm surprised they didn't make a hole in the floor. On the way home to drop me off at my dad's house, someone had to either pick up drugs or drop off drugs. I asked Patti, 'Is that what's going on? Come on, I'm not stupid. Why are we driving to Echo Park at one in the morning to run an errand?' She denied it. I think Kurt was frequently overcharged for drugs by his friends. Cali once remarked to me how those two would be getting charged $600 for $100 worth of drugs, naturally. It made them think they were doing a lot more than they were.

"I felt very trusted. They treated me like I was an adult and not like I was a weird kid. They welcomed me into their house and gave me real tea. There was a real air of domesticity underneath all the chaos, like 'Jessica is visiting.'

"I remember these weird skull and babies and limbs paintings: art that would show up in collections later. A dress being nailed up to the wall: collections of little doll heads and perfume bottles. I'd hang out on the couch while they played with Frances. They were still very much parents in the middle of all this weirdness. I definitely felt like they were trying to have a normal life somehow. Courtney made Kurt give me some of Eric's collection of Nirvana bootleg singles and a copy of 'Dive'."

In early March, shortly after Jessica's visit, Kurtney moved into their new home – at 11301 Lakeside Ave NE in Seattle, overlooking Lake Washington, with views of Mount Rainier and the Cascade mountain range. The house cost $2,000 a month to rent, and had three levels.

"Kurt had his MTV award, *The Astronaut*, in the bathroom," recalls Earnie Bailey. "You could either piss in the toilet or on the award. It was hilarious and appropriate. He had the broken K arch-top acoustic guitar from the start of the 'Come As You Are' video on his front door. I offered to fix it up for him."

In the garage sat two cars: Kurt's trusty Valiant, and a grey 1986 Volvo.

"One of his cars was held together by moss," laughs Earnie. "There was this cool classic car lot on Denny that had hip, oddball Sixties cars – and they had a pale blue Dart identical to Kurt's old rotten one. I think Kurt paid 4,000 bucks for the restored one, so he could have the pair."

By this point, Jackie Farry had had enough of nanny-ing. It wasn't so much looking after Frances Bean, whom she adored – it was more Courtney's habit of treating anyone around her as a menial. Frequently, Jackie would be asked to take business phone calls that Kurt wanted to avoid – also, she'd barely been given a day off since she started. Cali DeWitt took over. This changeover coincided with Frances being returned to her parents' unsupervised care on March 25 – which happened mainly because the LA court had no real jurisdiction in Washington State.

"They were like, 'We've made a decision to take Cali as our full-time nanny and you can follow us up to Seattle with Eric,'" says Rene. "So I became Eric's flatmate in Seattle. We went out a lot there – me, Courtney, Eric and Cali. It was a lot of fun. I was able to get the drug situation handled pretty quickly. I had a large amount of doctors from whom I could get any of the drugs needed for stabilising our habits. Then I moved into Lakeside Ave with them, and Cali and I assumed all domestic responsibilities. It was a little sketchy to have me with any sort of a title. Everyone mistook me for Cali. We both had coloured hair. We didn't talk about me too much. I kept around the house. They spoke through me a lot when they were cutting themselves off from the world. I did a lot of speaking with [John Silva's assistant] Michael Meisel trying to explain what was going on."

In April, Courtney flew to the UK to promote Hole's new City Slang single, 'Beautiful Son'[19], a song partway inspired by Kurt: he featured as a young child on the cover, and played bass wearing one of Courtney's dresses in the video (filmed before Kristen joined the band) – thus confirming the lyric, *"You look good in my dress / My beautiful son"*. She played a solo acoustic gig at London's Rough Trade records where she chain-smoked, and Hole appeared on *The Word.*

"When Courtney went to England, that was the first time me, Kurt, Dylan and Cali had a few days to mess around without her," reveals Rene. "We had so much fun. We would go into town, walk into a drug dealer's living room: Kurt, Dylan, Mark Lanegan and Layne Staley[20] coincidentally walking into the same basement at the same time. It was pretty amazing. Everyone had mutual admiration for each other. Now, looking back on it, there were all these great talented guys who were tainted forever because of their drug use."

On her visit, Courtney stopped by *Melody Maker* to help me edit the letters page. The look on our editor Allan Jones' face when I showed him her unexpurgated 1,000-word viewpoint was a joy to behold. Disbelief at her complete lack of grammar was followed by bemusement at the idea we should be giving over space to her ridiculous ideas, followed by anger.

"Everett, we are not printing this crap and that's final," he shouted at me. Allan was an unrequited old school music journalist. He comes from the era of Nick Kent, Charles Shaar Murray and Lester Bangs. By and large, though, he was remarkably tolerant of my escapades at *Melody Maker.* He loved the rock stuff I was championing, but wasn't so convinced by my infatuation with Grrrl-style feminism. Courtney editing a section of his beloved *MM* was pretty much the final straw.

Jones eventually relented. Courtney's letters page and editorial appeared in *MM*, with several explanatory interjections from myself. She used the opportunity to talk about two of her favourite topics of 1993, the Riot Grrrls and feminism. The singer had recently fallen in love with Susan Faludi's powerful feminist screed *Backlash: The Undeclared War Against American Women.*

"When Riot Grrrl began, I was very supportive of it," she wrote. "It seemed as though things were getting better . . . I gave a *Bikini Kill* fanzine to Everett, Kim [Gordon] and Thurston [Moore] and *Spin*, and I would have done anything to promote it, to help it."

That wasn't strictly true. I obtained my fanzine from Calvin Johnson, and probably passed it along to Courtney, but whatever. It is true that Courtney initially aligned herself with my flatmates Huggy Bear and Kurt's old girlfriend Tobi Vail. Hearing about the all-girl concerts that

Huggy Bear had been organising in England during 1992, she demanded that Hole should be allowed to play one.

By all accounts, it wasn't that well attended. Courtney, never one to bask in the glow of political correctness, called a female critic 'fat' from on stage. She talked about how weird it was to play a London show without me there. Indeed, she found it so odd that she took a £130 taxi ride back to my Brighton house afterwards. She soon tired of her new allies, however; especially when it became apparent that they weren't prepared to court fame the way she'd been trained to. Also, her attempts to ingratiate herself within the suspicious and closed world of Olympia, to seek approval from her husband's former peers, failed miserably.

This change of heart was reflected in her hastily written *MM* column.

"I feel plunged back into the Dark Ages," she complained. "Riot Grrrl celebrates the anarchy but also the clumsiness and incompetence of *femme* musicians. That's like giving women high-level corporate jobs even if they can't do the job correctly. I am *not* assimilationist. I am a populist. I believe that everyone, not just people that know Fugazi personally, has a right to revolution, but I'm not going to be dumb about it. I'm going to understand the mechanics of the Empire that I am going to fuck with. I am going to insinuate myself with the best of them."

Courtney's mistake here is rudimentary. She assumes there is only one way to write songs and judge 'competence' (her word) and storm the Empire. There are few parallels to be drawn between women making exploratory music and women holding down high-powered jobs. Maybe the fact Courtney thinks music equates with business might explain her musical direction in the late Nineties/the new century.

"I've worked too hard to put up with too much to be dragged down by the incompetence of a few spoilt elitists," she continued. "Most of us aren't rich and spoilt, drinking gourmet coffee with soymilk and dreaming up daily manifestos for the few. Most of us feel ugly and are lonely, and want to be pretty (or handsome). Maybe some of us want to be pretty because it was, and always will be, powerful. Maybe some of us want to feel good about ourselves, and negotiate the world and have children and even give the Patriarchal Empire a run for its money."

Enough. What Courtney is talking about in the above paragraph is peer approval, not beauty. The 'pretty' she is referring to can never exist because it is a false value placed upon the individual by an inconsistent society. The only 'pretty' that truly exists is on the Inside. So 'pretty always will be powerful'? Surely then, the way forward is to re-educate not reinforce stereotypes. What about wanting to be informed, intelligent,

funny, wise, smart, sassy, crafty . . . a goddess in other words, Courtney?
Or is buying yourself a new nose really that important?

On April 9, Nirvana played a benefit show for Bosnian rape victims at San Francisco's cavernous Cow Palace – support came from The Breeders, L7 and Disposable Heroes Of Hiphoprisy.[21] (Krist reverted back to the original spelling of his name around this time.) I remember sitting up top among the pigeons with Kim Deal and Jo Wiggs from The Breeders looking down on Kurt while the achingly poignant 'All Apologies' played.

Kurt looked so fragile, so vulnerable, one speck of humanity against a whole generation of curiosity-seekers, fans, the cynical, the bored and a whole bunch of cheerleaders – no tattoos – in butt-hugging sportswear. By the door, Shelli Novoselic was handing out leaflets, trying to make people think about why they were there. Some hope! The kids were there because MTV had told them to be there. Still, it's always better to attempt than accept: maybe one or two of the audience went away and thought about the Bosnian crisis because their favourite stars had asked them to. It's possible. After all, didn't Clinton ascend to the Presidency because of MTV's *Rock The Vote* campaign?[22]

> *"Let's go back a few years,"* I wrote in my review. *"Rock, as an innovative and thus creative form, is dead. I'll temper that. Rock, as created by men, is dead. Women? I think there's still some potential . . . There's nowhere left for rock music to go, no new barriers for it to cross, it's been too assimilated, too categorised, too absorbed. It has been a minority interest for years, like jazz, like soul . . .*
>
> *"So let's go with the theory that Nirvana's 'Smells Like Teen Spirit' was the last glorious death knell of a once vibrant art form and be done with it. (Although 'In Bloom' is a far better song, anyway.) But if rock's over and they killed it, why do I still love Nirvana? The free drinks? The kudos? The unlimited backstage access to arena shows like this? The payola?*
>
> *"No. Nirvana reach too deep inside me for theories. My only explanation is that they play the type of music I grew up loving and which I will always love. I love Nirvana for 'Rape Me', tonight's opener, a song as battle-scarred and shredding as any OV Wright soul-stirrer. I love them for putting on tonight's show (only about their sixth since Reading), the humanity at the core. Yeah, the humanity at the core . . . that's a pretty good reason to love a band. Guess that would explain Sebadoh – The Pastels, too.*
>
> *"I love Nirvana, for Kurt's peerless way with a pop melody. For the way the new album can sound like R.E.M. serenading* MTV

> Unplugged[23] *with acoustic guitars. Heaven forbid I should compare that gang of maudlin retro doomsters with such shimmering pop stars as Nirvana, but both recordings have the same dryness, naturalness and unadorned quality about them. But don't equate dryness with a lack of emotion here.*
>
> *"Why love them? For their encore, which is longer than their set used to be, for songs like 'Breed', 'Territorial Pissings' and 'Floyd The Barber', which still roar and buzz as they did before. For the way they don't play 'In Bloom' and 'Polly', thus avoiding the two songs that have the most potential for horrendous lighter-waving and clap-alongs, but still play 'Lithium' and 'Teen Spirit', because to have done otherwise would have been childishly churlish. For the way they have another 20 songs on standby, which are just as plangent, just as exquisite as the aforementioned."*

"At the very end [during 'Endless, Nameless'] Kurt climbed up on top of his amplifier cabinets," recalls Earnie Bailey. "All of a sudden, he jumped up and arced, and came down on top of Dave, who turned this weird red colour as he had the wind knocked out of him. Kurt fell on this drum kit with all these cymbal stands sticking out, and I'm thinking, 'How is he not going to impale himself?' – but he walks off without a scratch."

After the show, I ended up at Kurt and Courtney's rented apartment writing a strange joint article with Kurt about arena rock shows and being beaten up by bouncers. He'd tell me a paragraph or two to write, then I'd detail how I thought Nirvana's new songs shone, "As blue and battered as anything from the devastating, forthcoming debut album by Madder Rose[24], as raw and trembling as any Daniel Johnston live tape." Although of course I didn't say it aloud: more probably we both yawned and stretched our limbs as Courtney sat by the fire, reading feminist literature. As soon as I'd finished writing the promised 3,000 words on the couple's typewriter, we went to bed. We were tired.

"Word started to spread that I had a copy of *In Utero*," recalls Earnie Bailey. "People that I didn't know at all well – like Eddie Vedder – would call, asking if they could hang out and listen to the album. I told Eddie I'd loaned it out. You can't leak it to the other side.

"Dale Crover stopped by my hotel room at the Phoenix, and asked if he could hear the album," the tech adds. "I had a cassette copy, so I put it on. I was nervous when 'Milk It' came on, because it was very derivative of the Melvins' song 'It's Shoved'. When it started, I saw this puzzled look come across Dale's face, which gradually changed as he realised it was a compliment, ultimately.

"After the show," Earnie continues, "Krist and I went down to the North Beach area, the City Lights bookstore. We were chasing [Jack] Kerouac's ghost, visiting his old stomping grounds, trying to find some of the old rooms he used to read in. There was a closed liquor store right across from the hotel and we got in pretty late, but we paid a couple of hundred dollars to the man vacuuming for a bottle of Wild Turkey, which kept things going for a lot longer.

"Another time, Krist and Dave and I drove up to Vancouver to see Wool [Washington, DC rock band, ex-Scream] play a show. Beforehand, Krist and I went to a sports bar and got into this funny conversation about money and how the world might be a better place without it. So we took all the cash out of our pockets and threw it on the ashtray on the table and lit it on fire. These massive jock guys physically threw us out because we burned our cash in the ashtray."

**Addenda: Cali DeWitt**

"So time goes on and I'm spinning my wheels in LA and doing drugs and I want to get out of that lifestyle. Courtney was continuing to pressure me to work for them, and live with them. She said, 'Just do it for a couple of months.' She said, 'There's a show at the Cow Palace, we'll meet you there.'

"So they fly me to San Francisco to meet them for this show. It was a great show and I felt pretty good. I was excited. From there, we drove to Seattle. Officially, all of a sudden, I'm the nanny. I don't realise what that means until I start. I get to the hotel room, and Frances is put on my lap to see how she likes me. She likes me; we get along great. I spent a lot of time now with that baby under my arm. On the drive to Seattle it took a while because Courtney wanted to stop and shop at antique stores. They both were injecting the Buprenex still. It made me uncomfortable. It shouldn't have because I'd seen far worse things, but someone sitting next to you in the car injecting this Buprenex into their leg . . . I didn't say anything. Why would I? I'm not the type. People always say, 'You should have said something,' but it's like, hold on a second. The only reason you're in that situation in the first place is because you're the kind of person who wouldn't say anything.

"It hadn't come to the point for me where friends were dying. It didn't seem real. Now, 10 or 15 years later, I look at people who are still heroin addicts, and they don't have any teeth and they're having hip replacement surgeries and they're only 34 years old. People really do die. You really do destroy yourself completely. But at that point, it wasn't a reality. So it dawned on me the first day that I've basically got two people who are my friends. I get along really well with Kurt and Courtney. We can shit-talk about music all day long and it's funny and we feel comfortable."

That's an important point; there weren't that many people who got along with Kurt and Courtney.

"Yeah, I don't know why it was me . . ."

I can guess. You were a punk rock kid and you were young.

"I was also cool enough to keep it internalised. I didn't run around and tell everyone what I was doing. They were my friends, but they were older than me and I looked up to them, so I listened. Halfway to Seattle, I turned 20. The next day, we got to Seattle. I remember on the drive thinking, 'This is great, but I'm in for it here.' These people obviously needed taking care of. I felt like I needed taking care of, and I've got this baby."

Who was driving?

"I was."

Were you aware of the vast, almost mythical, management machine that surrounded them?

"No, not yet. I didn't understand the level of manipulation going on until much later."

Presumably you weren't even aware of the rest of Nirvana . . .

"Yeah, for better or for worse. It wasn't like I tried to make it happen, but all of a sudden I was in the secret circle. I was a kid with no money who had a backpack and a skateboard who had some incredible friends who gave me incredible opportunities. In New York and LA, I was running around like a squatter punk kid. I was certainly excited to live in Seattle, I'd never lived in Seattle; I was excited to go on tour outside of a van; I was excited about all of these things.

"There was a major thing that happened two days into being in Seattle. It was this big, brand new house they had rented on Lake Washington. I had the bottom floor and I thought it was cool. About two days in, I asked Courtney to keep drugs away from me. This is not to blame her because I would have found drugs anyway, but she tended to dumb things down and try to pull one over on people. She did this a lot, but you can't pull a drug thing over on someone who likes drugs; it's just too obvious. She introduced me to their friend Dylan who came over. At first I didn't like Dylan that much because he was a junkie. I had this image that I was not going to do that and I was naïve enough to think that Kurt and Courtney were not going to do that because they had Buprenex, and everything was going to be fine. Then I saw him and I knew.

"She said that she needed me to get some money out of the bank and go with Dylan to pick something up for the house. I knew right away. I got a stomach ache and I'm thinking, 'I can't do this,' but I go along with it. I'm sitting in the car with this guy Dylan. He has me park in this shitty neighbourhood. He goes and he comes back and he goes, 'I got it.' I knew it was drugs and the obsession to use drugs came over me, which was always what brought me down. When we got back to the house, I was yelling at Courtney. I go, 'You can't! I'm a drug addict. I'm younger than you in this.' Probably one of the reasons that I could get on with Courtney as much as I did was for whatever reason, where other people were afraid of her, I yelled at her all the time. She needed it. She was like, 'I'm sorry, fine. You should do some.' It was this thing that went on all day, this fight. We were both really loaded and we were both trying to hide it from each other, and Eric [Erlandson]'s there. I'm holding the baby, and it scared me. I'm like, I can't do this, be in this situation. This was April 15, two days after we got there."

What was Eric's role in this?

"Eric would often show up and try to fix things. Courtney was in some kind of turmoil and she had a last resort. Eric was always on Courtney's side and would come take care of things and clean up messes."

Did Eric do drugs?

"Eric was one of these amazing people who could take it or leave it. Eric was someone who didn't mind experimenting with drugs, but wasn't really interested in them. But it was a bad day, and I remember fighting with her for long enough where at some point I was crying and just saying, 'I can't be in this environment and do this for you.'"

Was Kurt around?

"No, I don't know where he was. He might have gone away with the band for a couple of days. When he wasn't around and she was, drugs were in the house – and vice versa. But that sort of changed it for me. I went there with a real strong . . . it would have failed sooner or later anyway. But I had to try to be a sober nanny – and on my nights off, I could go off and party and do drugs and be a 20-year-old."

What did your nanny duties entail?

"They were supposed to entail taking care of Frances. Courtney immediately tried to take advantage of that, and have me send faxes and answer phones and stuff. I told her pretty quickly that I wouldn't do anything else. She would say, 'God, don't yell at me.' She would always say, 'God, don't yell at me!'"

That's weird, that's how I was with Courtney for quite a while as well. I remember Courtney saying to me early on that one of the reasons she liked hanging out with me was because I was one of the few people who could make her cry.

"It's good if you can beat her at that. She likes to tell people what to do, and she likes it even more when they say, 'No.' I had the kid a lot, sometimes for a week. I didn't mind. I actually, much to my surprise, liked it a lot. I liked Frances and I was good with her and I had fun with her."

What would Kurt eat?

"Mostly junk food: frozen dinners, frozen pizzas. He had a favourite pizza place in Pioneer Square and sometimes I'd go pick up pizzas there. He and I shared a junkie love of food that was cookies and Lucky Charms. He found out what my favourite cookies were and bought me a case of them as a surprise. Around the same time, she came home with two bowls. She'd spend all this money that wasn't hers on expensive things. Some part of her, probably the part of her that wanted to get into a fight, couldn't resist telling him how much they were. They just looked like fancy bowls to us, but they were $600 each, there was real gold leaf on them. He was pissed off and yelled at her. He said, 'The money spent on those bowls could have paid my rent for three months, five years ago.' So he sat in my room in the basement and watched TV with Frances and me. He was fuming over these bowls and he went upstairs and asked me if I was hungry. He poured two bowls of Coco Puffs into these expensive bowls, brought them downstairs and said, 'Well, this is the best use we're going to get out of these bowls, isn't it?' "

He had some X-ray specs down there, didn't he?

"Yeah, all those cheap, shitty magic tricks and fake body parts. What he spent his money on was like what you see on the back of the *In Utero* record: expensive medical dolls. That's another thing. All these books talk about how tortured and unhappy Kurt was. I don't think he was that unhappy. I think he was very funny. He was everything people say about tortured and unhappy, but I also think he had a lot of joy at times. He used to make me laugh the same way she made me laugh, all the time."

Did Kurt ever mention his old girlfriends?

"No, not to me."

Did Courtney?

"Yeah, she'd bring it up and he'd shrug it off. I started a rule between them pretty quickly, probably in the first month I was in the house. I said, 'Look, this is not normal. I don't want you to bring me into the middle of your fights. Don't ask me who's right; don't yell to me in the middle of it' – because they would do that and I didn't need that."

## NOTES

1 Aerosmith and Led Zeppelin – both bands were considered beyond the pale to the punk rock librarians of Olympia, although some hipsters grudgingly admitted that Zeppelin, at least, could *rock*.

2 There were five in total lifted from the Dale demo: 'Mexican Seafood' as originally featured on the C/Z compilation EP *Teriyaki Asthma*, Vol 1, and 'Beeswax' from *kill rock stars*.

3 'Sliver' later got released in the US as a single to promote *Incesticide*. A video was shot in Kurt's garage, directed by Kevin Kerslake, filmed on grainy Super-8, featuring Frances Bean among others as the band played live against a backdrop of Kurt's collection of weird objects.

4 Daniel Johnston's felt-tip drawings are full of disconcerting, sometimes misogynistic, imagery: women with their heads missing, skulls, many-headed creatures and his alter ego Casper the Friendly Ghost. A former art student, Daniel was inspired by US comic book artists from the Sixties, particularly Marvel Comics stalwart Jack Kirby's larger-than-life visualisations.

5 The Stinky Puffs were a brilliantly elemental band formed by the Half Japanese singer's son – released an album on Shimmydisc, 1995's *A Little Tiny Smelly Bit Of . . .*, full of simple, scratchy pop songs.

6 A generation of indie kids lost their hearts to Mazzy Star singer Hope Sandoval's dispassionate, dreamtime croon: the LA duo's debut album, 1990's *She Hangs Brightly* is crystalline post-Velvet Underground perfection. Even better is guitarist David Roback's psychedelic pre-Mazzy Star outfit, Opal.

7 It was an interview Kurt arranged by himself, much to the annoyance of Geffen's press department.

8 The Pacific Northwest also has strong ties with *The Simpsons*. The first time I visited Sub Pop, I noticed a signed Matt Groening print on Bruce Pavitt's office wall. *The Simpsons* creator studied at Evergreen State College.

9 The inspiration behind 'Scentless Apprentice' was the Patrick Süskind book *Perfume* (1986), written about a maniac perfumer in pre-revolutionary France who has no scent, but whose advanced sense of smell means he is alienated from society.

10 No Pearl Jam – because "Pearl Jam, like, suck, heh heh," as Butt-head, the more intelligent of the pair put it.

11 "On the hotel itineraries," recalls Earnie, "Kurt and Courtney were often Mr And Mrs Simon Ritchie, while Dave went by Roy Rogers."

12 The title of 'Pennyroyal Tea' refers to a herbal abortifacient – "It doesn't work, you hippie," Kurt caustically remarked in his journal.

13 Frances Farmer's supporters felt she was demonised mainly because she wrote a poem entitled 'God is Dead' when she was 17 and thence visited the Soviet Union at the height of the Cold War.

14 Probably a reference to the AC/DC album *Back In Black*.

15 Drawn from her ghost-written autobiography *Will There Really Be A Morning?* In recent years, doubt has been cast on its authenticity.

16 Pat made up a great story about how the band set their pants on fire to celebrate the record's completion, a line that one journalist swallowed whole. Perhaps he should have remembered the old playground chant: "Liar, liar, pants on fire."
17 The engineer was renowned for walking around the streets of Chicago in a big 10-gallon Stetson.
18 Many people loved Evan Dando, particularly for his lazy and beautiful way round a pop/country cover, but his continued use of acid did make him very dopey. Kurt, on the other hand, found Dando's glad-handing irritating in the extreme.
19 Leslie Hardy has her picture on the EP, but doesn't play on it.
20 The Alice In Chains singer died from a heroin overdose in 2002.
21 Disposable Heroes of Hiphoprisy were an excellent politically motivated and witty San Francisco hip hop band, fronted by Michael Franti.
22 It's easy to underestimate the power of the media: Amnesty International, for example, benefits greatly when a band like U2 prints its address on their album sleeves.
23 It was the vogue for MTV to invite rock bands into a large studio and get them to perform acoustically, supposedly without amplification – but usually just a little quieter. With a few exceptions – Neil Young springs to mind – the format failed dismally, serving instead as one more smug, backslapping, industry exercise.
24 Madder Rose were a somnambulist, drug-tinted, Velvet Underground-inspired, pop band from New York – none of their albums really did their live shows justice, but 1993's debut *Bring It Down* is pretty gorgeous.

# CHAPTER 25

# Eyes Wide Open

*William recites a poem all about some kid, see, out on the street, see, meets up with a drug dealer, see, in a hotel room, see, there's a chopped-up body in a suitcase, see, he needs to score a hit of smack, see, he's only got three dollars, see, it's Christmas, see, the wind is grey outside, see, the kid grows ill, see, the images grow blurry, see . . .*

*. . . and a guitar destroys 'Silent Night', right, howls like it's the wind whipping along the street, right, coils in on itself like it's the kid himself hooked in the hotel room, right, lets burst with a scream of feedback like it's the 'priest' arguing with the bastard, right . . .*

*This pairing works remarkably well.*

*Whether you're prepared to listen to Burroughs' almost deathly monotone speaking of decay and distraction over Kurt Cobain's tortured guitar musings more than once is up to you.*

*There's something morbidly fascinating about the thought, though.*

(Review of 'The 'Priest' They Called Him', *Melody Maker*, September 11, 1993)

ON May 2, 1993, the King County emergency services received a phone call from 11301 Lakeside Ave NE. The police report stated that Kurt Cobain had been, "At a friend's house two hours earlier, where he'd injected himself with $30–$40 worth of heroin. He then drove home to the address of the incident and stayed in his room." After Kurt refused to unlock the door, Courtney dialled Wendy and Kim, who immediately set out from Aberdeen to try and help, but by the time they arrived his condition had worsened, and Kurt was vomiting and in shock.

It wasn't the first time this had happened – it's been rumoured Kurt overdosed several times during 1993. Courtney tried throwing cold water over her husband, and giving him various drugs – Valium, Buprenex, Benadryl, codeine – to counter the effects, but nothing worked. Eventually, the paramedics were called when Kurt started to turn blue. He was rushed to Harborview Hospital where he drifted in and out of consciousness, intermittently quoting Shakespeare to his sister.

"That time, he had cotton fever," explains Cali DeWitt. "When you shoot drugs you rinse it through cotton. If the tiniest strand of cotton gets on to the needle and into your bloodstream, it's not so much of an overdose as your body reacting to the cotton. You get really flushed and shaky and hot. It's physically uglier than an overdose."

But it's not so dangerous . . .

"Not compared to a real overdose," Cali agrees. "There was another overdose at that house around this time. Jackie [Farry] was visiting and I think Nils Bernstein [president of the Nirvana fan club] was at the house too. I carried Kurt upstairs and threw him into the Jacuzzi bathtub and turned the cold water on and that woke him up. I just wanted to get him walking around, but then Courtney cooked him food, and fed him in there. I was definitely starting to see how volatile this home life was going to be."

On June 1, Courtney staged a small intervention/rehab session in the house: she called in Krist, Janet Billig, Nils, Wendy and Kurt's stepfather Pat O'Connor. His friends and relatives all went through a number of reasons why Kurt should quit doing drugs – his own health and the welfare of his daughter being paramount among them. Courtney pointed out that she'd started attending Narcotics Anonymous, and was trying to quit smoking cigarettes.[1] He refused to listen, and stormed upstairs: this was the cue for his peers to start bickering among themselves over who was to blame.

Three days later, the emergency services were called to the house once more, and Kurt was thrown into King County jail for three hours for alleged domestic assault. Bail of $950 was posted. The charges were later dropped.

The police report mentioned an argument the couple were having over Kurt's gun collection. Courtney threw orange juice in Kurt's face, he pushed her and she pushed him back, someone scratched someone else . . . Kurt later strenuously denied all the allegations. In an interview with *Spin*, he claimed that all that happened was he and Courtney had been running round the house, screaming and wrestling, having a good time, when, "Suddenly, there's a knock on the door, and there are five cops outside with their guns drawn."

He added that the two of them argued over who should go to jail. Domestic dispute law in Washington State demands that police officers arrest someone before they leave the premises. The cops confiscated Kurt's guns – all three of them – after Courtney revealed their whereabouts.

"I don't think he assaulted her," says Cali. "They were arguing really bad and she was picking on him. In a fight, he could be vicious, but she would also pick on him until he exploded."

Don't you think Courtney had a tendency to wind people up so she could play the victim?

"Yeah," the former nanny laughs. "Courtney likes drama. She likes to be yelled at. I think she wants someone to dominate her."

She's told me that.

"Me too," he agrees. "It's a classic thing. Strong, aggressive people would like someone to dominate them at some point. It's like CEOs going to a dungeon to get whipped. I know other women who fit her description to a lesser degree and they like an aggressive man in their life. He doesn't have to be an aggressive asshole in public, but they want to fight and they want to argue, and they want to be slapped occasionally. This time, he was eating Spaghetti-O's and somehow the plate of them wound up on his face. I think Courtney threw them. He was happy that the cops were there, probably because it meant an end to the fight. It was almost like saying, 'Fuck you, the cops are going to arrest me. What are you going to do to get me now?' And he's sitting there on the stairs and his whole beard is filled with this awful sweet red sauce and it's caked in."

Presumably it was Courtney who called the cops.

"I'm sure it was her," he agrees. "Probably goading each other into it. One saying, 'I'm going to call the cops,' and the other saying, 'Go ahead; call the fucking cops. I just want to eat my dinner. Send me to fucking jail.'"

How would you describe them as a couple?

"I think they were volatile. I think they were bad for each other. Those couples that love each other, they can't imagine their lives without each other, yet they're going to kill each other. A couple of more stable people would have seen that and split up, or stayed away from each other. As a couple, it was like two people desperate to make something that can't work, work. I think he loved her very much and I think he was a lot more naïve than her."

Do you think his Olympia training clashed with her?

"Probably, but he was someone who liked to say 'fuck you' to everybody. Dating Courtney was his way of saying 'fuck you' to Olympia."

From what I remember, the management was scared of them.

"They didn't know what to do with them," agrees Cali. "They were used to dealing with people who wanted their career steered. At the core,

Kurt still had a lot of punk rock ethics. He wanted to be what he was, but he didn't want his songs used in a Nike commercial. Courtney was more on the management side when it came to selling music. A lot of the fights stemmed from that. That fight where the cops came was by no means the only one."

Were you aware of Kurt's gun collection?

"I wasn't aware that there were more than one or two," Cali replies, "but I can imagine anyone I know buying guns. It doesn't always mean suicide."

It's America, for god's sake.

"Yeah, it's America."

I remember Kurt telling me about the guns, that each one had a journalist's name.

"That's almost like pillow talk," the ex-nanny counters. "It was definitely said. There was a night that Courtney asked me, and she was serious, if I thought that Rene would kill Lynn Hirschberg's dog. Because I guess Lynn Hirschberg had this dog that she loved more than anything. For a couple of days Courtney was telling me, 'You get Rene over here. I'm going to send him to New York; I'll give him $5,000. I want him to kill that dog.' I never called Rene because what if he'd done it? I don't think he would, but I didn't want to get him involved. A few days later she had forgotten about it."

I definitely remember having a conversation with Kurt where he said, "If I ever go out, I'm going to kill some of those bastards first."

"Yeah. I've heard him talk angry like that. I'm glad he didn't. That would have changed everything."

The dispute over *In Utero* rumbled on through April and May.

Although Nirvana claimed they were under no pressure from Geffen and their management to tamper with Albini's recordings, privately it was a different matter. In his journal, Kurt detailed a smart compromise: first release the original version – "an uncompromising vinyl, cassette, eight-track only release" – and follow it up a month later with a remixed version entitled *Verse, Chorus, Verse*, with an advisory sticker stating 'Radio-Friendly, Unit-Shifting, Compromise Version'. Pity it didn't happen.

The solution was simple – alter the mix when the CD was mastered. Great store is placed on production: few bands realise when they first enter a studio to make a record that mastering is equally as important, and almost as pliable. So someone simply turned the vocals up on Albini's mix, and added more compression – end of problem. A month later, Geffen brought in R.E.M. producer Scott Litt to remix 'Heart-Shaped Box' and 'All Apologies' (from which he removed a long stream of feedback) at Seattle's Bad Animals studio – Kurt added an acoustic guitar and some backing vocals to 'Heart-Shaped Box', and everyone was happy. Well, perhaps not Albini . . . or me. But we didn't matter.

"You could put that band in the studio for a year, and I don't think they could come up with a better record," Albini told Michael Azerrad, annoyed. "If that doesn't suit their record company then the record company clearly has problems that go beyond this record. The record company has a problem with the band. The sooner everybody involved recognises this, the easier it will be on everybody."

Danny Goldberg refutes this: "The stress didn't come from the band or the record company, but from Steve Albini. Kurt wanted to work with Steve because he liked his work, and also he wanted to work with someone from the independent world to show his core audience he was still one of them. It was recorded quickly. The mixes were very muddy. Both Gary [Gersh] and I said you can't hear the vocals, and the words are a big part of the music. Kurt agreed. So we asked Scott Litt to do the singles. Albini later said Geffen was pushing Kurt around, and it was only him who respected his integrity, but Kurt had 100 per cent control on that record. He chose the person who did the remix, and approved the final versions."

In May, Kurt settled on the *In Utero* title – taken from some of Courtney's poetry – and conceptualised the album artwork. The front cover – a full-size model of a see-through woman with all her inner organs showing, holding out her hands in supplication, head slightly bowed – is taken from a classic schoolroom model entitled *Brunnhilde: The Transparent Woman* used by American children to discover facts about the female anatomy. Kurt added a pair of angel's wings. The album's back cover was a disturbing pink wash collage of dolls, intestines, foetuses, umbilical cords and flowers – "Suggesting the aftermath of a massacre," as the singer put it.

"Late on Sunday afternoon, Kurt called me up and says, 'I've got this thing I want you to photograph for the album,'" recalls Charles Peterson. "He's like, 'You've got to come over in an hour; they're all going to die if you don't.' So I cobbled together whatever film I had in my refrigerator and went over. He had set up on his dining room floor this collage of carnations and tulips and plastic body parts.

"There was a big screen television in a sunken living room that was permanently on," the photographer continues. "The house was kind of a pit, the way Kurt and Courtney lived their lives. While I was photographing this thing – it was difficult because I had to hover over it, and it's not my forte to do a still-life shot – Kurt played the *In Utero* recordings from a boom box on the 'island' in the middle of the kitchen. It was an actual mix, sequenced and everything. It sounded great. And he was like, 'What do you think of the mix?' He was really uncertain. Honestly, if I listen to it now on a good stereo it sounds like shit. You do have to turn up the bass and treble. But listening to it on a boom box then, it sounded like classic Nirvana."

Life went on as usual. Krist continued to speak out against homophobic and censorious statutes. Break-up rumours continued to surface, Kurt sometimes going public with his desire to form a group with Mark Arm or Mark Lanegan. Dave kept his distance. Kurt carried on taking drugs, not so surreptitiously any more – visitors to the house felt they needed to work their schedules around whether Kurt was high or not, something Kurt resented, figuring he was fully able to function anyway. And Courtney continued to shop, plot her own course for world domination and invite her friends over.

"People were behaving oddly towards me in Minneapolis," says Jessica Hopper. "So Courtney had Janet [Billig] buy me a ticket so I could hang out with them in Seattle for a week, under the guise that I was going to look at schools.

"That house was a weirdly inappropriate house for them," she continues. "It had a beige carpet, this so-called suburban den. Nice, new construction, just normal looking, coffee table and all that. Upstairs, there was a destroyed-looking room with all Kurt's records and guitars. The kitchen was pretty normal except there were tons of mail and faxes everywhere, and there was a huge collection of medical examples of embryos all over the dining room floor. There were things written all over the walls in markers and lipstick: upstairs, outside Kurt's art room Courtney had painted something like 'I fucking love you' on this nice clean wall and nice clean carpet. They'd punk-ed up this totally nice house, but it was like no one had really moved in. There wasn't anything on the walls. For a couple of days I was sequestered in the house. Sometimes I'd hang out with Frances and her nanny.[2] Kurt and Courtney would be locked in their bedroom: they'd come out and I'd run some errands with Courtney. I took a cab into Capitol Hill and did record shopping.

"One day they had me hold a microphone while they recorded some songs together. They did 'Pig Meat Papa' by Leadbelly, and I was holding the mic and Frances at the same time, and she was crying a little. You could hear it in the recording. They were singing it together. Kurt was playing. They did two Leadbelly songs, that other one they ended up doing on *MTV Unplugged* ['Where Did You Sleep Last Night?'] and then she tried to get him to play something else. They were both high. Everything I saw during that time, even though it was very taxing and tiring, was entirely responsible for me never doing drugs – seeing these people that I respected and liked barely communicating, or in their own world together.

"Courtney was the active one," Jessica continues. "Kurt was the withdrawn one, but he was always really funny. Any time he was around Frances he was really alive: he would talk about weird things he was obsessed with, a documentary about animals or children in another country. He seemed interested in phenomena. He was watching a PBS 40-part series on [Roman emperor] Caligula[3], something you'd check out of the library. They were both totally intellectual. They were also intensely private. A friend called me on one of the house lines, and they wanted to know how I knew him. I felt like I'd inadvertently breached their privacy.

"They didn't leave the house much. It was like a big incubator. Cali and I went out and ran errands for them."

On July 1, the day Jessica arrived, Hole played a show at the Off Ramp in Seattle – the same day the *Seattle Times* ran a story about Kurt's arrest. Courtney was in her usual captivating, sarcastic form, getting into scuffles, playing songs from *Live Through This* – including 'Doll Parts', performed on acoustic guitar[4] – and making reference to the newspaper story, saying, "Yeah, my husband is a total wife-beater. NOT!" Kurt and Krist turned up after the show ended, having been to see Leonard Cohen perform. "We hung out with Leonard Cohen's daughter Lorca, on the day after he played Seattle," says Earnie Bailey. "She was very sweet."

"Cali picks me up from the airport," recalls Jessica. "We get some food, hang out a little, he brings me to the house and leaves to go to do stuff, before him and Kurt go to see Leonard Cohen. *En route* to the show, Kurt drives Courtney and me up to Capitol Hill to make a stop at Kat [Bjelland] and Stu's [Spasm, singer with Lubricated Goat[5]]. Kat is not there – she hates me anyways – and sweaty, sweaty Stu in his glitter cowboy shirt answers the door. Immediately, I'm like, 'OK, I understand: *errand* . . .' So I'm deposited in the living room and told it'll only be a few minutes.

"Twenty minutes later, I'm sitting there reading a magazine and down the hall in the kitchen I can see something weird is going on. They call me in: Kurt is sitting in the invisible chair, nodded *way* out. Courtney, meanwhile, her arm is swelling up and looking spotty and discoloured –

whatever happens when some cotton gets in your blood – and is a total mess and a touch panicky. Stu is sweating, at once totally high and scared. None of them feel they are in any shape to go out in public, so they need me to run a few errands . . .

"I'm a little panicked myself. I'm being told I'll have to care for them and drive them to the show, even though I couldn't drive a manually operated car yet. Kurt was like, 'I'll guide you through it.' As soon as I'm out, I stop at every payphone, calling the house, hoping Cali is there to help me. I get to an ATM. Strangely; Mark Arm is behind me in line . . .

"On the way back, I'm crying I'm so freaked out, and finally I get through to Cali, and he comes and fixes everything. That was my first day in Seattle with them."

"Stu and Kat were total wing nuts," laughs Rene Navarette. "They were recently married, with a place on Capitol Hill. Kurt and Courtney would hang out at theirs a lot. Stu was a storyteller. It was always funny whenever he left the room, watching Kurt mimic Stu trying to promote his Crunt album – which I thought was great[6] – in his Australian accent. Stu had this pitch he'd do over and over; he'd say about being in Berlin and being stabbed, and being beaten up by 10 men and then ripping off their arms, and go into detail about being mugged for all of $10. It was almost cartoon-ish.

"Kurt being funny would either fall on deaf ears or be the funniest thing in the world. It was so hit and miss. It came from him being the cool kid in the country town. He was still really humble. He was very childish. He would mimic people and it was hilarious when it did hit. 'Stare hard, retard!' was one of his favourite sayings."

Also on July 1, Tim/Kerr records released 'The 'Priest' They Called Him', a limited edition 10-inch record featuring William S. Burroughs doing a monologue over Kurt's guitar. It was a one-sided single, with the two performers' signatures etched into the B-side. Burroughs was a bit of a mentor to Kurt, who had even offered the iconoclast a cameo role in the video for 'Heart-Shaped Box'. It's arguable how positive a role model Burroughs was for Kurt: by making his drug use and his junkie friends sound so interesting he made heroin a much more attractive prospect for the singer – something that sadly also happens every time Kurt's drug use is mentioned. The record was fine, if odd. The guitar part was lifted from the Laundry Room sessions in November 1992.

"He was probably really honoured to be doing something with Burroughs," comments Earnie. "He was a great hero of his."

Three days later, Dave Grohl played a reunion show with Scream, the start of a 10-date US tour – and Dischord released the Scream back catalogue on CD. *Los Angeles Times* wrote of the final night, "Dave Grohl supercharged the usual punk rock polka stuff with an extraordinary array of back-beat flams and paradiddles." No kidding.

Bearing in mind Scream's predilection for breaking up and re-forming as band members fell in and out of favour with one another, it was tempting to view this as a continuation of the Washington, DC band's career path. Grohl felt estranged from the Nirvana camp: he'd had a massive row with Courtney during the recording of *In Utero*, the band had played live just once during the first six months of 1993, and he was trying to release some of his own Laundry Room recordings on a Detroit label.

"Dave never came over to the house," says Cali. "It was apparent that Dave and Krist didn't like Courtney, but Krist really loved Kurt and was trying to make an attempt at being a friend, even though it was crazy at the house. Kurt was kind of nasty to Dave, like he was still the new guy.

"If Kurt and I were going out," the former nanny continues, "like if Kurt and I were going to a P.J. Harvey concert, then Courtney was definitely not in town. And when Courtney was not in town, we had a lot of fun. I'd wind up signing Dave Grohl autographs all night because I had long black hair. Kurt was nervous about the P.J. Harvey concert [Under The Rail, Seattle, July 9] because he liked her so much."

We all did. P.J. Harvey's first recordings (*Dry*, *4 Track Demos*) were characterised by their vivacity, viciousness and starkness. The English singer was able to cut to the heart of emotion with a raw incisiveness that set her apart. Polly is also an incredible blues guitarist – her songs feel simple, but the rhythms are original and very complex. Initially influenced by loads of blues guitarists, plus counter-culture heroes like New York poetess Patti Smith and Australian storyteller Nick Cave (whose dissolute Gothic look Polly once drew upon), she soon established herself as the equal of her peers.

"It was during the [P.J. Harvey's third album] *Rid Of Me* tour, and the place was half-full," continues Cali. "She was so great. He wanted to ask her to go on tour with Nirvana. So after the show, we went backstage and I know it took a lot for him to ask her. She was polite, but she turned him down. I think that made him love her even more."

"I heard that Courtney was very bothered by Kurt's interest in P.J. Harvey," comments Earnie.

Courtney was very bothered by any female in whom Kurt showed even the vaguest of interest – but right enough, as on the surface Polly fell right within the Olympia stereotype to which Kurt was attracted: dark-haired, soulful, moody, a musician and highly intelligent.

On July 17, *Nevermind* finally dropped out of the *Billboard* Top 200, after 92 weeks.

Six days later, Nirvana played their second gig of the year at the 4,000-capacity Roseland Ballroom in New York, as part of the annual industry bun-fest, the New Music Seminar. A queue snaked round the block as frustrated seminar attendees flashed their badges and tried to gain entry: no dice. Inside, support act The Jesus Lizard turned in a typically anarchic set of their voodoo blues: singer David Yow stagediving before even a note was played.

"The place was huge with a white linen VIP area, and my punk rock self hated it," notes German promoter Christof Ellinghaus. "I thought it was gross. It was full of jocks, the people Kurt was scared of, sports buffs."

"It was a secret show, but everyone knows about secret shows," recalls Cali. "They were going to try playing with another guitarist [Kurt's other guitar tech, Big John Duncan] and a cello player [Lori Goldston]."

Big John was previously noted for appearing on *Top Of The Pops* sporting a flamboyant Mohican haircut back in 1980, playing guitar with post-card punks The Exploited. Big John – a lovely fellow, but built like a barrel and not someone you'd want to cross – also had played guitar in dire Scottish band Goodbye Mr McKenzie alongside future Garbage singer Shirley Manson.

Lori was a classically trained cellist, a mainstay of Seattle's moody, jazz-influenced The Black Cat Orchestra – Nirvana came to know of her after she took part in a performance inspired by events in Sarajevo. "They said they were looking for a cellist to tour with them and do *MTV Unplugged*," Goldston recalls. "Kurt wanted to expand his parameters. He didn't think his way of singing was very sustainable. He thought his voice would get destroyed. His solution was to set his sights on being quieter, playing weird chamber music. He wanted an oboe. Kurt was very subtle. He would indicate the next song by just moving around. He liked talking in abbreviated ways. Coming from Long Island where everything was explicit, it was like everyone talked in codes.

"I was so nervous at that first show, I started smoking," she continues. "It was a great show. It was a little surreal."

It certainly was. Nirvana started with 'Serve The Servants' and 'Scentless Apprentice' from *In Utero* – two songs the audience was unfamiliar with, but massive surges of adrenalin – before stepping up a gear into 'Breed' and 'Lithium', the place going crazy, the rampant singalong not spoiled one bit by over-enthusiasm. Kurt wore a pair of Devo shades and his trademark, red striped bumblebee jersey. ("But I have to wear this, I have fans out there," he pleaded when Courtney attempted to smarten him up pre-show.) Krist looked spruce and dapper in a stiff-collared black shirt and short hair. Dave drummed furiously, grinning like the Cheshire cat.

'Rape Me' followed, tantalising and strangely apposite. Big John took the stage with his dark hair and trimmed blond beard to add firepower to the next four songs: 'Aneurysm', 'Territorial Pissings', an elegiac 'Heart-Shaped Box' and equally as beautiful 'All Apologies', Goldston's sweeping cello adding layers of texture.

"These are the sounds taking the music industry by storm," Krist called out. "It's called . . . alternative rock!"

The crowd was buzzing after 'All Apologies', expectant; eager to break into a riot of moshing like they'd seen on MTV. Instead they got . . . acoustic Nirvana! *Nirvana Unplugged*. Talk about confusion. Some folk laughed, some clapped, some grew disinterested exceedingly fast and started talking loudly – you wouldn't have thought these were the same rabid fans so eager to see the sainted Kurt Cobain only minutes before. It was a shame, because the middle section was both moving and a brave experiment on Kurt's part to move his band's sound on.

"It was awkward because the first part of the show was so powerful," Earnie suggests. "Krist was airborne. I couldn't get over how amazing the rhythm section sounded. The ending was almost anticlimactic, if only because I could hear people talking during the acoustic set. I couldn't tell if they were distracted or in awe. There were a lot of industry people in an alcove along the side wall that was formerly the stage where big bands used to play, and it sounded like that was where some of the noise was coming from."[7]

It was almost the reverse of Bob Dylan going electric in 1967: the kids hated the idea of their heroes changing tack. Haunting versions of 'Polly', 'Dumb' and 'Where Did You Sleep Last Night' followed, but all one could hear halfway back were scenesters loudly ordering drinks. Meanwhile, a handful of hardy dancers exercised their right to positive sarcasm, stagediving frenziedly during the softest moments.

And then . . . Nirvana stopped playing, packed up their instruments and left the stage. Gone. No one knew what to do. No one clapped or cheered. Silence. Muted talking. Eventually, the band returned for a perfunctory run-through of 'Smells Like Teen Spirit' and a noise fest, Kurt dropped to his knees in front of his effects board.

Afterwards, the mood backstage was oddly restrained. I made a joke to Courtney about Nirvana's new acoustic middle section sounding like U2 – I'd recently seen a live show wherein the pompous Irish band performed an acoustic set on a smaller stage. She nearly thumped me before she realised I was winding her up.

Bumping into Kurt, I started telling him about this great new rock band I'd seen the night before, Dayton, Ohio's Guided By Voices: "They're like a cross between Sebadoh, Swell Maps[8], Cheap Trick and Eddie And The Hot Rods[9]," I babbled. He barely feigned interest.

That seminar was eventful.

Later that night, Cali tried to convince the Nirvana entourage to accompany him to legendary Bowery club CBGBs where an unknown punk band called Rancid was playing. No deal. Anyone left standing wanted to check out the debut of Pavement's new drummer at the Matador records showcase – far hipper.

"They all made fun of me," Cali sighs.

The night after, I was sharing a taxi with Cali, also to CBGBs, to catch the Amphetamine Reptile showcase. Cali asked, "Can I smoke?" and when the driver replied no, he asked, "What the fuck is this doing in here then?", ripped the ashtray straight off the door and threw it out the window. I offered the driver 20 bucks, and prayed he wasn't packing a gun.

"If I'd done that now I'd be embarrassed," Cali laughs, "but then I was just excited because you'd mentioned some band or other. The same night Tom Hazelmyer [AmRep boss] picked me up over his head and threw me on to the roof of a car in front of CBGBs. He liked to do that. [Indeed he did. The same week, he threw Thurston Moore into a dumpster.] He said, 'Stay away from my wife.' I said, 'Well, she shouldn't be dressed that way.' We've been friends ever since. He liked the stupidity of my young, arrogant mind."

Another night, several of the Nirvana entourage caught a 'grunge' covers band playing live, much to our delight. All the songs were performed faithfully – Soundgarden, Pearl Jam, Spin Doctors, Red Hot Chili Peppers, etc – until it came to Nirvana. These were sung in a high-pitched squeal, the singer camping it up like he was a TV gay. The obvious inference was that Nirvana weren't real 'men' at all. Not like their peers. Krist and Dave were stoked when they found out.

"It all sounds so familiar," laughs Earnie.

At the same convention, Kurt and Courtney took a cab across town to

Wetlands at the unfashionable end of Hudson Street, to see TV Personalities play live. It was the usual mixture of desultory humour and bittersweet pop. Arriving at the venue, Kurtney espied Steve Malkmus, singer of Pavement. Not brooking any arguments, they placed themselves either side of Malkmus at the back of the club, remaining deep in conversation all night.

Later, I saw Kurt walking along the street dishevelled and distracted, on his own, having just argued with Courtney and been thrown out of the cab.

I said the mood backstage at Roseland seemed oddly restrained.

There was a reason for that: as Courtney explained when she grabbed me pre-gig from the increasingly crowded VIP area where I was rubbing shoulders with Sonic Youth, Beck, The Beastie Boys, Girls Against Boys, Urge Overkill, Babes In Toyland, Melvins . . . (and they were just the ones still speaking to me) – only a few hours before Nirvana played, she'd discovered her husband, dead, on the floor of their hotel room.

"Got to New York, got to the hotels," says Cali. "Of course, everyone being drug addicts, everyone wanted to get heroin. You know there's white heroin in New York as opposed to the brown heroin on the West Coast. It's black tar here on the West Coast and on the East Coast it's China White. Actually, if you're a drug user here and you do black tar all the time you kind of feel like you're almost not doing drugs if you do white heroin. It feels more innocuous. It's not the sticky stuff that you have to cook. It's in this nice little bag.

"We all had our hotel rooms on the same floor, but probably a good eight or nine rooms away from each other. The day of the show I could hear Courtney screaming for me across the floor. I ran down the hall and opened the door and Kurt was lying by the door in his underwear with the needle in his arm and his eyes wide open, not breathing. Basically dead with his eyes open. He was, as is well documented, very small, so I pulled the needle out of his arm and picked him up and started slapping him and punching his chest right in the sternum pretty hard. The second or third punch he blew out all of his air and started breathing again. He closed his eyes and opened his eyes and looked around, confused. The screaming had alerted a lot of people on the floor and we could hear other people running down going, 'What's going on?' – and security. I just said, 'Let's get him dressed.' He's asking what's going on, and she was like, 'You were dead, you were dead!' I took him out past everyone and got him some food, and we walked around Times Square a bit. Afterwards I was really shaken. I'm not trained in any kind of CPR [cardiopulmonary resuscitation], so it was a freak I hit him in the right place."

That's interesting because Anton Brookes has said how shocked he felt when he saw you and Courtney spring into action like "experienced medical aids". He was left with the impression you must have done it fairly often.

"If you do hard narcotics all the time, you wind up doing this fairly often," explains Cali. "By fairly often, I mean once a month. I don't mean just to Kurt, I can count eight or nine people I've been in that situation with. As far as 'experienced medical aids', I always chalk it up to like if a car falls on someone and someone gets superhuman strength. Your adrenalin goes and there's no time for fear. Images get burned in your mind. The image of a friend of yours in his underwear with a needle in his arm and his eyes open, but blue, and not breathing, is like a flash stain on your psyche. Kurt played a show that night to all these people and he did a really good job, but I remember thinking the whole time, 'He was dead four hours ago and none of these people know that.' It was scary. I think it scared him too."

That was the first time?

"It happened before in Seattle."

Do you remember anything else from the show?

"It was good," Cali smiles, "but Big John didn't belong on stage with them."

A couple of weeks after the New Music Seminar show, Nirvana played another secret gig. This time, it was a benefit for the Mia Zapata Investigation Fund at the King Theater in Seattle, on August 6. Tad and Patti Schemel's former band Kill Sybil also played. Zapata was a popular local figure, a singer with an astonishingly emotive voice, who fronted local punk band The Gits – she'd been found raped and strangled in Seattle's Central District neighbourhood in the early hours of July 7.

"Nirvana was the last-minute headliner," recalls Gillian G. Gaar. "So last-minute, that no one was sure if they were going to play or not. They started with 'Seasons In The Sun', Kurt's voice sounding all raw and scraped – and played the entire song. It was great."

There was a massive fight backstage between Courtney and Tad's wife, Barbara Beymer – rumoured to be as large as Tad Doyle himself. "She was someone Courtney shouldn't have been fucking with," commented Page Hamilton. "She could have ripped her limb from limb."

"It's pretty safe to say that a lot of people who lived in Seattle for a long time didn't like Courtney," comments Cali sagely.

I don't think you're giving away any secrets there, Cali.

"Courtney's ego didn't like to get beaten," he suggests. "I feel like Kurt was mad at Tad because of it. More like a husband's anger towards his assaulted wife."

The way he told it to me, he said Tad had been booked to play some of the *In Utero* tour, and they got dropped because of that incident. I remember him saying, "What can I do? Tad's my friend, but his wife attacked my wife. Am I supposed to just ignore it?"

"It was a reluctant anger, like, 'I'm supposed to stand up for my wife,' right?" Cali asks. "Even if he knows she's not in the right. She probably had it coming. When you're with someone who all your friends hate, it's a very uncomfortable situation. You want your friends to be your friends but if they're bad-mouthing your wife, you have to do something. It definitely contributed to his loneliness."

**Addenda: Frances Bean's first birthday**

"My second visit to Seattle coincided with Frances' birthday [August 18]," recalls Jessica Hopper. "Me and Cali [the pair were an item by then] were listening to Bad Brains and jumping on the couch with Frances like punk rockers. Kurt was on the next half-floor going through his records. He commented, 'I wish I could be this excited about music.' Frances was very much in our care: we'd given her a little Mohawk with Kool Aid and tinted her hair, and the next day we were reprimanded and told that a baby is not a dog – 'You guys. C'mon. She's a baby' – despite the fact she was a baby with a teeny tiny bomber jacket with a blue Germs circle on the back.

"I met Michael Azerrad during that visit: he'd come out to finish his book [*Come As You Are: The Story Of Nirvana*, sanctioned by Gold Mountain in a futile attempt to stop some of the more scurrilous reportage on the band]. Everyone thought Michael was safe because he was a dorky, jovial rock journalist – a nerd. He was there for a day or two doing interviews. There was a real air of secrecy and I was told, 'Don't look at papers.' They were strewn everywhere."

"Frances had her first birthday party in that house," says Charles Peterson. "It was a fairly good-sized affair. I took a couple of handfuls of Polaroids and gave them to Kurt at the end of the day. Everyone gathered in the sunken living room and was giving presents for this one-year-old. Somebody gave her a big red tricycle with a white anarchy symbol painted on the seat. There were tons and tons of gifts. I was sitting next to Kurt, and I've never seen anyone so sad and overwhelmed. It's supposedly this big, joyous moment, his daughter's first birthday, but I think a set of wooden building blocks would have been enough. It reminded me of the picture I took of him outside the record store where he's got his head in his hands. It was that same, 'My god, what is this monster?' "

"I remember the birthday party differently," comments Jessica. "The weirdness of the day was having people in the house – granted, it was like family, the closest thing they had to family: Nils, his brothers, Charles, Cali, Patti, maybe 10 people. I have picture after picture of Courtney and Frances smiling and playing, everyone smiling. Kurt was reclusive at best and the two of them together, they were in such isolation, they might of well have been on an ice floe. Paranoia was a huge part of the everyday. They were suspicious of even the closest people around them; no one came over except employees or one or two people here or there. I would say he was overwhelmed, not with Frances or her birthday, but merely from being around people."

## NOTES

1 Unsuccessfully. The claim Courtney later made that she was into 'juicing' (drinking freshly squeezed juice every day) can be taken with a pinch of salt. She didn't discover that fad until around 1997.

2 Cali would double up on duties with Nils Bernstein's mum Sigrid Solheim.

3 It was probably *I, Claudius*, the utterly brilliant 13-part UK TV series starring Derek Jacobi and John Hurt, made in 1976.

4 Acoustic guitar was a rarity in Hole songs – but that was how Courtney played 'Doll Parts' to me shortly after composing it, down the phone at 4 a.m., drunk and alone at a party. I told her the song was beautiful, and she shouldn't change it.

5 Lubricated Goat were an abrasive, nasty Australian grunge band from the late Eighties.

6 It was pretty damn good – heavy and *mean. Crunt* came out in February 1994, featuring Blues Explosion drummer Russell Simins.

7 On one bootleg recording of this show, Courtney can be clearly heard during this section, talking about Dave Grohl, and how her husband would be better off without the drummer.

8 Swell Maps were a killer ramshackle lo-fi band from the UK, who released some of the earliest independent post-punk singles, and were a major influence on Sonic Youth and Pavement, among others. The 1979 Rough Trade album *A Trip To Marineville* is the place to start.

9 Eddie And The Hot Rods were pre-punk pub rockers, best known for their 1976 call to arms, 'Do Anything You Wanna Do'.

## CHAPTER 26

# We Had Joy, We Had Fun

I HATE rock'n'roll.

How can I feel any other way? Look what it did to Nirvana. One moment they're cruising along happily, struggling to make the most commercial album they can to reach as many people as they can. The next, they've achieved their goal and realised that there's no way back, this is their life whether they want it or not.

No one ever tells you about the downside of hedonism: all the nagging headaches and colds and feelings of paranoia that exist for years afterwards.

In September 1993, 'Heart-Shaped Box', backed with 'Milk It' and the Dave Grohl composition 'Marigold'[1], became the first UK single to be lifted from *In Utero* – it entered the charts at number five. The front cover was a shot of one of Courtney's heart-shaped boxes of confectionary, framed by flowers on silver foil: the back was another Charles Peterson photograph of Kurt's montage of foetus-like dolls, petals and general debris, tinted blue. It was released to radio in the US, with accompanying video – but not as a single. Geffen, concerned that *In Utero* was uncommercial, refused to allow any singles to be lifted from the album for fear they'd detract from sales.

The video – directed by renowned Dutch photographer Anton Corbijn, but not without some controversy after director Kevin Kerslake filed suit in 1994, claiming it ripped off ideas from his original treatment – was littered with evocative, dark imagery: a little girl dressed as a Ku Klux Klansman, a crucified Jesus figure dressed as Father Christmas or perhaps the Pope, a field of poppies, a black crow, foetuses hanging from trees . . .

"I've always painted abstracts," Kurt explained to *Melody Maker*. "I love dreams that don't make sense. I'd much rather watch a film that doesn't have a plot. Most of my lyrics don't connect because I've taken lines from lots of different poems of mine and put them together. I'll make up a theme well after the fact, oftentimes while I'm being interviewed."

The situation with Kerslake dragged on through September: the director submitted several treatments before being informed his services were not required, despite the fact Nirvana were proceeding with a video that bore a marked similarity to his versions. It was an odd decision – Kerslake had directed four Nirvana videos ('In Bloom', 'Come As You Are', 'Sliver', 'Lithium') and helped Kurt sift through hours and hours of live footage and Super-8 movies of Nirvana for use in a full-length compilation video (released after Kurt's death as *Live! Tonight! Sold Out!!*). Kurt's decision not to use him and not tell him either, though, was classic Cobain passive/aggressive behaviour. (One detects the hand of Courtney in there, as well, not least because Anton Corbijn was a rock photographer of considerable prestige, who had worked closely with both David Bowie and U2.) Kerslake was even invited by the singer to attend the MTV Music Video Awards with him on September 2, because the 'In Bloom' video was up for an award.

"I went to the 'Heart-Shaped Box' video shoot," says Cali. "That was another interesting day as far as arguing goes. We were in LA at the Four Seasons. I think they'd been fighting a lot and Kurt had a vibe like, 'I wish Courtney would leave me alone.' She was picking at him in a Gold Mountain sort of way. She kept telling him, 'This is an important video for you, so don't fuck it up. You have to look good.' Him going, 'Shut the fuck up. I'll look how I look. I'll look like myself. Quit telling me how important this is.'

"That fight escalated over hours," he continues. "It was always a slow build. In a classic Kurt way of saying 'fuck you', he put a cigarette out in the middle of his forehead. There was a huge burn there and it looked really nasty. He goes, 'There, are you happy? Am I going to look fucking good enough for you now?' It took the wind out of her sails a little. If you watch the video, there's a lot of make-up on his forehead because it was a really bad scab, big and in the centre. In the close-ups, there's a strip of hair that never seems to move from the middle of his forehead. They had to paste some hair over it."

'In Bloom' won Best Alternative Video at the MTV Awards. The band attended, Courtney dressed like a minor Hollywood starlet in a low-cut white dress and perfectly tousled hair, clutching Frances Bean, waving to the media, almost unrecognisable from the way she looked when she first met Kurt two years previously. There was no controversy, aside from the van containing the band showing up late, and Krist nearly running over Jeff Ament from Pearl Jam in his haste to be there on time.

★ ★ ★

Six days later, on September 8, Kurt and Courtney played together for the first – and last – time on stage, at Club Lingerie in Hollywood. It was at a Rock Against Rape benefit, also featuring all-girl punk band 7 Year Bitch and [X singer] Exene Cervenka. Courtney played 'Doll Parts' and 'Miss World' solo before calling for her "husband Yoko", at which point Kurt got up on stage and the pair played together on 'Where Did You Sleep Last Night' and 'Pennyroyal Tea' (a staple of Hole's live set).

Nirvana were no longer the biggest rock band in the world – that dubious honour now belonged to Pearl Jam, whose new album *Vs* broke all records when it was released, going in at number one on *Billboard* and selling 950,000 copies in America, first week. In comparison, *In Utero* sold 180,000 in its first week when it was released on September 21[2] – although it too went in at number one. But those figures were affected by the refusal of two of America's largest chains, Wal-Mart and Kmart, to stock the album because of the foetuses on the back cover. They also objected to the title of 'Rape Me'. Geffen later revised the artwork so the fans could buy it at those shops – they deleted the foetuses, and altered the title of 'Rape Me' to 'Waif Me'.

"One of the main reasons I signed to a major label," Kurt explained, "was so people would be able to buy our records at Kmart. In some towns, that's the only place kids can buy records."

"The MTV Awards was the first of Courtney's 'trying to be somebody else' dresses," Cali comments. "That was around the time where the part of her personality that she already didn't like was turning into someone who would say, 'Don't you know who I am?' to waiters and stewardesses. She introduced me to Danny Goldberg and something about him epitomised everything I didn't like about the idea of a music-business person. Something about him epitomised something in that to Kurt too, and I think that Courtney liked that about him. Courtney liked the power she imagined Danny had. She would endlessly lecture us about why we were wrong about Danny."

I remember Courtney introducing me to Danny. He shook my hand but it was obvious he was thinking, "Why are you wasting my time with this person?"[3] A saying I really like is, "You judge a person not by the way they treat their equals or betters, but by the way they treat people who are in a less fortunate situation than themselves." Most record industry people wouldn't even begin to understand that.

"That's a good saying," Cali agrees. "I didn't like Danny Goldberg. I may have been only 21, but my immediate reaction to him was, this is one of the bad guys. I had the same feeling about John Silva. It was more real with Danny. My love for Courtney – and I did love her – started to come into question around the 'Danny is great' time. That was around the time she started to yell at waitresses."

That's the biggest problem I have with Courtney. If I apply what I just said to Courtney, I can't defend her. I always used to judge people by the way they treated me. Well, Courtney's done some pretty bad things by me on occasion, but on the whole she's been fine. We had a lot of fun. But if I apply that criteria . . .

"There's not much grey area," nods Cali. "With Danny I was like, 'Oh look, the devil's come over for tea.' I felt a kinship with Kurt about his dislike of industry people. I would order my Bikini Kill records through the mail and he'd be really excited when they came. He'd be like, 'I opened your package because I knew it would be some kind of awesome home-made records,' and we'd sit around and talk shit about people like that. His management made him uncomfortable. Courtney was always trying to tell him that he was one of them: 'You are one of the big boys now, and the losers you like are just that, losers.' That was commonly one of the things they fought about."

Cali's view of Kurt's relationship with his management may well have been influenced by Kurt's desire to appear punk rock in front of his younger, cool buddy. While objecting to the demands that Danny placed upon him and getting Dylan Carlson to look over Nirvana's accounts, Kurt clearly had faith in his manager. He drafted a will stating that if Courtney was to die, he and Rosemary Carroll should become Frances Bean's guardians.[4]

Or maybe he just needed a surrogate father figure . . .

"We were older people he knew that he felt had a relatively healthy family," explains Goldberg. "There weren't that many people who were married and had a kid that he felt comfortable with. I guess he didn't feel anyone in his direct family was appropriate in that scenario. We loved him. It was a thrill to be around someone who was so clearly a genius."

Nirvana's line-up at Roseland was a trial run for the forthcoming *In Utero* tour.

Kurt decided the time was ripe to feature another guitarist in the live show, and that the 'acoustic' middle section, with the addition of cello, was a step in the right direction. He began to look up old punk rock guitarists, but – he complained, seemingly heedless of the irony – "Most of them were junkies." Then Cali suggested he give Pat Smear a ring.

Pat was perfect. He was born and raised in western Los Angeles – real name Georg Ruthenberg – to mixed race parentage (an African-American/Cherokee opera singer mother and German/Jewish immigrant inventor father). In 1962, at the age of three, he ran away to a Jesus commune. As a teen, he attended the Innovative Program School in Santa Monica, a school designed for students who couldn't fit into the regular educational curriculum, where he met future singer Darby Crash. The pair formed The Germs in 1976.[5] Ruthenberg renamed himself Pat Smear after learning about pap smears in high school – because he thought they were so disgusting.

As a member of The Germs (and, later, as a solo artist and musician with artists like extrovert German singer Nina Hagen) Pat had impeccable punk credentials. Sonic Youth used Pat's name as the chorus of their 1994 song 'Screaming Skull'. The Germs' 1977 single, 'Forming'/'Sexboy (live)', is generally regarded as the first punk record from Los Angeles, and their debut 1979 album *GI*, produced by Joan Jett, is a highpoint of late Seventies US hardcore.

Pat had acted in films (*Blade Runner*, *Howard The Duck*), appeared on mainstream TV shows as an atypical punk and already been through a major junkie drama with Darby Crash, who killed himself in 1980 at the age of 22. Penelope Spheeris' cult LA punk documentary *Decline Of Western Civilization* – featuring performances from Black Flag, X, The Germs, Alice Bag Band and Circle Jerks – was filmed shortly before Darby's death.

Pat had a marked peculiarity on stage with Nirvana, of taking his shoes off just before playing, so he'd be standing in his socks. More importantly, he had a great sense of humour.

"There was a lot of painting our nails and putting on dresses – it wasn't like we'd go out and buy records or even leave the house," Rene Navarette says. "When you added Pat Smear to the mix, we were a real pile of pansies. We were pretty flamboyant. We liked drawing. We were having our glam period, and that's why Pat fitted in so perfectly. He was this punk icon who wanted to do the same as us, get loaded, put on make-up and tell jokes about it. When I found out Pat wasn't gay it made me feel more comfortable. It felt better to behave feminine and fool around with notions of sexuality, especially as it seemed to make the people we didn't like feel uncomfortable. As a group of guys, we were not promiscuous. As much as we'd joke about body parts, Kurt wasn't a pervert of any sort."

"Pat had been poor and living with his girlfriend for 10 years," says Cali. "Bands as big as Red Hot Chili Peppers had offered him a guitar-playing position [in early 1993], and he'd turned them down. He said the only new band he would play in was Nirvana. Pat was nervous and excited, and an excellent injection of fun and good times to the band. Kurt loved him."

"Pat was fun because he was an outsider coming into a stressful situation," explains Earnie Bailey. "He had the ability to not get drawn in – and I'm not sure if it was so much his personality or that he realised we were a bit in awe of him. I used to go see *Decline Of Western Civilization* at the midnight movies in Spokane, and one of my favourite sequences was The Germs part."

The first time Pat played with Nirvana was on *Saturday Night Live*, September 25, 1993. In marked contrast to January 1992, the show passed off without incident – apart from actor Adam Sandler threatening to do his Eddie Vedder impersonation, and Courtney throwing a fit because she thought Kurt would be blamed for it. The band turned in a couple of fine, soulful performances – 'Heart-Shaped Box' and 'Rape Me' – the two guitars tempered neatly by Lori Goldston's sweeping cello.

"They really had fun," comments Cali. "Pat's energy on stage was so different to what they were used to. He was nervous, but once it started he was going ape-shit like none of them ever did. They were all watching him – 'Look at this great guy having so much fun playing our music.' They all looked up to Pat because of his history in The Germs."

"Was that when The Breeders were playing upstairs with Conan O'Brien, and J. Mascis came backstage?" asks Earnie. "We saw Mike Myers come down the hall dressed for the first time as the coffee talk lady, and nobody recognised him. I remember thinking, 'Who is this woman with this really outlandish dress?' [Feted East Coast drag queen] RuPaul was a lot of fun; we hit it off with her instantly. John Silva had Converse hook us up with new shoes. Pat, Dave, Kurt and I all got Converse one stars, and Krist got low tops.

"Pat showed up with this Charvel Stratocaster [as used by poodle rocker Eddie Van Halen]," continues Nirvana's guitar tech. "It had a natural wood finish and a locking tremolo set-up – definitely not what Nirvana were at, guitar-wise. When he popped the case open there was this great silence. We were all just getting to know Pat, and we didn't know how to tell him he couldn't play that guitar. Kurt had this blue Mosrite [as used by Johnny Ramone – far cooler] with him that was one of the guitars damaged in his bathtub. I cleaned it up a little and got it working again, and we offered that to Pat to play instead."

*What ran through your head when Kurt asked you to join Nirvana?*

*"At first I thought it was my friend Carlos 'Cake' Nunez playing a joke on me, but Courtney*[6] *had called me a couple of days earlier and told*

*me Kurt was gonna call and ask me – so I was pretty prepared. Of course I accepted immediately! They were my favourite band at the time and 'Cake' was already trying to track down Kurt's phone number for me because I'd read an interview where he'd said that Nirvana was meant to be a four-piece. And I knew there was a new album and tour coming up. Anyway, I later heard that Michael 'Cali' DeWitt had suggested me, and it all worked out the way I'd hoped."*

*What were the first couple of weeks like?*

*"It was pretty intimidating. It took a while to get over the feeling that I didn't deserve it. But Kurt and Courtney invited me into their home and treated me like family and we sounded great at rehearsal, so I got comfortable real fast."*

*What are some of your favourite guitarists and greatest inspirations?*

*"I knew I wanted to play guitar when I was 12 and got Alice Cooper's* Love It To Death. *Not just because of the playing, but also because of that photo on the back of the white SG custom. Soon after, Bowie released* Ziggy Stardust *and had the coolest guitarist ever, Mick Ronson, who's equally great at rhythm and lead. And then Yes'* Fragile *came out, featuring Steve Howe, who is the best guitarist ever. A couple of years later, Queen released their first album that showcased Brian May who instantly became – and still is – my favourite guitarist. Joan Jett of The Runaways, Brian James of The Damned and Steve Jones of The Sex Pistols were the guitarists who inspired me to learn to play well enough to start a band. My parents forced piano lessons on me and it was really easy for me to play by ear, so I did the same thing with the guitar, learning the parts from my favourite albums."*

*Favourite guitars?*

*"Hagstrom! I never had my own guitar in The Germs but for some reason I decided to buy one for our farewell show. It was a red Hagstrom HIIN that set me back $125 and I've played it in every band I've been in. My second favourite brand is Gibson. I also love Japanese copies and counterfeits from the Seventies and other off-brand stuff."*

*Can you tell us more about your activities in the music world in between the end of The Germs and the joining of Nirvana?*

*"After Darby died I retired from music but was back soon enough. I played in lots of local bands and probably never took my career seriously enough, but I was able to have one without selling out. I've never been signed to a major label, never had a record 'advance' – so I've never owed 'The Man' anything – and I had never been on a full tour until I hooked up with Nirvana."*

(Interview by Rasmus Holmen, www.nirvanaclub.com, September 2002)

It was around this time the idea of Kurt collaborating with Michael Stipe[7] started to take hold. The pair met at a party at Krist and Shelli's house at 2253 N 54 St, Greenlake.

"The Fugazi guys were there as well," recalls Earnie. "We were down in the basement playing pinball with Michael when Kurt and Courtney arrived. You could hear Courtney upstairs asking, 'Where's Michael Stipe? I want to meet him.' We were nervous at first and being polite – and then she falls down the stairs into the room! I can still remember the look on Michael's face. It was an amazing entrance.

"Krist and Shelli lived in a great house, with a garage on the side," he continues. "In the basement, they had several pinball machines [Kiss, The Addams Family] and a jukebox, with records by [Sixties beat groups] The Count Five[8] and The Zombies[9], and 'Sex Bomb Baby' by Flipper. We would ride motorbikes to Second Time Around, this used record store in the U District, scouring for big hole 45s."

"It was such a change," Debbi Shane remarks, "from pooling together our food stamps [August 1991], to Shelli calling me and saying, 'Debbi, we just bought a house and we have a room for you!' They had a bar in the games room downstairs, with plants and flowers. They had a TV room with all the videos and records and stereos. They even had their old bed from Tacoma, and then they finally found a bed that Krist could fit his whole body on."

In the second week of October, Kurt flew out to Triclops Studios in Atlanta, Georgia to lend support to Hole's recording sessions for the band's second album *Live Through This*. Courtney wanted him to sing backup, but he was either unwilling or unable – a couple of numbers are said to feature his voice, but mixed so low as to be inaudible. Kurt was looking to expand his musical brief, however: every now and then, he'd jam with Eric Erlandson in the house. He felt frustrated at having to conform to the Nirvana template. It wasn't a comment on his bandmates, more at the expectations placed upon the three of them when they got together.

Kurt never did collaborate with Stipe – but really, Stipe was just another in a list of potential suitors that Kurt had shown interest in, interest that was more daydream than reality. More than anything, he wanted to play in the equivalent of Calvin and Tobi's 'project' bands . . . but whenever friends suggested doing anything like that, he'd grow suspicious, figuring they only wanted to join forces to exploit his fame. This may have been one of the reasons why he didn't sing on *Live Through This*.

"I never thought he was disenchanted with being in Nirvana," argues

Danny Goldberg, "but as an artist he wanted to play with other musicians. He wanted to stay alive creatively. He was going through a restless questioning period."

Oddly, almost all my memories of Nirvana live in 1993 are happy ones.

Much of this is down to Nirvana's road crew, a great bunch of people. Also, it helped that the band had a new collection of songs to tour, once they'd overcome their almost morbid fear of bootleggers. (Hey! There's nothing wrong with the odd live recording. It keeps money away from the record industry, and ensures the fans are happy. It doesn't stop anyone from buying the actual releases, either.) The fact that Geffen couldn't sell as many copies of *In Utero* must have pleased Kurt. Plus, Pat Smear had joined the band . . . and it's almost impossible to stay miserable while Pat's around.

There's no denying the situation wasn't ideal during Nirvana's final US tour, however. There was an obvious rift between Kurtney and everyone else: and also a developing rift between Kurt and Courtney themselves. Kurt's relationship with his management had deteriorated to such an extent that John Silva openly referred to Kurt as 'the junkie', while it was hardly a secret that Kurt hated Silva, and for most business dealings went through his assistant Michael Meisel. What didn't Kurt argue with his management about? The recording of *In Utero*, his home arrangements, his riders, his bandmates, his royalties, his drug use, his personal appearances, his press . . . he'd even stated categorically he wanted to take 1993 off from touring – and yet, here he was, embarking on the lengthiest Nirvana tour of all. On top of this, Kurt put down Dave in interviews; and his friendship with Krist had certainly seen better days.

"There was an incident where Kurt went crazy," recalls Rene. "We weren't sure if he'd got some ecstasy, because me and him had done some speed in secret. Round the back of the house someone had set up a load of little toy soldiers with some sticks tied together. He was super-paranoid. I confronted him about it – it was round the time he painted on the wall in red paint, 'You will never understand my real intentions' – because it seemed like he was trying to fit the 'crazy rock star' role. I'd tease him about it, which was part of the reason he liked having me around. Most people would stand back in awe: 'Oh, no one understands you, you're so complicated.' He really wasn't like that – he was a pretty simple, right-on guy, a little bit of a baby. In retrospect, you need to have a certain amount of self-pity to kill yourself."

Kurt's disgust with celebrity culture was growing unchecked, not helped in the least by Courtney's blatant love for it. Long gone were the days when he might have relished the idea of becoming a star, or looked forward to climbing into a van with Krist and Chad en route to another tiny club. Indeed, for the *In Utero* tour, two tour buses were hired – one for Kurt and Pat Smear, the other for the remainder of the band and crew members.[10]

"There was definitely a change," says Rene. "Courtney was finding her place among that higher level of fame, whereas the pressure got to Kurt a lot more. I went along to New York for *SNL*, and as soon as we got there, Cali and I claimed our vacation. They wanted us to stay at the Paramount, but we wanted to stay at St Mark's and do drugs with G.G. Allin; and we did, we woke up on the floor, covered with roaches . . . with G.G.'s brother, but that's still pretty good. Kurt OD'd while we were there – and they were mad with us because they couldn't find Cali or me. It wasn't a problem. We'd make fun of Kurt – 'Oh, did you OD on the body-bag?' – that's the different brands of heroin they sell in NY – 'Oh, you thought that was a really good idea, to buy a bunch of body-bag' – and he did, it was a joke most of the time. With his weird Pacific Northwestern twang, he'd tell us he liked the way it was working out, being a rich heroin addict. It seemed to bring him some happiness."

"Celebrity culture is so repulsive," comments Rosemary Carroll. "Kurt hated it. To see it like that, and then suddenly become it, must have been terrible for him. Courtney's response to it was different, she exploited and manipulated it and ran towards it. Left to his own devices, Kurt would have escaped it completely. It didn't bring him very much joy. He was convinced to tour by everyone who wanted him to tour – from his wife, to his managers, to his record company, to his band, to his fans. It wasn't an evil conspiracy. There was simply a tremendous demand to see Nirvana."

"There was a lot of tension and I didn't feel Nirvana were going to last much longer," Earnie says. "I didn't want to go on the *In Utero* tour. I felt it would be a nightmare. There was a lot of stress, combined with Kurt's escalating negativity towards Dave, which I felt was unjust. So I used my restaurant as an excuse to try and get out of it.

"Then Kurt put me in an awkward situation," he continues. "He said, 'Let me hire a manager for your restaurant so you don't have to work there any more.' I hemmed and hawed and said I couldn't do that. That's when he realised I was quitting Nirvana: and nobody had ever quit Nirvana, everyone had been sacked or whatever. Pat later said to me that Kurt thought it was amazing – that I could just walk away and say, 'Fuck it,' because he had wanted to, so many times. So they went out on the *In Utero* tour, and after a couple of days I got a call from Krist. Much to my surprise, he said it was going well. Once they got away from the outside distractions, they were having fun again."

The feeling was more upbeat than anyone expected. Most insiders attributed it to the fact Courtney was barely around: she was busy with other commitments, recording *Live Through This* and playing the occasional Hole live show. It was also rumoured she was sleeping with other men, particularly Lemonheads singer Evan Dando and old flame Billy Corgan.

"If Courtney was on the tour, the tour was not very much fun," states Cali. "The tension would be pretty thick. When she was gone, it would be back to everyone having a good time. But mostly it was fun. Alex [MacLeod] travelled with me and Pat and Kurt a lot. He was doing the best he could, tour-managing a madhouse. The shows were much bigger, and the audiences were not always the people they wanted to be playing to."

I didn't take notes on the dates I attended. The main condition Kurt placed on me when travelling in his tour bus was that I shouldn't write about Nirvana for *Melody Maker*. "You're always doing that," he complained. "Why can't you just come along as a friend? I don't mind if you want to do a book at some point in the future, but please no interviews or reviews." Of course, I complied with his wishes.

The *In Utero* tour started on October 18.

For support acts, Kurt chose several of his favourite bands – notably The Breeders, Half Japanese and The Meat Puppets – and consulted Cali on the others.

As both a solo artist and in Half Japanese, the astonishingly prolific Jad Fair has released countless albums of naïve, charming music: two types of songs – monster songs and love songs. I love Jad for his warmth, his spectacles, the way he cuts away the bullshit and strips music back to its essentials – humanity, a cracking good story and melody line. I love him for his boundless enthusiasm and shy genius. Maybe it's wrong to call Jad naïve because he certainly knows what he's doing, but he has a purity that to me is at the core of virtually any great music you might want to name.

Jad never tunes a guitar, believing such an action to be the antithesis of what rock'n'roll is about: spontaneity. He's never bought a guitar in his life: the ones other musicians throw away are fine. The guitar he played during a 1991 UK tour with The Pastels he picked up in a Glasgow junk shop for £28 the day after he arrived. He sings out of key, sometimes gratingly, always expressively. In his hooded parka and thick-rimmed spectacles he looks like an eccentric uncle. I've seen Jad play concerts with a rolled-up newspaper and upturned wastepaper basket for rhythm, with just his voice for colour. I've heard Jad improvise songs on the spot, songs that are heart-rending in their direct pleasure and emotion. And I've seen Half Japanese play stadiums in precisely the same fashion.

"With my headphones on, Jad and I share our little secret walking through shopping malls and airports," Kurt once wrote in a note to me.

"I like to listen to Jad Fair and Half Japanese in the heart of American culture," he explained. "It makes me feel like an alien, like I'm not actually walking, but floating like a dream. I just think that, if these people could hear this music right now, they'd melt, they wouldn't know what to do, they'd start bouncing off the walls and hyperventilating. So I need to hear that music really loud and pretend it's blasting through the speakers in the malls."

What can I tell you about The Meat Puppets? There are four early Eighties American hardcore albums you should own: the debuts from Flipper, The Minutemen, Minor Threat – and the taut, wired, explosive and downright funny 1981 self-titled album from the long-haired Kirkwood Brothers, Curt and Cris. Rarely have vocals sounded so skewed and manic, rarely have guitars seemed so hemmed-in and angular. Hardcore fans loved the Puppets for their breakneck speed – but there was more to the Phoenix, Arizona trio than intricate three-chord thrash. Curt's dislocated guitar style veered between hillbilly, heavy metal, psychedelic and Fifties country/gospel group The Oak Ridge Boys. His brother's bass sound was endearingly fallible. Their two mid-Eighties albums, *Meat Puppets II* and *Up In The Sun*, influenced a generation of musicians, from J. Mascis and Kurt Cobain onwards.

The Breeders, meanwhile, were the finest rock'n'roll band of their day. Kim Deal dressed like a mechanic and sang like a drowsy angel. Her voice oozed lasciviousness and *smouldered*, while her hedonistic bent rivalled Keith Richards. All I know is that there was something about the way she used to stand there on stage, cigarette hanging from her lips as she bent down to change another string. The former Mrs John Murphy wrote the finest pop songs of her generation, never pandered, did things by her rules – could turn out a mean country song, too – and got into bar brawls with Ohio truckers. And she never once apologised for her drug taking.

"Kurt let me pick a number of the opening bands," Cali says. "I picked Jawbreaker[11] and Chokebore. Having Jawbreaker on that tour caused huge drama in the punk rock world. People were like, 'Have they sold out or not? Can I still like them?' I enjoyed the freedom I had on the *In Utero* tour. Kurt would laugh because I'd go find the real punk kids and give them all-access passes, which infuriated Courtney when she was around. Sometimes I would go home because the argument ran that Frances couldn't be on the tour the whole time.

"Frances really liked being there," her former nanny continues. "She knew her dad's music and as soon as he started playing, she wanted to stand on the stage. She was only a little over one, so she wouldn't wear the ear-phones and she couldn't stay for the whole show. But she loved to be around."

The opening night was at the 15,000-seat Veterans Memorial Coliseum in the Arizona State Fairgrounds in Phoenix, with Mudhoney in support. The stage set was noticeably different – ornate, even: two full-size reproductions of *The Transparent Woman* from the cover of *In Utero*, angel wings intact, plus some odd-looking fake trees.

It wasn't as fancy as it might've been: "At the rehearsals at the soundstage in LA, they projected *Dante's Inferno* on a huge white screen behind the band," reveals Earnie. "It was so dramatic and powerful to watch them playing in front of that Twenties silent film. But someone calculated that it would cost too much to hire a crew and take it on the road, so they scratched the idea. They were uneasy about how well the tour would sell."

It was Nirvana's first major arena tour, and the musicians had difficulty adjusting to the size of the stages: "I felt like the bass-player from Aerosmith when they brought all the lighters out that first night," Krist commented to MTV news. In the same interview, Kurt lamented how he could no longer play in small clubs and stagedive with impunity; and also how he recoiled in horror from kids "trying to rip my flesh off for souvenirs". In response to their belligerent fans, the band would sometimes break into sarcastic refrains from stadium rock songs – in Phoenix, it was Aerosmith's 'Dream On'. In Albuquerque, New Mexico it was 4 Non-Blondes' 'What's Up' and a medley of Led Zeppelin riffs.[12]

"Before, we were just vagabonds in a van, doing our thing," Krist told *Musician* in October 1993. "Now we've got a tour manager and a crew and it's a production. We've got schedules and shit. It used to be an adventure. And now it's a circus."

Nevertheless, the first night went well – building to a climax with a storming version of 'Smells Like Teen Spirit' before finishing in mellow mood, with the cello-textured 'All Apologies'.[13] Not that you'd know it from the review that appeared in *USA Today*: "Creative anarchy deteriorated into bad performance art as the band overindulged a tendency towards willful chaos."

"Wow," Pat Smear remarked as everyone fell into an immense depression over the critique. "That journalist totally nailed us."

Before the gig in Kansas City on October 21, Alex MacLeod drove Kurt over to nearby Lawrence to meet his junkie idol William S. Burroughs. The 10-inch record the pair made together had been recorded separately. "Meeting Burroughs was a real big deal for Kurt," MacLeod commented. The two men chatted for a while before Kurt had to leave to go play his show: Burroughs later claimed the conversation didn't touch once on drugs. "There's something wrong with that boy," the literary giant remarked as Kurt drove away. "He frowns for no good reason."

The next night, in Davenport, Iowa, the crowd started slam dancing before Nirvana even took the stage. Afterwards, Kurt stopped at a taco place, two blocks from the venue, for a bite to eat. "Taco day was my favourite day at school," he told Geffen rep Jim Merlis as kids stood and stared at him, disbelief all over their faces.

In Chicago, Illinois, on October 23, the first of two nights at the Aragon Ballroom, the band played a previously unheard song – 'You Know You're Right'[14] – and Kurt waltzed off with one of the angels. The show was, by all accounts, a corker – certainly far superior to the second night there, where the band refused to play 'Teen Spirit' and Kurt lost his temper at fans throwing wet T-shirts on to the stage and shorting out his effects pedals board.

"Tonight's concert – Nirvana's second of two nights at the Aragon – is a real stinker," wrote *Rolling Stone*. "The venue's cavernous sound turns even corrosive torpedoes like 'Breed' and 'Territorial Pissings' into riff pudding, and Cobain is bedevilled all night by guitar and vocal monitor problems. There are moments of prickly brilliance: Cobain's sandpaper howl cutting through the Aragon's canyon-like echo in the tense, explosive chorus of 'Heart-Shaped Box'; a short, stunning 'Sliver' with torrid power strumming by guest touring guitarist Pat Smear. But there is no 'Smells Like Teen Spirit', and when the house lights go up, so does a loud chorus of boos."

"Chicago was bad because Bobcat [Goldthwait – American comedian, best known for appearing in the *Police Academy* series] made that joke," recalls Lori. "A friend was backstage with me, she was an actress, she was really on alert, and she made me pull myself away and look at it from the outside. The news story was Michael Jordan's father had got murdered, something like that. And Bobcat was opening, and he made a crass joke about it. The audience wanted to kill him. Things didn't pick up. Sitting backstage, people just didn't say anything for a really long time. The sound was bad."

Chicago was the nadir – not that it seemed to bother Kurt too much, who could be observed backstage happily playing with Frances. It was almost as if Nirvana had to get a truly bad gig out of their systems before they could start enjoying themselves. Certainly, the mood lifted after that night and the tour soon settled down into a comfortable routine: drive, hotel, soundcheck, hotel, gig, hotel, drive, hotel, soundcheck, hotel, gig, drive . . . with a few interviews thrown in, when Gold Mountain could convince the band it was necessary.

Nirvana would normally play 20–25 songs in 95 minutes, including the 'acoustic' section ('Dumb', 'All Apologies', 'Jesus Doesn't Want Me For A Sunbeam'[15], 'Something In The Way' *et al.* with Goldston on cello), and follow it with one encore usually ending on a noise/destruction sequence.[16]

"I travelled with the band," says Lori. "Everybody was really nice, polite and respectful – there was surprisingly little nutty partying. But it was so fucking boring! It felt like sensory deprivation to me, all the travelling, being told where to go, playing the same set every night. I liked the music and I watched all the bands every night, but the circumstances didn't suit me: to have the same set, same order, go home and watch cable TV. I talked a lot to Krist – he is, as you know, a hilarious guy."

He'd given up drinking by then?

"Not completely," the cellist replies. "But he wasn't playing drunk, and that was a big switch for him. There was talk about politics, and his family circumstances. Jennifer [Youngblood, photographer and Dave Grohl's fiancée] was around. Shelli was around. They were great. Earnie was really nice to talk to."

On October 26, Nirvana played the Mecca Auditorium in Milwaukee, Wisconsin. It was the final show with Mudhoney and Jawbreaker in support – Boredoms[17] and The Meat Puppets took over the following night in Kalamazoo, Michigan.

"That tour with Nirvana was horrible," exclaims Mudhoney guitarist Steve Turner. "It was the least fun we'd ever had, it was heartbreaking how fucked-up their organisation was and how, like, Krist was trying not to drink so the management was telling us we couldn't have beer in our room, yet at the same time their management would be coming into our room asking for a beer. They were spending all this money on hotels that they wouldn't even use sometimes, like thousands and thousands and thousands of dollars, yet they'd be worried about little things so they were firing people on tour almost every day, like crew members for saying the wrong thing. Kurt was miserable and secluded, it was so horribly sad . . .

"And then we were supposed to do this Pearl Jam tour a couple of months later," Steve continues, "and it was like, 'Oh my God. What's *this* gonna be like?' And it was great. Everyone's happy, their crew was all happy, big hugs with everybody, management was totally nice, but the decisions came from the band. It was night and day. It just made me hate . . . Nirvana's manager," he laughs. "Quite a bit. I just feel sorry for everything, and hate the world of big rock more than ever."

A show at the Michigan State Fairgrounds Coliseum in Detroit followed – Kurt stormed off stage after being hit on the head by a shoe – before two nights in Ohio. At the first, in Dayton, Kurt and Krist got it into their heads that Chad Channing was in the audience and refused to proceed until their old drummer came up on stage to play on 'School'. The show stopped for 10 minutes while the pair jammed on a version of The Stooges' 'Down On The Street' until they realised Chad wasn't present.

At the second, at the University of Akron on Halloween, the band dressed up for the occasion: Kurt as Barney, the big purple dinosaur, with a bottle of Jack Daniel's, Dave as a mummy, Pat as Slash from Guns N' Roses and Krist as a blackface Ted Danson from *Cheers*[18], with PC marked on his forehead (for Politically Correct). The party mood continued after another shoe was thrown, hitting Kurt on the head once more. Instead of storming off stage this time, he unzipped his flies, pissed into the shoe and hurled it straight back.

The tour moved across the border to Canada. After the sold-out show at the 8,500-capacity Maple Leaf Gardens in Toronto, Krist accompanied The Meat Puppets to an after-hours party where the four musicians jammed. They played noodling instrumentals, with Krist on guitar – but it's possible that Nirvana got the idea of asking the Kirkwood brothers to guest with them on *MTV Unplugged* from it.

On November 5, Nirvana played a tumultuous show at the University of Buffalo in Amherst, NY. Halfway through, Kurt stopped 'In Bloom' to shout at the security staff for holding their fans back from dancing at the front. "You guys in the yellow shirts, get the fuck out of here, you're spoiling the fun. They're not hurting anybody, so let them stay." Kurt then stagedived into the audience.

"There was a huge crowd at the show in Buffalo," remembers Cali, who was there with Courtney and Frances. "It was a lot of shirtless, thick-necked men screaming. For the encore, I went on stage with them and the Boredoms and The Meat Puppets. Kurt started to play 'Smells Like Teen Spirit' and then everyone made noise and the Boredoms screamed and blew horns and made a racket [with Boredoms' Yamatsuka Eye on vocals]. All those thick-necked, shirtless men started hurling stuff at us, and screaming, 'Fuck you!' Kurt liked that."

I remember the audiences being pretty respectful.

"There were good ones and there were bad ones," he replies. "There were shows where the entire arena would be flipping off the Boredoms and the next night everyone might enjoy them. It was really something else to watch the Boredoms play to that many people."

Two nights later, in Williamsburg, Virginia, The Breeders and Half Japanese joined the tour: "The Breeders were great," says Cali. "Kim [Deal] didn't change her clothes the whole tour. I'm sure it's an exaggeration, but as my memory serves, it's real. She dressed like a gas station attendant. She'd wear these dirty jeans and a dirty T-shirt. She would always have Jim Beam and a joint. She has grey hair – not totally, but she used to put grease in her hair before she went on stage so that you couldn't see the grey. It was funny to see someone be vain about that when they didn't change and they were drunk. One night the band started warming up without her. They were like, 'It's time to go on stage'. She went, 'Shit', and looked around, grabbed the ham off the deli tray and wiped it in her hair for grease and ran up the stairs. She left us all sort of speechless. I think it was Courtney who said, 'Her name now is Rawhide.' I was impressed."

I caught up with the *In Utero* tour on November 9, the same day that 'All Apologies' was released as a single in the UK. Once again, Geffen refused to release it in the States, fearing it would affect album sales.[19] It was backed with 'Rape Me', even more stark and unnerving when heard in isolation, and the totally excellent non-album track, the playful and heavy 'MV'.

I made it joint Single Of The Week in *Melody Maker*, alongside Bikini Kill's thrilling 'Rebel Girl', because:

> *"It's the most supremely resigned, supremely weary fuck you to the outside world I've heard this year. 'All Apologies' has the most gorgeous, aching tune, an emotionally draining* ennui. *Every time I hear Kurt break into that line,* 'Choking on the ashes of our enemies', *I grow close to tears, and I can't help but wonder at the stupidity of people who see Nirvana as a fashion accessory."*

That night, I can still vividly recall the scary ride from the tiny airport in Bethlehem, Pennsylvania to the Stabler Arena at LeHigh University, through endless miles of pitch-black woods – I'd stepped off the plane to find no taxi rank, no transport, nothing; just some bloke wandering up to me asking if I fancied a ride – and my feeling of relief when the bright glare of arena lights made itself known through the trees.

The sports arena itself was massive, cold and unwelcoming. Nobody was outside. There was no cause for anyone to be outside. It was in the middle of nowhere and I was late and freaked out by my mid-America surroundings. It seemed a very far cry from those early days spent thrusting my head into a bass bin in Seattle clubs or leaping off the Astoria stage in a blind frenzy, unconcerned with personal safety, as instruments worked themselves into a tumult of contrition around me. It seemed the total antithesis of everything I loved about rock music, loved about Olympia, loved about Nirvana. Where was the scope for spontaneity, for communication now? Was it on the faces of the thousand or so orange-coated security men directing me through a pointless chain of barricades? Was it in the echoing, cavernous sound of the venue itself, the brutal claustrophobia of rock unleashed into still, tepid evening air? Was it in the plastic seating, the rows upon rows of Aerosmith and Pearl Jam fans watching the band in MTV-led acceptance?

I sauntered up to the door and told the bullish hicks to let me in. I was Everett True! I was a fucking friend to the stars. One call to Alex MacLeod, and I was free to wander wherever I liked. I met my travelling companion, *Melody Maker* photographer Steve Gullick, who'd driven up from New York with eccentric Mercury Rev[20] singer David Baker. Steve amused us by burping the alphabet and enacting an entire kung fu movie with belched sound effects. Indeed, I recall that one reason Kurt took to Gullick so easily was the fact that, on one of the first occasions they met, Kurt belched loudly in Steve's face whereupon the photographer threw his head back and did perhaps the loudest belch I've ever heard. Kurt was suitably impressed.

"I got a picture of Kurt looking like Christ in Bethlehem," remarks Steve, "which was quite funny."

I later introduced David Baker to Kurt – when he'd gone, Kurt took me to one side and instructed me to, "Never let that man near me again." This was odd, because Kurt was usually tolerant of my strange companions and David was very likeable. Kurt could be intense and paranoid, though.

Despite the anaemic surroundings, I too recall this show – and the ones that followed it – as rare good fun, the best I'd seen Nirvana since 1991.

Tons of people in the vast hockey arena threw their shoes on to the stage, and walked home barefoot afterwards, in some strange Pennsylvania ritual. The mood was upbeat, Pat was clearly a tonic, Courtney most definitely wasn't around and everyone adored the Deal sisters (Kim and Kelley from The Breeders). Plus, it was such a thrill seeing Half Japanese warp and throw strange shapes on such a large scale, and Nirvana . . . Nirvana sounded amazing. I soon found a favourite spot to watch the show, just behind Earnie's massive rack of Kurt's guitars[21], to the side of the drum riser – either that or I'd be out the front, going crazy as the band hit the opening chords to 'Lithium', or 'Rape Me', or 'Blew', or 'In Bloom', or whatever.

From my vantage point, I watched Lori weave her magic on the cello, and exchanged constant grins with Pat Smear – both Pat and I still disbelieving at our good fortune at being allowed to be part of this – and shake my body around without fear of annoying the ever-stressed MacLeod too much.

The following day, Steve and I travelled up to Springfield, Massachusetts on Kurt's tour bus alongside Dave, Krist and Alex – the old gang, back together momentarily. We watched a *Cheech And Chong* movie. Dave was wearing a comedy Michael Jackson T-shirt, so Steve made a tasteless joke about Michael Jackson. Kurt suggested Steve shouldn't make jokes about people if he didn't know them.

"I'm just waiting to go to hell now," Steve comments, "so I can tell him some jokes about himself."

At the gig that evening, Kurt was standing at the side of the stage, watching Half Japanese, when a fan shouted over for a light – so Kurt ran into the crowd and obliged, freaking him out. The show once more was superb, 'On A Plain' sounding particularly poignant, and the noise finale of 'Scentless Apprentice' and 'Blew' so intense and extended that the only way anyone could drag Kurt off the stage was when Pat threw a bottle of Evian water over him where he knelt, hammering shit out of his guitar. Old songs such as 'About A Girl' and 'Sliver' seemed to be taking on new layers of resonance with every play – and anyone doubting Kurt's feminism should have caught his confused self-castration on 'Heart-Shaped Box' or fiery 'Frances Farmer' on this tour.

Other reports suggest that Kurt seemed pretty wasted at this show – that's possible. I recall the pair of us sharing a fair whack of whiskey beforehand. But it certainly led to an entertaining performance, with 'Territorial Pissings', 'Teen Spirit', 'Rape Me' and the searing refrain from the opening 'Radio Friendly Unit Shifter', *"What is wrong with me?"* in particular benefiting from his alcohol-fuelled spontaneity.

"Both gigs were great," confirms Steve. "They were a professional arena rock band. Both gigs were pretty much the same: really fucking tight and good. I enjoyed them a lot more than the Scandinavia gigs and Reading gigs in 1992, but *In Utero* is fucking amazing. I got the impression they'd worked out their problems."

Later, a handful of us threw a Queen party in Nirvana's other tour bus: Krist, Steve, Kelley Deal, Nirvana biographer Michael Azerrad and me. "The evening ended superbly in some car park," Gullick wrote in the Nirvana photo-book *Winterlong*. "Krist presented me with a bowling ball and a piece of broken TV screen that we'd been watching the Queen videos on. I think it was the prize for 'best Freddie impression'. They were Kurt's videos – he usually managed to hide his love for Queen from the press."

They had the following day off: Nirvana watched old school English punk band Buzzcocks play in Boston. I too departed, and hitched a ride back with Sebadoh/Folk Implosion[22] singer Lou Barlow and his future wife Kathleen Billus to the Fitchburg, MA show at the George Wallace Civic Center on November 12, where I introduced Lou to Kurt.

I knew the pair were fans of each other's work.

Can you remember the first time you met Kurt?

"Yeah, it was the only time I met Kurt," replies Lou. "They played that ice rink in Massachusetts. It was weird. We were mutual fans of each other, and had this uncomfortable conversation that people that are fans of each other's music generally have when they first meet. He was playing a show. People were hovering around. The first thing he said to me was he felt frustrated that Nirvana couldn't jam. He thought Sebadoh was more unfettered, like we were free. He was feeling self-conscious about Nirvana being locked into this rock routine and being in big buses."

What did you like about Nirvana?

"They were like Melvins but catchy," the singer says. "I felt bad for Kurt that he wanted the band to be experimental and radical, but they were a hit songs, catchy band. It was his voice. Black Sabbath meets Bay City Rollers, or whatever he said, that's how it worked for me. I didn't confuse them with being an experimental, indie, lo-fi band."

Do you think Nirvana opened a lot of doors?

"Not at the time," Lou sighs. "I just thought they were a really accessible sounding band, they wrote great sounding songs that were heavy, they produced their records in a way that translated to a larger audience. But it was great to have a metal band that doesn't have lead guitar and has a great screaming vocalist who doesn't sing about pulling chicks and taking drugs. He's singing impressionistic lyrics. That's a great combination. They're probably my favourite metal band other than Black Sabbath. They presented to me the best aspects of chunky, simple lyrics you can get behind, and a great vocalist. That was Nirvana. I know he was such a fan of indie rock, and he felt a little bit at odds with what he was producing, as opposed to what other people were producing. What he could do though, he did well. He probably did it effortlessly. Which probably really confused him."

The next night, in Washington, DC, I was standing at the side of the stage watching Nirvana encore, furtively drinking my whiskey, hiding it from the fiery glare of Alex MacLeod. I wasn't supposed to drink while I was travelling with Nirvana, management orders, for fear of being a bad influence. Frequently though, Alex would come up to me, check my mug of black coffee and give me a snifter from a bottle hidden inside his jacket when assured I'd been a good boy. Suddenly I became aware that he was shouting my name. "Oh fuck," I thought to myself. "What have I done wrong now?" I was a bit scared he might have discovered I'd had a hand in Pat Smear's prank of busting his hotel toilet with the aid of two towels earlier.[23] I look up, and see he's rushing towards me.

"Kurt wants you to sing the encore. Get on stage NOW!" he yells above the noise of the PA. On the live recording of the show, you can hear Kurt going, "Please don't throw your shoes," before screaming "Everett" down the microphone several times. It's spooky to hear your own name shouted with such passion.

I'd been joking with Kurt beforehand that he should get me on stage because the last time I'd performed live with Nirvana was at the 9:30 Club in the same city, two years earlier. I never expected him to take me seriously. So I rushed on, parka pulled up over my head, whereupon Kurt did his usual trick of shoving his guitar-strap over me amid confusion because he's left-handed and he's putting it on upside down and I can't fucking play guitar anyway. "Don't worry about it," he laughed. "It looks better with you wearing it. You can always smash it afterwards."

What did I sing and play? I have no idea: something to do with doughnuts. I kept chanting in a vague approximation of the beat and distorted guitar the band was playing behind me. As they continued, so did I. The audience looked . . . bamboozled isn't the right word. *Cheated.*

Did I smash Kurt's guitar at this show? Who knows? "If it feels good, do it," as Kurt himself said a few years earlier. And it feels fucking great to smash a guitar. They're also a lot harder to break than you might think.

"I don't think you did break that guitar," says Earnie Bailey – who should know. Hmm. It was probably because I could see Alex drawing a line across his throat, like he was going to murder me if I did any such thing. "Yeah," he laughs. "Still, I would have remembered that." Kurt grabbed the guitar from me, and started hurling it at a mirror ball hanging a few feet away – he never did manage to hit it. Eventually Krist had to climb back on stage and carry him off, tucked underneath his arm.

That night I clambered on to a bunk in Kurt's tour bus alongside Pat for the journey back to New York. We watched videos of puppet sex created by insane Midwest band The Frogs most of the way. It was a long drive, and no one was saying much.

When we arrived in New York at 6 a.m. I discovered I had no money, and furthermore my booked hotel room didn't come into effect until midday. Kurt offered me his floor to sleep on, and departed upstairs to go check the situation out. Confused, I wandered out on to the streets of New York with my rucksack and got caught up in the preparations for the NYC Marathon that were taking place across the block in Central Park. Kurt came back downstairs, surprised that I'd disappeared. "Where did you go, man?" he asked later on that day as we sat outside in the catering tent by the Javits Center Coliseum and I tried to nurse my ravaged voice back into health again with copious amounts of honey, herbal tea and hot lemon. "I looked for you for ages."

I couldn't reply. My voice had gone.

That Coliseum show – prestigious, Nirvana's first announced show in Manhattan since the Marquee Club in September 1991 – was even more surreal. I recall standing in the super-VIP area by the stage: there was only one other person in the enclosure, supermodel Naomi Campbell.[24] Huh? The whole time, I was thinking, "I'm going to be up there shortly" – but I couldn't croak above a whisper, I'd screamed myself so hoarse the previous night. I was suffering from nerves, mainly because I knew Kurt was going to call on me to sing again and for some reason I'd sworn off alcohol momentarily, probably because I couldn't speak. The sound was dreadful: echoing around the cavernous, circular venue like a disused aircraft hangar. Indeed, I so couldn't sing that Kurt doubled up for me, the pair of us doing some sort of deranged duet. "Kurt wasn't even singing," Jim Merlis told Carrie Borzillo-Vrenna (not quite true, as bootlegs prove). "It was Everett by himself. It was so terrible. Kurt brought him on stage and he just screamed into the microphone."

The following morning, Nirvana's management received calls from New York journalists wanting to know who the mystery 'rock star' on stage with Nirvana had been.

"I bet you were happy about that," comments Earnie.

I think it's funny as fuck. The fact that people like Jim hated me was the reason why Kurt asked me to get on stage in the first place. It was pretty obvious he wanted to piss the crowd off.

"Was that the show where Alex threw Kate Moss out?" asks Earnie. "She had come backstage with a friend of hers, and I heard there was something bizarre about that, like they approached the security guy and he let them in without being on the guest list. So Alex booted them out."

The Roseland Ballroom on November 15 was another great show although I was almost past caring as I'd pummelled my body so hard. It was another industry showcase – supposedly an intimate one at that – but I never did come to terms with the concept of a 5,000-capacity venue being 'intimate'. Surely intimate means you and Kurt's mum, and no one else? Or maybe one of the old house parties Nirvana played in Olympia when they were starting out.

"That show was amazing," comments Rosemary Carroll. "The intensity with which they played was one of the things that made them so great: the expression of pent-up anger and frustration, and the sense of solidarity with the audience that was wordless and wasn't pandering . . . Kurt had the ability to establish the connection with the audience that very few people have."

A whole load of us gathered on stage for the encore, an extended version of The Stooges' 'I Wanna Be Your Dog'.[25] Kurt played drums, Dave was wandering round with a bass, I was croaking out the occasional line that I could remember, Jad was shouting down a megaphone, Krist was beating a floor tom, and various members of Half Japanese were pummelling the hell out of their instruments. At the song's climax, Pat Smear handed Jad Fair's young stepson Simon one of Kurt's guitars, and nodded at him, encouraging him to break it – he took about a dozen attempts. By the time he'd finished, the whole ensemble was standing round cheering him on.

"At first, I was horrified at the way Kurt would smash instruments," Pat Smear told www.nirvanaclub.com's Rasmus Holmen. "But it was showbiz . . . certainly not as horrifying as Darby Crash smashing bottles on his head and slicing his chest up at every show. And then I learned about Earnie Bailey, who was a genius at putting them back together in ways that made them even cooler than they started out. Guitar smashing is pretty contagious, though – I did it myself sometimes. Fender would send us fresh guitars on tour and you'd have like three brand new guitars that were all identical. I almost needed to scar them up just to tell them apart. Overall, I think guitar smashing is as amazing and shocking as it was when I first saw it done by Marc Bolan at a T. Rex show in '73.[26] Who cares, it's just a piece of wood. Smash away!"

"In '92 and '93 I would bring a mixed bag of guitars along," recalls Earnie. "And you never really knew what was going to get it, and things got it for different reasons. By *In Utero* we were getting these more disposable Stratocasters and Japanese Mustangs, and I remember thinking, 'The Mustangs are going to be the first to get splintered,' because I thought they were terrible. I did a few basic modifications to them, to make them at least tolerable during the one song Kurt was going to smash them, and they turned out to be his main workhorses.

"It was strange because, in the early days, if Kurt only had one guitar and the time was right for smashing, he would smash it. It didn't matter how much he liked the guitar. I felt the destruction set should have been phased out by the *In Utero* tour. In a way I liked it, though, because it could turn unpredictable and it was a part of my purpose for being there. And they weren't smashing rare guitars that had survived four decades, but new, off the shelf things."

I didn't attend the recording of *MTV Unplugged* on November 18. I can't remember why. I was in New York, and I'm sure it would have been easy enough to go. Probably, I wanted no more part in the corporate crap surrounding Nirvana. Listen to those wankers cheering every note of each song's introduction on the CD,[27] like it's a jazz concert. Look at all those lilies, chandeliers and black candles, cameras and carefully framed screen shots on the sleeve. You tell me I was wrong to stay away. What did *MTV Unplugged* have to do with Krist or Dave, or even Pat?

Nirvana were a band, remember.

Why is it that American music critics think rock groups turn grown up the moment they go acoustic? It couldn't possibly be because they didn't like said rock groups in the first place, could it?

*MTV Unplugged* is not Kurt Cobain sharing an intimate moment with the world; you have intimate moments in the privacy of your own bathroom. You don't have intimate moments in front of batteries of soul-sucking video cameras and technicians. I'm not denying that when Kurt covers that Vaselines song ('Jesus Doesn't Want Me For A Sunbeam'), or David Bowie's 'The Man Who Sold The World' with its insistent guitar refrain, it touched a chord deep within me, and hundreds of thousands of fans. And the Leadbelly cover ('Where Did You Sleep Last Night?') is pure gold, Kurt's voice sounding so awesomely betrayed and world-weary, and when he screams . . . when he screams, my God, it's like a thousand years of blood-lust and disappointment and rejection, all encapsulated within a couple of bone-chilling moments. (It's pretty bloody obvious who the song is aimed at – especially considering Courtney wasn't present.) And yes, it was nice to hear Kurt experimenting with his songs, and giving them space to breathe and blossom.

It's just . . . Jesus! It's *MTV*, the absolute enemy, for God's sake.

How patronising was the whole concept of inviting Nirvana on to a show like that? The Kurt of old would have scorned it for the shallow façade it was.[28] The singer was in too deep to withdraw by this point, though. Myself and Gullick skipped across town to where old mates Chicago's Urge Overkill were sitting in a diner, dreaming of being swank rock stars on a par with Neil Diamond . . . or at least Nirvana.

There was crap surrounding *MTV Unplugged* right from the start.

As ever, MTV were being arrogant corporate assholes, thinking they knew how to judge a band's material better than the band itself – they wanted Nirvana to play the hits, no unknown songs. Kurt disagreed and announced he wanted The Meat Puppets to come on as guests, much to the disgust of MTV, who were expecting Eddie Vedder at the very least. Originally, the idea was that Nirvana were going to cover three Meat Puppets songs – 'Plateau', 'Oh Me' and 'Lake Of Fire', all from their second album – but, as Pat Smear explained, "Curt Kirkwood's playing style is so unique we could never make them sound quite right. Krist or Kurt suggested that we just have 'em come up and do it themselves."

It wasn't like the format itself was particularly successful, either: Stone Temple Plagiarists had done an *Unplugged* a few weeks earlier, and taken several hours to record a 45-minute, ostensibly 'live' set.

It wasn't even 'unplugged', come to that, as most bands – including Nirvana – played with their instruments amplified. They just played a little quieter.

"We did the rehearsals out in New Jersey," says Earnie. "I worked on two of Kurt's Mustangs that day, and his Jagstang as well. I could hardly look over at the stage. Every song sounded very rough and awkward, like hearing a band getting together for the very first time. I couldn't believe they were going ahead with this the very next day. It was looking like their first bad career move. There was one glaring mistake during 'Pennyroyal Tea'. On the video, it's apparent – but they went back and fixed it on the CD, and I almost wish they hadn't. 'The Man Who Sold The

World' was unbelievable, it gave you chills, but I didn't see the point of releasing the album. I liked The Meat Puppets' songs better than their own songs, but I didn't care for the guitar sounds on the record."

Others disagree with Earnie and me, though.

"Last time I saw Kurt was at the *Unplugged* show," says New York photographer Michael Lavine. "He specifically got us front row seats and came out and gave [video-maker] Steve Brown and me huge hugs. On stage, it was perfect. We went backstage and he was messed up, grumpy and distant, somebody had given him those green Converse with the white stars – those were the shoes he was wearing when he killed himself."

"That was an incredible show," remarks Janet Billig. "Kurt was so focused and in it, and this was a bit of a surprise as he was not in a good place emotionally by that point. He was angry that day, really shitty and moody at everyone around him[29], but when he got on stage he was incredible. He was *in* every song. He was so excited about the songs being taken seriously, that they were being properly crafted. I told him afterwards it was a career-defining moment and that he played guitar beautifully, and he retorted that he played guitar like fucking shit. You could comfortably say he didn't take a compliment that easily. And that was the path he was on, songwriting that was real and true."

"Kurt was extremely excited about it," comments Danny Goldberg.[30] "He was very proud of it and thought it would bring the band to a whole new audience. The fact it came out retrospectively doesn't mean it was someone else's idea."

"That was one of my only regrets," says Cali. "Here's exactly as it happened. It was a drug thing. Courtney and I were in Seattle and we both had been doing drugs for the weekend and didn't want to go to New York. We got to the airport; we got on the plane, but while we were waiting for the plane to take off, we talked ourselves into believing that the show would be better for Kurt if we weren't there – which actually might have been very true. Really, our reason for not going was that we wanted to go back to the house and get more drugs, and that's what we did. So I didn't see *Unplugged*. Instead, I got to hang around with scumbags on Capitol Hill.

"Talk about missing a great, great show," Cali laughs. "I didn't even think about it until a couple of weeks later when I heard a tape of it. It was just so good. Hearing them do 'The Man Who Sold The World' for the first time blew my mind."

* * *

A couple of days before *Unplugged* was recorded, an amusing incident happened outside the band's New York hotel, the Regis.

"There's a certain kind of New York kid that's crazy for famous people – all a little too old to be doing it, aged about 20–21, drama club kinda kids," states Lori Goldston. "There were three of them waiting outside the hotel, holding CDs. We came out, and they rushed over. 'Kurt, Kurt!' He was in a bad mood. They were like, 'Kurt, we love you!' – and he got out the van, stood up on the step and spat over the van on to these kids on the sidewalk. They looked shocked. Absolutely stunned, crestfallen, devastated, and it was really, really funny. I'm not a mean person, but it was hilarious. He was a really good spitter, and this was the only rock gesture I ever saw him make."

**Addenda 1: Steve Turner**

Why did Nirvana get big and not Mudhoney?

"It's pretty obvious!" exclaims the Mudhoney guitarist. "That record [*Nevermind*] is anthem after anthem. It's very deep music. We had songs that were serious too, but Nirvana sound totally legit and real and there's a desperation that cuts deep."

I always thought Kurt was a rotten lyric writer.

"He was, but he has one of those voices that could sing the telephone book and make it sound real and convincing. Nirvana frustrated me so much once they got famous: how could that band make as many mistakes as they made? Once they got a little bit of success, it was like, 'Oh my God, you're doing everything wrong!' I never liked the production on *Nevermind*, it sounded like Eighties big rock. I liked the demos better – great melodies, great songs, great voice. I don't like Grohl's drumming at all. He's a hard-hitting, pounding drummer. I like things with more finesse. I liked Chad's drumming for Nirvana, a little sloppier and a little looser. It swung more."

Do you think Olympia was a big influence on them?

"Sure. Well, Krist was always the guy that hung out with Melvins, from day one. I think the Olympia influence became negative towards the end – where Kurt kept trying to prove that he was real and 'punk rock', as opposed to Pearl Jam. One of the saddest mistakes they made was his inability to admit what they'd done with *Nevermind*, that they'd gone totally LA – and that's not bad, whatever. They made a pro, expensive record, they had people remix it for radio, they played ball completely and it worked.

"There was a lot of guilt and back-pedalling trying to prove they were still punk rock. They surrendered way too much control to their management and lawyers and people. It was almost like they were saying, 'If we don't care about what we're doing that means we're more punk rock than you.' What???" Steve shakes his head in bemusement. "Nirvana became stooges far more than – to use the opposite example – Pearl Jam. Pearl Jam were in control of their own destiny. Whereas once Nirvana got big, it was like, 'OK, now you have your money-hungry management making decisions for you.' Great! That's real punk rock!"

Going back to the Olympia influence . . .

"Olympia is a bit of a mystery to me. They played their first show in Olympia. In their early days it seemed like everything they did was organic and a lot smaller, like their scope was small: it wasn't about success, more about being with cool people, nice people and whatnot. Nirvana wasn't really from Seattle. They were closer to Olympia. Geographically, they were more aligned with the scene there and also to the Olympia lifestyle, both the college kids and the wastoid rednecks. Meeting some of the Melvins' and Matt [Lukin]'s friends in Aberdeen freaked me out. I was like, 'This is fucking *weeeeeird*.' That was not my world at all down there."

A lot of Kurt's ideas about punk rock . . .

"They sprung directly from Olympia and Calvin. Yeah. A lot of that stuff came from DC as well, the politics of it."

It's about setting up your own alternative lifestyle outside of society . . .

"Which is great! I'm all for it!"

But this is where things got fucked up with Nirvana because all of a sudden they decided they were a punk band – and punk has traditionally embraced the mainstream . . .

"Yeah, they were being pushed and pulled and they couldn't even admit some of their influences . . ."

I guess part of the problem is that Olympia is a very elitist town.

"People move there and become snobs. It's weird. They never liked Mudhoney down there."

That elitist attitude sat very uncomfortably with fame. You can't have both. You can't be ultra-elitist and make a record like *Nevermind*.

"Yeah, if they'd just admitted their ambition, if they could have reconciled the dichotomy somehow – and it's not a big stretch, it's stuff that doesn't fucking matter in the big picture. It's little insular in-fighting crap that doesn't apply any more."

The mystery person in this equation to me is Krist.

"Krist is very punk rock, but he wants everyone to love each other.[31] He's just a big . . ."

. . . old hippie.

"Yeah. Totally. Big fucking hippie. He was kind of the guy that was along for the ride. He did stuff but he was trying to make what Kurt wanted to happen, happen."

He got thrown quite a curveball in the shape of Courtney.

"Right," Steve laughs. "That kind of . . . messed things up a little bit."

You think?

"It's weird because they dropped the ball big time. That's the tragedy of the whole thing to me. They couldn't see that they'd outgrown any of their previous ideas. Everything that they were using to make decisions was irrelevant. If they'd only sat down and talked with Pearl Jam, I swear to God, it would have helped them *a lot.* They were in a powerful situation and they just handed it all to people like that manager guy [John Silva]. Fucker! And the thing that always blew my mind was that Sonic Youth used him. I just never could understand, like, even before Nirvana, I was like, 'Why is this guy your manager? He's a prick!' I never could figure out how they could deal with him."

**Addenda 2: Bruce Pavitt**

You know that The Legend! got up on stage with Nirvana several times on their last US tour. About five or six dates. We did the encore together, myself singing.

"I didn't know that!" exclaims Bruce.

Yeah, the Courtney-sanctioned version of history (*Heavier Than Heaven*) doesn't mention it.

"It seems Kurt and the band were able to maintain some creative ties, although it seems Courtney did her best to sever a lot of those ties. For the most part, it appeared that attorneys and managers and handlers surrounded Kurt in his final days, while many of his long-standing creative friends – and I would include myself in that, and Calvin and so forth – felt distanced. Courtney did not want any of those people around."

Mark Arm and Steve Turner say the same thing at this point. They can't figure out why Nirvana chose to absolve themselves of all power and give themselves over to just about the biggest management company going.

"That was the same management company that was working with Sonic Youth and The Beastie Boys."

But Sonic Youth took control of their own lives.

"Well, I wasn't familiar with the inner dynamics of that relationship, but that's the management company that all the large progressive acts were working with. It doesn't surprise me at all."

Again, Mark, Steve and Dan from Mudhoney all cite the *In Utero* tour –

they say it sucked in so many different ways. And they all draw a parallel with the Pearl Jam tour they went on shortly afterwards.

"I heard those stories, too, and at the time, it was not seen as a reflection of the management at all. It had everything to do with Courtney Love. It was like, 'Oh, we went on tour with Nirvana, and Kurt and Courtney had their own bus separate from the rest of the band.' Their management had nothing to do with this decision. It was Courtney separating Kurt from his own bandmates! I remember them coming back and telling me the same thing: 'And then we went on tour with Pearl Jam, and even though they are the corporate band, the energy and the connections and the culture that was cultivated with their group was inclusive, was human.' That was an interesting paradox. That the alternative band was behaving in a more grossly corporate way than they could possibly have imagined. It had nothing to do with John Silva."

Pat Smear travelled with Kurt.

"Pat Smear travelled with Kurt," the former Sub Pop boss repeats. "That's true, and that's interesting. Why him, and not Krist?"

Pat was from LA, so he was Courtney-approved. Also, Krist's wife had a major problem with Courtney, and Shelli's not the type to hold back.

"Right. Shelli's pretty cool."

## NOTES

1 Laidback, harmony-laden and based round an acoustic riff with a softened vocal from Grohl himself – 'Marigold' was to prove an incisive glimpse into Dave's future career as bandleader of the unit-shifting, radio-friendly Foo Fighters.

2 *In Utero* was released a week earlier in the US on clear vinyl only, a limited edition of 25,000. The UK release date (both vinyl and CD) was also September 14.

3 Having said that, I should add that Danny Goldberg has been very helpful and supportive during the writing of this book – and I have considerably revised my opinion of him.

4 The list ran: Danny and Rosemary, Kim Cobain, Janet Billig, Eric Erlandson, Jackie Farry, Nikki McClure . . . and then his own mother, Wendy. The will was never signed. Apparently.

5 One of The Germs' drummers was Dottie Danger aka Belinda Carlisle, who later formed all-girl chart band The Go-Go's, most notable for the bouncy number one 'We Got The Beat'.

6 Pat Smear and Courtney Love became friends after meeting on the set of Joel Silberg's 1984 hip hop movie, *Breakin'*.

7 Remember Courtney's Portland list of How To Get Famous? Number five: make friends with Michael Stipe . . .

8 It was almost certainly The Count Five's frenzied 1966 Top 10 hit, 'Psychotic Reaction'.

9 It was quite possibly The Zombies' sweetly melodic 1964 Top 10 hit, 'She's Not There'.

10 Craig Montgomery was no longer touring with Nirvana, having left after a disagreement over the sound on *Saturday Night Live*.

11 Jawbreaker were a second-generation hardcore band from Santa Monica. Their third album, 1992's brooding *24 Hour Revenge Therapy*, benefited from the almost obligatory Albini production. They signed to Geffen in late 1994, on the back of Nirvana's patronage. They shouldn't have.

12 With rich irony, Courtney Love later collaborated with 4 Non Blondes producer Linda Perry on her truly appalling solo album, 2004's *America's Sweetheart.*

13 The set ran: 'Radio Friendly Unit Shifter', 'Drain You', 'Breed', 'Serve The Servants', 'About A Girl', 'Heart-Shaped Box', 'Sliver', 'Dumb', 'In Bloom', 'Come As You Are', 'Lithium', 'Pennyroyal Tea', 'School', 'Polly', 'Milk It', 'Rape Me', 'Territorial Pissings', 'Smells Like Teen Spirit', 'All Apologies', 'Blew', 'Endless, Nameless'.

14 Courtney initially laid claim to 'You Know You're Right' by performing it with Hole on *MTV Unplugged*. It later resurfaced on DGC's 2002 'greatest hits' compilation *Nirvana*.

15 Contrary to reports in *Heavier Than Heaven*, Nirvana never once played a gospel song entitled 'Jesus Wants Me For A Sunbeam'.

16 For example, at the end of the Kansas City show, as 'Endless, Nameless' blew itself out in a orgy of distended guitar strings, Kurt informed the audience he was leaving his guitar switched on (where it was resting against an amp, feeding back) until they all went home.

17 From Osaka, Japan – Boredoms are a vivid explosion of colour and light and communal belching and feedback and blaring trumpets: brilliantly, bizarrely hilarious.

18 Ted Danson had been ridiculed a few weeks previously, for appearing in blackface with his girlfriend Whoopi Goldberg.

19 Later that month *In Utero* was certified platinum in the US (sales of one million), so it seems that perhaps Geffen could have relaxed *a little* about the sales. *Nevermind*, meanwhile, had just passed the five million mark.

20 I wrote that on NYC band Mercury Rev's second album, 1993's *Boces*, "Guitars meld, and fuse into one gigantic, multi-headed beast. Flutes whisper in and out like the wind on the Interstate 5. Drums echo cavernously and spring off on multiple paths of exploration. Listening to Mercury Rev is like slipping down a shopping mall of freaks and hairdressers, only to be confronted by wilderness."

21 Earnie had been convinced to join the tour by that point.

22 The Folk Implosion were Lou's peculiar chart crossover band – Sebadoh honed down and slightly cleaned up, basically – best known for 1995's hit single 'Natural One', taken from the raw *Kids* movie soundtrack.

23 Earnie Bailey: "MacLeod was charging for everything back then. It was only a year ago that Pat said he got his first cheque from Nirvana, saying he owed nothing."

24 Tennis star John McEnroe was later spotted looking decidedly out of place in Nirvana's dressing room.
25 Mudhoney also used to delight in inviting people up on stage while encoring with the same song.
26 Pat may be getting his Marc Bolan groups confused. In 1973, Marc was a heart-throb pop star. He actually used to smash his guitar with his first group, Sixties psychedelic pop stars John's Children. They got thrown off The Who's 1967 German tour for trying to upstage them in the destruction stakes.
27 *MTV Unplugged* was released after Kurt's death, the sound cleaned up and the between-song banter and occasional jam removed. Cash in? Of course.
28 MTV themselves only belatedly decided it was 'classic' music TV after Kurt died. Up to that point, they hadn't even screened it.
29 Kurt was in withdrawal, and incredibly nervous about playing acoustic.
30 Krist, on the other hand, referred to it as 'Nirvana lite' in the album's press release.
31 It's almost a prerequisite of being a bass-player: to try and stop the other musicians fighting.

# CHAPTER 27

# Fallen Angels

THE last conversation I ever had with Kurt was on Christmas Day 1993, when he and Courtney rang me up at my house in Brighton, England.

"You're the only person we could think of out of all our friends who'd be in today," Kurt explained, mindful of an anti-Christmas rant I'd given him and Kim Deal two weeks earlier in Seattle. "We haven't spoken to anyone all day, except for the postman. How are you? Still miserable? Merry fucking Christmas."

I tell this anecdote now, but I have a feeling the last time I actually spoke to Kurt may have been when Courtney called up and said, "Kurt wants to ask you something." This was odd, cos Kurt didn't usually call me on the phone. After half-a-minute of heated argument in the background, he picked up the receiver and mumbled something about how he wanted me to visit his 'doctor' in a nearby town, pick up some supplies and ferry them across to Seattle.

I told him – very politely, I'm sure – to fuck off.

*"What are you going to do on New Year's Eve, Kurt?" asks Kim Deal.*

*"Get drunk off my ass, and play with pyrotechnics," replies Nirvana's singer. "We're playing in San Francisco, and we're going to have pyro-technicians come and shoot off some fireworks. Isn't that cool?"*

*You're going to get drunk? You never get drunk before you play.*

*"OK," he admits. "Afterwards."*

*How about you, Kim? What do you normally do on New Year's Eve?*

*"Bang pots and pans," she laughs, stoned. "Go out on the streets. Yeah!"*

*Kurt wants to know if I smoke pot. I shake my head.*

*"No?" he continues, amazed. "Have you never smoked pot?"*

*I feel a distinct sense of déjà vu coming on. Maybe the tape recorder is stuck on a loop. Maybe the lack of sleep is finally getting to me.*

*Yeah, of course I have.*

*Kurt isn't satisfied.*

*"You don't have a pot-smoking period in your life?" he persists.*

*No. I squatted once, though. Do you know what squatting is?*

*"You lived somewhere where there's no electricity?"*

*Something like that. A guy OD'd in the room next to mine.*

*"But you can't OD on pot," he laughs.*

*We both look at Kim, who's sitting on the bed between us, lost, drifting in her own reverie.*

*No, you're right. You can't.*

*You just become . . . one more, sleepless in Seattle.*

*When I arrive in town, one of the first things I do is to call Kurt Cobain at home, where he's waiting for his wife to fly back from Atlanta where she's been remixing the new Hole album with R.E.M. producer Scott Litt. What do you talk about with someone you haven't seen for six weeks or so, and whose lifestyle is so different from your own?*

*We discuss the insecurity that emerges from the lack of sleep caused by jetlag and/or alcohol, how tired we feel, and how much we hate Jeff Ament of Pearl Jam. Such an all-American jock! Kurt, having just got back from another gruelling leg of the* In Utero *tour. Me, having flown for 13 hours straight to try and arrange this* Melody Maker *Christmas cover story.*

*"Do you still want to try to do this thing with Kim?" the singer asks at one point, as I struggle to keep my eyes open.*

*Sure.*

*Sure, I do.*

*"Just tell me when, then. I need to go to sleep now."*

*The feeling's mutual.*

*The MTV New Year's Eve spectacular,* Live And Loud, *featuring Nirvana, stoner rap band Cypress Hill, Pearl Jam and The Breeders, is being pre-recorded live at Seattle's Pier 48, a cavernous, freezing, ferry terminal. Kids have been queuing for up to eight hours in the pouring rain to bear witness to what looks to be a legendary reconciliation between two of the city's supposed leading exponents of 'grunge' – indeed, the two bands who have, between them, defined the genre, on MTV terms.*

*The rift between Nirvana and Pearl Jam has been well documented. Briefly, it started way back, in the days when Ament and Stone Gossard played in the ill-fated Temple Of The Dog and, before that, Green River. The friction between the bands was subsequently inflamed by their respective successes and the way they were inevitably bracketed together by the world press.*

*This has happened, despite the bands' clear differences. Pearl Jam have always played classic FM American rock. Nirvana are something more extreme and mould-breaking altogether. Matters weren't helped when Pearl Jam's success was perceived to have resulted from Nirvana's, or when sales of the new Pearl Jam album* Vs *far out-stripped those of* In Utero.

*Mr Cobain has told the press several times how much he despises Pearl Jam. Pearl Jam have tried to downplay any stories of a rift, perhaps conscious of a credibility gap, perhaps because life's too short.*

*Rumours had recently surfaced of a reconciliation between Eddie and Kurt but, even so, for MTV – even with all its immense corporate muscle – to get these two bands together on the same bill is a hell of an achievement.*

*The only problem is: where the hell is Eddie Vedder?*

*Eddie Vedder's presence (or lack of it) hangs heavy over the proceedings. Rumours abound as to why he hasn't shown. Maybe it's simply down to a rekindling of the old feud with Nirvana, although the presence of Stone Gossard and Jeff Ament on stage with Cypress Hill would seem to belie this.*

*Gossard tells* Maker *photographer Steve Gullick that Eddie is 'extremely ill' and his voice sounds 'terrible'. So what's new? But you can't help recalling the recent well-publicised punch-up Vedder had in New Orleans, add it to the fact that recently he's been drinking more heavily, and start wondering if this is evidence of something more serious.*

*Everyone's trying their hardest not to let Eddie's non-appearance get them down, however. Doubtless, MTV's people are furious, but the kids don't seem too bothered. And why should they? They got in free and have just witnessed one of Nirvana's best shows ever. None of the Seattle drinking fraternity ligging it up in the green room seems too put out, either.*

*To one side are Matt Lukin and Steve Turner from Mudhoney, plus their manager Bob Whittaker – the man who once drove me down a sidewalk in his Cadillac after a particularly fine party.*[1] *The Screaming Trees brothers are talking to Kim Thayil of Soundgarden. Krist Novoselic is wandering around with his hand in a sling, having injured it quite badly during Nirvana's apocalyptic encore. His brother's somewhere, too – just as tall, and looking identical: his sister, too. There's Kurt's mate, Dylan from Earth; the Sub Pop entourage; Scott Litt; someone from R.E.M.; the Chili Peppers in drag and in Irish costume and generally behaving like dickheads. Eric from Hole rushes around trying to film people in compromising situations. Kurt sings the Pearl Jam song 'Jeremy' with an Eddie Vedder mask on for him.*

*None of which concerns your reporter, however, who faces an organisational headache trying to bring Kurt and Kim together. Kurt has the distractions of a wife and baby he hasn't seen together for far too long, while Kim is content to chill with Cypress Hill – another band notable for their love of the weed. What I didn't realise was that, despite the musicians' mutual admiration, Kurt and Kim barely know each other.*

*What did you think of Kurt when you met him, Kim? (It was in New York, during the mixing of The Breeders'* Safari *EP, just when* Nevermind *was taking off. Nirvana were playing a show midtown, and, knowing how big a fan of The Breeders Kurt was, I took him down to the studio.)*

*"That's right!" she laughs. "I didn't know he was who he was anyway."*

*"You didn't know I was from my band?" Kurt asks, incredulously.*

*"I knew you were probably from Nirvana," she explains. "And somebody else probably was, maybe. But maybe you weren't. I didn't know anybody really – just that you [she points at me] were bringing some people from Nirvana."*

*What did you think of Kim, Kurt? You were in awe of her at the time, right?*

*"Well, I loved* Pod *so much that I was freaked out to meet you," he reveals to Kim. "Then, when I got there, you were really condescending. But, at the same time, you were so generous. I was right at the point of freaking out about being a rock star, and I thought everyone was making fun of me."*

*"It was just, 'I'm recording,'" Kim explains. "'It's my stuff on tape. You guys are listening to my shit. You know what I'm thinking about. What the fuck are you doing here?'"*

*"I understand," sighs Kurt. "I also felt like I was totally imposing on you, like the rock star come to hear a taste of the new album. I was under the impression that you knew exactly who I was."*

*Kim murmurs something about whether we can hear her clicking her gums like an old person – she's very stoned and very tired. We've been waiting for about three hours for Kurt to come out of a marathon MTV interview, covering Nirvana's entire history. Kurt's just very tired. It's been a long day.*

*Since you've gotten to know each other better, how have your perceptions of each other changed?*

*"But we don't know each other," Kurt exclaims. "This is a good way of meeting each other. Hi, Kim!"*

*"Hi Kurt!"*

*"I hardly ever show up in time to see their set, cos I'm so fucking lazy," he explains. "I've seen them only about six times on this tour. That makes me feel like a creep."*

*"I've seen them every night," Kim tells me. "Our bus leaves at*

*midnight usually, so it's perfect. It's so great! Nirvana do the best dumb songs in the world! They're dumb in a good way, like the Ramones."*

*Earlier, Kim revealed her favourite Nirvana songs to be 'About A Girl', 'Scentless Apprentice' and 'No Recess'*[2]*, and that she likes to watch them with a joint to hand, hidden behind a pillar. Kurt returned the compliment by telling me how The Breeders keep getting better – they have to, "because they're still learning to play their instruments. Which is great.*[3] *We have to be absolutely phenomenal to even play a good show, because we all know our parts so well."*

*Do you see any similarities between your personalities?*

*"No," replies Kurt. "Kim is way more upbeat and happy and friendly. I'm the pissy mean one. We're the opposite."*

*Sure. But you both have this thing that Courtney pointed out to me, where you know your stuff is really good and that you don't need to prove yourselves beyond that.*

*"Yeah, that sounds cool, doesn't it?" laughs Kim. "That's exactly what we think. You're right, Courtney, goddamn it!"*

*"Don't you have any questions about Christmas?" Kurt asks me, as he goes to gob out the window of his Four Seasons hotel room.*

*Sure I do. Here comes one now.*

*Do you hate Christmas?*

*"No," replies Kurt. "It holds good memories. I've always had really good Christmases with my family – I have a very large family. Everyone has always gotten together and had a great blowout, at least until my grandfather died. He was usually the highlight of the ceremonies. He'd get really drunk, put on wacky hats and sing for everyone."*

*Kim wants to know how many brothers and sisters Kurt has.*

*"I only have one real sister [Kim Cobain], and one half-sister [Brianne O'Connor]," he informs her.*[4] *"The rest of them are on my mom's side of the family. My mother had seven brothers and sisters and they all have children."*

*Do you find Christmas at all depressing, Kim?*

*"Nope!" she responds, perkily. "Everett, c'mon you can talk to us. You find it depressing, don't you?"*

*Yes, I do.*

*Kurt asks why.*

*Bad memories. But you don't want to interview me.*

*"Yeah, we do," he laughs. "That was the agreement, right? One question each!"*

*OK. I hate Christmas because it exaggerates all the emotions that are around. If you're lonely most of the time – as most people are – but can just about get by, it rubs it in. You don't need it. It's no coincidence the suicide rate goes up over the festive season.*

*"That's very true," Kim agrees, soberly.*

*"It's too bad that every lonely person can't have a good deed done to them on that day, although it would probably be kind of patronising," Kurt muses. "But there's always someone who gets left out – someone who doesn't get a free meal, or a present, or have someone say hello to them. Everyone's so extra-conscious."*

*Also, Christmas reinforces the traditional values that Western Civilisation was built upon. I don't like those values. I find them hypocritical. I don't see anything good in the family structure.*

*"I do," Kurt disagrees, "if it's a good family."*

*"You don't believe that, Everett!" Kim laughs in disbelief.*

*Sure I do. Fine, if it's a good family. But you wander out on to the street any day, and you can see for yourself that most families aren't good families – mothers whacking their kids because they're too tired to cope, fathers being men. Most of it is shit. Most of the people in the world shouldn't be alive today. Stupid people shouldn't breed.*

*A stunned silence follows.*

*"God!" exclaims Kurt, "didn't I once say that to you?"*

*"I thought I had a bad outlook!" exclaims Kim. "Man, I feel just like [US actress] Sally Field next to you! Jeez! Everett!"*

*Well, it just annoys me sometimes.*

*"I don't see any reason why a person should pretend to like their family," demurs Kurt. "You should not go and spend Christmas with your parents if you don't like them."*

*But that's what it does to you. It forces you into certain situations.*

*"I know," he replies, sombre now. "It does that to a lot of people."*

*There's a pregnant silence.*

*"Merry Christmas everyone!" Kurt suddenly roars.*

*"I have a really interesting question," announces Kim.*

*Go ahead.*

*"Kurt, do you smoke menthols?"*

*"Yes, I do," he replies. "I smoke Benson & Hedge's Deluxe Ultra-Light Menthols."*

*"Oh my god! I can't believe that you do that. That's so funny!"*

*"But it tastes good," he argues. "And it fools me into thinking that I'm smoking less, or taking more vitamins, or something. And my breath smells good."*

*Kim. Is there anything you really want to know about Kurt?*

*"Are you going to finish the rest of your meat?" she asks him, looking pointedly at his platter, sitting unfinished and cold on the side of the bed.*

*"Yeah!" he exclaims.*

*"What was that?" she wants to know. "A steak? Medium rare, medium medium, medium well? Well done. I see."*

*Do you have any favourite people in common? Name a few of your favourite people.*

*"OK," begins Kurt. "Let me think . . . I like Shabba-Doo, the breakdancer."*

*"Katrina Weiss," Kim states, firmly. "The Soviet Union ice-skater. That's her name, right?"*

*Yeah. You mentioned her to me earlier. You said she was your ideal woman, and we said that was because you didn't want to grow hairy and old, and that you have a little girl fixation.*

*"Hey, hold on," she stops me. "Aren't we supposed to ask you the questions? Why do you feel so depressed around Christmas time, Everett?"*

*Because it heightens the emotions – hey, I already answered that.*

*Kurt yawns. Closes eyes. Wakes up again.*

*"Hey brother," he jokes. "Can't you just remember the good times?"*

*Is there anything you really want to know about Kim?*

*"Yeah," he replies, "but I don't want to ask her in an interview."*

*We switch the tape off.*

*Across the room, Courtney is discussing her album with her manager and someone from Geffen. Over on this side, both Kim and Kurt are looking weary. I don't believe I've felt so tired in years. It must be time to leave.*

*OK. Finally. Could I have a Christmas message for our readers?*

*"I hate you!" laughs Kim.*

*What me, personally – or the kids?*

*"Whatever," she replies, confused.*

*"She hates something!" gloats Kurt, softly.*

*"Did I ever say that I didn't?" she asks, surprised. "Oh, really? Well, you [points at me] would be the correct answer, wouldn't it?"*

*OK. Kim. What would you give Kurt for Christmas?*

*"I don't know." She pauses. "Something home-made. Maybe a napkin – a crocheted napkin."*

*How about you, Kurt?*

*"A certificate to a hair salon, so she can get a perm," he jokes.*

*"I just want a good Christmas," he continues. "A nice, quiet, casual Christmas with Frances and Courtney."*

*"What do I want for Christmas?" Kim asks herself. "You know those reindeers that you can hang on shower-stalls and you have a radio while you're taking a shower? That's what I want for Christmas."*

(*Melody Maker*, December 25, 1993)

The *In Utero* tour rumbled on through November and December; four shows in Florida[5], Georgia, Alabama, New Orleans, two shows in Texas . . .

On November 23, while the band were recovering from *Unplugged*, the soundtrack album to the *Beavis And Butt-head Experience* was released, featuring Nirvana's 'I Hate Myself And I Want To Die' – Kurt was a fan of the show, figuring it was truer to life than any caricature had the right to be.

"I wasn't really aware of the business side of Nirvana," says Cali. "Sometimes Kurt would ask me questions – 'We've been offered $60,000 to have a song in the *Beavis And Butt-head* movie. I'm uncomfortable with the idea, but why do I feel that way? Do you think I should do it?' Discussions like that, where he was confused as to his punk idealism and the reality.

"We loved *Beavis And Butt-head,*" Cali continues. "It was funny. We'd watch that more than we watched anything. When we were in Athens, Georgia [November 29] hanging out with Michael Stipe, the biggest score was when we found *Beavis And Butt-head* dolls. A month later they were everywhere."

Kurt was a fan of all the same TV shows everyone loved back then – *Beavis And Butt-head, Ren And Stimpy, Married With Children, Mr Rogers, Roseanne, Wayne's World, The Simpsons . . .*

"We were watching the premiere of a *Wayne's World* special where they were playing their favourite new videos and they played 'Heart-Shaped Box'," recalls Cali. "It zoomed in on the part when Kurt says, 'Hey wait.' The video stopped and Wayne goes, 'Did he just say, hey Wayne?' Kurt just fell off the couch laughing. Wayne goes, 'Kurt, buddy, you don't have to write a song, just call me. I'll talk to you any time.' "

Boston band Come joined the tour on November 26, in Jacksonville, Florida – replacing Half Japanese as the second support. A lot more shoes were thrown that night.

Like Screaming Trees, Come touched upon a deep wellspring of Americana. In their raw, churning grind you could hear traces of the back-water Delta blues, maybe the ruthless poignancy of Patti Smith. Like the first few Hole singles, like Babes In Toyland, like those traumatic post-Beatles songs that John Lennon formulated out of primal scream therapy, you knew singer Thalia Zedek was giving all of herself. The art becomes the life.

It was the voice, mainly. The way it seemed dragged down by layers of hopelessness, the way it reached up to the heavens only to spiral down again into darkness, the way it cried *"I don't remember being born"* on 'Fast Piss Blues' and scared the life out of you. It was the rasp within the voice, its nakedness, the way it echoed those youthful moments when life spun crazily on its head and you were running wild and free, only for some shit-head to glass your mate in the face. It killed me the way Thalia sang a line like *"Just relax / Just relax / Just relax"* (from the opening track on 1992's debut album *Eleven: Eleven*, 'Submerge') with such urgency, knowing it was the one thing she'd never be able to do, unless she was sunk within a narcotic haze.

Kurt and Cali stopped over at Michael Stipe's house for a couple of days in Athens after Nirvana played Atlanta, Georgia. "We brought Frances along," recalls Cali. "That was a good time. Kurt was a bigger R.E.M. fan than you'd think. He liked Michael Stipe and got along with him. We hung around Michael Stipe's house and went walking around Athens, which is a great town – or was. I think they've built a highway to it from Atlanta, so it's a little more accessible now.

"There was a musician in Athens named Vic Chestnutt[6] who Kurt liked, critically acclaimed, but not that famous," the ex-nanny continues. "Michael was like, 'Let's go over and surprise visit Vic Chestnutt.' Vic Chestnutt is in a wheelchair. He answers the door and there's Michael Stipe and Kurt Cobain. He just went, 'Woo-wee, party, party,' and started spinning around. Athens had a nice small-town feeling. Kurt was like, 'I would like to live here.' We slept on the floor of Michael Stipe's other house, which was an unfurnished cool shack. We relaxed. Michael Stipe took a ton of photographs those two days. He sent some to Courtney and they get lost in a pile of shit by her bed and probably ended up getting burned."

Shonen Knife replaced Come on December 3 in New Orleans. It was noticeable the enthusiasm that had characterised many of the earlier dates had dissipated, Nirvana interacting with neither each other nor the audience. "At the most," wrote one reviewer, "Cobain would give a quick glance at his bandmates to see if they were ready before he plunged from one tune to the next."

Two days later, in Dallas, crap early Nineties pop star Vanilla Ice got turned away from the show: "Everyone was like, 'Shit! Go get him!'" laughs Lori Goldston, "but he was gone."

And the shows continued: Oklahoma, Nebraska, Minnesota . . . Kurt would sometimes ask his audience what they thought of the new Pearl Jam album, or stick a cord into his mouth and pretend he'd been electrocuted, or Krist would jump around so much he'd momentarily unplug his own lead mid-song, or there'd be problems over Krist's accordion on 'Jesus Doesn't Want Me For A Sunbeam', or Kurt would invite some kid up on stage to smash his guitar, or tell another kid off mid-song for groping a girl's breasts . . . but there was little to distinguish one show from the next. This was corporate entertainment, a well-oiled touring machine whose only discernible purpose was to help the record company shift product – Nirvana certainly weren't playing these shows out of pleasure.

As Kurt's Aunt Mari sagely put it to Gillian G. Gaar, "When Kurt became famous, music no longer was an escape for him. It was a nightmare of scheduled 'creativity' and harried performances. It was almost like he became a caricature of himself. Kurt's success only reinforced my suspicions of how the music business operates. By that, I mean the artist becomes a commodity, a can of beans if you will, merely a saleable product? Can anything drain the human spirit more?"

How about hooking up with MTV once more?

The taping of *Live And Loud*, on December 13, would be the last time I saw Nirvana play live. It wasn't the best of nights, although Nirvana's startling performance belied the thick mood of apprehension.

"I went down to the Pier 48 abortion," recalls Charles Peterson, "and I was on the list, but I wasn't on the list for cameras. I was so pissed because I had to go back and put my camera stuff in the car. I left two-thirds of the way through. I thought, 'This is not Nirvana.' It felt like they were going to break into an intermission during their set for television commercials. I hated the weird angel figures on the stage."

A close friend of Nirvana's stole Krist and Shelli's wallets from their dressing room to sell for his heroin fix. I sat around and waited for an eternity, sworn off alcohol again, while a girl I'd had a crush on for years suddenly indicated she might be interested in me. I never had the chance to find out. But Nirvana were superb: even though Kurt refused to allow me to run on stage wearing an Eddie Vedder face mask, the band seemed absolutely driven. One of the angels got decapitated during the final encore of 'Endless, Nameless' – wherein Kurt also invited a frenzy of kids up and the band entirely destroyed their equipment. And I mean entirely: monitors, amplifiers, guitars, mic stands, parts of the stage, leads, *everything*. Kurt was howling with fury through 'Serve The Servants' and 'Rape Me', and sounded almost otherworldly on the Bowie cover. 'Radio Friendly Unit Shifter' had never seemed so appropriate. Who knows what arguments he'd had with Courtney upon her return earlier that day (by this point, Kurt was convinced his wife was sleeping with

Billy Corgan, especially when Billy offered to take Courtney away on vacation), who knows what drugs he consumed and dark thoughts he brooded upon, but for once they transferred into a vivid, brutal approximation of his old energy, his old fire. Such a shame it had to be at an MTV screening . . .

"That was the last one I enjoyed," says Rob Kader. "It wasn't like the old days, but it was better than the arenas. If you look at that last tour they were playing the same effin' set list every night. In the early days Kurt gave every ounce of his energy. By *In Utero* it was gone. It wasn't Nirvana any more. It wouldn't have surprised me if the band had broken up."

"*Live And Loud* was bad," remarks Cali. "It was a great show, but Kurt was really fucked up. Courtney was really fucked up; I was really fucked up. I don't know what they were doing, but I'd been shooting speed and heroin for three days. I came there with a bunch of really scraggly people. The show was good, but I felt all this tension building in my life and in my house and with them. In the last four, five, six months, it was like being inside of a beehive – the energy was really intense and their fighting was really intense. He suspected her a lot of cheating at that point. There was tension all around that night. There was something powerful about the show, but it was more like a dark power. The way he was clapping [sarcastically] at the audience at the end. Things had started to turn weirder. They were apart a lot. He didn't want her to be on tour all the time, but it was also that desperate, 'I love you so much I feel like I'll die without you,' kind of feeling. It was a dark and tense night. All this negativity was based and directed at Courtney – from the whole band. If she was there, it was bad. If she wasn't, it was a lot lighter."

"That was the best time I ever saw them, aside from the Marquee in NYC," states Steve Gullick. "It was a short set, and short sets are generally better. They were on fire. Kurt seemed to have found some energy from somewhere again – the energy he'd lost at the end of 1991."

When it came to the photo shoot for the *MM* cover, Gullick set up a temporary Santa grotto at the side of the band's bus, draped a feather boa of Courtney's around the pair, and Kim and Kurt counted him down from an allotted 24 shots. Kim got bored and fucked off after four. "You see a lot of those shots around," comments Charles Peterson. "I really don't like the thing with the boa and sunglasses. It reeks of sadness. I'm glad now that my photo pass got rejected."

I waited 15 hours straight for that interview; Kim tried to walk out several times, and each time Courtney talked her out of it. So the interview was finally happening, the three of us sprawled out across Kurt's bed,

20 or 25 minutes in – and we were enjoying ourselves. Then I looked down and noticed I hadn't turned the tape on. Shit. Double shit. But Kim and Kurt thought it was hilarious. "Oh, that's just Everett, let's start again." So they did; I was lucky to get away with it.

"Do you remember?" asks Gullick. "We were drinking with The Breeders afterwards, and singing Bee Gees songs, and you were French-kissing Alex [MacLeod]. The band weren't around much because they had to watch the footage. That was the first time I saw one of those kids' vibrating toy balls, like a sea mine. Frances had one."

Melvins moved into the second support slot on the day after *Live And Loud*, and the tour continued.

Salem, Oregon. Tad's home town of Boise, Idaho. Ogden, Utah. ("Utah was really miserable," remarks Lori. "Creepy rednecks. The venue smelled like shit, like some rodeo thing.") Denver, Colorado. Sacramento, California – where The Breeders finally bowed out of the tour, as the entire machine took a short Christmas break. When it returned on December 29, in San Diego, Gibby Haynes' acid-fried Texas freaks Butthole Surfers were the main support, with AmRep band Chokebore[7] the openers. The two bands played the rest of the tour.

The next night, in Inglewood, California, speed-wank guitarist Eddie Van Halen turned up inebriated before the show, and was down on his knees trying to convince Krist and Kurt that he should jam with Nirvana on the encore. "No, you can't," Kurt said flatly. "We don't have any extra guitars."

"Well then," Eddie shouted, pointing at Pat Smear. "Let me use the Mexican's guitar. What is he, a Mexican? Is he a nigger? A black?" It was sad and deeply offensive: Eddie had picked on entirely the wrong person. Kurt probably found his mere presence in Nirvana's dressing room abhorrent, but Eddie had actually been one of Pat's musical influences. Kurt was disgusted. "Tell you what," he said. "You can go on stage after our encore and jam by yourself." Meanwhile, Courtney was next door, complaining to John Silva that her husband was treating Eddie Van Halen – *Eddie Van Halen*, for fuck's sake – meanly.

"Backstage wasn't like a big party scene," comments filmmaker Dave Markey. "It was very sparse, pre-show. Eddie was just hanging with himself and several bottles of wine. As he got more and more drunk, he got more and more rude. I had my camera with me and it was pathetic enough for me not even to have it turned on. Then he started making racist comments about Pat and it got uncomfortable. Everyone's had that experience with the really drunk guy at a party fucking with your friends, and it degenerates into a fight – but this was *Eddie Van Halen*. He also pretended he was coming on to Krist."

During the destruction at the set's end, Kurt used one of the dummies' arms to play his guitar. He then picked up a drill and started boring holes into his instrument before spinning it above his head. Meanwhile, Krist sang The Kinks' 'You Really Got Me'.

"I was on the whole California leg of the *In Utero* tour," says Jessica Hopper. "That was a little weird, because Cali wasn't working, and so he and Rene were totally on drugs. It was fucking freaking me out. Cali and I went with Pat in a limo down to San Diego. Chokebore were awesome. I remember Kurt saying after he heard the Chokebore record it was the sound he hoped for on the next Nirvana record: at the time, they were this dramatic loud/quiet, volatile, damaged outfit. Troy [Von Balthazar, Chokebore singer]'s vocals were almost like caterwauling. Abrasive.

"The whole tour was denial, denial, denial," the writer continues. "There were a lot of factions, caused mainly by the drug factor.

"There was definitely an air of Kurt being more reclusive," she adds. "There was a separation between people in the band. Even during the previous summer there had been more camaraderie. Kurt spent a lot of time with Frances.

"Kurt, me, Jackie Farry, Rene, Cali, Frances and Pat were all on one bus," clarifies Jessica. "Patti [Schemel] may have been with us at times too, if Courtney was along. On that bus it was a typical situation of no one talking about anything, terse silence and sporadic, light conversation only – Frances was the focus of everyone's attention by way of denying the pall that hung over Kurt, the band, the tour. Bad things were happening and it was never getting addressed; management and the rest of the band was seen as an enemy, there were castes to the inner circle. When I got back home, my mom was like, 'You're not allowed to be on tour any more. You're a mess.' "

On New Year's Eve, Nirvana played the Oakland Coliseum Arena in Oakland, California with Bobcat Goldthwait MC-ing. It was somewhat of a punk rock fest.

"At the time, the East Bay was the centre of punk America," explains Jessica. "*Maximumrocknroll* had a store called Epicentre that Matt Wobensmith[8] worked at. Cali and I went there and bought a bunch of zines and records, and Cali told Matt that he could have whoever he wanted on the list that night, with backstage passes. So all these people from [San Francisco/Oakland punk bands] Green Day, Spitboy, J. Church and

Monsula came down. Green Day had just been signed, and they were really star-struck, like, 'Whoa, we're backstage at the Coliseum.' There were probably about 30 of these punk musicians, sat at those dumb tables in the green room watching Nirvana, and at midnight Bobcat descended from the ceiling wearing a diaper, dressed as Baby New Year, and all these balloons and weird crap fell from the ceiling.

"That was probably the best Nirvana show I ever saw," Jessica finishes. "They were so insanely good. All these punk kids from this notoriously holier-than-thou scene were psyched to be there. Either Kurt or Cali remarked about what a coup it was to have all these ideological punk rockers going round saying how amazing the show was, despite having called them sell-outs before. It was the last thing these people expected – that they'd spend the New Year drinking Nirvana's beer."

The final leg of the American *In Utero* tour then moved on through Medford, Oregon, Vancouver[9] and Spokane before finishing up with two nights at the Seattle Center Arena on January 7–8. "The Seattle shows were kinda nice," comments Lori, who parted company with the band after the second night, "but everyone was exhausted by then."

The homecomings were ebullient: Kurt introduced 'Teen Spirit' at the first show saying, "This song made Seattle the most liveable city in America."

"It was fun backstage, like a homecoming scene," recalls Earnie Bailey (who had the advantage of having dropped out of the tour again after *Unplugged*). "Earlier, we were over at Krist's house, waiting to go down the venue, when a group of Kurt's relatives approached him, wanting Kurt to ride with them. He didn't want to get into conversations about the old days, and there was an awkwardness as it felt like so much had changed in the time since he last saw them. So as Krist and I were driving off, he ran up and asked if he could get in the middle seat of Krist's old pickup truck and ride down there with us."

The second night at the Center Arena was the last time Nirvana played in the States.

## Addenda 1: Pearl Jam

Many local musicians think Pearl Jam got an unfair press in '92–'94, in regard to their relationship with other Seattle bands. Maybe it's because people like myself didn't understand the place Pearl Jam came from – suburban metal.

"At least two-fifths of Pearl Jam came from punk rock," Mark Arm corrects me. "Well, Jeff [Ament] did. And Stoney [Stone Gossard] was a metal kid, but he played at punk rock shows. I think a lot of people locally – punk rock purists or whatever – saw a difference in intent with Pearl Jam from the get-go. Mother Love Bone had been pursuing a major label deal since the break-up of Green River. But fuck it, almost all of the original Sub Pop bands ended up on major labels. It's just retarded."

It's weird: why Pearl Jam and why not Soundgarden? They too were signed to a major label, almost from the start.

"Yeah," agrees Mark. "They were signed to A&M essentially, but decided to do an album on SST – which is more of a crass commercial move than just going to a major label, because they were doing damage control ahead of time. I know there was this big controversy between Kurt and Pearl Jam, but people weren't hammering on Alice In Chains! Alice In Chains was considered irrelevant in some respects."

I think it was because someone was trying to sell Pearl Jam as a hipster band. And they're not.

"But Pearl Jam probably did as much for unknown bands as Nirvana ever did," argues Mark. "And way more than Alice In Chains, or Soundgarden. We did the first few weeks of the *In Utero* tour in the States, and by this time Nirvana was a big machine and they had a roadie for each person in the band, they had a lighting crew and a sound crew – a separate bus load of people travelling with them. And that tour was fucking painful. It was one of the worst experiences in my life in a rock environment. The whole vibe that was going on – they'd surrounded themselves with so many gross management people. Just fucking sick, gross people that I would never want to associate myself with in any kind of relationship. And this is from a band that came up through Sub Pop, through punk rock roots! If you take any kind of care in what you do and who you deal with, you can make the hugest difference . . .

"One of the amazing things about Pearl Jam to me," Mark finishes, "is that at some point they realised, 'We're only on this treadmill the record label put us on for as long as we want to be.' You don't have to blow your brains out to get off of it. You just stop doing interviews, stop making videos . . . stop doing whatever you don't want to do. Pearl Jam totally closed ranks and helped each other out through a weird, difficult time."

**Addenda 2: Ben Shepherd**

"Last time I saw Nirvana was down on the waterfront in Seattle."

Yeah, I was there; I was having a bad day. I hated that MTV shit.

"I liked meeting Cypress Hill. You got used to that weird MTV world where stars are treated this way, and friends and family are treated another way. It was just weird that our town was suddenly . . . that. It's like, 'Why is all this shit here?' "

I remember being shocked at Pier 48 because I went into a bar outside the super-privileged backstage area and there were all the guys I knew. I thought, "Why are they all here and Nirvana's in there? That's retarded."

"It wasn't the same spirit at all."

I remember finding it really odd. It was the last time I saw them as well.

"I got to see them with Pat Smear, who I've always wanted to see because I love The Germs and he's one of my favourite guitar-players of all time. I love how loose and fluid his guitar playing is."

Did you speak to Kurt that day?

"The last time I saw Kurt, Frances was in the backseat, and we were mixing the [Ben's garage-stamped Soundgarden side-project] Hater record on 3rd Ave. I was walking with Kim [Thayil, Soundgarden] and someone else towards the House of Leisure and I saw Kurt and I ran up and said, 'Hi,' to him. He goes, 'Hey, get in here,' because he didn't want to talk to the other guys. We drove around the block, caught up real quick and said we'd get in touch with each other really soon. Through the grapevine I'd hear how he wanted to jam with me and Buzz [Osborne] and somebody else. I was like, 'Yeah, let's do it.' We tried to set it up, but that was the last I saw him. I got to meet Frances. I grabbed her little finger and put my finger in her hand."

## NOTES

1 We had a record company rep cowering in the back. At one point it was clear we weren't going to make it through the gap between a hedge on one side, and a lamppost on the other. So I started pummelling Bob, who was still driving. It was the only option. He took out half the hedge. Needless to say, Mudhoney didn't sign with the record company in question.

2 For some reason, I always used to refer to 'School' under this title: maybe it's an old working title of Kurt's.

3 Kurt is clearly referring to the credo of spontaneity being at the heart of all great rock music.

4 Kurt also had a half-brother Chad Cobain, born to his dad Don and stepmother Jenny Westby.

5 Sonic Youth showed up at the Miami date, where Kurt played a snippet of Led Zeppelin's 'Heartbreaker' – a song Nirvana covered many years earlier.

6 Vic Chestnutt is a a quadriplegic folksy musician. His direct, confessional and depressive songs sometimes draw parallels with Daniel Johnston.

7 Chokebore were a very male, hardcore band from Hawaii, with disturbing rhythms and an even more disturbing tendency to mutate into a less stadium-friendly version of the Chili Peppers.

8 Matt Wobensmith was responsible for the queer punk rock zine *Outpunk*, which mutated into a record label. In 1992, Outpunk released two great compilation EPs, *There's A Faggot In The Pit* and *There's A Dyke In The Pit*, the latter featuring Bikini Kill and 7 Year Bitch.

9 Two nights: on the first, someone kept screaming out for 'tourette's'. Kurt finally replied, "What am I, a fucking jukebox?"

## CHAPTER 28

# Lovesick

"I DON'T know how quickly [Nirvana] went to Europe after *Live And Loud*, but I think we went to LA pretty fast," says Cali DeWitt. "I was young enough that I got spoiled real quick by staying in expensive hotels and flying first-class. My ticket was first-class, and on the way out the door, Courtney handed me this handful of pills. She was like, 'Have a good flight, don't take all these at once, I know you always do.' I took seven or eight of them and I remember a bunch of stewardesses waking me up in the airport going, 'The plane is waiting for you, sir, you have to get on,' and being carried to my first-class seat."

Did you get paid well?

"I got paid well," Cali laughs. "Besides the fact that I got paid well, I could take money out, which I used for drugs and records. If I had $100 in my pocket, I felt pretty rich. It was kind of sad that I was the trusted one, and I was a drug addict. They both accepted it. I didn't do drugs with both of them at the same time because they were always trying to hide it from each other. If one was gone, the other would call me and ask me if I wanted to do it. It was fairly dysfunctional."

On January 19, 1994, Kurtney purchased a new home: a $1.13m 1902 three-storey, five-bedroom house, 171 Lake Washington Boulevard East, in the upmarket Madrona neighbourhood of Seattle. It had stunning views of the lake and was fairly secluded, except for a small park right next door. The garden was massive – three-quarters of an acre – and populated by gorgeous vegetation, magnolia trees, hollyhocks and rhododendrons. On the top floor was a large, chilly attic and several unheated storage rooms; the middle featured the bedrooms, including a master suite with its own bathroom; and the lower level was given over to a spacious living room, modern kitchen and a drawing room that doubled up as Cali's bedroom. A white staircase ascended from the middle of the living room. Outside the house was a greenhouse and garage, where Kurt's Valiant stood.

Most of Kurt and Courtney's neighbours were either old money sorts, or representatives of the new, increasingly affluent Seattle[1] – folk like Peter Buck from R.E.M. and Howard Schultz, the CEO of Starbucks.

"The house was incredible," says Cali. "It was a bit big for him. There was a little bit of, 'We're buying a fucking mansion. Do we really need this?' She talked him into it. It was more beauty than any of us were used to, but there was something scary about it as well. There was a big stone basement, a huge attic and a lot of space. The house was bought and we were moved in and then it was time for them to go [off on tour] again."

Did they unpack?

"Kind of," he laughs. "They unpacked the bedroom. I don't know if any house they ever lived in was totally unpacked."

And you still did most of the grocery shopping?

"Oh yeah," replies Cali. "I love grocery shopping. I bought soda and cereal, tons of it, and junk food, frozen dinners, ice cream, pop tarts."

By this stage, Cali's responsibilities were more as a live-in buddy to Kurt. Although he still looked after Frances on occasion, his drug use had escalated during the *In Utero* tour, and so other nannies were hired – some from agencies, who mostly lasted only a week or two, and some trusted confidantes like Sigrid Solheim and Jackie Farry (who would sometimes stop by to help out).

"Cali was the house-sitter," clarifies Jessica Hopper. "He was the go-between between Courtney and Kurt. He was 'using' a lot more than I was aware of. Kurt had given him a credit card with a $50,000 limit, something crazy. We weren't estranged, but how close can you be to someone who's strung out and miles away? I wasn't talking to Courtney very often – once I became Cali's girlfriend I was more ensconced in his world than their world. When I'd talk to him, it seemed there was a lot of drama: Nirvana was under a lot of pressure to do Lollapalooza, and Kurt didn't want to do it. He would have rather broken up the band."

The Lollapalooza situation caused considerable friction between Kurt and Courtney, Kurt and his band, Kurt and Gold Mountain, Kurt and DGC, Kurt and . . . everyone, really. It was reported Nirvana were offered somewhere in the region of $7 million to headline the travelling rock road-show, but Kurt had no interest in playing along with more corporate games, certainly not when he was in the middle of a massive tour: Nirvana were scheduled to play another 38 shows in 16 countries over two months on the European leg of the *In Utero* tour. Kurt didn't understand why it was necessary to go along with such gruelling schedules. Surely, rock music was meant to be a fun – a release?

Yet even with Kurt's violent objections to playing Lollapalooza, Nirvana got pencilled in to play the festival.

"It seemed like things were pretty dire between him and Courtney," continues Jessica, "and also for both of them individually. I remember Courtney telling me that Kurt was doing heroin and cocaine, and it was making him really paranoid."

It was necessary that Cali was around: back home, Kurt became even more reclusive – seeing only Cali, Rene, Dylan Carlson, Eric Erlandson and, occasionally, friends like Pat Smear. Kurt spent most of his time in the month off between the American and European legs of the *In Utero* tour taking drugs with Dylan.

"It seemed like they were always looking for an appropriate friend for Kurt," says Rene Navarette. "Someone inspiring, to be all the things Courtney wanted for him, someone who wouldn't take advantage of him. All he wanted to do was joke around. That was what he had going with Dylan: not a lot of brain science going on, just a comfortable friendship."

Every so often, Courtney became sanctimonious about Kurt's drug use, conveniently forgetting the fact she took a ton of pills herself, and so Kurt would ask friends to hide the drugs outside in the bushes . . .

"I can see them both doing that," comments Cali dryly. "That part of the story where Courtney claims she attempted to stop drug dealers coming over – I'm not sure it's the entire truth."

"Those three weeks at the start of 1994," Rene explains, "were a dark time. I was not staying around the house so much because of the situation with Cali. [Cali had slept with Rene's girlfriend Jennifer Adamson, the 'lost' Culkin[2] sister. Famously, she posed nude for a Mono Men record sleeve.] Kurt and I would joke about it. He thought it was funny that I swore vengeance on Cali and never carried out my threat. He would joke around in front of both of us: like, 'When are you going to kick Cali's ass?'

"Cali and I took care of everything around the house," he continues. "Having two junkie teens taking care of the baby and the shopping, it was a beautiful mess. I would stay at Caitlin's house. [Caitlin Moore, one of Kurtney's drug connections.] I was seeing her at the time. There was one nanny who was a bag of emotions. She didn't last very long. Me and Cali had become so jaded by all the stuff that was going on, if she complained about seeing a syringe in a bathroom we'd say something like, 'That's not a baby bathroom. You wouldn't take a baby into an adult movie, would you? So don't take a baby into an adult bathroom.' Frances slept in the same bed between Cali and me, so we didn't have any drug paraphernalia around. There were many areas of the house that were off-limits because it was a junkie's house – and the baby wasn't allowed in any of those parts.

"Just before we moved out of the Lakeside Ave house, the Northridge earthquake happened in LA [pre-dawn, January 17, 1994]," adds Rene. "Cali and I and Frances were asleep in our room downstairs. Kurt and Courtney came down and woke me up, brought me upstairs and said, 'Look dude, we just want to tell you we love you and everything's going to be OK, but everyone you know in LA is dead' – and they turn the TV on and it's showing fire and water shooting everywhere like Armageddon. Then they follow me downstairs to go fetch Cali. I start to shake him, and he's like, 'Look, there's a baby here, and if the baby wakes up there's going to be Armageddon right here, right now. If there are people dead they will be dead in the morning. Now turn off the light and go back to sleep.' It was a sweet gesture because they said we could live with them forever. It was like we were the kids they would take care of."

In the middle of all this turbulence, Nirvana returned to the studio for what would be their final recording session – at Robert Lang's in North Seattle on January 28–30.

"I did the session at Bob Lang's with them," says Earnie Bailey. "Krist and Dave and I showed up . . . Dave brought his drums down, I think he was driving a black suburban around that time, Krist brought his bass and a Marshall amp. We got set up, and started waiting . . ."

Kurt didn't show up that day or the next. On the Sunday, he materialised and started playing around with a few ideas – the first time Nirvana had been in a formal recording setting for almost a year, since *In Utero*. Basics for 11 songs were recorded in 10 hours, but only one was finished, the stunning 'You Know You're Right'. It was a deeply sarcastic and mesmerising summation of Kurt's situation; pointed lyrics sniped sharply at Courtney in a passive/aggressive manner, while a bell-like guitar chimed and feedback and drums swirled round in a maddening eddy of emotion and frustration. It followed the quiet/loud Nirvana template, but weirdly so: caught in a middle ground between *In Utero* and something even more disturbing.

*"Nothing really bothers her/ She just wants to love herself,"* Kurt intones, anguished, before bursting into one last mighty sarcastic roar: *"Things have never been so swell/ I have never felt so well."*

"On the first day, we took this lengthy tour of the studio," Earnie continues. "On the second day there was more waiting, but then it got busy recording some of Dave's material. The third day, Kurt finally showed up towards the evening, wearing his corduroy jacket, and he hadn't bothered to bring a guitar or amp. He assumed we'd go get it for him, and we thought he would be bringing it, as there was no phone call or contact from him regarding what he would use. Krist and Dave were pissed that Kurt hadn't been around for the last couple of days, and now he was upset at them for not tracking down his guitar and his amp! It wasn't a good situation. Kurt was pretty down when he showed up.

"He wound up using my pedal board, a recently modified Univox guitar that was out in my car, and an amplifier that belonged to the studio. After getting things worked out, we all went out for pizza. We were laughing and relaxed; we had a great time. But when we got back to the studio, all of a sudden Kurt became quiet again and it felt tense. They recorded the instrument tracks quickly, and then it came time to do vocals . . .

"So I left and went to my car. I was about to turn the ignition over when I had this creepy feeling that this was it. It was terrible. So I thought: I need to break that. I walked back inside and started to pick up cables or something. I didn't say anything to Kurt because I didn't want to disturb him, but I looked at him as he was playing guitar with his back turned and thought, no, that's ridiculous, that's nothing. I went out and got into the car and left, and that was it. That was the last time I saw him."

On February 2, Nirvana flew out to Europe.

With them was Melora Creager, from the gothic NYC-based cello trio Rasputina, who'd been recommended to Nirvana by Michael Lavine as a replacement for Lori Goldston. Creager's band had a predilection for playing their instruments while dressed in Victorian corsets and bloomers. The other main change was that Pat Smear was singing back-up harmonies, not Dave Grohl.

For the first performance – three songs on a variety TV show in Paris – the entire band dressed in open black waistcoats over white shirts, in homage to late Seventies pop band The Knack.[3] The effect was somewhat disorientating: whereas the other three musicians had short, neat, cropped hair, Kurt had an unruly blond mop – and taken altogether, it looked like a bad version of the glorious style exhibited during the 'In Bloom' video. Kurt looked supremely disinterested, while Krist was mugging it up a little *too* much during 'Pennyroyal Tea'. Halfway through the final song, 'Drain You', Kurt threw his guitar to the floor and – grasping the mic stand – stood there screaming into the microphone, looking uncannily like a miniature version of Mark Arm.

Both Dave and Krist's partners were on the tour. Not Courtney, though – throughout the entire European tour it seemed like she was on the verge of flying out, but she never did. There wasn't a chance of recapturing the camaraderie on the American dates a few months back: Kurt was in a deep depression, resenting being dragged away from his house and his drugs and his wife. Once again, he was in withdrawal – and on morphine. "He looked so worn out," Shelli Novoselic commented. "It was so sad."

The tour opened in Cascais, Portugal on February 6 with Buzzcocks in support.[4] Buzzcocks were a genius art-punk band from Manchester who mixed lovelorn, spiteful lyrics with jagged guitar riffs and rampantly incestuous pop hooks as they stormed the British charts during the late Seventies. They split up following three, wonderful albums and then – after singer Pete Shelley spent an unsuccessful stint pursuing a solo career – re-formed in 1989, a pale shell of their former energy. Kurt was in love with Seventies punk rock as championed by magazines such as *Creem* and *NME*, though – and it was enough for him to have his former heroes playing on the same bill. Buzzcocks continued on the tour until February 18.

Kurt was missing Courtney badly, but consumed with jealousy at the thought she might be sleeping with someone else. He called her after Nirvana's second show in Madrid; crying, telling her how much he hated everyone, everything, wanting to cancel the remaining dates. Courtney later claimed in *Rolling Stone* that Kurt had told her that he'd walked through the audience and his fans were smoking heroin off tinfoil, crying out 'Kurt! Smack!', giving him the thumbs up – like he was their junkie idol. It's very possible someone is guilty of embellishment here, but what is fairly certain is that – as ever – the conversation disintegrated into violent argument. Courtney later claimed the quarrelling was caused by her concerns about his drug use. It's possible. But it's much, much more likely the fighting was caused by his worries about her fidelity, and Courtney placing constant pressure on Kurt to play ball with Gold Mountain and go along with whatever they 'suggested'.

"I think he suspected her of cheating on him with Evan Dando and Billy Corgan," sighs Cali. "Was she? I think so. I mean, define cheating. Did they get fucked up and make out one night? That counts to a husband who's wondering. Was it a real affair? No, maybe not. The one intense moment, and we're jumping ahead here, is he called me from Italy, and I was in London with Courtney. We were late to see him. We were three weeks late. He was really serious and really calm and he was like, 'I know that you don't get in the middle of our stuff and I know you don't take sides, but can I ask you something as your friend?' I was like, 'Yeah.' He goes, 'Is she cheating on me?' It was serious, no nonsense. I remember thinking, 'I think that she is,' but I didn't say that. I said, 'I don't think so, and if she is, I don't know it.' I didn't know for sure and what if I had said, 'I think, maybe?' I don't think I could have saved him from anything if I did say yes.

"We had been putting off going to Europe," he continues. "We came down to LA for a couple of days because she had to do something. She immediately got two bungalows at the Chateau [Marmont, very high-falutin hotel in Hollywood] – one for me and Frances, and one for her. She rented a car for me the second day and all this stuff. After what felt like a couple of weeks, I stopped asking when we were leaving every day. She kept putting it off and I was like, 'Well, tell me when you want to go.' I don't remember how long we were there, but I remember he was calling going, 'Are you coming or what?' I'd be like, 'Hey, I'm coming. When Courtney's ready to come, I'm coming.' I don't remember how long we were there, but I do know that I saw the bill when we did leave, and it was $37,000."

For the record I think Billy, yes, Evan, no.

"I think Evan was always a friend to her, but a real affair, probably not," agrees Cali. "Billy, yes. So I didn't know what she was doing. I shacked up in the hotel and I had a fine time. I had Rene with me a lot during this time. It was me, Rene and Frances. By the time we finally got there [to Europe], Nirvana were on break on tour and he was in Rome waiting for us. He asked me if she was cheating on him and I said no."

Kurt tried to cancel the tour, asking production manager Jeff Mason what the consequences of such an action would be. The answer came back that Nirvana were liable for all costs, hundreds of thousands of dollars. So the tour ground on, Kurt barely speaking to Krist and Dave – lost in a defeatist, sullen daze.

While the band were in Paris on February 13, Kurt posed for a series of shots with a French photographer, messing around with a sports pistol – in one of them, Kurt, high on drugs, posed with a rifle in his mouth, the barrel pointing upwards. If it was a joke, it was in pretty bad taste. It was around this time that Kurt started losing his voice: years of screaming and drug and alcohol abuse were taking their toll. Throat spray was purchased, but it only alleviated the problem temporarily, and so Alex MacLeod would take Kurt along to see doctors at whatever city Nirvana was playing – Barcelona (February 9), Toulouse and Toulon, France (February 10 and

12), Paris (February 14–15), Rennes and Grenoble, France (February 16 and 18). That didn't help either. The doctors would simply advise Kurt to lay off singing altogether for two months and learn to sing 'properly'. Kurt's response was typically punk rock – "Fuck that."

On February 19, Nirvana played Neuchâtel in Switzerland, where the audience threw toilet paper rolls at the stage. Support came from Sub Pop's French hardcore group Les Thugs (who, coincidentally, sounded enormously influenced by the Buzzcocks). Before the show, Krist and Dave and their respective partners, along with Melora and some of the crew, went ice-skating at a rink adjacent to the venue. "Kurt didn't go," Melora remarked to journalist Carrie Borzillo-Vrenna, "because he was, you know, kind of depressed." The next day was Kurt's 27th birthday. His manager John Silva gave him a packet of cigarettes.

And so the tour ground on. On February 21, in Modena, Italy, Melvins took over as the opening act. Someone threw a drawing of Kurt's face on to the stage during 'In Bloom' and he briefly pretended to wear it as a mask. But his spirit had pretty much gone: it was apparent to everyone his heart wasn't in it, that he was going through the motions and yet everyone seemed unwilling or unable to do anything about it: "People acted like nothing was wrong," Melora told Borzillo-Vrenna. "It was weird. They talked around him, or through him. I didn't know what the details were, but I felt like, 'Excuse me, this guy is miserable.' The band didn't talk much. I felt like Krist cared a lot about Kurt, but whatever happened over the years that I wasn't privy to . . . he just seemed sad about Kurt's state."

Kurt looked like shit – skin a mess of craters and pockmarks, skin tone a ghastly pallor, eyes barely focused – during Nirvana's performance on the Italian TV show *The Tunnel* on February 23 in Rome. The band played just two numbers, 'Serve The Servants' and 'Dumb', but it was clear his voice could barely cope. The first song was sung in a weird baroque undertone recalling the infamous *Top Of The Pops* appearance.

The following day was Kurt and Courtney's second wedding anniversary. The couple celebrated apart, Courtney in LA hanging out with Cali (not in London, as she later claimed), still promising to fly out any moment, Kurt alone in Milan: just him and a few thousand rabid fans singing along with every miserable word. Afterwards, everyone was hanging out in the Melvins' dressing room having a good time . . . everyone except Kurt, who just lay there on the couch, not saying a word.

The second night in Milan, Kurt tellingly played the riff to The Cars' monster New Wave smash 'My Best Friend's Girl' in the middle of the intro to 'Radio Friendly Unit Shifter' – the song may seem upbeat, but its sentiments are very dark, depressed, concerning a girl that the narrator is in love with, but who has been seen walking around town with his friend. Kurt spoke to Krist after the set, and told him he wanted to cancel the tour right there, there was no point continuing – but the next date, on February 27, was in Ljubljana, Slovenia and many of Krist's relatives would be attending. So he played a few more shows.

"He hung on there for me," Krist told Charles Cross. "But I think his mind was made up." Kurt spent the entire three days in Slovenia closeted in his room while his bandmates went out and explored the countryside.

Nirvana's final show took place in Munich, Germany on March 1, at Terminal Einz, a small (3,050-capacity) airport hangar. There was a deep sense of foreboding hanging over the day. None of the band liked the acoustics of the club – too echo-y – and Kurt's depression had deepened. He skipped out after soundcheck having asked for an advance on his *per diems* from Jeff Mason. On his return, he phoned Courtney, got into a fight, and immediately called his lawyer Rosemary Carroll to tell her he wanted a divorce.

"Did he ever say that to me?" asks Rosemary. "Yes he did, but I don't know how serious he was. He loved her very much. He was besotted with her, but at the same time it was very difficult for him. In any relationship, there's a honeymoon period of excitement and wonder and joy, and then you're left with a period where the two people have to figure out if they're companionable and can coexist together, and Kurt was maybe figuring out that Courtney was not companionable. The defining moment of Kurt's life was his parents' divorce, and he would have done anything to avoid that same situation rather than put Frances through it – and to the degree he thought divorce was inevitable, the pain of that was unbearable, unbearable."

"He was lovesick and crazy, and he didn't know what to do with all the emotions going on," says Cali. "I didn't know anything about a prospective divorce. I just knew that he was done fighting and he believed she was cheating on him. He didn't want to believe those things, but they were eating him up."

On top of all this, Kurt was extremely ill. The next day, a doctor diagnosed him as having severe laryngitis and bronchitis.

"Kurt was sick," Melora told Borzillo-Vrenna. "He didn't want to play. They were looking for herbal cures and doctors. They didn't seem to be getting along with management either."

The show started with a full, deeply sarcastic version of 'My Best

Friend's Girl', which segued straight into 'Radio Friendly Unit Shifter', Kurt sounding absolutely tormented as he screamed out the refrain of *"What is wrong with me?"* The set finished with 'Heart-Shaped Box', the love song Kurt had written for Courtney, back before he had been so thoroughly disabused of all his notions of romance.

The following day, Nirvana cancelled the rest of the first leg of the European tour (two more shows in Germany). Dave stayed on in Germany to work on the soundtrack to *Backbeat*, the Beatles/Stuart Sutcliffe movie. Krist and Shelli flew home to Seattle. And Kurt and Pat Smear flew to Rome, where they checked into the sumptuous Excelsior Hotel and awaited Courtney, Frances and Cali's arrival.

"So we went to London for a couple of days," says Cali. "We were supposed to stop in London at the airport on the way from LA and go directly to Rome, but Courtney had to get out and go shopping – and maybe do a little press [for Hole's second album, *Live Through This*, which was due out at the start of April] – which turned into a two day thing."

Yeah, you visited me. You came to the *Melody Maker* offices, and Courtney helped me review the singles. Among the records was Lou Barlow's solo Sub Pop seven-inch, the stark 'I'm Not Mocking You': "He's the kind of guy you'd fuck and the next day would be hanging from a tree in your backyard," commented Courtney. "Lou Barlow and Steve Malkmus [Pavement singer] . . . which one is hotter? Which one would you marry and which one would you fuck on the side?"

She projectile vomited into bins while you changed Frances Bean's nappy on our art editor's desk. The baby pissed on the page layouts.

Cali laughs: "The night before, I went to see Pavement by myself. You were the only person that I could possibly have known who'd be there, but you weren't around. So the next day we went to Rome. We were spoiled. We'd been staying in the nicest hotels in America, but this hotel in Rome, the Excelsior, was the most palatial thing any of us had ever seen. We get there and Kurt's approach . . . he's not angry or anything . . . he really tried to make it a romantic thing for him and Courtney. Their room [room 541] was all set up and there were flowers [red roses] everywhere and these giant $500 candlesticks. [Kurt also purchased some three-carat diamond earrings.] They had champagne sent up. [Kurt didn't drink any.] He was like, 'I missed you so much,' but she just took some pills and went to sleep. He was visibly unhappy and bummed."

Kurt had wanted to make up and make love. That much was apparent to the most insensitive of observers – but not to Courtney. She later admitted to *Rolling Stone* journalist David Fricke, "Even if I wasn't in the mood I should have just laid there for him. All he needed was to get laid."

"Some hours later I woke up to her screaming – it was a common thing," Cali grimaces. "Our rooms were connected and I ran in there and he was on the floor, dressed, with his eyes open, blood coming out of his nose. She was like, 'Kurt took all these Rohypnol[5] and Kurt drank champagne.'"

Courtney had woken up sometime between the hours of 4 and 6 a.m. to realise her husband was no longer in the bed next to her. He was fully dressed, with $1,000 in his pocket and a three-page note in his hand. "The note was on hotel stationery," she told *Spin* in 1995, "and he's talking about how I don't love him any more and he can't go through another divorce [a reference to his parents]."

The note quoted Shakespeare: "Dr Baker [Kurt's doctor at a previous detox attempt] said, like Hamlet, I have to choose between life and death," Kurt wrote. "I'm choosing death." It also mentioned the names of the people Kurt thought Courtney was cheating on him with.

An ambulance appeared at around 6.30 a.m. and took Courtney and the still-unconscious Kurt to the Umberto 1 Polyclinic Hospital in the city centre, where he was placed on a life support machine. He had the contents of his stomach pumped – 60 Rohypnol pills according to some reports, which he would've had to remove individually from their plastic containers – but slipped further into unconsciousness. By midday, stories had started filtering through in London about a suspected overdose, while CNN actually stated that Kurt had died.

Gold Mountain countered with a statement reporting that Kurt had, "Inadvertently overdosed on a mixture of prescription medicine and alcohol, while suffering from severe influenza and fatigue."

"He was . . . it was scary," says Cali. "Pat Smear was there, too, and he ran in. The ambulance came and took them away, and he was in a coma. I couldn't believe how fast the press works. I couldn't believe how fast they were knocking on my door. They were calling my room and knowing my name, people from everywhere. I think he had a bunch of cash in his pocket, he had written a note, but the note alluded to leaving. It said he was leaving and some people say it was another suicide note. As far as I could tell it was a 'running away' note. It was also bizarre for him to drink; he never drank alcohol. He really took a lot of Rohypnol.

"It was one of those things like, 'Was it or wasn't it?'" Cali continues. "You could mistake massed depressed consumption for a suicide attempt. I wonder why he was all dressed and why he had all that money. Maybe he just had all that money . . . you could speculate about these kinds of things all day and all night. It's hard to say, although if I remember correctly she did hide that note."

She burned that note . . .

"As far as I remember it, she didn't burn that note until after he died."

She told me that something weird happened when she burned it.

"When she threw it in the fireplace it exploded," Cali confirms. "That's what people who were there tell me, some kind of thing – if you believe in stuff like that. I do, in a way. On my 21st birthday, when the real part of this journey started [when Kurt died], they had all fallen asleep and I was on the freeway. The biggest owl I've ever seen in my life flew straight towards the car and put its wings out. It flew right at the windshield screaming. I remember thinking, 'I'm sure that's a bad omen.' "

According to Courtney's version, Kurt woke up the next day – on March 5 – after 20 hours of unconsciousness, wrote a note that said, "Get those fucking tubes out of my nose," and, when he was well enough to speak, asked for a strawberry milkshake.

"He actually said, 'Get this fucking catheter out,' " Cali corrects me. "It wasn't his nose. It was a catheter. I came there right after and that's what they said he said. It was crazy. Pat and I were trapped in our hotel room, but we decided to go out anyway. We put big coats on and stuck Frances under one of them and went to run around Italy. Kurt was in a coma, but it also didn't seem that unusual that it was happening. We had fun. Pat dyed my hair pink. When we went to hospital Kurt just smiled and looked happy and was like, 'Punk rock!' It was sort of back to normal. Then we went back to Seattle."

Can you remember Courtney's reaction?

"She just talked about it like it was an accident."

Janet Billig called me up that weekend to tell me that it wasn't a suicide attempt, just an accident. "Kurt's fine, he's sitting up in bed, talking and joking." Maybe he was by that point.

"He was," Cali smiles. "He was happy to see me and Pat and Frances. The plane ride home was funny. Pat Smear and I both got hepatitis A around that point and we turned yellow, maybe on the plane ride home. We got sick."

Kurt left hospital on March 8, and flew home four days later – on the plane, he could be heard arguing loudly with Courtney to give him a Rohypnol. She told him she'd flushed them down the toilet. He was carted off at Sea-Tac airport in a wheelchair.

Even after all this, it seemed like some of Gold Mountain were living in a dream world – Melora Creager reported being sent on to Prague on March 11 for the start of the second leg of Nirvana's European tour and being told to wait there. "Even when I got back to New York, they still didn't want to cancel anything," she told Borzillo-Vrenna. "They finally said Europe's not gonna happen, but be ready for Lollapolooza because we were still planning to do that."

"Cali called me when Kurt OD'd in Rome," says Jessica Hopper. "It was the middle of the night, and he was crying and really upset. He said Kurt's dead. He tried to kill himself. It was two or three in the morning, and then by the time it was light he called again and said Kurt wasn't dead and he was going to be OK. After Rome, there was definitely much more of a pall, a much heavier vibe. There were a lot of things that people weren't talking about. No one was capable of truly intervening; the status quo was already so fucked in the first place. Everyone felt that something bad was going to happen, that someone was going to die. There were a lot of quiet, unwritten rules. Everything revolved around Kurt's moods, an egg-shells kind of situation, much more so than before."

> *You've been quoted as saying the final show in Munich was 'totally amazing'. What do you remember about the show?*
>
> *"Kurt and I were suffering from bronchitis," replies Pat Smear, "and his voice became noticeably more trashed with every song. When we sang together we sounded like cats fighting. His voice was sooooo gone, but instead of trying to conserve it, he seemed to delight in pushing it to the, 'I won't be able to sing for days,' limit. After a while it was a bit much."*
>
> *There's been much talk about the sessions at Cobain's residence on March 25, 1994 with you, Kurt and Eric Erlandson. What can you tell us about this?*
>
> *"There was some jamming and some four-tracks made. Kurt played drums and sang, Eric played bass and I played guitar."*
>
> *Which songs were recorded other than 'Do, Re, Mi'?*[6]
>
> *"None that I remember."*
>
> *Do you know if Kurt was planning on making another Nirvana record? If so, had any songs been targeted for it?*
>
> *"It was mostly all about touring at that point. Compared to what was left, we'd barely started . . . more Europe dates, Japan and the Far East, South America, Lollapalooza, etc. The only thing that I knew about the next record was that Kurt was writing for it and he'd mentioned some ideas about its direction. He sometimes asked me to help him write while we were touring Europe, but it was really intimidating for me and impossible for us to get acoustic guitars for our [hotel] rooms. I told him*

*how good Dave's tapes were, and that he should write with him, but I don't know if he ever had the chance to ask him."*

*During the final few months of Kurt's life, how was the general vibe in the band? Critics argue that Kurt hated his bandmates and that Nirvana had essentially broken up.*

*"All bands go through the same bullshit. I've seen it over and over, and I try not to take it too seriously. I'd assumed we were just on a temporary break and that we'd finish up Europe and move on to Lollapalooza. Even when I heard it was cancelled, I didn't believe it."*

*What's your favourite, or fondest, memory of Kurt?*

*"He cracked me up."*

(Interview by Rasmus Holmen, www.nirvanaclub.com, September 2002)

"I talked to Kurt every night while he was in Europe," says Rene. "I talked to him before Rome. I remember him waiting for Courtney to get there from London – he was asking me what was going on with her. I didn't know. I was at the house by myself. I talked to Cali right after he found his body, and heard the madness going on. Cali didn't know what to do, he had the baby and the baby was crying. Cali found the suicide note from Rome.

"I felt instinctively that maybe Kurt had found out Courtney had cheated on him," Rene continues. "Knowing her, and the way she does things, who knows what happened? I know they loved each other and they had a crazy relationship. I was more worried about him finding some sort of peace. When they came back from Rome, I knew he was suicidal simply from the way he did drugs. I could sense the feeling of darkness, of death around him. If you're a drug addict, you can tell when something is going to happen to certain people who are using. It was brewing. I didn't think he necessarily meant to kill himself so much as he didn't care. As long as he was on dope I knew he was OK, but I also knew there was a point where it stopped working."

After Kurt returned home, Rene called Kurt's mum, Wendy O'Connor, to come over to the house. It was decided Kurt needed some home-made cooking, to help him feel comfortable again. Wendy cooked a couple of dinners of Kurt's favourite food – fish sticks.

"I didn't talk about the suicide attempt too much," says Rene. "Cali and I talked about it, but we tried to keep everyone else cool. We tried to operate from a basis that everything was OK. If something heavy went down, Kurt would go into his room. The only ones that would go in would be Cali or myself or Eric [Erlandson], and based on our demeanour people would judge what was going on. There wasn't much time between that and when Kurt left with me – two days. It's pretty blurry."

"Once we got home, their fighting started again, really bad," Cali says. "Nothing in particular, just a lot of hostility. Gold Mountain was pressuring the fuck out of him not to cancel Lollapalooza. [Kurt finally confirmed he was cancelling Lollapalooza in the second week of March. "The band was broken up," Krist bluntly stated to Charles Cross.] In the middle of this turmoil, Courtney was yelling at him about money, like, 'All the money you're losing! How can you do this to your daughter,' which is always a good one. He was only 27 years old, walking around with like the weight of the world on his shoulders. If you are sensitive and have all these people yelling at you, 'Why are you ruining our lives?' It doesn't make you feel good. He felt backed into a corner."

His father called up a couple of times. Do you remember taking those calls?

"I took the calls and said he wasn't there, I'm sure," Cali replies. (It's been reported that his father did manage to get through to Kurt once, and had a 'short, but pleasant' conversation.) "I remember at the house before that on Lake Washington, his dad coming to the door, unannounced. Kurt was right there saying, 'Not here.' I felt really in a corner. I was just staring at his dad going, 'He's not here, you can't come in.' I don't know him, but I know I'm in the middle of something I shouldn't be in the middle of.

"But the bigger argument around that time was to do with guns," he continues. "It was Kurt locked in his bedroom with guns, threatening to kill himself, saying, 'Get away from me, just leave me alone.' But even at that point I didn't imagine that he was actually going to do something to hurt himself. I thought it was just bluffs and bad arguments."

It was March 18, just two weeks after Rome. Courtney called 911 again, and police showed up within minutes. She told the cops that Kurt was suicidal. Kurt told them he had no intention of killing himself, and that he had just locked himself in his room to keep Courtney away. The police confiscated four of Kurt's guns – a Beretta .380, a Colt AR-15 semi-automatic rifle and two Taurus's – and 25 boxes of ammunition, plus a bottle of "assorted, unidentified pills". Under further questioning, Courtney admitted to the police that she hadn't actually seen Kurt holding a gun, but that she was concerned for his safety knowing he had access to guns.

(This version contradicts a more histrionic story Courtney told *Spin* journalist Craig Marks in 1995, that after she got inside the locked door, she saw guns, laid out around Kurt: "I grabbed the revolver and I put it to my head and I said, 'I'm going to pull this right now. I can't see you die again.' He grabbed my hand. He was screaming, 'There's no safety. You don't understand. There's no safety on that. It's going to go off. It's going to go off.'")

The police took Kurt downtown to the jail, but didn't book him.

"He was always happy when the cops were there," states Cali. "He would start joking. The cops were probably into it, too."

There's some missing days in the final weeks of Kurt's life. One such period occurred a few days after Kurt and Courtney returned from Rome, some time between March 12 (when police received an anonymous 911 call from the Lake Washington residence, later rescinded) and March 18. Terrified more than anything by Kurt's seeming indifference to his own fate, and knowing that the Rome incident was a botched suicide attempt (even if this fact was kept a secret until after Kurt's death), Courtney ruled that no drug taking should be allowed inside the house. She even banned Dylan from visiting because she was worried that he was Kurt's main drug connection. Ironically, Dylan also supplied Courtney.

His wife's hypocrisy was the last straw for Kurt – how dare *she* lecture *him* over drugs. The couple had a violent argument and, accompanied by Rene, Kurt walked out. It was the last Courtney would see of Kurt for several days. The drug buddies skipped all familial responsibilities, and checked into various cheap hotels along Aurora Avenue – the Marco Polo, the Crest, the Seattle Inn.

"We were walking down Denny Way," begins Rene. "It was like Kurt wanted his last run in the city. It was our little adventure out. It was night-time and he didn't know where anything was. We went into [trendy Capitol Hill hang-out] Linda's Tavern, which was still brand new, and everyone gawked at him. Seattle is a very tight-knit place. Then we saw Nils Bernstein and went and sat at his table, but it wasn't like his home-town scene. Kurt felt alienated.

"We didn't have any cash and all Kurt's credit cards were cancelled, but we had a Western Union cheque from my mum for $100. I didn't have any ID, so we had to use Kurt's. We walked into this 'all cheques cashed' place, and it was like being in one of those 'surprise' TV shows when someone famous walks in. There was a stoner guy praising Kurt, but in a funny way that Kurt could appreciate. All of a sudden, it seemed like he was in touch with the city again, but it was short-lived.

"We were staying at a motel on Aurora, the Marco Polo. We'd been stopped a few times on Broadway. A group of kids scuttled around us. Kurt would always say how he wanted to be in touch with the kids, but when it came down to actual interaction he felt uncomfortable. We went into Urban Outfitters where Kurt bought some funny glasses and a hat and a funny coat – that was our disguise for the day.

"We'd left because he and Courtney had had a fight. Cali had just left with Jennifer [Adamson], and I was the only one home. Courtney arrived home, and then I heard this huge argument. It was the only time I ever saw Courtney punch Kurt. They were arguing over some pills. Someone had hidden someone else's Rohypnol. I walked in on them punching each other, and before he went to reciprocate, I grabbed him, put him over my shoulder and walked away. I kept on walking, out the front door. When we got to the top of the driveway, I ran back and got his jacket, and we continued walking. We walked from the house to the city. We were out for five nights. First night, we still had the credit cards. The incident at Linda's happened on the third or fourth night. It was a frustrating time for Kurt. He usually never wanted to be away from the house.

"We went to our friend Caitlin's house [on the intersection of 11th and Denny]: usually, that was our main objective. We'd score there. We hung out there, scarfed up some food and took a cab to whichever hotel we were staying at. We stayed at three different hotels – motels – altogether. We were mainly walking around, like teenage runaway types. It was a lot of fun. After the first night, I was worried we'd get into trouble. I'd call the house and talk to Eric to try and get a feeling of what was going on, but he'd be like, 'Don't involve me.' We ran into Dylan at Jennifer Adamson's on Capitol Hill – she wasn't dating anyone at the time. Dylan and Cali and myself would stay at her apartment and listen to records. We had a lot of fun there. There was the occasional visitor, but it was fairly private.

"I kept Kurt out that week because he reacted with such a good attitude. It seemed healthy for us to be away from the house, get some air. We were all trying to get him to wake up a little after he came back from Rome."

"Jennifer Adamson was my girlfriend," says Cali. "I had Jessica Hopper and Jennifer Adamson. Jessica was the good girl. Jennifer wasn't a bad girl, she was a drug girl and Jennifer is dead. She died four or five years later [in 2000] of a drug overdose. I was living at the house and Jessica was there, but I would go and do drugs with Jennifer. I remember one very surprising night when I was at Jennifer Adamson's house. All of a sudden Kurt showed up there, buzzing the buzzer. I looked, because I wouldn't let most people in, and I was like, 'What are you doing here?' He was like, 'I just had to get out of the house. There was a fight. Can I come in and listen to records with you guys?' He was really into Elastica.[7] I had just gotten their first single."

Several of Kurt's friends – such as Krist and Dylan – were beginning to wonder if Kurt's lengthy coma in Rome hadn't caused some adverse effects. They were concerned he may have been left with brain damage. "He didn't seem as alive," Dylan commented to Charles Cross. "After Rome, he seemed monochromatic."

"He seemed a little bit more himself while we were away," continues Rene. "We had an opportunity to have some 'bro' time. I'd joke with him how he never got to sleep with any of his favourite girls, and how he could probably do that, and how Courtney would probably enjoy it.

"It was strange. I'd never seen him walk very much before – or be physical – except for when he was on stage. Sometimes he'd get dispirited about how he was spending so much money on crap, or he'd make fun of Courtney for doing that – like somehow they'd end up broke. He never really grasped how wealthy he was. We tried not to be too serious, and there were a lot of times when we were out of it. Courtney had rules there was no drugs in the house – no cocaine or speed, no white drugs – and I'd go, 'What about your pills?' So we were trying to find crack, because we never did it. We smoked some speed out of a light bulb instead, and thought it was funny, irreverent.

"I wasn't expecting the credit cards to be stopped. It was Courtney's way of forcing his hand. She was good at that. She knew we needed money and that I didn't have any, and she wanted him to come back because she'd heard he was out enjoying himself and that hurt her feelings. The way Courtney dealt with having hurt feelings was by unleashing this tornado of frustration on you. I remember being shocked by her cancelling the cards, but I wasn't surprised by the severity of the action. Kurt and I said to each other, 'That's your money,' but we were scared at the idea of going into a bank to deal with it ourselves. We didn't want to create a big situation. I was under 20 and felt illegitimate, and Kurt didn't feel much more legitimate.

"The morning that Courtney cancelled the cards, he'd picked up a paper that had a story about Nirvana cancelling something he didn't even know about. He made a phone call; he wasn't shocked, but he was pissed off. He made phone calls the whole time we were gone, most likely to Courtney. I didn't understand why he did it because he'd complain about her to me, and go on about how he didn't care what she thought, but then he'd call her and talk sweetly.

"Kurt OD'd pretty bad at the Marco Polo. It happened from time to time. One reason they kept me around was because I was good at reviving people. My job description was 'personal assistant' but it was more like to make sure he didn't die, or that somebody didn't rob him, or he didn't OD. It took me 20 minutes that day to get him up and on his feet: it was the first time in a while I felt that scared. I didn't tell anyone, but it was a bad number.

"The next day was when he found that paper and got upset. The day ended with him calling Rosemary Carroll to specifically change some things about his will. That freaked me out, because there was always the underlying fear he would try and kill himself. We'd joke about it: how he'd take all the money from Courtney's name and leave it to Frances, and leave Cali and me some money.

"I got him to call Krist, and Krist came by. He was going to take Kurt out to some cabin of his so he could withdraw – his van was full of sleeping bags and instruments. But when we were on our way, Kurt started shifting his story, that maybe he should go back to the house. I found out later that Krist was supposed to be taking Kurt back for an intervention, but he was trying to be a double agent – it would have been so fun if we'd gone to his cabin. Maybe it would have changed everything. But we were pretty tired, having been out all those days."

This last paragraph doesn't quite tally with other versions of the events. One story has Krist meeting Kurt for the first time that week at the Marco Polo on March 21 – three days after the incident with the guns – so Kurt and Rene couldn't have been missing at that point. Apart from that, the stories are fairly close. There was a 'tough love' intervention planned on March 21, but it got cancelled after Krist tipped Kurt off. Krist felt that, far from helping Kurt, such a course of action would merely have added to his paranoia and sense of alienation.

At the Marco Polo, Krist reported Kurt as being delusional – and that he wanted to buy a motorcycle. He didn't understand what Kurt was on about, and suggested that the two of them should go away on holiday together (presumably without Rene). First, though, Kurt was hungry – Krist wanted to take him to a fancy restaurant, but Kurt suggested Jack In The Box. It was only when the car was halfway to Capitol Hill that Krist realised what Kurt was up to. His dealer's flat was right next door to the burger joint. The two friends yelled at each other, and Kurt left.

## NOTES

1 Amazon, Microsoft and Starbucks are all based in Seattle, or nearby. The original Starbucks is down in Pike Place Market, a couple of blocks from Sub Pop.

2 As in *Home Alone* star, Macaulay Culkin.

3 That night, the riff at the start of the opening song, 'Rape Me', even sounded a little like the stuttering guitar on The Knack's 'My Sharona'.

4 Nirvana's set list ran: 'Radio Friendly Unit Shifter', 'Drain You', 'Breed', 'Serve The Servants', 'Come As You Are', 'Smells Like Teen Spirit', 'Sliver', 'Dumb', 'In Bloom', 'About A Girl', 'Lithium', 'Pennyroyal Tea', 'School', 'Polly', 'Very Ape', 'Sappy', 'Rape Me', 'Territorial Pissings', 'Jesus Doesn't Want Me For A Sunbeam', 'The Man Who Sold The World', 'All Apologies', 'On A Plain', 'Scentless Apprentice', 'Heart-Shaped Box', 'Blew'.

5 Rohypnol is a drug used to treat severe insomnia, and also an aid for heroin withdrawal. Courtney always used to refer to it as a 'baby sedative' to me. I took a couple once, for a flight to Japan, and they knocked me out for the entire 27-hour duration.

6 An acoustic demo of 'Do, Re, Mi,' surfaced on 2004's *With The Lights Out* box set. It sounds oddly like a Paul McCartney song – or perhaps something Kurt would have sung on KAOS radio in Olympia – the voice cracking and soaring off into the stratosphere. It's very poppy, and heart-rending.

7 Elastica, a female-led, mid-Nineties, Britpop band, owed more than a passing debt to old school angular art-punks Wire.

# CHAPTER 29

## Spring Rain

"PEOPLE were always muttering about Kurt's heroin use," says Rosemary Carroll. "I heard rumours, maybe from the first time I was aware of him. I don't know. Towards the end, it affected his relationship with everybody: it gave people something to pin their own anger on; their frustration and inability to deal with a genius, because he was a drug addict. That's what angered me most [about his death], he had so much more to do and say and create – but he was also under a huge amount of pressure. And more than what the heroin may have done to him physiologically, it was the way it gave everybody an excuse to dismiss him that was so wrong. His legitimate grievances were dismissed as the ravings of a junkie.

"There was that big intervention," Kurt's former lawyer continues. "I did not go to that. During the last weeks of his life, he did call me two or three times. I tried to tell him he had options – and the pressures he was feeling that were unbearable could be alleviated. That all the paths facing him that were horrible could be avoided. He could have altered his life. He didn't have to stay in Nirvana. He didn't have to stay in any relationship that was paining him. But I told him that to get out of these situations he had to be straight, because as long as he was a junkie he was providing an alibi for everyone that was controlling him.

"The only times I'd talk to him was when he'd call me, because he was not reachable. One time, he talked to my daughter who he really liked and she asked him to come down and visit us. I wanted to get into a room with him and tell him he could be protected. It all seemed so unbearable to him and so enormous. I wish we'd all done a better job of protecting him."

So there was an intervention planned for March 21, but Kurt got tipped off . . .

". . . and left," adds Cali.

Krist Novoselic told him, because he thought it was a stupid idea.

"Krist was sensible throughout the whole thing, the best he could be," says Cali. "Kurt said cruel things to Krist, but he didn't mean them. He was just full of misery and wanted everyone to get away from him. You don't want people who really love you there, trying to help you. Or people like the people who were at the actual intervention [Friday, March 25] – a few friends and a lot of business people."

Assembled in the Lake Washington house that day for a 'tough love' session were Courtney, Danny Goldberg, John Silva and Janet Billig from Gold Mountain, Pat Smear, Cali, Dylan Carlson, Mark Kates and Gary Gersh from DGC, and a presiding counsellor, David Burr. Wendy was absent, looking after Frances in Aberdeen.

'Tough love' sessions are supposed to wake the user up to the reality surrounding them: each person present was told to confront Kurt with the consequences of what would happen if he didn't stop taking heroin. Geffen would drop Nirvana; Nirvana would split up; Courtney would divorce Kurt; Gold Mountain would refuse to work with Nirvana. Kurt must have known most of the speeches were bullshit. Most of those present didn't feel they had the authority to confront the individual upon whom a large proportion of their livelihoods depended. "He had such an aura around him that day," remarks Goldberg, "that it felt like we were walking on eggshells."

"When I arrived and saw Dylan was there," recalls Rene Navarette, "I knew something weird was going on because Courtney had recently exorcised him from the house. But by that point Kurt wasn't listening to me. I was saying we needed to get out of there, but Dylan was already making him high and there was no talking to him. I was concerned for Kurt's state of mind. I knew it would be a mess – plus, Courtney was using dope to keep him there. I knew that Kurt's attitude was that he didn't care if he died. Any change that was going to happen wouldn't happen by having his hand forced.

"Dylan had dope so we all got loaded together," Rene continues, "but I knew something was going to go down. Soon as I saw Eric, I told him, I've got to get out of here – that's when Eric lent me money for a plane ticket to LA. Before I left, I went to Kurt and told him I was leaving, and told him it was my birthday soon – and that if he was going to rehab, he'd be there for my birthday on March 30. I called the house that night. Pat Smear gave me a play by play. He told me the intervention was ridiculous."

Courtney was the only one who spoke for any length of time: she implored Kurt to go to treatment at the Exodus Recovery, a drug rehabilitation centre in Marina del Rey, CA. She threw at him the one threat she knew he couldn't shrug off: that if she divorced him he wouldn't be able to see Frances very often.

Kurt listened to all his peers in silence, and then in venomous terms pointed out the hypocrisy and faults of many of those present.

"In my memory, it feels like there were like 20 business people there," says Cali. "There was probably more like eight. There was Danny Goldberg and people from Gold Mountain – all these people who don't really have anything to do with what was going on and hadn't been friends to him on a personal level. What were they doing here? He was acting really, really fucked up. He was acting too fucked up to stand. It wasn't my place, but I was getting annoyed, it was bothering me. It was this weird attention everyone was giving him. Courtney or someone kept saying, 'Cali, walk him around.' I was walking him around the backyard and it dawned on me how stupid it was. We were out on the lawn and I was like, 'Buddy, you don't really need me to walk you around.' I dropped him and he fell down to the floor. He smiled and looked up at me in a way, like, 'You understand that I don't need you to walk me around. I could totally walk.' It was almost like he thanked me with his eyes for dropping him."

It's been written that Dylan refused to take part . . .

"Dylan was there," Cali replies. "Dylan tried to appeal to Kurt as a friend. This is the other instance of Kurt throwing it into the faces of people he cared about. He started yelling at Dylan. Dylan was too fragile to handle it. He was like, 'What the fuck are you doing here? You're just as bad as all these other people!' He threw a recycling bin at Dylan, filled with glass, and all this glass broke and Dylan started crying and left. At that point Courtney had been picking on Kurt for so long and so much, he felt trapped. And now she had brought basically what he considered the enemy into the house to tell him what he was doing wrong.

"The only reason to have an intervention is to show someone that you're hurting people you care about, and not in a tough love way," Cali explains. "A few close friends of mine, and my dad, did an intervention on me and it had an effect because they were all people I respected. They weren't yelling at me. An intervention that would have been successful would have been like Tracy and Tobi, people Kurt had known for years – Ian Dickson – people who don't have a vested interest in his success. I feel like I can remember them talking about, 'You need to clean up and do Lollapalooza,' at the intervention. That was missing the point completely. It should have been, 'Why don't you not go on tour for a year, never record again, just get together with your daughter and leave this all behind?'"

Courtney tried to convince Kurt to fly with her to LA – where she was checking into the $500-a-night Peninsula Hotel to detox herself – but he refused, flipping through the Yellow Pages instead, trying to find a 'proper' psychiatrist, so she left the house in a car with Janet Billig. It was the last time she saw her husband alive. One by one, the others followed . . .

"Yeah, it happened and they all left," says Cali. "We were left in the house like, 'What the fuck? What just happened?' "

Kurt retreated to the basement, and played around with a few ideas on guitar with Pat and Eric. The following day, Jackie Farry came by and took Frances away to LA to be near Courtney.

"Jackie had to take Frances at this point," Cali says. "I was like, 'Will you come take Frances because my drugs have gotten out of hand in the face of this madness in the house right now.' I've got Courtney saying, 'You have to stick to Kurt like glue right now. Don't let him do anything.' She wants me to shadow him and call her and tell her what he's doing. I'm really in the middle of this thing now."

Having turned his back on the intervention, Kurt had no one to hold him in check – and the inevitable happened once more. He OD'd, alone on the back seat of his Valiant, where he'd been placed by other users scared that if a famous rock star died in their apartment, they'd be in trouble with the police.

He didn't die. He woke up the next day, aching all over. He returned home, ignored any phone messages from Courtney, and called Rosemary. She convinced him that he should try treatment one more time, and so reservations were made for Kurt to fly out to LA on Tuesday, March 29. Krist was asked to drive Kurt to Sea-Tac Airport, but on the way there Kurt once again changed his mind. He attempted to leap from Krist's car while it was driving along the Interstate 5 and, once at the terminal, he punched Krist in the face. The pair grappled and Kurt broke loose, sprinting away across the concourse.

It would be the last time Krist saw him.

On Wednesday, March 30, Kurt had a change of heart again. He would get treatment, after all.

Before he left, he got loaded and drove over to Dylan Carlson's condominium where he asked his old friend to do him a favour. He wanted Dylan to buy him a rifle, "For protection and because of prowlers" – the police had taken away all his other guns. So the pair drove over to Stan Baker Sports on 10,000 Lake City Way NE, and purchased a six-pound

Remington M-11 20-gauge shotgun and a box of ammunition for $308.37, cash. "Kurt seemed normal," Dylan remarked. "Plus, I'd loaned him guns before. If he was suicidal, he sure hid it from me." Dylan offered to hold on to the gun for Kurt, knowing he was on his way to Exodus, but Kurt insisted on keeping the gun himself.

At LAX, Kurt was met by Pat Smear and John Silva's assistant, Michael Meisel, who drove him to the centre. The singer checked into room 206 and enrolled in a 28-day programme. During the next couple of days, several psychologists visited Kurt, none of whom suspected he was suicidal. He voiced his concerns about the forthcoming Kevin Kerslake lawsuit (over the 'Heart-Shaped Box' video), fearing it could bankrupt him – and when Jackie Farry came to visit with Frances, told her about the arguments he'd been having with Courtney over Lollapalooza. But generally he seemed in good spirits, and when Jackie and Frances came back the following morning, he was in an upbeat mood, showering Jackie with compliments and playing with his daughter, throwing her up in the air.

It was April 1 – the same day that the second leg of Nirvana's European tour, due to restart in Birmingham, England on April 12, was officially postponed.

Later that day, Kurt was sitting outside in the smoking area joking with Butthole Surfers singer Gibby Haynes about one of Gibby's friends who had escaped Exodus by jumping over the six-foot rear wall. Such an action wasn't necessary as the front gates were always left unlocked, but there was a certain romance to it. "What a dumb ass," the two musicians laughed. (Gibby was also going through rehab at Exodus. It was that kind of place.) Later, Pat Smear dropped by with a friend, Joe 'Mama' Nitzburg. The three men walked out to the back patio and sat and chatted for an hour with Gibby.

At some point in the afternoon, Courtney managed to call Kurt – she'd already tried several times to reach him – and had a brief conversation. "No matter what happens," she claimed he told her, "I want you to know that you've made a really good record [Hole's album, *Live Through This*]." She asked him what he meant.

"Just remember, no matter what, I love you."

At 7.25 p.m., Kurt walked out of the back door of Exodus and scaled the wall. A couple of hours later, he boarded Delta flight 788 to Seattle – arriving at Sea-Tac at one in the morning. He was now officially missing: as soon as she heard the news that he'd left Exodus, Courtney started scouring LA for him, calling drug dealers and friends, convinced he would overdose.

"Here's where I'm in the picture where I'm not supposed to be," says

Cali. "I was supposed to go down to LA right after him. They're both in LA, I'm in Seattle, and I decide to stay in Seattle [at the Lake Washington house]. I'm a drug addict, I'm in Seattle – what do I want to come down there for? I'm glad they're out of the house. Jessica [Hopper] is staying at the house with me [Cali's 'straight edge' girlfriend had flown out to join him for spring break a couple of days earlier], I'm leaving to go get drugs or go get food or do whatever I do every day. So he runs away from Exodus, and no one knows where he is. Every day when I come into my room, which is downstairs, my phone rings. I answer it; it hangs up. In retrospect, I think that was him in the house, calling to see if it was me. [Courtney had placed a restriction on Cali and Jessica that they weren't allowed in most of the other rooms when they were alone in the house.] I had a collection of metal toys on my shelves and one day I came home and they were all facing in the wrong direction. I was like, 'Did I do that?' I think that was just him messing with me."

On the morning of April 2, Kurt took a Graytop cab ride over to 145th and Aurora. He was on the lookout for more dope and ammunition, having already disposed of his first lot – he purchased some 20-gauge shotgun shells from Seattle Guns that day. Once again, Courtney cancelled all of Kurt's credit cards. The next day, increasingly desperate, she hired a private investigator straight out of the Yellow Pages. But Kurt had gone to ground. There were reports that he'd spent a night with an unidentified friend at the other Cobain residence – the house in Carnation – where police later found a blue sleeping bag and an ashtray filled with two brands of cigarettes. But, despite a handful of scattered sightings of Kurt hanging around in the park near the house and on Capitol Hill, nobody knew where he was.

Wendy O'Connor filed a missing person's report with the Seattle Police Department on April 4, stating that Kurt had "bought a shotgun and may be suicidal". The report also listed Caitlin Moore's address as a possible hang-out location.

Sunday passed, and then the Monday . . .

"He did see me when he got home, for a minute," says Cali. "He kicked open my bedroom door and saw me in there. He was like, 'What the fuck are you doing here? You were supposed to go to LA yesterday.' I was like, 'I didn't want to. What are you doing here? Everyone is looking for you, Courtney thinks you're dead in a ditch.' He goes, 'OK, well I'll call her.' I didn't really have any reason to think that he was on the lam and hiding. But that was the last time I saw him."

* * *

At some point on either Tuesday, April 5 or Wednesday, April 6, Kurt Cobain killed himself. He walked up to the greenhouse above the garage, locked the doors, propped a stool up against the French doors, wrote a one-page suicide note in red ink addressed to his imaginary childhood friend Boddah, and shot himself in the head with the shotgun, one bullet, dying instantly. A cigar box lay by his side, full of drugs and drug paraphernalia. A wallet lay wide open on the floor. Kurt had taken 1.52 milligrams of heroin – more than enough to kill most heroin users outright. His body lay there for two or three days, while his friends continued to search high and low for him.

Courtney sent Eric over to the Lake Washington house to help look for Kurt. He seemed furious with Cali, and instructed Cali and Jessica to look everywhere, especially to find a secret compartment in the closet in the master bedroom. But they didn't search the grounds.

"Courtney had gotten a private detective – the brilliant Tom Grant – to keep an eye on the house," recalls Cali. "I was staying at Jennifer Adamson's house and I had searched high and low for him and I had searched for this gun she had told me about, and I couldn't find it. I was feeling pretty paranoid when she told me there was a detective watching me because I was on drugs all the time. [Courtney was still in LA at this point.] The end result was I said, 'I'm going to come to LA and see you, I'm on my way.' "

On April 6, Lollapalooza organiser Ted Gardner issued a press release, officially confirming that Nirvana would no longer be headlining the festival – "Due to the ill health of Kurt Cobain." With a richly bitter irony, the headlining slot was passed along to Smashing Pumpkins.

On April 7, management at the Peninsula Hotel placed a 911 call to police. When the cops arrived, Courtney was taken to Century City Hospital for a suspected heroin overdose – she was booked and charged with heroin possession and receiving stolen property. She posted $10,000 bail and was later cleared of all charges.

The same day, Cali and Jennifer Adamson carried out another search of the house at 2.15 a.m. – Jessica had flown back to Minneapolis two days before. They discovered the bed unmade in the master bedroom, cold to the touch – with MTV playing, muted. The pair returned again at dusk, with a few other friends. Cali was seriously spooked. He didn't want to enter the house.

After checking every room, Cali left Kurt a note on the main staircase – "Kurt, I can't believe you managed to be in this house without me noticing. You're a fuckin' asshole for not calling Courtney and at least not letting her know that you're OK. She's in a lot of pain, Kurt, and this morning she had another accident and now she's in hospital again. She's your wife and she loves you and you have a child together. Get it together to at least tell her you're OK or she is going to die. It's not fair, man. Do something now."

"Do you remember the wax old lady that we had?" Cali asks. "It was a life-sized replica of Lizzy Borden.[1] I would put it in windows facing out to scare people, or put it in front of guests' bathroom doors for when they opened the door. I was always afraid of that thing. That day, Bonnie [Dillard, Jennifer Adamson's friend] and me and some other people went over there to get some food or money or something. On our way out the driveway, Bonnie turned around and said she saw someone looking out the attic window. I turned back and it was gone. In my memory, that was Kurt watching us leave. I imagined it was the wax lady she saw, but it was probably him. I talked to his mom afterwards. She was like, 'He could be so quiet if he wanted to be. He could just sit there.' It was a huge house. So I'm loaded, and I don't think he's in there. If I hear a creak of the floor-boards here and there, I'm sure he was there a lot of the time. Was he going over to Caitlin's house? Maybe. He had a car. There's so much crazy speculation."

Police records show a cab leaving the Cobain residence with a young man answering to Cali's description at 4 p.m. that day.

Early that evening, Cali took a flight down to LA.

"When I got to LA, I was so paranoid," Cali continues. "I went to this girl's house. She was like a high school girlfriend. I was like, 'Someone's watching us.' Rene was there. I remember the night so clearly. I was so crazy and I felt so afraid. I found out a couple of years later, that her dad had hired a private detective to watch her on a whole separate issue. She was a drug addict, a dominatrix, and she was a rich Jewish girl from a really wealthy family. So I was being watched in both cities."

The following morning – around 8.40 a.m. on Friday, April 8 – electrician Gary Smith discovered the body of Kurt Cobain while he was carrying out some routine work on the house's alarm system. He called 911, but not before first calling his boss at Veca Electronics, who promptly called Seattle talk radio KXRX with "the scoop of the century".

The official police report stated: "Smith arrived at 171 Lake Washington Blvd East to carry out some electrical work. Smith walked on to the west facing deck of the garage and observed the victim through the windowpanes of the French door. The victim was laying on the floor, with a shotgun across his body and a visible head wound."

KXRX broke the news at 9.40 a.m.

"In the morning, Rene and I got a phone call from Rene's mom telling us what had happened," says Cali. "They'd found the body that morning. I just turned around and went back to the airport and went back up there. I didn't sleep at the house ever again. It was so surreal. Your friend is dead, and it was on the front page of all the newspapers. It took years to digest. It was too much. The day of the funeral was my 21st birthday. It was too much to handle. I just remember the phone ringing all those times."

**Part One: Jessica Hopper**

"I don't think I realised how bad it was until I got to Seattle during spring break," states Jessica Hopper. "Cali was a complete fucking mess and Courtney was in a hotel in LA, and Kurt was in rehab in southern California. And Cali was using as much as $400 to $500 a day could buy him. He was like, 'Don't answer the phone, Courtney calls every one or two hours.' He was only talking to her intermittently because she was calling constantly. There was a real drama, but it was a manipulated situation. It was during the course of Kurt going missing. I think I'd been there for two days – the house was empty, no one else except for Cali and me. It was the first time I'd been to the new house. They had some really nice furniture but it looked like the other house, like they'd never quite moved in. It was a lot bigger, and there were records and knick-knacks and stereos in every room, but Cali's room had a terrible vibe, from being in it, smoking cigarettes and getting high and making mixtapes every day.

"At one point I accidentally picked up the phone because I was expecting a call, and it happened to be Courtney: had I heard from Kurt, what was Cali doing? She said, 'Get Kurt to call me.' Cali was furious with me for taking the call. There was a real bad atmosphere over everything. There was a real vibe of fundamental chaos. It felt like somebody was going to die, the whole time. I didn't want to leave because it felt like Cali was going to die. I'd been around people using, but I'd never seen anyone strung out like that.

"The night before I left, Cali went out for two hours to get drugs and hang out with his girlfriend [Jennifer Adamson] or whatever it was, and I heard somebody in the house and I thought I saw somebody walk through the hall. I assumed it was Kurt. I went, 'Hello? Who the hell is here?' I stood in the doorway, and later I heard something creaking upstairs: after that was when Cali took a note up. I told him that I thought Kurt was here. That was towards the end of my stay.

"Oh, and at some point, Eric showed up at the house because he was going out to the Cavern, this other house they had in the woods. He was looking for Kurt, and he was also looking for Kurt's gun. And there was a locked room next to Kurt and Courtney's bedroom, and he was trying to find the key to that room because there was a padlock on it, a big lock. He was looking around the house, really urgently, asking us if we'd seen Kurt. That day Cali had to find something in the basement, and he made me come into the basement with him; he was so freaked out because we'd heard someone in the house and he thought Kurt might be down there. The house was so creepy at that point. I don't remember the chronology. The house was really cold. There was nothing to eat in the house. There was an air like I wasn't even supposed to have been there. I should have just stayed in Cali's room. Everyone was totally on drugs. Kurt's missing, or they think he has the gun and he's missing. I vaguely remember Cali thinking that maybe Kurt would show up at their dealer's. He wanted to find Kurt.

"Right around that time was when Courtney cancelled all of Kurt's credit cards, and that included Cali's credit cards, so he couldn't get drugs and he started to freak out. He was supposed to buy me a plane ticket home and all of a sudden he couldn't and I was panicking. I had to call my dad, and say, 'I can't tell you the situation, but it's really bad and I have to get out of here and I need a $600 plane ticket the next day.'

"The last morning I was there [Tuesday, April 5 – although it might have been the Monday], right about 6.30, 7.00 a.m., I woke up and Kurt was standing next to the bed. He was like, 'Hi,' totally normal. I talked to him for a few minutes and he made a joke about my head. It was shaved at the time, so he made a joke, something to do with that Unrest song, 'Skinhead Girl'. Cali woke up, and we told Kurt, 'You've got to call Courtney, she's freaking out, you have to call her.' We gave him the number in some little address book, and he sat towards the end of the bed and tried to call, but they wouldn't put him through to her room. [Kurt had forgotten the assumed name his wife was staying under.] He was trying to do that for a while, and I fell back asleep. I woke up, maybe an hour later, and he was sitting at the foot of the bed, looking at a copy of *Puncture* magazine. I said something like, 'Did you get through to Courtney?' and he said no.

"The TV was on. It was a Meat Puppets video on MTV. I don't think he said anything about it. He was just watching. I don't remember him being dressed like he'd been out – although it was probably warm enough that you could be out with just a sweater – but I got the impression he'd just gotten there, like he'd just walked in. He was casual. He didn't seem more high or sedated than normal. He seemed normal and he was being jovial with me. I hadn't seen him since New Year's. So then I fell back asleep and he was gone.

"I woke up, and a few hours later Cali had called a limo service to take me to the airport. That might have been around 11 a.m. I got up. I'd been eating Diet Coke and bananas for days. I'd been sick while I was there, and I remember leaving, but I was so freaked out at leaving Cali to die there, I threw up in the driveway before getting into the limo. It was from the anxiety. I could tell something really bad was going to happen. There was a TV tray next to the bed with this pre-prepared syringe of Narcane[2] wrapped in masking tape. Death was in the house waiting.

"Cali was a mess. He'd nodded off while he was carrying a flaming log to the fireplace. He dropped it on the carpet. A couple of my friends were there, the girls from my band, it happened when they were leaving . . . Cali was trying to pretend everything was normal, wearing pyjamas at three in the afternoon, dropping flaming logs on the carpet and they asked me to leave with them, and I was like, I can't.

"I left and went home to Minneapolis. That was midweek. I was sick for two days when I got back because I was such a mess. I'd spent the previous week watching Cali shoot up in front of me. I think I came back to school on Thursday and then as I was leaving school on the Friday somebody said that they'd heard on the news, someone with blond hair had been found dead in the house. I assumed it was Cali, he'd been talking all week about bleaching his hair, and I passed out right there in the parking lot. I went inside school and I called Cali's parents and they told me it was Kurt, not Cali. And that was it. I remember talking to Courtney for a minute or two.

"Jackie Farry called me for my rundown on events because we realised I was the last person to see Kurt. They all wanted to know what I'd saw and heard. Cali was no use at all. He thought Kurt showing up was just a dream. He debated so hard whether I'd seen him. The only other thing I remember about talking to Jackie was that she said Kurt's ghost was in the house and everyone could feel it."

**Part Two: Rene Navarette**

"The day of my birthday [March 30], I got a call from Kurt from a payphone that didn't say anything, just 'Hey . . .' Kurt was missing, I believe. I got home and listened to my messages, and there was Kurt's message, and all these insane messages from Courtney. She'd be screaming, 'I know he's there' – and it was the same for the next few days. A lot of people thought he was with me. He wasn't. I remember calling Cali, and he was there with Jessica in the house. He told me that he'd had a dream that Kurt showed up holding a big white bag [like a gym bag]. I told him it sounded creepy to me, that he should get the fuck out of there. He came home [to LA] that night. We were looking for Kurt. Courtney had us calling places, threatening people, wanting me to strong-arm people she thought might have been hiding Kurt – I wanted to do it, to clear my own name. People thought it could have been me.

"Cali found out Kurt was back in Seattle, left a note for him, and took off to LA. My mom and I picked Cali up from the airport. We went to my friend Candice's. At the airport, someone was following my mother's car. We had to do some quick manoeuvring to lose them. We thought it was a PI. We went over to Candice's house, and my mom called to let us know that someone had died, and that Cali should call his parents because everyone thought it was him. It was surreal.

"At that point, I hadn't talked to Courtney as a friend that whole last couple of weeks, she was so crazy. Someone called us at Candice's, someone from Gold Mountain arranged for us to take a flight from LA up to the house in Seattle. The plane we were on was full of people going there for the same reason, via Gold Mountain. We got off the plane and people were taking pictures. When we got to the house it was weird. There was someone from MTV reporting from in front of the house, someone else draping black plastic over the trees to stop people coming in. There were so many people in the house. We were just looking for Frances.

"Cali and I went into a room and there were people there. We'd hear the occasional scream let out, Courtney was screaming. It was all really weird. We all didn't know how to act. We wanted to make sure Frances was OK. We were like, 'We've got to get the hell out' – I remember blacking out, going to the funeral, hanging out with [Hole bassist] Kristen Pfaff. Little did we know, but Cali and I were really sick. We'd gotten hepatitis. We went back to the Roosevelt hotel downtown, after the funeral, still on drugs – and the manager came up and told us the credit cards we were on had been cancelled. Gold Mountain flew us back to LA. Everyone was like, 'You've got to get off drugs.' My mom drove us out to El Paso, Texas to try and help us get clean. It was when we were there we noticed we were bright yellow from the hepatitis. We drove back and got hospitalised. It was a blur after that for a while.

"There was this one guy who found me through my brother, came at me with this whole conspiracy theory – the idea that Kurt was killed. It's ridiculous. He himself had told me a couple of times that if he was going to kill himself that would be the way he'd do it, exactly that way. We'd joke about it. We'd joke about the process, doing such a big enough issue of dope that we could get the gun to our heads and that was what happened. That was the humour we kept with him, later – childishly making fun of people or things."

**Part Three: Earnie Bailey**

"In early 1994, Kurt had a second Telecaster, a Sunburst model that I modified by putting two humbucker [pickups] in it and several hardware upgrades. I overhauled it for him, thinking the Tele could be the next place for him to go, guitar-wise. Krist took it to him and said, 'God, he just loves that guitar.'

"When Krist came by to take him to the airport that day, Kurt grabbed his coat and his guitar without the case, and left. Things turned pretty sour at the airport, they got into a scuffle and Kurt threw the guitar at him. He made it clear the band was over. So Krist came over to my place afterwards and he said, 'Fuck him, I'm done with that guy.' He explained what happened and said, 'We should work out some songs.' I said sure. I figured we would stay busy until they made up, but it did seem like he was relieved and that the break-up was final . . .

"Krist and I were at a show the night Kurt died, but we left about halfway through. We were really fidgety and uneasy. MTV had leaked that the band had broken up, or word was getting around that the group was over, and we felt uncomfortable every place we went. We headed down the street to the Crocodile and stayed there for a bit, but called it an early night. He took off for the farm [Krist and Shelli had purchased another property by this point] to go clear his head, and Shelli stayed back at the house in Seattle.

"I was working one morning at the restaurant, and the phone rang, and it was Krist. He said, 'Hey, guess what? Kurt's dead. Do you want to go up to the house and hang out with Shelli until I get home?' I assumed he'd overdosed. I said OK, so Brenda [Earnie's wife] and I locked the place up and went up there. We were sitting with Shelli watching CNN and MTV news and the reports started coming in that Kurt had been found at his house – and about an hour later, they began reporting it was a suicide. And it was just unbelievable, because you couldn't even imagine that. I couldn't process it.

"It was really difficult after that. There was the memorial and Krist had asked me to put together a tape to play after the service, so I put together a list of songs I thought Kurt would like. There was a Vaselines song on there. And I think The Beatles' 'In My Life' was the first song on the cassette.

"Krist, Dave, our partners and I all rode down to the service in Krist's Toyota. The toughest part was walking in, and on the pews was this picture of Kurt, the photo of when he was a boy, with the dates of his birth and passing on it. It's almost like you black out at that point. You can see your shoes and that's about it. We walked over to our seats and sat down, Lanegan was sitting behind me and he had his head down, and I started sobbing, and I don't think I stopped until it was over. I was quiet, almost frozen, but I couldn't stop. I looked over across the aisle from me and there was a man who was in the same position, hunched over and crying, and I realised it was Kurt's dad.

"The next day, or whenever, *Seattle Times* ran a photo of Kurt lying in the greenhouse on their cover and it was so horrible to see. What if that was the editor's son laying there, how would they feel? I put in a quarter and threw every single one in the dumpster."

**Addenda: Everett True**

I was in Cincinnati, Ohio on April 8, 1994 with Steve Gullick when I first heard the rumour that Kurt Cobain had killed himself.

We were in town to interview Beck, then one of Gold Mountain's rising stars with his slacker anthem 'Loser'. I'd got to town the previous night, in time to catch Tacoma, WA skate-grunge band Seaweed at a local venue that also served as a Laundromat. Despite two members being down with the flu, the ex-Sub Pop act were in fine thrashing form, reminding me of all the energy and massive power hooks that first attracted me to the Seattle sound. Steve had flown in the following morning and we were sitting around waiting for his room to become ready. It was one of those days you sometimes get while travelling: grey, dull and stretching on forever. We were looking forward to hooking up with the Cheap Trick-loving Guided By Voices in neighbouring city Dayton later that week, though.

Already, we'd been informed that Beck also had the flu, and might have to pull out of both that night's show (at the Laundromat, with skewed LA female pop band That Dog in support) and our interview. So we were sitting around in my hotel room, relaxing, watching MTV and CNN, looking at magazines. Hole's album *Live Through This* was about to come out and Steve, being faintly prudish, was shocked at some of the photographs of Courtney. "I wonder what Kurt would think of this?" he asked me a couple of times. Despite the weather, though, we were happy; bringing each other up-to-date on the last few hectic weeks, when the phone suddenly rings. It's about 11 a.m.

Steve picks it up. It's Paul Lester, my features editor from *Melody Maker* – not always the most sensitive of fellows. "So what's all this about Kurt Cobain being dead then?"

"I don't know what you're talking about," Steve replies. "You better speak to Everett."

I look at Steve. There's obviously something wrong, I can tell by his manner.

"It's Lester," he says. "He says there's a rumour going round that Kurt has killed himself."

I speak to Paul and tell him that neither of us knows anything but that I'd ring around, find out and ring him back as soon as I could. He asks me to hurry, as there's a whole load of *Maker* journalists waiting in the office late in case the story is true. Steve and I look at each other: it's about then that the façade crumbles and . . . don't ask me how . . . but we both know it's true. Kurt has killed himself.

I don't know what made us feel so certain. It wasn't as if either of us had realised up to that point that Kurt was suicidal. Both of us had thought the Rome incident had been a genuine accident. I thought this despite the fact Courtney had called me up shortly afterwards, asking whether I thought that treating Kurt to a 'tough love' session to help him kick his heroin addiction was a good idea. I had no idea what such a session entailed but I figured anything that helped Kurt sort his life out had to be worth trying. Also, Courtney's personal manager, Janet Billig from Gold Mountain, had phoned me up personally after Rome to reassure me there was nothing mentally wrong with Kurt.

The next 30 minutes were spent in a bad haze of uncertainty as I phoned every number I could think of – Gold Mountain, Bad Moon (Nirvana's UK press agents), my contacts at Geffen, Kurtney's house – to no avail. Eventually I was forced to call Nirvana biographer Michael Azerrad in New York City. I didn't want to. I didn't like the man. I felt he'd been chosen to write the Nirvana book by Kurt's management simply because he had a 'safe pair of hands'.

"Yes, it's true," he told me. "We're all on our way out to Seattle. I'd advise you to do the same."

It struck me then as an odd statement. It still does. What earthly good could I do by going to Seattle? Perhaps Michael was making reference to that selfsame job description I'd had screamed at me on a Brighton–London train all those years ago and that I'd vehemently denied: "You're just a fucking music journalist." Is that all it came down to after years of passion: I had a job to carry out?

I told Steve the news.

I threw the remnants of my bottle of Maker's Mark down the sink, figuring that the worst possible thing I could do at that stage was to get trashed. Steve asked me to inform *Melody Maker* he didn't want any of his photos used in the inevitable tribute that would follow . . . I think that when I called back up I must have spoken to my editor, Allan Jones. He told me that I should just go and do whatever I needed to do, "Plane tickets, whatever, it doesn't matter, we'll cover the cost, you don't have to write anything if you don't feel like it." It's a conversation I'll remember with gratitude forever.

I can't remember accurately what followed. It wasn't real. We sat there dazed. I didn't know what to do or where to go. I didn't want to fly to Seattle to confront a future that I knew would come crashing down around me as soon as I arrived. For the last five years of my life I'd managed to leave my past behind and not deal with the bad side. I wanted to be anywhere but in America, in Seattle, in Ohio . . . I started thinking of all those times I'd refused to call Kurt or Courtney, thinking that famous people didn't need friends, not when they had so many managers around them. I knew that if Kurt had just managed to hang out with Steve and I, see a band like Guided By Voices a few times, get trashed with Kim Deal, he'd never have been driven to such an extreme . . .

Yeah, right.

The phone rang again. It was my friend Eric Erlandson, calling from an airport. "Courtney wants you to come to Seattle." So it was I found myself walking through the sterile, anaemic aisles of Cincinnati airport with Steve, clutching a bag full of vinyl albums that I'd bought only the day before. We didn't know what to say to each other. I gave Steve the records to take back to England with him.

So it was that I came to be flying into Seattle on the afternoon that Kurt Cobain's body was discovered, tears streaming down my face, the refrain to a Hole song spiralling crazily round inside my head. *"Live through this with me,"* the lady sang. *"And I swear that I will die for you."*

Eric had informed me that when I arrived at Seattle, if I called the house they would arrange for a limousine to pick me up from the airport. It was necessary. By the time the car had got to the gates of the Cobain residence in Lake Washington it was crazy outside. Police tape and small scrums of reporters and the curious lined the secluded road. No one was being allowed in unless they'd been expressly invited. I couldn't help feeling I was being allowed access to the rock journalist's ultimate dream: a guest list to die for. Sorry about the black humour, but you fucking *know* we liked it that way.

Inside the house, it was curiously silent. Mark Lanegan was standing in one corner, not speaking to anyone. He looked alone and I felt alone, both of us separated from everyone else by our natures and the situation. It seemed natural we should hang out together.

There was virtually no one else there until Krist and Dave turned up with a few friends and family and went and stood on the other side of the room. Courtney and Eric's camp turned up a little later . . . or perhaps it was earlier. I remember some record company types briefly having a fit at my presence there – I was a journalist – and thinking, "You stupid, stupid fuckheads. I'm not the one being paid to pretend I'm a fucking friend."

At one stage, Krist came over and asked if I wanted to come to a wake being held for Kurt that evening by a few of his old Seattle friends. I declined because . . . well . . . I was in Courtney's camp that day, and there was no getting round it. My loyalties had been sorted out a while before. Even though I wanted to speak to Krist, I couldn't because of the politics around Nirvana that didn't die away for one second upon Kurt's suicide, only intensified.

Mark and I stuck around the house after almost everyone else had departed. There were some terrible arguments going on between Courtney and Eric, and the nanny Cali, but that was nothing unusual. Some of the people there wanted to take drugs to hide the terrible sudden pain, and others equally as vehemently didn't want them reintroduced into the house. We were introduced to Kurt's mom, Wendy, by Courtney the following way, Courtney using my real name – "This is Kurt's friend Mark and this is my friend Jerry." Both of us were shown and read the suicide note.

And that's almost all I'm going to tell of that terribly sad weekend. Mark and I stayed in the whole time at his apartment, somewhere near the start of the Monorail, downtown. We didn't go out except for perhaps one cup of coffee round the corner. We barely spoke. I was mostly concerned with making sure Mark was all right, and I'm sure he was the same back. We turned on the television once: there was talk of Nirvana and the fans' vigil, and we turned it off again straight away. Some Sub Pop hipsters were holding their annual party, which had turned into a wake at the Crocodile Club. Fair enough, but Kurt hadn't exactly got along with his former peers in recent years. We played a few records, walked around the house, tried to pretend to each other that we hadn't been crying. Mostly, however, we just sat there and waited for Courtney to call, in case she needed us.

When it came to the day of the funeral service, we realised that I had no appropriate clothes to wear. My only pair of jeans had holes in their knees. We knew that Kurt wouldn't have given a fuck but I still didn't want to look disrespectful. So I borrowed a pair of Mark's black drainpipes and turned up to the service with the top three buttons undone.

It was a gloriously sunny day as we left Mark's apartment to go down to the church – the sort of day when Seattle becomes the most beautiful city in the world, bar none, with Mount Rainier and the Olympics in shimmering crisp detail behind the skyscrapers and Space Needle. It had been raining the whole of the previous week, as is the Pacific Northwest's wont.

"I swear that Kurt would never have killed himself if the weather had been this nice last week," Mark remarked thoughtfully.

Initially, I felt a sense of betrayal at Kurt's suicide. That rapidly disappeared over the following months. People say that suicide is the ultimate act of cowardice, but you know what? It's far more cowardly to let your life disappear into nameless years of drinking and drugs, whiling away the days of your life in a bleak TV-satiated depression because you're too scared to make a change. Sure, I blamed his management for placing too many demands on him while he was feeling so fragile. I soon outgrew that, though. They didn't mean to kill him! They were only trying their best to accommodate everyone, do what Courtney and Kurt and Krist and Dave were asking of them.

Kurt's death was such a shame, such a shame. At one point it had really felt we could've changed things, but with his suicide it was finally proved to me, irrevocably, this is what happens when you try to fuck with the system. There it was in plain black and white. The system kills you.

I know others that the system has killed also: people with fragile, unique voices that became overpowered by the boorish chants of the grey masses – friends and acquaintances and others even closer. They too were unable to cope with the demands placed upon them of everyday life. Maybe someone they loved left them, perhaps they never managed to adjust to everyone else's normalcy. Who knows? It's not difficult to imagine nothing when you sink into such total depression. Anything is preferable to loneliness: especially death. Kurt happened to be the most famous friend who'd killed himself. He was also the hardest to mourn. Who could I call? Who could I speak to about his death? Anyone I knew that might be able to relate was thousands of miles away and had sorrows of their own. I already felt bad enough about the contradictions of my position as part of the voyeuristic rock press. Had I somehow contributed to Kurt's death? Maybe the only reason we hung out together was because his glory reflected upon me and gave me that illusion of glamour I'd been searching for all my life.

We had talked about changing things with Nirvana. What would we have replaced the old order with, though? We wanted something *better.* What did that mean? We wanted something less macho, more female-led, more sensitive and spontaneous and fun and exciting: Jad Fair and Courtney Love and Kim Deal, Kathleen Hanna, Daniel Johnston and Dan Treacy. We wanted our friends, our peers, our dreams and our heroes in positions of authority; is that such a crime? We wanted a place where bullies and braggarts didn't automatically rule. We wanted a place where women aren't automatically second-class citizens because they – we – are already part of us. A place where commercial radio counted for shit.

What did we want? Not much: just Nirvana.

I returned to England after a couple of days.

Danny Goldberg had given a speech at Kurt's funeral service that had made me realise precisely why the singer had finally given up. This speech had no grounding in reality, no relation to any man I've known. In it, Kurt was referred to as, "An angel that came to earth in human form, as someone who was too good for this life and that was why he was only here for such a short time." Bull-fucking-shit! Kurt was as pissy and moody and belligerent and naughty and funny and dull as the rest of us, it just so happened he was a little too sensitive for the situation he found himself in, too. After the service I left the church and started walking – to anywhere, anywhere but where all these self-righteous prigs revelling in their own fame and importance were sitting.

I forced myself to return, remembered there were people like Lanegan there, and Calvin Johnson, and Jon and Bruce from Sub Pop, and The Breeders . . . people I loved dearly. Yet in all the days that followed, I only ever found one other person who had been equally as upset by that speech: Kristen Pfaff, bassist with Courtney's band and formerly bassist with great Minneapolis hardcore trio Janitor Joe. (I'm sure there were others, but I wasn't in communication with many people right then.)

We chatted about Nirvana that summer as Kristen rejoined her old band for a tour across Eastern Europe alongside fellow Amphetamine Reptile act, Hammerhead. There were nine or so of us all crammed into a dirty old van, talking of love and laughter and life and those small, but so significant, details in between. Everything seemed so right again: punk rock like I'd always loved it, practised by two bands for whom it was their natural birthright. The venues were tiny, sweating, crammed with enthusiastic faces and blistering power chords. At night, we would all sleep together in a dormitory, enlivened by whatever cheap alcohol we could lay our hands on. It was like being born again: Kristen was so lively and full of optimism about the future and music and life.

"The rhythm that you hear is the pounding of our hearts," as one poet put it.

A couple of weeks later, Kristen was found dead in the bath in her Seattle apartment. Strangely, that evening was the first time I'd spoken to Courtney since leaving Seattle. She thought I'd heard the news somehow when I called. It wasn't that. It was just that I'd had another premonition of death, similar to the time an Angel of Death had visited me while driving down the freeway between Boston and New York after I'd been out drinking the night before with NYC musician, Charlie Ondras from Unsane – and he died the exact same time I saw it.

The craziness didn't stop there.

I still travelled to America and Australia and Europe, drinking even harder. What else could I do? It wasn't real, was it? I was sure that somewhere along the line I'd receive a phone call from Anton or Janet telling me that it had all been a ghastly Dwarves-style joke. (Sub Pop's scum rock band Dwarves once put out a press release stating that their bass-player had been murdered in a back ally in Middle America. The outrage was considerable when it transpired the whole story was made up.) It was absurd to feel that way, especially as Courtney had taken me into the garage where Kurt's body was found, where she had lit some candles in homage, but sometimes the massive events are the hardest to come to terms with. So I continued out-drinking bands and PRs and passers-by in vain attempts to regain my feeling for life; so I became even more desperate in my writing, searching for replacement bands.

It wasn't until my passport got stolen from my hotel room in Chicago while I lay comatose on the floor on the other side of the bed, vomit dripping from my mouth, that I finally stopped travelling to America. Instead, I continued beating myself up on the other side of the Atlantic, reverting to the bleak acceptance of being down the pub beyond chucking out time every night of the week, not even bothering to attend shows.

Music had failed me.

## NOTES

1 Lizzy Borden was a New England woman tried and acquitted for the brutal axe murders of her father and stepmother in the late 19th century. Her trial inspired a children's skipping rope chant: *"Lizzie Borden took an axe/ And gave her mother 40 whacks/ When she saw what she had done/ She gave her father 41."*

2 Narcane is a drug used by paramedics to counteract the effects of heroin overdose: "It's like an adrenalin shot; very uncomfortable but a potential lifesaver," comments Cali. "That particular shot was stolen from a parked ambulance."

## CHAPTER 30

# The Aftermath

"THE last time I saw Courtney in person was when she was up here for the *Rockrgrl* Music Conference in 2000," says Gillian G. Gaar. "She was with Kurt's sisters, Brianne and Kim. It was eerie how much Kim looked like Kurt. What really got me was she smoked a cigarette the same way he did, just sitting there. It was like watching his double. And she had the same quiet way of talking. We went up to a hotel room and we were passing around beers from the mini-bar. Kim opened her beer and she took a sip and she just muttered, sort of an aside to herself, like, 'Ahhhh . . . that takes me back to high school.' "

What are your feelings on Nirvana now?

"It was a pretty cool thing that happened," replies Chad Channing. "It's nice to say that I had a hand in bringing that kind of music to the public. It was definitely enjoyable to be able to play with Krist and Kurt, and we built a really good friendship."

Do you find this whole myth making . . .?

"Bullshit?" interrupts the drummer. "Yes I do. It is bullshit. Why people want to put people on stands, like gods, it's just a joke. It's wrong. Why in the world would you put anybody so high up like that anyway? Kurt was a regular guy who just wrote music, wrote good songs and was in the right place at the right time. If we'd done it five years earlier, it wouldn't have happened."

**January 2005**

"I feel now like if he could have lived two more months, he'd still be alive," says Cali DeWitt. "I think of Kurt now as someone who was in the early stages of bad drug addiction. I've known so many people in the first two or three years of drug addiction who let it overtake them and committed suicide. I've also known so many who got past that. It's one of those silly, tragic things. It was early drug addiction coupled with rampant, lovesick craziness. He was too smart to have died this way.

"Kurt's been made into this miserable person in the history books, and he wasn't," the former nanny continues. "A sick part of myself, one of the first things I thought when I found out how he killed himself was, 'You really said what you wanted to say. There's really no stronger way to say "fuck you" than what you did.' I wish he hadn't, but I was proud that he was able to do what he wanted to do. It was a very confusing feeling for me. My friend, who was also my hero, had killed himself and there's all this press . . . I didn't know how to digest it."

What did you do?

"I went back to LA and my parents were really, really afraid," Cali replies. "They said, 'Look, we've denied it to ourselves, but you're obviously on drugs.' My parents were so supportive. That's probably what saved my life. I stopped doing drugs for a little while, but I couldn't deal with it. I went out again and I was running around. I didn't have access to the kind of money I had when I was with Kurt and Courtney. It was a different game – back to hustling in LA. I ran into this girl who I was obsessed with when I was a teenager. She was 35 and I was 21, and she was [a famous rock star's] wife. I saw in her eyes a beautiful, self-destructive person. She had $50,000 and we spent it in six weeks. Both of us were trying our damnedest to die. I wound up in a Scientologist rehab in Oklahoma. When that didn't kill me, the rest was easy. There was a moment five or six years later where I woke up and I felt like, 'I'm starting to digest what happened when I was 20.' I got sober just before I turned 28, so it'll be four years in March.

"I followed it in the press," Cali continues. "It was kind of a big deal. There's a lot of big 'I don't knows'. All I've been able to digest is he had a lot of heartache and he was pretty new to drugs and he didn't know how to digest that kind of depression. That part of him that wanted to say 'fuck you' to the world succeeded. I don't think that was him at his core. Most of the people that I was hanging out with back then are dead.

"As for Courtney, I slowly stopped calling her. As a drug user, I was lazy and I slowly tore myself away from the idea that she would dangle in front of me: if you stay with me as my employed friend, you'll be fine. I just had to look into the future: when I'm 30, do I want to be Courtney's live-in friend? Living with someone who yells at waitresses all the time, I can't handle it. She feels like I abandoned her, and in a way I did. I care about her; I want her to be OK. I couldn't live with that weird, 'I'm going to be a Hollywood actress' life. I definitely feel like she lost her way, or maybe she was never going the way I imagined she was."

Me too.

"I don't think about it an awful lot any more. I'd like to have spent more time with Frances in the last 10 years, but I would have been useless for most of it. Over the years it became more difficult to call. Whoever the new assistant would be on the phone like, 'Yeah, I'll tell Frances you called.' But I saw her on her birthday about a year and a half ago. It was great and I hung out with her all day and I hadn't seen her in awhile and she had pictures of me on the wall. I wish that I was a little closer to the way that I am now than I was in my early twenties so I could have been with her all of the time."

I'm thinking of starting off the book with a copy of the fax that was sent out the day after Kurt's memorial, lampooning Danny Goldberg's speech, because I think it draws a line in the sand. I'm trying to reclaim Nirvana for the punk rock kids, away from the industry.

"Which is good," nods Candice Pedersen. "That's an interesting, relevant path to go down, but it wasn't accidental that Kurt was with the people he was with. He chose them because he was very ambitious and those people didn't do anything to him that he didn't wish. He made adult choices. What I will say is that he recognised he was in a situation he couldn't get out of."

I still haven't seen the fax. I wonder that if I had, it would have made me feel less alone.

"I only read the fax at the time," says Rich Jensen, "but it made an impression on me. It referred to the fact Danny Goldberg – being the professional that he is – understood Kurt's interests better than Kurt did. The best example, and this comes from the fax, was the time that Kurt didn't understand how important it would be to his career to attend the MTV Music Awards [September 1992]. He thought that perhaps he should stay in the hospital. Instead, he was convinced to sign a waiver to release himself from the hospital to attend the awards. It was only with the kind of professional advice that Danny Goldberg could provide that Kurt could see where his true interests lay. The fax was very critical and very angry and cutting, but precise. It was very impressive. We talked before about the complication of Nirvana as being both a participant in, and antagonistic to, the major label music business that was really part of what made Nirvana interesting and compelling socially. That fax was one case where a voice seemed to get inside that complication and open it up emotionally in an impressive way.

"It went to a number of different places," continues Rich. "It came into the fax machine at Sub Pop anonymously. [To this day, it's never been made clear who sent the fax – but the finger of suspicion rests on one of Kurt's former Olympia friends present at the memorial service.] It caused a stir, we all looked at it. People were calling each other all day to figure out who did it. But in fairness to Danny Goldberg, it's a difficult thing to be a music business executive. For example, when Kurt died, I had a position of some responsibility at Sub Pop. That day I was out of town and I took the bus from the airport and I was carrying my bags to work. I was about a block away from the offices when I heard the news. We had a little shop – the Sub Pop Mega Mart on 2nd Ave – and I called and said, 'Shut the shop.' I knew that it would be a place where cameras would go. It wasn't anything that anyone should have to be paid eight dollars an hour to be responsible for.

"Then what happened was everything Kurt Cobain touched became 10 times more valuable. All the records start selling like crazy and the companies who put out their records become valuable commodities. You find yourself sickeningly attached to the destruction of the possibility of the creative process that drew you there. It's the most evil, most ironic success possible. So I offer that in defence of Danny Goldberg. Kurt wasn't the only one. Danny Goldberg is a smart, articulate guy who means well and who's done well. Not only has he done well personally – he's made a lot of money – but he's done good things for a lot of people. It is a complicated situation to be in.

"So when we're talking about this fax . . . I probably would have reacted exactly the way the person who prepared this fax reacted to Danny's speech, but you need to bear all that in mind."

"I always had this feeling I would talk to him again – why wouldn't I?" asks Carrie Montgomery. "I figured I'd wait it out. Two years later, I felt I had waited it out long enough, so I called their house . . . the day before they found his body. It was bizarre, because I called Dylan out of the blue, like, 'I was thinking about calling Kurt today,' and he's like, 'Why? Do you know where he is?' So I started calling his house and left two or three messages. Then I find out the next day that he was laying there dead while the phone was ringing.

"After he died," she continues, "I felt like I had lost *my* husband. He was so adamant that he didn't want to be famous forever, he didn't want to be in the public eye and I was like, 'Go buy a castle in Scotland and paint and write a book, I mean, shit, it's not like you're going to have to earn a living.' But he always had this insane fear of being poor."

"I thought Kurt was going to start his own record label, or do a lot more creative type things," says Debbi Shane. "He didn't. He got married; he had a baby. I remember this happy-go-lucky kid. He was a really funny, goofy kid who liked Kraft Macaroni and cheese and Kool-Aid and Cheez Whiz, and Peanut Butter Cap'n Crunch."

Do you think Nirvana were better than 10,000 other bands?

"I don't know," says Tobi Vail. "Billy Childish says, 'Music is about sound and performance as well as good songs. If it wasn't, every time someone played The Kinks' "You Really Got Me", it would sound good.'

"Nirvana not only had the songs, they had the sound and the performance aspects down. Even from the beginning – playing dorm rooms or makeshift halls with inadequate vocal PAs – they had the sound figured out and they gave 100 per cent, even if there were only 10 people there. Sonically, they were generally the best band on the bill of any show they played, and most crowds they played to could see that immediately. When they opened for Sonic Youth with Dale drumming it was clear to everyone who saw them that they had the potential to be huge. That's when the songwriting started matching their sound and performance level. There are bands that I personally like better, but they were an objectively good band on all fronts."

Here's something that confuses me. People say that Nirvana changed everything; but precisely *what* did Nirvana change? They made it easier for Smashing Pumpkins, Bush, Pearl Jam, Silverchair and a bunch of crap bands to sell a load of records. They made Courtney Love rich.

"That's how it always is," Slim Moon agrees. "Look at all the emo bands that we can blame Rites Of Spring for, and all the straight edge bands that we could blame Minor Threat for, or all the hideous, jangly indie rock bands that we can blame Pavement for. The main legacy that great bands have is a whole bunch of shitty bands. The reason people talk about Nirvana with a crazy gleam in their eye, different from other bands, is that there's no glitch in Nirvana that makes people feel like they were fed something that wasn't real. There's still a fantasy that a great rock'n'roll band should be able to just set up over in the corner of your living room and blow your mind. Most people know that on some level Nine Inch Nails can't do that. And when people think of Kurt's expression – his songwriting and his interviews – they see him as being completely honest and not contrived. Even our favourite rock stars, we usually suspect of a certain amount of contrived-ness."

There's an obvious reason for that. People are surprised I never liked The Smiths. The reason for that is because if Morrissey actually meant what he was singing about in the early Eighties, he wouldn't have been on stage. Kurt, you can't ever doubt because he fucking killed himself.

"There's no later days or cheesy records," assents Slim.

It doesn't have to take suicide for validation, though. I would point to Neil Young as a musician who always came across as someone who stayed true to himself.

"Maybe 30 years from now, Neil Young will still be seen as big of an influence on the history of rock as Nirvana, but right now Nirvana's presence is so . . ."

People say they're a big influence, and I don't see it. Show me any influence at all.

"Certain people started changing their voices to sing like him, certain people started researching their songs. In particular, Stone Temple Pilots and Bush . . ."

I don't mean in the really obvious, musical, way.

"If the thing that was special about them was their genuineness, it is really remarkable how much genuineness is missing," Slim agrees. "That's not carried over as an influence. You don't now see legions of bands trying to be totally real. It seems like bands are more contrived now than they were."

Why do you think Nirvana have such resonance now? – I mean with teenage kids.

"Easy answer," replies Bruce Pavitt. "Because it's good. It's timeless music. Same way that Neil Young still sounds great. Nirvana's music has emotional integrity, I would say, as much as style."

Do you think it's partly because Kurt never grew past that stage of being incredibly confused about life?

"That's a good point, yeah," agrees Bruce. "He does express a lot of angst and confusion, which is what being a teenager is all about. I agree. I have nephews and nieces that are all listening to Nirvana and totally connecting with it."

Why are people still talking about *Nevermind* in 2005?

"Because everything that's come since then is half as good and completely derived from *Nevermind*," retorts Steve Fisk.

How so?

"The form," explains the Seattle producer. "The lyrics. The loud/soft/

loud. The rasp in the voice. It's really embarrassing, but there haven't been any new ideas since Nirvana. Puddle Of Mud, 'She Hates Me'. Play that next to 'Rape Me'. It's the same beats per minute, it's the same chords, the same phonics."

"I'll tell you three things," says former Thrown-Ups guitarist Leighton Beezer. "One of them is, I bet we had the same impression and another one, I bet we don't have the same impression. Did you see the *Time* magazine cover [October 25, 1993] with Eddie Vedder on it that said 'Grunge: All The Rage'? When I saw that I was like, '. . . Oh, GAWD!!! Somebody completely missed the boat on this one!' Grunge was all tongue-in-cheek. I mean, *ma-a-a-aybe* Eddie did have some issues to express to the masses, but . . . people were not 'angry' here in Seattle. There was no violence or anger or angst involved in grunge at all."

Which is where Nirvana went wrong. They got too serious . . .

"OK, but that's my . . . oh, wait now, OK, this is, then I'm right, you won't agree with my second statement," Leighton laughs. "My second statement was that Kurt's suicide was the ultimate punchline. On the order of, 'Ha ha! Made you look!' Yeah! He set it up that he had to keep topping himself, in this style, and he had gone as far as he could go without doing that. In fact, he had long since gone as far as he could go without doing that. So it was, do you want to move forward and take this to its logical conclusion or not?"

By that logic, Courtney Love is the ultimate grunge icon.

"Oh yeah. Well, marrying her was probably the last really obnoxious thing he did before . . . that. I think he was definitely in love with her, which blows my mind . . . pardon the expression . . ."

No problem.

"I'm in the software business, right?" the former Thrown-Ups guitarist says. "So I know some software people who are really, really rich. One of them bought Kurt's old house, and she threw a party before she renovated the place, so we could see what it used to look like. It wasn't that spectacular, except for up in the little baby's bedroom, Kurt had painted little cherubs and angels around the top of the wall, reminiscent of the Sistine Chapel, only with Courtney's face on them! [It was actually the work of singer/comic book artist Dame Darcy in 1996.] She said she was going to take it all out, and I implored her not to. I'm sure Kurt was very happy for a while there."

**Addenda: Sleater-Kinney**

(Sleater-Kinney are included here as a modern-day example of the sort of band Olympia was once synonymous with – articulate, passionate, female-led rock music.)

"I remember going to parties at Tobi Vail's house," says singer Corin Tucker. "It would be Bratmobile, Nirvana, in that order. They were an Olympia band, and it was people screwing around. There wasn't a hierarchy of, 'Oh, this person is famous, and this person is a better artist than that person.' It was more about people who wanted to hear what other people were doing, and were really respectful about it. It was so liberating to me, as a young person who wanted to be an artist."

Why Olympia?

"It has a lot to do with the convergence of many things," replies Corin. "[The Olympia lifestyle] gave people who didn't have a lot of money, and people in Oregon and Washington, the ability to be working class and still be able to move around and have aspirations of going to college and achieving a more intellectual job, not just working in a supermarket their entire life. In Olympia, there were all these people from different economic backgrounds, and this intensely ideological college happening. It was very intellectual and such a utopia because it wasn't just about playing music to get rich. It was more about exploring what you wanted out of life."

Also, Olympia is associated with female artists: and that seems to me one of the main reasons why Nirvana were so different – and more interesting – than the rock bands that went before. Kurt was clearly influenced by his female peers.

"There are so many references in their lyrics," agrees co-singer Carrie Brownstein. "Like in 'Been A Son', it's like he's saying, 'If I ever met a wise man, it would be a woman.' It was like, whoa, you're speaking the same rhetoric as Bikini Kill or Heavens To Betsy, but you're couching it from a different perspective. They were from the longshoreman town, government town, hippie college town, drawing from all of that. All the bands in Olympia borrowed from those influences, but in some ways, Nirvana did it the best of all. They did it in a way that transcended Olympia. There are numerous amazing bands from Olympia, but Nirvana spoke to millions of people. If you compare them to other bands, they're similar. Obviously the Riot Grrrl bands were a little more obvious in what they were doing, but there were a handful of male bands that were also doing what Nirvana was doing, but they didn't have that . . . *thing*. Not so many people heard Some Velvet Sidewalk or Beat Happening or Unwound."

"Calvin [Johnson] is super-educated about feminism and a total feminist," explains Corin, "but Kurt was able to write about women in a way where you thought about their experiences. I thought it was emotional."

"Kurt seemed to be soaking it in, like it was osmosis," adds Carrie. "In Olympia, they don't care about awards, not at all. Whoever is playing the most obscure show in Olympia is everyone's favourite band that week. It's intense to make music in a town where the smaller you are, the more revered you are. It's like a reverse pull."

Small shows are fun.

"Small shows *are* fun," Carrie agrees. "I think that everyone's trying to hold on to that purity there, that moment where it's, 'Just me and 10 other people saw this and it's never going to be on the Internet and nobody took any pictures, it's just a memory that we have.' It's an antiquated way of thinking about art and experience. Everyone leaves Olympia with the sense of knowing that maybe the best thing you ever did was the show that only 10 people saw. Whether or not you can continue to get validated by more and more people, it's hard to forget that some of the people you really cared about liked you better when only 10 people saw you."

# DISCOGRAPHY

(Compiled by Enrico Vincenzi, www.sliver.it)

## SINGLES

**Love Buzz / Big Cheese**
**1988 – USA**, Sub Pop (seven-inch SP23)
1,200 copies, black vinyl, twofold paper sleeve. 1,000 copies were hand numbered in red ink on the back sleeve, the remaining 200 had a thick red marker slash in place of the number. Several counterfeits exist, in black and in coloured vinyl.

**Sliver / Dive / About A Girl**
**1990 – USA**, Sub Pop (seven-inch SP72)
First release: a total of 3,000 copies in black, marbled blue and clear pink vinyl. Threefold paper sleeve with a Sub Pop Singles Club card attached. Yellow labels. Some leftover clear pink copies were later distributed in a twofold sleeve, without the card.
Second release: pressed in various vinyl colours (black, clear, clear pink, clear marbled blue, clear pale yellow, marbled opaque pink, marbled opaque peach). A very limited quantity was pressed in white vinyl and was only available to the bands, Erika pressing plant employees, and Sub Pop employees.
Housed in regular cardboard sleeves, the name of the manufacturing plant (Erika) is mentioned on the back sleeve, or on the yellow record labels. Counterfeits exist in black vinyl.
Third release: black vinyl, black labels. Twofold or regular sleeve.
**Sliver / Dive / About A Girl** – live (CD and 12-inch only) / **Spank Thru** – live (CD only)
**1991 – UK**, Tupelo (seven-inch TUP25, 12-inch TUPEP25, CD TUPCD25)
The seven-inch was pressed consisting of 2,000 copies; lime green vinyl, gatefold sleeve.
The 12-inch was pressed in marbled blue and in black vinyl.

**Molly's Lips** – live
**1991 – USA**, Sub Pop (seven-inch SP97)
4,000 copies in marbled green vinyl and 3,500 in black vinyl. Threefold paper sleeve with a Sub Pop Singles Club card attached. This is a split single, the Nirvana track is on the B-side. On the A-side, there is 'Candy' by The Fluid. Counterfeits exist in black vinyl.

**Here She Comes Now**
**1991 – USA**, Communion (seven-inch COMM23)
The number of copies printed is still unknown, but should be a total of 1,000, in different vinyl colours: black, blue, purple, pink, green, grey, yellow, red. Except for the black, all vinyl copies have a marbled appearance, and for some of the 'main' colours there are variations (light and dark blue, three or more shades of purple, etc). Some other colours were used in just a handful of copies (orange, mustard, muddy white). Looks like the manufacturer used all the leftover vinyl bits he had lying around . . .
Threefold paper sleeve. This is a split single, the Nirvana track is on the A-side. On the B-side there is 'Venus In Furs' by the Melvins. Both tracks are Velvet Underground covers.
Counterfeits exist in black, red, green and purple vinyl.

**Smells Like Teen Spirit / Even In His Youth / Aneurysm** (CD only)
**1991 – USA**, DGC (seven-inch DGCS7-19050, CD DGCDS-21673, MC DGCCS-19050)
The seven-inch were intended for jukebox use, and have a plain blue or grey DGC sleeve.
Two different promo 12-inch copies: the first (PRO-A-4314) includes 'Aneurysm'; clear yellow vinyl and picture sleeve.
The second (PRO-A-4365) plays only the title track, on both sides; black vinyl and plain white sleeve with a title sticker.
Promo CD (PRO-CD-4308) in card sleeve, including the title track only (album and radio edit). Some regular CDs were also used as promos, adding a red 'PROMOTIONAL' print on the discs. Two different promo cassettes (no code), both including the title track only.
**Smells Like Teen Spirit / Drain You / Even In His Youth** (12-inch and CD only) **/ Aneurysm** (CD only)
**1991 – UK**, Geffen (seven-inch DGCS 5, 12-inch DGCT 5, 12-inch picture DGCTP 5, CD DGCTD 5)
The CD was first released with the UK tour dates on the back, then reissued removing the dates and adding a blue border on the front. The seven-inch has silver painted labels. Copies with unpainted labels and large hole were meant for use in jukeboxes. Promo cassette (no code), with the radio edit of the title track.

**Come As You Are / School** – live (CD only) **/ Drain You** – live
**1992 – USA**, DGC (seven-inch DGCS7-19120, CD DGCDS-21707, MC DGCCS-19120)
The seven-inch copies were intended for jukebox use, and have a plain blue or grey DGC sleeve.
Promo 12-inch (PRO-A-4416) with the title track on both sides; black vinyl and plain white sleeve with a title sticker.

Promo CD (PRO-CD-4375) in gatefold card sleeve, including the title track only. Some regular CDs were also used as promos, adding a red 'PROMOTIONAL' print on the discs.
**Come As You Are / Endless, Nameless / School** – live (CD only) / **Drain You** – live (12-inch and CD only)
**1992 – UK**, Geffen (seven-inch DGCS 7, 12-inch DGCT 7, 12-inch picture DGCTP 7, CD DGCTD 7)
The seven-inch has black paper labels or silver painted labels, copies with unpainted labels and large hole were meant for use in jukeboxes.

**Lithium / Been A Son** – live / **Curmudgeon** (CD only)
**1992 – USA**, DGC (CD DGCDM-21815, MC DGCCS-19134)
Promo CD (PRO-CD-4429) in plain card sleeve, including the title track only. Some regular CDs were also used as promos, adding a red 'PROMOTIONAL' print on the discs.
**Lithium / Been A Son** – live / **Curmudgeon** (12-inch and CD only) / **D-7** (CD only)
**1992 – UK**, Geffen (seven-inch DGCS 9, 12-inch picture DGCTP 9, CD DGCTD 9, MC DGCSC 9)
The seven-inch has silver painted labels, copies with unpainted labels and large hole were meant for use in jukeboxes.
Promo CD (WDGCT 9) including the title track only, no artwork. Promo cassette (DGCDM 21742) including all four tracks.

**In Bloom**
**1992 – USA**
No commercial releases. Promo CD (DGC, PRO-CD-4463) in plain card sleeve.
**In Bloom / Sliver** – live (CD only) / **Polly** – live
**1992 – UK**, Geffen (seven-inch GFS 34, 12-inch picture GFSTP 34, CD GFSTD 34, MC GFSC 34)
The seven-inch has silver painted labels, copies with unpainted labels and large hole were meant for use in jukeboxes.
Promo cassette (no code) including all three tracks.

**Oh, The Guilt**
This is a split single. The Nirvana track is on the B-side. 'Puss' by The Jesus Lizard is on the A-side.
Released in a total of 100,000 copies worldwide.
**1993 – USA**, Touch & Go (seven-inch TG83, CD TG83CD, MC TG83C)
**1993 – UK**, Touch & Go (seven-inch TG83, CD TG83CD)
Blue vinyl seven-inch, some copies included a poster.
Two versions for the CD release: card sleeve or jewel box.

**1993 – Australia**, Insipid Vinyl (seven-inch picture IV-23)
Picture disc seven-inch in clear plastic sleeve with red or black title sticker; limited to 1,500 copies.

**Heart-Shaped Box**
**1993 – USA**
No commercial releases. Promo 12-inch (DGC, PRO-A-4558) in picture sleeve, with the title track and 'Gallons Of Rubbing Alcohol Flow Through The Strip', otherwise available only as a bonus track on the non-US CDs of the *In Utero* album.
Promo CD (DGC, PRO-CD-4545) and promo cassette (DGC, no code), both with the title track only.
**Heart-Shaped Box / Milk It** (12-inch and CD only) **/ Marigold**
**1993 – UK**, Geffen (seven-inch GFS 54, 12-inch GFST 54, CD GFSTD 54, MC GFSC 54)
The seven-inch has silver painted labels, copies with unpainted labels and large hole were meant for use in jukeboxes.
Promo cassette (no code) with the title track only.
**1993 – UK/France**, Geffen (seven-inch GES19191)
Red vinyl, made in the UK for the French market. 5,000 copies, numbered on the front sleeve.
**1993 – Germany**, Geffen (seven-inch GES19191)
Limited edition, red vinyl.

**All Apologies / Rape Me**
**1993 – USA**
No commercial releases. Two promo CDs: the first (DGC, PRO-CD-4581) has the title track only, the second (DGC, PRO-CD-4582) includes also 'Rape Me'.
**All Apologies / Rape Me / MV (Moist Vagina)**
**1993 – UK**, Geffen (seven-inch GFS 66, 12-inch GFST 66, CD GFSTD 66, MC GFSC 66)
The seven-inch has silver painted labels, copies with unpainted labels and large hole were meant for use in jukeboxes.
The 12-inch includes two prints with the cover artwork with different background colours.
Promo CD (NIRVA1) including only 'Rape Me' and 'All Apologies', no artwork.
Promo cassette (no code).

**Pennyroyal Tea** – Scott Litt remix **/ I Hate Myself And I Want To Die / Where Did You Sleep Last Night (In The Pines)** – *Unplugged*
**1994 – UK**

Seven-inch, CD and cassette were scheduled but never released. A few copies of the promo CD (NIRPRO) were distributed; title track only, no artwork.
**1994 – Germany**, Geffen (CD GED21907)
Recalled and destroyed immediately after the release. A few hundred copies later surfaced on the European and Korean markets, shortly followed by a nearly perfect counterfeit.

**About A Girl** – *Unplugged*
**1994 – USA**
No commercial releases. Promo CD (DGC, PRO-CD-4688)
**About A Girl** – *Unplugged* / **Something In The Way** – *Unplugged*
**1994 – France**, Geffen (CD GED21958)
Card sleeve; two versions were released, with a slightly different track timing.
**1994 – Australia**, Geffen (CD GEFDS21958)
5,000 copies in numbered card sleeve. 200 unnumbered copies were used for promotion.

## EPs

**Blew / Love Buzz / Been A Son / Stain**
**1989 – UK**, Tupelo (12-inch TUPEP 8, CD TUPCD 8)
The 12-inch was pressed in black vinyl only. Fakes exist, in black vinyl, coloured vinyl and picture disc.
The CD has also been heavily counterfeited.

**HORMOANING**
**Turnaround / Aneurysm / D-7 / Son Of A Gun / Even In His Youth / Molly's Lips**
**1991 – Australia**, Geffen (12-inch GEF21711, CD GEFD21711, MC GEFC21711)
"Exclusive Australian '92 Tour EP"
The 12-inch is in red and blue swirl vinyl. 4,000 copies. Several fakes have been made, in black, white and many other vinyl colours.
Two versions exist for the CD, they have the same inlays and differ only for the disc: a first pressing (black text on silver background, the code DGCDS21711 is printed on the disc) was made in the USA and sent to Australia. A second pressing (red and white text on blue background) was later made locally. The blue version has been counterfeited.
A thousand copies of the cassette have been released.
**1991 – Japan**, DGC (CD MVCG 17002)
The graphic is different from the Australian release. It is one of the most heavily counterfeited Nirvana items.

## ALBUMS

### BLEACH

**Blew / Floyd The Barber / About A Girl / School / Love Buzz (not on all releases) / Paper Cuts / Negative Creep / Scoff / Swap Meet / Mr Moustache / Sifting / Big Cheese (not on all releases) / Downer (not on all releases)**

**1989 – USA**, Sub Pop (12-inch SP34, CD SP34b, MC SP34a)
'Big Cheese' and 'Downer' aren't included on the vinyl releases.
12-inch first release: 1,000 copies, white vinyl. Some copies have a black and white poster.
12-inch second release: 2,000 copies, black vinyl. May have a Sub Pop Singles Club card. Some copies have a black and white poster.
12-inch third release: coloured vinyl (clear red, clear pink, marbled pink, marbled blue, marbled purple, marbled green, red and white swirl). 500 copies of the red and white swirl pressing were sold as a numbered set, shrink-wrapped with a blue vinyl 'Sliver' seven-inch single.
12-inch unreleased: a small number of copies were pressed in greenish white marbled vinyl, and never released for fear they could be passed for the first white limited release. Most copies ended up in the collections of Sub Pop employees or band members.
12-inch fourth release: reissued in 2000 in black vinyl only, recognisable by the presence of a barcode on the back sleeve.
The CD was first released around 1990. A remastered version was used for all reissues. A few copies were packed in long cardboard boxes.
'Big Cheese' was missing from the first cassette release, and was added in the remastered reissues.
**1989 – UK**, Tupelo (12-inch TUPLP6, CD TUPCD6, MC TUPMC6)
'Love Buzz' and 'Downer' aren't included on the vinyl releases, on the first CD release and on the cassette.
12-inch first release: 300 copies, white vinyl. Second release: 2,000 copies, lime green vinyl. Third release: black vinyl.
The first CD release had only 11 tracks. Then it was reissued with 13 tracks.
**1992 – UK**, Geffen (CD GFLD 1929, MC GFLC 19121)
Remastered version.
**2002 – UK**, Warner Music (12-inch 9878400341)
White vinyl, picture inner sleeve and a 'Back to vinyl' sticker on the front. First release, limited to 2,500 copies, 13 tracks. Second release, 11 tracks only ('Big Cheese' and 'Downer' aren't included).
**1989 – Australia**, Waterfront (12-inch DAMP 114)
'Big Cheese' and 'Downer' aren't included.
Eight different vinyl colours, housed in matching sleeves. Allegedly 500 copies were made for each version, but some appear much less frequently than the

others, so even this number may not be correct.
Black vinyl, black background with silver titles on front sleeve.
Yellow vinyl, black background with yellow titles on front sleeve.
Purple vinyl, purple background with silver titles on front sleeve.
Red vinyl, red-orange background with silver titles on front sleeve.
Red-orange vinyl, black background with silver titles on front sleeve.
Light blue vinyl, blue background with silver titles on front sleeve.
Blue vinyl, black background with blue titles, or black background with silver titles on front sleeve.
Green vinyl, green background with silver titles on front sleeve. This is a "1992 Australian Tour Edition, limited to 500", as written on the outer sleeve. Includes a poster with the sleeve design, and an outer sleeve in white cotton fabric, silk-screened in green and red with the titles and the tour dates.

**NEVERMIND**
**Smells Like Teen Spirit / In Bloom / Come As You Are / Breed / Lithium / Polly / Territorial Pissings / Drain You / Lounge Act / Stay Away / On A Plain / Something In The Way / Endless, Nameless (only on some CD and cassette releases)**
**1991 – USA**, DGC (12-inch DGC24425, CD DGCD24425, MC DGCC24425, DCC DGCX24425)
Promo copies of the 12-inch have a 'For promotion only' gold stamp on the back sleeve.
The first copies of the CD were housed in a long cardboard box, and missed the last track 'Endless, Nameless'. It was later added on the reissues, then omitted again, then re-added . . . The same happened with the cassettes.
Three different promo cassettes (no code).
**1995 – USA**, Mobile Fidelity Sound Lab (12-inch MFSL1-258, CD UDCD666)
Reissue from the original master tapes, on 12-inch (5,000 copies numbered on the back sleeve, high definition vinyl and gatefold sleeve) and CD (Ultradisc II golden CD).
**1991 – UK**
German releases (Geffen, 12-inch GEF24425, CD GED24425, MC GEC24425) were distributed in the UK. Only promo cassettes (DGC, no code) were made locally. Two versions: one includes the full album. Another has four tracks only.
**1998 – UK**, Simply Vinyl (12-inch SVLP 0038)
Audiophile release on 180g virgin vinyl. Two pressings, with silver or golden stickers on the outer clear plastic envelope sleeve.
**1992 – Czech Republic**, Globus (12-inch 2101101311, 12-inch picture 0235)
Green vinyl. A few promo copies were pressed in black vinyl. This first

(official) pressing has black labels with silver titles and very glossy sleeves. In 1999 (unofficial?) reissues were made in black, green, blue, clear with multicolour spots and green with multicolour spots. These reissues have silver labels with black titles.
The picture disc has a blue rim, and there is also a first and second pressing, distinguishable only by the presence of some extra numbers on the matrix.

**INCESTICIDE**
**Dive / Sliver / Stain / Been A Son / Turnaround / Molly's Lips / Son Of A Gun / (New Wave) Polly / Beeswax / Downer / Mexican Seafood / Hairspray Queen / Aero Zeppelin / Big Long Now / Aneurysm**
Compilation of rare and unreleased tracks
**1992 – USA**, DGC (12-inch DGC24504, CD DGCD24504, MC DGCC24504)
Blue marbled 12-inch vinyl, 15,000 copies.
The first copies of the CD were housed in a long cardboard box, and included extra pages on the booklet with Cobain's liner notes. These were removed and then re-added on the reissues. Some copies were used for promotion with a black 'PROMOTIONAL' print on the disc.
Three different promo cassettes (no code).
**1992 – UK**
Dutch (Geffen, 12-inch GEF245040) and German (Geffen, CD GED24504, MC GEC24504) releases were distributed in the UK. Only a promo cassette (DGC, no code) was made locally.

**IN UTERO**
**Serve The Servants / Scentless Apprentice / Heart-Shaped Box / Rape Me / Frances Farmer Will Have Her Revenge On Seattle / Dumb / Very Ape / Milk It / Pennyroyal Tea / Radio Friendly Unit Shifter / tourette's / All Apologies / Gallons Of Rubbing Alcohol Flow Through The Strip** (CD only, not on US releases)
**1993 – USA**, DGC (12-inch DGC24607, CD DGCD24607, MC DGCC24607)
Clear light green 12-inch vinyl, 15,000 copies. Promo copies have a 'For promotion only' gold stamp on the back sleeve.
Some copies of the CD were used for promotion with a white 'PROMOTIONAL' print on the disc.
Three different promo cassettes (no code).
**1993 – USA**, DGC (CD DGCD24705, MC DGCC24705)
Censored version, for sale in Wal-Mart and K-Mart shops: 'Rape Me' is re-titled 'Waif Me' and the back cover graphic has been modified. The Scott Litt remix of 'Pennyroyal Tea' was used.
**1997 – USA**, Mobile Fidelity Sound Lab (CD UDCD690)

Reissue from the original master tapes, on Ultradisc II golden CD.
**1993 – UK**
Dutch (Geffen, 12-inch GEF24536) and German (Geffen, CD GED24536, MC GEC24536) releases were distributed in the UK. Only a promo cassette (Geffen, no code) was made locally, including the extra track.
**1998 – UK**, Simply Vinyl (12-inch SVLP 0048)
Audiophile release on 180g virgin vinyl. Two pressings, with silver or golden stickers on the outer clear plastic envelope sleeve.
**2001 – Germany**, Geffen / Universal (12-inch 424 536-1)
For this reissue the original Albini mixes have been used, instead of the remixed versions used on all other releases.

**UNPLUGGED IN NEW YORK**
**About A Girl / Come As You Are / Jesus Doesn't Want Me For A Sunbeam / The Man Who Sold The World / Pennyroyal Tea / Dumb / Polly / On A Plain / Something In The Way / Plateau / Oh Me / Lake Of Fire / All Apologies / Where Did You Sleep Last Night**
Recorded live for MTV's Unplugged at Sony Studios, New York, on November 18, 1993.
**1994 – USA**, DGC (12-inch DGC24727, CD DGCD24727, MC DGCC24727)
The 12-inch was pressed in white and in black vinyl.
Some copies of the CD were used for promotion with a black 'PROMOTIONAL' print on the disc.
Numbered promo cassette (no code).
**1994 – UK**
German releases (Geffen, 12-inch GEF24727, CD GED24727, MC GEC24727) were distributed in the UK. Only a promo cassette (Geffen, no code) was made locally.
**1998 – UK**, Simply Vinyl (12-inch SVLP 0053)
Audiophile release on 180g virgin vinyl. Two pressings, with silver or golden stickers on the outer clear plastic envelope sleeve.

**FROM THE MUDDY BANKS OF THE WISHKAH**
**Intro / School / Drain You / Aneurysm / Smells Like Teen Spirit / Been A Son / Lithium / Sliver / Spank Thru / Scentless Apprentice / Heart-Shaped Box / Milk It / Negative Creep / Polly / Breed / tourette's / Blew**
Compilation of live tracks, collected from different concerts.
**1996 – USA**, DGC (12-inch x2 DGC2-25105, CD DGCD25105, MC DGCC25105)
On side four of the vinyl release there is compilation of stage banter, not available on CD and cassette.
Some copies of the CD were used for promotion with a red

'PROMOTIONAL' print on the disc.
Two different promo cassettes: the first (no code), 57 minutes long, was meant for the album launch on radio stations, the second (DGCC-A-25105) contains all album tracks.
**1996 – UK**
Dutch (Geffen, 12-inch GEF251052) and German (Geffen, CD GED25105) releases were distributed in the UK. Only a promo cassette (Geffen, no code) was made locally.

**NIRVANA**
**You Know You're Right / About A Girl / Been A Son / Sliver / Smells Like Teen Spirit / Come As You Are / Lithium / In Bloom / Heart-Shaped Box / Pennyroyal Tea** – Scott Litt remix **/ Rape Me / Dumb / All Apologies** – *Unplugged* **/ The Man Who Sold The World** – *Unplugged* **/ Something In The Way** – *Unplugged* (only on 12-inch) **/ Where Did You Sleep Last Night** – *Unplugged* (not on US CD)
'Best of' compilation, including one unreleased track: 'You Know You're Right'.
**2002 – USA**, DGC (CD 0694935072)
**2002 – EU**, Geffen (12-inch x2 439 523-1, CD 439 523-2, MC 439 523-4)

**SLIVER – THE BEST OF THE BOX**
**Spank Thru (*)** – from Fecal Matter demo; 1985 **/ Heartbreaker** – live **/ Mrs. Butterworth** – rehearsal demo **/ Floyd The Barber** – live **/ Clean Up Before She Comes** – home demo **/ About A Girl** – home demo **/ Blandest** – studio demo **/ Ain't It A Shame** – studio demo **/ Sappy (*)** – 1990 studio demo **/ Opinion** – solo acoustic radio appearance **/ Lithium** – solo acoustic radio appearance **/ Sliver** – home demo **/ Smells Like Teen Spirit** – boom box version **/ Come As You Are (*)** – boom box version **/ Old Age** – *Nevermind* outtake **/ Oh, The Guilt / Rape Me** – home demo **/ Rape Me** – band demo **/ Heart-Shaped Box** – band demo **/ Do Re Mi** – home demo **/ You Know You're Right** – home demo **/ All Apologies** – home demo
Compilation of tracks from the *With The Lights Out* box set, plus three unreleased tracks **(*)**.
**2005 – USA**, UMe (CD B0005617-02)
Advance promo CDr (no code), individually numbered and watermarked to prevent unauthorised use. Custom inlays.
**2005 – UK**
Made in EU (Geffen, CD 602498867181) CDs were distributed in the UK. Only a promo CDr (no code) was made locally, individually numbered and watermarked to prevent unauthorised use. Custom inlay.

## BOX SETS

### SINGLES

**1995 Germany**, Geffen (CD x6 GED24901)
Re-pressings of all six CD singles from the *Nevermind* and *In Utero* albums, contained in a picture cardboard box:
'Smells Like Teen Spirit' / 'Come As You Are' / 'Lithium' / 'In Bloom' / 'All Apologies' / 'Heart-Shaped Box'

### WITH THE LIGHTS OUT

**Audio tracks:**
**Heartbreaker** – live / **Anorexorcist** – radio performance / **White Lace And Strange** – radio performance / **Help Me I'm Hungry** – radio performance / **Mrs Butterworth** – rehearsal recording / **If You Must** – demo / **Pen Cap Chew** – demo / **Downer** – live / **Floyd The Barber** – live / **Raunchola/Moby Dick** – live / **Beans** – solo acoustic / **Don't Want It All** – solo acoustic / **Clean Up Before She Comes** – solo acoustic / **Polly** – solo acoustic / **About A Girl** – solo acoustic / **Blandest** – demo / **Dive** – demo / **They Hung Him On A Cross** – demo / **Grey Goose** – demo / **Ain't It A Shame** – demo / **Token Eastern Song** – demo / **Even In His Youth** – demo / **Polly** – demo / **Opinion** – solo acoustic / **Lithium** – solo acoustic / **Been A Son** – solo acoustic / **Sliver** – solo acoustic / **Where Did You Sleep Last Night** – solo acoustic / **Pay To Play** – demo / **Here She Comes Now** / **Drain You** – demo / **Aneurysm** / **Smells Like Teen Spirit** – demo / **Breed** – rough mix / **Verse Chorus Verse** – outtake / **Old Age** – outtake / **Endless, Nameless** – radio appearance / **Dumb** – radio appearance / **D-7** / **Oh, The Guilt** / **Curmudgeon** / **Return Of The Rat** / **Smells Like Teen Spirit** – Butch Vig mix / **Rape Me** – solo acoustic / **Rape Me** – demo / **Scentless Apprentice** – rehearsal demo / **Heart-Shaped Box** – demo / **I Hate Myself And I Want To Die** – demo / **Milk It** – demo / **Moist Vagina** – demo / **Gallons Of Running Alcohol Flow Through The Strip** / **The Other Improv** – demo / **Serve The Servants** – solo acoustic / **Very Ape** – solo acoustic / **Pennyroyal Tea** – solo acoustic / **Marigold** / **Sappy** / **Jesus Doesn't Want Me For A Sunbeam** – rehearsal demo / **Do Re Mi** – solo acoustic / **You Know You're Right** – solo acoustic / **All Apologies** – solo acoustic

**Video tracks:**
**Love Buzz – Scoff – About A Girl – Big Long Now – Immigrant Song – Spank Thru – Hairspray Queen – School – Mr Moustache** – December 1988, Krist's mother's house, Aberdeen, WA / **Big Cheese** – June 1989, Rhino Records, Los Angeles, CA / **Sappy** – February 1990, Bogarts, Long Beach, CA / **In Bloom** – Sub Pop video / **School** – September 1990, Motor

Sports International Garage, Seattle, WA / **Love Buzz** – October 1990, Olympia, WA / **Pennyroyal Tea – Smells Like Teen Spirit – Territorial Pissings** – April 1991, OK Hotel, Seattle, WA / **Jesus Doesn't Want Me For A Sunbeam** – October 1991, Paramount Theatre, Seattle, WA / **Talk To Me** – October 1993, The Crocodile Café, Seattle, WA / **Seasons In The Sun** – January 1993, BMG Ariola Studios, Rio De Janeiro, Brazil
Compilation of rare and unreleased tracks. Three audio CDs and one video DVD in a threefold container, with a printed metal plate on the front. A 60-page booklet with extensive notes is housed in an inside pocket. The 'dark' surfaces of the box are printed with heat-sensitive ink, which reveals hidden pictures when lightly heated.
**2004 USA**, UMe (BOX B0003727-00)
**2004 EU**, Geffen (BOX 0602498648384)

## OTHER MISCELLANEOUS PROMO-ONLY RELEASES

### NEVERMIND IT'S AN INTERVIEW

**1992 USA**, DGC (CD PRO-CD-4382)
Promo CD intended for radio airplay. Contains an exclusive interview conducted by Kurt St Thomas, with complete live tracks from the October 31, 1991 live concert at the Paramount Theatre, Seattle ('About A Girl', 'Aneurysm', 'Drain You', 'On A Plain', 'School') and other clips of studio and live tracks playing in the background.
This item has been counterfeited.

**On A Plain**
**1991 – USA**, DGC (CD PRO-CD-4354)

**I Hate Myself And I Want To Die**
**1993 – UK**, Geffen (MC no code)

**All Apologies** – *Unplugged* / **All Apologies** – LP version
**1994 – USA**, DGC (CD PRO-CD-4618)

**The Man Who Sold The World** – *Unplugged*
**1994 – USA**, DGC (CD PRO-CD-4704)

**Where Did You Sleep Last Night** – *Unplugged*
**1994 – UK**, Geffen (CD NIRVPRO 1)

**Lake Of Fire** – *Unplugged* / **Where Did You Sleep Last Night** – *Unplugged*
**1994 – Australia**, Geffen (CD PROCD-4265)

**Aneurysm** – live
**1996 – USA**, DGC (CD PRO-CD-1033)
**1996 – UK**, Geffen (CD PRO CD 1033)

**Drain You** – live
**1996 – USA**, DGC (CD PRO-CD-1070)

**Smells Like Teen Spirit** – live
**1996 – France**, Geffen (CD MCA F0010) Card sleeve

**You Know You're Right**
**2002 – USA**, DGC (CDR INTR-10853-2) Custom printed CDr
**2002 – UK**, DGC (CD INTR-10853-2)

## SELECTIONS FROM WITH THE LIGHTS OUT

**White Lace And Strange** – radio performance / **Blandest** – demo / **Polly** – demo (US CD only) / **Lithium** – solo acoustic / **In Bloom** – Sub Pop version (US CD only) / **Heart-Shaped Box** – demo / **You Know You're Right** – solo acoustic
Selection of tracks from the *With The Lights Out* box set
**2004 – USA**, UMe (CDR no code) Seven tracks, custom printed CDr
**2004 – EU**, Geffen (CD NIRVBOXCDP1) Five tracks, card sleeve

## NIGHTLY NIRVANA

### WEEK 1

**Smells Like Teen Spirit** / *Cobain: inspiration for name 'Smells Like Teen Spirit'* / **Even In His Youth**
**Serve The Servants** / *Albini: work ethic* / **Rape Me** – live at *SNL*
**Sliver** / *Novoselic: exposing the underground* / **Oh Me** – *Unplugged*
**On A Plain** / *Vig: hearing Nirvana's first record* / **About A Girl**
**Heart-Shaped Box** / *Full band: absurdness of bands like Extreme* / **Spank Thru**

### WEEK 2

**Lithium** – acoustic / *Cross: Kurt was a songwriting genius* / **Aneurysm**
**Dumb** / *Cobain: how I write lyrics* / **You Know You're Right**
**In Bloom** / *Vig: hooking up with Sub Pop . . . then Nirvana* / **Immodium (Breed)** – Smart Studios 04/90 **(*)**
**Verse Chorus Verse** / *Cobain: selling out* / **Polly** – live. Rome, February 22, 1994) **(*)**
**Stay Away** / *Albini: people latching on to Kurt* / **Pennyroyal Tea**

### WEEK 3

**Drain You** / *Vig, the importance of Krist and Dave* / **Marigold**
**Come As You Are** / *Cobain: right album, right time* / **Verse Chorus Verse** – outtake
**Love Buzz** / *Cross: Cobain wanted fame* / **I Hate Myself And I Want To Die**
**Jesus Doesn't Want Me For A Sunbeam** – live, soundtrack from the DVD / *Cobain: 'All Apologies'* Unplugged / **All Apologies** – *Unplugged*

**Something In The Way** / *Poneman: I knew two different Kurt Cobains* / **Seasons In The Sun** – soundtrack from the DVD

**WEEK 4**

**Negative Creep** / *Cobain: writing songs for* Bleach / **Downer**
**Ain't It A Shame** / *Endino: the Jury explanation* / **Where Did You Sleep Last Night** – *Unplugged*
**Lounge Act** / *Vig: Kurt's mood swings* / **Old Age**
**Lithium** – live / *Krist: tossing the bass at the VMA's* / **Territorial Pissings**
**Breed** / *Endino: Dave Grohl was too loud* / **Milk It**

**WEEK 5**

**School** / *Endino: Frances Bean on 'Rape Me'* / **Rape Me** – demo
**Dive** / *Cross: Kurt's icon status* / **The Man Who Sold The World** – *Unplugged*
**Been A Son** – live / *Cobain: stagediving* / **Aneurysm** – live
**Pay To Play** – demo / *Vig:* Nevermind *touched a nerve* / **Come As You Are** – *Unplugged*
**Opinion** / *Endino: last second tapes on box set* / **Token Eastern Song**

**WEEK 6**

**All Apologies** / *Albini: his opinion of Nirvana going into recording* / **Frances Farmer Will Have Her Revenge On Seattle**
**Heart-Shaped Box** – demo / *Jerry Cantrell on Kurt Cobain* / **Something In The Way** – *Unplugged*
**Aero Zeppelin** / *Krist: we thought 'Teen Spirit' was a Pixies rip-off* / **Smells Like Teen Spirit** – Butch Vig mix
**Turnaround** / *Grohl: 'You Know You're Right'* / **You Know You're Right** – demo
**Pennyroyal Tea** – solo acoustic / *Endino: more Nirvana music out there* / **Curmudgeon**

**WEEK 7**

**Dumb** – radio appearance / *Endino: no hits on the box set* / **Return Of The Rat**
**Oh, The Guilt** / *Cobain: choosing the HSB video director* / **Heart-Shaped Box** – live
**Molly's Lips** / *Cross: Kurt was a troubled guy* / **tourette's**
**Lake Of Fire** – *Unplugged* / *Endino on 'Do Re Mi'* / **Do Re Mi**
**Breed** – live / *Vig: the legacy of* Nevermind / **D-7**

**WEEK 8**

**Plateau** – *Unplugged* / *Cross: Kurt was a troubled guy* / **Jesus Doesn't Want Me For A Sunbeam** – rehearsal demo
**Mexican Seafood** / *Endino: Nirvana's first recording session* / **If You Must** /
**About A Girl** – *Unplugged* / *Vig: favourite song on* Nevermind / **Smells Like Teen Spirit** – live

**Come As You Are** / *Cobain:* Nevermind *was recorded perfectly* / **Lithium** – live at Reading Festival **(*)**
**Here She Comes Now** / *Endino: 'They Hung Him On A Cross'* / **They Hung Him On A Cross**

**WEEK 9**
**On A Plain** / *Novoselic:* Nevermind *is a rite of passage record* / **Polly** – live
**Sappy** / *Endino: making of a box set* / **Where Did You Sleep Last Night** – solo acoustic
**Son Of A Gun** / *Rollins: on Nirvana and Kurt* / **Radio Friendly Unit Shifter**
**Old Age** / *Vig: early* Nevermind *recordings* / **Dive**
**Sliver** / *Cobain: where did he get the content for some lyrics?* / **MV**

**WEEK 10**
**Hairspray Queen** / *Vig: Kurt's mood swings* / **Scentless Apprentice**
**Serve The Servants** / *Cobain: old school dinosaurs needed to be weeded out* / **The Man Who Sold The World** – *Unplugged*
**Even In His Youth** / *Cross: the underdog winning* / **Been A Son**
**Very Ape** / *Poneman: Seattle sound at the time* / **Negative Creep**
**All Apologies** – solo acoustic / *Endino: everything is not on the box set* / **Endless, Nameless**
**2004/2005 – USA**, UMe (CDRs no code)
Weekly radio promos for the *With The Lights Out* box set. Starting at end of November 2004, when the box was released, the series lasted for 10 weeks, until the end of January 2005.
Each CD contains a complete radio programme, with interviews and a selection of tracks, some of which are unavailable elsewhere (*). Custom printed CDrs with accompanying cue sheets.

## SLIVER – THE RADIO SPECIAL

**Smells Like Teen Spirit** – boom box version / *Cobain: where the title for 'Teen Spirit' came from* / **Old Age** – outtake / **Lithium** – solo acoustic / *Jack Endino: Frances Bean on 'Rape Me'* / **Rape Me** – band demo / **Sliver** – home demo / *Butch Vig: 'About A Girl' . . . favourite song from* Bleach / **About A Girl** – home demo / **You Know You're Right** – home demo / *Grohl: recording studio version of 'You Know You're Right'* / **Ain't It A Shame –** studio demo / *Steve Albini: people latching on to Kurt* / **Heart-Shaped Box –** band demo / **All Apologies –** home demo / *Jack Endino: 'Do Re Mi'* / **Do Re Mi** – home demo
**2005 – USA**, UMe (CDR no code)
Radio promo for the *Sliver: The Best Of The Box* album. The CD contains a complete radio programme, with interviews and a selection of tracks. Custom printed CDr with accompanying cue sheets.

## TRACKS ON COMPILATIONS

**SUB POP 200**
**Spank Thru**
**1988 – USA**, Sub Pop (12-inch x3 SP25)
Three 12-inch records contained in a black cardboard box, 20 page booklet with photos and info on the bands. 5,000 copies.
**1989 – UK**, Tupelo (CD TUPCD4)
**1991 – USA**, Sub Pop (CD SP25b)
**1995 – USA**, Sub Pop (CD SP25-2)
Reissue, black cardboard box and 20-page booklet, as a replica of the vinyl box set.

**SUB POP ROCK CITY**
**Spank Thru**
**1989 – Germany**, Glitterhouse (12-inch GR0052)
German release of the *Sub Pop 200* compilation, without some tracks. Gatefold sleeve.

**TERIYAKI ASTHMA Vol. I**
**Mexican Seafood**
**1989 – USA**, C/Z (seven-inch C/Z009)
Silk-screened twofold paper sleeve. 1,000 copies.

**TERIYAKI ASTHMA Vols. I–V**
**Mexican Seafood**
**1991 – USA**, C/Z (CD CZ037, MC CZ037)
**1991 – Holland**, C/Z (12-inch x2 CZ037)
Gatefold sleeve.

**HARD TO BELIEVE**
Kiss covers compilation
**Do You Love Me?**
**1990 – USA**, C/Z (12-inch CZ024, CD CZ024, MC CZ024)
Initially the front sleeve featured a distorted picture of the Kiss members' faces, then, fearing legal action from the band, CD and cassette were re-released with a different graphic on the front sleeve.
Different track lists were used on the various releases, but the Nirvana track appears on all.
The 12-inch was first released in purple-red vinyl and gatefold sleeve, then in black vinyl, both in gatefold and single sleeves.
**1990 – UK**, Waterfront / Southern Studios (12-inch DAMP 121, CD DAMP 121CD)
The 12-inch was released in a gatefold sleeve.

**1990 – UK**, Waterfront (12-inch x2 DAMP 121)
Double 12-inch release, pressed in red and in black vinyl. Gatefold sleeve.

**HEAVEN AND HELL Volume 1**
Velvet Underground covers compilation
**Here She Comes Now**
**1990 – UK**, Imaginary (12-inch ILLUSION 016, CD ILL CD 016, MC ILL CASS 016)
**1991 – USA**, Communion (12-inch 20, CD 20CD, MC 20)

**HEAVEN AND HELL Volumes 1–3**
Velvet Underground covers compilations
**Here She Comes Now**
**1992 – UK**, Imaginary (CD x3 ILL CD 016 / ILL CD 017 / ILL CD 022)
Collection of the three volumes, in a numbered cardboard box.

**KILL ROCK STARS**
**Beeswax**
**1991 – USA**, kill rock stars (12-inch KRS-201, CD KRS-201)
12-inch first release: 1,000 copies in hand-screened sleeve. Hand signed and numbered on the front by the sleeve designer. Blank back sleeve.
12-inch second release: regular sleeve, not silk-screened or numbered. Track list and bands' pictures on the back sleeve.

**THE GRUNGE YEARS**
**Dive**
**1991 – USA**, Sub Pop (CD SP112b, MC SP112a)
On the front CD inlay is ironically written, "Limited edition of 500,000".

**EIGHT SONGS FOR GREG SAGE AND THE WIPERS**
Wipers covers compilation
**Return Of The Rat**
**1993 – USA**, Tim Kerr (seven-inch x4 TK 917010 TRIB2)
Cardboard box containing four seven-inch vinyl records in individual picture sleeves, and an info sheet in textured paper.
10,000 complete boxes. 4,000 boxes contain black vinyl records. The other 6,000 contain coloured vinyl records.
Each single was pressed in several different colours then randomly put inside the boxes. It's not known how many colours were used for each single, and how many copies were pressed for each colour. Probably the pressing plant used all the leftover bits of coloured vinyl they could find . . . The Nirvana single has been printed in clear, grey, clear red, clear blue, marbled green (different shades), marbled blue-green (aqua). Other colours also used (not for the Nirvana single) are: marbled pink, marbled red, marbled peach-red, white,

clear yellow (gold), clear green, clear orange, marbled light blue, marbled dark blue, marbled light purple, clear dark purple.

**FOURTEEN SONGS FOR GREG SAGE AND THE WIPERS**
Wipers covers compilation
**Return Of The Rat**
**1993 – USA**, Tim Kerr (CD TK 91CD10 TRIB2)

**NO ALTERNATIVE**
**Sappy**
Two different front sleeves, with a picture of a young boy or of a young girl. The Nirvana track is 'hidden', and the title isn't mentioned anywhere. For this reason, until the release of the *With The Lights Out* box set, which defined the official title, it had also been called 'Verse Chorus Verse' or 'Another Rule'.
**1993 – USA**, Arista (CD 07822-18737-2, MC 07822-18737-4)
**1991 – UK**, Arista (CD 07822-18737-2)

**THE BEAVIS AND BUTT-HEAD EXPERIENCE**
**I Hate Myself And I Want To Die**
**1993 – USA**, DGC (CD GEFD-24613, MC GEFC-24613)
Some copies of the CD were used for promotion with a red 'PROMOTIONAL' print on the disc.
**1991 – UK**, Geffen (12-inch picture GEF24613, CD GED24613)
12-inch picture disc in a clear plastic sleeve.

**DGC RARITIES Vol. 1**
**Pay To Play** (early demo version of 'Stay Away')
**1994 – USA**, DGC (CD DGCD-24704, MC DGCC-24704)
Advance promo CD ((DGCD-A-24704) with custom back inlay and 'ADVANCE CD' printed in red on the CD.
Some copies of the regular CD were also used for promotion with a white 'PROMOTIONAL' print on the disc.

**GEFFEN RARITIES Vol. 1**
**Pay To Play** (early demo version of 'Stay Away')
**1994 – UK**, Geffen (12-inch GFL-19247, CD GFLD-19247, MC GFLC 19247)

**FIFTEEN MINUTES**
Velvet Underground covers compilation
**Here She Comes Now**
**1994 – UK**, Imaginary (CD ILLCD 047P)

**FENDER: 50th ANNIVERSARY GUITAR LEGENDS**
**Come As You Are**
**1996 – USA**, Pointblank / Virgin (CD 7243 8 42088 2 0)
A limited number of copies contain a commemorative guitar pick.

**HOME ALIVE – THE ART OF SELF DEFENCE**
**Radio Friendly Unit Shifter** – live
**1996 – USA**, Epic (CD x2 E2K67486, MC x2 E2T 67486 ET 67487)

**HYPE!**
**Negative Creep**
The CD releases contain a short synth version of 'Smells Like Teen Spirit' as a hidden track.
**1996 – USA**, Sub Pop (seven-inch x4 SP378, CD SPCD371)
The vinyl release is a cardboard box containing four seven-inch singles in different vinyl colours (the Nirvana one is green marbled) in individual picture sleeves, and a black and white poster.
**1996 – UK**, Sub Pop (CD SPCD371)

**SNL 25 – SATURDAY NIGHT LIVE The Musical Performances, Volume 2**
**Rape Me** – live
**1996 – USA**, Dreamworks (CD 0044-50206-2)
On the back inlay there are only the band names. A sticker with the track list is attached on the box or on the wrap, but the Nirvana track name has been removed (censored).
Promo custom printed CDr (no code)

**KURT COBAIN'S SIDE PROJECTS**
**FECAL MATTER – Spank Thru / . . .**
**1995**
The line-up on this pre-Nirvana band was: Kurt Cobain (guitar, vocals, percussion), Dale Crover (vocals, bass, drums), Greg Hokanson (drums).
In December 1995, Cobain and Crover recorded a demo tape on a four-track recorder, at Cobain's aunt's house. Cobain then edited and dubbed the tracks on cassettes he distributed to friends. Of the 15 or more tracks recorded, only 'Spank Thru' has found its way on to an official release, Nirvana's *With The Lights Out* box set, 2004.

**THE JURY – Where Did You Sleep Last Night / They Hung Him On A Cross / Grey Goose / Ain't It A Shame**
**1989**
The band's line-up was: Kurt Cobain (guitar, vocals), Mark Lanegan (guitar, vocals), Krist Novoselic (bass), Mark Pickerel (drums).

In August 1989 the four musicians recorded four blues tracks in Jack Endino's Reciprocal Studios. 'Where Did You Sleep Last Night' was then included on Lanegan's album *The Winding Sheet*, 1990. The other three have been included on Nirvana's *With The Lights Out* box set, 2004.

**MARK LANEGAN – THE WINDING SHEET**
Cobain sings background vocals on 'Down In The Dark', and plays guitar on 'Where Did You Sleep Last Night'. Novoselic plays bass on 'Where Did You Sleep Last Night'.
**1990 – USA**, Sub Pop (12-inch SP61, CD SP61B, MC SP61A)
The first 12-inch release was of 1,000 copies in red vinyl. It was then reissued in black vinyl.

**MARK LANEGAN – Down In The Dark / I Love You Little Girl**
Cobain sings background vocals on 'Down In The Dark'.
**1990 – Germany**, Glitterhouse (seven-inch GR0101)
Twofold paper sleeve in two versions, with the credits positioned differently on the back sleeve.

**THE GO TEAM – Scratch It Out / Bikini Twilight**
The Go Team was a project by Calvin Johnson, leader of K records. On this single the line-up was Calvin Johnson – guitar, Kurt Cobain – guitar, Tobi Vail – drums. Cobain plays on 'Bikini Twilight'.
**1989 – USA**, K (seven-inch GTJL 89)
Black vinyl seven-inch, in a plain white die-cut paper sleeve. According to Calvin Johnson, around 700 copies were made. The band name and credits are printed in red ink with a rubber stamp on one side of the sleeve. Some copies have been printed on both sides. Both tracks are on the A-side. On the B-side, there is a blue silk-screened band logo. A few copies miss the logo and have a white label instead. A very few copies have small logos printed on the white label and on the vinyl.

**EARTH – EXTRA-CAPSULAR EXTRACTION**
The band's line-up is Dave Harwell, Dylan Carlson and Joe Preston. Kurt Cobain and Kelly Canary are credited as 'specialists'.
Cobain features on vocals on the track 'A Bureaucratic Desire For Revenge'.
**1991 – USA**, Sub Pop (CD SP123B)
Card sleeve, may include a card inlay with the front sleeve artwork, and an 'Earth featuring Dylan' sticker on the front.
**2002 – USA**, Sub Pop (12-inch SP 123, CD SPCD 123)
Reissue of 1,000 copies of the 12-inch, and 3,000 copies of the CD, in a regular jewel box.

**EARTH – SUNN AMPS AND SMASHED GUITARS LIVE**
Originally released on Blast First in 1995, then reissued with added tracks. One of them, 'Divine And Bright', features Cobain on vocals.
**2001 – USA**, No Quarter (CD nqr001)

**EARTH – Divine And Bright** – demo **/ Divine And Bright** – live
The demo version features Cobain on vocals.
**2003 – USA**, Autofact (seven-inch FACT 01)
First release, 1,000 copies in clear plastic sleeves. According to the label owner, 700 copies were pressed in black vinyl, 276 on white vinyl (may have faint black stains) and 24 on clear green vinyl. A few extra copies were pressed while changing the vinyl colour, and resulted in marbled black and white. The picture sleeves weren't available, so the records were distributed in plain clear plastic sleeves.
Second release, 500 copies in picture sleeves, made in 2004. Pressed in literally tens of different vinyl colours, all more or less marbled/swirled. Black, white and clear green are between the colours used, but copies from the second pressing can be distinguished because they are slightly 'muddy', while the colours of the first pressing are pure and bright. The picture sleeves were ready, and could be used. Allegedly this reissue, even if made using the same pressing plates as the first, wasn't authorised by the label owner.

**WILLIAM S. BURROUGHS – KURT COBAIN – THE 'PRIEST' THEY CALLED HIM**
Burroughs reads one of his dark novels, over a guitar feedback noise background provided by Cobain. Novoselic posed for the front sleeve picture.
**1993 – USA**, Tim Kerr (10-inch 9210044, 10-inch picture 9210044, CD 92CD044)
On the 10-inch records the track is recorded on the A-side. The B-side is blank, with etchings of the artists' signatures.
First pressing: black vinyl.
Second pressing: picture disc with black B-side. 5,000 copies, numbered on the A-side from 1 to 5,000.
Third pressing: picture disc with yellow B-side. 5,000 copies, numbered on the A-side from 5,001 to 10,000.
Fourth pressing: picture disc with photos of Burroughs and Cobain on the B-side. 5,000 copies, not numbered.

**MELVINS – HOUDINI**
**Hooch / Night Goat / Lizzy / Going Blind / Honey Bucket / Hag Me / Set Me Straight / Sky Pup / Joan Of Arc / Teet / Copache / Pearl Bomb / Spread Eagle Beagle** (CD only) **/ Rocket Reducer #62 (Rama Lama Fa Fa Fa)** (12-inch only)
Cobain helped produce and mix some of the tracks, and also played guitar on

'Sky Pup' and additional percussion on 'Spread Eagle Beagle'
**1993 – USA**, Amphetamine Reptile (12-inch 532-1)
Gatefold sleeve, 5,000 copies. May include a sticker with the band name written in the same style as the Kiss logo.
The track 'Spread Eagle Beagle' was too long for inclusion, so it was substituted with 'Rocket Reducer #62'
**1993 – USA**, Atlantic (CD 7 82532-2, MC 82532-4)
The print on the CD may vary in the number and combinations of the colours used.
Promo cassette (7567-82532-4 CA 491) with custom inlay.

**MELVINS – Hooch / Sky Pup**
Cobain helped produce both tracks, and also played guitar on 'Sky Pup'
**1993 – USA**, Rise (seven-inch picture RR76)
Picture disc, design by Kozik. 1,000 copies. Five-colour silk-screened multi-fold sleeve. It's a "hard to open package" (as written on the sleeve), and once (if) you manage to open it without damage, you better not close it again . . .

**HOLE – LIVE THROUGH THIS**
Kurt sings barely audible backing vocals on 'Asking For It' and also co-wrote the outtake 'Old Age', released on the 'Beautiful Son' single (City Slang, 1993) and on the compilation album of rare Hole tracks *My Body The Hand Grenade* (City Slang, 1997). A version of 'Old Age', recorded solo by Cobain, has been included on Nirvana's *With The Lights Out* box set, 2004.
**1994 – USA**, DGC

# ACKNOWLEDGEMENTS

Nirvana. Kurt. Krist. Dave. Chad. Thanks for existing.

Great chunks of narrative have been taken from my previous 'grunge' book, *Live Through This: American Rock Music In The Nineties* (Virgin, 2001). Apologies to anyone who may have bought that and realised the marked similarities. I just felt the story deserved a wider audience.

Most of my articles quoted first appeared in *Melody Maker*; and also *The Stranger*, *Uncut*, *NME*, *Hit It Or Quit It*, *Plan B* and a handful of other publications. Some are original transcripts of tapes that have lain dormant for over a decade. I am grateful to IPC Magazines for granting me permission to quote extensively from the articles concerning Nirvana and Kurt Cobain that I wrote for *Melody Maker* between 1989 and 1994. And I would like to thank my commissioning editors – particularly Allan Jones – for giving me the opportunity to travel so extensively during the early Nineties.

The following people were gracious enough to agree to be interviewed for this book: Dawn Anderson, Julianne Anderson, Mark Arm, Cheryl Arnold, Earnie Bailey, Lou Barlow, Leighton Beezer, Ruud Berends, Danny Bland, Kurt Bloch, Anton Brookes, Carrie Brownstein, James Burdyshaw, Kelly Canary, Rosemary Carroll, Chad Channing, Peter Davis, Mikey Dees, Cali DeWitt, Ian Dickson, Christof Ellinghaus, Jack Endino, Eric Erlandson, Jennifer Finch, Steve Fisk, Gillian G. Gaar, Danny Goldberg, Lori Goldston, John Goodmanson, Kim Gordon, Steve Gullick, Tom Hazelmyer, Jessica Hopper, Megan Jasper, Rich Jensen, Barrett Jones, Rob Kader, Wally Kempton, Al Larsen, Michael Lavine, Mary Lou Lord, Dave Markey, Nikki McClure, Jim Merlis, Carrie Montgomery, Craig Montgomery, Slim Moon, Thurston Moore, Rene Navarette, Joe Newton, Bruce Pavitt, Candice Pedersen, Dan Peters, Charles Peterson, Jonathan Poneman, Lee Ranaldo, Janet Billig Rich, John Robb, Debbi Shane, Ben Shepherd, Aaron Stauffer, Stephen Sweet, Corin Tucker, Steve Turner, Tobi Vail, Carlos van Hijfte, Kim Warnick, Rusty Willoughby. Thank you.

I'd like to particularly thank Gillian G. Gaar for permission to quote at length from her numerous articles on Nirvana. Also, I wish to publicly acknowledge the support and friendship I have been offered while writing this book, particularly from Tobi, Craig, Jack, Earnie, Eric, Jessica and Cali. It's meant a great deal to me. Thank you.

The Dave Grohl quotes in Chapter 12 are taken from a 2005 interview conducted by *Mojo* journalist Stevie Chick. Used with permission.

The Pat Smear quotes in Chapters 26 and 28 are taken from a 2002 interview conducted by Rasmus Holmen, www.nirvanaclub.com. Used with permission.

The following people have been supportive, even if no interviews have transpired: Ryan Aigner, Nils Bernstein, Calvin Johnson, Courtney Love, Krist Novoselic, Joe Preston, John Silva, Kim Thayil, Bob Whittaker. Cheers.

I also want to thank the following: *Plan B* Editor Frances May Morgan, for her incisive and thorough proofreading, without which much of this book would be crap, frankly; my main Seattle intern, Natalie Walker, for transcription way beyond the call of duty, any amount of research and quote checking and not least for providing the original version of the Aberdeen travelogue that appears in Chapter 1 – cheers; my Omnibus editor Chris Charlesworth for his patient, good-natured support; Johnny Rogan for his excellent index and comments; Emily Graham, Laura Wright and Victoria Hogg in Brighton, and Beth Capper and Melissa Bradshaw in Chicago and London, for further proofreading duties, transcription and generally kicking my ass; my other Seattle interns, William 'Bill' Bullock, Katie Shaw, Ari Spool and Abby Waysdorf for their enthusiasm and selfless hours spent transcribing tapes and sitting in on interviews; Alex Roberts at www.livenirvana.com for her suggestions, contact lists and never-ending stream of live Nirvana DVDs; Carol Clerk and Andrew Mueller for making me laugh; Ben Myers, Rasmus Holmen and Mike Zeigler for research; Lance Bangs; Enrico Vincenzi at www.sliver.it for his kick-ass discography; Craig and Eve for providing me with a place to stay in Seattle; my fellow workers at *Plan B* magazine – particularly Chris, Andrew and Frances – for bearing with me so long; my mother, Margaret Thackray, for baby-sitting her grandchild Isaac through the last few crucial months.

Finally, I am indebted to my patient, supportive and beautiful wife Charlotte Thackray for continuing to put up with me and encourage me, even as the book dragged into its 16th overdue month. I love you. And I really do promise never to put you through this again.

www.planbmag.com
everett_true@hotmail.com

# INDEX

Albums are printed in italics, singles in roman